Ro & Joe

Thanks for your Support

I Hope you enjoy.

Samuel S. DiPaolo

To Ro & Joe –

Best wishes!!

[illegible]

A COP'S MEMOIR
THE UNHOLY MURDER OF ASH WEDNESDAY

THE STAINED LIFE & RUDE TIMES OF MOB WANNABE "BOLO" DOVISHAW

BY

DOMINICK D. DIPAOLO
AS TOLD TO JEFF PINSKI

Published by Global Roman Publishing
Division of D&P Erie, LLC
Erie, Pennsylvania
www.mmweriepa.com
Mobsters, Murderers and Wannabes, Erie, Pa.

ISBN: 978-0-9960535-0-1

Library of Congress Control Number: 2014936914

Printed in the United States of America.

Dedication

To my family:

THIS WORK COULD NOT HAVE EXISTED WITHOUT THE CONTINUED support, patience and love of my wife Janet and our children Patrick J. DiPaolo and Dawn DiPaolo Romeo. They have been there for me through my many years of police investigations, through all of life's joys or tribulations, and will forever continue to be my source of great pride and strength.

With much love,
Dominick

Dedicated in loving memory
of our beloved son,
Patrick John DiPaolo.

1969-2013
"Our Hero"
Thank you for being our son
WIEITOT

Acknowledgments

Chronicling the complex details of the Frank "Bolo" Dovishaw murder and related offshoot crimes could not have been possible without help along the way. The authors gratefully acknowledge the assistance they received from many sources, public and private, and express their sincere thanks to the following:

Larry Kisko, for his resource assistance; Rose Alo and Jean Farkas, for their superior typing skills; Eileen Romeo and the late investigative journalist Carol Pella for their proofreading, critiques and productive input; authors Don Lewis, Esq., a former federal prosecutor, and Rick Porrello, an Ohio police chief, for their wise counsel; Rick Klein of Van Tuil Photo and Imaging for his photographic reproduction expertise; Laurie Rogan, for her investigative skills and court documents; Chris Sigmund, for his talented graphic map creations; and Daria Reymore, for her enthusiastic copying and production efforts.

Also, the authors thank Jamie Mead, Esq., for permission to use a photograph published by the Times Publishing Company; Janet Colao DiPaolo and Dawn DiPaolo Romeo, for their tireless editorial assistance; Erie Police Chief Randy Bowers, for police photos; Erie Police Captain Frank Kwitowski, Lieutenant Chris Crawford, and Detective Sergeants Ken Kensill and Jay White, for their assistance with issues under their jurisdiction; Kim Hersch, of First Niagara Bank for photographic assistance; Tony Ciecierski, for his technical expertise and advice in creating our web site; and Doris Stawniak Pinski, for her lifelong patience.

Also, our thanks to the Pennsylvania Department of Corrections, Pennsylvania Department of Probation and Parole, Erie County Adult Probation Director Jeff Shaw, Kim Kwitowski, of the Erie County Clerk of Courts office, Erie Bureau of Police, and Michigan State Parole Board for information each agency provided.

The authors also acknowledge that their collective work could not have reached publication-ready stage without the insightful and critical edits of retired Erie School District Teacher and national writing coach Mary Jane Koenig.

Dom DiPaolo
Jeff Pinski

Sourcing, methodology & opinion vs. fact

Factual information contained herein was culled from police records, court documents and transcripts, statements of victims, witnesses and defendants, notes, newspaper clippings and other sources of public and private information. Public sources are identified. At times material was obtained from Dominick D. DiPaolo's memory.

Opinion and private thoughts have been clearly identified as those of the authors, or are obvious to the reader. On rare occasions where no written or oral record, or gaps in the storyline exist, dramatic license is taken and reasonable supposition employed.

As always, every person charged with or suspected of a crime is considered not guilty until proven otherwise through court conviction or guilty plea. Also, rare instances involving individuals not identified in photographs do not connote negativity about those individuals; none is intended.

Authors' note: Post-World War II Erie, Pennsylvania

Erie, Pennsylvania, was no different than any other city or town in sending its sons and daughters to far-flung duty stations, ships and battlefields during World War II.

When Erie's warriors returned, the same post-war culture of prosperity that swept the nation took hold. In many cases this new middle-class economy grew because the GI bill created millions of first generation college graduates who moved into jobs that were not only family-sustaining, but also created discretionary income. In other cases, veterans prospered because the war had cut short the Great Depression. Those who did not avail themselves of higher education returned to their family retail businesses, farms, or factories that now converted back to peace-time manufacturing. Every family needed at least one car, a washing machine and dryer, refrigerator, television set, high fidelity phonograph, and myriad other big ticket products. The nation flourished, and Erie along with it.

It was an amazing time of growth in northwestern Pennsylvania for the next generation. Jobs were plentiful on the industrial front in industries such as General Electric, Hammermill Paper, Zurn Industries, Lord, American Sterilizer, Kaiser, Bucyrus Erie, Marx Toys, Continental Rubber, just to name a few, and literally hundreds of smaller "shops" that dotted Erie's east and west sides, the bayfront and the 12th Street "Industrial Corridor." The dairy and agri-business thrived, as did commercial fishing in a city situated on the shores of Lake Erie, halfway between Cleveland, Ohio, and Buffalo, New York. In those pre-shopping mall days, retail jobs were available in many family-owned businesses that lined State Street, heart of the city's Central Business District, a wide corridor with pedestrian aisles, which ran south from the Public Dock, and separated east Erie from west Erie.

Erie remained a town of about 130,000, occupied by various cultural ethnicities that reflected the successive waves of immigration from the mid-19th century to the mid-20th. Two of the largest groups – Italians and Poles – were often divided according to eastside Polish and westside Italian, although intermarriages were frequent. Catholicism was the predominant and common faith of each group and both thrived in the professions, in education, law enforcement and in politics. Most individuals were hard-working, second generation Americans who raised families, paid taxes, obeyed the laws of the land, and led otherwise productive lives.

Yet, Erie was no different than other similar-sized or larger cities in growing its own ugly subculture of crime. Some of these overt blemishes were connected to nearby "family" controlled mob venues of Buffalo, Cleveland, Youngstown and Pittsburgh, while another dimension was more loosely organized among home-grown societal misfits. Such criminal activity often focused on obtaining an easy buck through burglaries, robberies, illegal drugs and even occasional killings. But gambling – illegal gambling in this time before state-sanctioned daily numbers games and the burgeoning casino business – was king. From the professions to retail stores to schools to shops to even grandmothers with their pennies, nickels, dimes and quarters, thousands of dollars were bet each day on the illegal daily "number," usually appearing in "code" on the newspaper's financial pages, where one and all could see and there could be no misleading bettors. Sports betting was also a huge component of Erie's illegal gambling empire. One who took the risk to facilitate such unlawful gambling was called a "bookmaker," a person who makes "book" on the betting, or in slang, a "bookie." Bookies made their huge profits usually not by betting themselves (although some did), but by charging a commission, or fee, on clients' bets. The commission was known as vigorish or vig. When an occasional bet involved too much money for the local bookie to comfortably handle, it would be "laid off" to a larger illegal gambling operation in a bigger market, such as Pittsburgh or Buffalo. This was the gambling network that existed in Erie and elsewhere following World War II. And what a lucrative business it was! Even after Pennsylvania established the "legal" daily number in the 1970s, the illegal gambling industry found a way to stay in business by increasing clients' profits on successful bets, with payouts greater than those offered by the state.

In this climate, illegal gambling in Erie not only existed, but thrived for decades after the war. This is a story focusing on one such gambling operation, but also on many peripheral illegal activities, the slimy tentacles of this subculture spreading throughout Erie and often beyond during the career of one police detective. Why those from similar backgrounds, those raised in homes emphasizing religious and moral ethics, went in opposite directions either honorable or afoul of the law, is a societal issue best left for sociological debate. But the authors hope you derive as much thought-provoking information about an era and bygone culture as they did in telling about it.

May 2014

Who's Who

The listing below contains the names of every person identified within the following pages according to the positions they held or were known by during the time frame referenced, generally prior to 1990. Although many on this list clearly have been involved in criminal activity, many others are respected laborers within the criminal justice system, or are mentioned in passing with various connections to the central theme, some important, some innocuous, as the story unfolds through the many twists and turns of a lengthy murder investigation. Readers should not infer wrongdoing merely because an individual is listed below, because no such inference is intended unless specifically stated in the accompanying brief descriptors. Many of those listed below also have been included to demonstrate over-arching relationships and non-criminal connections between individuals and families within the City of Erie and Northwestern Pennsylvania; thus, degrees of separation are often far less than six. The authors' sole intention is to provide readers with a positive resource, helpful in identifying the many individuals who occupy the following pages.

A

Abbatto, Isabella – Ricky Cimino's aunt
Adiutori, Dominick "Dee" – Ties to Buffalo mob; store owner
Adiutori, Lidano "Junior" – Erie bookie
Agresti, Thomas – Chief U.S. Bankruptcy Judge
Agresti, Joseph – Erie lawyer
Agresti, Richard – Erie lawyer
Agresti, Charles – Erie lawyer
Allen, Eddie – Erie Detective; Youngstown, Ohio & Santa Anna, California Police Chief; Mafia expert
Allessie, Louie – Convicted murderer
Allessie, Carlo – Erie bookie

Alo, Egilio "Gido" – DiPaolos' friend
Alo, Rose – DiPaolos' friend
Ambrose, Leonard III – Criminal defense attorney
Amendola, Diane DiRenzio – Bank teller
Anderson, Bill – Convicted bookie
Angelo, Gus – Service station owner
Anthony, Fred – Erie County Judge
Aquino, John – Sports Page bartender
Arduini, Angela – Singer
Arkelian, Art – Erie Charity Sports Banquet founder
Armstrong, Richard – Marjorie Diehl's "ex"
Arnone, Anthony "Niggsy" – Convicted bookie, gambler, murder defendant
Arnone, Bernadine – Anthony's wife
Arnone, Liborio "BoBo" – Anthony's father
Arnone, Rose Giamanco-Altadonna – Liborio's wife; Anthony's mother
Auerbach, Arnold "Red" – Boston Celtics owner

B

Bagnoni, David – DiPaolo's Erie detective partner
Bagnoni, David, Jr. – David's son; DiPaolos' Godchild
Bagnoni, Mario "Bags" – Deputy Chief; City Councilman; David Sr.'s father
Baumann, Norman "Bo" – Convicted bank robber
Bellomini, Robert "Bells" – State Representative; convict
Berardi, Arthur – State trooper; Erie Police Director
Berlin, Daniel – Racetrack employee
Berry, Bill – Times Publishing Co. printer; murder victim
Bilotti, Al – Erie School District police officer
Bird, Larry – NBA Hall of Fame
Bizzarro, Lou – Restaurant owner; pro-boxer
Bizzarro, John – Used car lot owner; pro-boxer
Bizzarro, Paul – Towing company owner
Bocci, Bob – Convicted felon
Borowicz, Adam – Frank "Ash Wednesday" Dovishaw's step-father
Borowicz, Flora Gama Dovishaw – "Ash Wednesday's" mother
Bourjaily, Billy – Convicted felon

Bowers, Charles Sr. – Erie Police Chief; Bank Security Chief
Brabender, Robert Jr. – Erie lawyer
Breslin, Jimmy – Author
Bressan, Joseph – Certified Public Accountant
Briska, Karen – Darrell Steiner's girlfriend
Brooks, Dennis – DiPaolos' friend
Brooks, Lucille – DiPaolos' friend
Brasington , J.C. – Erie police officer
Bruno, Dominick – Shoemaker; City Squire Club treasurer
Buchanan, Mary Beth – U.S. Attorney
Bundy, Ted – Convicted serial murderer
Buto, Nick – Erie police officer

C

Caccamo, Carl – Montevecchio gang member
Calabrese, John – Convicted drug dealer
Calabrese, Merchie Sr. – Erie alderman
Calabrese, Merchie Jr. – Convicted bank robber, drug dealer
Calandra, John – Cleveland mobster
Cambra, David – Found Erie Police Cpl. Robert Owen's body
Carabbia, Charles "Charlie the Crab" – Youngstown mob
Carabbia, Orlie – Youngstown mob; hired Dorler for mob hit
Carabbia, Ronald "Ronnie Crab" – Youngstown mob; convicted murderer
Carideo, Richard – Sports Page co-owner
Carlo, Mavis Thompson Montevecchio – Caesar Montevecchio's first wife
Carney, Edward – Erie County President Judge
Ceraso, Thomas – Greensburg, Pa., criminal defense lawyer
Charboneau, Joe – Major league baseball star
Chase, Robert – Erie County District Attorney
Chism, Donald – Erie convicted mass murderer
Cimino, Ricky – Convicted hired arsonist (Pal Joey's)
Cimino, Robert – Ricky's father
Ciotti, Anthony "Cy" Jr. – Convicted felon;
Ciotti, Anthony "Tony" Sr., – Cy's father

Cisternino, Pasquale "Butchie" – Ferritto's Greene murder accomplice
Clanton, Melvin – Murder victim
Clark, Ramsey – U.S. Attorney General; DiNicola defense counsel
Claus, Lawrence – Pa. Attorney General's office
Colograndе, Sebastian "Bashi" – Convicted bookmaker
Colograndе, David – Arnone, Dovishaw convicted faked robbery participant
Concilla, Condita "Candi" Montevecchio – Caesar's sister
Connelly, Shad – Erie County Judge
Connelly, Jeff – Cambra's lawyer
Connelly, Bill – Pa. Attorney General's office
Cononico, Jim "Peeps" – Ohio murder victim
Corleone, Vito "Don" – "The Godfather"
Costello, Donna – Joe Scutella Jr.'s girlfriend
Coughlin, Wally – Catholic Youth Organization basketball coach
Cousey, Bob – NBA Hall of Fame star
Cousins, John "Jack" – Erie Police Detective Chief
Covelli, Sam – Entrepreneur

D

Dahmer, Jeffrey – Convicted serial killer
D'Alba, Jay – Theresa Mastrey's lawyer
Daley, Chuck – Pennsylvania State Police Task Force
Dalton, Joy – DiPaolos' friend
Dalton, Kevin – Pat DiPaolo's friend
Dalton Ron – DiPaolos' friend
Damore, Al – Restaurant owner; convicted bookie; cocaine dealer
Damore, Art – Restaurant owner
Damore, Lundy – Restaurant owner
D'Andrea, Donald "Jungles" – City Squire Club employee
Darrow, Clarence – Widely known defense attorney
DeBello, Alfred – Convicted bank robber
DeDad, Sam – Store owner
DeDad, Tony – Store owner
DeDionisio, Paul Jr. – Erie Police Chief
DeDionisio, Raymond – Deputy Erie Police Chief

DeFranco, Anthony "Tone Capone" – Convicted murderer
DelSandro, Alfred "Big Al" – Major Erie convicted bookmaker
DelSandro, David – "Big Al's" son; convicted bookie
DelSandro, Rose – "Val's" wife; DiPaolo's Godmother
DelSandro, Roseann "Roe" Giamanco-Altadonna – Convicted bookie
DelSandro, Valdo "Val" – Tavern owner; DiPaolo's Godfather
DeMauro, Tony – "Ten percenter"
DeRose, Joey Jr. – Ohio murder victim
DeRose, Joey Sr. – Ohio murder victim
DeRose, Renee – Dawn DiPaolo's friend
DeSanti, John "Johnny D" – Longtime Erie school teacher
DeSantis, Billy—"Fat Sam" Esper gang member
DeSantis, Frank – *Erie Daily Times* sports editor
Detisch, Father John – Parish priest
Diehl, Marjorie – Convicted murderer
Dillinger, John – Mobster; referenced by Montevecchio in court
Dillon, Leo – Assistant U.S. Attorney
DiMarco, Dino – Bookie; Dovishaw numbers writer
DiNicola, Ron – Attorney; brother of Louis
DiNicola, Louis – Convicted, then acquitted of triple murder
DiNicola, Marian Schwartz Mello DeSantis Maggio – Convicted bookie
Dinsio, Amil – Convicted felon; bank break-in specialist
Dinsio, James – Convicted felon; bank break-in specialist
DiPaolo, Dominick – Erie Police Detective Sergeant; District Judge
DiPaolo, Janet – Dominick's wife; hair stylist
DiPaolo, Mary "Babe" Pallotto – Dominick's mother
DiPaolo, Pasquale "Pat" – Dominick's father
DiPaolo, Patrick – DiPaolos' son
DiPasquale, Vinnie – Convicted drug dealer
Dodd, Charles – West Va. Sheriff; convicted drug dealer
Dominick, Chico – Pool hall owner
Dominick, Mike – Pool hall owner
Dominick, Sam – Pool hall owner
Dorler, Robert – Two-time convicted hit man
Dovishaw, Frank "Bolo" "Ash Wednesday" – Bookie; murder victim
Dovishaw, Frank Sr. – "Ash Wednesday's" father
Dovishaw, Joan Szczesny Bachofner – "Ash Wednesday's" wife

Dunford, Donald – Erie Police Identification Unit officer
Dunlavey, Michael – Erie County Judge; U.S. Army General
Duran, Roberto "Hands of Stone" – boxing champion

E

Earll, Jane – Assistant District Attorney; State Senator
Ebert, M.L. "Skip" – Pa. Attorney General's office; prosecutor
Erickson, Charles Sr. – Erie Police Captain
Esper, Samuel "Fat Sam" – Convicted felon; witness protection program
Esposito, James – Lawyer; convicted drug dealer
Euliano, Gerry – DiPaolos' friend
Euliano, John – DiPaolos' friend
Evans, Elmer – Erie County Judge

F

Faraha, Ronnie – Cleveland mobster; convicted drug dealer
Farbo, Michael – "Fat Sam" Esper gang member
Fasenmyer, John – Charged with bribery, illegal wire tap
Ferrante, Armand "Peppy" – Dovishaw, Ferritto friend
Ferrare, Frank – Arnone employee
Ferritto, Raymond "Ray Marciano" – Admitted Erie hit man; bookie
Ferritto, Bernie – Ferritto's wife
Ferritto, Roseann – Ferritto's daughter
Ferritto, Victor – Ferritto's son
Fillinger, Halbert "Homicide Hal," M.D. – Forensic pathologist
Fischer, Sister Nancy, SSJ – Sacred Heart Church
Fischer, Roger – Erie County Judge
Fitzgerald, Judith Guldenborth – Assistant U.S. Attorney; U.S. District Judge
Fleming, Harry – Convicted murderer; burglar; fence
Folga, John - Erie County deputy sheriff
Forte, Fabian – 1950s/1960s teen singing idol
Fossesca, Samuel "Skinny Sam" – Ohio mobster; hit man
Foulk, Bradley – Erie County District Attorney

Frantino, John – Pittsburgh mobster
Fratianno, Jimmy "The Weasel" – Calif. mobster; West Coast "Don"
Freeman, Donald – Michigan Circuit Court Judge
Frye, Evelyn – Louis Nardo's girlfriend
Fuller, Lee – Erie attorney
Funt, Daniel – Convicted murderer

G

Gaeta, Joseph "The General" – DiPaolo friend
Gajewski, Walter "Butch" – Erie Detective Sergeant; DiPaolo's partner
Gama, Mary Fabian – "Ash Wednesday's" Aunt
Gama, Debbie – Teenaged murder victim
Gambatese, Anthony "Tony Gams" Jr. – Bookie
Garfield, Allen – Beating victim
Garhart, John – Erie County Judge
Gemelli, Samuel – Erie Police Chief
Giacalone, Anthony "Tony Jack" – "Made" mob member
Giacalone, Joseph – Montevecchio crime partner
Giamanco-Altadonna, Amelia "Maya" – Convicted bookie
Goodwill, Robert "Goodie" – Erie Police officer
Grassi, David – Erie Police Detective Sergeant
Gravano, Sammy "The Bull" – John Gotti's "capo"
Greene, Daniel "The Irishman" – Ferritto murder victim
Gross, Charlie – Business owner
Grybowski, Clara – City Squire Club board member
Grybowski, Pearl – Convicted bank robber; drug dealer
Guaranti, Bobby – Montevecchio gang member
Gunter, Donald "D.C." – DiPaolo's Erie police detective partner

H

Hamilton, Billy – Youngstown, Ohio, FBI agent
Harkins, Bernard "Babe" – Erie City Councilman
Haskins, James – Erie County deputy sheriff
Hazen, Gene – Calif. wise guy
Herbstritt, Rick "Snowy" – CYO basketball coach
Heuser, Craig – Deacon; DiPaolos' friend

Hirsch, Irvin – Michigan jewelry store owner
Hoffa, James "Jimmy" Sr. – Vanished union leader
Hooker, George – Pennsylvania State Police Trooper
Hunter, David – Cimino's former Erie attorney

I

Iannello, Frank "Frankie Day" – Joe Rotunda associate
Iesue, Emilio "Mickey" – DiPaolos' neighbor

J

Jabo, Harry – Pennsylvania State Police Task Force
Jellison, Virgil "Butch" – Pennsylvania State Police ballistics expert
Jolly, Loren – Montevecchio gang member
Jiuliante, Jess II – Erie County Judge
Juarez, John "Chino" – Montevecchio gang member

K

Kennedy, John F. – U.S. President
Kennedy, R. Gordon – Erie County District Attorney
King, Raymond – Erie Police Identification Unit officer
Kinnane, James "Jim" – Longtime Erie FBI agent
Kinsman, Charles – Montevecchio gang member
Kovalesky, Raymond – Erie school teacher
Kownacki, Joseph – Erie County Public Defender
Kozak, David, Ph.D. – Gannon University professor; political analyst
Kroto, Frank – Erie County Assistant District Attorney
Kuhn, Norman – Erie Police Detective Sergeant
Kupczyk, Jenny – Dawn DiPaolo Romeo's friend
Kwitowski, Frank – Erie Police Detective Captain

L

LaRocca, John – Pittsburgh crime family head
Laskaris, John Peter – Convicted felon
Lawrence, David – Pennsylvania governor
Leamy, William "Bill" – Erie Police officer

LeFaiver, Elliot – Erie Alderman
Leone, Fiore – Longtime Erie County Councilman
Levin, George – Erie County Judge
Levis, Donald – Erie Police Detective Lieutenant
Lewandowski, Vincent – Erie Police officer who often assisted DiPaolo
Lewis, Donald – Crawford County District Attorney; Asst. U.S. Attorney; author
Liberatore, Tony "Lib" – Cleveland, Ohio, "wise guy"
Licavoli, James "Jack White" – Cleveland crime family leader
Ligambi, Joseph "Uncle Joe" – Philadelphia mobster
Logue, Tony – Erie County Probation Officer, Public Defender; DiPaolo's friend
Logue, Anthony Jr. – Tony's son; DiPaolos' Godson
Lombardo, Carl "Warpie" – Convicted bookie
Lonardo, Angelo "Big Ange" – Cleveland mob leader
Lucas, Tim – Erie County Assistant District Attorney
Luppino, Giacomo, D.M.D. – Erie dentist
Lupu, John – Convicted felon

M

MacDonell, Herbert, M.D. – Nationally recognized blood spatter expert
Maggadino, Stefano – Head of Buffalo, N.Y., crime family
Maggio, Michael "Jazza Mike" – Convicted bookie
Maggio, Fredrico "Freddie May," aka Bill DeMarco – Convicted felon
Manendo, Louis – Erie city employee
Mannarino, Gabriel "Kelly" – New Kensington mobster
Mantle, Mickey – New York Yankees baseball star
"Marcoline" Brothers – Dorler's claimed Ohio firearms supplier
Marino, Carmen – Cuyahoga County prosecutor in Danny Greene murder
Marnen, Ted – Erie Police officer
Maruca, Steve – Montevecchio gang member
Mastrostefano, Donald (Mastrey) – Convicted bookie; Dovishaw numbers writer
Mastrostefano, Theresa (Mastrey) – PennBank official
Matson, Augustine – Certified Public Accountant
McCammon, Christine (Chastity) – Dovishaw's girlfriend

McClelland, Lindley – Erie County Judge
McCurdy, Charles "Cubby" – Erie Police Detective Captain
McShane, Gerald – Erie Police Detective Sergeant; DiPaolo's partner
Meeks, George – Convicted armed robber
Michails, Aziz – Cleveland mobster; attempted murder victim
Mifsud, Jerry – School administrator; Erie City Councilman
Miller, Grant – Jack Miller's son
Miller, Jack – Convicted bookie; armed robbery victim; business owner
Miller, James "Mills" – DiPaolo's friend
Miller, Jean – Jack Miller's wife
Miller, Ralph – Jewelry store owner
Miller, Theresa "Tree" Giamanco-Altadonna – Convicted bookie
Minedeo, Victor – Burglar
Mischler, Forrest, M.D. – Examined Pal Joey's arsonist
Monroe, Marilyn – 1950s/1960s movie star
Montevecchio, Albert – Caesar's brother
Montevecchio, Bonnie – Caesar's wife
Montevecchio, Caesar – Convicted burglar, armed robber, murder set-up man
Montevecchio, Carmen – Caesar's brother
Montevecchio, Carmine – Caesar's father
Montevecchio, Tilba Sambuchino – Caesar's mother
Moore, John – Criminal defense attorney (Dorler)
Morabito, Dominick – Business owner
Morabito, Patsy – Business owner; DiPaolo's uncle
Murphy, Tom – Pittsburgh mayor

N

Nagosky, Richard – Millcreek Township police officer
Naples, Joey – Ohio murder victim
Nardo, Louis "Nardino" – Burglary/armed robbery victim
Needham, Janet – Murder victim
Northrup, Cindy – Ricky Cimino's girlfriend, caregiver; perjurer
Nuara, Kelli Scutella – Joe Jr.'s daughter
Nuara, Ron – Kelli's husband; provided Pal Joey's arson fire information
Nygaard, Richard – Erie County Judge; U.S. Circuit Court Judge

O

Oligieri, Art – Ruby Port band member
Orlando, Michael – Erie Funeral Director
Orlando, Q. Gregory – Erie County Court Administrator; DiPaolo's friend
Orlando, Quentin, Dr. – Erie City Councilman; Pennsylvania State Senator
Owen, Robert – Erie Police corporal; murder victim
Owen Jane – Corporal Owen's wife

P

Padovani, Dominick "Uncle Paddy" – Convicted bookmaker
Palermo, Nick "Fat Nicky" – Convicted bank robber
Palilla, Anna Giamanco-Altadonna – Theresa Mastrey's mother
Palilla, Frank – Theresa Mastrey's father
Palilla, Salvatore – Theresa Mastrey's brother; Arnone employee
Pallotto, Peter – Sports Page co-owner
Palmer, Edward – John Laskaris' partner
Palmisano, Michael – Erie County Judge
Paolello, Anthony – Convicted murderer
Pape, John – Garage owner
Paradise, Alice – "Blackie" wife
Paradise, John "Blackie" – Convicted multiple felon
Parry, Thomas – Erie school teacher; football coach; convicted bank robber
Payne, Raymond – Erie school teacher; convicted murderer
Pella, Carol – Longstanding WSEE-TV investigative reporter
Perfetto, James "Doc" – Erie police K-9 officer
Petro, Julius – One of hit man Ray Ferritto's murder victims
Pfadt, William – Erie County Judge
Pfannenschmidt, Dennis – Pa. Attorney General's Office attorney
Piesacki, John – Pa. Attorney General's Office agent
Pietrzak, Ellen – Convicted drug "mule"; Robert's wife
Pietrzak, Robert – Erie police officer; convicted drug "mule"
Polito, Bob – DiPaolos' friend
Pollock, Donald – Erie police officer
Presley, Elvis – Recording & film superstar

Provenzano, Anthony "Tony Pro" – Mob "made" member/wise guy
Puckett, Glenn – Convicted murderer
Puskar, Julie – Dovishaw bookie

R

Raffa, Louie "Lumpy Lou" – Cleveland mobster
Remek, Renee – Dorler trial defense attorney
Renault, Louis – *Casablanca* police captain
Riazzi, Rollo "Rags" – Convicted bookie
Richmond, Hyle – Longtime WICU-TV news anchorman/reporter
Ridge, Tom – Lawyer; Congressman; Pa. governor; Homeland Security Secretary
Rieger, Billy – Montevecchio gang member
Rigazzi, Toby – Erie police officer; Erie County deputy sheriff
Robbins, Greg – Patricia's son; DiPaolo's nephew
Robbins, Patricia DiPaolo – DiPaolo's sister
Robbins, Tim – Patricia's son; DiPaolo's nephew
Robinson, Edward G. – Star of movie, *Little Caesar*
Romeo, Dawn DiPaolo – DiPaolos' daughter
Romeo, Frank A. – Barber
Ross, Bobby – Erie Police Detective Sergeant
Ross, John "J.R." – Erie County Detective
Rothstein, William – "Set-up" man; educator
Rotunda, Frank – Erie police officer; convicted felon
Rotunda, Joe – Multiple convicted felon
Rotunda, Joseph "Jimmy" Jr. – Convicted "con" man
Rotunda, Tim – Convict
Rotunda, Tommy – After-hours club operator; bookie
Rowley, James – Pa. Superior Court Judge
Russell, James – Esper gang, convicted felon
Russell, Peter – Esper gang, convicted felon

S

Salamone, James "Westfield Jimmy" – Reputed mobster
Salarino, Arlene – Ricky Cimino's friend
Salarino, Mike – Ricky Cimino's friend
Santaguida, Joseph – Philadelphia defense lawyer (Arnone)

Santorma, Mary – Florida police officer
Satelli, Silvio "Si" – Drug dealer
Scarfaro, Nicodemo – Philadelphia crime family head
Scalise, Frank "Foops" – Bookie
Scalise, Frank C. – Business owner; armed robbery victim
Schlosser, Kara – Dawn DiPaolo's friend
Schneider, Tom – Cleveland-based ATF agent
Schwartz, Frank – Erie police detective sergeant
Sciarrilli, Ron – Ricky Cimino's cousin
Scutella, Dan – Convicted felon
Scutella, Ernie – Pa. state employee; Joe Jr.'s nephew
Scutella, Frank – Assistant Erie County District Attorney
Scutella, Giuseppe (Joseph Sr.) – Convicted of indecent assault; Joe Jr.'s father
Scutella, James, Jr. – Son of James, Sr.; Los Angeles, Calif., police officer
Scutella, James, Sr. – Brother of Joe Jr.; forge worker
Scutella, Joseph Jr. – Convicted drug dealer; arsonist; RICO charges
Scutella, Joseph III – Son of Joe Jr.; listed as Pal Joey's owner
Scutella, Margie – Wife of Joe Jr.
Senger, Bill "Dutch" – School teacher, bartender
Senzarino, Dominick Jr. – Ohio murder victim
Serafini, Charles "The Hawk" – Montevecchio gang member
Serpico, Frank – NYC police officer
Shanahan, Pat – Erie police detective sergeant
Shatto, Linda – "Cy" Ciotti's girlfriend
Siegel, Bernard "Bernie" – Asst. Erie County DA; DiNicola prosecutor
Simpson, O.J. – NFL superstar; convict
Sinatra, Frank Jr. – Singer; superstar Frank Sinatra's son
Sinito, Tommy – Reputed Cleveland mobster
Sisson, Charlene – City Squire Club officer
Skonieczka, Alois – Erie police officer; Erie County Prison Warden
Skonieczka, Richard – Erie Police Chief
Smith, Charles – Convicted bank robber
Soccoccio, Michael "Mike Sockett" – Bookie
Soffredine, Ralph – Michigan probation officer
Spadafore, Anthony "Donald" – Convicted drug dealer; RICO Act
Spadafore, John – Convicted drug dealer; RICO Act
Spadafore, Ralph—Convicted drug dealer; RICO Act
Stanley, James "Shorty" – Murder victim

Stanton, Thomas – Erie police captain
Steiner, Darrell – Ricky Cimino's driver
Stellato, Carl "Satch" – Nardo burglary "middleman"
Stuck, Ronald – District Court Judge
Szumigala, Ben "Benny Zoom" – Deli owner

T

Taft, Mark – Murder victim
Taft, Roger – Erie lawyer
Thomas, Charles – Police informant; victim, attempted murder
Thomas, Frank "Frank Romeo" – Greene murder immunity; witness protection
Thomas, James "Fizz" – Convicted drug dealer
Thomas, Jeannie – Dovishaw/Ferritto convicted bookmaker
Thomas, Ronnie – Convicted drug dealer
Thompson, Jim – *Erie Daily Times* reporter
Tobin, Dennis – Erie police deputy chief
Tomassi, Dana – Fredrico's daughter
Tomassi, Fredrico "Freddy Thomas" – Restaurant/business owner
Tomassi, Dr. Rick – Fredrico's son; podiatrist
Tomassi, Susan DeSantis DeMichele Murosky Ferritto – Erie city employee; escort
Timko, Andy – Co-owner, Tim & Del's
Torrelli, Phil – Dovishaw bookmaking partner
Tracy, Walter "Skip" – Esper gang member
Travers, Dickie – DiPaolos' friend
Travers, Sue – DiPaolos' friend
Troop, Jimmy – Convicted felon
Troop, Larry – Convicted felon
Tullio, Louis – Longtime Erie mayor

V

Valachi, Joe – Mobster turned informant
Valli, Frankie – Four Seasons lead singer
Vella, Peter – Convicted felon
Vendetti, Alex "Jiggs" – Convicted bookmaker
Vendetti, Chester – Erie lawyer

Vendetti, John – Alex's son; District Court Judge
Vendetti, Richard – Erie lawyer
Veshecco, Michael – Erie County District Attorney
Vorsheck, William – Hypnotist

W

Wandless, James – Frank C. Scalise's son-in-law; DiPaolo's friend
Ward, Hank – Strip bar owner
Ward, Bruce – Two-time convicted murderer; death row
Weber, Gerald – U.S. District Court Judge
Wecht, Cyril, M.D. – Nationally known pathologist
Weichler, William – Criminal defense attorney ("Tone Capone")
Weindorf, Joseph – Erie police detective sergeant; District Court Judge
Wells, Brian – Murder victim
White, John "Pigeon" – City Squire worker
Wieczorek, Robert "Wizz" – Pat DiPaolo's friend
Willis, Hobie – Bank robber
Winiecke, Tammy – Perjurer
Wisinski, Kenneth – Newspaper carrier Michelle's father
Wisinski, Michele – Newspaper carrier
Wood, Merle – Longtime Erie County Coroner
Woolis, Rito – Erie police detective sergeant

X

Xenakis, Manuel "Mike the Greek" – Bookmaker; Ferritto's later partner

Y

Yacobozzi, Andrew "Booty" – Erie police officer
Yoculan, Paul "Paul Younger" – Performer
Young, Patty DeSantis – Drug convict

Z

Zimbalist, Efrem, Jr. – Actor; starred in *FBI* TV series
Zimmerman, LeRoy – Pennsylvania Attorney General

Part One

THE CRIME – *"BOLO DON'T WANT THE PAPER NO MORE"*

CHAPTER 1

CHASTITY WAS PISSED.

Bolo was late. Again.

And now her anger was tempered only slightly by worry. Was she about to be blown off by her one and only repulsive sugar daddy in this God-forsaken icebox of a town?

Not only had business been slow at the Bootlegger Lounge, but the few regulars who bothered to show up seemed more interested in the Monday night football game blaring from the smoke-stained wall-mounted color television set than in her augmented, Size 38, triple-D breasts – even minus the pasties.

Not that their attitude was all that surprising. Chastity had long-known she was no knock-out. Missing a tooth or two from a motorcycle club brawl in Buffalo several years earlier, Chastity's only remarkable feature was a small tattoo of a scrubby marijuana plant on her now flat ass. She always knew she'd never be a strip-joint headliner in a major city, or even a back-up chorus-line girl out west.

But she had the moves, slow, seductive pole-dancing moves that drew more than appreciative cat-calls, as well as all those one-dollar tips knowingly stuffed into her thong. At least she usually managed to land short gigs in small towns.

Plus, if she was lucky and played her cards right with the potential one-night-standers, she'd find a sugar daddy in the pack to shack-up with, one who would gladly supplement her twenty-five dollars a night, plus tips. Not bad. And maybe even score some local white powder to boot. No, not bad indeed. Only tonight, with frigid air and threatening snowfall keeping most of the die-hard regulars in front of their home RCAs, the tips had been minimal at best. And Hank Ward's cheap well booze and tap beer seemed even more disgusting to her cocaine-numbed tongue than usual. God, how did she end up in the asshole of the world, she thought, wallowing in pity for herself, her surroundings, her predicament, her life.

Still, despite Erie's reputation for long winter nights and some of the cheapest customers around, 28-year-old Chastity wasn't all that worried. At least not yet. It was a new year –1983 – and she had a brand new squeeze to go with it. At least for a short while. Overweight and sweaty with bad breath and a gross birthmark in the center of his forehead, there was little about Bolo Dovishaw that Chastity actually enjoyed. He was only a wannabe wise guy, just a street punk who never got made by the mob.

At five feet eight inches in street shoes, Dovishaw tipped the scales at 240 pounds and, at 46, was 18 years her senior. He was a fat, old slob. His so-called friends called him "Porky Pig," often ridiculing him to his face and also behind his enormous back. Aside from his overall physical unattractiveness, he was a lifelong shameless braggart, the kind most individuals simply can't stand being around for long.

Chastity had been around the horn and back since she was 15 and had seen his type before. Many times. Bolo talked the talk, sure, but with little or no substance or stature behind any of his words or frequent boasts. Yet, if an occasional unsatisfying toss in the sack with the fat prick would help pay the bills, then so be it, Chastity thought. After all, she had been with worse. Indeed. Much worse.

Besides, if there was even a little truth to his bragging about having stashed away several hundred thousand grand from his betting business, then, who knows, maybe she could get her hands on some of it before her gig in Erie ended and she moved on to the next dump of a nightspot in Rochester or Akron or Youngstown.

Bolo had promised to call immediately after kickoff and the betting had stopped. That was more than an hour ago. It started snowing again since then. Frigging "Lake Effect" snow, she thought. Ah, but maybe she would soon score a gig that would be way down south.

Maybe Norfolk with all the sailors. Or Savannah. Or anywhere. Anywhere but fucking Erie.

Now it was almost 11. Chastity was growing more furious by the minute. No poontang for him tonight, she smiled to herself. Zero. Zip. Nada. Still, she waited. Christine McCammon, "stage" name, Chastity, waited.

Five hours earlier and several miles to the south of the Bootlegger Lounge, Kenneth Wisinski, an impatient man at best, once again drove his car slowly past Frank "Bolo" Dovishaw's West 21st Street house. Wisinski had been obsessing over Dovishaw for days now. On this night, he was chauffeuring his son and a neighbor kid to a Boy Scout meeting. But Wisinski had more on his mind this night. Much more.

Wisinski had been slowly cruising past Bolo's house for several weeks, trying to catch the local reputed bookmaker at home, but never succeeding. Wisinski's daughter, 13-year-old Michele, was Bolo Dovishaw's newspaper carrier. The girl had been having a difficult time collecting the $21 Dovishaw owed her. Like any good father, Wisinski decided to take matters upon himself.

"Everyone knows this guy is a gangster," Wisinski mused. "But, y'know, fuck it, pay the kid! He's got all kinds of money." No sir, not even a gangster would be allowed to stiff *his* kid.

Wisinski knew Dovishaw drove a big, green Cadillac and each time he drove past Bolo's house, he looked for the familiar status ride, but apparently either the car was in the shop or Bolo was hardly ever at home. Now, as he slowly wheeled past the house for the umpteenth time, the green Caddy passed Wisinski's car in the other direction. The good father, in his rear view mirror, watched with some satisfaction as the Caddy pulled into Dovishaw's driveway. *Gotcha!*

After dropping off the boys at the nearby Blessed Sacrament Church for their scout session, Wisinski vowed to head back to Dovishaw's to collect the money owed Michele. Gangster or not, Wisinski wasn't prepared to come away empty-handed.

Bolo Dovishaw would never know about Kenneth Wisinski's determination.

At exactly 6 p.m. that evening, Bolo guided the big car into the driveway and entered his home with three hours to spare before the last NFL Monday night game of the season. Despite the modest digs in the heart of Erie's famous "Little Italy" neighborhood, Frank "Bolo" Dovishaw appeared to be a happy fellow that night. He lived rent-free in a house once owned by his mother. He drove a late-model, green Cadillac Deville. He was still on fairly good terms with Joan, his wife, although they had been separated for years. He ran one of the most successful and lucrative sports-betting books in Northwestern, Pennsylvania. And, he was banging that weird broad, Chastity, at Hank Ward's strip joint. Weird or not, Bolo thought, there definitely would be more Chastity banging later that night.

As if life wasn't already terrific enough, Bolo, always hungry, was about to scarf down one of Al Damore's awesome meatball subs. Al Damore's Pizza Shop carried the traditional cheese and pepperoni fare, along with wings, salads and subs. For Bolo, Al always stuck in an extra meatball or two. Cocaine, however, was a special order.

At the midway point of his 5th decade, and after serving a stint in prison for robbery, albeit a staged phony one, and later a gig with the Federal Witness Protection Program after turning snitch, life was finally turning good for the previous life-long loser. Too bad for poor Bolo, he'd have only a few minutes to enjoy Damore's sub – and, for that matter, the rest of his life.

At least, Bolo would not die hungry.

CHAPTER 2

Less than a block away from Bolo's digs, a well-dressed figure stepped out of the car and into the dark, brisk, cold night, tugging up the collar of his topcoat – black, velvet collar, the same kind you'd see the characters wearing in the Godfather movies. But this one was playing no movie role. This guy was real. Deadly real.

He moved slightly away from of the car, but did not close the door. His raspy voice as frosty as the air, he whispered to the driver, "Meet you later." Then he slammed shut the door, turned and slowly walked away, trying hard to keep his black, pointy wing-tips out of Erie's filthy street slush.

The driver breathed deeply for a few moments, smiled, then jammed his right foot hard on the accelerator, the wheels spinning in the snow and slush, and quickly sped away, headed in the direction of a nearby Erie sports bar. After all, it was Monday night and there was football to watch. But football this night was the last thing on this driver's mind. There was an alibi to establish.

Meanwhile, the ominous figure in the black overcoat was already familiar with West 21st Street, even in the dark. For a week he'd scoped out and cased the street – and the house numbered 1634. He buttoned his coat over the black suit and tie, then jammed his gloveless hands into the overcoat's deep pockets. In his right pocket, his fingers surrounded a familiar object, a .32 caliber Italian Beretta semi-automatic pistol. The metal was still warm to the cold touch of his fingers. He relaxed, almost comfortable. He had done this before. This won't take that long, he thought, already fantasizing over how he might spend the blood money.

In front of 1634 West 21st Street, the figure with the menacing aura paused for only a second. Even in the mostly dark neighborhood, the nearby streetlight illuminated his steamy breath in the cold night air. The Caddy was in the driveway. Inside the house, the lights were on. It looked welcoming. Warm and cheery on a cold night. He checked his watch. 6:15 p.m. Then he smirked. The professional hit man climbed the three unshoveled front steps, kicked the snow from his shoes, took a deep breath and rang the doorbell.

Several minutes earlier, having dropped off his book-making partner at the partner's home, Bolo had arrived at his own West 21st Street house an even three hours before kick-off. His "clients" were already starting to phone in their bets, and Bolo knew he'd only have a few minutes at most to devour the sub before Monday Night Football's pre-game betting got so fast and furious that he'd be able to do little else than take those bets until just before kick-off.

It had been a good weekend for college football gambling, given the holiday bowl games and propensity of Erie's bettors to try to score big at the end of the season to make up for their earlier, sometimes massive, seasonal gambling losses.

This night's pro game between the Cowboys and Vikings, the last regular season game, meant nothing in the standings, but it would be a great warm-up for the coming weekend's NFL playoffs, Dovishaw thought. The off-the-field action would be good, very good. His take this night could be in the thousands, even after pay-outs to the winners. First, though, there was Al's meatball sub to enjoy, but not savor. Like everything else he did, Dovishaw savored little, exploring life through crude gulps, belches and gross flatulence.

The phone rang.

Bolo didn't answer. His mouth was stuffed with a half-chewed mush of bread, ground beef, provolone cheese and Al's tangy marinara sauce. But that was okay. He knew he wasn't losing money by not answering. He knew that on the fourth ring, the call automatically would transfer to a house several blocks away. That kid, Victor, would take the bet. What a perfect set-up! The phone was on a relay system, high-tech for the time. The General Telephone Company only charged him an extra couple of bucks a month for the service. Ha. If they only knew, Dovishaw thought with typical greedy satisfaction.

He also chuckled over his set-up with Ray. Who would have thought, or even believed it? Bolo Dovishaw in partnership with Erie's most notorious hit man – the ice-blooded Raymond Ferritto. It was why Bolo could afford to feel so brave. With Ray as his bookie partner, who'd mess with Bolo? Who would ever fuck with Ray? No one. That's who.

Bolo's noisy chomping, an idyllic reverie to him, was broken, however, not by the ringing phone, but by the intruding door bell. What the hell, Dovishaw thought. Now what?

Still wearing the rubber overshoes from his earlier outing with Ray Ferritto, Bolo padded to the front door. Through the window he could see it was a well-dressed man wearing an expensive topcoat. It could not have been a new client. Bolo never allowed clients at his home. They were to make book by phone, not in person. Dovishaw was not pleased. And, if this was a shill or salesperson, well, he'll send this meatball sub intruder packing quickly.

Bolo opened the door a crack.

"Yeah?"

"You Frank Dovishaw?"

In typical fashion, he responded, "Who the fuck wants to know?"

Frank "Bolo" Dovishaw would never find out.

Kenneth Wisinski dropped off the boys at the church, told them he'd be back at 8 o'clock, then swung his car north from West 26th Street to West 21st Street – Bolo Dovishaw's street. Wisinski was both confident and determined. As he drove, he thought about just how pleased Michele would be when he forked over the money Dovishaw owed her. Just the thought of his daughter's smile made him drive faster.

CHAPTER 3

HOLY MOTHER OF GOD!

Bolo Dovishaw thought he might have actually shrieked the words. But in reality, no sound had come out.

"I said – *inside*! Now!" ordered the well-dressed guy at the door as his gun's barrel almost touched Bolo's horrified face.

Smirking again, the gunman delighted, in a purely sadistic way, in pushing the terrified Dovishaw back into his house. The man was a born bully at heart. A bully with a gun. It always worked. And he was having fun.

"Please don't hurt me," Bolo pleaded as the gunman forced him to the floor, spread-eagled, and patted him down.

Funny, the intruder thought. Big wheels were all the same. Phonies. They all behaved the same way in the face of fear: Whining. Begging. Pleading.

"On your feet," the gunman ordered, making his voice even more ominous. With the Beretta to Dovishaw's head, he was clearly enjoying himself as he now forced the trembling fat man down the cellar stairs and into the typically dank basement.

"On the floor," he motioned.

Face down on the cold, hard concrete, Dovishaw now began to whimper and sob.

"Please, take whatever you want!" he cried out. "Just don't hurt me! Please!"

With a rack of women's dresses nearby, perhaps those having once belonged to Flora, Dovishaw's deceased mother, the man pulled two flowered belts and quickly bound Bolo's hands and feet with a sailor's degree of knot-tying expertise. Yes, he had done this before.

"Please!" Dovishaw again begged. "Take anything! My money is in my pocket. Take it all. But please don't hurt me!"

The cruel-faced man in the black top coat was now really enjoying this part. He always did.

"Any other money in the house?" the man demanded, his voice almost a growl.

"No, no – nothing." Bolo was now bawling.

"Don't fuck with me, Dovishaw! What about your bathroom vanity hiding place?"

Dovishaw's pounding heart almost skipped a beat. Bolo felt the cold barrel of the gun against the back of his neck. Despite his terror, he thought of another robbery three years earlier where the gunmen knew about his bathroom vanity hiding place. It had been an inside job. And now in a sudden epiphany moment, Dovishaw knew with a chill that this was, too.

"Oh, yeah. There. Maybe a couple of bucks. That's all."

"And what about your car keys?"

"On the table near the front door."

"Where are your bank safe-deposit box keys?" the man demanded.

"They're around, somewhere," Bolo stupidly ventured, now angering the intruder.

"I told you not to fuck with me, Fatso." It was almost a whisper. "Where are the keys!"

It was a loud demand.

"In my other pocket!" Bolo quickly caved. "Just take them!"

The man let out a breath, reached into Bolo's trousers and smiled. How easy it had been!

Dovishaw began to allow himself to think that now everything would be okay.

He had cooperated. The stranger had what he wanted and would now just leave. Bolo would soon be back to taking bets from his real "clients." And he would report this intruder to Ray, his protector. Ray would handle it from there.

"Nothing personal, Bolo," the man broke through Dovishaw's daydream. "But get on your knees."

Dovishaw seemed to grasp what was coming. Openly weeping, he complied.

Now the gunman looked around the dank basement. Ah! He saw what he had been searching for. He grabbed the worn throw-rug at the bottom of the basement stairs, folded it several times and placed it against the back of Bolo's head with the .32 Beretta actually touching the rug.

Sweet Jesus!

"Please!" Dovishaw wailed. "Don't! Please! Don't!"

The stranger smiled, almost sardonically – he had what he had come for. He easily pulled the trigger.

Watching with almost detached satisfaction as Dovishaw crumpled to the floor in a clump with an ugly thump, the shooter smiled again.

The killer covered Bolo's unmoving body with a sheet from the laundry basket, then unfolded the rug and placed it over Dovishaw as well.

Back upstairs, the man found Dovishaw's secret bathroom money stash, pocketed several thousand dollars, then searched the home for more. Finding nothing else worth his interest, he grabbed the Caddy's keys, then returned to the basement and pulled the rug and sheet from Dovishaw's body.

Fuck.

Suddenly, the intruder had the uneasy feeling Bolo was not yet dead. Although he had no formal medical training, from past experience the shooter had come to understand that the "hit" was not dead until he had urinated and defecated. Dovishaw had done neither.

Trudging back upstairs again, he found a rusty paring knife in a kitchen drawer, then returned to the basement, hurriedly stomping down the staircase.

Lifting Dovishaw off the floor by his hair, the killer quickly and expertly plunged the knife deep into Bolo's right eye. Black goop ran down Bolo's pudgy face.

And then the killer waited.

A few minutes passed and the stranger finally got what he wanted from Frank "Bolo" Dovishaw. The air filled with the rancid and putrid odor of human excrement and urine. It was Bolo's last humiliation. And the killer now knew for sure Bolo was dead.

Suddenly, the man's satisfaction dissipated into the cool basement. A chill went through the killer and he froze. He wasn't alone. He clutched the Beretta and held his breath.

Someone was banging on the front door.

Aha!

Finally Kenneth Wisinski was going to get his daughter's money! He had wheeled his car behind the green Cadillac in the driveway on West 21st Street, trapping the gas-guzzler. There would be no escaping, now.

Wisinski walked to the front door and knocked. Nothing.

He knocked again. Still nothing.

The lights were on. The Caddy was in the driveway. But nobody was coming to the door. *What the fuck*?

Now Wisinski was getting upset. Believing Dovishaw was inside, but ignoring him, Wisinski began banging on the door and then actually kicking it!

"Open the door, you cocksucker!" he yelled. "You stuck my daughter and I want the damned money!" He banged and kicked again. Again, nothing. Pissed, reluctantly he left, stomping in through the unplowed driveway to his car.

But now on a determined mission, he vowed he wouldn't be denied. He would be back.

Inside the modest, two-story frame dwelling, the killer, tightly grasping the handgun, waited for the banging to stop. Then he waited endless minutes longer to make certain no one was coming in. Convinced he was finally alone, the killer set out to complete the plan he had already put in motion. The next step was to get the dead Dovishaw out of the house.

Minutes earlier, perhaps in a dreamily, eerie sort of way, Bolo Dovishaw might have been aware he had been shot. If such was the case, although there was no pain, he couldn't move. Numbed, he somehow knew he was still alive. And now there was a spark of hope as he sensed his intended-killer was leaving. He heard the footsteps retreating away from him on the cellar stairs.

He probably prayed, *Oh Jesus, please, let him be gone.*

And perhaps Bolo allowed himself to think that he would be safe now.

Moments later the thumping sound of heavy footsteps on the stairs returned. He somehow would sense the killer was back. Dovishaw felt pressure on top of his head, as though his hair was being pulled from his skull. Through a blur, he thought he caught a tiny glint of shiny metal reflected in the bare-bulb basement light.

And at that exact moment, Bolo Dovishaw might have thought his one and only final thought. Like hearing a horrible whisper, it was a single word and image:

Caesar.

CHAPTER 4

Less than a mile away in a small, but popular watering hole called "The Sports Page," the driver of the car carrying the hit man to Dovishaw's home that night sat at the bar smiling to himself. Everything was going perfectly! Soon, fat Bolo would be dead, his body ironically hidden in the trunk of his own car. A soon as the killer passed along the coveted safe deposit box keys, the Caddy with Dovishaw inside would be on its way to Cleveland, Ohio, to be abandoned at the huge Hopkins Airport Parking lot.

The smiling bar patron surveyed his surroundings. Already, locals were starting to fill up the place, ordering their pepperoni pizzas and wings and pitchers and getting seats facing the TV for the Monday night game. As a past local high school football star of sorts in another lifetime decades earlier, the man nodded pleasantly to acquaintances as they wandered into the bar, recognized and greeted him. What an incredible alibi! A cast of thousands, all swearing to his whereabouts at the time of the killing! And he couldn't help smiling again.

While he waited to be joined by a cokehead from Cleveland trying to score a packet or two of white powder, his thoughts drifted back to events that unfolded only a short time earlier.

The greedy killer from the Cleveland area looked more like he was dressed for a business dinner than to score a hit. Suit and tie, top coat and dress shoes, all black. The killer could have been a banker or stodgy Republican, the middleman in this killing almost laughed. He had arrived on time at the pre-arranged pick-up point, a West 38th Street Laundromat not too far from Bolo's place, dropped off there by his dutiful wife, who silently and promptly turned the car around and headed back to Ohio without so much as a question or even an inquiring glance. Apparently, she knew better.

The two men had cased Bolo's house earlier, so the Ohioan knew exactly what to expect. In fact, this would be the second time the hit on Dovishaw had been attempted. The first was several weeks earlier, in December, also on a Monday night when the take from the weekend gambling would have been heavy. But when the middleman checked out Bolo's house just a short time before meeting the killer, he spotted the vehicle of another Erie wise guy parked in the driveway. These co-conspirators didn't want company there. Not that night! They needed Bolo alone. The middleman sent the grim-faced hit man back to Cleveland, and the event was rescheduled for January 3 – this night.

To eliminate any more risks with an unexpected visitor, the middleman arranged for the earlier intruding wise guy to be away that night. And even the weather was cooperating, he thought. Sure it was frigid and a little snowy, but, hell, it could have been worse in Erie, Pennsylvania in early January. Much worse.

Continuing his thoughts of earlier that night, he recalled that after the killer's wife drove off, the well-dressed man climbed into his car. They drove in silence for several minutes before they reached Bolo's block. The arranger slowed down, then brought the car to a stop to allow for the killer in black to get out.

"Meet you later," he said, almost too softly for the driver to hear. And then he was gone into the cold night. Gone in the direction of Bolo's house.

That was 30 minutes ago.

By now, Bolo was history.

Tough shit. The fat asshole won't be missed.

With the sports bar steadily growing more crowded , the middleman understood his involvement tonight was serious business. No stranger to criminal activity almost his entire adult life, he'd been involved in plenty of shit before. But, he seemed to rationalize with himself, he wasn't the killer. Not this time. Actually, he was merely just the conduit between the real planner and the killer. He made the arrangements, sure. He found the hit man, of course. He did the negotiating, drove the man to Bolo's, but his hands were clean. No messy stuff for him. Or so he kept telling himself.

While the middleman was still lost in his thoughts, a red-faced, overweight bar patron wearing a bright green bowling shirt with the words, "Bizzarro's Towing" on the back and carrying a pitcher of Bud back to his table, stopped briefly to greet the smiling alibi-establishing guy at the bar.

"Hey, Caesar!" Mr. Red-Faced Overweight Bowler beamed.

The seemingly happy guy at the bar looked up. Everyone thought they knew Caesar.

Caesar Montevecchio just nodded with a sense of contentment.

After all, it *was* the easiest ten grand he'd ever make. And he continued to smile.

Less than a mile in the other direction from Frank "Bolo" Dovishaw's house, Raymond Ferritto was pacing the floor at his Brown Avenue residence.

At first he was pissed. But now the anger had subsided and he was actually beginning to get concerned. Where the hell was Bolo? He was supposed to be at home, taking bets, just like any other Monday night during pro football season.

It was 7 o'clock and Ferritto tried checking in with Bolo, as he always did, to learn how heavy the action had been before kick-off shortly after 9. Bolo had dropped off Ferritto at home before 6. They had stopped at Damore's for a meatball sub. The fat pig Bolo was always hungry, always eating.

Why he had agreed to partner with Dovishaw was a mystery to many – after all, they were nothing alike, had nothing in common – but it wasn't all that strange for Ferritto. Bolo's book was already well-established when Ray returned to Erie from that fucking stint in jail at Chino, California. (Later, Ferritto, Dovishaw and Ferritto's nephew, Frankie Thomas, had served in an aborted witness relocation program.) Bolo, the perennial fucking coward, wasn't about to give any shit to Ray, so it was an easy and convenient way for Ferritto to re-enter Erie's underbelly. And, after only a few years, Ray was doing okay, thanks in large part to dumb fucking Bolo. Bolo worked while Ferritto reaped the monetary rewards.

Ferritto, the confessed hit man, was feared by nearly everyone. He didn't seem to mind the characterization that followed him everywhere. If the truth were told, he liked it. He wore it like a badge of honor. His reputation as a cold and cruel bully and mob hit man had gotten him through life unchallenged. No, nobody would fuck with him. And because he was Dovishaw's partner, nobody fucked with Bolo, either.

But where the hell was the fat shit? Ferritto thought. Perhaps it was again time to slap the nitwit around a bit.

No fucking way, the out-of-breath killer thought.

No fucking way was he going to get this heavy prick's body up the stairs, out the door and into the Caddy's trunk.

The well-dressed man from Ohio was huffing. Huffing and sweating. Huffing and sweating and swearing.

He had tried several times to move Bolo's body, but quickly learned it would take more than just him to accomplish that task. *Bolo weighed a ton!*

A ton of *dead* weight, the killer almost chuckled.

Sure, that had been the plan: Kill Dovishaw. Get the keys to the safe-deposit boxes. Clean out the bathroom vanity. Put the body in the trunk of the big, green Caddy. Meet his contact. Deliver the keys. Then drive the body to Cleveland and abandon the car in the middle of the massive airport long-term parking lot, where it was not likely to be discovered for weeks, maybe even months.

But he hadn't counted on this. Bolo's huge, flabby body was immovable. And, the killer had to admit he was plain out of shape when it came to doing anything requiring physical strength. Why risk a fucking cardiac for a dead bookie? Besides, he didn't want to spend another minute in Dovishaw's damned house.

Someone had been banging and kicking the front door. Another minute and he would have whacked the door-banger as well. And the fucking phone, it rang incessantly, never stopping. As each minute passed, with each ring of the phone, the once calm killer was becoming increasingly jumpy.

What he needed was a new plan. Easy. Cover the body. Get the fuck out. After all, hadn't he accomplished all he set out to do? Who would blame him for leaving now? And if anyone did, tough shit. What could they do about it now? Nothing. The deed was done.

The killer found another bed sheet in the basement laundry basket and placed it over Bolo, whose lifeless body was still oozing dark maroon blood from being stabbed in the eye. He took the throw rug, the same one used to muffle the .32's report, and covered the sheet with it. Finally, he tossed clothes from the laundry basket around the big lump on the floor for good measure. Checking his surroundings, he determined it would be difficult for anyone peering in a basement window to ascertain a body was on the floor.

Leaving on the house lights as he departed the home with the dead body on the basement floor, the killer got into Bolo's late-model Caddy, backed out of the driveway, and drove away. He was headed for the Station Restaurant parking lot on nearby Peach Street, the pre-determined after-the-hit meeting place where he would pass along the safe-deposit box keys to his contact. Shit, he smiled. It had been *so* easy.

CHAPTER 5

CAESAR MONTEVECCHIO WAS SMILING, TOO, WHEN THE OHIO cokehead arrived at "The Sports Page" bar a few minutes late.

The drug deal was another potential alibi, that is, if he should actually need a second one, but scoring coke for the guy was barely an afterthought on this night. For his part as the hit's arranger, Montevecchio would collect $10,000. The shooter would get $20,000.

Funny, the shooter had wanted the money before the hit.

"Put the money up front. Sure I'll do it. Why not?" the killer told Montevecchio.

But later, when Montevecchio met with the Erie businessman who Caesar maintained ordered and engineered the hit, that request was quickly nixed.

"I've got someone, but he wants the money upfront."

"Fuck him," Caesar recalled the businessman telling him. "When it's done, he gets paid."

The killer had agreed, especially after learning there was another $10,000 in it for him if he also killed Raymond Ferritto at the same time he whacked Dovishaw. Another Erie wise guy had put up the bonus cash for the Ferritto hit. Two birds with one stone, so to speak. End the Dovishaw/Ferritto partnership once and for all. All the more gambling money to split up for those who remained.

Montevecchio had another drink with the cokehead from Ohio. He tried phoning his cocaine contact. The contact's daughter answered.

"Daddy's not home," she said when she recognized Caesar's voice. "But he'll be home shortly."

"Okay, honey. Tell him I called. I'll call back."

Turning to the cokehead, he simply said, "No go."

A few minutes later, the two left "The Sports Page." But Caesar had a sudden premonition that something just might be amiss. It was a premonition that would be confirmed, as Montevecchio would soon learn.

"Follow me in your car," he instructed. "I need to make one stop at the Station Restaurant. Just take a minute." The premonition paid off. At least for that night.

Traffic wasn't as heavy as the killer expected on the usually crowded upper Peach Street, the main approach to Erie's huge retail shopping mall, actually situated outside the city limits in the adjacent Millcreek Township. It took only a few minutes to get from Bolo's house to the Station Restaurant.

Swinging the huge Caddy into the normally popular night spot's parking lot, he quickly realized the area was virtually empty. It was Monday night. Erie folks weren't big at dining at fashionable restaurants on weeknights, he thought. Maybe a good thing. Why have too many people around?

The killer's mind focused just once on Bolo. The dumb shit was still wearing rubbers on his shoes, too fucking lazy to even take them off before eating his disgusting meatball submarine sandwich. The keen-eyed killer spotted the telltale scrappy remains of the sub here and there on the living room table near the front door. He smiled that sardonic smile and thought, *Some last supper, Bolo.*

Those images of Bolo did not last. His new thoughts were of something far more important. His $20,000 payday. He easily guided the big car into a space in the middle of the lot, turned off the engine, climbed out and peered around at his lonely surroundings.

Where the fuck was Caesar?

He'd soon find out. And, he'd learn Caesar wasn't alone.

When Caesar Montevecchio arrived at the Station Restaurant a short time later, he didn't immediately spot the killer in the empty, darkened parking lot. But soon after finding his own parking space, his eyes adjusted to the dim light. First he spotted Bolo's green Cadillac and thought, *Ah, everything's going perfectly!*

Then he spotted the killer. *He fits the profile*, Montevecchio thought to himself. Just standing there in the cold, not moving, eyes narrow and piercing. But without emotion. Just waiting. Icy as the weather itself.

Caesar got out of his car and approached the shooter. But before they even began to speak, the Ohioan spotted the cokehead – a man he knew to be also from Ohio – as this new intruder got out of his car and began walking toward them. The killer was upset, but not enough to kill again, mostly just irritated.

"What the fuck is he doing here?" the killer demanded.

"On a coke deal," Montevecchio replied. "Never the fuck mind about him. What happened with Bolo?"

Now the second man was upon them, and, being more than moderately curious, he wanted to know what was going down between Caesar and the killer.

"Bolo is dead," the killer almost dead-panned the words. "Here are the fucking keys." He handed both safe-deposit box keys to Caesar.

"I couldn't lift that big fat fuck. So I left him there."

Montevecchio felt his heart skip a beat. He was incredulous!

"What?" It was more of a exclamation than a question. "What the fuck!" he could only shake his head. "Jeezus, you fucked everything up!"

"What the hell do you want from me?" the killer finally showed defensive emotion. "I should have brought help. I couldn't lift him, that's all. But I covered him with a rug and clothes. We're all right."

What followed was a quick conference that culminated with the unanimous decision to get the killer and the other Cleveland man out of town as quickly as possible. But first, they would have to dispose of Dovishaw's car, all present readily agreed.

With the killer behind the wheel of the green Caddy and the second man from Ohio following in his own wheels, they drove off toward the Holiday Inn South. The hotel was situated on Interstate 90, a major east-west thoroughfare just south of the City of Erie – and the most direct route from Pennsylvania to Cleveland, Ohio. With Bolo's car hidden in the parking lot behind the popular hotel for travelers and locals alike, the two men departed Erie for Cleveland on that cold winter night in the cokehead's car.

Driving as fast as they dared without attracting the attention of the Pennsylvania State Police, they headed westward.

Erie, Pennsylvania, is often referred to as the nation's biggest small town. Or, America's smallest big town. Its civic leaders are less than progressive, its natives often lacking the vision and foresight required to move the city forward. Whatever the locals call it, however, folks are happy to generally get from most anywhere in town to anywhere else in the lakefront city within five or ten minutes.

It had taken Caesar Montevecchio only minutes from the Station Restaurant to reach a Laundromat on West 38th Street. In those pre-cell phone days, he dropped a quarter into the slot at the corner telephone booth and dialed the number he had long ago memorized. When a man answered, Montevecchio uttered only four words.

"I'm at the Laundromat," he said. Then he hung up.

Within minutes, an Erie businessman with a dark complexion, seemingly well-tanned, arrived, or so it would be recounted by Montevecchio later. Despite the "tan," Caesar would later say he knew the man hadn't been on a cruise or a Caribbean vacation. It was his natural coloring, the coloring of descendants of those who arrived during the early part of the century from Mediterranean nations. And, it was how the businessman got his nickname.

"Take the bank-box keys," Montevecchio said before breaking the unwelcome news about the dead Bolo Dovishaw's whereabouts. "Bolo is dead. But he's still in the house," Montevecchio simply explained. "Couldn't move him."

The businessman blanched – and almost lost his tan-like look. He was as unnerved as Montevecchio had been with the killer when told the body was left behind in the basement.

"We're all going to wind up in jail, you know that!" the businessman stammered in disgust, it would later be alleged. But Caesar Montevecchio had had just about enough for one night of fuck-ups.

"Look, you've got the fucking keys. Just go do your thing and let me worry about Bolo."

When the men departed the secret meeting site, the Laundromat was empty. In silence, they drove away in different directions.

Perhaps at the exact moment Montevecchio and the businessman were parting company at the Erie Laundromat, the two Ohio men were some 50 miles west of the City of Erie, and about 30 miles into the so-called Buckeye state. When they reached Interstate 90's Youngstown exit – considered by most to be the halfway point between Erie and Cleveland – the passenger tersely directed the driver to veer southeast onto Ohio's State Route 11.

They drove in silence into Mahoning County, home to many of the Northeast's most notorious underworld figures. As the car crossed the Meander Lake Bridge, not far from Youngstown and the famous Niles, Ohio, night life strip, the driver slowed to a crawl. Traffic on the secondary highway was almost non-existent late that Monday night.

The killer rolled down the passenger window. And, with a mighty toss, he first hurled the .32 caliber clip, and then the weapon itself into the black, still unfrozen water of Meander Lake.

Thrown separately, both bullet magazine and pistol instantly sank to the lake's bottom, now part of the infamous and unofficial weaponry underwater graveyard depository that included hundreds of guns and knives and shell casings. Most of them, not surprisingly, were wiped down of fingerprints.

The two men continued their drive west in silence. They drove into the dark, cold night without exchanging a word. True to form in their business, they never looked back.

CHAPTER 6

Ray Ferritto had the look of a killer.

Even with his premature full head of silver-gray hair and slight, wiry frame, his cold, clear eyes belied the appearance of any grandfatherly or patriarchal image. But tonight, the cold look was gone.

He wasn't sure if he was more worried or more pissed. Either way, the outcome was the same: Bolo Dovishaw – known as Ash Wednesday to some because of the unsightly birthmark blemish on his forehead – was missing. An inner sense that had gotten Ferritto through a life of murder and mayhem told the admitted hit man something was amiss, something maybe seriously amiss.

After he tried to telephone Bolo at 7 o'clock when the call was automatically transferred to Victor's house phone, he tried again at 8. Then at 8:30. Then just before the kick-off. The results were the same: No Bolo.

Ferritto recalled Bolo's weekend pattern. Recently, on Saturday and Sunday nights, Dovishaw could be expected to be hanging out at Hank Ward's strip joint, known as the local "titty bar" in its patrons' jargon, the Bootlegger Lounge on West 8th Street. Ray knew Bolo was hot for one of the out-of-town strippers. But it was a stretch to think he would have gone to the Bootlegger on an important game night.

If anything noble could be said for Dovishaw, he usually put business first. Work now, play later. Usually.

Ferritto watched the televised game all the way through the midway point of the fourth quarter. Finally, about 11:30, his concern took over. He needed to know what was up with Bolo. He left his house and drove less than a mile to Bolo's.

Shit. Lights on, but no car in the driveway. Ferritto swung around and headed in the opposite direction toward Damore's Restaurant on East 10th Street, near State Street, Erie's main drag. The restaurant was owned by Al's brother, Lundy, who was at the bar with the few remaining patrons, mostly wannabe wise guys. Ferritto took him aside and quickly cut to the chase.

"You seen Bolo?" Lundy hadn't. Not that night. Not for a while.

Using Damore's bar telephone, Ferritto dialed the Bootlegger's number and got the same answer. No Bolo – and some pissed off broad named Chastity waiting for him to show up or call. None of this had a good feel to it, the hit man thought. But whatever was up with Bolo, it could wait until morning. Then there would be time enough to show the missing fat ass who the fuck was in charge.

An irritated, tired Ray Ferritto drove home and went to bed.

Hank Ward was always the last one to leave the Bootlegger Lounge. Once a respectable restaurant and popular gathering place, it was now just another strip joint. But restaurant or strip bar, either way, business had been horrible this Monday night.

It was just before midnight, and the place was empty. Only the goofy stripper Chastity remained, probably waiting for that jerk-off Bolo, Ward thought to himself.

"I'm closing," Ward told her. "Go home. Or go wherever the hell you go."

Chastity tossed her classy discount store fake fur, tinted purple/lavender and pink, around her shoulders, pulled the collar up to her chin, and tippy-toed in spiky heels through an inch or so of fresh, new snow to her '75 Ford Pinto, the same model seen on all those exploding gas tank videos. She hoped it would start.

Fuck Frank Dovishaw, she thought. Fuck 'em all.

She went home.

Raymond Ferritto was 54, but easily could be taken for at least 20 years older.

Those high cheek bones gave his cold, dark and deep-sunken eyes a chilling sinister look. His premature gray, almost white hair didn't for a single moment soften or mitigate the extremely harsh effect of his deeply lined face. As Ferritto aged, he merely grew uglier.

This Tuesday morning obviously was no exception. It surely didn't help in the beauty department that Ferritto didn't sleep very well the previous night. Upon rising, he frowned when he thought back to Monday night. Once again, he tried phoning Bolo Dovishaw at home. Again, he had no success. Now truly concerned, but not yet panicked, for nothing could actually put the hit man in a panic, Ferritto began calling around to Dovishaw's established hangouts. Many of them were the same ones visited by Ferritto in vain the night before. The answer at each one had been the same. It seemed no one had seen Bolo for several days. It was beginning to appear that only Ferritto had seen Dovishaw the previous day. Ferritto was getting that gut feeling that something was very much amiss. Bolo might be so dumb that stupid pills would not even work on him, but he was, up to now, at least consistent and predictable.

Early that afternoon, Ray Ferritto finally called and reached Phil Torrelli. Not very bright, Ferritto thought, but with connections to Erie's underbelly, Torrelli was the third member of this bookmaking trio's partnership.

"Check out Bolo's house," Ferritto ordered Torrelli. It was clearly established in such matters just who was the boss and who was subservient. Normally, Ferritto would have had a key to the house, but he had given it to Cy Ciotti, perhaps Erie's best-known set-up man, after Ciotti temporarily moved in with Bolo several weeks earlier. Ciotti – and Bolo's house key – however, were now in Pittsburgh for a few days. Torrelli promised to stop in at Dovishaw's house, then immediately report back to Ferritto.

About four o'clock that afternoon, Phil Torrelli telephoned Ferritto to report he had been to Dovishaw's west Erie home. Although Bolo wasn't home, Torrelli said, it appeared that nothing was out-of-place. More and more, Ferritto was thinking, none of this was like Bolo Dovishaw. He was an asshole, yes. But he was a mostly reliable asshole. Where the hell was the fat fuck?

Ferritto called Vinnie DiPasquale, another local wannabe wise guy and coke dealer (now doing 30 years in Florida for cocaine trafficking).

DiPasquale knew how to reach Ciotti in Pittsburgh. At present, that's all Ferritto was looking to do, hook up with the reputed Erie gangster and find out just what the hell was going on. Once Ferritto had the Pittsburgh telephone number, he quickly called Ciotti.

"Something's up with Bolo. I can't find him," Ferritto said with more urgency in his voice than he had intended.

"I'll come home right now," Ciotti, told his pal, Ferritto. But, in truth, he didn't sound all that concerned.

At about the same time Ferritto was expressing his Bolo concerns to his other bookmaking partner, Torrelli, Caesar Montevecchio was said to be phoning an Erie importing business.

"I have something for you," the dark-skinned businessman told Montevecchio. "Stop right over."

Caesar hung up. Montevecchio immediately telephoned the shooter somewhere in the state of Ohio. A meeting was arranged for 7 p.m. at Mr. C's Pancake House along Interstate 90 at Exit No. 34 in Ohio, just about halfway between Erie, Pennsylvania, and Cleveland, Ohio. A few more chores, Caesar thought, and it will all be over. As was often the case, Caesar was wrong.

That night, while Caesar Montevecchio was arriving at the Ohio pancake house, at exactly 7 p.m., in Erie, Ray Ferritto and Cy Ciotti met in Frank "Bolo" Dovishaw's driveway. The West 21st Street house lights still were on, burning brightly and illuminating the dwelling from within on the dark wintry night. But Bolo's Caddy was gone. Cy, who had earlier driven the 120 miles from Pittsburgh to Erie, and Ray tried to figure out where Bolo might have gone, or, better yet, who might know of his whereabouts.

Ferritto wanted to enter the house right away, but Ciotti was now claiming he had given his key to his girlfriend, Linda Shatto, who was out of town and probably would not be back in Erie until the following day. The two men drove to Dovishaw's wife's house, a short distance away.

Although Bolo and Joan Dovishaw had been separated for years, they still maintained a close friendship. Ferritto thought – hoped – Joan might have a key to Bolo's house. As luck would have it, the men found Joan Dovishaw at home that evening. But there, the luck would end. She hadn't spoken with Bolo since New Year's Eve, four days earlier, when he stopped by for a visit. And, not only hadn't she heard from Dovishaw, she didn't have a key to his house, either.

Frustrated, Ferritto and Ciotti telephoned Phil Torrelli and ordered him to meet them back at Dovishaw's. They drove back to West 21st Street in silence, where Torrelli arrived a short time later. Now they'd find out what was going down, Ferritto was certain.

After using Phil Torrelli's key to enter the west Erie home, it was obvious to all present that the house had been ransacked and trashed. In the bathroom, the vanity hiding place for the money was exposed and open, the scene indicative of either a robbery or a burglary or perhaps both.

"You're so fucking stupid," Ferritto shrieked at Torrelli. "This looks like 'nothing' is wrong?" Ferritto was now convinced Torrelli did not check on the house as he had earlier claimed, but lied about driving there and not finding Dovishaw. Torrelli knew better than to argue with the hit man. Avoiding Ferritto's chilling stare, his gaze centered with fascination on his shoelaces. Then, in silence, the three men searched Dovishaw's house. Nothing.

Eventually, they had gone through the entire structure, room by room, space by space. All, that is, except the basement, the only place not yet checked out by the trio. It was Ferritto who dutifully tugged open the door with Ciotti and Torrelli peering over his shoulder. There, at the bottom of the staircase, was what appeared to be a pile of clothing. But Ferritto, the killer, the mob hit man, knew better.

Frank "Bolo" Dovishaw was no longer missing.

CHAPTER 7

Several hours earlier, Caesar Montevecchio had arrived at the importing business on Erie's west side, later records would show. It was in a corner building smack in the heart of the city's Little Italy district, known throughout Erie as *the* place to acquire any fashion of Italian food from extra virgin olive oil to wedding soup to all variety of pastas. But Montevecchio wasn't there for ethnic culinary delights, not that night. No, on this night it was finally time for the pay-off.

The business was located on the first floor of the two-story brick building, its upstairs having been divided into individual housing units and apartments, rented out by the businessman to supplement his income and help support a gambling addiction that already had him tens of thousands of dollars in debt, court records would later ascertain. By the time Montevecchio got there, the businessman had already visited Dovishaw's west Erie bank next to the Super Duper grocery market and looted the dead man's safe-deposit boxes.

From his jerky movements, Montevecchio could tell the businessman was beginning to freak out. Silently, the man indicated to Montevecchio to follow him to a vacant second-floor apartment. When they were alone, away from business' employees and customers, the businessman said, "The pig had less than I had expected in the boxes."

Montevecchio wasn't surprised. Actually, he had come to expect as much from this guy.

The Erie businessman paused for just a brief moment, then, almost reluctantly, he handed Montevecchio a small, brown, paper bag. It was stuffed with cash.

"That's for the shooter. Twenty grand. I'll get the rest to you later. This has already cost me $37,000, for Christsake!"

Although the room was chilly, the businessman was sweating profusely. Next he held out two safe-deposit box keys.

"Put them into Bolo's car, wherever the fuck it's stashed. I don't want to know."

Montevecchio felt a need to plan further, but the businessman cut him off short.

"Just get the fuck out of here," he directed. "I'm fucking nervous enough. Just leave!"

Caesar Montevecchio, still waiting for his $10,000 cut, knew he would have to wait a little longer. He could wait. But now, there was an appointment at an Ohio, roadside restaurant he needed to keep.

For a Tuesday night in January, Mr. C's Pancake House along Interstate 90 was a surprisingly busy place. Or, perhaps not so surprising. The thriving business was situated along the major interstate highway intersecting Erie, Cleveland and Youngstown. Located at the Ashtabula, Ohio, exit, it had long been an easy off-on stop for travelers and over-the-road truckers. Standard food fare – all-day breakfasts, burgers and fries lunches and cheap turkey, ham and meatloaf dinners – Mr. C's was for a long time an adequate alternative to the fast-food joints littering the interstate highways. And, it was a perfect meeting place for Caesar and his Ohio cohorts. No, they wouldn't be ordering the short stack blueberry pancake special on this evening. Hell, they wouldn't even be going inside the establishment.

Montevecchio arrived at the crowded restaurant alone, a few minutes before 7 p.m. He saw that the parking lot was packed, but eventually he found a space in back, next to a medium-sized pick-up truck with Indiana's "Hoosier" vanity plates.

The killer was already there, still with his Ohio "chauffeur," the cokehead, who had shuttled him home to Medina, Ohio, just west of Cleveland, the previous night.

Without even a greeting, the killer climbed into Montevecchio's front seat.

Montevecchio, who had been coveting the contents of the brown paper bag, knew better. He quickly handed the bag to the Ohioan.

"It's all there," he said. "Count it if you want."

The killer took the bag and, hefting it up and down as if to check its weight, but without actually counting for accuracy, opened the car door to leave.

"Just a minute," Montevecchio said. "Take these, too." He held out to the killer two small objects.

"What? That guy's bank-box keys? No fucking way!"

"Just take them and put them back in Bolo's car!" Montevecchio insisted.

"You put them back," the killer said. "I'm not driving into Erie. You know just where that car is. It's at the Holiday Inn, just off I-90. You take the risk, not me."

"Hey, fuck you, asshole!" Montevecchio roared. "You know that was part of this deal. And you also know I can't go around that fucking car. You know that!"

Reluctantly, the killer took the keys and, without a single word, got out of Montevecchio's car, closed the door, and silently disappeared into the frigid Ohio night.

Minutes later, Montevecchio was speeding back to Erie on Interstate 90, while the killer and his driver were also on the same highway, heading in the same direction.

Back in Erie, Ray Ferritto, Cy Ciotti and Phil Torrelli knew indeed they were in a quandary. They were among the most well-known of Erie's underworld, Ray and Cy with long rap sheets. Ferritto had even attained instant global fame when he had deftly confessed just five years earlier to being a mob hit man. Torrelli had never been pinched, but had been a perennial suspect in the illegal numbers business. Tonight, however, they found themselves in an extremely uncomfortable and unenviable position. They were confronted with a body. Not just an everyday, garden-variety body, but the rather viciously brutalized body of one of their own. None of the three had a thing in the world to do with this killing. At least it appeared that way. Or did they?

What's more, they didn't even know what to do about it. Not the faintest notion of how to handle the situation. Torrelli, however, was the first to comment.

"Fuck. Now what do we do?"

There were several moments of silence while together, their combined brain-power mulled over and pondered the limited alternatives.

Call the police? Hardly. These were not respectable citizens, for sure.

Get rid of the body? Not exactly. If they were discovered, how could they explain?

Just leave and ignore the whole situation? Too late for that. They were already involved. What to do? They fretted.

Finally, it was Cy Ciotti who came up with what all agreed was, if not the perfect solution, at least one that would get the trio off law enforcement's hook.

"Let's call Frankie! Let him call it in!"

After a few more moments of contemplation and nervous hand-wringing, it seemed like the best solution available. Ferritto made the call.

"We're at Bolo's," his raspy voice said into the phone. "We think there's a problem. Get over here now." It was far more than a request. Without waiting for a reply, Ferritto hung up.

Frank Rotunda was one dirty cop. A detective with close ties to Police Director Arthur Berardi and Mayor Louis Tullio, he dined at times with Berardi, and although Berardi once recommended that Rotunda be suspended and demoted, neither occurred. Rotunda not only dealt in illegal drugs, but wasn't bashful about participating in house burglaries, or whatever it took to make a quick buck over and above what the citizens of Erie paid him to serve and protect. He must have owed this unholy trio big time for him to immediately respond to their order. Frank Rotunda would follow orders. He would be there as directed.

While the worried trio waited impatiently at Bolo's digs, another call was placed, this one to Joan Dovishaw, Bolo's estranged wife, also requesting that she meet them there. And then they paced as they waited for Erie Police Detective Frank Rotunda to show.

Meanwhile, not very far away from the West 21st Street house, Kenneth Wisinski was on a mission. That asshole Dovishaw owed his 13-year-old daughter $21 – two months of daily and Sunday newspaper deliveries, by Wisinski's reckoning. For two days now he had been regularly trying to find Bolo at home to collect for his daughter. The previous night, in fact, he damn near kicked down the front door when the man he knew as a local gangster wouldn't answer his incessant knocking and doorbell-ringing – even though that fucking Cadillac was in the driveway and Dovishaw, the flaming asshole, was obviously home! Earlier drive-bys that Tuesday revealed the Caddy had disappeared, and, probably, so had Bolo. But he wasn't about to give up. Not now. Hell, not ever. Not until he got the $21 bucks.

Now it was 7:30 p.m. The house lights were still blazing and although the Caddy was gone, there were several other vehicles lined up in the driveway. Why not see what's up, he thought. Kenneth Wisinski quickly parked at the curb in front of the house, got out, strode up the few icy stairs, then pounded authoritatively on the front door.

"That can't be Frankie already," Torrelli offered his startled companions. "What the fuck, you just hung up on him a minute or two ago. Now what?"

Without saying a word, Raymond Ferritto walked through the living room and answered the door.

"Yeah?"

Wisinski immediately recognized the silver-haired man from Dominick's Restaurant, a place he considered to be an all-night greasy spoon on East 12th Street where Wisinski's wife had been employed.

"I want to talk to Dovishaw," Wisinski managed to demand, but not quite with the previous authority of his door-pounding. After all, this guy at the door wasn't your average hood.

"What for?" Ferritto asked.

"He owes my daughter for the newspaper."

"What?"

"Hey, you tell Bolo I want my daughter's money."

Ferritto sighed. He was pissed and exasperated and frustrated. But mostly, he just wanted this fucking unwelcomed intruder at the front door to go away.

"How much?"

Wisinski told him.

Ferritto reached into his pocket and pulled out a wad of bills. The smallest was a twenty.

"Hey," Ferritto yelled, turning to Ciotti inside the door. "You got a buck?"

Wisinski recognized Cy Ciotti from Dominick's as well. What a gang he had happened to bust in upon this night!

Ferritto took the one-dollar bill from Ciotti, peeled the twenty off the inside of the cash wad, then handed the two bills to Wisinski, who was now shifting back and forth, from one foot to the other, eyeing his nearby car in case he needed to make a hasty retreat.

"Here," Ferritto's icy eyes froze Wisinski even more than the chill in the January night air.

"Tell Bolo my daughter will start delivery of the paper again," Wisinski weakly offered.

"Bolo don't want the paper no more," Ferritto said.

Wisinski beat a hasty retreat as Ray Ferritto slammed the door. And he whispered to himself, "Cheap fucking gangsters couldn't even give her a tip. Them mother-fuckers."

Later, however, the exchange between the two men that night, combined with Wisinski's recollection of his visits to Dovishaw's home the previous evening, would do much to establish the actual time frame of Dovishaw's slaying for investigators.

But on that Tuesday night, Wisinski could only feel good. After all, his bull -dog persistence had paid off. He had his daughter's money. And that's all that seemed to matter.

A few minutes after Wisinski drove off with the $21 for his daughter, Detective Frank Rotunda finally showed up. Ciotti took the lead in explaining to Rotunda that Bolo was missing and that they were concerned since Dovishaw hadn't been seen for several days. It just wasn't like ol' Bolo to just take off like that without telling someone, especially Ray. Rotunda looked confused over what his expected role would be.

"Look, Frankie, you're a cop," Ciotti said. "You know what to do. We just didn't want to touch anything around here, given that the place looks like it's been ransacked and trashed. That's why we called you – 'cuz you got professional expertise in these matters." Cy delivered his "sincere" compliment, managing to keep a straight face.

Rotunda quickly eyed the interior of the house. It didn't take much deduction power to convince him that while Dovishaw might not have been the perfect housekeeper, it appeared far messier than what even Bolo was known for.

"So, what do you think?" Ferritto asked.

"How the fuck am I supposed to know?" Rotunda shot back, a little more forceful than he actually intended. But the comment had the effect of quelling any guilty misgivings the three might have harbored about drawing the not-too-astute police officer into the murder. Yeah, it was time to stick it to him, the other three simultaneously thought.

"Hey," Ciotti offered, hitting himself in the forehead with an open palm, as though he just had a brilliant thought. "We didn't check the attic or the basement. Why don't I go ahead and see what's in the attic. Frankie, why don't you check out the basement?" Ciotti didn't bother to wait for a reply as he headed upstairs and toward the attic stairs in the drafty old house.

Shrugging nonchalantly, Frank Rotunda found his way to the cellar door, opened it, and noisily clomped down the stairs hurriedly. He was anxious to wrap up whatever was going on and get the hell out of Dovishaw's house. Besides, he was having spooky feelings. The ace detective didn't need to possess a keen sense of observation. His discovery of Frank "Bolo" Dovishaw's lifeless body took him only moments.

"Holy fuck!" Rotunda yelled up the basement stairway. "It's Bolo! He's dead!"

The three smiling faces on the first floor nodded knowingly to one another. They had their patsy, alright. God, they thought, Frankie is so fucking dumb. How did he ever become a cop? How the hell he didn't realize he was being set up would always amaze them.

Within minutes of Rotunda's frantic telephone call to Erie Police Headquarters to report the crime, three black-and-whites, lights flashing, screeched to a stop in front of the house in the normally serene West 21st Street neighborhood.

Ten miles west of Mr. C's Pancake House, traffic was light on Interstate 90 on their return trip from Erie. The killer in the passenger seat was totaling the bagful of cash. Twenty thousand. The agreed upon amount. He smiled. An easy night's work. After driving back to Erie and stashing the safe-deposit box keys in Bolo's car – an unexpected move insisted upon by that wacko Montevecchio that didn't thrill the killer – he and the driver had agreed to quietly disappear for at least several months. No calls. No contact at all. That suited him just fine.

Inside the car, the killer slowly counted out $15,000 for himself. He gave his driver the remaining $5,000.

"Thanks for the rides," he said.

They continued to drive west in silence.

On his way to Mr. C's Pancake House earlier that night, Caesar Montevecchio couldn't resist driving past the Holiday Inn just off of Interstate 90, if only to satisfy his morbid curiosity. It was a crisp evening, not as cold as the previous night, and there was no snow falling.

From the east-west interstate highway, he had a clear view of the Holiday Inn's sparsely populated parking lot on the south side of the road, and of the recently late Frank "Bolo" Dovishaw's abandoned green Caddy. Nothing. All quiet. All good.

Who knows, maybe it wasn't so bad after all that the killer hadn't dumped the vehicle at Cleveland's Hopkins Airport, Montevecchio thought. Maybe this would be just as good and the Caddy wouldn't be discovered for days or even weeks.

Now returning from his pay-off encounter at the Pancake House with the shooter in Ohio, Montevecchio once again drove past the Holiday Inn's back parking lot and viewed it from his vantage point along Interstate 90. Ha! So far, so good, he thought. The longer Bolo's whacking goes undiscovered, the colder the trail becomes. You didn't have to be a cop or CSI investigator to know that. The colder the trail became, the better for everyone involved, especially for Caesar.

He wondered whether the killer had dropped off the keys yet. Caesar continued on, not wanting to be around the site when the Ohio hit man arrived.

Montevecchio arrived back in Erie about 11 o'clock that night, his round-about route taking him through the west side of town and along Greengarden Road. As he passed the West 21st Street intersection, the urge to look became just too powerful! He was compelled to at least take a quick glance toward Bolo's house. He slowed down and twisted his neck sideways for a clear view of the house. What he saw both frightened and excited him.

Police cars. Police cars with flashing lights everywhere.

Fuck, he thought. Oh, fuck!

And then he drove on into the night.

CHAPTER 8

THE COP ON THE COUCH GRINNED APPRECIATIVELY AS THE VIDEO-TAPED images of thinly clad teenaged cheerleaders pranced around the television screen.

Debbie Does Dallas was perhaps the most popular porn flick of the 1980s, so it wasn't strange that even a cop would take time out to admire and appreciate a pirated VHS offering of those supple young bodies at play. Only this cop, lounging on Frank "Bolo" Dovishaw's well-worn couch with its perhaps fake leather upholstery and hidden holes from cigarette burns, was taking his porn break in the middle of a crime scene.

What a fucking load, the detective sergeant arriving upon the scene thought.

"Take out that fucking tape!" ordered the veteran investigator, Dominick DiPaolo. "Shut off the damned TV. Take a ride. We'll call you back when we leave."

The grossly overweight uniformed officer looked more offended than ashamed as he lumbered away.

Earlier, after the discovery of the grisly murder was reported to police headquarters, the patrol division officer had been assigned to "stand by" at the house to protect the crime scene. But now, being unceremoniously kicked out, the cop knew better than to protest. Complying with the detective's order, he mumbled a few unintelligible words and left the warmth of Dovishaw's house for the cold January morning that was taking forever to dawn outside.

DiPaolo, long the Erie Police Bureau's foremost homicide detective, had been through this drill many times before. He and his partner, Detective Don Gunter, had arrived at 1634 West 21st Street only minutes earlier. It didn't take DiPaolo very long to size up the chaos he had witnessed so many times during past crime scene examinations:

Cops – uniformed and plainclothes – were in every room. They peered through doors, windows and closets. They pulled open kitchen cabinet and dresser drawers and examined papers, underwear, whatever was inside them. Like kids in a toy store, it seemed to DiPaolo, they were somehow compelled to not just touch, but handle everything they saw.

Jesus! Protect the crime scene? What a joke. More like they had orders to destroy the immediate environment.

Surveying the disorganized chaotic activities that more than disrupted the murder scene, DiPaolo exhaled deeply, then loudly raised his voice for all to hear:

"Everyone! Listen up!"

When he had the attention of the house-roaming hoard, he directed:

"Everyone in the living room! Now!"

When the last cop – there were perhaps 10 spread out into every room in the small Dovishaw house – had straggled into the front room, DiPaolo was terse:

"Detectives Weindorf and Kuhn will brief us. Everyone else, out! Do not touch anything – anything! – more! Now, as quickly as you can, please leave the premises."

More typical grumbling from typical cops, many of them who got their jobs the old-fashioned way – through Erie's not-too-thinly veiled political patronage system. Despite Civil Service requirements, it had always been an "open secret" in Erie. Who you "knew" was always the determining factor when searching for a city job – including on the police force or in the fire department. But like the "stand-by" patrol officer before them, these officers at least now knew this was Dom DiPaolo's case, DiPaolo's crime scene until he said otherwise.

It took several minutes before the last cop finally had trudged out, leaving DiPaolo, Gunter, and the two night shift detectives alone in the house. Detective Sergeant DiPaolo took another deep breath, then surveyed his surroundings. *Shit. What a fucking mess.* Created by his own department's inefficiency? He recalled the December 1980 Corporal Robert Owen murder crime scene, also destroyed by Erie Police Department shoddiness and inefficiency, and thought, "They never learn." Or was the victim, Frank "Bolo" Dovishaw simply the pig DiPaolo had always sized him up to be?

Either way, the house was a colossal disaster. Probably ransacked by the perp – or the perps, he thought.

Wow! Bolo "Ash Wednesday" Dovishaw, DiPaolo thought. Dead. Murdered. Is anyone surprised?

Less than an hour earlier – at 7:45 a.m. on Wednesday, January 5, 1983, Detective Sergeant DiPaolo had reported for work at Erie City Hall eager to follow up on a string of burglaries and robberies he suspected were tied to the heavy hitters of northwestern Pennsylvania's organized crime underworld.

Before he had the opportunity to sip his first cup of murky detective division coffee, he was summoned into the presence of Detective Captain Charles McCurdy, a veteran, but garden-variety, by-the-book cop who on occasion acknowledged he mistrusted everyone, including his own mother. McCurdy, who lived until age 86 when he died in retirement in 2012, was another who had advanced through the ranks of the long-established political patronage system, based not on what he accomplished as a police officer, but how many votes he could muster for the party without making waves. In this case, the "party" was the Democratic political machine of Mayor Louis J. Tullio, now in his fifth four-year term.

Tullio's iron grip over everything and anything that went on in City Hall was legendary. With Lou Tullio, who initially built his power base as secretary/business manager of the equally-politicized Erie School District two decades earlier, you either loved or hated the gregarious guy.

Dom DiPaolo? He loathed him. And he made no secret about his dislike for the mayor.

Still, despite the indisputable smut of Erie police politics, DiPaolo considered Charles "Cubby" McCurdy to be a straight shooter, albeit an almost comic book caricature of the universal police tagline, "To Protect and Serve."

"EVERYONE'S a liar, cheat and thief," McCurdy, with the look of a scolding parent, was often fond of telling anyone who would listen. "Everyone!"

"Even your mother?" someone would inevitably ask with a smirk.

"Everyone," McCurdy would coyly smile. On this morning, McCurdy was wearing his well-weathered brown checkered sport coat, shiny-seated blue serge trousers, tan shirt and dark blue, perhaps grease-spotted tie. With heavy, black work shoes and white tube socks, McCurdy never made anyone's best-dressed list. Nearing the end of an unremarkable career, he was seeking neither glory nor additional criminal cases for his résumé. Now approaching his pension, McCurdy operated on one speed: coast. But at heart, he was a good cop.

DiPaolo found the detective captain in a rather foul mood as he entered McCurdy's closet-sized office and initially learned of Erie's first recorded homicide for 1983. Tersely, without emotion, McCurdy broke the news to DiPaolo: The body of one Frank "Bolo" Dovishaw, a major sports-betting bookie and wise guy wannabe, had been found the night before in his basement. He had been shot once in the head. His hands and feet were bound. He was covered by a rug and dirty laundry.

"That's all I know for sure," McCurdy said.

But McCurdy wanted DiPaolo to know in no uncertain terms that the chief of police himself, Richard Skonieczka, had ordered McCurdy to assign DiPaolo to the case and authorize him to pick his own investigative team. Somehow, the chief's vote of confidence offered DiPaolo little solace or comfort. The chief, who died in 2012, wasn't a bad cop, not really. But DiPaolo knew he was close pals with Mayor Tullio. After World War II, Skonieczka was one of several high-ranking police officials who had played football at Gannon College for Lou "The Coach" Tullio, himself a former star at Holy Cross College.

"Look, you know all those guys," McCurdy offered, as though DiPaolo and the wise guys all belonged to the same restricted country club. "I'm thinking the wise guys – they've got to know something."

No shit, DiPaolo thought. But he never actually said it out loud. McCurdy got enough ribbing from the troops. Why should DiPaolo add to the torment?

"Oh, yeah, there's one thing more," McCurdy suddenly remembered, his recollection coming in almost hushed, conspiratorial tones as to make sure no one walking by the office would overhear. Erie cops were often a funny bunch when it came to "their" personal cases. Many, though not DiPaolo, were territorial, never wanting to share vital information that would give anyone else *their* collar.

"Yeah? What's that?" DiPaolo asked.

"Frank Rotunda's involved."

"What do you mean 'Rotunda's *involved*?'" DiPaolo almost choked on his coffee, incredulous Captain McCurdy had failed to mention that little tidbit earlier.

"Hey, what I know is just sketchy stuff," McCurdy said, somewhat apologetically. "Apparently the wise guys actually called Rotunda to Dovishaw's house when they found Bolo's body. It was Rotunda who called it in to the station last night."

DiPaolo knew all too well of Rotunda's reputation, or lack of it. Rotunda, not very effective as a detective, had loose personal ties to the underworld, ties that somehow never resulted in arrests or solved cases. DiPaolo had long suspected Rotunda was one of those rare "dirty" cops, but he could never prove it.

"Look," McCurdy said in a conciliatory fashion, "Joe Weindorf and Norm Kuhn are still at Bolo's house. They'll give you a run-down on everything they have. They're thorough guys. Then the investigation is all yours. Just get over there."

At least DiPaolo respected Detective Sergeants Weindorf and Kuhn. DiPaolo collected his partner, Gunter, and together they headed to the West 21st Street home of Frank "Bolo" Dovishaw. What DiPaolo could not have known at the time, however, was how long this murder case would dominate his life, how far its tentacles would stretch into Erie's organized crime fraternity, or how it also would reach into the highest echelons of the bureau of police and even some in Erie's banking community. But at that moment, he was ready to begin.

CHAPTER 9

THE DRIVE FROM ERIE POLICE HEADQUARTERS TO WEST 21ST WOULD take the detectives less than 10 minutes. It was enough time for DiPaolo to ponder the life of Frank "Bolo" Dovishaw. What an ugly life it was. DiPaolo already knew much about Bolo.

Francis Donald Dovishaw – aka Frank, Francie, Frankie, Bolo, Ash Wednesday – was born to a Romanian father, Frank Dovishaw, and Romanian mother, Flora Gama Dovishaw, during the leanest, hardest years of America's Great Depression. Bolo grew up as many second generation Americans of the era, neither impoverished by the hard times that swept the country, nor wealthy, but "poor" by later standards of the prosperous post-World War II America.

His father was a forge worker, while his mother, as was customary when her son was born in 1936, stayed at home to run the household. Like so many of that era, DiPaolo knew from a career of dealing with common street hoodlums always looking for the big score, Dovishaw was a perfect fit for the well-established small-time, criminal mold. From the beginning, he appeared to be hard-wired for laziness and the easy score.

It was clear from the start for those who knew Bolo: He would not labor in the 100-degree plus heat of the forge that sent his father to an early grave, nor would he spend his life buried in the obscurity of one of Erie's dozens of industrial factories, small or large. The daily drudgery of the shop life was for others, not for Bolo Dovishaw. Very early on in life he decided his fortune would not come from toil or hard work, but at the expense of others. Rather than work, if there was an easier way to get rich, he would find it.

As a result, few found it surprising that Dovishaw would grow into manhood occupying his free time – and there was an abundance of free time – hanging out on street corners, shooting craps for pennies and dimes, playing poker through the long nights, and finding himself in frequent, though minor, skirmishes with the law.

Dovishaw was raised in the Roman Catholic Church. Starting at age six in 1942, Bolo Dovishaw was destined to become an average student at Holy Rosary School on Erie's east side. Three years later, his father died unexpectedly of a massive heart attack when Bolo was only nine. But, by 1950, when Dovishaw completed the Catholic parish grammar school at the age of 14, his mother had remarried. This time it was to Adam Borowicz, a Polish immigrant. The family moved across town, from the east side to 1018 West 18th Street, part of Erie's famous "Little Italy" neighborhood. Yet, tragically for the still struggling family, Borowicz would die accidentally 11 years later on April 1, 1961, when, at the age of 52 he drowned after falling from a fishing boat in Lake Erie.

Whether the loss of the two dominant male figures in his life by the age of 25 contributed to what Bolo's life would later become is unknown. Perhaps, some say, the die was cast for Dovishaw by other factors and dynamics, environmental, societal, emotional. In either of the ways, Dovishaw's life remains a matter for speculation.

As a self-contained, intimate community with a shared culture for many, "Little Italy" was at the same time both famous and notorious. The neighborhood produced many who contributed mightily to the quality of life in Erie, Pennsylvania – priests, physicians, cops, teachers, politicians and others who often labored in anonymity, but were honest, hard-working and productive citizens. The houses were impeccable, most with rose gardens, the aromas emanating from the homes tell-tale of what was simmering on the stoves inside. Dovishaw's parents and step-father, for example, never achieved fame, but they never had brushes with the police, either, and were highly-respected in their community.

Conversely, the same neighborhood steadily served as an incubator for crime and the most heinous of criminal behavior and activities. Dovishaw, from young adulthood, chose the latter option.

A rose might still be a rose by any other name, but even Dovishaw's nickname – Bolo – served to portend his personality and what those who knew him best not only thought of him, but also what incredible lack of potential they saw in him. It was the young men who frequented the Midway Pool Hall in the heart of Little Italy in the 500 block of West 18th Street, owned by the Dominick brothers – Chico, Sam and Mike – who dubbed young Frank Dovishaw as "Bolo." Detective Sergeant DiPaolo thought the name to be ironic. It's often used by police as an abbreviation for "Be on the lookout."

That Dovishaw was deemed from the beginning to be so untrustworthy – even by those with similar reputations – was more than telling. That he was destined for a violent death that would mirror what had become his criminality was perhaps anti-climatic to his start in life, DiPaolo thought.

For it was a life that began almost typically for many first and second generation Italian-Americans, as well as other immigrants of varied ethnicity, whose families settled in the northeastern United States communities and the industrialized cities along the Great Lakes just before and following the turn of the 20th Century. They came to build new lives in a fresh, new country, and that's exactly what they did. The majority of these non-English speaking immigrants to the new world toiled with their sweat and blood to create the so-called "American Dream" for themselves and for their families and those future generations of Italian-Americans and others who followed. For most, their hard-wired culture was to work unflinchingly, no matter how hard. Eventually they began to take their places in virtually every occupation and profession, and in every nook and cranny of American life.

Some, like Bolo, and like Caesar Montevecchio, Cy Ciotti, Ray Ferritto, Joey Scutella, Merchie Chris Calabrese Jr., Niggsy Arnone and others of the new loose and fast generation, took much different tracks.

So it was here in Little Italy where Dovishaw, although not Italian, formed his earliest and most indelible relationships with those who would come to dominate Erie's slimy underbelly for decades to come in crimes both petty and horrific. In Little Italy during the 1950s and 1960s, young Bolo Dovishaw quickly found his way to many other unsavory joints besides the Midway Pool Room. They were places owned and frequented by wannabe wise guys who, at the time, were simply labeled "hoods" or "thugs;" these were places like the A-K Lunch on

West 18th Street, owned by Sam and Tony DeDad, The Black Window, also on West 18th, owned by set-up man Cy Ciotti, and Carlo Allessie's Ticker Tape in the same neighborhood, as well as the famed Monarch Club. The Black Window was one of the more notorious of Bolo's haunts. A four-lane bowling alley originally owned by Charlie Gross, it was sold to Ciotti, who immediately painted the front window black to ensure that passersby – as well as nosy cops – couldn't see inside, where there was said to be far more gambling than bowling.

After graduating from the former Academy High School in 1954, Bolo enlisted in the U.S. Navy. Following boot camp, he became a hospital corpsman and worked as an X-Ray laboratory technician as well as in the pharmacies at each of his duty stations. Did these service occupations provide a glimmer of hope that Dovishaw would someday embark in a meaningful civilian career? Fat chance. After his four-year Navy stint, Bolo was honorably discharged – perhaps the first and only time the word "honorable" would be applied to him or used to describe his activities. Following separation from the service, he eventually found work in 1960 as a laborer with the locally-respected Mayer Brothers Construction Company.

Mayer Brothers, situated in Little Italy not far from Bolo's homestead, was known for hiring young, tough men from the neighborhood. It was the hardest of labor, yet it was honorable. Back-breaking work produced much sweat and, at the time, little pay. Dovishaw, to no one's surprise, lasted two weeks. Easier money was more in tune with his preferences. And he was determined to find it. In the meantime, however, he signed on for a softer job at what was called "The Monkey Works," Erie's globally-famous Marx Toys Company situated directly in the heart of Little Italy and again where many young Italians worked. Bolo, as was his past practice, enjoyed being a big shot with the younger workers at Marx, always showing off the wad of cash he constantly carried.

Johnny "D" DeSanti, a respected school teacher who worked summers while in college, later said Bolo liked to tell stories to young guys, always trying to puff up his image. Everyone at Marx, however, knew Bolo was a blow bag, always bragging about his money. Dovishaw's bragging, aside, where *did* all Bolo's cash come from? Few knew. And those who did weren't talking. But, as usual in Little Italy, there was plenty of speculation.

Less than a year later, at the age of 24, Dovishaw found a new job, one more suitable to his temperament, lack of occupational training, limited ability and scope, and over-all laziness. Becoming a clerk at the popular Dee's Cigar Store was a primer for Bolo Dovishaw on the inner-workings of Erie's dark underworld of illegal betting. It also introduced him to Erie's big-time gambling figures who occupied that narrow universe, and reconnected him with several childhood chums who got their start in Little Italy.

It is said that at that time literally hundreds of illegal bettors frequented Dee's Cigar Store daily. The cash take was awesome. And Bolo wasn't about to be left out. Dee's sold tobacco products, newspapers and magazines, but existed then in that capacity mainly in name only.

The State Street landmark was owned by Dominick "Dee" Adiutori, the longtime, well-known king of Erie's illegal gambling industry. His empire was run from Erie's main drag cigar store and newsstand, where Dovishaw now clerked. Dee's partner in the Erie Coin Vending business was James Salamone, fondly known in underworld circles as "Westfield Jimmy" Salamone. With close connections to Buffalo and Cleveland mob families, Adiutori and Westfield Jimmy were widely considered locally as the "Big Boys" of Erie's lucrative illegal numbers and sports betting kingdom. Prior to his death in the mid-'70s, Stefano Maggadino, the head of the Buffalo, New York, crime family, is said to have visited with them regularly.

Both Adiutori and Salamone had been arrested and pleaded guilty to gambling charges. "Westfield Jimmy" was probed by the Pennsylvania Crime Commission in 1979 for allegedly being a lieutenant in Buffalo's Stefano Maggadino crime family.

Unknown to Dovishaw, his first attempt to get rich by taking from others – even his fellow thieves – would be a precursor of what would eventually lead to his gruesomely violent death, a grisly execution even to the most hardened, that some believe might have been predestined some 23 years earlier.

While Dovishaw clerked at Dee's front for Erie's illegal numbers racket, he firmly established himself as a minor, yet nonetheless laughable crime figure at the age of 24, masterminding what would later become known to Detective DiPaolo as Bolo's great botched phony robbery.

The era was the beginning of what would later become known as "The Turbulent '60s." Dovishaw, it seemed, was highly determined to get a jump start on the decade. Enlisting a pal from Erie's Little Italy neighborhood where Bolo got his start, Bolo set out to effect the "perfect" crime. Sadly, he just wasn't that cerebral.

Anthony Arnone – crudely nicknamed "Niggsy" for obvious reasons relating to his dark, Mediterranean complexion – along with Bolo, had found themselves in dire need of $8,000 to pay off gambling debts. Gambling debts in Erie or elsewhere were like U.S. Savings Bonds, DiPaolo would come to learn. The longer they went unpaid, the more they matured. Unlike savings bonds, however, a maturing gambling debt could lead to a serious head laceration from a Louisville Slugger or even worse.

As result of this need for money, Dovishaw and Arnone began their professional illicit careers less than auspiciously. They saw the daily gambling receipts at Dee's as a quick and easy way to pick up the needed cash. A last-minute "walk in" participant in the plan was David Cologrande, not one of the wise guy wannabes, but one of the "crowd," one susceptible to peer pressure. Cologrande also clerked with Dovishaw at the local numbers and gambling headquarters. By chance, he just happened to walk into the store as the "perfect" crime was being launched. As a result, the others – Dovishaw and Arnone – quickly cut him in on the deal.

According to Bolo Dovishaw's original script, Arnone would be the "robber," while Dovishaw himself would be the poor, hapless robbery "victim." With clock-like precision late that cold night – December 9, 1960 – Arnone, the "robber," strolled into the cigar store and calmly confronted Dovishaw who equally calmly handed him $10,000 in illegal numbers receipts of the day. And at that exact moment, as the unknowing Cologrande walked in on the "robbery," he was immediately clubbed nearly senseless by the Coke bottle-brandishing Niggsy Arnone.

"What the fuck are you doing?" the stunned Cologrande managed to stammer. He had already seen too much, knew too much. The others promised to cut him in on the take from their fake robbery. Bolo waited for Niggsy to "escape" into the night before sounding the police alarm. So far, so good.

Meanwhile, at Erie Police Headquarters – about a mile away – officers there received the alarm with, well, alarm! They were much more alarmed than they would have been for merely a normal run-of-the-mill robbery. That's because they knew Detective Sergeant Nick Buto was at the center of the nightly big-stakes poker game in the hidden downstairs room at Dee's. Buto's fellow card sharks included the first round draft choices of Erie's slimy underworld, all convicted felons with ties to organized crime throughout the northeast. Not good for Buto or any police officer.

Rather than rushing to the scene of the "crime," the winking and nodding cops opted instead to give their boss ample time to collect his winnings and make a stealthy, but strategic departure, before sending a squad car with lights flashing, sirens blaring.

The "hold up" would be investigated. Eventually. Ah, the perfect crime. An integral component of Dovishaw's plan of action called for the trio to stash a large chunk of their booty in a bank safe-deposit box at Security People's Trust Company, then remain cool and nonchalant until they believed it was finally safe to divvy up and spend the ill-gotten phony robbery loot, including the satisfying of their gambling debts.

Dovishaw had officially reported the robbery to – who else? – but the card-playing Sergeant Buto, saying $10,000 was taken. The investigation remained open for months. But following the robbery, instead of depositing most of cash in the bank box, the co-conspirators kept for themselves just enough to raise the collective eyebrows and suspicion of police and bookies alike when they began spending in uncharacteristic style – just as typically as high rollers would have.

It wasn't until later that a young detective named Mario Bagnoni got a tip from one of his many street sources that the Dee's robbery actually was phony. Bagnoni, later rising to the rank of deputy police chief and elected to Erie City Council for more than three decades, was assigned to the case. He made quick work of it.

Bagnoni teamed up with Detective Sergeant Bobby Ross (whose son, John "J.R." Ross, became Chief Erie County Detective and later a fraud investigator at Erie Insurance Exchange). First, Bagnoni and Ross grilled Dovishaw, who promptly gave up his pals Arnone and Cologrande. Next, the street-savvy cops visited Arnone at his parents' home. Arnone approached a desk drawer, reached in and came up with $2,000 in robbery proceeds. When Bagnoni and Ross showed up at Colograndes home, the third member of the trio quickly confessed, having no qualms about implicating the other two. More robbery money was later turned over to Bagnoni and Ross by Niggsy Arnone's then girlfriend. The detectives, acting on information from the robbers, also found money buried at Mercyhurst College in southeast Erie. The remainder of the stolen cash was recovered from Bolo's safe-deposit box at Security Peoples Trust Co., 18th and State Streets.

All three "robbers" were sentenced by Erie County Judge Elmer Evans to serve 6-to-23 months in Pittsburgh's Allegheny County Work House. Some perfect crime, DiPaolo recalled from reading yellowing police files during his rookie years.

While Bolo was doing time at the Allegheny County Work House, his stepfather, Adam Borowicz, died unexpectedly in the April 1961 fishing accident. As was the custom at the time, Bolo was escorted to the Erie funeral home by prison guards to pay his respects, and then returned to the Allegheny County Work House. Later that same year, he was released on parole.

For Dovishaw, his first serious brush with the law involving Niggsy Arnone wouldn't be his last. But the next time, they would not be on the same side. According to police, they would be far from it.

Dominick DiPaolo remembered well all he had read in those old files. Soon after Dovishaw's release from prison, Bolo moved quickly to try to establish himself as a player. Hanging out now at Dante's Cigar Store in the 500 block of West 18th Street in the heart of Little Italy, he quickly bought into the Veteran's Club at West 18th and Chestnut Streets. The club was run by Erie cop Toby Rigazzi and future Erie County Councilman Fiore Leone. Leone was quick to get out when Bolo arrived, leaving Toby and Bolo. From his base at the Vet's Club and Dante's, Dovishaw began an association with the infamous and ill-fated City Squire Club in downtown Erie. The City Squire was a popular after hours spot for the elite of the local underworld, a hangout and watering hole for wise guys and wannabes alike.

At the City Squire, Bolo met wise guys from Buffalo, Pittsburgh, Cleveland and especially from Youngstown, Ohio – a post-World War II hot-bed of Mafia activity because of its strategic location situated between the major cities of three populous states.

Youngstown, and the Niles-Warren, Ohio "strip" would become infamous as well because of the geographic location's known hospitality to organized crime. (A former Erie detective made his name in Youngstown, trying to clean up organized crime. Eddie Allen, who later became chief of a metro California police department, also authored what was considered the first definitive mob book, *The Mafia: Merchants of Menace.*)

It was at the City Squire where Bolo hooked up with Erie's John "Pigeon" White and Donald "Jungles" D'Andrea, who ran the club for him. ("Pigeon" and "Jungles" later left the club and purchased a downtown hotspot called "The Shamrock Café.") Dovishaw also got involved with "made" men from the Youngstown mob who were associated with the Buckeye Ribbon and Carbon Company, a firm dealing in typewriter ribbons and carbon paper. Bolo became the company's Erie representative. The company's Erie branch immediately became a front for Dovishaw's new gambling enterprise. Dovishaw's alleged partners in both business and bookmaking were Donald Mastrostefano, who also went by Don Mastrey, and Dino DiMarco. Although Buckeye Ribbon and Carbon would go out of business a few years later, Dovishaw found himself in his element. His illegal gambling business quickly grew to one that reportedly netted the partners more than $2,000 a day, a staggering sum for smalltime bookmakers of the early 1960s. They felt they were literally rolling in money, and some, with their black, velvet-lapeled overcoats, played the role to perfection.

Dovishaw's purchased interest in the City Squire Club was with his pal, set-up man Cy Ciotti, who was known to police to frequently set the stage for robberies and burglaries. In October of 1970, the club at West 3rd and Peach Streets, was destroyed by a sensational five-alarm fire. The building was gutted, the blaze eventually ruled the result of what some of that day, including cops, called "Italian Lightning" or, in correct terminology, arson. Typically, there were no arrests in the arson fire. It wouldn't be the first time that Bolo would skate. But with the fire ruled arson, the insurance claim was denied. Even so, the City Squire Club managed to move to a new and larger location on Brown Avenue on Erie's west side bordering Little Italy.

Bolo was calling the shots, now. It was a one-man operation, but he needed good guys on his board to secure Pennsylvania Liquor Control Board approval. So he had his pals Dino DiMarco installed as president and Armand Ferrante, also known as "Peppy," as vice president. Charlene Sisson, a longtime political supporter of Mayor Lou Tullio, became the club's secretary-treasurer, while Clara Grybowski, the mother of the infamous Pearl Grybowski, and Dom Bruno, became directors.

Frankie Thomas, nephew of admitted mob hit man Ray Ferritto, and who later would be involved in Cleveland's Danny Greene hit, was named to manage the new City Squire Club.

Business was good at the City Squire and it was especially good with gambling. But by 1973, Bolo Dovishaw's illegal numbers operation began drawing serious attention from law enforcement officials. In April, officers of the Pennsylvania State Police Organized Crime Division arrested Bolo and Dino, as well as Donald Mastrey, who worked for Frank's Cleaners, delivering dry cleaning to homes, a perfect scenario for taking numbers. It would be Dovishaw's last arrest. For it was then he decided to become a snitch for the Feds, but not without remuneration. In return for turning on his pals, Dovishaw got protection from law enforcement at all levels. The gambling and co-conspiracy charges against him were dropped, officially *nolle prossed* in legalese. But most important, as part of the ongoing deal, he was given carte blanche to operate his illegal business freely and without hindrance from the cops. Other bookies, it seemed to many, were arrested with much frequency. But Frank "Bolo" Dovishaw, aka "Ash Wednesday," was never again charged with a criminal offense.

During this wildly successful period of Dovishaw's "professional" life, many of his "pals" were indicted on federal bookmaking charges. Among those arrested were Frank C. "Foops" Scalise, Lidano L. "Junior" Adiutori, Alfred "Big Al" DelSandro, Michael "Jazza Mike" Maggio, Rollo "Rags" Riazzi, Marian DeSantis, Sebastian "Bashi" Cologrande, Michael "Mike Sockett" Soccoccio, Big Al's son, David, Alex "Jiggs" Vendetti, and Carl "Warpie" Lombardo. No one even suspected it was Dovishaw feeding the Feds all the information they could handle. Or did they? Some of these bookies would later figure in Dovishaw's miserable life, perhaps leading to his demise. But at the time, Bolo had complete freedom from prosecution.

His "book" had grown so large that Bolo was now butting heads with Al DelSandro, Carlo Allessie and Bill Anderson, previously uncontested and said to be among the hottest bookies in Erie.

Bolo's snitching even got him immunity in the Danny Greene murder trial in 1977 – a killing later admitted by his eventual partner, Raymond Ferritto. The stooling resulted in continued total freedom from prosecution. Combined with the arrest of so many others, by the early-1980s Francis "Bolo" Dovishaw found he had near exclusivity in the illegal gambling business.

Bolo was king of illegal gambling in Erie, Pennsylvania. Who would have ever thought it? Not the cops. Not even Dovishaw's contemporaries at that time. Because of his successes, this period demonstrated Dovishaw's willingness to truly establish himself as one of Erie's major organized crime figures for the first time.

On October 5, 1977, Bolo and Frankie Thomas, manager of the City Squire, helped Thomas' uncle – the admitted hit man Ferritto – in the bombing murder of Cleveland mobster Danny Greene. Greene's body was blown apart as he approached his car in the East Cleveland suburbs when Ferritto, with a little help from his Erie pals, detonated a radio-activated bomb. All three were eventually arrested, but after turning evidence for the government, all were given immunity from prosecution, an act that forever amazed Detective Sergeant Dominick DiPaolo, especially as he set out to investigate Bolo's murder.

As the underworld saying goes, DiPaolo thought, they "shit the bed" on the Cleveland mob. In police talk, they stooled on their pals. After the Danny Greene trial in Cleveland, Dovishaw, Thomas and Ferritto were placed in the federal witness protection program and relocated to Texas, where Dovishaw took the new name, Frank Fabian. He chose Fabian partly because his idol had been the 1950s' flash-in-the-pan teenage sensation Fabian Forte, and partly because it was his grandmother's – Mary Fabian Gama's – maiden name.

Federal witness protection didn't agree with the three men. Within a year, they were all back in Erie. Ironically, their reputations as mob hit men gave them new status, working in their favor in Erie's racketeering nether-world.

Bolo's life had changed. He'd come a long, long way from Little Italy's pool halls and cigar stores.

Since 1967, when he was 31, he had been married to Joan P. Szczesny Bachofner, a divorcee. They lived at 3021 Elmwood Avenue in a well-kept middle-class neighborhood only a few miles, but a world away from Erie's Little Italy. The marriage was rocky and often stormy because of Dovishaw's hide-and-seek gambling lifestyle.

As a result, it was no surprise to anyone who knew them that Bolo and Joan separated in 1977 after Dovishaw entered the federal witness protection program with the Danny Greene murder/conspiracy case still ringing in Joan's ears. Although they no longer resided together, their relationship could still be described as cordial, it was said. To the day he was slain six years after the separation, the couple had not divorced.

Dovishaw ran his gambling operation out of this mother's house since 1973. But when Flora Gama Dovishaw Borowicz died in 1979, Bolo actually moved into and took over her home at 1634 West 21st Street for good. He not only ran his illegal sports betting business from there, he now lived there. The name listed in the phone book, DiPaolo learned that first morning of the murder investigation, was none other than "Frank Fabian," an inside joke appreciated only by Dovishaw and shared with a chosen few. Yet now, DiPaolo thought with a grimace, Bolo Dovishaw was no longer laughing.

But there was more in the records that DiPaolo had read and reread dozens of times.

By the early-1980s, Dovishaw was known as Erie's undisputed gambling kingpin – even to street-savvy Erie news reporters. He was also known to frequently associate with Pittsburgh mobsters, often laying-off bets that were too big for him to handle with Pittsburgh's larger and more sophisticated gambling operation.

Friends and acquaintances in illegal gambling enterprises have never been known for their customer or product loyalty. One evening in 1980 clearly demonstrates the cut-throat ruthlessness of Bolo's supposed friends. On the night of March 13, after "Ash Wednesday" had completed collections on his gambling route, he returned to his West 21st Street home only to be confronted by two masked men who had been hiding inside.

The men, according to later statements to police, were believed to have been Norman "Bo" Baumann of Detroit, boyfriend of alleged hooker Pearl Grybowski, who was passed around the wise guy circuit like a library book, and Charles "The Hawk" Serafini, also later to become another police target. They were alleged to have beaten and robbed Bolo Dovishaw.

"The Hawk" thought he was untouchable because one of his pals was Erie City Councilman Jerry Mifsud, DiPaolo recalled. Mifsud, a one-time star football and baseball player for Erie Cathedral Preparatory School, was considered to have been a council ally of Mayor Lou Tullio.

The connection for Serafini was an important one. (Baumann would later hang himself while in a Michigan penitentiary awaiting extradition to Erie for a Halloween bank robbery he pulled with Pearl Grybowski.) Serafini was then seeing a young Jane Earll, a college student waitressing at Bechto's Café on the west side. She later would become an assistant district attorney, respected state senator and even Republican nominee for Pennsylvania Lieutenant Governor. Important to note that Earll, then and later in life, was never involved in any criminal or even untoward activities.

Bolo's robbers knew exactly where to look for the gambling proceeds stashed in the secret bathroom vanity hiding place because Caesar Montevecchio, who set up the robbery for the two participants, told them. But they didn't want to tip off Bolo with their inside knowledge. Just to make it look good and protect Caesar, they bludgeoned Bolo, threatening to kill him if he didn't tell them where the money was hidden. The masked robbers took Dovishaw's car, which he later discovered just several blocks from his home. Despite the attempt to deceive him, Dovishaw was convinced the robbery was the result of inside information supplied by those who knew of his operation, and knew where he kept his money. Bolo often told his cronies he knew the robbery was the work of Caesar and "The Hawk." He believed he was right, but he could never prove it.

Although the robbery victim Dovishaw reported the crime to police, the amount listed was "undetermined." Word on the street, however, was that the robbers made off with between $25,000 and $50,000 in illegal sports betting receipts.

What DiPaolo could not know during this extremely early phase of the murder investigation was the irony he would later discover. It would again be Montevecchio who would make another attempt at wiping out Bolo's gambling stash – but one that would also claim Dovishaw's sorry life.

During these years of relative success, despite the robbery – or maybe because of it – Dovishaw had hooked up with hit man Ferritto and

Phil Torrelli. Sadly for Bolo, his protective support system didn't work. They became partners and in so doing they created one of the largest, if not *the* largest, illegal gambling books in Northwestern Pennsylvania.

Only "Big Al" DelSandro was left to compete with Bolo's book. But DelSandro was no dummy when it came to figuring out Dovishaw's success was the result of his relationship with the federal authorities. DelSandro was convinced Dovishaw was capable of taking the heat off himself by putting it on others, including Big Al DelSandro. Eventually, DelSandro found himself getting grabbed by police more and more. And he began to blame Dovishaw.

DiPaolo would always smile when he remembered Big Al's crazy ravings.

"I got grabbed by the city police, state police, the FBI, the army, navy and marines and that fucking fat pig Bolo is still out walking around," DelSandro once stormed to DiPaolo. "He ain't seen the inside of a cell in 20 years. He got a legal license to book."

Such was still apparently true on that cold, wintry morning of early January, 1983, DiPaolo thought. Frank "Bolo" Dovishaw was hated by his competitors in the illegal gambling business, and by his supposed friends, who cared not for Bolo, but only for his stash. Now, all bets were off, DiPaolo thought. No more protection for Bolo Dovishaw. No more protection for anyone. This was now DiPaolo's case. And he vowed to see it through to the end – no matter where it took him.

CHAPTER 10

IT HAD TAKEN DETECTIVE SERGEANT DOMINICK DIPAOLO ONLY A FEW minutes to drive with his partner, Don Gunter, from Erie Police Headquarters to Bolo Dovishaw's West 21st Street house. But it was plenty of time, in DiPaolo's analytical cop's mind, to recount the uselessness and human futility of Dovishaw's wasted life and especially his death. Few would mourn him, the police officer was certain.

It had taken Erie's top homicide cop even less time to survey the Dovishaw house and hastily clear the premises of all unwanted cops, many of whom had seemed to be lingering in virtually every room, almost systematically and by design destroying evidence in what once might have been a pristine crime scene.

Now alone in the house with Gunter and the pair of 3rd shift detectives, DiPaolo could start the process of not only determining *what* had happened – but even more importantly, *why* it had happened. And once he learned the *why*, he was confident that sooner or later the "*who*" would emerge.

After the uniformed officers left, Detective Sergeant Joseph Weindorf, along with his partner, Detective Sergeant Norman Kuhn, began their briefing. DiPaolo listened intently, methodically checking out the house as Weindorf led him to an apparent bathroom hiding place – a wooden, built-in vanity – for Dovishaw's lucrative sports betting business' ill-gotten proceeds. What he saw was the result of an obvious crime. A three-foot section of wood had been removed from the side of the bathroom vanity. It was painted the same antique cream color as the main vanity. The now gaping hole in the bathroom facility revealed hundreds of ledger sheets and numbers slips that Dovishaw had painstakingly hidden there. The find confirmed what most cops already knew.

Frank "Bolo" Dovishaw had operated one of the largest numbers and sports betting games in the largest numbers and sports betting town in northwestern Pennsylvania. The old numbers racket, thanks to the Commonwealth of Pennsylvania's governor and legislators, actually had gone legal years ago. The profits in the state's "Daily Number" game went to benefit senior citizen services. But the illegal numbers trade and those who operated it had not fretted for long once the state got into the act. The state actually made it easy for the criminal underworld to continue the numbers business – let the state handle the details, such as publicly selecting the numbers on live TV each day, while the bookies simply increased the payoffs for their illegal transactions. Combined with sports betting, the take was enormous, even in a mid-sized town like Erie. Bolo was handling $2,000 a day on the three-digit number. Over a good, solid sports betting weekend, the handle could reach $200,000.

It had been roughly 12 hours now since police were informed of Erie's latest gangland-style murder. Joe Weindorf would fill in whatever sketchy details he was able to assemble overnight for DiPaolo.

Joe Weindorf was a straight cop, DiPaolo always believed, and, with a Criminology degree from Mercyhurst College, he was one of the few members of the Erie Police Department who could boast a higher education sheepskin. Another was DiPaolo's ex-partner and good friend, David Bagnoni, who had a Master's Degree in Criminology. Weindorf would later go on to become a district magistrate, just as DiPaolo would. After that, Weindorf was Erie County's public safety director. But for now, the homicide investigator's job was to listen carefully as Joe Weindorf ran down the few details known at that time to police. Both Weindorf and Kuhn were good with details, DiPaolo thought.

At 8 p.m., Weindorf explained, Detective Frank Rotunda had telephoned Detective Captain Tom Stanton to report that longtime Erie bookie Bolo Dovishaw had been murdered. Hell, DiPaolo thought,

Rotunda had been pushing the envelope with his pals in dirty places for years. DiPaolo had long suspected that Rotunda was getting his extra discretionary cash by having close ties to Erie's major numbers racketeers. For years, Rotunda had met regularly in City Hall's 2nd floor cafeteria with two city workers, both known to be taking numbers from city employees or anyone else who wanted in.

DiPaolo took a quick mental departure from his briefing, recalling well when he and David Bagnoni pinched one of those two city workers, Louie Manendo, and his political friends. The Sears and Roebuck Warehouse had been broken into and more than 50 25-inch color television sets were grabbed. DiPaolo and Bags learned the identity of the burglar and quickly arrested him. The burglar, in an attempt to save himself, DiPaolo recalled, told the cops he could give up "some big people" in Erie, those who frequently bought the stolen merchandise from him. Once DiPaolo was convinced the burglar just might be telling the truth, he recruited a female police officer to assist with the investigation by accompanying the burglar undercover on his mission to sell the TVs at steep discounts. Assistant Erie County District Attorney Frank Scutella okayed the plan, and the pair – burglar and undercover cop – set off to unload the merchandise.

Dr. Giacomo Luppino, a well-known Erie dentist in Little Italy, John Pape, one of Lou Tullio's big-time supporters, cop Frank Rotunda's uncle Joe Rotunda, who lived with the mayor's sister and owned Al-Dente's Restaurant and the Liberty Club, Frank Iannello, aka Frankie Day, one of Rotunda's employees, and Louie Manendo, the city worker who was said to be one of Tullio's lackeys, were all targeted for the discounted TVs – and all purchased the stolen merchandise. Did they know the TVs were hot? For twenty bucks each? Hello? Manendo had met the undercover cop and burglar behind a grocery store at night, as Manendo had requested. He was found to be in possession of a .38 caliber handgun and twelve grand in cash. Not bad for a city job, DiPaolo thought. All the proud new owners of the 25-inch color television sets were quickly locked up. And then, as DiPaolo recalled, the proverbial manure hit the Westinghouse.

The next morning, Deputy Police Chief Jack Cousins called the two young detectives into his office.

"Are you two fuckin' out of your minds? Do you know who you locked up?"

"Yeah," DiPaolo said. "Dirt bags. Why?"

"These are all friends of the mayor, that's why!"

Now it was Bagnoni's turn.

"Does the mayor or his friends have immunity?" Bags asked with no small amount of sarcasm. "Some kind of immunity we don't know about?"

Now Cousins was almost beside himself in his stuttering response.

"You know I want to become the Chief! And now the mayor yelled at me and said, 'You can't control them two guys! How are you going to control the entire department?'"

It was all DiPaolo and Bagnoni could do to stifle laughter.

"Didn't you know that Rotunda is like the mayor's brother-in-law?" Cousins continued.

"Yeah, so what?" the detectives beamed in near unison.

"Well you embarrassed me! You should have told me what you were doing!"

"Yeah, right," DiPaolo said. "When we take a black kid down on a job, we don't tell you. Why is this different?"

"Leave! Now!" Cousins ordered.

Joe Rotunda, the cop's uncle, had an impressive criminal background, having been arrested for rape and corrupting the morals of a minor, a 15-year-old girl, and pleading guilty to a lesser charge of fornication. He also had been arrested on bribery charges, pleading guilty, as well as a number of arrests for bookmaking, charges in which he was found guilty. He also pleaded guilty to counterfeiting, and was in and out of state and federal pens. With his mayoral connection, he thought he was invincible, but learned the hard way he was not. DiPaolo always found it incredible that the Guiseppe Mazzini Society, an Erie Italian civic group, once named Rotunda as its Italian-American Man of the Year. DiPaolo recalled men such as Attorney Richard Agresti, who founded Boys Baseball in Erie, Dr. Quentin Orlando, a city councilman and state senator, Mario Bagnoni, the former deputy police chief and city councilman with 35 years of service, and Fiore Leone, a county councilman for 37 years, as those who so much more deserved the recognition than Rotunda. Rotunda was also was inducted into the Metropolitan Erie Chapter of the Pennsylvania Sports Hall of Fame, yet few, if any, could figure out what sport he played or coached, lest it was for a prison team. Even recently, one inductee served time in a federal prison for selling cocaine. Some committee members, DiPaolo asserts, were aware beforehand of the inductee going off to jail. As a result, DiPaolo has questioned the organizations' credibility. Still, DiPaolo acknowledges, there were also many deserving awardees who were honored by both groups. But now DiPaolo's boss, Cousins, was questioning why the detective team arrested Rotunda?

(DiPaolo recalled this Rotunda incident more than 30 years later when learning Joseph J. Rotunda, aka James and Jimmy, Joe Rotunda's then 71-year-old son, who, along was his wife, was charged with filing false police reports, conspiracy to commit retail theft and several summary violations. Rotunda was accused of reporting to police that he and his wife were carjacked at gunpoint, an incident later determined to be phony. He eventually pled to a lesser charge. "Still trying to scam the system, just like his old man," DiPaolo thought.)

Weeks after the TV arrests, Assistant DA Scutella phoned the pair of detectives and requested that they meet him at the Nicholson Restaurant across Perry Square Park from City Hall in downtown Erie, and a short walk from the Erie County Courthouse on West 6th Street. At the restaurant, Scutella told the cops, "We got fucked. Tullio, Cousins and Elliot LeFaiver (then 5th Ward minor judiciary alderman where the charges against the mayor's pals had been filed) met with Bob Chase (then the District Attorney and Scutella's boss). Chase called me into his office and told me to withdraw the charges because they represented entrapment."

Scutella said he argued with his boss, but Chase insisted the charges be dropped.

"What could I do? I work for him!" Scutella told the cops.

"That's total bullshit," DiPaolo fired back.

"I know," Scutella said. "How do you think I feel?"

Cousins, however, never again mentioned the pinch to the detectives. But about a month later, without notice or warning, DiPaolo and Bagnoni were split up as detective partners. They were told that the powers that be wanted one of them on the first shift and another on the second shift, allegedly to take responsibility over high profile cases. They were convinced the separation was over the stolen TV busts, but they couldn't prevent the split.

Several weeks later, new departmental rules and regulations were implemented in the Erie Bureau of Police. Any officer from any division requesting a warrant for any defendant was supposed to meet first with the officer in charge of the shift and, using controlled identification numbers, would be issued blank warrants after giving the defendant's name and address on a warrant sheet. This had the same impact of notifying all the department's and the city's top officials of who was about to be arrested. The so-called "DiPaolo-Bagnoni Rule" was employed for many years to follow.

About a year after the split-up of the successful detective team, a young man, Melvin Clanton, was killed in his home, having been shot five times. For a week, the dicks working the case had no leads and were at a standstill in their investigation. Cousins called for DiPaolo and Bagnoni.

"How about taking this case over? We're getting a lot of heat from the black community and from the news media. If you can solve this, I'll talk to the mayor to get you back as partners."

Four days later in Cleveland, Ohio, the detective pair locked up four suspects for the murder, two Clevelanders and two from Erie. All were later convicted.

Later, Cousins told the detectives, "Sorry, but the mayor won't go for it. He's still pissed at what you did to his brother-in-law."

But DiPaolo and Bagnoni knew they never would be a permanent team again. They took the case, not because of Cousins' promise, but because they were professionals who were more concerned with and motivated by solving a murder.

DiPaolo would later think, why would Lou Tullio even wonder why the cops disliked him with such a passion.

Now DiPaolo was back to being transfixed on Detective Weindorf's briefing of all that had transpired the previous evening – especially the part about the cop Frank Rotunda's involvement. Sooner or later, DiPaolo thought, Rotunda would get his. Apparently, Weindorf continued his briefing, Rotunda had been summoned to Dovishaw's house by none other than one Raymond Ferritto. Everyone knew Ray Ferritto. Ferritto, the master of brutality. An admitted mob hit man for hire who had left the federal witness protection program several years earlier – his second departure from the government program – to return to Erie and his wise guy friends.

Ferritto had telephoned Rotunda, saying he was concerned because he couldn't find Dovishaw. He asked that Rotunda meet him at Bolo's house. The gullible Rotunda complied. When the cop arrived, Weindorf explained to DiPaolo, he searched the house and eventually found Dovishaw's body in the basement. *Oh, really?* DiPaolo thought! He immediately smelled "set-up." And the cop sensed that Rotunda never knew he was set up. It had to have been the second discovery of the body that night. Ferritto and his buddies quite simply could not have missed the corpse in the cellar. For Christsakes, even a cursory search of the house would have turned up Dovishaw's body! But it had been carefully planned that the dumb Erie cop Rotunda find the body, DiPaolo quickly guessed, and then "officially" inform police of the gruesome discovery.

When Detective Sergeant Weindorf arrived at the house a short time after Rotunda made his call to Captain Stanton, he found Ferritto and the other heavy hitters of Erie's criminal underworld, Anthony "Cy" Ciotti and Phil Torrelli, along with Joan Dovishaw, Bolo's estranged wife, now his widow. With the other four in the living room, it was left to Rotunda to conduct Weindorf on a guided tour to the basement. There, Weindorf observed the outline of an obviously huge body, with one leg sticking out from beneath what appeared to be an old, well-worn throw-rug.

Weindorf's further examination showed Dovishaw was fully clothed, with "rubbers" still on his shoes. Both of his hands and feet were bound. Beneath the Erie gambling king's head, a large pool of dark red blood still slowly expanded. As specified in standard police operating procedures, Weindorf immediately called for the Identification Section unit – akin to but certainly not similar to today's modern crime scene investigators of television fame. Weindorf supervised the taking of photographs while the throw rug was carefully removed from Dovishaw's body.

As DiPaolo continued to listen, asking a pointed question here and there, Weindorf explained that the initial examination revealed one hole in the rug, roughly the size of a bullet. A white sheet covered Dovishaw's body, but the sheet had been placed under the throw-rug. Police had also discovered that the killer had used pastel-colored green, flowered belts, the same kind used on women's dresses, to bind Bolo Dovishaw's hands and his feet together.

An array of women's clothing items, including dresses, slacks and blouses, were neatly arranged and hanging from nearby clothes racks. The belts appeared to nicely match two dresses that were hanging on the rack. The dresses, investigators speculated, were those of an older woman. They further speculated the clothing probably once belonged to Dovishaw's mother, Flora, who formerly lived in the West 21st Street home, but had died several years earlier.

Weindorf also showed DiPaolo a paring knife with a broken brown handle that had been found near the body. The blade was blood-covered. When ID Section cops laboriously rolled over Bolo's heavy body, Weindorf continued, they could not detect any apparent stab wounds or slashes from a knife. They all agreed they would have to await the coroner's autopsy report to determine whether Dovishaw had been stabbed as well. According to Weindorf, it appeared Dovishaw had been shot at least once in the back of his head on the right side, and close to his ear.

That was it? Nothing else to report?

Weindorf had ordered the wise guys at the scene to appear at Police Headquarters to give formal statements at 10 a.m., in about an hour.

Shit! Talk about not having much to go on, DiPaolo thought. The detective knew he needed to use his precious time there, when the scene was still relatively fresh, to carefully, systematically survey his surroundings.

There was nothing distinguishable or remarkable about the house that seemed to come from the same cookie-cutter model as so many others in Erie's expanded Little Italy neighborhood. It was like most of the others, a two-story, frame house constructed in the early part of the 20th century. All were built in close proximity, with only a narrow driveway separating the houses. During summer months, with windows open or screened, if someone sneezed in one house, neighbors responded with, "God bless you!" If one family was having spaghetti for dinner, all the neighbors knew about it. The entire neighborhood inhaled the aroma of sauce.

Living room, small kitchen and smaller dining room downstairs. Three bedrooms and a bath upstairs. Storage was in the attic, or the basement, where the laundry was also generally done and the furnace was located. Most of the houses in the neighborhood had natural gas heat that was blown inefficiently from their huge old coal-converted furnaces. Water was heated the same way.

From the looks of things, the interior of Bolo Dovishaw's house surely appeared to have been very thoroughly ransacked by his robber/murderer, or was it robbers/murderers?

What a fucking mess, DiPaolo again whistled.

Bolo Dovishaw might have been simply an undisciplined, messy slob of a man. But no one was that messy. Someone had been searching this house. Searching for something besides the hidden bathroom vanity? And did they find whatever it was they were looking for? DiPaolo wondered.

Radioing the assigned patrol officer – the one fond of porn flicks – to return to secure the house from intruders – DiPaolo took some small comfort knowing the Identification Unit officers were still there photographing and otherwise processing the entire structure, top to bottom, and compiling whatever evidence that would become the basis for his search for Dovishaw's killer.

He checked his watch. Already it was 9:45 a.m. Just enough time to make it back to the station to interview the wise guys. As he turned to leave, a metallic glint on the basement floor caught his trained eye. It was a spent shell casing that was resting against a carton of empty soda bottles, undiscovered until now.

"Check that out!" he alerted Identification Section Sergeant Don Dunford, pointing to the shell on the floor. "Make sure it's dusted for prints and preserved." The casing, DiPaolo knew on sight, was part of a .32 caliber bullet. It was the first real evidence in a case – DiPaolo couldn't have known at the time – that would take him years to break. Nor could he have known the many roads on which this case would travel, or the large number of additional crimes he would encounter along the way. But now, there were wise guys to interview.

Part Two

"BELIEVE ME, YOU REALLY DON'T WANT TO DO THAT!"

CHAPTER 11

"I SEE THEY'VE GOT THE *ACE* ON THE CASE," RAY FERRITTO SAID WITH a wry smile, more of a smirk. He almost spit out the words, after learning DiPaolo was assigned to the homicide.

The hit man had arrived at Police Headquarters just shortly ahead of DiPaolo. He was already waiting, somewhat impatiently, in one of the three mostly barren interrogation rooms, the ones wired for sound and with the tell-tale see-through mirrors that generally fooled no one, especially not the bad guys.

"What's up, Ray?" DiPaolo cut through the amenities. Why screw around with niceties with this low-life of Erie low-lives, the detective thought.

"You better find who whacked Bolo," Ferritto said. It was more of a demand, but not a threat. How very typical of Ray Ferritto's arrogance, DiPaolo thought. Ray always wanted to play the role, always sought to be in charge, or give the appearance of being in charge, even at police headquarters. Especially with the cops. What the hell, Ferritto must have been thinking; after all, he was feared in many circles. He had killed – murdered – many times, casually, indifferently, and always gotten away with it. Almost with a stamp of approval from the government. As far as Ferritto was concerned, why shouldn't he be arrogant?

Now it seemed to DiPaolo that Ferritto thought he was doing the detective a personal favor just by being there. But DiPaolo knew Ferritto well and wasn't about to eat any shit from this guy.

"Start from the beginning," DiPaolo said. "Tell me what you know. Everything."

Ferritto slouched down in his chair. Then he complained.

"Shit, I already told my story last night to the cops at the station. If they don't remember, that's probably because maybe they were drunk."

That wasn't a surprise. DiPaolo and Gunter were amazed at the statement taken from Ferritto the night before, misspelled words, words that did not even exist in any dictionary! The detective who took the statement was known to have a pop or two while on duty. (DiPaolo recalled several years earlier that he and Gunter were called at their homes at 2 a.m. to investigate the homicide of a McDonald's maintenance worker who was shot to death while taking out the garbage. The street sergeant at the crime scene telephoned the chief at home to advise that the detective working the homicide had one too many and that perhaps it would be wise to call in a fresh team. The detective's drinking was condoned for many years until he left the force, not surprisingly *before* his normal retirement. Although that cop was once given a suspension for drinking and a bar fight, DiPaolo knew he was the kind of cop who always gave the good guys bad names because of his actions.)

"Drunk or sober, I want to hear it from you," DiPaolo said, staying calm, refusing to get visibly upset with this asshole and especially refusing to back down.

Ferritto gave DiPaolo one of those cold, disgusted stares that would have withered most wise guys and cops alike. But DiPaolo wasn't buying it. He went back too far with Ferritto. He knew too much about him. And for his part, Ferritto knew that DiPaolo knew. So, it was a wash, a draw, and there was a momentary stand-off, just seconds really, but enough time for DiPaolo to mentally process the Ferritto file.

In January of 1983, Raymond Ferritto, 54, had been a long-established and confessed hit man for a regional mob that for years spread its venom-saturated tentacles from Cleveland to Buffalo to Pittsburgh and Youngstown, with Erie, Pennsylvania, conveniently situated directly in the middle. Ferritto was even known as a journeyman killer in California. With literally no conscience and lacking even a single decency gene in his entire body, Raymond Ferritto is said to have killed at least 15 victims on contract hits.

Ferritto, DiPaolo knew, was prominently featured in a tell-all book by Jimmy "The Weasel" Fratianno, a West Coast Mafioso who broke the honor code of silence. Now in the same federal witness relocation program that once protected Ferritto, Fratianno was never bashful about betraying colleagues and even friends to his own financial advantage. Fratianno, however, was indeed apt in his description of Ray Ferritto, calling him a young, strong guy from the East Coast who had ice for blood. "Killing someone was like writing a bad check for him," Fratianno had written. But DiPaolo didn't need Fratianno to know about Ray Ferritto's peculiarities, and even about Ferritto's now-outed public penchant for killing.

His first run-in with Ferritto had come nearly 20 years earlier. It was an experience he would not forget. Ever.

It was the summer of 1965.

Young Dominick DiPaolo, the ink on his diploma from Technical Memorial High School still wet, had landed a dream summer job with the City of Erie's Parks Bureau as a playground supervisor at Columbus School in the heart of Little Italy.

His playground partner was an attractive, dark-haired girl named Roseann Ferritto, Raymond Ferritto's only daughter.

It was one of those idyllic summer jobs that most kids of that relatively innocent time would die for. Every Erie elementary school had a similar playground. And every one had at least two playground attendants to make sure the hundreds of post-World War II Baby Boomer kids didn't have the opportunity to kill themselves or each other. Minimum wage aside, the hours were good. The time was spent outdoors. And there was little or no stress. At least none at playgrounds where a Ferritto kid wasn't employed.

That summer, among other daily duties at the Columbus School Playground, the teenaged co-workers Dominick DiPaolo and Roseann Ferritto were supposed to monitor the water's chlorine level in the little kids' wading pool every hour. And that's what led to DiPaolo's first encounter with Roseann's dad, Raymond.

DiPaolo and Roseann had just returned from a lunch of giant Italian "Hero" subs at Morabito Brothers Grocery Store at West 16th and Cherry. The store was owned by DiPaolo's uncle Pat Morabito and his brother,

Dom. DiPaolo and Roseann had lunch at the popular "Little Italy" grocery store almost every day. After lunch, on this scorching, 95-degree day in early July, as DiPaolo was leaning over the pool, making the hourly chemical test, Roseann playfully gave him a friendly shove, just enough to send the future Erie cop toppling into the pool with a whopping splash.

The kids loved it and laughed. Roseann laughed. Even DiPaolo laughed, having found the prank – typical of summer staff goings on at playgrounds around the city – refreshing.

Several days later, when DiPaolo saw the opportunity to even the score – he seized upon it. Moments later, when Roseann climbed from the pool, she was drenched. And this time it was DiPaolo's turn to join the kids in laughter, but at Roseann Ferritto's expense.

Suddenly DiPaolo was accosted from behind in what could only be described as a vicious attack. He was caught by the neck in a vice-grip choke-hold and struggling for breath. DiPaolo and his assailant both hit the ground, but the grip around his head and neck only tightened. Gasping for breath, DiPaolo struggled mightily to escape when he heard Roseann's shouting.

"Daddy! Daddy! It's okay! Please! We were just goofing around!"

And then DiPaolo heard yet another voice, but this one was definitely male.

"Ray, let him up! You're going to kill him, for Christsakes. Just let him up!"

The attacker loosened his grip and finally let go. DiPaolo, still on the ground, frantically sucked in air, then stood up and punched the attacker in the face. They both landed on the ground again before the second man again separated them.

Roseann was pleading with her father, trying to tell him that playground staffers routinely played jokes on one another. But Ray Ferritto, in cold, deliberate tones, with index finger cocked at DiPaolo, merely whispered, "If you hurt my daughter, you're dead."

The second voice DiPaolo heard that day belonged to Merchie Chris Calabrese, Jr., another neighborhood wise guy who would later in life rob banks, get convicted, and finally, after being released, get further involved with heavy duty cocaine distribution in Florida and Erie. Eventually, he headed back to a federal penitentiary. Calabrese, the son of Erie's Third Ward Alderman, Merchie Calabrese, Sr., had helped pull DiPaolo to his feet that day.

Afterwards, DiPaolo and Roseann watched in silence as the two men turned and walked toward a large, black Cadillac, both doors open, that had stopped directly in the center of West 16th Street.

"Your father . . . is fucking nuts . . . " DiPaolo managed between huge gulps of air. "If he ever comes around me again . . . I'll break his head . . . with a baseball bat!"

"Forget about it, please!" Roseann urged. "Believe me, you really don't want to do that!"

Before DiPaolo could respond, they were approached by a third man. It was becoming a very busy day for grown-ups at the west Erie school playground. This time, it was Raymond Ferritto's nephew, Frankie Thomas, who had played baseball with Dom DiPaolo in high school. Frankie Thomas was laughing. He had just come from Ferritto's car.

"My uncle and Merchie were driving over 16th Street and saw you push Roseann into the water," Thomas said. "He didn't know what was going on. He thought you hurt her."

"Oh, yeah?" DiPaolo blurted back. "Well, fuck him. I just might hurt him."

"Oh, you don't want to even think of doing that," Thomas shook his head, now serious. "He's nuts, y'know. He would definitely kill you. I'm serious, Dom. Don't you fuck with him. He just got out of The Joint. And he's a changed man. So just forget it."

DiPaolo had forgotten about the stint in the slammer. The word on the street was that Ferritto was recently released from a state prison for hard-core offenders after serving a time on burglary convictions. Prisons do have a way of changing people. But DiPaolo felt Ferritto was just as cold-blooded when he entered prison as when he was finally released and set free to again ply his bullying.

Several days after the choking incident, DiPaolo's neck still smarted when he turned his head back and forth, and ugly black-and-blue bruises were evident about his shoulders. But it was his day off and playground supervisors had opted for a trip to the beach, Presque Isle State Park. Roseann Ferritto had asked that DiPaolo pick her up on his way to the popular Erie summer fun spot.

That morning, pulling into the Ferritto's driveway, DiPaolo was more than aware of the big, black Caddy parked there. He pounded on the horn several times. Roseann's step-mother, Bernie Ferritto, suddenly appeared at the front door and beckoned to him.

"C'mon in, Dom. Roseann isn't quite ready yet."

Oh, Fuck, he thought. *Oh, Fuck!* Mrs. Ferritto was insistent. Reluctantly, DiPaolo entered the Ferritto household, immediately declining Mrs. Ferritto's offer of coffee, juice and doughnuts.

"Oh, gee, no thanks," he shrugged off the offer.

As DiPaolo's extraordinary luck would have it that morning, Ray Ferritto was seated at the kitchen table, his newspaper held in front of his dark, creased face.

"Ray, you know Dom?" Bernie asked.

"Yeah, I know him."

He didn't look up from the morning paper.

Silence.

DiPaolo shuffled from foot to foot.

"About the other day," Ferritto said. "Roe told me you both joke around like that all the time. I didn't know."

"Yeah."

The last thing DiPaolo wanted was to talk. Where the hell was Roseann, anyway?

"Your neck okay?"

"Yeah. Fine." DiPaolo wouldn't give him the satisfaction of saying otherwise. Even if his friggin' neck had broken, he wouldn't admit it to Ferritto that morning.

Suddenly, Roseann Ferritto magically appeared. Finally.

As they left, Ferritto called out, "Hey, Dom, sorry about that. Really I am."

"Yeah. Okay."

As they got into DiPaolo's car, he remarked to Roseann, "I still want to crack open his skull."

Roseann was laughing.

After the summer of '65, DiPaolo lost track of Roseann Ferritto and her father.

His path with Ray would cross again. Many times. And now, 18 years later, DiPaolo was again face-to-face with Raymond Ferritto. DiPaolo wondered if Ferritto remembered attacking him so long ago at the Columbus School playground, and later apologizing at Ferritto's house. Made no difference now.

This time it wasn't a playground. It wasn't Ferritto's house. It was DiPaolo's house. There had been a murder. This time there would be no talk of baseball bats or cracked skulls. But this time Ferritto would talk.

"Well?" Ferritto questioned as menacingly as he could muster. "Are you going to ask about last night or not? I got things to do. I ain't got all day, y'know."

Although there was now nothing Ferritto could do that would intimidate the cop, the question nonetheless brought DiPaolo back from that inner-city neighborhood playground 18 years ago to the here and now.

Ferritto's impatience was ironic. Things to do, my ass, DiPaolo thought. If those things meant getting dead Bolo's illegal gambling book in order and collecting bets, they sure as hell could wait. DiPaolo had a few "things" to do himself.

"Talk," DiPaolo directed with some authority. "Just tell me what you know about Bolo just before he was whacked."

Slowly, cautiously, Ferritto began. As he spoke, a snapshot of Erie's underworld gambling operation began to emerge. Not that DiPaolo didn't know the routine. But it was far more interesting to hear it from one of the central participants as opposed to reading about it in someone's impersonal rap sheet.

According to Ferritto's account, the former mob hit man spent most of his days with Bolo Dovishaw on the numbers collection route. It's where they bagged the illegal gambling money from the bettors, large and small, and smaller bookies alike. On Monday, January 3, Dovishaw, driving his distinctive green Caddy, picked up Ferritto around noon and they proceeded to make several stops along their customary route.

"Where?" DiPaolo demanded.

Ferritto was suddenly concerned.

"Hey, I don't want to bring no heat to these people," the mob killer said.

More irony. Pseudo honor among thieves, DiPaolo thought.

"I'm not looking at people for gambling," the cop calmly responded in a matter-of-fact tone. "I'm trying to find out who hit your buddy."

"Okay, okay," Ferritto said. "I just wanna make sure."

He continued, "We stopped at Ronnie Thomas' house, Niggsy Arnone's warehouse and Julie Puskar's house."

Ferritto was thoughtful for a moment, as if he was retracing their steps that day.

"Oh, yeah, we ended up at Al Damore's Pizza Shop. Bolo got a meatball sub."

"What time was that?"

"I dunno. Maybe around six. A little before, a little after."

"Then what happened? Then where did you and Bolo go?" DiPaolo probed. It was almost like pulling teeth, these kind of interrogations, DiPaolo thought.

"He dropped me off at my house," Ferritto said.

DiPaolo knew where Ferritto lived on Brown Avenue, about a mile east of Dovishaw's West 21st Street house where his lifeless body was found, shot and mutilated in the basement.

"He just told me he was going to head home, you know, to eat his sub and then start taking action for the Vikings/Cowboys game that night."

"So that's been your normal routine on most Mondays?" DiPaolo asked.

"Yeah, pretty much."

Sounded like an exhausting work schedule these bookies have, the detective thought. Get up at noon. Finish by 6 o'clock. What a joke.

More teeth-yanking.

"Then what happened?"

"I tried to call him a little later," Ferritto recalled. "I dunno, maybe about seven or so. But the damned relay switch just transferred the call to another location where the phones are manned 24 hours a day."

It was the standard operating procedure for bookies to prevent them from losing business when they were not at home or unable to take the betting calls. Simple. After a few rings, the automatic relay activates, sending the call to another location where a real person waits to take the bet. No automatic answering machine or electronic betting or online action in this analog, pre-internet gambling world.

"Where?" DiPaolo wanted to know.

"Where what?"

Clearly, Ferritto was playing games.

"What the hell. Where was the call transferred to, Ray?"

"Why?"

"Let's get something straight. I ask the questions. You answer. You don't lie. You don't conveniently forget facts or to tell me something. You don't hold back. If you *really* want me to find your pal's killer, if you *really* want me to do this right, this is the way it goes. My way. The only way! Got it?"

"Fuck. The house is up on Hazel Street. Jesus, Dominick, it's my kid's house for Christsakes. Victor. He mans the phones."

"So you must have talked to your kid. What did he tell you?" DiPaolo was persistent.

"He said he was taking action all night. He said Bolo wasn't home at all because the calls kept coming through."

"This was somewhere around seven o'clock?" DiPaolo asked.

"Yeah, I called him at seven, eight and then at 8:30. All the way up to kick-off. Bolo just never answered," Ferritto recalled.

"Then what?"

"The only thing I could think of was that on Saturday and Sunday nights, Bolo would hang out around Hank Ward's titty bar. You know the one, right?"

DiPaolo knew of the Bootlegger Lounge on West 8th Street. It had once been a respectable, upscale restaurant. Now it was a cheap strip joint, often frequented by men like Dovishaw and his pals.

"What was the attraction at the Bootlegger?" the Erie cop asked, as if he couldn't easily speculate on Bolo Dovishaw's sexual preferences.

"What do you think? Bolo was fucking one of the broads from out of town."

"What's she go by?"

DiPaolo knew that the strippers, many of them underage, used phony or exotic names.

"Trixie or Bambi, something like that." He was silent a moment. "No, it was Chastity. That's it, Chastity. She was one of the older ones. Kind of a dog. You know."

Always such a classy guy, this Ray Ferritto, DiPaolo thought. "No, I don't know," DiPaolo smiled. "So, what do you know? Is that where Bolo went?"

"I don't think so," Ferritto continued.

Then he thought for a moment. "But it was a stretch for him to do something like that. On game nights, he was always work now, play later. He rarely screwed around when there were bets to be taken. That's the way he was."

Ah, such a work ethic would make his ancestors proud, DiPaolo smiled to himself.

Ferritto said he watched most of the televised game. But the later it became, the more concerned he became about Dovishaw's whereabouts. Finally, about 11:30, Ferritto left his house and drove to Dovishaw's on West 21st Street, he told DiPaolo.

"His car wasn't in the driveway, but the house lights were on," Ferritto explained.

He drove past Dovishaw's and continued to Damore's Restaurant near State Street, Erie's main drag, and owned by Al Damore's brother, Lundy. Ferritto parked nearby, went inside, and immediately asked Lundy whether Dovishaw had been around at any time during the night.

"He hadn't been there. So I called Bootleggers. Same thing. No Bolo. But that dancer, that Chastity, was still waiting for Bolo to call."

"What next?" DiPaolo continued to press.

"Nothing. I went home and went to bed."

"That's it?" DiPaolo asked. "There's gotta be more."

"There is," Ferritto acknowledged grudgingly. "When I got up Tuesday morning I tried calling Bolo again, but still there was no answer."

Ferritto said he began to get really concerned and then telephoned around to Dovishaw's various hangouts and haunts, but with no success.

"No one saw or heard from Bolo for a couple of days," Ferritto said.

"Then what?"

Extracting teeth again.

"Early yesterday afternoon I called Phil."

"Torrelli?" DiPaolo knew Phil Torrelli was Ferritto's and Dovishaw's partner in the bookmaking business, mostly a go-fer and bag man.

"Yeah, Torrelli, Phil Torrelli. I told him to check out Bolo's house."

Ferritto had given his key to the Dovishaw house to Cy Ciotti, another wise guy and longtime set-up man who DiPaolo knew from his earliest days on the force.

Ciotti was temporarily living with Dovishaw, but was now in Pittsburgh for several days, according to Ferritto.

"Phil promised to stop at the house, then call me back," Ferritto continued. "He had a key."

"Did he actually check out the house? Did he get back to you?" DiPaolo asked.

"Stupid Torrelli calls me about four. He says Bolo wasn't home, but the house was okay. Everything was fuckin' fine there. Jeezus!"

Next, Ferritto told DiPaolo, he telephoned Vinnie DiPasquale. DiPaolo knew DiPasquale as a street cocaine dealer and wise guy who later was sentenced to 30 years in a Florida prison for cocaine trafficking.

"Vinnie gives me Cy's number in Pittsburgh. I told Cy that Bolo was missing, and Cy says he's coming right away."

"So that's when you all met at Bolo's?" Detective Sergeant DiPaolo probed further.

"Not all. Just me and Cy. We tried to figure out where the fuck Bolo could have gone to, but we kept striking out. So we went over to Joan's house."

Ferritto told the detective he knew Bolo still maintained a friendship with his "ex," and that maybe Joan Dovishaw had a key to Bolo's. Ciotti, Ferritto said, was claiming he gave his key to his girlfriend, Linda Shatto, and Shatto was also out of town until the next day. They found Joan at home, but she hadn't spoken with Dovishaw since New Year's Eve, four days earlier, when he stopped by for a holiday visit. She did not have a key to the West 21st Street house, either.

"So we called Torrelli and then met him at Bolo's," Ferritto said. "When we went in we could see the fucking place had been trashed. Everything was messed up. I told Torrelli he was fucking stupid and a fucking liar. The asshole never checked the house like he said he did." Torrelli later admitted he was tied up and never checked out Bolo's house. Ferritto said the three men then searched through Dovishaw's house.

"We didn't find nothin' until we opened the cellar door. I could see a pile of clothes at the bottom of the steps. But I think I knew right then it was Bolo."

When they cautiously descended the steps, Ferritto said, his suspicion was confirmed.

"What the fuck," Ferritto said. "We knew we couldn't phone it in to the cops, right? How would that look?"

"If no one did anything wrong, why not?" DiPaolo asked. "What did you have to hide?"

"Gimme a break, dammit. You know my record. And Cy's. Who the fuck was going to believe us – the drunken cop from last night?"

Ferritto had a point.

"So that's when you brought in Rotunda?"

"Yeah."

"And?"

"Cy says let's call Frankie. Let him find the body and call it in to the cops. So we called Frankie, and then Joan and told her to meet us at the house."

DiPaolo was starting to figure Ferritto's story was better suited for Jimmy Breslin's *The Gang Who Couldn't Shoot Straight*, but he kept his thoughts to himself and instead probed further. "How the hell did you ever manage to pull this off with Frank Rotunda? Is he that dumb?"

"Shit," Ferritto almost laughed. "It was easy. We just told him Bolo was missing and we found the house trashed and didn't want to touch anything.

"Then Cy tells him we didn't check the attic or cellar and offers to go to the attic while telling stupid Frankie to head down to the cellar."

"And Rotunda fell for it?" Dom DiPaolo fought back an urge to smile.

"Fuckin'-A he did! He goes down the stairs and in a few seconds he yells back up that he found Bolo – he was real fucking excited – and that Bolo's dead. What a dumb shit!"

As planned and almost on cue, Rotunda phoned in the murder to police headquarters.

"That's all I know," Ferritto said. "Now don't be bringing any shit down on my kid. I swear that's the truth to everything I know about this."

DiPaolo was tempted to believe him. The story had the ring of truth to it. But if he knew one truth about Ferritto, it was this: He could not be trusted. Period.

CHAPTER 12

Dom DiPaolo knew Ray Ferritto and Cy Ciotti well. With Ferritto, it had begun with his memorable encounter with the mob hit man during the summer of 1965. With Ciotti, it began five years later during DiPaolo's rookie years with the City of Erie police department.

DiPaolo remembers that day as well.

Early in 1970 he took a call from his father, Pasquale "Pat" DiPaolo, whose love of politics had elevated him to a behind-the-scenes kingmaker in local Democratic circles. The senior DiPaolo not only knew every powerful figure in the local Democratic Party, but was long-respected among Erie's Italian-Americans, in particular in a community where so many immigrants had their start in Erie's "Little Italy." There, in Erie's Third Ward, Pat DiPaolo was chairman of the county's Democratic Party for more than a quarter of a century.

The elder DiPaolo told his son that Tony Ciotti, president of the Calabrese Club, in the heart of Little Italy, needed weekend security at the club, which was beginning to be *the* Erie venue for young crowds to dance and drink. Second tier, but nationally known musical acts, played there, too. There had been several fights that went along with crowds, the senior Ciotti told the senior DiPaolo, and the junior DiPaolo, now a police officer, would be welcome weekends to pick up extra cash.

Indeed, the crowds were huge there. This was *the* place to be in Erie in the early '70s. Ruby Port and The Younger Brothers, with Paul

Yoculan, also known as Paul Younger, the Frankie Valli of the Erie music scene, was the house band. Art Oligieri was excellent on trumpet, and Angela Arduini, the female vocalist, was without a doubt the best singer in Erie for many years. Dom DiPaolo agreed to take the part time job. What the hell, with a young family to support on a cop's salary he could use every extra dollar he could squeeze out of legal moonlighting.

Nine months after DiPaolo began working security at what was nicknamed "The Cally Club," Ciotti's son, "Cy," was released from the federal penitentiary at Leavenworth. The younger Ciotti quickly made the Cally Club his number one hangout. Before long, DiPaolo recalled, almost every local wise guy and wannabe – including Ray Ferritto – were regulars there as well. DiPaolo had not seen Ferritto since that summer five years earlier, but he never forgot either the incident or the threat, especially Ferritto's hard features and icily frigid eyes.

Upon Cy's return, DiPaolo quickly learned that father and son did not see eye-to-eye. They disagreed about most everything. The younger Ciotti wanted to take over the club. He had illusions of grandeur about bringing national headliner, Las Vegas-type floor shows to Erie. But most of all, he wanted to install Barbute, a fast-moving Italian dice game, on the second floor. As part of the rake, the younger Ciotti would claim a share of the pot in the high stakes game. Even as a beginning cop, DiPaolo wasn't naive. He understood this game was illegal and he wasn't about to condone it.

"Look," he warned the older Tony Ciotti. "I know you're friends with my father. But that makes no difference now. Because if you allow Cy to start his illegal shit here, then I'm out of here. And if Cy does that shit in front of me, so help me I'll lock up his ass."

DiPaolo's concerns, however, were short-lived. At least for the short-term. Two months after his warning to the senior Ciotti – on July 30, 1971 – Cy was arrested and then convicted on federal mail fraud charges. Cy was gone from the Cally Club. And so were most of the wise guys. DiPaolo was relieved. The money wasn't exactly decent. At $3.25 an hour, DiPaolo's six hours netted him a grand total of $19.50 for a night's work. He figured he'd be further ahead and earn more if he was paid by the fight, rather than by the hour. But the work was tolerable. And it was legal.

Nearly a year passed. It was now April of 1972, a time of hippies, more intense Vietnam War protests and the presidential primaries. The national Watergate scandal was still two months off when Cy Ciotti came home from "college," as he was so fond of calling his home away from Erie.

While Dom DiPaolo was working "security" at the Cally Club about the time Cy was released from prison, Cy's old pal, John Paradise, also known as "Blackie," was hired to work at the club. Everyone in that element knew Blackie. He was a funny, but simple guy, sort of like the Paulie Walnuts character on *The Sopranos*. DiPaolo recalls that Blackie wanted to make everyone think he was one of the tough guys, but actually had many hang ups. Apparently, because of a stroke Blackie suffered as a young man, his mouth was twisted, distorting it to the extent that he told his many stories out of one side of his mouth. Meanwhile, Tony Ciotti, Sr., who couldn't stomach any of his son's wise guy wannabe friends, told DiPaolo that Blackie "talked like that" because he once got his hands caught in a cash register drawer while trying to steal money and when he screamed out in agony, "his mouth just stayed that way."

It was while DiPaolo was still a kid, however, that an event occurred with Blackie that was widely known, repeated and laughed about throughout Erie's "Little Italy."

In August 1957, Cy Ciotti, Ray Ferritto, Victor Minedeo, Blackie and John Lupu of Warren, Ohio, were involved in a burglary at Gus & Gene's Auto Garage, owned by Gus Angelo, on Peach Street. They pulled a safe from the popular auto repair shop, but all were quickly apprehended by authorities. Minedeo, who owned "The Letto" night spot next to the garage and set up the job, quickly caved on his pals, forcing all to plead guilty.

Just prior to sentencing, Minedeo suffered a fatal heart attack. The others, no longer confronted with the Minedeo snitch to testify against them, tried to withdraw their guilty pleas, but old Judge Elmer Evans wouldn't hear of it. January 12, 1958, Ciotti, 29, Ferritto, 29, Lupu, 31, and Blackie Paradise, 47, stood before Evans in his stately courtroom for their day of reckoning. Blackie, having twice before been convicted of felonies, was now a three-time loser, while the others were "only" going down for the second time. Evans sentenced Ciotti, Ferritto and Lupu to serve three-to-six in a state prison. Then, he turned to Paradise and ordered him to serve four-to-eight. Immediately, Ciotti began sobbing.

Blackie, standing next to Cy, said, "Hey, whatsa matter? What are you crying for when it's only three-to-six and four-to-eight months? We can fuckin' do that standing on our heads!" Ciotti glared at Blackie through his tears and said, "You dumb fuck – those are *years*, not months!" Blackie, fully grasping what Ciotti was saying, promptly fainted, hitting his head on the wooden railing in front of the judge's bench. An ambulance was called to take the passed out tough guy to the hospital. The foursome served their time and were ultimately released.

Just several years after that, Blackie Paradise was walking along West 18th Street, the heart of Little Italy, on his way to purchase a loaf of Italian bread to go with the macaroni his wife was preparing for dinner that night. Suddenly, a car pulled up alongside Paradise. Inside, were two out-of-town cons who had been with Blackie in the joint. After a few moments, Blackie entered the car and drove with them to Florida. He returned three years later.

"The story goes that when he finally returned home," DiPaolo explained, "his wife, Alice, hit him in the head with the dish of macaroni that was in a box that she had saved for three years. When Blackie told the story, he said, 'I probably had it coming.'"

But now, with Cy home from "college," life was not so funny and the battle for control of the Cally Club resumed in overdrive. Tony Ciotti, aging and frail, finally gave in to his younger and stronger son. Cy got his way. He began bringing in headline acts, including Frank Sinatra, Jr. On any given night, the club resembled the famous Appalachian meeting of the top Mafia families of a decade earlier. Within several days of Cy's takeover, security officer Dom DiPaolo quit.

There had been talk of an illegal Barbute game that was going to be started upstairs. Not only did DiPaolo know when to call it quits, but he advised all of those who worked for him – all moonlighting Erie cops – that it was in their own best interests to leave as well. Chuck Erickson, Bob "Goodie" Goodwill, Billy Leamy, Greg Orlando, Don Gunter and David Bagnoni, all departed the club with DiPaolo. Only one chose to stay. "If the illegal game goes upstairs," DiPaolo warned the cop, "you're on your own."

"Fuck it," the cop replied. "Cy's giving me a raise."

"I've got a wife and kids and a mortgage, too," DiPaolo said. "But this shit isn't worth it."

The cop failed to heed DiPaolo's advice. Many years later, DiPaolo's warning would come back to haunt him. For DiPaolo, however, his brief employment encounter with Erie's underbelly was over. Still a uniformed street cop, there would be no more Cy, Ray, Bolo or wise guys. Or so he thought. In the ensuing years, Ferritto would make a name for himself far, far from Erie's infamous Cally Club and northwestern Pennsylvania, and especially with a cop named Dominick DiPaolo.

And as for DiPaolo, even a crack homicide detective in Erie, Pennsylvania needed to complement his income from time to time with moonlighting jobs – but jobs that wouldn't raise eyebrows or questions about the cop's integrity.

Take the now famous, or infamous, Mickey Mantle encounter, for example! Instead of the Cally Club, DiPaolo took gigs, "clean" jobs that did not jeopardize his reputation or tax his ethics. One was head of security for local media wizard Art Arkelian during Arkelian's annual extravaganza, the Erie County Sports Banquet. Each winter for decades, radio station owner Arkelian, brought to town the very top names in virtually every professional sport. His charity banquets continue to this day. These events attracted "SRO" crowds to see the best of the best. Arkelian put DiPaolo in charge of security for the dinner, and DiPaolo hand-picked five trusted officers to help him watch over the sports legends.

The banquet of February 10, 1981 at the old Erie Shrine Club in downtown Erie will long be remembered. That winter, Erie got wacked every day with not inches but feet of snow. On banquet night, the weather was just as horrific, but like mostly everything else in Erie, this event would not be cancelled. Snow or no – Arkelian's banquet would go on. It was destined to be a banner year for the headliner of all headliners: the New York Yankees incomparable Mickey Mantle. DiPaolo – no star-struck kid – knew his baseball better than most, and like so many others who came of age in the 1950s and 1960s, Mickey Mantle was idolized by most as the greatest of his generation. For DiPaolo, who played organized sports his entire life, this was to be a dream come true. Not only was he going to meet his idol – DiPaolo had managed to wear Mantle's Number 7 on all his uniforms – but he was getting paid for it!

The big night arrived with even more snow. But the weather could not prevent the Shrine Club from becoming a sea of dark blue pinstripes on white, banners, photographs and signs paying tribute to the Yankee Great. Men in the audience who grew up idolizing the Yankees and their home run star brought sons and daughters or grandkids. Despite the snow storm, it was the largest crowd in the sports banquet's history. They waited in breathless anticipation for their hero – Mickey Mantle – to arrive. The electric excitement in the air could not have been greater for a rock star or the president. It was Mantle they all wanted to see. Fathers told their children to remember they would come face-to-face with an American sports icon.

Now, because of the snow, the Greater Pittsburgh Airport – where Mantle and several other stars were to catch the short flight to Erie – closed for the afternoon and evening. Instead, they boarded a stretch limo Arkelian sent earlier in the afternoon to bring them north to the even snowier Erie.

Meanwhile, at the Shrine Club on East 8th Street in downtown Erie, security chief Dom DiPaolo was advised by Arkelian that he just then received word the limo – with its precious cargo – was now in the small city of Meadville, Pennsylvania, about 35 miles south of Erie. When the limo hit Meadville, Mantle informed the driver that he needed to make a pit stop. The limo had pulled into Sandalini's Supper Club about 4 p.m. It was now 6:30.

Mickey, the star of the evening, was having a wonderful time at Sandalini's entertaining the bar patrons, regaling them with jokes and inside baseball stories.

The patrons, in return, were generous with their hero, too, buying Mantle drink after drink for several hours before the group again hit the road and short drive straight north to Erie.

In Erie, as the stormy night wore on with the program already underway, a roar that could be heard for blocks went up from the audience as the Mighty Mick finally strolled into Erie's Shrine Club. The legendary New York Yankee, it was obvious to all, was quite loaded. Still, Dominick DiPaolo, felt honored to escort his idol Mantle to the dais. It was a moment he would never forget – at least that's how he felt until another equally unforgettable moment quickly arrived.

As the program progressed, Mantle became increasingly obnoxious, loudly laughing and rudely chatting and cracking jokes while those on the dais were addressing the crowd. Even some audience members were getting concerned over Mantle's disgusting behavior in his highly intoxicated state. But it was about to get even worse. Without warning, Mantle rose from his chair and approached the two emergency exit doors situated immediately behind the dais while one of the sports stars was speaking. Opening the doors, the slugger walked outside into the cold, howling, biting wind and blizzard conditions. All eyes were on him.

Artie Arkelian signaled DiPaolo to follow Mantle outside, if for no other reason to keep watch over him. DiPaolo first grabbed a cloth napkin from the head table, positioning it in the door jamb so that the door could be closed, keeping the blizzard outside from blowing in, while at the same time allowing re-entry to the downtown Erie Shrine Club.

Now outside, the cop found himself in the club's parking lot. Peering around, squinty-eyed in the raging white out, DiPaolo spied Mantle straddling a snow pile between two parked cars.

"Mickey? Are you okay?" asked DiPaolo, who was also in his full Erie Police uniform.

Mantle looked up, then grabbed his groin and said, "I'll be better when you come over here and hold it." He was urinating in the snow between the two cars.

So much for baseball idols. At least a little respect for law enforcement, the cop thought while retorting to his idol, "Fuck you." The cop turned and re-entered the Shrine Club, smiling as he made sure he took the napkin away from the door jamb so that the door not only easily closed, but locked. None of this drama went unnoticed by most in the audience. First they saw Mantle abruptly leave. Next, a uniformed cop followed him out, making sure the door did not lock behind them. Then, the cop returned alone, making sure the door was locked behind him.

Several minutes later, there arose such a banging on the emergency doors that startled not only the audience, but also anyone who might have been outside and within shouting range on that blustery evening. Eventually, one of the athletic stars arose from his dais seat to open the door. As Mantle stumbled, returning to his seat covered in snow, the audience went into wild hysterics. But then, the *real* tragedy of the evening began.

As Mantle was being introduced, he walked to the podium wearing a brown denim jacket, jeans and western-style boots.

"I have never seen so much fuckin' snow in all my life," he began. "How do you people live here? You gotta be fuckin' crazy!"

Silence from the audience, most spectators with mouths agape.

Launching into an often rambling and incomprehensible tirade, his expletive-laden talk lasted perhaps 10 minutes, DiPaolo swears Mantle dropped the F-bomb at least 100 times. The cop remembers men getting up from their tables and pulling their kids from the room in disgust. Only half returned when Mantle finished doing his worst.

"It looked like the room had emptied during a fire drill," DiPaolo later recalled. "It was embarrassing for everyone there. Poor Artie. He never imagined a public figure would stoop so low."

After the crowd cleared out, Arkelian noticed a muscular, well-dressed young man alone a table, head in his hands. The man was sobbing as Artie and DiPaolo approached. "What's wrong?" Arkelian asked.

"I have a knot in my stomach. Wish I never saw him like that. For all he did for baseball, I'll always remember him for this night." It was Joe Charboneau, sensational Cleveland Indians rookie.

The annual sports banquet – featuring the late Mickey Mantle – is now a part of Erie history and lore, undoubtedly the worst event for Artie Arkelian. Finally, when it was over, DiPaolo related to Arkelian what had earlier transpired in the parking lot.

"I should have locked him up then," DiPaolo said with a smile. "It would have saved you all this embarrassment."

In the days and weeks that followed, the Erie media – newspaper and television sports reporters – tore into Mantle with a flurry. Men wrote letters to the editor and sports writers to proclaim they had discarded banners, photos and clippings that they had long collected that were associated with Mantle. Most were simply devastated.

A few years later, Mantle would die following complications from liver transplant surgery – his liver destroyed by his heavy drinking. In most regions of the country, the Triple Crown winner whose number was retired, who appeared in 12 World Series, who was inducted into baseball's Hall of Fame during his first year of eligibility, was mourned and honored after his death. But not in Erie.

Now, several years later at Erie Police Headquarters, DiPaolo would soon follow up on the Ferritto interview by taking statements from

Ciotti, Torrelli, Joan Dovishaw and the questionable cop Rotunda. Still, he didn't expect much difference in their stories. As anxious as he was to move on in the investigation, he couldn't help but ponder over how Erie's Raymond Ferritto managed to gain national notoriety.

It probably started much earlier for Ferritto, but the actual national notoriety began in the mid-1970s. By 1977, Danny Greene, an Irish mobster in Cleveland, had finally decided to make his move on Cleveland's mob-related Licavoli Family. The move failed before it even began. Greene ended up dead, the victim of a car-bombing as he left his dentist's office in Cleveland's east suburbs. It was then when DiPaolo finally believed Frankie Thomas's earlier ominous warning about his uncle Ray Ferritto a dozen years earlier: "*I'm serious, Dom. Don't fuck with him.*"

But it was Frankie Thomas who eventually failed to heed his own words. Ray Ferritto, Frankie Thomas and Bolo Dovishaw were all arrested in connection with the made-for-media sensationalist hit on Danny Greene. It was Erie, Pennsylvania's own Ferritto who detonated the bomb in the car parked next to Greene's in the parking lot along Brainard and Cedar Roads in the affluent section of East Cleveland adjacent to highly-traveled Interstate 271. When Greene departed from his dentist's office and climbed into his vehicle that fateful day, Ray Ferritto, by his own admission in open court, was carefully watching Danny from the nearby Interstate 271 Exit Ramp.

DiPaolo could imagine the cool and calm Ferritto calmly pressing down upon the remote control button, eyes as cold as ice, instantly ending the life of Cleveland's Irish mobster. And, for the immediate moment at least, the Licavoli Family's problems with the Irish mob, thanks to Erie's homegrown killing machine, were over. The "button man" had succeeded.

Frankie Thomas, Ray's nephew, was now in the big time with Uncle Ray, his idol. Ray had Frankie handle the cars used in the bombing. The "Joe Blow" car, for example, the vehicle where the bomb was actually placed, had been stolen elsewhere in Ohio, as was the getaway car. Through a mechanic pal in Erie, Frankie had both vehicles titled in Pennsylvania, and both received Commonwealth plates and state inspections. Frankie drove the "Joe Blow" car to Cleveland, while Bolo Dovishaw drove the getaway vehicle there on Ferritto's orders.

Ferritto and Ronnie "The Crab" Carabbia took off in the getaway car when the "Joe Blow" car exploded, killing Greene. As their bad luck would have it, a bystander wrote down the plate number and helped a sketch artist come up with a composite drawing of the driver – Ferritto. He was easily made by the Cleveland cops, who traveled to Ray's Erie home several days later. Over the visor on the passenger side of Ferritto's personal car, Cleveland's finest discovered the getaway car's state registration. The not very astute Frankie Thomas had kept the registration. In addition, the getaway and Joe Blow cars bore sequential registration stickers and the same hand-writing of a certain Erie garage mechanic.

Ah, once again *The Gang That Couldn't Shoot Straight* all over again, DiPaolo mused.

But, surprise of surprises, in a stunning plea arrangement to save his younger sister's son, Ferritto agreed to become a state government witness. Another motivation was probably that Ferritto believed he was double-crossed by the Licavolis, who weren't coming up with cash for Ferritto's defense. Ferritto's take for the Greene hit was supposed to be 25 percent of the Warren-Youngstown, Ohio gambling profits, and full-fledged membership in the mob. But when he was arrested, the organization not only didn't arrange for an attorney for Ferritto, but instead put out a contracted hit on him. That was enough for Ferritto. And that's when he flipped on the Cleveland mob.

He was famously quoted as saying, "All my life I've been one way. I always did what I was supposed to do and now all of a sudden I did them the biggest favor that they wanted done and they were talking about killing me and here I am in jail awaiting trial . . . " Ferritto felt the only avenue left was to make a deal.

"It wasn't because I saw God or read a Bible," he was later quoted. "It was just that I thought at that time that I had to look out for me . . . And I thought that would be my best move."

He cooperated fully with the Cleveland Police Department. So much so that 12 members of the Licavoli crime family – all from the mob's elite upper echelon – were implicated by Ferritto's very detailed testimony. In addition to pleading guilty to killing Danny Greene, he also admitted to the Julius Petro hit at LAX (but only because Jimmy "The Weasel" Fratianno talked on him). But there were many, many more Ray Ferritto murders.

Those men in the Cleveland crime family Ferritto gave up included James "Jack White" Licavoli, a reputed Mafia boss; Angelo "Big Ange" Lonardo, a Mafia underboss; Ronald "The Crab" Carabbia, a

Mafia hit man; Pasquale "Butchie" Cisternino, another mob murderer; "The Weasel" Fratianno, Tommy Sinito and John Calandra.

After a 79-day trial, Cisternino and Carabbia were convicted, while the others went home. Ferritto and Fratianno had pleaded guilty. A "back-up" team had been led by Tony Liberatore, who also pled. But to save Ferritto, Thomas and Dovishaw from retribution at the hands of the Licavolis, they were all enrolled in the Federal witness protection/relocation program. Ferritto became Ray Marciano. Thomas was Frank Romeo, and Bolo became Frank Fabian, taking his mother's maiden name, all sponsored by Carmen Marino, the state prosecutor. Yet, within two years, they became bored with their new lifestyle. To a man, they were anxious to return to their storied wise guy status and the three came back to Erie.

Were they worried about the Licavolis? No, not much. That's because fate, through all its tricky and weird twists and turns, intervened favorably for them. Since none of the Licavolis were jailed, Ray Ferritto was, if not entirely in their good graces, at least officially off their radar screen and hit list. Although he had admitted to a premeditated, cold-blooded murder, the cops, in their haste to get to the Licavolis, had too quickly granted him immunity from prosecution.

What a sweet deal, DiPaolo thought. Or perhaps, DiPaolo had to ask during those early hours of the Bolo Dovishaw murder probe, was hapless Bolo's professional, execution-style killing just the beginning of a mob payback? And if it was, would there be more paybacks to come?

It was obvious that if Ray Ferritto was worried about that, he wasn't showing it, at least not to Dom DiPaolo. Ferritto was just finishing buttoning up his black top coat. But DiPaolo stopped him before he could leave the interview room.

"What do you think?" DiPaolo questioned. "A payback from Cleveland? C'mon, Ray, time to really talk to me."

Ferritto seemed to freeze for just a slight moment.

"I don't know. Fuck, man, I would like to know. Maybe I'm on the list? Who the fuck knows?"

He turned and walked out.

Ferritto is the only one left, DiPaolo thought. Of all the locals involved in the Danny Greene hit, only Ferritto had survived. Frankie Thomas, at the tender age of 31, died five years earlier of a cerebral hemorrhage. And now Bolo had been murdered, executed in his own home. Maybe Ferritto was right. Maybe he *was* on the list. Wouldn't that be something? DiPaolo smiled.

A clear illustration of DiPaolo's tenaciousness to stay with cases until ultimate resolution was launched the same year as the Greene hit in Cleveland. In Erie in April 1977, the partially clothed corpse of Janet Needham, 32, was discovered by a woman walking her dog between two houses. Human bite marks were on the victim's face, and she had been raped after death (necrophilia). Within hours, Detectives DiPaolo and David Bagnoni arrested 20-year-old Bruce Ward. Ward told officers he couldn't remember what had taken place, but wanted to help them.

"Fine," DiPaolo said. "We'll help you remember." At 1 a.m., the cops took Ward to the home-office of Bill Vorsheck, a local certified hypnotist. Vorsheck applied his talents to cases for all Erie County law enforcement agencies; such findings at the time were admissible in court. Vorsheck put Ward into a chair, explaining he was going to help him regress to the time of the killing. Ward, however, quickly told Vorsheck, "I don't think this is necessary. I did it. I will tell them." Apparently Ward was too frightened of being put under, and gave a full statement on his involvement in the heinous crime. On September 17, 1977, he pleaded guilty to a general charge of murder and was sentenced to life by Erie County President Judge Edward Carney. After that, DiPaolo told Vorsheck the detective would bring all his suspects to the hypnotist.

On appeal, however, Ward got a new trial, was convicted of manslaughter, sentenced to five-to-ten years, and after more brushes with the law was paroled in 1989. Soon after, he was charged in Arkansas with killing an 18-year-old convenience store clerk, who had also been raped. DiPaolo twice testified against Ward in Arkansas, leading to a conviction and death sentence. DiPaolo was to be a witness at Ward's August 2011 execution, but a last minute stay stopped the penalty from being carried out. No new date has been scheduled. DiPaolo's tenacity was again underscored by his sticking with the Ward cases for so many years.

But now in 1983, as expected, Cy Ciotti, Phil Torrelli and Joan Dovishaw all provided similar stories. The dirty cop Rotunda, dumb shit that DiPaolo knew he was, still hadn't figured how he had been set up.

While DiPaolo still knew he couldn't trust any of them, in this case all seemed to be giving the same basic, truthful facts about finding Bolo's body. And all seemed rattled with the discovery.

But DiPaolo also knew he couldn't rule out any of them. They were all still to be classified as "persons of interest," as cops like to say. No suspects, not yet, just tons of "persons of interest."

Every cop who goes through Detective Training 101 knows they must uncover three factors in solving murder cases: First, motive: a reason to stimulate a person into taking the life of another human being. Next, opportunity: the right circumstances must exist to pull off the murder with reasonable expectations of escaping detection. Finally, means: the weapon or weapons of choice and wherewithal to snuff out a life.

DiPaolo knew Bolo Dovishaw's killer had all three elements in place and working in his/her favor. DiPaolo already had identified two of the elements: opportunity and means. But he now needed to figure out motive. When that happened, he was certain, he would identify the killer. But that didn't mean it was going to be easy. DiPaolo instinctively knew from previous experience there was a ton of grunt work to accomplish: calls to be made, alibis to check, shoe leather to be worn off. What he needed first at this juncture was determining the actual time of the killing.

The Erie police detective was reasonably certain Raymond Ferritto was the last person, other than the killer, to see Bolo Dovishaw alive. The task at hand, he calculated, was to now determine events that transpired after Dovishaw arrived home that Monday evening with his cherished meatball sub. Dovishaw died sometime between Monday evening when he was last seen and Tuesday night. Likely, given Ferritto's statement, it was shortly before the start of the nationally-televised football game. But how to be sure about the time of death? The coroner's report would narrow the timeline, the cop knew, but DiPaolo wanted more.

His answers, as it turned out, would be from an unlikely source: A 13-year-old girl and her father. Shortly after the interviews with Ferritto, the wise guys, Mrs. Dovishaw and Frankie Rotunda, Detective Captain McCurdy approached DiPaolo.

"A supervisor in the circulation department at the *Erie Times* called to say one of their newspaper carriers might have some information about your murder investigation," McCurdy told DiPaolo.

It was a good break. What transpired next would fix in DiPaolo's mind the time frame for Dovishaw's death to within two hours.

CHAPTER 13

IT WASN'T THE NEWSPAPER CARRIER, PER SE, BUT HER FATHER WHO would help DiPaolo the most in determining when Frank Bolo Dovishaw swallowed his final meatball and drew his last breath. DiPaolo and his partner, Donald Gunter, immediately left police headquarters for the 10-minute drive to Bauer Lane and the Wisinski family.

Bauer Lane was a short, west Erie street of modest, public housing look-alike homes. It was one of Erie's many typical, working class neighborhoods with that cookie-cutter appearance, postage stamp front lawns, a few shrubberies, no attached garages, yet within easy walking distance to public and Catholic schools. Several west side factories, including the pollution-belching National Forge, were only a few blocks away.

It was in one of Bauer Lane's three-bedroom dwellings that the two detectives found the Wisinski family. Headed by Kenneth, an impulsive, shoot-from-the hip, often angry man whose temper would later lead him to jail, the family could have been stereotypical of thousands of others who financially struggled during those last-gasp days of Erie's industrial glory. Wisinski's temper, it would be later determined, came close to rudely ending his life the night of Monday, January 3.

Meeting and talking with Wisinski and his 13-year-old daughter, Michele, one of hundreds of young. self-contracting newspaper carriers with the *Erie Daily Times* and *Morning News*, the detectives quickly pieced together a plausible time frame for Dovishaw's murder. The facts were simple, indisputable:

Dovishaw's house was on Michele's newspaper route. She hadn't been paid by the customer in several weeks and was absorbing this business loss at the expense of her own meager profits. Finally, she told her dad, and the elder Wisinski was upset the man the neighborhood knew to be "a gangster" had stiffed his teenager for $21.

For several days since the first of the year, Wisinski, dedicated dad that he was, had tried without success to catch this Dovishaw fellow at home.

But on Monday, January 3, shortly before 6 p.m., Wisinski thought he finally caught a break. While driving along West 21st Street, hauling his son and neighborhood kids to a Boy Scouts meeting at a nearby church, he saw Dovishaw pulling "his big green Caddy" into his driveway.

"Now I got you, you prick," Wisinski thought at the time.

After dropping off the boys at Blessed Sacrament Catholic Church, Wisinski sped back to Dovishaw's, he recounted to the two detectives, and parked behind Bolo's car in the driveway. It was no later than 6:15 p.m. when Wisinski loudly banged on the front door. No response. With Bolo's car in the driveway and the house lights burning brightly that January evening, Wisinski knew Dovishaw was still inside, obviously avoiding him, obviously avoiding his newspaper payment obligation, and in the process sticking his daughter with the $21 tab.

Wisinski was pissed. He banged on the door again, this time even harder, he said. Nothing. So he began kicking at the door. Still nothing.

"You fat pig fucker!" he yelled.

He continued to shout out demeaning obscenities, as if that was going to resolve the issue. But still no response. Now, even angrier than before, Wisinski offered a final loud and mighty kick at the door before leaving. He was more determined than ever to recover his daughter's money, by God!

Less than two hours later, while heading back to the church to collect the boys, he drove past Dovishaw's house and observed that while the lights were still on, "son-of-a-bitch, that damned green Cadillac was gone!" Wisinski told the detectives he then vowed to return, as often as it took, to collect that damned $21. After all, it was now a matter of principle – that, and his poor daughter's honor.

While the missing Cadillac could have had no meaning for Kenneth Wisinski at the time, it provided DiPaolo the key piece of information needed in establishing the time line in Bolo's murder. Before meeting with the Wisinskis, detectives had learned Bolo's car was discovered in the parking lot at the Holiday Inn South along Interstate 90. The hotel once had been a popular night spot among the locals, but was now mostly just a good place for weary travelers to spend the night. About three miles south of Erie, also along Route 97 in Summit Township, with an often full or busy parking lot, DiPaolo knew it was a clever location to dump a hot car. It wouldn't be noticed for hours, maybe days.

The cops also knew it was highly unlikely Dovishaw drove the car there himself and still ended up slain back in his basement. No, the killer must have taken the car after whacking the numbers king in his home. But which direction had Bolo's murderer headed – east or west on I-90, or north or south on Route 97? While that would be determined later, at least now the investigators had a pretty accurate time frame.

Wisinski had watched as Bolo pulled into his driveway shortly before 6 p.m. At 6:15 p.m., there was no answer to Wisinski's repeated hollering, banging and kicking on the door. And around 8 p.m., the car was gone.

DiPaolo also knew Ferritto had first tried reaching Dovishaw by phone about 7 p.m., but with no success. It could be assumed, then, the killing likely occurred between 6 and 7 p.m., and quite possibly at the exact time Kenneth Wisinski was making a commotion at the front door.

Neither Wisinski nor DiPaolo could have known at the time how correct DiPaolo's assumption was – or how close Wisinski had come to meeting the same fate as Dovishaw while the bookie's killer waited impatiently for the banging and kicking to cease.

It was Wisinski who also managed, albeit unknowingly, to confirm much of Ferritto's wise guys' version of events that occurred that Monday and Tuesday. The pissed off father told detectives he made drive-bys past Frank Dovishaw's house at least several times on the next day, Tuesday. And still, he insisted, the lights were on, but no car in the driveway. Early that Tuesday night, however, Wisinski said he encountered several cars in Bolo's driveway. Still determined to get his kid's money, he parked and went to the front door. This time when he banged on it, two men known as hoods to Mr. Wisinski – one Raymond Ferritto and one Anthony "Cy" Ciotti – came to the door. The two did not tell Wisinski where Bolo was, but they paid him the $21 without debate or comment. With great conviction, they also instructed Wisinski to have his daughter stop future deliveries.

"Um, Bolo don't want the paper no more," Ferritto's deep baritone intoned.

If Wisinski thought the sudden loss of a newspaper customer was unusual, he didn't say. His only concern was the $21 owed to his daughter. And now that the debt had been satisfied, he couldn't care less about Dovishaw or his hoodlum pals.

Veteran cops know the first 48 hours in any murder investigation are critical to solving the case. When murders are not solved within those first two days, detectives understand it's likely the homicides might not ever be. If there are arrests, they are often months and sometimes even years in coming. Trails grow cold. New cases take precedence. And, ultimately, murders end up as cold case files.

DiPaolo knew the trail to Dovishaw's killer indeed was rapidly cooling off. From the start he was in the hole; Bolo's demise was not even reported until more than a day after the killing. Another truth to murder probes well-known to DiPaolo was this: In more than 90 percent of all homicides, the murderer had previously known the victim. Since all of Dovishaw's acquaintances were either wise guys or wise guy wannabes, it wasn't difficult for DiPaolo to begin to advance the theory that Dovishaw died at the hands of one or more within the local mob's realm. The old adage was true: Live by the sword, die by the sword; live by the mob, die by the mob. But who? And why?

Back at Dovishaw's digs, a thorough search of his house didn't turn up much more than the splintered bathroom vanity hiding place for some cash and numbers sheets. But now, upon reflection, DiPaolo had to wonder: Did Bolo give up the hiding place to the killer or killers?

Or, did the murderer have inside information about what to find and where? And what more, if anything, was Dovishaw's killer searching for? And, did the murderer find it?

With no forced entry visible to investigators, how did the killer get inside? Did Dovishaw leave the door unlocked? Considering his vocation, that was doubtful. Did he voluntarily open the door to the killer? More likely. Did he know the killer? Possibly. Or, was the killer simply a stranger, but one brandishing a weapon? Also possible, DiPaolo thought.

From Ferritto, Ciotti and Torrelli, DiPaolo learned that in 1980, less than three years earlier, Dovishaw had been the victim of a home invasion and robbery. He'd opened the door to a man who had knocked, and was struck on the head and robbed. Dovishaw told his pals he thought the perp was either Caesar Montevecchio or Chuck "The Hawk" Serafini. He was right. Montevecchio had set up the job for The Hawk and Bo Baumann, Pearl Grybowski's squeeze, who Caesar ran with in the Michigan slammer, and who would later hang himself. Some names seem to never go really away, and even if not apparently present at the moment, they're always lurking, shallowly floating beneath the surface.

Based on the previous invasion, however, DiPaolo surmised Dovishaw would never open a door to anyone with whom he was uncomfortable, unless the person happened to be leveling a firearm point blank at Bolo's face. More and more probable.

CHAPTER 14

ON TV, THE LIFE OF A COP IS GENERALLY DEPICTED AS GLAMOROUS and uncomplicated. Television murders get solved within a 60-minute time-frame, including 14 minutes of commercials. TV cops work on only one investigation at a time, rarely multiple unrelated cases, and certainly never summary or misdemeanor offenses. Imagine Kojak, Columbo or the *Criminal Minds* crew probing shop-liftings or hub-cap thefts for an hour or two. In real life, however, working on just one investigation is a luxury most municipal police detectives cannot afford. Even major investigations require the less-than-exciting mundane drudgery of routine, labor-intensive and time-consuming detective work. Working the phones, checking endless records and following leads that more often than not go nowhere, all come with the turf.

Detective Sergeant Dominick DiPaolo, temporarily putting his other cases in a brief holding pattern, more akin to a juggler's balancing act, ordered the Police Bureau's Central Records Division to pull all accounts of recent home robberies where victims were bound, especially reports that might include known bookies, gamblers or wise guys. But he also knew such occupations were not always noted in police reports. DiPaolo went through the many reports, eventually identifying and singling out gambler Frank Scalise, bookie Jack Miller, and Louie Nardo – all who would later figure to some degree in the Dovishaw murder probe.

Also of interest: During the search of Bolo's house, detectives found paperwork for two local bank safe-deposit boxes. Paperwork yes, but *no keys* to the bank boxes.

Another find at the West 21st Street crime scene was an identification card with Bolo's photo, but with the name "Frank Fabian." Fabian was Dovishaw's mother's maiden name, DiPaolo knew, the name Bolo used while he was under the Federal Witness Protection program in Dallas, Texas.

Police searchers further discovered a mere $28 in cash, with a rubber band around it, in Bolo's bedroom, and another $40 in a trousers pocket. What's more, the victim's solid gold watch was still on Dovishaw's right wrist. Although the presence of the money and watch seemed to rule out robbery, it didn't represent a great stash for a loose-spending, illegal numbers king, DiPaolo was forced to acknowledge. Where the hell was his numbers bank? Where did he keep his gambling stash? The answer came from an unlikely source. Mob killer Raymond Ferritto.

When DiPaolo got Ferritto on the phone, he didn't waste time or mince any words.

"Ray, where the hell did Bolo keep his bank?" the detective demanded.

Ferritto, also interested in Dovishaw's finances, or what was left of them, but for far different reasons than DiPaolo, was quick to respond.

"Bolo worked out of the box."

"The safe-deposit boxes?" DiPaolo asked.

"Yeah. The boxes."

Now, DiPaolo was beginning to catch on. As in all initial capital crime investigations, myriad theories form, are discarded, replaced by more theories, which in turn are replaced by others and then advanced as far as the cops can carry them. It's part of the investigative process. Initially, nothing, no theory so advanced, is ruled out. Good cops keep open minds and let the evidence do the talking, whether physical, circumstantial or eye-witness. But even at this early stage in the probe, patterns were beginning to take shape, DiPaolo realized. Records of safe-deposit boxes were found at Dovishaw's house. But no keys. Was a motive beginning to emerge?

DiPaolo quickly prepared and executed a search warrant for the two safe-deposit boxes assigned to Frank Dovishaw at Erie's PennBank branch next to a large local grocery supermarket appropriately named "Super Duper" on West 26th Street just beyond Erie's city limits in Millcreek Township. At the bank branch with former Erie Police Chief Charles Bowers, now the bank's security chief, and a vault company representative present, Detectives DiPaolo and Gunter directed that Bolo's two safe deposit boxes be drilled open.

The assistant branch manager, Theresa Mastrey, was helpful and talkative, almost too gabby, DiPaolo thought to himself at the time.

"Mr. Dovishaw was really a big mouth," she told the police investigators.

"Really? In what way?" DiPaolo asked.

"You know, he was always bragging to the tellers about his money," Mrs. Mastrey volunteered.

"Interesting," DiPaolo said.

Mastrey advised, "If I pick up anything from the tellers or the customers about Mr. Dovishaw, I will call you immediately." Mastrey not only promised to cooperate, but also volunteered that she had known Bolo Dovishaw for many years.

"That so?" the detective probed.

"Oh, yeah. He was really a nice guy," she said.

DiPaolo thought the "nice guy" comment didn't reconcile very well with the earlier "big mouth" disclosure, but also kept that thought to himself. There was something odd about this bank official's behavior, DiPaolo was coming to believe. But the cop kept that to himself as well.

When the detectives inventoried the drilled open bank boxes, they learned Dovishaw's last entry to both boxes had been December 28, 1982, about a week before he was slain. Bank Box No. 424 contained some $28,000 in cash, $40,000 in Certificates of Deposit, and another $38,000 in other investments, along with insurance policies that declared his wife Joan as his only beneficiary. Bank Box No. 449's contents were similar. The box held $18,000 in cash, $60,000 in CDs and another six thousand dollars in various investments. Also in the box was a log containing the names and nicknames of bettors, as well as special code numbers known only to Frank "Bolo" Dovishaw and perhaps maybe a chosen few others.

Although the cash was substantial, it seemed to DiPaolo that given Dovishaw's status as running Erie's most lucrative gambling operation, there should have been more hard cash there, much more. The $46,000 didn't appear to be worthy of a major sports-betting operation. With a few lucky betting hits, Dovishaw could have been wiped out of his assets. Were there more boxes somewhere else? Unlikely. Had there been more cash in these boxes? DiPaolo wondered. And where the hell were Bolo's keys to them?

It was a question being asked in other circles as well. Circles that held no legitimate ties to law enforcement. The answer, however, would soon become known.

In early 1983, law enforcement's use of technology as a crime-fighting tool was limited at best. But in Erie, Pennsylvania, such use was nearly non-existent.

DiPaolo had long known there was much to be desired about the work of the Erie Police Identification Section, the evidence-gathering branch of the department. Officers of the ID Section, unlike today's forensic-trained crime scene investigators, attained very little in the way of available technological training. They did the best with what they had, which wasn't much.

Bolo Dovishaw's green Cadillac sedan, discovered in the parking lot at the Holiday Inn South, was towed to the basement of the Erie Municipal Building for processing by the ID Section. Even though the car had been searched and processed by other officers, DiPaolo and Gunter returned to the City Hall basement, where they began a final, systematic search of their own before releasing the vehicle. The Caddy, it had already been determined, was clean of fingerprints, even Dovishaw's, wiped down by a professional. While examining the Cadillac, DiPaolo suddenly recalled that another bookie had once told him that Bolo unwisely kept a stash in his car. The detective popped open the trunk. It appeared clean. Almost too clean. Just a spare tire, a case of whiskey and five empty, but neatly folded, brown paper bags. But why would Bolo Dovishaw keep empty paper bags in the trunk? DiPaolo wondered.

The cop quickly determined that the ID team had not pulled down the felt-like lining around the trunk's interior. For if they had,

DiPaolo knew from previous experience, the trunk's soft lining would not have been replaced. DiPaolo grabbed at the lining and tugged. He ducked as stacks of money hidden beneath the lining rained down upon him.

Phoning Sgt. Raymond King, the officer who ran the ID Section, DiPaolo demanded that an Identification officer immediately report to the basement garage, and this time tear the car apart in search of new evidence that might have been overlooked during the previous inadequate search.

"I mean right now," the angry DiPaolo roared before hanging up.

Eventually, that second, more thorough Identification Section search of Bolo's Caddy unveiled $8,400 from the trunk hiding spaces and another $6,800 that had been pushed up and under the luxury automobile's dashboard.

"A total of $15,200 in a murder victim's car and the Identification Section's inspection missed it all," DiPaolo whispered to Gunter.

"Heads will roll," DiPaolo predicted. That's what the brown paper bags were for! To transport the cash and then hide the cash in the trunk. Not only didn't the original search discover the cash, but ID officers initially failed to report to DiPaolo perhaps the most significant finding of all: In the dashboard's ashtray, two safe deposit box keys had been found. But DiPaolo didn't have to examine them to predict the box numbers. 424 and 449. Reporting the keys would have saved much work, also the unnecessary box drilling. The cops had been about to release the car to Bolo's wife – and DiPaolo would not have known about the keys.

CHAPTER 15

WITHIN DAYS OF THE DISCOVERY OF BOLO DOVISHAW'S BODY IN the basement of the West 21st Street house, the murder probe turned even more bizarre. On Saturday, January 8, Dom DiPaolo got what turned out to be one of the most startling telephone calls of his long police career. Just when DiPaolo was starting to believe he had seen it all, that nothing could surprise him, he was once more dumbfounded by unpredictable human behavior.

The call came from Michael Orlando, director at Orlando's Funeral Home at West 22nd and Raspberry Streets in Erie's Little Italy. Bolo's family selected the funeral home not far from Bolo's house to handle Dovishaw's funeral and burial arrangements. That Friday night before Orlando's call to DiPaolo and nearing the conclusion of calling hours, Raymond Ferritto had approached Orlando, he told DiPaolo.

"And?" DiPaolo asked when Orlando paused. "What did Ray want?"

"I want to stay after everyone leaves," Ferritto said to the funeral director. It was obvious to Orlando that Ferritto's remark was not a request.

"Well, I would like to close at 9 p.m. It's been a long day," Orlando weakly responded. Most funeral homes ended calling hours at 9 o'clock.

"I'll only be a few minutes," Ferritto assured Orlando. "I just want to check out Bolo's body."

Now, funeral directors and undertakers are often accustomed to being on the receiving end of strange requests from families and friends of the deceased. But this one was clearly off the grid. Orlando blanched. Finally he managed to stammer to Ferritto, "Well, ah, er, don't you think we better check with his wife?"

"It's okay. She knows," Ferritto snapped.

The mob hit man was getting impatient with the funeral director. And Orlando knew better than to argue with an acknowledged killer. With a silent sigh, the funeral director resigned himself to staying after hours. Yes, undertakers, as a built-in occupational hazard, experience many weird activities. But during all his years in the bereavement business, even Orlando was not prepared for what came next. Neither was Dom DiPaolo.

It was part fascination, part horror, part revulsion. The three strong emotions kept contradicting themselves within Funeral Director Michael Orlando's mind as he watched mob hit man Raymond Ferritto systematically examine the murdered man's body. With much exertion and great effort, Ray Ferritto managed to lift Frank "Bolo" Dovishaw's heavy remains from the satin-lined coffin. Ferritto then, in a rolling movement, maneuvered the body onto the open coffin lid. No one will ever know, but Ferritto might have been thinking to himself at the time that his effort with Dovishaw's lifeless body was giving an extremely accurate meaning to the term, "dead weight."

Slowly, and with purpose, Ferritto began to undress the corpse. First Bolo's shoes came off, then his socks, then the blue suit – the jacket and the trousers – and then the natty tie and starched white shirt. Finally, Ferritto stripped the bloated body of its underwear. And then, Frank "Bolo" Dovishaw, in all his unholy and frumpy and embalmed glory, was stark naked as Raymond Ferritto stood over him.

Orlando could only squeeze shut his eyes, rather than watch Ferritto examine the body with almost the precision of an overly-eager pathologist. When the undertaker opened his eyes, Ray Ferritto, apparently not finding whatever it was he had been searching for, was attempting to re-dress Frank Dovishaw's lifeless and dead weight body. And not doing a good job of it. Orlando, now too shaken to even speak, simply helped with the re-dressing in silence.

When they had finished the task at hand and Bolo was re-dressed and comfortably back inside his final resting place, Orlando managed to breathe a deep sigh of relief.

"Hey, I just wanted to check Bolo," Ferritto attempted to reassure him. "Thanks for your help."

Orlando could only stand there and nod weakly. When Ferritto was gone, Orlando looked around to make sure all was as it should have been, then turned off the funeral parlor's lights and left. Most others, probably, would not have handled such a situation as well as Orlando managed to. The next morning, fulfilling what he knew to be his civic duty, Michael Orlando telephoned DiPaolo to relate this very strange tale.

Even though it was Saturday and a rare day off, DiPaolo was not about to wait for Monday morning to confront Ferritto about this new development. He drove to Ferritto's Brown Avenue home.

DiPaolo didn't beat around the bush. There were no pleasantries as the veteran cop got immediately to the point.

"Ray, you've got to figure I have surveillance on the funeral home," DiPaolo bluffed. There had been no such surveillance, but the funeral would be photographed later that morning. DiPaolo knew it made sense to let Ferritto think the cops were watching everything and everyone – especially Ferritto. Besides, at this point it would have served no purpose to bring Orlando's telephone call into the conversation.

"Why the hell did you stay so long last night after the funeral home closed?"

Ferritto smirked that famous, snide and withering Ray Ferritto smirk.

"Fuck, you don't miss a trick, do you?"

"No games, Ray," DiPaolo cautioned.

He needed to let Ferritto know who was in charge of the investigation.

"I told you from the start I was going to do this right. Why were you there so long?"

Ray Ferritto actually seemed to soften somewhat, perhaps as much as was humanly possible for him, and then he just shrugged as he was thinking it wouldn't harm anything to tell DiPaolo what had happened. At least his version of what had happened.

"Hey, I just wanted to check out Bolo. You know, to see if he was tortured. If he was, that might have been meant as a message to me, y'know?"

"And? What did you learn?"

"No, he wasn't tortured. But, you know, I had to fuckin' see for myself," Ferritto nonchalantly shrugged again, as though he was accustomed to and completely comfortable tampering with corpses.

Ice for blood, the detective so very aptly remembered the description. DiPaolo did not mention that it was Orlando who came to him with the story about Ferritto's body search. And as far as DiPaolo knew, Ferritto never discovered Orlando had been the source of the information, and not any police surveillance. But Ferritto wasn't done talking, either.

"Y'know, now I'm thinking maybe it was that punk Caesar and his buddy, The Hawk," Ferritto began to speculate about the killing.

That Ferritto would finger Montevecchio and Serafini, even in a hypothetical, speculative way, didn't surprise DiPaolo. Both names had made the cop's short list several days ago. Ferritto then related a meeting he had with Montevecchio in a basement sitting room of the Orlando Funeral Home several days earlier.

"Fuckin' Caesar tells me he had nothing to do with the hit because he liked Bolo." When DiPaolo raised his eyebrows, Ferritto added, "I told him, 'If I knew you had something to do with it, you would fuckin' know. Because you'd be upstairs – and you wouldn't be standing up.'"

Weeks passed. As DiPaolo had feared, the trail grew faint and cold. Detectives branched out in their search for clues, any clues, anything that might help to get the murder investigation back on track. The official autopsy report showed that Bolo had died from a single bullet wound to the right side of the back of his head. There also were minor cuts and bruises on the right side of Dovishaw's plump face. The presiding forensic pathologist, Halbert E. Fillinger, Jr., M.D., speculated the facial abrasions and contusions might have been sustained during a struggle. Yet, no actual "defensive wounds" were found. In the initial autopsy report, the stab wound to Dovishaw's left eye was not even reported. It was only later, much later, when DiPaolo learned the truth that Fillinger, a world-renowned medical examiner from Philadelphia nicknamed "Homicide Hal," would amend his post mortem report to read: "Laceration of left eye consistent with stab wound of eye." But that wasn't until four years later in 1987.

In any event, the official cause of death was still listed as "gunshot wound of head." Dovishaw's was the only blood found at the scene, including the blood on the broken paring knife. The shell casing DiPaolo found on the scene was from a .32 caliber pistol, with Norma brand ammo. Norma ammo was extremely rare as criminals' preferred ammunition of choice, DiPaolo knew. Perhaps the uniqueness of the ammo would now make it easier for police to eventually find a match and ultimately, Bolo's killer. The time of death, according to the pathologist, was pegged at 24-to-28 hours before Dovishaw's body was discovered – roughly 6:30 to 7 p.m. on January 3. Based on his interviews with the Wisinskis, DiPaolo believed he already had ascertained a much more accurate time of death – 6:15 p.m.

Detectives DiPaolo and Gunter now set about the mundane tasks of contacting virtually every firearm dealer in Erie County. They learned none stocked Norma brand ammo. Too little interest in the brand, the dealers said. The reason, they said, was that Norma ammunition cost at least double, probably even more, than that of the most popular ammo available to customers. Norma ammo was made in Sweden, distributed to only one wholesale dealer in the U.S. located in Dayton, Ohio. But the wholesaler did not send any Norma to retail dealers in Ohio, leading DiPaolo to suspect the ammo was taken in a break-in.

The days turned to weeks and weeks became months as the murder probe bogged down in futile dead ends and hopeless interviews with every Erie wise guy, along with all the wannabes. Sadly, what DiPaolo had learned was what he already knew: Bolo Dovishaw ran the biggest and most lucrative gambling book around. He also had the largest capacity for bragging. Eyewitnesses, as the cop expected, were non-existent, either at Dovishaw's house or the hotel parking lot where his car was found. One day, in frustration and just to prove a point, DiPaolo drove from Bolo's house to the Holiday Inn, a distance of 2.3 miles. The trip meter on Bolo's Caddy had recorded seven miles. From Ray Ferritto's statement, DiPaolo knew that before they stopped at Damore's Pizza that Monday night, Bolo filled the tank and reset the trip odometer. What DiPaolo learned from this exercise was that Bolo's murderer most likely drove directly from the house to the Holiday Inn.

If there had been another stop, it would have had to have been between Dovishaw's house and the hotel. It appeared that the location to ditch the vehicle was chosen in advance. But, was it?

With leads running out, the time was now for the dreadfully tedious examination of the many recent home robberies and burglaries in Erie and surrounding northwestern Pennsylvania. From the large stack of cases before DiPaolo, he narrowed the possibilities and focused on only seven robberies/burglaries from May 1978 to May 1982, the most recent crimes fitting his criteria. Maybe surprising to DiPaolo, in retrospect, was that Caesar Montevecchio's name did not appear in any report as a possible suspect. Not only was Montevecchio not charged, but he was not even mentioned in any of the crimes examined by DiPaolo.

Montevecchio. While Caesar might not have been on the cop's radar scope, somewhere in the recesses of DiPaolo's mind the name would always have a familiar ring to it. As DiPaolo labored on this case, he began to develop an instinctual feeling deep in his gut. He still had no real evidence. But his gut was rarely wrong.

CHAPTER 16

LIKE FRANK "BOLO" DOVISHAW, CAESAR DAVID MONTEVECCHIO WAS brought up on the hard streets of Erie's Little Italy during the height of the Great Depression. "Hard Times" became an era of American history that defined a generation of Caesar Montevecchio's peers – some of them using the experience of growing up during the Depression to go on to greatness and fame, others heading in the opposite direction to infamy.

A hit movie a few years earlier, *Little Caesar*, might have been an accurate predictor of the soon-to-be life of this unknown Caesar from Erie, Pennsylvania. But Caesar Montevecchio was no Edward G. Robinson, although the character actor's role as one of the first "Public Enemy" genre of movies might have been suited for the Erie hood.

Caesar's father, Carmine D. Montevecchio, was born in Erie and attended local schools. Like many of his early 20th century generation, he rarely left the familiar confines of Little Italy, where there were ample bars and private clubs, opportunities for skilled and non-skilled laborers, and an abundance of Catholic churches. According to Pennsylvania State Police intelligence reports, Carmine was known to have frequented Little Italy clubs and was a moderate drinker. Carmine, unlike his son, Caesar, kept steady legitimate jobs, starting with the Hayes Manufacturing Company, where he worked as a die-setter, and later at Marx Toys, "The Monkey Works" situated in the heart of Little Italy on

West 18th Street. Carmine labored long hours as a machinist. Earlier, he was known to have been a skilled brick-layer.

Caesar's mother, Tilba S. Sambuchino Montevecchio, had a remarkably similar history as her husband, Carmine. Also born and educated in Erie, she was raised in a devout Catholic home. Described in police intelligence reports generated in the 1960s as a "social drinker," Tilba, too, had previously worked at the Hayes Manufacturing Company with Carmine, and also at "The Monkey Works."

In their life together, Carmine and Tilba were typical of the time. They had a strong work-ethic and true to their Catholic roots, they produced four children. In addition to Caesar Montevecchio, there were Albert, Condita (Candi) Concilla, and Carmen.

How Tilba raised the couple's brood was her business alone, Carmine had decided. She ran the household and was responsible for all familial duties, a role she apparently relished, without the interference of her husband. It was a fairly typical arrangement among the highly ethnic families of that era. Mama ran the roost. Papa supported the roost. Not surprisingly, neither Carmine nor Tilba had contact with police, nor did they have criminal records.

In this environment, young Caesar would grow up in Little Italy, almost exactly as Bolo Dovishaw had. Whereas Dovishaw had suffered the involuntary loss of male role models through untimely deaths, Montevecchio's similar loss of a strong male figure in the home was by his parents' mutual consent. While Carmine lived there and supported the family, it was Tilba who was in charge of the household. Unlike Dovishaw, Montevecchio grew up with both brains and brawn. Perhaps, had he applied his many talents in other, more meaningful endeavors, Montevecchio could have chosen virtually any of life's many roads to great success. No one ever doubted his mental capacity. His value system, however, would not allow for such personal success – at any level. Caesar was not hard-wired that way.

Police, with some irony, are fond of noting that young Caesar Montevecchio served as an altar boy in his parish church – St. Paul's in Erie's "Little Italy" – for more than 10 years. The question – what happened? – then becomes even more puzzling to ponder. But, by pre-ordained design or choice, something did happen to Caesar Montevecchio.

Born two years before Bolo Dovishaw on March 27, 1934, Montevecchio was not only smarter than most of his streetwise contemporaries, but he possessed an extraordinary athletic prowess. He was a jock. And a relatively smart one. Unlike the pudgy, bloated slain bookie of Eastern European descent, Montevecchio was blessed with classical-Italian chiseled good looks. Even in his late teenaged years, at five-feet 10, his 180 pounds contained far more muscle than fat.

Looks, however, never equate with human behavior. While still in high school, Montevecchio is alleged to have pulled his first "job." It was a 1951 burglary mentored by Giuseppe Scutella (Joseph Sr.), who took Caesar and Joey, Jr., along, as any thoughtful, nurturing parent would do, according to police reports. Carmine Montevecchio had taken no active interest in raising the family, leaving most of the child-rearing to wife, Tilba. And with no truly dominant and guiding male figure at home, Caesar turned elsewhere. Elsewhere was the Scutellas.

The threesome burglarized a house at West 22nd and Cascade Streets, situated in Erie's familiar Little Italy section, according to what DiPaolo later learned. The home was the dwelling of an elderly German-born resident. It was a nice haul for the first-timer Caesar. The trio reportedly made off with $7,000 in cash. For his efforts, Montevecchio's first score netted him $500. Ol' Man Scutella and Junior reportedly kept the remainder. Although the three initially were considered prime suspects in the caper, they were never arrested for this crime. The case was never solved.

The event – how easy money could be made if one had the guts to take it, and now knowing how easy it was to get away with it – appeared to have a lasting impact on young Caesar Montevecchio's life to come. Montevecchio, in less than an hour, had made more than his father brought home in a month. With that kind of logic, why not give serious consideration to such an easy life?

Without Carmine Montevecchio in the picture, the senior Scutella's influence on Caesar's life and criminal career path can never be fully measured. But at some point it seems clear, as one examines Giuseppe (Joseph) Scutella's background, that the older man was destined to make a deep and lasting impression on Montevecchio's psyche during Caesar's most impressionable early years. To say Giuseppe had the same impact upon his own son, Joey Jr., is again stating the obvious. In this case, the old tree/apple cliché was true.

To get into Caesar Montevecchio's head, one must first understand the significance of Scutella's early influence on the enthusiastic, and bright and brawny kid from Erie's Italian neighborhood.

Giuseppe Scutella was born in Italy, migrating to the United States at an early age at the start of the 20th century. Immediately, he began living the "American Dream" – that is, the "dream" as he saw it. He spent his early years in various Western Pennsylvania communities, some rural, some urban – Ridgway, Kane, Bradford, New Kensington – taking advantage of the times, becoming deeply involved in illegal bootlegging during the Prohibition Era. Eventually, after disgracing his heretofore respectable family through numerous criminal activities, Giuseppe was asked to leave those communities. He soon found his way to Erie, where Italians were firmly established in the growing lakefront city's community life. At first, Scutella found legitimate employment at the Erie Foundry, and then the Firch Baking Company, producer of the locally-famous Sunbeam Bread.

Soon, working for others – hard work at low wages – bored him. He had enough cash to purchase two lunch-counter restaurants, popular in the day, where he did a mighty illegal numbers business in both. With profits from the restaurants and numbers, Scutella bought the Tally Ho Bar at 18th and State Streets – not far from Dee's Cigar Store, the establishment long suspected as one of the city's biggest numbers fronts.

Giuseppe's wife, Josephine, was also born in Italy, and, like her husband, arrived here as a youngster. A passionately religious, ardent Catholic, she's credited with holding together the large family of eleven Scutella children. But, as the Pennsylvania State Police observed in an unflattering 1968 intelligence report distributed to local law enforcement officials, ". . . she succeeded in bringing up the girls (four) as young ladies. However, several of the males of this union became involved in many illegal activities."

Some of Joey Jr.'s brothers, through political patronage hiring, common for years in Erie, ended up working for the City of Erie, but some, according to state police investigators, "had police contact within the three-state (Pennsylvania, Ohio, New York) area."

One brother, Jimmy Scutella, worked hard for 40 years, molding a family of good citizens. Then his son, James Jr., became a police officer. Ironically, James Junior and DiPaolo were friends since grade school and Jimmy never ever condoned the efforts of some others who had turned to lives of crime in the Scutella family. Jimmy Jr.'s son is now a police officer in California.

Caesar Montevecchio's mentor, the senior Scutella came ever-so-close to losing his "American Dream" forever. Close, but – somewhat mysteriously – not quite.

In 1958, the Italian immigrant was accused of indecent assault stemming from separate incidents with two 14-year-old girls. He was indicted. Joseph, Sr., eventually pleaded guilty to the charges and was fined $250 while being sentenced to serve 23 months in the Erie County lock-up. Although Erie County, Pennsylvania's criminal justice system was not nearly as overcrowded and overburdened as it would become in later years, Joseph Scutella, Sr. was nonetheless immediately paroled. However, because of the conviction, proceedings were quickly launched to deport Scutella back to his native Italy. Once there, Italian authorities would be forced to deal with his criminal behavior.

Inexplicably, after first petitioning the Erie County Court to issue a ruling against the deportation, the prison sentence was suddenly commuted by Pennsylvania Governor David Lawrence and Giuseppe Scutella was saved from being sent back to his homeland. But because of the crime, he was still forced to divest himself of his Tally Ho tavern. Caesar's role model and mentor died of natural causes two years later.

While Joseph Scutella Senior's life of crime in his adopted country was ended through his death, Caesar Montevecchio's career was just getting rolling.

Coming of age during the post-Depression and post-World War II prosperity of the late 1940s and early 1950s, Montevecchio, attended both public and Catholic Schools. Montevecchio excelled athletically at Cathedral Preparatory School, a private Catholic high school for boys, a facility directly responsible for spawning doctors, lawyers, professors, CEOs, statesmen, journalists, judges and even Tom Ridge, a

Pennsylvania governor and the first Secretary of the U.S. Department of Homeland Security. But Caesar Montevecchio would not become a poster child for Cathedral Prep. In fact, Montevecchio would become to his high school what Ted Bundy and Jeffrey Dahmer symbolized to their alma maters.

During those impressionable high school years, Montevecchio still managed to earn fair academic grades and, because of his natural athletic aptitude and ability, he became a wildly-popular football and baseball star. Cathedral Prep records indicate no school infractions during his time there, and, more important, no criminal activity of record. According to those school records, as a student he was better than average academically, but did not apply himself.

Despite his first, at that time undetected criminal endeavor with the Scutellas a year earlier, he was named Erie's High School Athlete of the Year in 1952.What's more, Caesar Montevecchio's athletic prowess was responsible for the high school sports star being heavily recruited by regional colleges as well as universities and colleges at the national level. After graduating 137th in his Prep class of 173 that year, he carefully weighed his many college options before selecting the full scholarship offered to him by the prestigious University of Detroit. It was another of those life-altering decisions that would impact Montevecchio's criminal career.

Detroit, Michigan, at the time of Caesar Montevecchio's inauspicious arrival, was known for much more than cars. Since the Prohibition Era 1920s' "Purple Gang" Detroit was not only the nation's undisputed automotive capital, but had grown into one of the country's leading cities for harboring organized crime activities.

Long before the Michigan city became famous for its innovative Motown music, the tough street-thugs who once made up Detroit's famed Purple Gang were now replaced by the equally vicious eastern Syndicate. While Detroit might not have had a reputation as the nation's organized crime capital, it could still hold its own with the midwest's Chicago, the east's New York, and dozens of smaller cities, like Youngstown, where the mob ruled.

Montevecchio's childhood was not angelic, yet the Motor City was perhaps the worst town Caesar could have selected to pursue higher education. Detroit was ripe as a training ground for the next generation of thugs. Had Caesar chosen, say, a smaller suburban or rural school in the South, New England, the West Coast, or even in his own native Western Pennsylvania backyard, where a dozen smaller institutions thrived, his life, despite the negative influences established by the Scutellas, might have gone in a much different direction.

But Caesar chose Detroit. And Detroit is where Caesar found all the action he could handle – and then some. It was Detroit where the hard-core criminal mentality of Caesar Montevecchio would develop, be honed, and eventually fully emerge. Before long, college man Montevecchio was playing more than football for the Titans.

In the early-1950s Detroit, where America's powerhouse automotive industry had refitted and re-energized itself in the years following World War II's lack of domestic car production, Caesar Montevecchio wasted little time in finding his way to the Michigan city's slimy underbelly. For Caesar, it was exciting and far different than anything he ever experienced in Erie. He met new people, but more important, he developed powerful relationships with the worst of Michigan's criminal underworld.

Caesar was not a dean's list honors student. Rarely attending classes, he made neither the college grades he needed to keep his scholarship intact, nor did he even compete well on the playing fields. As a result, it wasn't long before Montevecchio left the University of Detroit and returned to Erie in search of other, less noble pursuits. Eventually, some of these opportunities would be with his new-found pals.

With his college deferment from the U.S. military draft no longer valid, he needed to complete standard military obligations. He knew there was no way out, and enlisted in the U.S. Army, where he served a three-year stint. In those post-World War II and Korean War days, military service was considered much more patriotic than it would be with the generations of Americans who would follow. Military service, because of the hundreds of thousands of Americans killed in the two world wars, was considered highly honorable, and veterans were generally revered. However, whatever patriotism Caesar Montevecchio experienced in uniform was quickly converted to a more narcissistic and self-centered mentality more typical of those who would grow up in the materialistic world decades later. Upon discharge, he reverted to his Michigan mob contacts.

His closest partner in crime would become a Michigan wise guy he met not in Detroit, but actually after Montevecchio returned to Erie. This new friend was Joseph Paul Giacalone of Flint, Michigan. "Joey" was a true wise guy from an early age. His father and uncles, including Anthony "Tony Jack" Giacalone, who would later figure into the disappearance of Teamster boss Jimmy Hoffa – long reported to be taking a "dirt-nap" – were well-established within the Detroit mob.

Through his good pal, Tom Parry, teacher and highly unsuccessful football coach at Erie's Technical Memorial High School, Caesar Montevecchio met Bobby Guaranti of Flint, Michigan. It was actually through Guaranti that Montevecchio became close with Joey Giacalone.

Erie's legendary underworld family leader, James "Westfield Jimmy" Salamone, had a hand in much of the action in the tri-state area between Erie and Buffalo to the east, Cleveland to the west, and Youngstown to the south.

But Erie was still Salamone's home base. Low-key and quiet, Salamone controlled the underworld of wise guy wannabes from behind the scenes, allowing the more flamboyant figures to dominate the headlines while in apparent silence he pulled their strings. It was Westfield Jimmy's connections with the Detroit mob, including the Giacalones, that also helped establish and cement the very close friendship between young Caesar and Joey. And from Joey, Caesar Montevecchio would learn and hone another kind of team-play, a group sport of sorts very much different from springing hither and forth across a 100-yard playing field. The "elementary" education Caesar picked up from Giuseppe Scutella was supplemented with the "higher" education guidance now provided by Giacalone.

In the next decade and a half to come, new best friends Joey Giacalone and Caesar Montevecchio were picking their "teams." These were separate, but connected gangs that would later terrorize the East Coast with their brutal crime sprees, leaving dozens of hapless victims in their wakes. For his team, Montevecchio selected his longtime Erie pals, Anthony "Cy" Ciotti, Carl Caccamo, Tom Parry, Billy Rieger, and his original burglary co-conspirator, Joseph Scutella, Jr. Also recruited was the wise guy wannabe John Fasenmyer. Giacalone, for his part, selected Loren Jolly, John "Chino" Juarez, Bobby Guaranti and Steve

Maruca, all tried and true veteran thugs from the streets of nearby Flint, Michigan. A thug from Boston was also said to be part of this group. The new games would soon begin. Points in this sport were not listed on any scoreboard, but in the number of illegal dollars raised through crime. Victims terrorized by these games were of Olympic proportions.

By the middle of the 20th century, Erie was still a blue-collar, shot-and-a-beer town, no different from the rest of the nation in experiencing unprecedented post-war prosperity and rapid growth of the new middle class. If legitimate and legal business was booming, then so was the underworld.

For Caesar, at least for the time being, love was in the air as well. After returning to Erie in the mid-1950s, before enlisting in the U.S. Army and prior to joining forces with Joey Giacalone, Caesar Montevecchio began in 1955 what the Commonwealth of Pennsylvania calls "Common Law Marriage" with Mavis Thompson, a native Erieite.

"Before her marriage," a Pennsylvania State Police intelligence report of 1967 relates, "she played the local hoodlum element very hard and was known for her being in company with the local . . . professional men.

"She has been very productive and five children were born to this union (with Montevecchio)," the report continues. "A check with the local courthouse records failed to locate an application for marriage." The report did acknowledge, however, that since her common law marriage to Montevecchio, "She spends most of her time at home with the children, attends church, and is seldom seen or observed in her former hangouts."

While police found no evidence of a marriage certificate, Montevecchio would later insist he was married to Mavis on December 3, 1956. Mavis, on the other hand, says the date was actually January 3, 1955. This nearly two-year discrepancy was never fully explained. But a State of Michigan probation officer's report would later observe, "According to the wife, at no time have they had any serious marital problems or separations. Montevecchio appears to be a family man, although, it is felt that like his father he has left the rearing of his children up to his wife."

The official record about the life of Caesar Montevecchio grows somewhat murky during the decade he was producing offspring with Mavis Thompson, wearing Army green and engineering the beginnings of what would become a memorable crime spree with Joey Giacalone.

Here's what is known from a court-ordered pre-sentencing report submitted on December 13, 1968 by Ralph L. Soffredine, a probation officer with the Michigan Department of Corrections, Bureau of Probation:

"Caesar enlisted in the U.S. Army in July of 1955 and was given an Honorable Discharge on October 17, 1958. The highest rank he held was that of Specialist 4."

Soffredine's report goes on to say that Montevecchio was employed by Erie's Marx Toy Company for five years before working for the Fenestra Corporation for six years. By the mid-1960s, police had long suspected an East Coast crime wave was created by the "teams" selected, organized and ruled by Caesar Montevecchio and Joseph "Joey" Giacalone.

"He spends most of his time loafing around various clubs and taverns along West 18th Street . . . ," one Pennsylvania State Police intelligence report of the period observes about Montevecchio. "He must be classified as about the top contact man in Erie and is suspected as being the set-up man for the large stick-ups."

The same report further speculates, "On the date of March 20, 1967, there was an armed robbery at Ralph Miller's Jewelry Store, 7th and State Streets, Erie, Pennsylvania, where a total of $75,000 worth of jewelry was taken. It is suspected that he (Montevecchio) was involved in this crime."

Being suspect is one thing. Being able to prove what you think is another. As such, Montevecchio was never charged with the Miller's job.

About the same time, the John Hancock Insurance Company office at West 37th and Poplar Street, was another target of the Erie gang in which Montevecchio was said to be involved. Ron Dalton, an insurance agent at the company, told DiPaolo, Bob Polito, Gido Alo and Joe "The General" Gaeta while golfing one day that when the robbery went down, Ron was in a back room doing paperwork. Dalton came out of the room, not knowing what was happening, as his co-workers were face down on the floor and the robbers were running out the front door.

Dalton said it was a good thing he was not in front since he had played football with Montevecchio at Cathedral Prep and would have been easily recognized by his former classmate. Dalton shudders to imagine the possible consequences had he been in the front room.

Further police speculation existed at the time that indicated Montevecchio "was involved in robberies in the State of Michigan" as well as many in Erie. Surprisingly, there is only one "official" rap sheet reference to actual criminal activity. The State Police intelligence report confirmed, "Caesar was arrested once in Erie, Pa., and that was on Nov. 5, 1966 and for visiting a disorderly house. He was arrested with a number of card players at the Monarch Club, West 18th Street, when it was raided by Erie city police. He (Montevecchio) paid a fine of $10 and costs and was released. He was not photographed, nor was he fingerprinted at that time." The alderman who presided over the case was Merchie Calabrese, Sr.

By the turbulent mid-60s, Montevecchio's and Giacalone's "teams" weren't protesting the war in Vietnam or racial injustice at home, as did so many of their generation. No, Caesar and Joey and their gangs were out for only themselves and what their unique brand of capitalism brought them. Banks, jewelry stores, insurance companies, other merchants. All victims. Nothing was taboo, nothing off limits, nothing too small or too big, in their rash of armed robberies along the East Coast. Caesar Montevecchio was considered the "brain" of the teams. He set up the jobs in Erie while Joey Giacalone and his Flint gang drove to Pennsylvania from Michigan and staged the many stick-ups. That was for the Erie jobs. In return, Joey did the same in Michigan and Massachusetts for Caesar's team.

It was said many Erie business owners were clearly in the know of the availability of Caesar and Joey Scutella to torch any establishment for a fee. For the arsonists' efforts, some local business owners with such a pioneering spirit, collected huge insurance payouts from the fire claims. Caesar Montevecchio also was suspected of a business-type arson in New Kensington, Pennsylvania, not far from Pittsburgh, where he was hired by Kelly Mannarino, alleged head of the local mob there.

Since Giacalone had been well-connected in Boston as well, the teams quite easily operated there, at least as long as their robbery spree lasted. Police long suspected one of Giacalone's connections, Hobie

Willis, owner of Boston's New Deal Café, was instrumental in setting up many of the East Coast bank jobs. According to police, it was believed Willis accompanied Montevecchio's "team" and Joey Giacalone in many of these pursuits.

But by 1967 – the year of America's pot-hazed "Summer of Love," hippies, war protestors and social upheaval – the team concept that had worked so well and for so long for Montevecchio and Giacalone was about to end. At least temporarily.

It had taken law enforcement agencies many years, but during that "Summer of Love," the Federal Bureau of Investigation and local and state police in Erie and Detroit began comparing notes. Finally, they got it. The Montevecchio-Giacalone team games ended, but only after 11 bank robberies and many lesser hold-ups. For police agencies, it was anything but a love fest that summer as they hammered Montevecchio and Giacalone – as the "team" leaders – hard and mercilessly. (Merchie Calabrese, Jr., son of the alderman, and Hobie Willis were arrested in Boston.)

The team leaders had been suspects for years in multiple East Coast bank jobs. Dozens of charges were filed against them, ranging from bank robbery, armed robbery, conspiracy and even attempted murder. But the crime that ultimately did them in was an armed stick-up at the Irvin Hirsch Jewelry Store in Flint, Michigan on August 16, 1967. The robbery netted the teams $40,000 in jewelry, all of it fenced in Erie by Montevecchio. Caesar and Joey were arrested that November and taken before the Genesee County Court in Flint, where after another year in the criminal justice system they were found guilty following a jury trial by their peers. The police report was telling:

"Caesar Montevecchio and Joseph Giacalone were two members of a group of several men belonging to a gang that pulled armed robberies in the east and Midwest. Caesar Montevecchio and Joseph Giacalone had an arrangement whereby Giacalone would set up jobs here in Michigan and Montevecchio would set up armed robberies in Pennsylvania," the document concluded.

The pre-sentencing report authored by local Probation Agent Ralph L. Soffredine to Genesee County Judge Donald R. Freeman was pivotal in determining what would come to be a devastating sentencing outcome for this modern day version of the James gang:

"Montevecchio appears to be very worried as to the sentence the court might impose. *He has stated that if they give him a lot of time, when he gets out he will make Dillinger look like an altar boy.*" It was perhaps the most inflammatory, unthinking comment one could make prior to facing a sentencing judge. It was a comment, given Montevecchio's intelligence, that even his most ardent detractors would not have expected to come from the boastful Caesar. Soffredine also wrote:

"According to information from Erie Police . . . he (Montevecchio) has been maintaining close associations with known racketeers in the eastern section of the United States. . . . Montevecchio has acted as a set-up man and contact man for gangland operations. Police officials indicated that they consider Montevecchio the more professional of this group of men and stated that he should be considered dangerous."

(Montevecchio, Joe Giacalone, Charles Kinsman, John "Chino" Juarez, and Loren Jolly had been arrested at a Pittsburgh hotel during the attempted murder of police informant Charles Thomas. Shot twice in the head by "The Shooter" Jolly, Thomas somehow ran from the room and escaped. The Montevecchio gang was part of a crime ring imported from Flint to try to kill a prosecutor. Later, DiPaolo, in a very personal way, would come to know all about Flint "shooters.")

More details followed. But Judge Freeman had heard enough. If he had intended to be lenient in the sentence he was to mete out to Montevecchio, Soffredine's report completely eliminated any previous tendency toward mercy the judge might have harbored. In this case, he would create no manic John Dillinger. Instead, he would do his judicial best to make sure Caesar Montevecchio never would have the opportunity to make anyone – let alone Dillinger – look like an altar boy.

And so it was on that chilly November 10, 1968, that the handsome, still youthful-looking 34-year-old Caesar Montevecchio was sentenced to serve 50-to-70 years at the Michigan State Prison at Jackson. Serving just the minimum would mean Montevecchio wouldn't see freedom until he was into his eighties. Serving the maximum meant life. His pal, Joey Giacalone, of Flint, got the same sentence.

Putting his own jurisprudence exclamation point on the sentencing, Judge Freeman further ruled that neither man would be even eligible for review for parole until they had served at least 22 years each in prison. *John Dillinger, indeed!* But judicial sentencings, even more than four decades ago, were just as they are now and not written in stone.

The former Erie Catholic Church altar boy who once held so much promise would eventually get the opportunity to carry through with his Dillinger threat. Sooner than anyone in the criminal justice system would have believed or even imagined, Caesar Montevecchio, like the clichéd cat with nine lives, got his second chance.

Released in 1978, not 70, 50 or even 22 years later, but after serving less than 10 years in the state prison – where he would learn new tricks to complement those already gained from his Erie and Michigan teachers – Montevecchio quickly resumed his criminal career. This time, however, it was in stolen cars, grand larceny, and whatever else that would generate quick, relatively easy income.

On July 30, 1975, while Joey Giacalone was still serving time for the jobs he pulled with Caesar Montevecchio, Joey's uncle, Anthony "Tony Jack" Giacalone, the well-known Detroit mobster, and New Jersey Teamsters boss Anthony "Tony Pro" Provenzano, were on their way to a lunch meeting with national Teamsters union leader Jimmy Hoffa at a suburban Detroit restaurant. Hoffa mysteriously disappeared from the restaurant's parking lot that day, never to be heard from again. Federal investigators have long speculated Giacalone and Provenzano had Hoffa killed to prevent him from regaining the Teamsters' Union presidency.

As for Detective Sgt. Dominick DiPaolo, he could easily understand how Joey Giacalone was influenced by his mobster uncle. It was also clear how the younger Giacalone passed along that influence to Montevecchio, that Caesar combined with influence he had already gained from his pals, the Scutellas.

The 50-to-70-year sentence in Michigan should have been the end of Caesar Montevecchio. It should have been another Erie punk bites the dust in a state pen. *Tutti Finuto*! Unfortunately for all of Montevecchio's many future victims – including a portly, Erie bookie, it was far from the end of Caesar Montevecchio. Instead, it was the beginning of a new and arguably the most violent chapter in Montevecchio's life.

Through 10 years of appeals and court motions, Montevecchio managed to successfully challenge and eventually beat the system as well as what would have been a life-sentence. With his final successful appeal, Montevecchio – who ironically had served as sports editor of the Jackson, Michigan State Prison newspaper – was given his freedom in 1978.

It was a decade later. The turbulent 60s had passed. The Vietnam War was over. The Civil Rights movement had mellowed. And the "Summer of Love" was but a brief footnote among the now aging hippie generation. But the mob – no matter where its social cancer erupted or how it morphed – was still flourishing. It was a time when Ray Ferritto was giving up the Cleveland mob in the Danny Greene bombing murder, and, along with his pals Bolo and Frank Thomas, was about to do a restful stint under federal witness protection in Texas.

When Bolo Dovishaw was whacked, Caesar Montevecchio had been back in Erie for four years. Yet, for DiPaolo, with each passing day, more and more signs pointed toward the former altar boy who once had the chutzpah to compare himself with John Dillinger.

CHAPTER 17

DETECTIVE SERGEANT DIPAOLO HAD LONG SUSPECTED LOCAL underworld figure Samuel "Fat Sam" Esper might be helpful in solving the Dovishaw murder. His pal was Caesar Montevecchio. And if not directly involved, DiPaolo believed Fat Sam would have inside information about the murder. Esper could very well be the key in this investigation, DiPaolo believed. If DiPaolo's suspicions were correct, starting at the bottom with Esper could eventually lead the detective to where he wanted to go – to the planners and the killer.

At six feet four inches tall and tipping the scales at 350 pounds, Fat Sam was more a comical figure than he was an imposing one. Not bright, but always good for a laugh among the real wise guys, Esper had been relegated to being a go-fer and runner for reputed old-time Erie bookie Joe Rotunda and his brother, Tommy Rotunda. The brothers ran two illegal after-hours clubs in Erie, both of them hangouts for Fat Sam. One was the Liberty Club on 26th Street in east Erie; the other the Sons of Italy on West 18th Street in the heart of Little Italy.

Esper had a long record. Nothing serious, mostly petty crimes. But still, Esper could have been working below law enforcement's radar on much more significant illegal activities. Fat Sam, it would turn out for DiPaolo, was perhaps the most logical starting point in the probe. Just as DiPaolo thought, it would be the overweight, gold-chain flashing Fat Sam Esper who would lead the cop to not one killer, but a Rogue's Gallery of Pennsylvania and Ohio criminal misfits. DiPaolo hoped Fat

Sam would served up his pal Montevecchio on a platter. But before DiPaolo could even begin to ensnare Samuel Esper, events transpired that not only threatened DiPaolo's life, but the lives of his wife Janet, and two young children, Patrick and Dawn, as well.

The threat surfaced in 1984. It was barely a year since Bolo's body was discovered. With the trail running cold, DiPaolo was straining to develop whatever leads he could. One frosty January night, perhaps as frigid as the evening a man in a black overcoat shot Frank "Bolo" Dovishaw to death a year earlier, DiPaolo's former detective partner, David Bagnoni, telephoned with startling news. "Bags," the son of powerful City Councilman Mario Bagnoni, said to be the only member of council not politically obligated to longtime Mayor Louis J. Tullio, had over the years developed a close relationship with DiPaolo, on and off the job.

Perhaps it was Councilman Bagnoni's acrimonious relationship with the mayor, or perhaps it was the two young detectives' refusal to adhere to Tullio's political agenda and cronyism. Whatever the reason, despite leading all others in arrests and cleared cases, Bags and DiPaolo were frozen at patrolman and detective sergeant rank respectively until they retired. And for David Bagnoni, the absence of promotions was also in spite of his advanced degree, a Masters in Criminology.

So close was this friendship that DiPaolo and his wife, Janet, were chosen as godparents for the younger Bagnoni's only son, David Jr. On the job, as undercover vice and drug squad officers, the two had developed a reputation of no-nonsense toughness, particularly within Erie's drug-culture community. They were seldom seen apart. And they had developed an even stronger relationship as the lead investigators probing a horrific mass murder eight years earlier during which Erie's Donald Lee Chism used a high-powered rifle to shoot to death his wife, her adopted father, and the couple's three young children.

So it was not entirely unusual for DiPaolo to receive an evening phone call from his on-and off-the-job pal, David Bagnoni, or vice versa. But when Bagnoni telephoned that January evening just a year after the Dovishaw slaying, it wasn't for social reasons or to exchange cop shop talk or personal scuttlebutt. This call was serious. Deadly serious.

"I ran into that asshole, the Hawk," Bagnoni began, almost breathless, referring to smalltime hood Chuckie "The Hawk" Serafini. It was immediately obvious to DiPaolo that whatever happened between Serafini and the cop had greatly disturbed Bagnoni. As Bagnoni began to relate the conversation, DiPaolo quickly understood why his friend was so unnerved.

It had been a chance meeting between the two with Serafini speaking first.

"How's your buddy, Dominick?" he sneered at Bagnoni. "Y'know, he's making this town pretty hot doing that fucking Bolo investigation," Bagnoni related The Hawk's comments to DiPaolo. Bagnoni could tell The Hawk wasn't merely making small talk. It seemed obvious Serafini was attempting to deliver a message.

"Dominick still live in the same house?" Serafini asked almost too innocently.

"Why?" Bagnoni answered with a question of his own.

"Just wondering. Do me a favor. Tell Dominick I said hello. Make sure."

Later pondering over the strange, almost cryptic comments, Bagnoni came to believe they were meant as a threat – a serious one – against his cop pal and maybe even his family. Listening to the story had the same chilling effect on DiPaolo as it initially had on Bagnoni.

"Watch your ass," Bags warned his friend. "You know these fucking guys are nuts."

DiPaolo understood the warning all too well. But he wasn't about to alter the way he lived or did his job because of it. Besides, it could have been just so much hot air. Unfortunately for DiPaolo, it wasn't.

Threats were nothing new to veteran cops. They seemed to come with the territory. Most of the time, threats amounted to much noise and no action. But each threat had to be evaluated separately, vetted and taken seriously. Cops know that bad guys and fruit cakes rarely act on such threats – but it's those rare cases that give one pause to worry. With nothing definite to follow up on, DiPaolo focused on the Dovishaw investigation, yet the threat remained fixed in the back of his mind. It wouldn't be long before DiPaolo learned just how real this threat actually was.

Shortly after Bagnoni's call to DiPaolo, a wise guy informant, a longtime state police snitch at the Uthman Chor Club where the fast-moving Italian dice game Barbute was played, telephoned the Pennsylvania State Police Troop E headquarters in Erie with an ominous tip that would become a warning to most in the local law enforcement community, including DiPaolo. The informant reported he overheard Caesar Montevecchio and The Hawk talking about sending a "message" to DiPaolo – "for good." Combined with Bagnoni's comments, the stoolie's information was enough for Assistant Erie County District Attorneys Shad Connelly and Tim Lucas to apply for court authorization for a hard wire on Montevecchio's home telephone where every call would be monitored by law enforcement officials. (These were pre-mobile phone days. Home phones and land lines, despite law enforcement's wire-tapping capabilities, were nonetheless the communications tools of choice employed by the underworld to conduct business.)

The ADAs presented the application petition, along with the probable cause affidavit, to Pennsylvania Superior Court Judge James E. Rowley in Pittsburgh.

On January 21, 1984, Judge Rowley gave his approval to deploy the hard wire. From that day on, Pennsylvania State Police investigators monitored all Montevecchio's calls, the regular, the frivolous and the potentially criminal. It took only a week before investigators hit pay dirt. DiPaolo was summoned to meet with State Police Trooper George Hooker, who played back a tape recording of a phone call Montevecchio placed from his Erie home to Joseph Giacalone in Flint, Michigan. Giacalone had also been released from his long prison term and was still relative, still one of Montevecchio's partners in crime.

"I want you to come down next weekend and take care of that problem I talked to you about," Montevecchio told Giacalone. "But the shooter has to come with you."

Giacalone was compliant, saying he'd check with the shooter and get back to his longtime pal, Caesar, in just a few days.

From the conversation, it seemed apparent, perhaps even obvious, that DiPaolo was indeed the target of a planned hit. From Serafini's remarks about the DiPaolo and the Dovishaw investigation, it was not difficult for police to begin to connect the dots between Bolo and Caesar.

DiPaolo's home, and his wife and children, were quickly placed under 24-hour police surveillance. So fearful were law enforcement officials of this unfolding situation that Erie Police Chief Richard Skonieczka authorized the use of 10 special detail officers for the around-the-clock surveillance. As a result, the coming days and nights would become tense ones for the veteran Erie cop. Finally, while police listened in on the bugged telephone, Joey Giacalone telephoned Caesar Montevecchio:

"See you Saturday at noon at your house," Giacalone said. "Have the spags (spaghetti) ready."

The Friday before the scheduled meeting at Montevecchio's home, police began to employ every available precaution: Montevecchio's house was now under surveillance and being watched 24/7, with an undercover tail constantly following Caesar. Police also tailed DiPaolo and his family for protection, while major routes leading into Erie from the west were closely watched at the Ohio-Pennsylvania line for Giacalone and his so-called "shooter."

After what seemed an eternity, Saturday finally dawned. Police waited. DiPaolo waited. But then, as nerves collectively tightened, there was a breather. About 10:30 a.m., Joey Giacalone placed another call to Caesar Montevecchio's home. According to the state police recording, Giacalone's car had broken down in Ann Arbor. He told Caesar repairs would take too long for the men to complete their trip that weekend.

"Cancel," Giacalone said. "Going back home. Will call."

That night, Pat DiPaolo, the cop's 14-year-old son, asked his father why policemen were following him and his sister Dawn to school. When DiPaolo asked what he was talking about, Pat explained he was playing baseball with his cousins, Greg and Tim Robbins, along with his pals Kevin Dalton and Rob "Wizz" Wieczorek and noticed two plainclothes officers there the entire time. After the game, Pat said the policemen followed him home. Oddly enough, Pat played for a team sponsored by Arnone's Importing – a name that would later play a significant role in DiPaolo's investigation into Dovishaw's murder. When pressed by his son, however, DiPaolo did what most fathers facing similar circumstances would have done. He lied. He told the boy his imagination was playing tricks on him, that no one was following him. But after the conversation with his son, DiPaolo told police he didn't want Janet and the children to know of the possible danger.

"Do me a favor," DiPaolo told Chief Skonieczka. "Move the surveillance back somewhat. It's really starting to alarm my family." DiPaolo hadn't told his wife or children of the threat. He told the chief, "My 14-year-old picked up the tail."

More time passed. One spring evening while DiPaolo was working the streets trying to turn up leads on Caesar Montevecchio, his police radio crackled to life. It was one of the members of the surveillance team covering his home. He was radioing for the district car:

"We have a guy walking down the subject's driveway," the surveillance officer calmly spoke into his mike. "I will be out of my car. Send a back-up ASAP."

DiPaolo, normally heavy on the accelerator on good days, now literally flew to his west Erie house. When he arrived, there was his neighbor, Emilio "Mickey" Iesue, face down, spread-eagle, on the ground next to DiPaolo's driveway. The surveillance officers had guns drawn – all pointing at Emilio, a gentle man in his seventies who lived next door to DiPaolo. Iesue's mother, still living, had a home across the street. After visiting his mom, Mickey strolled across the street toward his house, taking a shortcut through DiPaolo's driveway.

"He's my neighbor!" DiPaolo told the officers while helping Mickey to his feet and brushing him off. The neighbor was shaken, as one might expect. That led DiPaolo to confide in him about the threats and surveillance – but he also urged Mickey to keep the information strictly to himself. DiPaolo would later think about that night, thankful his family was not at home to witness the taking down of Mickey. He also felt safe, knowing fellow cops had his back.

More time passed. Days become weeks. The weeks became to a month and a half.

The wire remained up and manned 24/7 by state police investigators. Slowly, everyday life for DiPaolo returned to normal. It was at this time that Detective David Bagnoni took matters into his own hands.

At a local club, the Pratola Peligna Society, often called "The PP Club," Bagnoni approached Chuckie "The Hawk" Serafini. Bagnoni could not control his temper. He later related this conversation:

"I know what you and your fucking buddy Caesar are up to," Bagnoni menacingly waved a finger in front of Serafini's huge nose. "If anything happens to Dominick or his wife or his kids – if even they happen to trip and get a bloody nose – both you and Caesar are dead. I'll kill you both."

"What the fuck are you talking about?" Serafini was all innocence, surprise and bravery.

"You know what's up," Bagnoni countered. "And that's a promise!"

"I swear. I don't know what the hell you're talking about. You got some beef with Caesar? You want to talk with Caesar. Hey, be my guest. Tell him yourself."

After the Bagnoni-Serafini exchange, it didn't take long for word of the bugging to make its way to Erie's mean streets and political circles. But meanwhile, Pennsylvania State Police Trooper Hooker, who had been monitoring the hard wire, phoned DiPaolo, requesting his presence to hear the latest conversation. What he heard was a 1:15 a.m. call from Serafini to Montevecchio, with Serafini explaining his exchange with Bagnoni and the P.P. Club.

"Now where would Bagnoni get that information?" Montevecchio is heard saying.

"I don't know!" Serafini yelled.

"I know!" Montevecchio shot back. "From your big fucking mouth! When you drink too much, you're so fucking stupid! I don't know why I even talk to you!"

DiPaolo and Hooker were cracking up. Not that the planned hit was funny, but listening to Montevecchio and Serafini shouting at each other was.

"We don't have enough heat on us without you bringing more with your big fuckin' mouth?" Montevecchio screamed before hanging up.

After that, DiPaolo had no doubt the hit was cancelled because of Bagnoni's intervention. Serafini had gone straight to his pal on Erie City Council, Jerry Mifsud, and reported Bagnoni's threat. Councilman Mifsud, who would later lose his seat in that august body after reportedly trying to have the motorcycle cop who ticketed his wife demoted, went to Chief Skonieczka to complain.

But not before there was a third confrontation at the PP Club. It occurred one night as Bagnoni walked into the club and Serafini called him out to the center of what had been a dance floor. In a loud voice, as Bagnoni related to DiPaolo, Serafini reportedly said, "Go ahead! You want to hit me – go ahead!" Sitting nearby at a table watching, Bagnoni later recalled, was Councilman Mifsud.

"Go fuck yourself and your buddy," Bagnoni said, walking away. "I can see Peewee sitting over there."

But by now the alleged threat and the electronic eavesdropping at Montevecchio's home were out in the open. And investigators believed the Hawk was telling anyone who would listen that Bagnoni threatened to kill him because he thought Caesar Montevecchio was planning a hit on DiPaolo or the cop's family.

The surveillance and wiretap were finally stopped. But the threat was ended, thanks in large part to Bagnoni's bold, if somewhat unorthodox methods. DiPaolo told Bags he didn't know how he could not have cracked Serafini under the circumstances. There are those on a lengthy list who sustained timely head lacerations who could easily vouch as to the cop's veracity and penchant for evening the score, as well as his long memory. That, combined with Dom DiPaolo's undying dedication to his family, job and service to the citizens of Erie is probably best told through a series of incidents that actually began two years before he began his law enforcement career.

It was September 1967, the end of the summer love fest. As DiPaolo recalls, Nick Palermo, an alleged Erie building contractor and wannabe wise guy, attempted to take out a $10,000 loan at Marquette Savings and Loan, a local lending institution known for its "hometown" service. Palermo told officials at the thrift he needed the cash for his business – but DiPaolo believed the money was actually meant to finance a drug deal. Whatever the bank officials knew or not, the loan was denied.

Shortly after, on a Saturday morning when Marquette opened at 9 o'clock, a lone gunman barged into the newly opened Liberty Plaza branch at W. 36th and Liberty Streets and confronted the frightened teller, Patty Robbins. Robbins was seven months pregnant, her condition more than visible to the gunman.

"Gimme all the money in your drawer or I'll kill you!" the robber demanded.

The teller complied by emptying her cash drawer, handing over some $3,000, upon which the robber left the bank and sprinted to a waiting car. It wasn't a good day for robbers, but a great day for civic involvement. A quick-thinking passerby jotted down the get-away car's plate number. When police checked the number against motor vehicle registration records, they learned the car belonged to "Fat Nicky" Palermo.

At six feet three inches tall and weighing 350 pounds, Palermo, the driver of the get-away car, was hard to miss behind the wheel. When police finally found him, DiPaolo recalls, he flipped on Charles Smith, the bank robber and member of the God's Children motorcycle gang, and Smith's partner in crime, Alfred "Al" DeBello. DiPaolo recalled DeBello as one of Erie's perennial low-lives and also a member, along with Palermo, of the "Children." All three were arrested in the bank job. But prior to the trial, Smith was shot and killed in Cleveland, Ohio, over a fouled drug deal. Palermo and DeBello, however, both went to jail.

Two years later, rookie cop Dominick DiPaolo was at roll call when information about an escapee from a pre-release center was given to officers beginning the 2nd shift. The "wanted" person was Alfred "Al" DeBello. DiPaolo stiffened at hearing the name. Although the young cop did not know DeBello, he still coveted finding and arresting the fugitive. Early in the shift, the police dispatcher advised patrol cars via the police radio that DeBello was spotted along West 11th Street.

DiPaolo and his partner that night – J.C. Brasington – responded to the call and found DeBello hiding in the attic of his girlfriend's house. As DiPaolo took DeBello into custody, the cop later recalled, the prisoner resisted arrest, not once but several times. It meant DiPaolo was required to use reasonable force, as cops occasionally must do, to subdue the suspect. DeBello, who was knocked unconscious, was taken to a local hospital emergency room, treated, released, and transported to jail on the parole detainer.

When DiPaolo and J.C. Brasington were back on the street, J.C. asked his partner, "What the fuck was that all about?" But after DiPaolo explained, J.C. said, "You should have told me! Now I understand why you wanted the collar so bad!"

On the other hand, "Fat Nicky" Palermo managed to get out of the slammer in the early 1970s and was quickly back to drug dealings, passing bad checks, and ripping off unsuspecting customers who contracted his building construction business. Before long, DiPaolo had the opportunity to investigate Palermo in connection with a series of local thefts, leading to Palermo's arrest. The suspect wanted a break. He was willing to give up those who were also involved in the thefts – as always when cornered – in hopes of shaving off time from his sentence. But this time, his pleas went unanswered. DiPaolo refused to deal or plea-bargain.

After meeting with the Erie County District Attorney and getting support from the prosecutor, DiPaolo made sure Palermo went to prison without a deal. Why so tough on DeBello and Palermo? Because the young woman teller at Marquette Savings and Loan, the one who had so much trouble with her pregnancy after she was threatened with being shot – well, that woman was DiPaolo's only sibling. Patty Robbins was Patty *DiPaolo* Robbins. No one but J.C. knew. Not until now.

As for the robbers, Smith was already dead. In the early 1990s, DeBello is believed to have passed. In the late 1990s, Palermo died in prison, where he was serving time on the latest charges against him. DiPaolo was pleased. As he would describe it, his town was rid of "three more dirt bags."

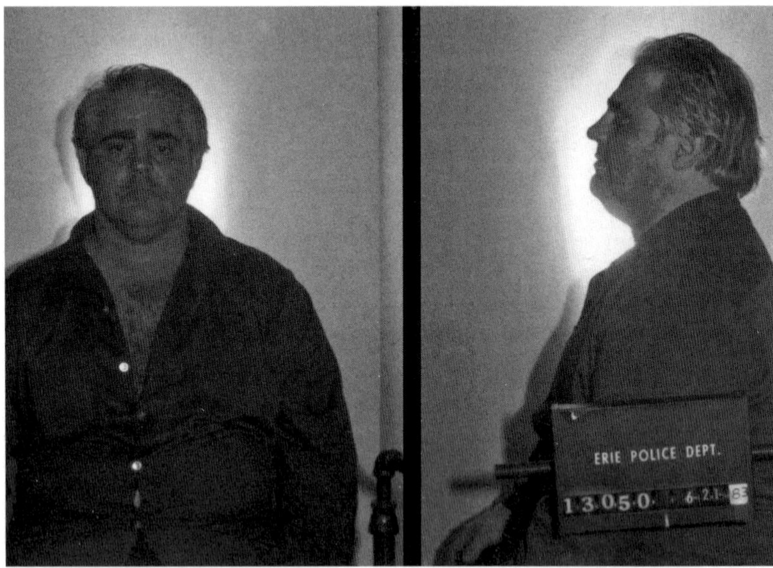

Samuel "Fat Sam" Esper belonged to two organized crime groups ultimately responsible for more than $1 million in burglaries, armed robberies and thefts. A key grand jury witness, he's in the witness protection program. (Courtesy of Erie Police Department)

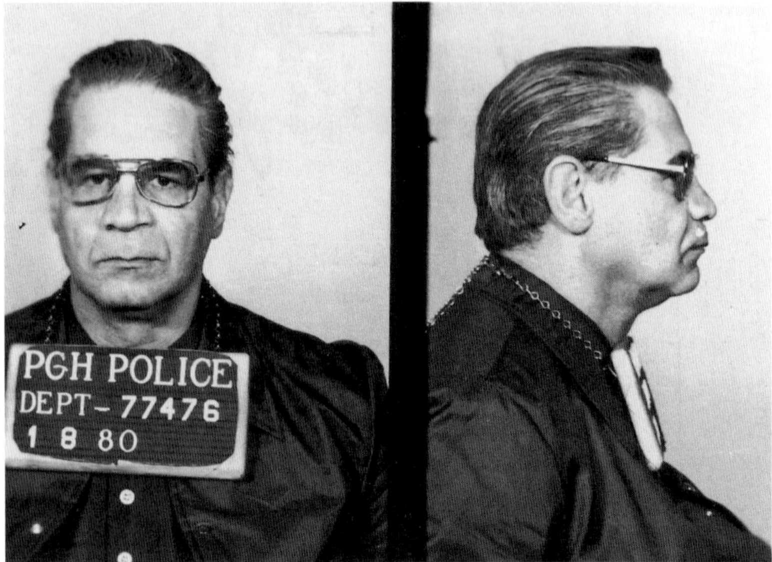

Fredrico "Freddy May" Maggio of Pittsburgh was sentenced to serve 15-to-30 years in prison. (Courtesy of Pittsburgh Police Department)

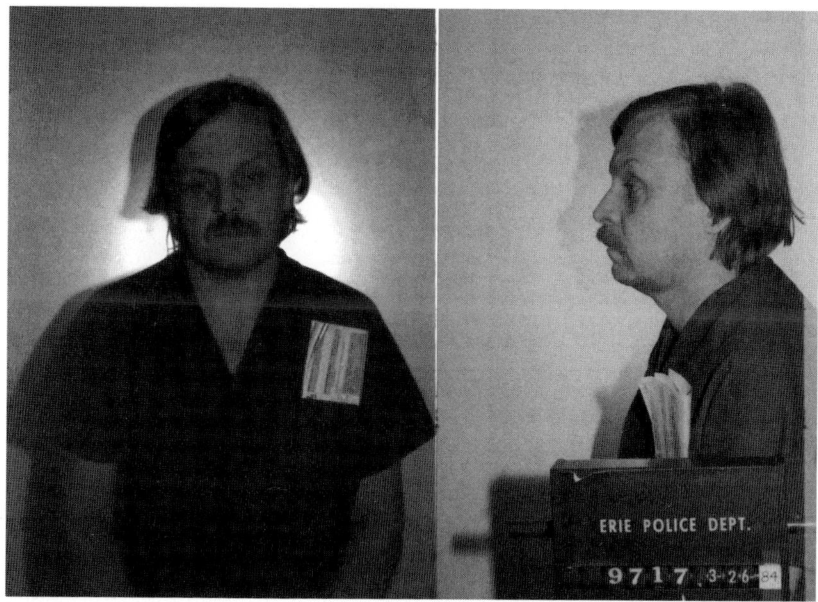

Walter "Skip" Tracy was convicted of state and federal criminal violations. His 10-year sentence was later reduced. (Courtesy of Erie Police Department)

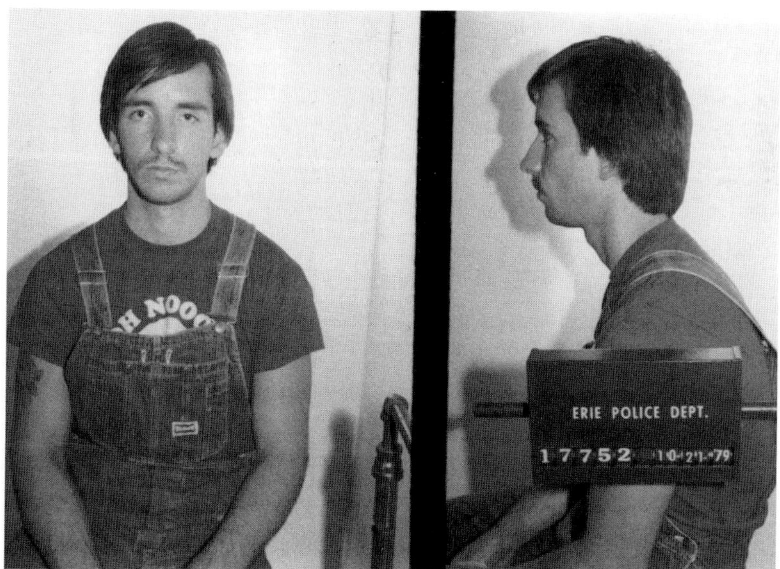

William "Billy" DeSantis pleaded guilty to burglaries and robberies with a net take of $100,000 in cash and goods. He served a probationary term. (Courtesy of Erie Police Department)

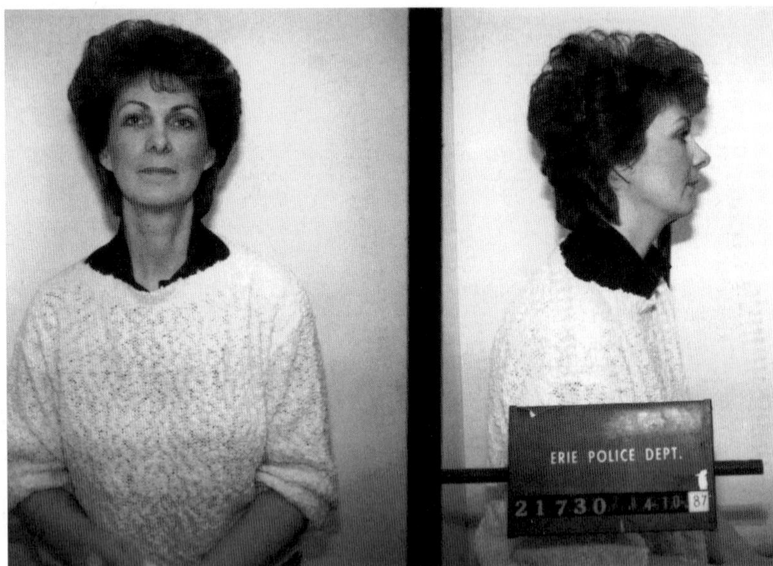

Susan DeSantis DeMichele Murosky Ferritto Tomassi, "Billy's" sister, later married to hit man Raymond Ferritto. She had been charged with burglary set-up, but "Fat Sam" changed his testimony about her and the charges were dismissed. (Courtesy of Erie Police Department)

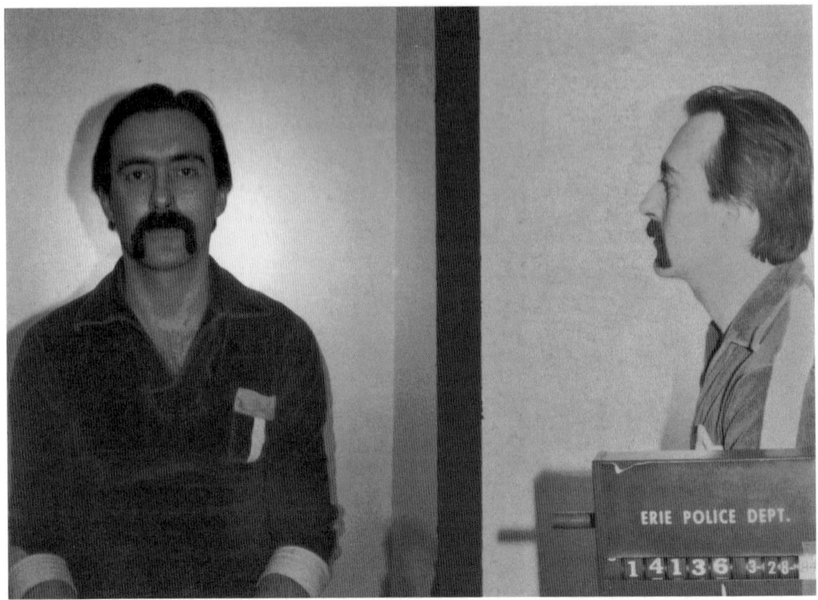

Peter Russell left a suicide note on the beach to avoid prison. He was found in Las Vegas 10 years later and went to jail on the original charges, plus new ones. (Courtesy of Erie Police Department)

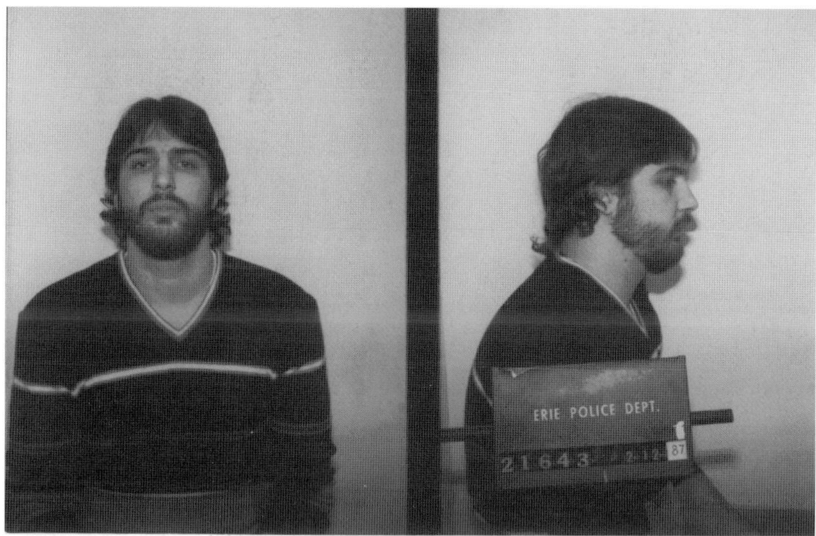

Michael Farbo pleaded guilty to two burglaries, but committed suicide prior to making promised disclosures about the Corporal Robert Owen murder. (Courtesy of Erie Police Department)

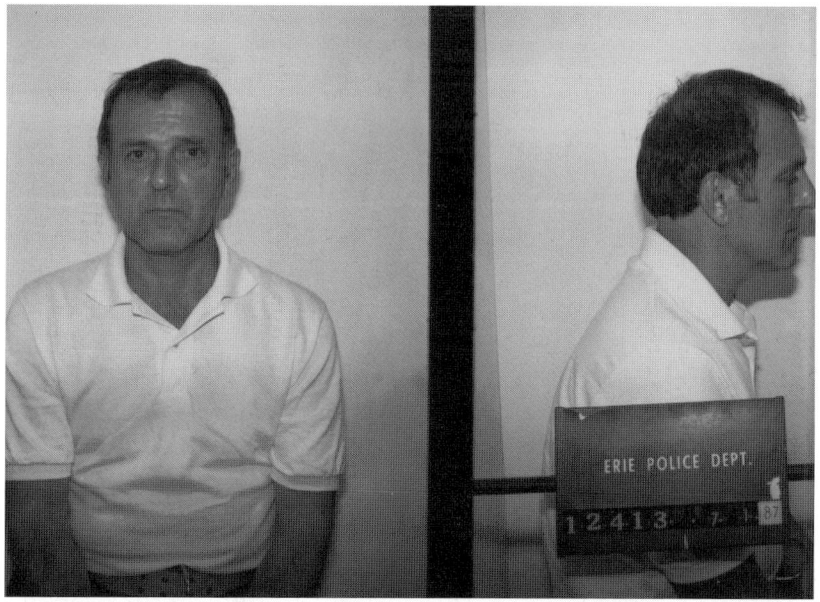

Caesar Montevecchio, Erie's career criminal and John Dillinger wannabe, was convicted of multiple felonies, including murder. While breaking in a house, he was arrested, along with "Fat Sam" Esper, by a police squad led by Detective Sergeant DiPaolo. (Courtesy of Erie Police Department)

"Fat Sam" is escorted to court by Detective Sergeant Dominick DiPaolo. Pictured from left to right are Erie County Sheriff Deputy James Haskins, Sam Esper, Det. Sgt. Dominick DiPaolo, Det. Sgt. David Grassi, Officer Donald Pollock, and Erie County Sheriff Deputy John Folga. (Author's Personal Collection)

Part Three

INVESTIGATIVE TASK FORCE – MINUS THE FBI

CHAPTER 18

THE PLOT ON DOMINICK DIPAOLO'S LIFE OBVIOUSLY HAD BEEN A major distraction in the Frank "Bolo" Dovishaw's murder investigation, as well as myriad other cases assigned to DiPaolo. The months since Dovishaw was slain had dragged on with painstakingly little progress in the high profile murder investigation. It was now approaching a year and a half since the killing, with leads virtually gone.

DiPaolo and his partner, Detective Donald Gunter, now worked the case only when time permitted among the more current, immediate police investigations. Those new cases included a recent rash of local bank robberies the detective duo cleared with arrests. But while probing the bank jobs, DiPaolo was required to attend frequent meetings with the Assistant U.S. Attorney, Don Lewis. During one such meeting and out of pure, unmitigated frustration, DiPaolo asked the federal prosecutor for guidance in the Dovishaw murder case.

Lewis was a tough government prosecutor and one of the few in the federal criminal justice system DiPaolo actually trusted enough to share sensitive information about his cases and seek advice. The Erie cop came to believe over the years that Feds, especially the FBI and other government agencies, couldn't be trusted with sensitive information, at least in DiPaolo's eyes they couldn't. He found, in his experience with them, that federal investigators were more inclined to not only shoot from the hip, blaming the locals for their own failures, but also quickly accepting credit and glory for the grunt work and labor of others when the investigations proved successful. Dominick DiPaolo wanted no part of the Feds.

But since he trusted Lewis without reservation, and since the Dovishaw case was causing many sleepless nights, DiPaolo sought out the federal attorney's counsel. Specifically, he told Lewis the case was not only growing cold, but those who might have vital and relevant information were fearful of talking to detectives, frightened of retribution from Dovishaw's killer or killers. Lewis suggested DiPaolo lay out the entire investigation from the beginning to the frozen-in-place point where it then stood for the federal prosecutor.

"The only way to make reluctant witnesses talk," Lewis sagely observed, "is to present the case to a federal grand jury where they would be compelled by law to testify."

But for federal grand jury involvement, obviously, there first needed to be a federal connection, prosecutor Lewis told the police detective. DiPaolo's trust in Lewis paid off. After reviewing every component and aspect of DiPaolo's initial and ongoing investigation, Lewis saw the very real possibility of organized crime involvement. It was one of those epiphany moments. Lewis saw a potential federal connection with the Racketeering Influenced and Corrupt Organizations Act – or, as the cops and feds simply love to call the legislation: RICO. RICO provides for extended penalties for crimes committed as part of a criminal organization, such as the Mafia, mob, syndicate.

With Lewis and DiPaolo now in deep conversations about RICO's possible impact on the Dovishaw investigation, it was the federal prosecutor who speculated it actually might be possible for him to sell the concept of a grand jury probe to his superiors in Pittsburgh.

"Let's go for a task force that includes the feds, state police, city police and Pennsylvania's Attorney General's Office," Lewis suggested. If the plan flew, Lewis said, it would be DiPaolo's case to lead.

The next step for DiPaolo was to win approval from his own superiors, especially Erie Police Chief Richard Skonieczka. With his ducks in order, DiPaolo approached the chief with the plan and laid out the possibilities. Skonieczka, son of the longtime Erie County Prison Warden Al Skonieczka, also a former Erie police officer, enthusiastically supported DiPaolo's plan. And now, with the blessing of Erie's top cop, the other law enforcement agencies quickly bought into the concept.

Yet, DiPaolo still harbored hugely nagging doubts about federal involvement. Even with this potential new avenue of attack and tool to help break open the Bolo Dovishaw case that was growing colder by the day, the cop was uncomfortable with even the thought of collaborating with the Federal Bureau of Investigation.

"No offense to you," DiPaolo told Prosecutor Lewis, "but I never met a fed I could trust. They seem to be programmed to lie to the local police and then they try to take all the thunder for themselves."

Lewis was empathetic with the Erie police detective.

"Hey, pal, look, it's your game. You call it as you see it," Lewis said. As a result, it didn't take DiPaolo long to eliminate the FBI from the mix.

"They were out faster than I could say Efrem Zimbalist, Jr.," DiPaolo would later recall, in reference to the 1960s' popular television series called *The FBI*. "This wasn't about the FBI or any law enforcement group. This was about forming a tight, cohesive task force," he later said.

In short order, the new special investigative panel was formed. Named to the group were Pennsylvania State Police Troopers Harry Jabo and Chuck Daley, Agent John Piesacki of the Pennsylvania Attorney General's Office, and DiPaolo and Gunter. In addition to probing the apparent underworld killing of Frank "Bolo" Dovishaw on January 3, 1983, the Task Force also was charged with re-opening the investigation into the death of Erie Police Corporal Robert Owen, who was murdered in December 1980. Owen's killer was still at large, the case unsolved.

DiPaolo remembered every detail so well, the Owen killing forever linked with a prominent house break-in a month earlier that year. It was the Thanksgiving weekend of 1980 that would prove to be a memorable one for Louie Nardo and his wife. Actually, the entire holiday season that year would be memorable for Erie police, especially DiPaolo.

The Nardos had returned home after celebrating the holiday with their out-of-town daughter, only to find their upscale home in Erie's Glenwood Estates burglarized. This was no bush-league job. The alarm system was disarmed. In the basement family room, Nardo's six-by-four foot walk-in safe was ransacked and his valuable possessions stolen.

DiPaolo knew Nardo to be a gambler who often bragged about his finances, making him a prime target for Erie's notorious bad guy burglars. Nardo bragged often at card games about how he acquired his many rings and watches – the reason DiPaolo suspected he was targeted not once, but twice!

Not only the safe, but the entire Nardo house was ransacked. Empty ring boxes were found throughout the house. Erie police were mystified. Veteran investigators had never before seen a large safe opened in quite that bizarre way. They had seen entire safes stolen. They had seen safes with the combination locks pulled, drilled or knocked out. But this was a first. In the basement, police found Nardo's outdoor garden hose. Apparently, the burglars first drilled a hole large enough to insert the end of the hose inside the safe. Then, they turned on the water, filled the safe, and placed a blasting cap on the opening. The blasting cap was hooked to a car battery, then set off, the resultant explosion covering everything in the immediate vicinity with water – boxes, papers, furniture, the room was soaked. The water had a secondary and practical purpose: It prevented paper money in the safe from catching fire and burning from the flying sparks.

After Louie Nardo telephoned Erie police to report the burglary, among the many officers responding to the crime scene was one motorcycle officer named Robert Owen. Also called to the scene was the Erie Police Identification Unit. Like today's modern crime scene investigators, it was the IU's job to process the area for evidence or clues that would lead police to the perps. It was while officers roamed throughout the house that Nardo, who was in a room directly off the basement family room, began yelling loudly.

When Nardo arrived at home that night, he was yelling, one of the ring boxes scattered on the floor still contained an expensive men's diamond ring. The burglars apparently missed that treasure, leaving it behind in the small box. But now, the box on the floor was gaping wide open and, surprise of surprises, the diamond ring was gone. And Nardo was screaming that the missing ring was taken by a police officer!

Sergeant David Grassi, the senior officer, a nephew of Erie Mayor Louis Tullio, actually Nardo's cousin, had the presence of mind to immediately order all officers scattered throughout the house into one room. Once there, he told the cops to empty their pockets. It must have been a bizarre sight. But, according to those who witnessed it, not one officer complained. All complied with Sergeant Grassi's order. No ring was found.

But Nardo was not mollified. He was angrier. Seething, this first cousin of Mayor Tullio telephoned the mayor at his home, complaining bitterly about Tullio's police department and the burglary investigation. Now, there were two investigations in progress: One dealt with the initial Nardo safe job. The second dealt with the possibility of a police thief.

Captain Charles McCurdy – "Cubby" to his pals – was considered a straight shooter as far as Erie cops went and was assigned to the missing ring probe. Immediately, McCurdy began an Internal Affairs investigation of the police officers present in the Nardo home. McCurdy not only set up interviews with the officers, but he also ordered polygraphs. Of the three officers whose initial lie-detector test results indicated they had failed, one was Corporal Robert Owen.

Owen had a reputation of being a tough guy. He had been an iron worker prior to joining the Erie Police Department, and, on the side, he operated his own vehicle-towing business.

Detective Sergeant DiPaolo had always been suspicious of Owen. For one, DiPaolo knew of the cop's association with those DiPaolo considered less than reputable. He had no proof, just suspicions. The public did not know about the three officers who failed the polygraph test. Not at that time. The few who knew weren't talking. But there was nonetheless much speculation in Erie's aggressive news media, print and broadcast, about the Erie Police Department's handling of the Nardo home burglary. Some could have easily speculated that while the officers present that night had been ordered to empty their pockets, boots – especially motorcycle officer's boots – would have been an easy hiding place for a small ring. But, that was only unfounded speculation.

The official investigation plowed ahead with no suspects or even good theories being developed in the Nardo job. Nor was there any concrete information or evidence in the stolen ring probe.

But McCurdy's Internal Affairs investigation had scheduled the three officers who failed the first Polygraph to undergo another lie-detector test during which additional questions were to be asked of the policemen. The re-testing was scheduled for Monday, December 29, 1980, with the three officers set to undergo polygraphs at 9 and 11 a.m., and 1:30 p.m.

For years, Dom DiPaolo had chosen not to take summer vacations, but instead to use his accrued yearly vacation time at the end of the calendar year. He looked forward to being off from the Wednesday before Thanksgiving to the first Monday in January spending quality time with his family. But at exactly 6 a.m. on Monday, December 29, 1980, DiPaolo's vacation was rudely interrupted by the shrill and persistent ringing of his telephone.

He finally answered with an irritated, "Yeah?" Little surprised the veteran cop, but what he heard was shocking. It was Police Chief Richard Skonieczka on the line with a good reason for interrupting DiPaolo's cherished time off. Corporal Robert Owen was dead. Owen, who was among the three suspect cops under investigation in the missing ring case, was found shot to death in full uniform early that morning. Would DiPaolo come back to work and take over the murder investigation? Skoniezcka asked in a combination plea and order.

DiPaolo sighed. This wasn't just a case. This was a cop. Dirty or not, a cop. And DiPaolo was obliged. Vacation be damned, of course he would return to work.

The next few months, DiPaolo later admitted to himself, would change the image of the Erie Police Department for years to come. The events of the coming months would also have a profound impact on the homicide detective's career – and his life.

Corporal Robert Owen's untimely death marked the first time in more than 30 years that an Erie Police Officer had been intentionally killed on duty. Three cops had been shot to death in 1949 by a crazed World War II veteran – but there was nothing mysterious about the case, another tragic example of how the war haunted many of those who had served in combat zones. But the Owen case was indeed a whodunit, especially at this early point in the probe. It was a horrific mess of an investigation from the start.

The initial police officers called to the Erie warehouse parking lot in the 1300 block of West 18th Street, where Owen's body was found, had destroyed the crime scene of any and all evidence. DiPaolo knew this wasn't done intentionally, but only out of an ignorant desire to be of help. But it didn't mitigate the mess and the destruction of potential vital evidence that now could never be fully recovered. Even though they wanted to help, these cops trampled down the crime scene, destroying anything of value to investigators. Even more incredible, an Identification Unit officer told Detective Sergeant DiPaolo that he called for an Erie Fire Department rig to hose down the entire scene. The officer told DiPaolo, "There was blood all over and the media was taking pictures – and, damn, it just wasn't right for the public to see a policeman's blood!"

As a result, with Erie's December temperatures dipping into the single digits, blood and other crucial evidence at the scene was washed into a huge ice rink. And with the crime scene evidence mostly gone, police were limited to concentrating on what they knew to be factual:

Owen's body had been found next to his police cruiser (motorcycles were not used during winter months) with the driver's door still open and the motor still running.

Owen had a gunshot wound to his chest. His holster was unsnapped, and his Smith and Wesson .38-caliber service revolver with the six-inch barrel nowhere to be found. It had simply disappeared. Stolen by the killer? Washed away? Nobody knew. Suicide, which might have been suspected had the gun been found at Owen's side, was quickly ruled out.

The area was well-known to police as it was hidden from public view from the street, and often was a good location for cops to take a rest-break during their shifts.

The grisly scene was discovered by a young neighborhood man walking his dog about 1 a.m. David Cambra, 24, who police would characterize as being somewhat mentally challenged, ran home after he spotted the dead officer in the trucking warehouse's parking lot, he told police. It was Cambra's mother who had telephoned police from home, and officers converged en masse on the scene, much like a cattle stampede.

Now it was left to DiPaolo and his partner, Gunter, to sift through the reams of written reports from those first officers to arrive on the scene. They also interviewed Erie cops who might have had vital information about Owen's last hours, even his last minutes alive. The detectives determined Owen had worked the second shift on Sunday, December 28, the "three-to-eleven" shift. DiPaolo also knew from his own early days as a patrol officer that any Sunday in late December was bound to be a slow day for cops.

He was right. During the entire shift, Corporal Owen had only two radio transmissions. One was a code from the radio dispatcher for

Owen to telephone his wife shortly before 4 p.m. Jane Owen confirmed she had telephoned the police station and that her husband later returned her call at home. During the conversation, she said, she asked whether Owen was coming home for dinner, which he did around 6 p.m. In the second radio transmission at 7:30 p.m., the police dispatcher asked Owen to telephone Sergeant David Grassi at Grassi's home.

Grassi confirmed he had contacted Owen during the shift to ask whether Owen would meet him for coffee. Grassi knew Owen was worried about taking the second polygraph test in the missing Nardo ring investigation the following morning. The re-test had been scheduled for 9 a.m. Grassi told DiPaolo he wanted to calm Owen down over coffee. DiPaolo knew the two officers were close, on and off the job.

"I don't care what Internal Affairs thinks of this," Grassi had insisted during the interview with DiPaolo. "Bob Owen did not take that ring. Dominick, I told Bobby to give me the ring and I would take it to my uncle (Mayor Louis Tullio) with a bullshit story. You know, someone mailed it to me. And it's over. Nardo gets his ring back." However, Grassi told DiPaolo that Owen denied the theft, saying, "David, I didn't take it! I don't have it!"

DiPaolo believed that if Owen did in fact have the ring, he would have given it to Grassi in a heartbeat to be done with the ordeal. Owen trusted his pal implicitly.

Although Grassi's offer for coffee was extended in good faith, Grassi said Owen declined meeting with him because he said he would be playing poker later at Paul Bizzarro's house. Paul Bizzarro, like Owen, also had a towing business and the two were close friends.

DiPaolo learned there were five men playing poker that night, most of them from the Bizzarro family. When interviewed later by DiPaolo, Paul Bizzarro acknowledged Bob Owen dropped by his house while Bizzarro, his nephews and friends played poker at the kitchen table. According to Bizzarro, it was about 7 p.m. when Owen arrived and immediately jumped into the game. Owen was still on duty, but it was not unusual for some Erie cops on slow Sunday nights to engage in non-official activities. Shortly after Owen arrived, Paul Bizzarro told DiPaolo, the officer received a radio transmission from headquarters instructing him to telephone Sergeant David Grassi at his home. This served to confirm what DiPaolo had already known. Owen got up from the table and used a wall phone in the kitchen to call Grassi. Bizzarro overheard Owen tell Grassi he couldn't make it for coffee that night. Owen returned to the poker game, but about 11:30 p.m., Bizzarro said, Owen left the table between hands to make another call from the kitchen. This time, Bizzarro overheard the officer say, "I'll see you later," before returning to the poker game. Bizzarro believed at the time the call was to Owen's wife, but learned later it wasn't.

A short time later, just before midnight, the game broke up. Bizzarro suggested to the group they go out for breakfast, but Owen begged off, saying he had to get his police cruiser back to Erie Police headquarters in downtown Erie. When he left Bizzarro's house, it was the last time anyone, save for the murderer, saw Corporal Robert Owen alive.

Within the next several days, DiPaolo and Gunter interviewed and took official statements from cops, from Bizzarro's card-playing buddies, and from two out-of-town truck drivers who that night had been looking for a warehouse and observed a police car in the warehouse lot from a distance. The truckers saw two individuals in conversation near the police car about 12:40 a.m., they told DiPaolo. They learned via news media reports of Owen's death in the west side warehouse parking lot, then volunteered their eye-witness information, for whatever it was worth.

Meanwhile, David Cambra, whom police initially believed quite accidentally stumbled upon the scene, now stubbornly refused to submit to a polygraph – further arousing detectives' suspicions. Cambra also declined to submit to hypnosis, which was then successfully employed to help witnesses with recall.

"Lawyering up," as the cops called it, refusing to talk to officers, only managed to bring heat onto Cambra, now making him the prime and only person of interest in the investigation. Perhaps he wasn't so innocently walking his dog after all, police began to speculate.

But several days later, Jeff Connelly, a young Erie lawyer, brother of Assistant District Attorney and soon-to-be Judge Shad Connelly, telephoned Dom DiPaolo to say Mr. Cambra would indeed cooperate with the police investigation and submit to the lie detector test. DiPaolo was more than willing to set up the polygraph.

On the day of the test, Cambra arrived first. DiPaolo couldn't help but noticing how unnerved and upset Cambra seemed as he waited for

Connelly. Finally, when the lawyer showed up, Cambra made a beeline toward him. Within minutes, DiPaolo could hear the lawyer yelling at his client. Then, Connelly approached DiPaolo, waiting with Gunter and members of the DA's office, and asked to speak alone with the lead investigator. When the two were away from the others, Connelly acknowledged that Cambra confessed coming upon Owen's body and stealing his service revolver, hiding it close to the railroad tracks not far from where the policeman was found.

But Cambra insisted to his lawyer that he did not kill Owen. According to Cambra's new statement, he was walking his dog near his home and saw the police cruiser with the lights on, the engine running and the driver's side door open. He also saw Owen laying on the ground "with blood all over him." His big shiny (chrome-plated) gun was on the ground about three feet from his body. Cambra said he yelled to Owen several times before determining the officer was dead. He said he grabbed the officer's gun and quickly ran home.

At first, Cambra placed the gun in a towel and hid it in an old garbage can in his garage. Next, he told his mother he found a dead cop while walking the dog.

Cambra's mom immediately called the police. David Cambra was now saying that he was worried that if he had told police that he had the gun, detectives would assume that he was the killer. It was a game changer, and DiPaolo could tell that after Cambra confessed up about the gun, his demeanor changed. He wasn't nearly as nervous and wasn't speaking in rapid bursts as he had been. Now much calmer, Cambra told DiPaolo that several days after the murder, he moved the gun from his garage and buried it near the railroad tracks. He offered to take DiPaolo there, then voluntarily took the polygraph and also underwent hypnosis, after which all agreed he was now telling the truth, that his only involvement was boosting the weapon found near the dead police officer.

Later that night, DiPaolo unearthed the weapon exactly where Cambra said it would be. The gun was towel wrapped, just as Cambra said it was. Examining the revolver, DiPaolo found only one spent shell casing in the cylinder. After the weapon was given to the Identification Section, officers learned it had been wiped down, containing no fingerprints, again confirming Cambra's account. Ballistic tests determined "the very strong possibility" it was Owen's own weapon that had been used to kill him. Although the case has not been solved, at least not yet, many theories were advanced over the three decades that have since passed:

One was that Owen stole Nardo's ring, hiding it in his motorcycle boot. But, knowing he could not pass the polygraph test, he killed himself. Another was that it was Cambra who killed Owen after the officer discovered Cambra trying to break into the trucking company warehouse and Owen confronted him there. Another was that one of the card players, angry Owen had won his money at Bizzarro's, followed Owen to the warehouse, quarreled with him, managed to get his service revolver and killed him during a struggle at the isolated spot. But none of these theories ever panned out.

One theory DiPaolo long advanced in the mysterious Corporal Robert Owen death involved others as well as it involved criminal activity. But it had nothing to do with the missing Nardo ring. DiPaolo is almost certain he knows the identity of the ring snatcher. A cop? Absolutely. But the statute of limitations, if not the dirty cop or libel laws, has long expired. DiPaolo believes it was plausible Owen and his car towing business were involved in illegal activities, and that he ultimately might have been killed to silence him. But not by any of those previously discussed on these pages. This was especially plausible since Owen would have had access to many abandoned cars and in particular their titles, which easily could have been switched for use on other vehicles.

Shortly after the killing, DiPaolo visited Owen's widow, Jane, at her home.

The detective asked and was given permission to examine Owen's room.

"Whatever you need, or want to do, just do it!" she said.

In the bedroom, in Owen's dresser underwear drawer, beneath the newspaper drawer-liner, DiPaolo discovered 96 "open" vehicle titles. Jane Owen said she had no idea they were there.

DiPaolo later determined all 96 cars had been salvaged and crushed, with documentation sent to the Pennsylvania Department of Transportation stating no titles were found. Thus, DiPaolo's theory of removing the Vehicle Identification Numbers from stolen cars and replacing them with the VINs from the open titles and selling the stolen autos would seem to represent a lucrative business.

Years later in 1987, while leaning on a number of underworld types in the Caesar Montevecchio investigation, DiPaolo again came across similar information about Robert Owen – that he might have been involved in a stolen car ring that called for the use of legitimate titles. A person who DiPaolo believed had information about the killing was Michael Farbo, arrested by DiPaolo as one of "Fat Sam" Esper's burglary cronies. Farbo was represented by Attorney Robert Brabender, Jr. Dom offered Farbo a deal made-in-heaven. He would plead guilty to two felony counts of burglary that normally carried maximum sentences of 10-to-20 years each in connection with a February 17, 1982 break-in at the home of Louis Manendo on Royal Avenue during which some $65,000 worth of coins, jewelry and cash was taken. In return for the plea, DiPaolo would seek to arrange with the sentencing judge for Farbo get only two years of probation with no jail time. Such a wrist slap, however was contingent upon one condition.

Farbo must give DiPaolo a full statement on what he knew about the killing of Corporal Robert Owen six-and-a-half years earlier. For there to be a plea deal, Farbo must talk about Owen. Otherwise, no deal. Take it or leave it.

What if his client didn't know anything about the Owen killing? Brabender asked DiPaolo. "Just ask him," DiPaolo confidently told the lawyer. After consulting with Farbo, Brabender telephoned DiPaolo. "He has what you want," the attorney said. "Set it up."

The deal was simple: Plead guilty to the burglaries counts. Talk about Owen. Get probation. So it was that on July 2, 1987, at 2 p.m. one Michael Farbo pleaded guilty to two counts of felony burglary in front of Erie County Judge William E. Pfadt. Sentencing was scheduled before Pfadt September 7 at 9 a.m.

According to the handshake in the courtroom on the day the plea arrangement, one day later, on July 3, 1987 at 9 a.m., Farbo and his lawyer were to report to Erie Police Headquarters where Farbo would give a detailed statement about the Owen killing. It appeared DiPaolo was finally about to move considerably closer to solving the Owen case! Ah, but how matters can change in the blink of an eye.

It was a warm summer evening, that July 2, 1987, several hours after Michael Farbo pleaded guilty to the Manendo job. DiPaolo was content his persistence and dogged pursuit in the Owen case was about to pay off. Then DiPaolo's efforts came to a screeching halt! At 5:55

that afternoon, the Erie Police radio crackled to life as the operator dispatched a car to the 300 block of East 8th Street after neighbors in the area reported hearing gunshots. Police officers Frank Kwitowski and Ted Marnen answered the "shots fired" call. There, they found the mortally wounded Michael Farbo, who was rushed to a downtown hospital.

While the newspaper, in its sanitized description of what transpired, called the injury "a self-inflicted gunshot wound to the head," police shrugged it off as another crook using a firearm to blow out his brains. Farbo languished in critical condition in the intensive care unit for several more days. His July 3 interview was delayed, DiPaolo hopeful his source would recover. The postponement, however, would be a forever cancellation. Michael Farbo succumbed to his injury. On July 8, 1987, he was dead. And with him went whatever Owen death information that might have gone to DiPaolo.

Still, DiPaolo believes he knows what Farbo had to give up in the Owen case. But he also believes Farbo could not carry out his part of the plea deal because of another interpersonal relationship, that a close relative was involved. That's all DiPaolo is prepared to say – at this point – about his theory. As for the missing Nardo ring – DiPaolo believes crime paid for the Erie cop who got away with it while leaving Bob Owen's reputation to take the rap. As for the Owen murder case, several attempts to revive the investigation under the premise of "cold case" probes were launched over the years. Erie County DAs concluded there was no evidence to shed new light on the case.

On the 30th anniversary of Owen's death, the Erie newspaper ran a lengthy article that mostly rehashed already known facts and rehashed theories without providing new information. Yet, as late as early 2011, the Erie County District Attorney's Office and the Pennsylvania State Police, seemingly without any solid foundation to begin another "cold case" probe and obviously in response to newspaper pressure, began one anyway. DiPaolo, at the time, speculated that David Cambra would once again be needlessly singled out as a person of interest – but without evidence against him.

He also still grimaces when he recalls what Jane Owen related to him more than 30 years after her husband's killing. It was early 2011 when she told DiPaolo, whom she still calls the only cop she trusted, that she was awoken about 1:30 a.m. on December 30, 1980, when Police Chief Richard Skonieczka, Deputy Chief Ray DeDionisio and

Deputy Chief Jack Cousins rang her doorbell. When she answered the door, she said, it was DeDionisio who said, "We're sorry to tell you that Bob was found shot to death just now. He committed suicide." Then, she amazingly was told, no gun was found. The young wife was aghast with the contradictory information. Some 30 years later she told DiPaolo, "Can you imagine that an hour after Bob was found, these three come to my house and tell me Bob killed himself, but there was no gun found next to him!" It was obvious to Mrs. Owen at the time that the police brass believed Owen had stolen the Nardo ring and killed himself because he couldn't pass a polygraph – so easy for the Police Bureau to have the death ruled a suicide, thus closing its internal investigation.

Erie Police Corporal Robert Owen was found murdered December 30 1980. His murder is still unsolved. (Courtesy of the Owen Family)

"Wrong, so wrong!" DiPaolo said at the time of the death, during his meeting 30 years later with Jane Owen, and even now.

Now, in 1984, DiPaolo finally had gotten his wish for the creation of an independent Task Force and federal grand jury to probe the Dovishaw killing. With the Task Force now in place, on a warm June 17, 1984, nearly 18 months after that frigid January night at Bolo's West 21rd Street home, DiPaolo was sworn in by the Director of the U.S. Marshall's Service in Pittsburgh as a Deputy U.S. Marshall in charge of the new federal investigatory Task Force. For DiPaolo, this new tool – the ability to compel reluctant witnesses to talk, no matter how fearful they might be – came as a godsend. For the first time in many months, creation of the federal Task Force was a positive indicator, at least in DiPaolo's mind, that now the stalled investigation would again move forward. The coming weeks and months were demonstrative of just how important this new development was to the success of the Dovishaw murder investigation, specially as it applied to one Caesar Montevecchio!

Montevecchio was dropped into Dom DiPaolo's waiting grasp almost by accident. For more than a year, since very early on in the investigation, the veteran Erie detective suspected Montevecchio, Erie's number one crime figure, of being a key player in the gangland-style hit on bookie Frank "Bolo" Dovishaw. In mid-1984, 18 months after gambling king-pin Dovishaw was taken down, the trail to the shooter had grown almost non-existent. The distraction of the wannabe wise guys' intended contract "hit" on DiPaolo himself had also resulted in an unnerving disruption of the "Bolo" probe. But now, he was back in the saddle, especially with the new empowerment of the federal grand jury. And DiPaolo was not above using whatever pond scum was available to lead him to Bolo's executioner. The major break in the investigation came from an unlikely source – "Fat Sam" Esper.

DiPaolo's gut long told him Fat Sam – a minor figure in the underworld pecking order – would at least know something about Dovishaw's murder. DiPaolo had yet to figure out a way to get to Esper, let alone a way to make him talk. Then it happened, that one decent break DiPaolo had been waiting, hoping, even praying for. The break came from Patrol Officer Vinnie Lewandowski, a dependable street cop who, unlike a handful of others on the force, Dom DiPaolo trusted implicitly. Lewandowski, who worked with DiPaolo on surveillance or when the detective surreptitiously needed a person of interest checked out, was frequently DiPaolo's eyes and ears on Erie's streets. Lewandowski knew it was DiPaolo's intent to break "Fat Sam" Esper.

"I tailed 'Fat Sam's' car last night," the street cop told DiPaolo. "Guess who was with him?" The detective, interested at the mention of Esper's name, shrugged.

"Caesar!" Lewandowski smiled. "I followed them for a while, but hung back so they wouldn't make me and eventually lost them in the upper west side."

"Caesar?" DiPaolo asked. "Vinnie, don't break my balls. That's too good to be true!"

Lewandowski nodded, again with a knowing smile like cops so often use when they know what you don't. DiPaolo was well aware that

"Fat Sam" was on the periphery of heavy hitters in Erie's crimc world. But he could not begin to imagine smart Montevecchio hooking up with Sam Esper. The two mixed like Sunnis and Shia. What a surprise, DiPaolo thought.

Quickly, DiPaolo devised a plan. Fat Sam Esper was a weakling, DiPaolo believed, akin to an infant when left alone. The way to crack "Fat Sam" was intimidation and isolation from his more dominating pals. Officer Vinnie Lewandowski was just the cop to delight in such an assignment!

Over the next few weeks, strange things began to happen in Sam Esper's life. Wherever Esper's car was parked – his home, the many sleazy Erie clubs he frequented, anywhere and everywhere – ominous messages began to appear. These signs of misfortune – garbage, dog feces, a eerie black cemetery wreath – were left with equally disquieting messages, such as: "It's a matter of time!" or "You're going down!" or "We know what you're doing!" The intimidation was beginning to wear on Esper, but it was basic police procedure that would ultimately twist the metaphorical knife in "Fat Sam's" very large gut.

Although many might not have thought it at the time, compared with today's ingenious, almost magical world of electronic gizmos and wondrous computerized, digitalized devices, the year A.D. 1984 could was not a banner one for technology.

While perhaps not emblematic of society's technological Dark Ages, electronic tracking and computerized record-keeping were nonetheless still barely in their infancies, especially as it applied to law enforcement techniques, and even more especially within the confines of the Erie Bureau of Police. Yet, through this analog world's laborious process of manually checking local, state and federal records, investigators eventually learned "Fat Sam" Esper's Pennsylvania driver's license had been suspended, thanks to too many traffic offenses to mention. And after Lewandowski's unrelenting intimidation tactics and constant tailing, it was now time for the law enforcement investigators to step in and act:

It was on that tepid July 18, 1984 day at 9:30 a.m. after pulling one of his all-nighters at Tommy Rotunda's Sons of Italy Club on West 18th Street that "Fat Sam" sleepily climbed into his aging automobile, shakily ignited the engine, and began unsteadily to weave away. Lewandowski, the cop of the hour, was there to make the traffic stop and arrest. The charge was driving a vehicle while under suspension. Esper protested. And as Officer Lewandowski provoked him even more, "Fat Sam" became more belligerent, just as the cop knew the small-time hood would be. What should have been a routine summary traffic offense now led to Esper's incarceration at Erie Police Headquarters. DiPaolo arrived there within minutes and, after consulting briefly with Lewandowski, directed the street cop to Esper's cell.

"I'm taking you to an interrogation room to be questioned by Detective Sergeant DiPaolo," Lewandowski calmly told "Fat Sam."

"Fuck you," replied Esper. "I ain't talking to him. He wants to fuckin' kill me."

Lewandowski, feigning compassion, asked, "What do you mean?"

Esper explained that word on the street was that DiPaolo was threatening to shoot him if the detective caught "Fat Sam" illegally entering any building or home. "Fuck him," Esper said with a somewhat limited vocabulary that nonetheless got his message across.

After Lewandowski reported back to DiPaolo, the detective called in Sergeant David Grassi, who had previously successfully dealt with "Fat Sam."

"Hey, Sam," Grassi began, "I gotta tell you that you've got Dom DiPaolo really pissed. He's going to charge you with burglaries he knows you pulled. And he's going to get bond set so high you won't ever be able to post it. And then you're going to the county lock-up. Shit, is that what you want, man?"

"Fuck him!" Elocution deficiency or not, Mr. Esper was beginning to sound like a broken record. Grassi shrugged and left. Best to let Esper alone to stew and fret over his fate. However, it didn't take all that long for the weak-willed grossly overweight thug to cave in.

Esper almost frantically called out to the security officer on duty that morning, Patrolman Andrew Yacobozzi (aka "Booty"), "Hey! Send Grassi back here!" Esper bellowed. "I want to see him – now!" Yacobozzi, not about to be ordered about by any prisoner, let alone this low life, deliberately shuffled slowly away. But he did promptly advise Grassi and DiPaolo of the "request."

"How do I stay outta jail, for Christsakes?" Esper pleaded.

Sergeant David Grassi, who had dutifully trudged back to the prisoner holding area at Esper's panic-stricken urging, paused briefly for maximum effect. "Well, Sam, I guess you talk to DiPaolo," Grassi suggested. Then, he added, "In fact, you *better* talk to DiPaolo. He's in charge of the investigation, y'know. He's already pulling reports of burglaries he knows you did."

"Fat Sam" Esper was silent for several moments, as though he was pondering his limited options, none of which at the moment appeared too promising. "So then I don't go to jail?" he asked, somewhat hopefully and with that pathetic wounded doe look.

"Depends," Grassi said, playing "Fat Sam" all he could.

"On what?"

Grassi again paused for dramatic effect, making a profuse sweater perspire even more. "It depends on what you can give him. Exactly what *can* you give him?" Grassi probed further. "Give us a proffer."

"How about Caesar for 30 years? I'll give him everything we did. Plus more."

Caesar Montevecchio!

For the next year, "Fat Sam" Esper would become Detective Sergeant Dominick DiPaolo's new very best friend. Before it ended, "Fat Sam" would give DiPaolo 17 burglaries, 12 robberies and street thefts, and more than 25 thefts from homes, cars and boats. Esper would wear a wire on his pal Montevecchio, and record conversations with Caesar Montevecchio about Frank "Bolo" Dovishaw and even about the murdered Erie cop, Corporal Owen.

Finally, DiPaolo thought, *finally a break*. But first there was a run of bad luck, the kind that's inevitable when things seem to be going well.

That July of 1984, Montevecchio and Fredrico Maggio, aka, Freddy May, a convicted felon from Pittsburgh, along with "Fat Sam" Esper, planned a break-in. The burglary was to occur at a widow's home in one of Erie's more affluent suburbs, Millcreek Township, located just west and south of the city. According to the plan, the thieves would grab the widow's large cache of diamonds. Now, with "Fat Sam's" cooperation with police, all was in place July 28.

DiPaolo had arranged for surveillance on the home, and Esper was wearing a wire. For DiPaolo, the bust couldn't come soon enough. All he needed was just one chance to break Caesar Montevecchio. *Just one*! But events unfolded to the contrary. The trio of burglars found the woman home that evening and the break-in was called off.

After parting company with the others following the aborted burglary, Esper met with DiPaolo, who removed the wire. "Fat Sam" told of tentative new plans for another break-in on the following night. Back at police headquarters, DiPaolo played Esper's tape from hours earlier.

On it, he heard a conversation he thought he would never hear. "I wanted to ask you something for a long time," Esper could be heard saying to Montevecchio.

"Yeah? What?" It was clearly Caesar's distinctive, gravelly voice and knock-this-chip-off-my-shoulder style that had long-intimidated so many others.

"Why didn't you at least throw me a bone on Bolo?" Esper seemed to nonchalantly ask.

"Because I didn't get that much," Montevecchio shrugged. "Besides, it got all fucked up." DiPaolo let out a slow, long breath. *Finally.*

As they had pre-arranged the night before, Esper contacted DiPaolo the next afternoon with details for that evening's criminal activities. Caesar telephoned "Fat Sam" earlier. They were going to hit the house across the street from Louie Nardo's place – the scene of a home-invasion robbery a year earlier and situated in one of Erie's better-off neighborhoods near the border with Millcreek Township.

This time, however, DiPaolo knew he wouldn't leave any detail to chance. He'd be giving Caesar Montevecchio and his cronies a little boost, making sure the home burglary definitely would take place. DiPaolo led other Erie police investigators to the woman who owned the house, an executive secretary at a large local insurance company.

"We need you to leave home at 6 p.m.," DiPaolo explained. "And please make sure to leave the side door unlocked." The detective explained to the would-be victim that police officers would be stationed inside the house, waiting for the burglars. Leaving the cops a phone number where she could be reached later, she had little choice but to agree to the plan. With all the preliminary arrangements completed,

DiPaolo made sure two Erie Police officers were inside the home, while four surveillance cars were positioned away from the house, but still nearby.

Now, all DiPaolo needed were the burglars. They waited. Several hours after darkness fell, Montevecchio drove to Esper's digs and picked up "Fat Sam," who once again wore a wire for DiPaolo. Maggio had returned to Pittsburgh, so this time, it was just Caesar and Esper. Inside the car, Montevecchio and "Fat Sam" discussed the intended victim and how Montevecchio had learned about her considerable stash of wealth.

"I'll drop you off near the house," Caesar instructed while Esper listened patiently "You make entry. And make sure you look around good." Esper had been through the drill before. Many times. But still he listened in silence to Montevecchio's instructions. "Do the normal," Montevecchio continued. "Just fill pillow cases. Then come out and hide in the bushes. Put the hanky on the curb and I'll know you're waiting."

After he left the car, "Fat Sam" gently strolled to the house, but, losing confidence, he began to get cold feet. Approaching the house, Esper spoke low in hopes police officers inside would hear him. "Hey! It's me!" he said in a loud, stage whisper. "I'm coming in now. Don't shoot! It's me!" DiPaolo had earlier briefed Esper with very explicit instructions for entering the woman's house.

"Make sure you go in through the *side* door," DiPaolo instructed. "It will be unlocked." But even the simplest, most direct directions appeared to be lost on "Fat Sam." He headed straight for the *rear* door.

"The fucking door is locked!" Esper whispered into the wire. Now taking matters into his own hands, Esper put his shoulder and the 350 pounds behind it to the door. With one booming, shattering implosion, the door splintered off its frame and together, "Fat Sam" and the door crashed inside the house in a heap of wood and flabby flesh. (Later, the City of Erie would pay $600 for door repairs.)

Meanwhile, Dom DiPaolo, after observing Montevecchio wheel his car around the neighborhood in circles for several minutes, decided to make his move. As Caesar's car approached the nearby intersection, DiPaolo maneuvered his plain, unmarked cruiser in front of Montevecchio's. It appeared now that Montevecchio was attempting to back up. DiPaolo, not wanting Caesar to get away this time, fired a shot from his .38 caliber revolver into the air. It had the effect of cutting off the other car, forcing the shook-up Caesar to a screeching stop. In the blink of an eye and before Montevecchio could react, plainclothes cops and uniformed officers, weapons drawn and aimed, surrounded Caesar's vehicle. The group included Sgt. Jim Perfetto, aka "Doc," from the K-9 Unit, along with his dog, "Dino." DiPaolo had had "Doc" and "Dino" assigned to this surveillance in case someone decided to run. Then, Dino would have gotten his daily workout.

Within seconds, DiPaolo had pulled the stunned Montevecchio from his car, slamming him to the ground. The one thought running through DiPaolo's mind was the content of Montevecchio's tape-recorded call to his pal Joey Giacalone in Flint, Michigan. Montevecchio's calm, but chilling words were seared into DiPaolo's consciousness: *"Bring the shooter."*

Now the shoe was on the other foot, DiPaolo felt. Let him suffer just like DiPaolo had. Still, DiPaolo was cool. "Did you think you were going to get away with this shit forever?" the cop smiled at the man sprawled on the ground as uniformed men cuffed him. Caesar didn't answer.

CHAPTER 19

DiPaolo finally had Caesar Montevecchio. Or so it seemed. But, as the cop would learn, the road to nailing Montevecchio for the Frank "Bolo" Dovishaw hit would still be long and winding, often with unexpected twists and detours.

At Erie police headquarters, Montevecchio was left alone in a holding cell to stew and ponder his fate. It was time-tested successful police SOP. The pondering didn't take long, however. Less than an hour after Montevecchio was printed and processed, Caesar told Security Officer Andy Yacobozzi, "Hey! I want to talk with DiPaolo."

Joined by Detective Don Gunter in the small interrogation room with the standard two-way mirror to another viewing room, DiPaolo "Mirandized" Montevecchio. Caesar had been read his Miranda rights so many times in the past, he might have rattled off the warning by heart and with more precision than many cops.

"Listen up," Gunter growled. "We want to make sure you know what you're doing."

"I understand," Montevecchio replied. "I will talk."

Before the detectives could begin their questioning, Montevecchio looked straight at DiPaolo and said, "Look, I just want you to know I never wanted to hurt you." It was Serafini, not him, who had hatched the plan for the hit, he said.

"If you're going to lie to me again, I'm going to knock you off that fucking chair!" DiPaolo roared. "I know who hatched what. And I'm not in the mood for any of your bullshit. Just tell us about the burglary you're here for."

"Okay, okay! I did it. What do you want me to sign?"

It was the easiest and quickest confession DiPaolo ever extracted from a suspect. Yet, despite the ease, the cop wanted more.

"Nothing. Not yet," DiPaolo said. "Tell me how you ended up there."

"Listen," Montevecchio almost pleaded. "You let me out and I'll give you all the cocaine coming into town."

"I'm not here to talk about cocaine," DiPaolo could play hardball well. "I want you to start with this burglary. And then, I want you to tell me all about Bolo."

"'Bolo?' You let me out and I'll work on 'Bolo' for you, too."

Security Officer Yacobozzi, as well as assistant Erie County District Attorneys and other members of the Task Force, were in the next room, also anxiously wanting to learn more about the Dovishaw murder. But DiPaolo jerked open the door and barked orders to the Security Officer. "Get this piece of shit out of here. Take him back to the cell where he can rot as far as I give a damn!"

"C'mon, Dom! Give me a break!" No mistake about it now. The tough guy definitely was pleading. Even the toughest whine, DiPaolo thought.

"Fuck you! You got a break when I didn't shoot you tonight, you piece of shit."

Later that night, DiPaolo stashed Esper in a "safe house" with around-the-clock police protection. No sense in taking any chances with his star witness.

As "Fat Sam" gave up many crimes, DiPaolo recalled there had been an Erie County probation officer, a heavy gambler who was involved with "Fat Sam" and his pals. The P.O. became a 10 percenter, giving "Fat Sam" and the others information on houses and businesses ripe for break-ins. DiPaolo thought at the time that many of the P.O.'s visitors were not on probation. Another P.O., this one younger, was suspicious of the activity and reported the comings and goings of the hoodlums to DiPaolo while keeping tabs on the rogue officer and his boys without any of them having had a clue. The younger P.O., Tony

Logue, later became an attorney and then Chief Erie County Public Defender. He had provided DiPaolo with necessary intelligence and they remained friends ever since. DiPaolo and his wife, Janet, are godparents to Little Anthony, Logue's son.

It seemed "Fat Sam" could provide nothing about Bolo Dovishaw, and especially nothing about the bookie's execution a year-and-a-half earlier. DiPaolo became painfully aware the only link he currently held between Montevecchio and the Dovishaw killing was the recent single recorded wire conversation between "Fat Sam" and Caesar. It was a clear indication Montevecchio had some knowledge of "Bolo's" murder, it wasn't nearly enough to seek an indictment. Still, DiPaolo's gut told him Caesar Montevecchio was key to the Dovishaw slaying. And this cop's gut was rarely wrong. Despite the break-in confessions from Esper and Caesar, the Dovishaw murder investigation was again looking bleak.

Even the initial inventory search of Montevecchio's vehicle, impounded the night of his arrest, had annoyed the Erie police detective. In the trunk, DiPaolo found a new set of expensive, designer golf clubs. It aggravated the cop that Caesar was a one-handicap player, while DiPaolo was still a considerably higher 10. But then, fate struck a blow for the good guys.

CHAPTER 20

As DiPaolo begrudgingly fumbled with various compartments of Caesar Montevecchio's spanking new golf bag, he suddenly became aware there were more than tees and balls in one neatly zippered storage area. Inside that compartment was a small, innocuous, brown paper sack. In it was another bag, a plastic one; and inside the little plastic bag was pure, snow-white powder. Dominick DiPaolo, who had formerly worked the narc beat, held his breath. *Please don't let this be bleached flour,* he prayed silently as he field-tested the powder. *Please just let all this routine drudgery pay off.*

The cop exhaled, expelling his breath in one satisfying whoosh. The field-test confirmed the contents of the plastic bag: Cocaine. One full pound, thank you. *Yes!* A cop's prayers had been answered. DiPaolo allowed himself a brief smile. That and a single thought: *Goodbye, Caesar.*

At the time DiPaolo collared Montevecchio on the burglary job with "Fat Sam," Caesar was still serving an 18-month probationary sentence on a reduced charge of the unauthorized use of a motor vehicle. The charge stemmed from an arrest a year earlier in mid-1983 when Montevecchio was seen getting out of a car stolen from the Hammermill Paper Company's massive parking lot along Erie's lower eastside. There was no doubt the car was being used by Montevecchio and his cronies, perhaps "Fat Sam," DiPaolo thought, for burglaries and home-invasion robberies.

Caesar Montevecchio's lawyer, however, with help from a cooperative Erie County judge, had the stolen car felony count reduced to unauthorized use of a motor vehicle, a misdemeanor offense. The man once claiming he would make John Dillinger look like a choir boy drew only a probationary sentence. But now, with these new burglary charges – and especially the cocaine find – DiPaolo had enough on Caesar to force the judge to revoke Montevecchio's probation and resentence him to a full 22 months in jail on the unauthorized vehicular use alone!

It was indeed the cop's most fervent dream! DiPaolo would have Montevecchio under wraps for nearly two years! What's more, the detective, through prosecutors, insisted that bail-bond be set at $100,000 cash, further ensuring Caesar would be kept on ice for the duration. Even if the Dovishaw murder trail grew colder, Caesar was still behind bars. And there, DiPaolo would have ample opportunity to work on him.

Leonard Ambrose III, Esquire. Attorney Ambrose, a nattily, impeccably-dressed criminal lawyer with a taste for the finest suits, shirts and ties, shoes, had a reputation for taking on the biggest and most publicity-worthy cases, including some with suspected links to organized crime. DiPaolo had known Lenny Ambrose since their grade school days at Sacred Heart. In his early days as a lawyer, Ambrose had enjoyed a modicum of success that enhanced his reputation throughout the1970s and beyond. Tall, with slicked-back inky black hair and a wide, engaging smile, Ambrose could have been a network TV anchorman in another life. During his earlier years in the practice of law, Ambrose was an intense student of courtroom demeanor and behavior. It was during those early years, with many major cases in Erie County Court, observers could find young Attorney Ambrose sitting in one of the rear rows of the spectator section, intently taking in the work of various district attorneys and their assistants, as well as the county's best criminal defense lawyers. Ambrose also studied judicial rulings and seemed to have kept a book on the local judges. He knew how far he could go with each jurist before exhausting their patience.

Many attorneys knew that in Erie, Pennsylvania, practicing criminal law wasn't likely to get them rich. Yet Ambrose made an art of such a law practice and became a favorite of the local underworld, as well as garden variety criminals who made the big-time with their capital offenses. Ambrose also knew how to work the media well. Among the regular newspaper and television reporters covering the courthouse, he was a favorite, always highly-quotable for reporters in need, always prepared for an interview with print or broadcast journalists. Ambrose, by the 1980s, was perhaps Erie's best-known criminal defense lawyer.

Ambrose succeeded in practicing criminal law, easily surpassing many of his contemporaries. DiPaolo never forgot that early in Ambrose's career he used what the cop described as a legal technicality over a questionable, or defective search warrant to win acquittal for two young men who had been charged by Cleveland, Ohio, police in a major cocaine case. Ambrose also represented reputed wacko Marjorie Diehl, who killed her live-in boyfriend. The attorney, employing the relatively new defense of domestic violence, won her an acquittal. Having had run-ins with Diehl over the years on assorted narcotics investigations, DiPaolo believed that the domestic violence defense in the murder case appeared to have been a sham. "She'll kill again," DiPaolo thought at the time. She did.

Years later, Marjorie Diehl was charged with slicing apart the body of her latest boyfriend and sticking the pieces in the freezer. She was also charged in another capital crime, Erie's nationally-known "Pizza Bomber" case. She wouldn't skate this time, but her mental capacity is still being questioned.

DiPaolo recalls a memorable case that appeared to highlight Ambrose's sense of self-confidence. It was 1974 while Ambrose represented a major heroin dealer, James Thomas Sr., also known as "Fizz." Once the case got to court, Erie County District Attorney R. Gordon Kennedy, who only several months later would tragically die of an insidious, fast-growing stomach cancer, decided to personally prosecute Fizz Thomas. After Ambrose's barrage of pre-trial motions were disposed of by President Judge Edward Carney and Judges Lindley McClelland and Fred Anthony, a jury was finally selected February 13.

Testimony began and ended the next day. After the jury began deliberations, DiPaolo and his partner, Detective David Bagnoni, waited in the DA's office with Kennedy for the verdict. Minutes later, DiPaolo recalls as though it were yesterday, a beaming Leonard Ambrose entered the office, looked at DiPaolo, and said, "No hard feelings? I have to represent this guy like he was my father."

"Yeah, sure. Okay, Lenny. You do what you have to do," the cop shrugged.

Ambrose turned to Kennedy with a smile. "What do you think, Gordon? I kicked your ass pretty good, you have to admit!"

"Pardon me?" Kennedy shot back.

"Well, you tell me," Ambrose replied. "How do *you* think I did?"

Kennedy studied Ambrose coldly, then smiled and said, "Let me tell you something. If I were you I would make a citizen's arrest on the dean of my law school and have him charged with theft, and then see if you can get your father's money back as they didn't teach you anything there." After a moment of silence, a roar erupted from the DA's staff while Ambrose left.

The wait for the jury didn't take long. The panel took less than an hour to convict Fizz on all charges. As the jury filed out of the courtroom, Kennedy smiled at Ambrose, "They must not have caught the ass-kicking you gave me." Ambrose later appealed the guilty verdict all the way to the Pennsylvania Supreme Court. And after all the appeals were denied, his client was sentenced by Judge Anthony to serve 10-to-20 years in a state penitentiary.

Now, Ambrose's star client was Caesar Montevecchio. Montevecchio's brother, Albert, owned a successful electronics business in Rochester, New York, so money was available for Caesar's legal bills.

As a sub-plot to the Dovishaw case, the battle of wits was on. It was as much between Dom DiPaolo and Len Ambrose as it was between the cop and Montevecchio.

Along with Montevecchio, DiPaolo burned up the arrest books with the collaring of nine others as a result of the snitching "Fat Sam" Esper. Booked and charged with burglaries and home invasion robberies were many of Detective Sergeant Dominick DiPaolo's usual suspects. But it was Chuckie "The Hawk" Serafini who DiPaolo took particular satisfaction in collaring. DiPaolo, Gunter and Lewandowski waited late one night at West 16th and Cherry Streets outside the Circolo Nazionale Club, anglicized to "National Club," and with great fanfare dragged Serafini from his car.

Not that they intentionally roughed him up, but Serafini would later claim they "beat the crap out of me" as the suspect, the cops reported, lost bowel and bladder control during what appeared to be the use of force against a suspect officers said somewhat resisted arrest.

Serafini, like the others arrested on April 10, 1987, was brought in front of Erie County Judge William E. Pfadt for arraignment. Local Attorney Lee Fuller, who DiPaolo had on surveillance tapes attending Barbute and poker games with "the boys," represented Serafini. Prior to the setting of bail-bond, Fuller asked Judge Pfadt to take notice of his client's face – cuts, bruises, dried blood.

"Yes, I can see it," the judge, a former prosecutor said. "Now what?"

Fuller said, "My client did not look like that prior to his arrest."

"Okay, Mr. Fuller. $100,000 cash bond. Next case," Pfadt said. Later that month, Pfadt refused to lower Serafini's bond.

Susan DeSantis DeMichele Murosky was next before the judge. She had no attorney to represent her. But after she told Judge Pfadt that she worked for Lou Tullio at City Hall, he released her on her own recognizance. DiPaolo at once became suspicious. She was the daughter of a prominent Erie newspaper sports editor, the late Frank DeSantis, and DiPaolo believed phone calls had been made prior to her arraignment.

DeSantis DeMichele Murosky, DiPaolo thought, was streetwise at an early age, part of a large family growing up in Erie's "Little Italy." Some of her siblings were familiar with the inside of jail cells. Susan started off for a year in a correctional facility for girls, DiPaolo recalls. After working various jobs, including one in downtown Erie's Richford Hotel Velvet Room, she took her talents to Las Vegas where she became involved with the heavy hitters of the strip. Returning to Erie, Susan hooked up with mob hit man Ray Ferritto. She appeared to live the high life for a time, but was arrested after "Fat Sam" Esper stooled on her and one of her brothers. Susan was the only defendant of the six released on her own recognizance. Later, she claimed in her book she met with the judge after her arraignment in the privacy of his chambers and told him not to worry, that she took his name out of her black book. Judges, politicians, attorneys, physicians, all supposedly were inscribed in said black book, she claimed.

By the time her preliminary hearing rolled around, "Fat Sam" had forgotten his lines, claiming it wasn't Susan who gave up the house burglary – the home of a woman Susan was working for at the Richford – but maybe it was her sister; he was confused, he said. The charge against Susan was dismissed. After the hearing, DiPaolo was all over Esper, reminding him the deal was for him to testify truthfully – and that if he did not, there was no deal and "Fat Sam" would spend the rest of his life rotting in the slammer.

"Hey, she was just a little player and I felt bad seeing her in court," Esper said. "She always treated me really good when I called her – you know what I mean. And anyway, her brother, Billy, went down. I told the truth on him."

"I'll determine who the little players are!" DiPaolo roared. "Do this one more time and you're gone."

"I just wanted to help out Susan, the only reason I said it was her sister, Patty, was because I know she's going away on a cocaine charge."

DiPaolo yelled at his witness: "You lied on the stand! You keep doing that to help out your friends after you gave them up and you will do more time than anyone else." DiPaolo later said, "This was Fat Sam's one and only fuck-up." (Several months later, Esper was proven correct on his earlier assumption. Susan's sister, Patty DeSantis Young, was sentenced to serve two years in a federal penitentiary for dealing cocaine.)

After Ferritto died, much of Susan's meal ticket was gone. Freddy Tomassi, aka Fred Thomas, an 88-year-old well-known Erie figure, had operated restaurants, and owned many apartment complexes. Freddy's wife had died years earlier, and his mind was deteriorating. DeSantis began as his caregiver/nurse, then Fred married her. So as not to let his grown children know, the couple traveled to Meadville, just south of Erie in Crawford County, to obtain their marriage license. Only a year after such wedded bliss began, Fred passed away. Just before he died, according to his family, his second wife attempted to have him change his will, signing over significant assets of wealth – which were to go to his daughter and son, Dana Tomassi and Dr. Rick Tomassi, respectively – to her. But the family protested in court and it was determined Freddy simply was not of sound mind to do so. Then the Tomassi family approached the late District Attorney Brad Foulk, asking that she be charged. Foulk declined, prompting the always suspicious DiPaolo to question that decision.

Susan DeSantis-DeMichele-Murosky-Ferritto-Tomassi again sought a pay day. She authored her own book about mob hit man husband Ferritto. The section about the "Bolo" Dovishaw hit, DiPaolo knew, was pure fantasy. If it's a pay day she wanted, DiPaolo suggested, she'd have more luck with Pennsylvania Powerball.

Meanwhile, in the burglary case at hand, Serafini entered into a deal with the Attorney General, who allowed the defendant to plead no contest to a reduced charge of theft by deception prior to jury selection for his trial. Serafini caught only four years of probation, the plea and sentence particularly annoying DiPaolo.

However, it was Attorney Leonard Ambrose's efforts in his defense of Caesar Montevecchio that especially aggravated the Erie police detective sergeant. In the Commonwealth of Pennsylvania, the criminal code requires suspects be brought to a trial within 180 days of arrest, the so-called speedy trial rule. Whether or not it was because of his full calendar, Ambrose was known for delaying. In his representation of Caesar Montevecchio, Ambrose used his legal ability to delay whenever he could, DiPaolo believed.

The criminal lawyer sought evidence and alleged rules violation suppression hearings at the pre-trial level, first claiming illegal arrest, then entrapment, then illegal search, then failure to secure probable cause as well as other issues. As these tactics continued, the Erie County District Attorney's office was required to sign continuances under Commonwealth Rule 1100, the state law designed to preserve the 180-day limit. Ambrose was also required to sign-off on the continuances, so as to keep the case from being dismissed for not going to trial within the 180 days.

In January 1985, Ambrose petitioned the court to dismiss the charges against Montevecchio, allegedly because the District Attorney violated the 180-day rule. The 180 days, Ambrose argued, had expired without Montevecchio having been brought to trial. The district attorney objected. A hearing was scheduled. During the hearing, Ambrose successfully demonstrated that after the previous appeal of the evidence, the subject of the DA's objection, no Rule 1100 had been issued.

As a result, at 12:01 a.m. on January 23, 1985, two years after Frank "Bolo" Dovishaw's murder, Caesar Montevecchio was released from jail. Not only was Caesar free, but he was now also off probation as well. Assistant District Attorney Tim Lucas told DiPaolo he believed Judge Richard Nygaard was wrong in dismissing the charges and that he would appeal at once, believing the higher courts would reinstate them. In addition, Lucas said that when he told District Attorney Michael Veshecco he was appealing, Veshecco said he was wasting his time. The first appeal was to Nygaard, who denied it. Lucas said Veshecco responded, "What did I tell you." Lucas appealed to the Pennsylvania Superior Court.

DiPaolo, upset with Veshecco, thought back to when "Fat Sam" Esper first began snitching. One Saturday morning, DiPaolo, along with Assistant DA's Shad Connelly and Frank Scutella, arranged to have Esper meet with Veshecco. The plan was to get Esper to give Veshecco information about Montevecchio.

When DiPaolo brought Esper into Veshecco's office, Esper sat and said, "Good morning." To which Veshecco said, "Go ahead, Fatso . . . talk."

DiPaolo stared hard at Veshecco and said, "What the fuck are you doing?" Veshecco, according to DiPaolo's recollection, remained silent.

Esper shrugged, "Fuck him," and walked out. From that date in 1984, DiPaolo never again spoke to his former good friend Veshecco. Meanwhile, ADAs Connelly and Frank Scutella later told DiPaolo that Veshecco would not believe anything Esper would say. Turned out Veshecco was wrong about Esper.

Dom DiPaolo was frustrated. "Fat Sam" Esper was still under protective custody of the Erie Police, costing taxpayers thousands of dollars a month. Thousands more had been spent attempting to prosecute Caesar Montevecchio. A grand jury had been convened. Ten others who were arrested and charged with various crimes associated with Montevecchio had pleaded guilty and were sentenced to time in prison. And Caesar had gone home!

DiPaolo had sent all the "little" players to prison. But the big fish had swum away without homicide charges being filed. And now DiPaolo knew he was no closer to solving Frank "Bolo" Dovishaw's murder than he had been two years earlier.

ADA Tim Lucas, who had been working with DiPaolo on this case from Day One, told DiPaolo, "I know this fucks up your game plan. But believe me, Nygaard fucked up and Lenny got away with one for now, but I am appealing this to the Superior Court and I know it will come back. Look what the Superior Court did on the Gemelli case. Nygaard threw out all the gun charges, but on appeal all were reinstated." Former Erie Police Chief Sam Gemelli had been charged with 29 counts of theft, but Nygaard had dismissed them all. But, as Lucas said, they came back. "Nygaard gets a little nervous with these high profile cases," Lucas said. "Don't worry, these cases will be back, too."

But now what? DiPaolo thought. The answer again came from unexpected quarters.

This time, DiPaolo's savior was a young woman. It was Judith Guldenborth, an eager lawyer with impressive credentials who was recently named Assistant U.S. Attorney for the Western Pennsylvania District of Pennsylvania in Erie.

Just about the time Guldenborth received her appointment to the Erie office in the old U.S. Courthouse on Perry Square in the heart of downtown Erie, DiPaolo found himself pulling at straws to get to Montevecchio and resolution of the Dovishaw murder case. During his initial meeting with the new assistant U.S. Attorney, DiPaolo laid out the facts, then asked her to research the law and the cocaine case against Montevecchio. Would such a case fall under federal jurisdiction? And, if so, would she prosecute? DiPaolo's premise, as explained to the new federal prosecutor, was that ingredients for Caesar's pound of cocaine were transported across state lines. Could those facts alone place the case under federal jurisdiction? It's big-time coke, the cop figured. Why wouldn't the feds want it?

Guldenborth was intrigued. Yes, she would research the case. But she made no commitment to prosecute. But she had given DiPaolo hope when other avenues of hope were diminishing.

While the Feds were deciding whether to prosecute Caesar's cocaine case, DiPaolo's "Bolo" Dovishaw murder investigation again was interrupted. This time the delay came from a few of Caesar Montevecchio's best pals and wannabe wise guys. This delay, however, would have positive results on many fronts. Including the "Bolo" investigation. And especially Caesar Montevecchio. And it would come as no surprise to DiPaolo that the Scutellas were involved, heavily involved.

CHAPTER 21

FIRST THERE WERE SEVERAL MUFFLED EXPLOSIONS. NEXT, THE CORNER building in downtown Erie was ablaze. While the frenetic scene had nothing to do with the murder two years earlier of Frank "Bolo" Dovishaw, it had everything to do with leading police to those they considered to be the primary suspects in the slaying. But this would take time.

Pal Joey's Restaurant was fairly popular for tourists and native Erieites alike, especially those without, as the Feds are fond of saying, visible sources of income. The restaurant was situated at downtown Erie's southeast corner of 11th and State Streets when reputed wise guy and titular owner Joe Scutella is said to have arranged to have it torched.

It was a frigid February 1, 1985, not unlike the night Bolo was whacked, when the establishment, formerly known for years as the Erie Restaurant, went up in flames. DiPaolo was again called in to work the morning of February 2. Chief Skonieczka told him, "I hate to do this to you, but I want you to take this. The fire inspector is at the scene now. It looks like it was set."

Even before the chief's assignment, with Scutella having been such a longtime and literal partner in crime with Caesar Montevecchio, DiPaolo immediately suspected what some cops crudely called "Italian Lightning" as the cause of the spectacular general alarm fire. It also didn't take the cop too long to determine Scutella was the holder of a $600,000 insurance policy – issued in the name of Scutella's wife, Margie – on his eating and drinking establishment.

However, as Dominick DiPaolo dug deeper into the arson probe, familiar names popped up – the same names that filled the hundreds of reports in the Frank "Ash Wednesday" Dovishaw murder investigation of two years earlier. And now, DiPaolo was fairly certain, based on past experience with this Who's Who of Erie's underworld, if not directly involved in the arson and the Dovishaw hit, they would certainly have at least inside information about both high-profile crimes.

As he worked the suspected arson case, DiPaolo got a phone call from the Federal Drug Enforcement Agency operating in West Virginia. Agents there told DiPaolo that Joe Scutella Jr., unofficial owner of Pal Joey's, and another man, Bob Pietrzak, had been indicted on federal drug charges. Pietrzak was an ex-cop from Erie who had been DiPaolo's Little League baseball coach. *What a piece of shit he turned out to be,* DiPaolo thought after learning Pietrzak's wife, Eileen, also was indicted on the narcotics charges.

Scutella and the Pietrzaks, DiPaolo learned, were "mules" in a multi-million-dollar illegal drug operation between Peru and West Virginia. The Pietrzaks traveled to Peru, then returned with llama pillows filled with powdery cocaine. Donald Spadafore of the West Virginia mob was also indicted as the operation's kingpin, as were a local deputy sheriff, Charles Dodd, and two West Virginia lawyers, including James Esposito. Spadafore, envisioning a long spell in a federal penitentiary, was flipping on his contemporaries, Federal Alcohol, Tobacco and Firearms agents told DiPaolo.

The Erie cop couldn't believe his good fortune when ATF agents told him Spadafore ratted on Scutella, indicating Joe Scutella "blew up his Erie bar." It was all DiPaolo needed to hear. Within hours, he and partner Gunter were en route to Clarksburg, West Virginia, about 160 miles south of Erie. There, in the land of coal mines, steel mills and mountaineers, for the first time they met another new best informant – Donald Spadafore.

Spadafore, for a supposed mob kingpin, proved to be one of the most cooperative witnesses DiPaolo ever interviewed. Spadafore seemed almost pleased to give up anything and anyone to help his cause, meaning, save his sorry mob posterior, and he quickly gave up

Joseph Scutella, who, the West Virginia career criminal said, admitted torching his business.

"He said his joint got hit by Italian Lightning," Spadafore babbled on to the Erie detectives. "The asshole actually boasted that it was a 'family affair,'" he said. All was later testified to in open court.

Joe Scutella hired Attorney Tom Ceraso, and the dirty cop Pietrzak and his wife, Eileen, hired Attorney Leonard Ambrose, who traveled to Clarksburg to represent the Erie connection at the trial. DiPaolo said Ambrose's crisp shirts reminded him of an encounter with Ambrose several years earlier at a local dry cleaner and laundry establishment when Ambrose was picking up shirts. He told DiPaolo of his 90-day rule – having shirts laundered only three times before discarding them. "The starch ruins them," Ambrose explained to the cop. "Then don't have them starched," DiPaolo smiled back.

DiPaolo and Gunter sat in on portions of the Scutella/Pietrzaks Clarksburg trial, DiPaolo observing the far-from-Erie demographic make-up of this West Virginia jury. The movie *Deliverance* at times came to mind. Still, DiPaolo observed, jury members did not appear overly impressed with the defense attorney.

In legal circles, when cops win a major case against all defendants on all counts, they call it getting "Midas-sized." This trial represented classic Midas-sizing, all found guilty.

Joseph Scutella, represented by Attorney Ceraso, Ambrose's friend, and Robert and Eileen Pietrzak, represented by Ambrose – guilty. Anthony Donald Spadafore, John and Ralph Spadafore – guilty. Attorney James Esposito – guilty. Deputy Sheriff Charles Dodd – guilty. All for cocaine distribution under the R.I.C.O. Act.

Pietrzak and his wife got five years each, not terrible considering the severity of the drug charges and the maximum sentences available at the time. But Joey Scutella was recipient of the stiffest sentence of all – 25 years!

A month after the West Virginia experience put Scutella on ice for what would become the rest of his life, Detective Sergeant Dominick DiPaolo received the one phone call he had been awaiting. It was from Assistant U.S. Attorney Judith Guldenborth, later to become U.S. District Judge Judith Fitzgerald. DiPaolo held his breath as he listened to her announce that the feds were going to take their best shot at Caesar Montevecchio. He exhaled. *Finally.*

With the racketeering tentacles of burglary, robbery, drug trafficking, gambling and murder entwining all facets of the Dovishaw investigation, Pennsylvania Attorney General LeRoy Zimmerman had now turned over the complex probe to a federal grand jury. It was May 1985. Time now for "Fat Sam" Esper's grand jury performance.

Ever since "Fat Sam" blew in Caesar Montevecchio on multiple burglaries and robberies – and wore a wire which captured Montevecchio implicating himself at least to some degree in Dovishaw's murder – DiPaolo thought it best to keep his rising star in protective custody to keep him from meeting Bolo's fate.

Although "Fat Sam" had been stashed in a safe house, the night prior to Esper's May 25 appearance before the federal grand jury, DiPaolo had his star witness carefully and cautiously moved to the Hilton Hotel in downtown Erie, about four blocks from the federal courthouse along the town square on State Street. That's when DiPaolo realized Esper had serious physical appearance issues, especially with grooming and attire. Even on his best day, Esper was a slob.

He apparently bought his clothes at the discount house called Value City and if Value City officials had had their druthers, he probably would have been paid not to wear their outfits. Esper hadn't had his hair cut for months, ever since being stashed away. Aside from being grossly obese, the shagginess and shabbiness did not add to his appearance – and appearances in court *do* matter when it comes to credibility. DiPaolo wanted Esper looking, if not sharp, then at least presentable. The cop knew from prior experience that "presentable" often translated into "credible" in the eyes of many grand jurors.

But DiPaolo couldn't take Esper from the hotel to a barber or stylist. He could not risk it. The dangers involved far outweighed the benefits. Nor could DiPaolo risk bringing in an outside barber. The cop knew Montevecchio and his crowd had "ins" in virtually every quarter. Ill-appearing or not, it just wasn't worth the gamble. But that's when the detective sergeant suddenly thought of his wife, Janet, a state-licensed cosmetologist!

Janet had been cutting hair, women's and men's hair, for years. She was perhaps the only person at the moment that he knew he could trust with such a confidential situation. The more he thought about it, the more the idea appealed to him. But getting his wife to groom "Fat Sam" was going to be an extremely tough sell, DiPaolo knew. He was right.

At first, there was a definite "no" from Janet DiPaolo. But eventually, after much coaxing, pleading, and promising Esper would never know her relationship to DiPaolo or even her true identity, Janet DiPaolo softened and began to give in. It still wasn't a done deal, and DiPaolo knew he had more convincing to do.

With Janet definitely not pleased and still balking, DiPaolo assured his wife he himself would be there the entire time "Fat Sam's" hair was being cut. After much assurance and reassurance from her husband that she would be totally safe, Janet DiPaolo eventually consented, albeit reluctantly, to cut the fat man's hair. Before she could change her mind, DiPaolo quickly drove Janet to "Fat Sam's" hotel.

Tentatively entering Esper's room with no small amount of trepidation, Janet carried the standard shears, clippers and a barber's cape. Prior to her appearance there, DiPaolo had phoned the cops watching over "Fat Sam," warning them not to acknowledge Janet. DiPaolo, now putting on a serious face, introduced his wife to Esper as "Sally," as Officers Bill Leamy and Don Pollock sat nearby.

As hair stylist "Sally" busily clipped away at Sam Esper's shaggy mop, DiPaolo nervously flipped through the television channels. Esper broke the conversation gap.

"How long you been doing this?" he asked "Sally." She responded with an innocuous answer, just as her husband instructed – but she wasn't pleased with this entire scenario.

"Well, where do you work?" Esper pressed further. If Janet/Sally was unnerved by the experience, she certainly did not wear her anxiety on her sleeve. Whatever nervousness she felt, she didn't show it to Esper.

"Janet never missed a beat," DiPaolo would later recall. "She knew how to bullshit the bullshitter."

"Thank you very much," Esper said to Janet when she had finished the snipping. She managed a half-smile. Inspecting his new do in the mirror, he added, "Nice job, honey!"

Looking directly at DiPaolo, Esper said, "Don't forget to give this good-looking girl a big tip for doing such a nice job."

The next morning, DiPaolo picked up Esper at the hotel, where he was guarded by police 24/7, for their short trip to U.S. District Courthouse and the federal grand jury. DiPaolo was quiet. But not so Esper.

"Hey!" Esper started in right away. "Is that 'Sally' married? She looked pretty good." "Fat Sam" then made several references to "Sally's" anatomy. DiPaolo, now annoyed, silenced his witness.

"Never mind about her! Think about Caesar and the boys you're going to court to talk about," DiPaolo snapped.

When they arrived at the courthouse bordering Perry Square Park, they found security as tight as it had ever been before in Erie testimony of a police informant. Officers carrying automatic rifles were positioned in plain sight; marksmen perched high on the rooftop of Erie City Hall directly across State Street. They were all there to shield "Fat Sam" Esper. And he was loving it.

The investigation was back on track, at least from DiPaolo's perspective. Not only was Caesar Montevecchio indicted by the federal grand jury for possession of cocaine stemming from the golf bag search, but DiPaolo believed he had caught another break when Montevecchio's brother again hired Ambrose as defense counsel. Ambrose filed a barrage of motions claiming double jeopardy, illegal search, whatever was available in his arsenal of defense moves.

DiPaolo had recalled Sam Esper from the witness relocation program to testify against Montevecchio. Surprisingly, it was Esper and his new-found knowledge of the law that would prove to be Caesar Montevecchio's undoing. "Hey, how can Lenny represent Caesar?" Esper asked the cop. "He represented me one time and I told him I was doing coke with Caesar."

DiPaolo knew a good point when he heard one and passed it along to federal prosecutors, who filed a motion to have Ambrose removed from the case because of the alleged conflict. Serving a larger purpose, without Ambrose the proceedings would now be expedited. DiPaolo could not envision another attorney forcing the prosecution to jump through so many hoops and legal entanglements.

Following a hearing on the motion in November 1985, Ambrose was off the case. Esper had been correct about the legal conflict. The Erie lawyer, however, again arranged for his friend, Attorney Tom Ceraso of Greensburg, Pennsylvania, not far from Pittsburgh, to replace him and the trial was scheduled for December 5.

The trial had been moved to Pittsburgh on one of Ambrose's earlier motions for a change of venue, based on excessive media coverage in Erie. Following a suppression hearing on the coke, the defense motion was denied and the trial was to begin December 5. But on December 4, while DiPaolo was in his Pittsburgh hotel room prepping his trial testimony, U.S. Attorney Guldenborth telephoned.

"Good news, Dom! Caesar is going to plea tomorrow at 10 a.m.," she said.

DiPaolo was suspicious. After all, it was his nature. "What's the deal?" he asked.

"None!" the federal prosecutor said.

"I don't understand," DiPaolo pressed further, eyebrows still arched.

"That Judge Weber said to Ceraso and me before we left his chambers during pre-trial instructions, 'Work something out! Don't waste my time.' So, I guess Ceraso's strategy was not to piss off the judge and not waste his time. He probably figured he couldn't win it anyway and that maybe he'll get a break by copping."

Gerald Weber, appointed to the federal bench for life, was a no-nonsense jurist from Erie who often struck fear into the hearts of local lawyers practicing before him. Few attorneys before the federal bar wanted Weber hearing his or her case.

True to their word, the next morning, Caesar Montevecchio entered a plea of guilty in open federal court in downtown Pittsburgh. Leonard Ambrose, seated in the back of the courtroom, whispered to DiPaolo, "Best way to go. Maybe he'll get a kiss." (Read: Light sentence.)

Since the maximum sentence for such a plea was 15 years, the defense team was hoping – perhaps, praying – that by pleading guilty, Caesar Montevecchio would get a reduced sentence. Any reduction from the max would have been welcome. It was not to be.

"I have looked over your criminal history since your first conviction in 1967 some 18 years ago," Judge Weber told Montevecchio from the bench on January 21 prior to sentencing. "You have only been on the street for five years. During that time period, the rest of the time, 13 years, you have been incarcerated. And in that time period, you haven't been rehabilitated."

The judge, a bearded big man, paused for effect. None of the spectators spoke. Then Weber took up where he left off, discussing Montevecchio's refusal to be rehabilitated.

"In fact, I don't think you ever will. It's the order of this court that you spend 15 years in a federal penitentiary . . . starting now." Total silence from the back of the courtroom. But DiPaolo recalls Ambrose's shocked, ghost-liked expression.

Detective Sergeant Dominick DiPaolo knew a gift when he saw one. And he knew Montevecchio's lengthy prison term would at least buy time in the Bolo Dovishaw murder investigation. Later, the anticipated appeal was denied.

For the next year, as DiPaolo worked the Pal Joey's arson and other investigations, the cop picked up occasional bits of information about Bolo's murder, but not nearly enough to bring criminal charges. And surely not enough to make such charges stick. He often felt as though the case would never be solved.

Caesar and Scutella were both away at "college," hit man Raymond Ferritto had suffered a serious heart attack, followed by open-heart surgery, and Cy Ciotti had been on the lam for three years. Ciotti had been ordered to report to prison for a 15-year-sentence on a narcotics conviction, plus another two and a half to five years for robbing the Record Bar, a popular music store on State Street, but instead, Cy took off. Serafini, meanwhile, was still serving his four years of probation on a reduced charge from burglary, and "Fat Sam" Esper was basking somewhere in the sun, never knowing DiPaolo hadn't a shred of evidence with which to charge him on a traffic ticket on the day he flipped and turned government witness. All in all, not bad police work.

But the big one was still out there. And DiPaolo was having difficulty patting himself on the back while Dovishaw's killer or killers were still walking around free. But the cop's luck wasn't about to run out. Not yet.

September 7, 1986 would become a memorable day for DiPaolo. It was not only his wife's birthday, but the day an Ohio connection presented itself in the Bolo Dovishaw murder investigation.

DiPaolo was preparing to head home early. He had been at Erie Police Headquarters long enough, and he and Janet had plans to drive to Buffalo, New York, about 100 miles east of Erie, for a special birthday dinner with close friends, Sue and Dick Travers. Dick was also celebrating a birthday and all were looking forward to a grand celebration at Salvatore's Italian Gardens with friends John Euliano (Godfather to Dom's son, Pat), John's wife, Gerry, Dennis and Lucille Brooks, Egilio (Gido) and Rose Alo, and Ron and Joy Dalton.

When the phone rang, he paused a moment to grimace. The phone at DiPaolo's desk never failed to erupt in loud rings whenever he had family plans. On the other end was Tom Schneider, a federal ATF agent in Cleveland. When DiPaolo advised Schneider he was on his way out the door, the federal agent quickly got to the point. He was investigating one Robert Dorler in the bombing of a Cleveland warehouse. Dorler, Schneider said, was also the prime suspect in an attempted murder in which Aziz Michails of Cleveland was shot 11 times with a Mac-10 machine gun. In an attempt to win bargaining points with the prosecution, Dorler spilled information about an Erie guy in connection with at least several armed robberies. The Erie guy was named Caesar. Schneider told DiPaolo he couldn't pronounce the last name, it was long and Italian.

DiPaolo's heart rate upped significantly.

"So, this Caesar guy? You ever hear of him?" Schneider asked.

"Are you kidding me?" DiPaolo nearly shouted into the telephone. "I've been chasing him for years! This is unbelievable! Tell me everything!"

Robert Dorler of Medina, Ohio, near Cleveland, was now incarcerated at the Rochester, Minnesota, federal prison on arson and charges related to Lebanese terrorist groups, and was doing five years hard time, DiPaolo learned from the ATF agent. Something suddenly clicked in the Erie cop's gray matter. DiPaolo recalled "Fat Sam" telling him about Montevecchio's pal from Medina, Ohio, a hood named Bob he met at a 1982 Barbute game, a guy who dealt in hot diamonds and who owned Medina Vending. The birthday celebration was now on hold for several hours while DiPaolo collected and absorbed every word Agent Schneider was imparting.

Two days later, an excited Dominick DiPaolo and Assistant Erie County District Attorney Tim Lucas drove to Cleveland to meet with Cuyahoga County Prosecutor Carmen Marino. Coincidentally, it was

Marino who had prosecuted the Danny Greene execution-style car-bomb murder investigation involving Erie hit man Raymond Ferritto, the hit after which Ferritto easily gave up his Cleveland mob buddies in exchange for freedom.

"Do you know that asshole Ferritto?" Marino wanted to know right off. Funny, DiPaolo thought, almost laughing out loud, it was almost incestuous the way these hoods were all interconnected. *Maybe that's why they called it a crime "family,"* he thought, – *they'll all fucking each other.*

With the ATF's Schneider, two investigators from the Cleveland Police Department's Arson Unit and one from Organized Crime Investigations, DiPaolo and Lucas were brought up to speed on the Robert Dorler investigations. They listened intently as each of the others spoke, learning Dorler was indeed well-connected to Ohio's organized crime mob. And now Dorler was prepared to plead guilty within the week to arson, cocaine dealing and armed robberies, all occurring within the Cleveland area.

His plea arrangement with authorities called for Dorler to give up any other crime with which he was involved, or even had passing knowledge of. If authorities later determined Dorler had intentionally withheld information from them, the carefully negotiated sentencing deal would not stand. He'd be on his own to face significantly more hard time in addition to the wrath of his former mob buddies.

That's why the Ohio local and federal authorities were so keenly probing the Erie connection – just to make sure Dorler kept his part of the deal by relating all he knew about crime in Cleveland and anywhere else. Anywhere else, DiPaolo realized with a smile, would be Erie, Pennsylvania. DiPaolo instantly recognized this might be the opportunity awaiting, the one chance that would allow the detective to put the squeeze on Caesar Montevecchio and perhaps others, and for good.

Now it would be up to Robert Dorler to provide answers to key questions. DiPaolo, for the first time in years, allowed himself hope. And now, the Erie cop was not prepared to waste any time.

That very afternoon, DiPaolo accompanied the ATF and the Cleveland Police Department group to Cleveland's Justice Center. Lucas stayed behind with Prosecutor Marino. Although DiPaolo had been to the massive Ohio complex before, it would be his first actual meeting with Robert Dorler, one of the Cleveland mob's most celebrated go-to guys for virtually every style of criminal activity.

Dorler, wearing a bright orange prison jump suit, was soon brought before the group of Pennsylvania, Ohio and federal government crime fighters. Immediately, although it was their first meeting, DiPaolo recognized Dorler as one of those who had emerged from an Erie Barbute game the cop had staked out several years earlier. Dorler's cold, steely demeanor was unforgettable.

ATF Agent Schneider made the introductions.

"I want to read you your rights first. Then we talk," DiPaolo quickly got down to business.

"I'm not signing nothing or talking until I know the deal," Dorler responded. The suspected killer had long ago learned the keen art of plea bargaining and now he wanted his assurances provided upfront.

"I'm here in Cleveland with a district attorney from Erie," DiPaolo said. "He has given me the authority to make deals with you on anything – anything at all – except murder and cases involving children."

"Yeah? So where is this DA now?" Dorler snarled, warily looking around his sparse surroundings.

"He's with Mr. Marino," DiPaolo said. "He's in his office."

"Sir, not that I don't believe you – as I don't even know you. But I want to hear it from him." Dorler was adamant that he get the deal directly from a DA.

With a reluctant sigh, DiPaolo returned to Marino's office, retrieved Assistant District Attorney Lucas, and the two returned to the Justice Center to meet again with Dorler. There, Lucas verified to Dorler that Erie law enforcement authorities were interested in any involvement Dorler might have had in criminal activities in northwestern Pennsylvania – and, even more importantly, with whom Dorler had been associated with in Erie. The deal Lucas offered Dorler was actually a good one for the career criminal:

Dorler would be charged with each Pennsylvania crime to which he admitted pulling, but the eventual sentences would then run concurrently with whatever time he received in Ohio. Time now was of the essence, as Robert Dorler was scheduled to be sentenced for his local crimes by the Ohio court the following week. Assistant Erie County District Attorney Lucas spelled out the exceptions in no uncertain terms: The deal would in no way apply to any violations of the Commonwealth of Pennsylvania's child-molestation or murder statutes.

"If you're involved in any of those types of crimes," the Erie prosecutor underscored with emphasis, "then you best not talk with us."

Dorler thought a moment, then said he understood the offer. He insisted he was not involved with either homicides or with children. But he also said he did not want to testify against any of Erie's criminal figures. That appeared to be okay with Lucas, who told Dorler he and DiPaolo would gather information about the Erie crimes independent of what Dorler provided. Dorler's information would merely set the local investigators in the right direction. But Lucas also insisted, "If we need you to take the stand, you have to do it. But that would be a last resort."

Dorler was pensive another moment. "Does Carmen Marino know I'm cooperating?" he asked.

"Yes, he's very much aware of it," Lucas replied.

"No tricky shit?"

"None at all," Lucas smiled. Then, directing his attention to DiPaolo, he said, "Sarge, no tricky shit."

"Not from me," DiPaolo promised. "But that works both ways. I catch you in one lie or you send me on a wild goose chase, then no deal. Got it?"

Dorler nodded his understanding of the parameters of the plea bargain. But to further underscore his point, DiPaolo added, "If that happens, everything you admit, you get charged with and you're totally on your own. We know where you're coming from. Now you know where I'm coming from."

"Okay," Dorler shrugged. "Fair enough. Ask me what you want."

"First, your rights."

"I know what they are, for Christsakes. But I'm still not signing. I just don't like doing that."

"Fine, have it your way," DiPaolo said. "But I'm going to read them to you. Just tell me you understand, but refuse to sign. Then, Mr. Lucas here, and Agent Schneider of the ATF, will be witnesses."

"Fine," Dorler exhaled. "Let's just get on with it."

And that they did.

Robert Dorler's tale was both compelling and tantalizing for Erie Detective Sergeant Dominick DiPaolo. At that moment, however, he could not have even begun to guess how very close Dorler had been to the Frank "Bolo" Dovishaw murder. As Dorler spoke, DiPaolo listened intently.

It was April 1982 when Dorler was approached by Cleveland's Billy Bourjaily, a man Dorler described as being of Lebanese descent "but running with the Italians." Bourjaily had a pal in Erie, Pennsylvania, a guy named Caesar who Bourjaily met through Cleveland set-up man, bookie and fence Louie Raffa, also affectionately known as "Lumpy Lou," Dorler said. This Caesar guy, Dorler said, had telephoned Bourjaily for help with "some scores in Erie" that had turned out to be the Scalise, Miller and Nardo robberies and home invasions. Bourjaily, if he was interested in helping out, Caesar had promised, was to get "someone solid" to participate in the Erie, Pennsylvania endeavors.

"Yeah, why the hell not," Dorler told the recruiter Bourjaily, who made arrangements for Dorler to meet Caesar Montevecchio at the Holiday Inn situated in the East Cleveland suburbs, just off Interstate 271 and across from the popular Thistledown racetrack. During that first meeting between Dorler and Montevecchio, Bourjaily was also present, Dorler said. It was there at the Holiday Inn that Caesar told Dorler of "targets" in Erie who were gamblers and Barbute players. Montevecchio was certain the targets would not go to the law if they got robbed.

"We talked about the robberies for at least three hours," Dorler said. At one point, he said, Montevecchio told them he was "having a beef" with an Erie cop who had been tailing him day and night and might need "outside" help in eliminating this big nuisance. Montevecchio promised Dorler and Bourjaily he would do all the research, and the Ohio men could pull off the actual stick-ups and possibly help him out with this troublesome Erie cop problem.

"Fuck you. I'm not doing any cop!" Dorler claimed he told Montevecchio.

Again, as Dom DiPaolo listened to Robert Dorler's first-hand account, his blood began to boil at Montevecchio's earlier deception and all the worry and concern Caesar had put DiPaolo through over his family's safety. This would not be the end of it, the Erie detective silently vowed to himself. Montevecchio would one day get all that was coming to him. DiPaolo would make sure of it.

As for Dorler, he had no idea DiPaolo was the cop to be hit. Or did he? But now, DiPaolo needed to focus carefully on what Dorler was telling him about the unsolved Erie crimes, the Nardo, Scalise and Miller jobs. Montevecchio could wait until later. But his turn would come.

As they listened, Dorler outlined each robbery, how each went down and who were involved in the capers. The Medina, Ohio, hood named all of his accomplices, and in so doing he gave DiPaolo information only a participant could have known.

Robert Dorler's statement to law enforcement contained in DiPaolo's official report and dealing with both Montevecchio and William Bourjaily, dated October 30, 1986, are as follows:

- Dorler stated that they talked about armed robberies and some burglaries. He said Caesar had cased out the locations and when the time was right he would call. Dorler said it was two days later when Billy came to him with news that Caesar had called and was ready. He said they drove to Erie in Bourjaily's 1980 Oldsmobile, and went to the Green Side Trucking Place, off of Interstate 90 where they met Caesar. When I asked if he was referring to the Green Shingle, he said, "Yeah that was the name of it."
- Dorler said they talked for a while in Caesar's car, and then they were told that the hit for the armed robbery was a guy who owned a beer distributor and that he also made book. He said Caesar directed them to follow him in their car so that he could show them where to stash it, and said he would then take them to the house to be hit and drop them off there. Dorler said they parked Billy's car in a plaza, and then got into Caesar's car. The house was nearby. Dorler said Caesar took them past the house first, so he could point it out, and then dropped them about a block away. He said they were supposed to meet Caesar back at the Green Shingle when they were done. The plan called for them to take the victim's car (to get away) and then dump it in the plaza and take Billy's car to meet Caesar.

- Dorler said that he went to the front door and knocked. When a young man of about 20 answered at the door, he said he asked if Jack was in and the kid said "no." Dorler said he then pulled out an automatic and pushed the kid back into the doorway, putting the gun in his ribs and saying this was a hold-up. He said that Bourjaily, who had been walking along the street, then approached the front door and they both entered. Dorler said they asked the kid whether anyone else was in the house and the kid responded that his mother was upstairs. Dorler said that Billy held the gun on the kid while he went upstairs and got the woman. He said that once downstairs again, he directed the woman and her son to sit in the kitchen area and they wouldn't be hurt. He said Billy held the gun on them while Dorler tossed the house.
- While Dorler was upstairs searching, he said that Billy yelled up that the "old man was coming home." He said that he came downstairs and that as the "old man" was coming in, he hid behind the door and grabbed him as soon as he entered. He said he told the guy he wouldn't get hurt, but he wanted the money. But the man told him they did not have any money, and that any he did have was in a safe at the office – and it wasn't much.
- Dorler continued, saying that he had the old man sit with the others in the kitchen. While Billy watched them, Dorler finished tossing the joint. He said he found some jewelry and that was it. When he came back downstairs, he said he had the old man and the kid empty their pockets. They got some cash from the old man, and that the kid had tickets to a concert, but they did not take them.
- Next, he said, they cut the phone wires and tied them up and left in the old man's Caddy, driving to the plaza and dumping the Caddy, then driving with Billy to meet Caesar. When they met, Caesar took the jewelry and they split the money three ways. Caesar was going to get back to them after he fenced the jewelry. After that, Dorler said he and Bourjaily drove back to Cleveland. Dorler said that several days later he spoke with Billy, telling him that he had talked with Caesar and that Caesar relayed to him that the woman had on a diamond ring worth over

$20,000 and they had missed it. He also told Billy that Caesar told him that the newspaper had a composite picture of Billy and that it "fit him to a tee."

- Dorler said Billy "got real nervous" about the composite and that he immediately went to Jimmy Marino's Barbershop in Cleveland and had Jimmy cut his hair and give his eyebrows peak to try and change his appearance. Dorler said Billy was very concerned about these people getting that good of a look at him. He said Billy was also pissed at "fuckin' Caesar" as he told them that these people would not go to the cops, and they did. Dorler said several days later, Billy called him again and told him that the jewelry was junk and that he did not get anything for it. Dorler said he knew that Caesar was ripping them since one piece had been solid gold.
- I then asked Dorler what they did get. He said a solid gold man's bracelet, a woman's necklace, man's wrist watch and money. I asked about the man's diamond ring. Dorler said, "I never saw it, unless Billy scooped it on me."
- Dorler then stated that it was maybe a week later that Billy came to him, saying that Caesar called and that he had another score for them. He said that again they traveled in Billy's car and met Caesar at the Green Shingle and that they were told that a guy named Si, who ran a Barbute game, was the target. He said that Caesar told them that he would take them to this guy's house and that Si would be at the Barbute game. They were to go into the house by breaking in and then they were to wait for the guy to come home and stick him up. Dorler was wearing the toupee and glasses, while Billy was again bare-faced, but now with the eyebrows peaked. Caesar had given them what Dorler thought were the same two automatic weapons.
- Dorler said there was a ditch off to the side of the road and a stake near the ditch. Caesar told them that when they came out, they were to put a hankie on the stake, lay in the ditch, and that Caesar would then pick them up.
- Dorler said he and Billy went to the back of the apartment and forced open the door and went inside. He said they tossed the house and got five wrist watches, including two Rolexes. He

said they stayed in the apartment for hours, waiting for "Si" to return. When it was daylight, they decided to leave. Dorler said they went through the woods to the stake and tied the hankie on the stake, then lay in the ditch waiting for Caesar.

- Dorler said it was about 10 minutes later that Caesar came by and picked them up. Both Dorler and Bourjaily were "hot" with Caesar since they had waited all night for "Si" and that they had to lie in a ditch when it was cold and raining. Dorler said he thought to himself, "Fuck Caesar with these scores. I'm not risking getting caught or shot for pocket money and watches." He said Caesar drove them back to the Green Shingle and then he and Bourjaily drove straight back to Cleveland. But before leaving, he said they were "mother fucking Caesar all the way back to the Green Shingle."
- I asked him who took the watches, and he said that he did as he was so hot that Caesar was afraid to ask for them. He said he did not get much for them, but couldn't remember the exact amount. He gave Billy his share and also gave Billy Caesar's share. I asked Dorler whether he ever learned the last name of "Si." He said, "Something like Citoli and Cillia." I said, how about Satelli. He acknowledged that was the name as he did something with the guy later on in the year.

(Silvio Dante Satelli, born in 1934 in Italy, later served 10 years in the federal prison at Allenwood for distribution of cocaine. He was paroled in 1998.)

- Dorler said it was then a few weeks later when Billy came to him and said that Caesar had called him again and that he had another job set-up in Erie. Dorler said he told Billy, "Fuck you and your buddy, Caesar. There is no way that I'm going to go back to Erie and get skunked again."
- But he said Billy Bourjaily told him this one was a "sure thing" and that Caesar had hit this guy before and "got a ton of gold out of it." This target was a retired "jeweler or coin dealer or something like that." Dorler said he told Bourjaily, "No, I'm not interested."

- The next day, Dorler said, Billy told him that Caesar was in town and that he wanted to meet and talk with them about the score in Erie. Dorler said that he told Billy that he did not care how good Caesar was going to make it sound, he wasn't going. "Billy then said that they were supposed to meet later that night and if I didn't want to go, try to find somebody and we could bring him to introduce to Caesar." Dorler stated that he asked Billy, "How about George Meeks?" Dorler said that he had served time with Meeks in Marion, Ohio, and that he was "a good armed robber." Billy knew Meeks, too, and said, "Yeah, he would be a good guy – get ahold of him."
- Dorler said he told Caesar that George Meeks was willing to go along on the job and that he would also go. He said the four of them sat around and talked about "this guy in Erie who was retired and had a ton of money." Dorler said Caesar was staying that night with his brother and that they made plans to go to Erie the next day. Dorler continued, saying that it was two days later when Meeks came to him in Cleveland with a suitcase full of pocket watches that he said they got "from this guy in Erie." Dorler said that Meeks told him after the score that Caesar wanted the watches. But Meeks told him, "Dorler sent me here for him, so he gets the watches and what they're worth we all split."
- Then Dorler said that Meeks told him that he and Billy Bourjaily were dropped off by Caesar at the intended victim's house and that they waited in a garage for him to come home. When he did get there, his girlfriend was with him. They took the couple in to the house and placed both of them into the bathroom and then made them get into the bathtub. He said they then tossed the house and got money and the watches and some chains, and then took the guy's car back to where Billy had parked his and later met with Caesar. Dorler further stated that Caesar had given them the weapons they used. They also wore nylon stockings over their heads as Billy was getting a little scared. He was still a little paranoid about the police composite photo from the first job.
- According to Dorler, he gave Meeks a number of the watches, which he sold for about $25 to $50 each, and that whatever

Meeks got for whatever was sold was divided up, with Billy getting his share plus Caesar's. Several days later, Dorler said he spoke with Caesar, who was pissed off, as Billy and Meeks had totally missed the safe the Erie guy had in his house. Dorler said that a few days later, Billy came to him again and said that Caesar had another one set up for them. He said that Meeks and Billy went to Erie and that a few days after that he saw Meeks and Billy and they talked about "this guy who owned a grocery store that they had grabbed and something about getting him while he was going to his van." Dorler said that was all he knew about this job, even whether or not they got anything or what else might have transpired.

- Dorler then said that it was probably about that same time that Caesar was in Cleveland again that they talked about Caesar having an "in" with some cocaine. Dorler said that he told Caesar that he would not mind getting into that with him and would have many outlets. He said it was then that he started to deal in drugs with Caesar. Dorler said that he would either drive to Erie or that Caesar would go there to Cleveland. He said the majority of the time he would meet Caesar at the Green Shingle, but he also started meeting with him at the Holiday Inn along Interstate 90 just outside of Erie.
- I asked him what arrangement he had with Caesar on the coke, and he said that was given to him on the "arm" (on credit or good faith). After he sold the cocaine, he would give Caesar $1,900 for it. He responded that he dealt with Caesar on at least 12 different occasions.
- Dorler then went on to say Caesar was "stepping on it" and "what a profit he was making" and that he was seeing a $2,100 to $2,600 profit on each pound. When I asked Dorler whether he knew where Caesar was getting the coke, he said, "Yeah, it was from a fence in Pittsburgh, a big fat guy" that Dorler himself had once met while he happened to be in Erie. Dorler then said that he couldn't remember exactly when, but Caesar's coke connection eventually dried up. Soon after, Billy Bourjaily and Ronnie Faraha found a coke connection in Miami, Florida.

(Ronnie Faraha was a "made" man in Cleveland with the Licavoli Family.)

- He said Billy then became the "mule" for the operation and he started to sell Caesar their portion of the cocaine take. He said that Billy would go to Miami at least twice a month and that he was bringing back cocaine to Cleveland. Then Billy and Ronnie would split it up and some would go to Youngstown and Warren, Ohio, and one pound would go to Caesar in Erie. He said that he never picked up money from Caesar. That would always go through Billy. All Dorler was doing was the delivery.
- I then asked Dorler if he knew of any other armed robberies or about any other criminal activity that he was involved in, or knew of Meeks, Bourjaily, or anyone else involved with Caesar in Erie. He said it was during the cold winter months that Billy told him that Caesar had something going in Erie for them. At that time, Dorler said that Billy never asked him to go anymore as he knew that he (Dorler) wasn't interested, and also knew that he (Billy) was "doing coke pretty good." Dorler said it was shortly after that when he saw Meeks and he was told that he and Billy went to Erie. He said that Caesar set them up in the Holiday Inn along Interstate 90 and they stayed there for a couple of days before doing a job.
- Caesar gave them gloves, stockings and weapons. But when they were in the house, something went wrong and Caesar wasn't outside to pick them up, so they stole a car. Dorler said that was all he remembered about that particular job. I tried to get a little bit more out of him about that incident, but he claimed that that was all he could remember Meeks telling him about it.
- He then went on to say there was another time shortly after that when the same three went to Erie, stealing a car and bringing it back to Cleveland.
- He said that Meeks took the car down to his uncle in West Virginia, and that they did the serial number alteration and then sold it. Dorler did not know what kind of car was stolen as he never saw it. Dorler then began to talk about the cocaine again, stating that when he was coming to Erie he was bringing Caesar

four to five ounces every two weeks and that he was making out pretty well. I asked him when the last time was that he brought Caesar cocaine. He stated that he could not remember the exact date, but it was probably sometime around 1983. He said he was having heart problems at the time, and that he had learned later through Billy that Caesar had been arrested in Erie.

- I asked him how Billy had learned of the arrest. He said that Caesar's wife had called Elaine, Billy's wife, and told her. He said that Billy and his wife are "real close" to Caesar and his wife and that they go out socially "all of the time" both in Cleveland and also in Erie.
- I then asked him whether he had talked with or had seen Caesar since that time when Caesar had been arrested and he said that it was in March of 1986 that he received a call from Caesar and that Caesar wanted to meet him at the Holiday Inn along Interstate 71 in Cleveland. He said that he did meet at the Holiday Inn with Caesar, who wanted to know what Dorler was in to. Dorler said he told him he wasn't really into anything. He said Caesar was trying to figure out a way to "wash" dollar bills, but Dorler did not tell him he could help. He said that Caesar told him that he was flat broke and was looking to get a little action. Dorler said that he told him that he couldn't help him and that was the end of their contact, and that he hadn't seen or talked with him since.
- It was then when I asked Dorler what he knew about a certain homicide in Erie. He said, "You mean 'Ash Wednesday'?" Dorler then said that he had done a little work for Billy Hamilton of the FBI in Youngstown, Ohio, and that after "Ash Wednesday" was hit, Hamilton called him. He said that Hamilton told him that he knew through the Erie FBI Office that Dorler knew Caesar, and that Caesar was a suspect in the case. Hamilton wanted Dorler to see what he could find out about the murder, Dorler said. Dorler said he thought of a story he could run by Caesar to try and find out. He then called Caesar and arranged to travel to Erie, where he met Caesar at the Green Shingle.
- After talking with Caesar awhile, he asked him what he knew about "Ash Wednesday." He said that Caesar asked back, "Why?

Who wants to know?" Dorler said he told Caesar, "The 'Family' in Cleveland." He said Caesar then asked again, "Who?" Dorler said he told him "Mute." He said he knew at the time that Mute was in the joint, so he used his name, knowing that Caesar did not know him. At this time, Dorler said he could not think of Mute's real name, but that he was sure he was one of the Lonardo ("Big Ange") soldiers.

- He said that Caesar told him that Ray Ferritto is the one who found and killed him and that he sat on him for a day. He said that Ferritto did not know how to call the cops, but that he was working with this one city detective, so he called him and when the cop came over he saw the body.
- Dorler said Caesar told him that Ferritto cleaned up the place and took all the numbers papers out and then it wasn't until the next day after everybody got their stories straight that they called the law. He said that Caesar told him that Ray Ferritto had wanted to take over all the numbers and sports bets in Erie and that is just what he did. Dorler said that was all Caesar said about it and that they talked a little more about cocaine dealings and that he went back to Cleveland. He said they then got in touch with Hamilton and told him what Caesar had told him, and that that's all he knows about "Ash Wednesday."
- I asked him whether Caesar ever said anything to him after that, and he said, "No, not a word."
- Again, I asked him if there was anything else that he recalled about (criminal activity) in Erie. He said, "Yeah. Once again the others tried to get Satelli and that Meeks and Billy waited for Si outside the Barbute game one night, but nothing happened because someone spotted them. So they never did it and that was another of Caesar's failed scores."
- I then asked Dorler about a hit that Caesar put on Michails in Cleveland. He said that Caesar did not have anything to do with that.
- But I told him I remembered that on July 29, 1983, at about 3 a.m. that I saw Dorler at Sam Esper's house with Caesar and Sam, and that this was when Caesar solicited Dorler to do the hit on Michails the next day in Cleveland. He remained quiet for a few seconds and then he asked again, "Who?"

- I then described Sam and his home, and Dorler said, "Yeah, I do remember that. He was fucking huge!" He then described Sam's house and also said he remembered a friend of Caesar's getting into the back seat of Caesar's car and that they talked about it. I told Dorler I could not remember verbatim the conversation. But I said I did have the conversation recorded on the wire about Sam going to Cleveland and Dorler going to supply him with an Uzi to take this guy off.
- He said, "You're right. It was an Uzi, but I really can't remember that. But if you say it happened, then it did." He claimed that this was all he remembered of this particular incident.
- Dorler continued to say that when he did have the hit put on Michails, he got a "black male" from the east side of Cleveland, a man named Peewee who lives near Euclid and Ivarone Streets in an apartment there.
- Dorler said that Peewee owed him about $5,000 for coke, so he called it even with the hit, which he said "Peewee fucked up." According to Dorler, the weapon was an Uzi and that it had a silencer attached to it. I asked him where he got this gun, and he said it was from the Marcoline brothers in Cleveland. He said they had "a basement full of them (Uzis)." I then asked Dorler again if he could remember anything else that he did with Caesar in Erie.
- He said he remembered that at one time, while he was doing the coke with Caesar, that Caesar asked him if he wanted to do a couple of hits in Erie. Caesar told Dorler he felt he could move into something big and he would be living on "Easy Street." Dorler stated that that he told Caesar that he wasn't interested since he was doing well in the coke business.
- I then asked Dorler whether he had suggested anyone for the jobs to Caesar. He said, "No, I just didn't want to be bothered with them." When I asked him whether Caesar had ever mentioned who the hits were on, Dorler answered, "No. Other than the cop. But I told him 'No way!'"
- He then said that Caesar had a tray of phony emeralds that he brought into Erie from Gene Hazen on the West Coast. He said

that Caesar talked to Si Satelli about them and that Si bought them for $80,000 in cash, but that they were only worth about $500, if that. I asked how much Caesar got for the deal and Dorler said he couldn't remember the exact amount, but that it was probably about $10,000. Dorler said that when he reported back to the Fed Billy Hamilton, about "Ash Wednesday," he also told Hamilton about the emeralds.

- "I *do* remember something else," Dorler then said. It was when he met Caesar in March 1986 and they were talking about getting lucky when Caesar told him about a connection that he had in Cleveland for coke. Caesar told Dorler that after talking with his Cleveland connection he told him if he could get something going, he would call him. But he never did.
- I asked him whether he remembered who this guy was. He said that Caesar told him his first name, but never gave Dorler the connection's last name. It was at this time in the interview that I had asked as much as I could possibly think of asking Dorler, and it was then that the interview ended. Prior to us leaving Dorler, he asked ADA Lucas, "What's next for me?"
- Lucas told Dorler that we would take his information back to Erie and check it out, and, if we proceeded with charges, he would be charged and he would have to testify if necessary. Then, he would plead and the sentence would run concurrent with his time in Ohio. It was the same deal that Lucas had explained to him before. Lucas also said that if we caught Dorler lying or could prove he was involved in a homicide, there would be no deal.
- Dorler then said, "Well, I told you everything I know and I told you before I wasn't involved in any homicide." At that point, we left, telling him that I would probably be getting back with him.

DiPaolo would have a lot of checking to do.

CHAPTER 22

NOW BACK IN ERIE, DOMINICK DIPAOLO PULLED ALL THE ORIGINAL crime reports from the Erie Police Department's Central Records room and began comparing notes on the jobs Dorler had detailed. Dorler's confession, DiPaolo soon confirmed, became a lesson in professional criminal activity not ever taught in any university criminal justice program. *Amazing*, the cop thought of Dorler. *He had definitely been around the block and back.* The police records confirmed all that Dorler had spoken of – and more. And they would provide a surprise even DiPaolo could not have imagined at the time.

The first robbery had occurred on April 19, 1982, a short time after Dorler's initial, get-acquainted meeting with Caesar Montevecchio at the Holiday Inn. Jack Miller, an Erie bookie and owner of a local beer distributorship, had been robbed at his home. Miller, his wife, Jean, and son, Grant, were bound by two robbers who had used guns to gain entrance, then telephone cords to tie them. Dorler had been right in every detail of his account of the Miller robbery, including Grant's comment about the tickets. There were more as well: Less than a month later on May 7, 1982, apparently the same two men robbed Louie Nardo in his home. Nardo and his girlfriend, Evelyn Frye, were bound and placed in a bathtub. Nardo actually saw one of the robbers, and heard other voices as well. Gold watches, cash and jewelry were stolen from his house. Added together, the robbery take was reportedly worth more than $100,000.

But it was the third robbery that would prove to be the eye-opener for the Erie detective. Five days after the Nardo job on May 12, police records again confirmed Dorler's account of what had transpired. Frank Scalise, a grocer and reputed gambler, was driving his van home when he was held-up by two armed men. Somehow, Scalise managed to drop his four moneybags to the ground and subtly kick two of them underneath the van when exiting the vehicle. The two armed robbers viciously pistol-whipped Scalise into submission, then fled with two cash-filled bags, leaving the bloody Scalise at the scene, and, of course, the two additional moneybags still out-of-sight under the van. In the Scalise robbery report, however, something remarkable caught DiPaolo's trained eye that obviously had been earlier overlooked, or, at least the significance of the discovery had not been appreciated.

DiPaolo was incredulous as he read in the initial offense report that the uniformed officers at the crime scene found one live round of ammunition beneath Scalise's van, along with the two hidden moneybags undetected by the robbers. It was a bullet. More precisely, it was a .32 caliber automatic Norma brand bullet.

A chill ran up DiPaolo's spine. He immediately understood that it was only the second time in his long police career that he had heard or read the name "Norma" as it applied to ammunition. The first time, he recalled with almost youthful, joyous excitement, was at Bolo Dovishaw's home in early January of 1983. That bullet was found in very close proximity to Dovishaw's cold, dead body. For a moment, DiPaolo sucked in deep gulps of air. Then he held his breath.

What was in reality a very short period of time seemed to take forever. DiPaolo immediately directed the ID Section to send the live Norma round found under Scalise's van, along with the shell casing DiPaolo discovered at Dovishaw's house, to the Pennsylvania State Police Ballistics Laboratory for scientific comparison testing. The evidence was designated as "priority" and "rush." And then he waited impatiently for the return of the ballistic comparison results.

When the report returned and DiPaolo ripped open the manila envelope, his eyes rested on the only word that mattered: "Match." Both the Norma live round found under the van and the shell casing from Dovishaw's house had the same ejection markings. The live round had been inside the .32 pistol used to beat Scalise, the impact causing the round to accidentally pop out, leaving ejection marks on it. The same identifying marks were found on the shell in Dovishaw's home. Thus, both bullet and casing had come from the same weapon. It was an extraordinary discovery, one that could not be mere coincidence, the cop knew. DiPaolo now had solid physical evidence linking not just Dorler and Bourjaily to Frank "Bolo" Dovishaw's killer, but also Erieite Caesar Montevecchio, thanks to Robert Dorler giving up a few local robberies.

DiPaolo already knew Bolo's hit involved an A.C.P. Norma brand .32 caliber bullet from an automatic pistol. He now also knew beyond any doubt that Miller, Nardo and Scalise were all robbed by out-of-towners, working with Caesar Montevecchio, who apparently used the same weapon months earlier. For murder.

Caesar, DiPaolo thought. *It was Caesar's M.O. from day one.*

And the enormous break in the Dovishaw murder had been handed to DiPaolo by criminal figure Robert Dorler without Dorler even knowing it. Or did he?

Once again, however, the existence of a real-life municipal police detective manifested itself in the reality of an unrelenting caseload. Crime, like life, went on. Crime didn't stop while detectives cleared their caseloads. Wouldn't it be terrific, DiPaolo often fantasized, if detectives could be assigned just one case at a time and work exclusively until it was solved?

As usual, luxuries of working one case at a time didn't happen in DiPaolo's world. DiPaolo's plate was not just overflowing; it was buried. For those reasons, shortly after his amazing interview in Cleveland with Robert Dorler, just as the cop began the tedious process of verifying this new ballistics information in the Bolo Dovishaw murder case, an informant's telephone tip led him in another direction. Even that direction was not too far afield from the ongoing Dovishaw probe.

"You still want to some make arrests in the Pal Joey's arson fire?" the informant had asked. Pal Joey's. Arson. Joe Scutella. Oh, yeah. DiPaolo found himself compelled to temporarily shift gears, at least slightly, from the murder probe to the arson investigation, which had stalled. Yet the detective knew anything involving the Scutellas would not be a waste of time. "All the usual suspects," as *Casablanca's* Captain Louis Renault was fond of saying, as well as the many cases they were involved in, they seemed overarching like concentric circles.

DiPaolo mentally reviewed the facts of the unsolved arson case. On February 1, 1985, Pal Joey's Restaurant at 11th and State Streets in downtown Erie was destroyed in a spectacular conflagration. Determined by fire marshals to have been the work of an arsonist, DiPaolo was assigned the case even as he labored over Dovishaw's murder. DiPaolo ascertained the failing restaurant business, run by some members of the Scutella family and suspected wise guys and wise guy wannabes, was hemorrhaging money and therefore dying. Always suspect and suspicious, especially when it came to some of the Scutellas, DiPaolo had arranged for the insuring company to have the huge claim payment held back.

When the informant called DiPaolo with the tip, the Scutellas were in the process of filing a lawsuit against the insurance carrier to force payment on the business' $600,000 policy. Although no one was officially connecting the family with the fire yet, DiPaolo was continuing to advise the carrier, Donegal Insurance, that the Scutellas were under investigation in connection with the arson. Since DiPaolo could not prove his suspicions at that moment, and not yet in court, he advised the carrier to hold off on its payment for as long as possible while police developed and collected new evidence. As a result, Donegal continued to deny the claim and the Scutellas filed suit in Erie County Court to collect on their policy.

The confidential informant, a fellow wise guy in the know when it came to Erie's slimy dark side, confidently assured DiPaolo that it was Ricky Cimino, a low-level bit player in the local underworld's grand scheme, who actually set the fire on orders from the Scutellas. Furthermore, the source insisted, it was Darrell Steiner, another in Erie crime's unheralded low-life cast, who drove Cimino to and from the scene. It was also claimed that Cimino had been accidentally severely burned as he attempted to flee what had become a raging inferno that February night. He had dashed out of the building screaming, the back of his clothing still smoldering, and disappeared into a waiting car, or so DiPaolo was told. The informant told DiPaolo that word on the street was that the Scutella family was behind the arson.

That the Scutellas were involved in destroying their own business for the insurance money came as no surprise to the veteran detective. Just a day after the blaze, a source from one of Erie's television news departments told police he'd picked up reliable information about the Scutellas' likely involvement in the Pal Joey's fire.

DiPaolo knew the TV news source to be reliable, and considered vital the information provided: Ron Nuara, director of the news programs at WJET television, Erie's ABC affiliate, was at the time dating Kelli Scutella, one of Joe Scutella's daughters. Nuara, who since married Scutella, told station employees that Kelli's brother, Danny, had called her at midnight, February 1, shortly before the destructive fire, instructing her to bring the key to the building's second floor "right away." Soon after she delivered the key, the restaurant and the entire building went up in flames and smoke. DiPaolo would include all of the information in his official police reports, and also later testify in open court about the information he received from the confidential sources, and ultimately, so would Cimino.

The information did not provide hard evidence that DiPaolo would need, but enough to at least initially connect some members of the Scutella family to the arson fire, while further holding up the insurance pay-out. And besides, there was a link to Caesar Montevecchio. *Wasn't there always?* DiPaolo mused to himself.

DiPaolo knew both Ricky Cimino and Darrell Steiner by reputation, and from his personal police investigatory experience.

Cimino long had had cocaine connections with Joey Scutella and with Merchie Calabrese, Jr., and Merchie's kid, John. The connection, it came as no surprise, was Caesar Montevecchio. But DiPaolo was having difficulty ascertaining exactly where Steiner fit in. He had arrested Steiner several years earlier on a theft charge, so the detective was at least familiar with Darrell as a member of Erie's vast, but relatively insignificant, criminal underbelly. DiPaolo would not have previously speculated that the garden variety low-life Steiner would have been involved with Montevecchio, Scutella or Calabrese. But it didn't take long for DiPaolo to make the all-important connection between Ricky Cimino and Darrell Steiner.

After checking with his street informant sources, DiPaolo learned that Cimino was running an after-hours dive called the Pickwick Club at the time of the Pal Joey's fire. Steiner tended bar at the Pickwick Club. That connected the two of them. It was that easy.

Next, DiPaolo learned another wannabe wise guy, Peter Vella, a convicted felon with a criminal history dating back several decades, was now running the Pickwick. Vella had taken over the club's management responsibilities immediately following the fire. It coincided with the time Cimino and Steiner dropped off everyone's radar. The Pickwick was shut down late in 1985. Cimino and Steiner seemed to have vanished. Flipping a coin to decide between which of the two he would actively pursue, DiPaolo chose the less-connected and thus more easily intimidated Darrell Steiner. It was a plan that worked.

Before setting out to find Steiner, DiPaolo learned that the night of the fire – January 31, 1985 – just before midnight, Joe Scutella and his much younger girlfriend, Donna Costello, were seen by many at The Sports Page. Scutella had hardly ever frequented "The Page," but this night he was buying drinks for other patrons.

Bill "Dutch" Senger, a school teacher and a legend in Erie high school basketball and baseball, and star at Findlay University, was moonlighting, along with John Aquino, as a bartender at The Page. He got a $100 tip from Scutella as Scutella and his *comare* ("girl on the side") left the establishment. There was no doubt in DiPaolo's mind that Scutella was making extra sure of establishing an alibi the night of the fire. In Erie, who could forget a C-note left as a bar tip?

To find Steiner, DiPaolo cast around in his collection of sources and informants until he located one who clicked. It was an elderly woman who had known Steiner, a friend of Darrell's family. First time luck, she provided the detective with the answers he was seeking. Steiner, she said, had moved to Miami, Florida, shortly after the fire in February 1985.

What a coincidence, DiPaolo thought. A State Street building landmark that had once housed the popular Erie Restaurant burns to the ground and Darrell Steiner simultaneously skips town. It only took several calls to the Miami Police Department for DiPaolo to locate Steiner's whereabouts. The Erie man was living in a not quite life-threatening residential area of Miami.

Serendipitously for DiPaolo, Miami police patrol officers had ticketed Steiner for running a red light just a week earlier. He hadn't paid the ticket within the time period allowed, resulting in police issuing a warrant for Steiner's arrest. Lucky break or perfect timing, DiPaolo didn't care. It was all working to his advantage.

A short time later, DiPaolo and a special agent from the Pennsylvania Attorney General's Office in Pittsburgh caught a red-eye flight to Miami.

Miami police, extending all the professional courtesies expected between law enforcement agencies, were helpful and cooperative, even transporting the two Pennsylvania law enforcement officials to Steiner's new digs.

Unfortunately for them at the moment, it appeared Steiner was out. And DiPaolo had no way of knowing for how long. But Lady Luck struck again, this time in the person of an elderly female neighbor who helpfully volunteered that Darrell Steiner had earlier walked to the nearby Publix Supermarket. The friendly neighbor told the officers she knew Steiner would be returning from the store directly because Darrell was picking up groceries for her as well.

The officers parked their vehicle just a short distance from Steiner's Miami residence and watched – and waited – a mini stake-out of sorts. DiPaolo was no stranger to long and boring stake-outs. Although he would have waited for hell to freeze over, this one turned out to be one of the shortest of his entire career. Five minutes after parking the car, the Erie cop spotted Steiner strolling along the street ironically named "Lucky Lane."

Nonchalant and carefree, Steiner was dutifully toting what appeared to be a brown paper bag chock full of groceries from the popular Publix supermarket. The officers started the car and slowly edged out onto Lucky Lane. When they pulled up alongside Steiner as he walked, the Miami cop asked, "Darrell Steiner?"

Steiner slowed somewhat. "Yeah?" It was more of a question than a confirmation.

"I have a traffic warrant for your failure to appear in court," Miami Police Sergeant Mary Santorma said. Peering deeper inside the car, Steiner broke out into a nervous laugh.

"What the fuck! Dom DiPaolo comes all the way to Miami from Erie to help you serve a traffic warrant? No fuckin' way. I want a lawyer!"

It was much more than a simple demand for legal counsel, DiPaolo knew. Steiner, despite his bravado, had guilt written all over him. He was scared. *Good.*

Although it was an inauspicious means toward an end, DiPaolo thought, at least it was a start. Darrell Steiner would be as good a place as any to begin. And now DiPaolo had Steiner in his sights.

DiPaolo and the other officials allowed the transplanted Erieite Darrell Steiner to deposit his groceries in his Miami apartment and then hand over milk and bread to his elderly, friendly and helpful neighbor lady. Then police drove Steiner to the main headquarters building of the Miami-Dade Metro Police Department. In the car, the officers' intentional silence became deafening for Steiner. Finally, he asked, "Dom, c'mon, man, what's up?"

"At the station, we'll talk," the tight-lipped DiPaolo said.

When they arrived at police headquarters and led Steiner to an interrogation room, Sergeant Santorma told Steiner, "I'll hold off on booking you on this warrant. I'll let Sergeant DiPaolo talk with you first. Then we'll see what happens."

After ticking off from memory in quick order the all-so-familiar Miranda warnings, DiPaolo got straight to the point with Darrell Steiner.

"Are you willing to talk with us about the arson fire at Pal Joey's Restaurant in Erie on February 1, 1985?" he asked, skipping the unnecessary lead-up to the big question.

"Oh, so that's why you're here?" Steiner simultaneously asked and stated, not showing too much surprise.

"Sign the waiver. Then we talk."

"If I do talk, do I get a deal?"

"Just sign the waiver," DiPaolo instructed, his poker face stern, yet unrevealing.

Now Steiner was starting to actually show the fear he was feeling. It was clear he wanted out from under the pressure that initially sent him scurrying to the Sunshine State. And he wasn't going to be too particular about negotiating a deal for himself. *Wow!* the Erie cop thought to himself. This was one of the quickest breakdowns and confessions in Dominick DiPaolo's vast array of knocking out, figuratively, confessions. DiPaolo could only shake his head in amazement. If only they all could be this easy, he thought.

Darrell Steiner was as candid and forthcoming as anyone who was facing potential felony accomplice charges had ever been with the police. He laid out for authorities the Pal Joey's arson fire in the greatest of details that even Detective Sergeant DiPaolo could not have anticipated.

Ricky Cimino, Steiner began, had needed a driver to take him to and from Pal Joey's on that night. In return for the rides, Ricky promised Steiner half – some $12,500 – of the 25 grand Cimino would be getting from the Scutellas to torch their restaurant. Late the night of January 31, Steiner said, he drove Cimino to the restaurant, parking the car on East 11th Street, not far from Pal Joey's. Cimino left Steiner waiting in the car, while Ricky first went in the restaurant's front door, then came out, going straight to the building's side door leading to the second floor. But the door was locked. So he went back to the front door and entered.

A short time later, Cimino came out, motioned for Steiner to get out of the car and approach him. From there, they walked to the nearby Plymouth Tavern, where Cimino explained to Steiner that the side door leading to the second floor was locked and nobody there had a key. He also told Steiner that a call was made to Kelli, Joe's daughter, and she was coming with the key. Some 15-to-20 minutes after that, the two left the Plymouth and walked north on State Street until they got to Pal Joey's. Cimino went inside while Steiner walked directly to his car.

When Cimino came out, Steiner continued, he went to the side of the building and immediately entered through the now unlocked door. Five minutes later, he said, the bar and restaurant lights went out and three people emerged from the front door. One locked the door and all three left the building in the dark. Steiner, unfortunately, could not I.D. any of the three. Within moments, Steiner heard two distinct explosions from nearby, then watched red flashes of light coming from the building's second floor windows. Seconds later, flames were shooting from those same windows.

Almost immediately, a panicked – and flaming! – Ricky Cimino sprinted from the same side door he had earlier entered. Ricky was on fire! But he at least had the presence of mind to roll himself, crazily, in the snow to extinguish the flames that were wildly shooting from his clothing. Steiner, previously mesmerized by the horrific scene unfolding in front of him, suddenly concluded it might be a good idea to rescue his burning buddy. Stepping hard on the gas pedal, Steiner accelerated the vehicle, navigated the car the short distance to where Cimino was still repeatedly rolling in the snow, then got out and helped to ease the smoldering Ricky into the car.

"Ricky just kept screaming that he was burned," Steiner said. "His back, neck and hair were all singed."

DiPaolo, at one point, bit his lip to keep from grinning. It was such a visual description that the cop was able to imagine the scene well. Another scene from *The Gang That Couldn't Shoot Straight*, the cop thought as he again bit down on his lower lip.

Steiner continued. His first impulse was to drive Cimino to nearby Hamot Medical Center, just a few blocks away from Pal Joey's burning restaurant, for treatment.

"I was going to drive him to the hospital and just dump him off there," Steiner said.

"But he was screaming, 'Take me to Cindy Northrup's.' That was some broad that he was seeing at the time. She lived at 26th and Sassafras Street and late at night I was able to get us there in just minutes."

Once they arrived at Cimino's girlfriend's apartment, Steiner said, "I helped him into her house. She was there with Tammy Winiecke, the girl she lived with, and they were both screaming as they took off whatever was left of Ricky's still smoking clothes." (Later, both women lied about it when brought before a Grand Jury. Later, they were charged with and pleaded guilty to perjury.)

When the women took Cimino to a second floor bedroom, Steiner remained in the living room listening while Cimino continued to scream out in pain. Steiner quoted Cindy as repeatedly yelling at her boyfriend, "Ricky, please let Darrell take you to a hospital." But Cimino, fearing being identified as the arsonist more than he feared the burning pain, steadfastly refused. After another hour of yelling and screaming, Steiner could take no more and left Ricky at the apartment in the care of the two impromptu nurses.

"He was on his stomach when I last saw him. His back and ass were all burned and he had salve or something all over him. That and wet towels. He was a mess."

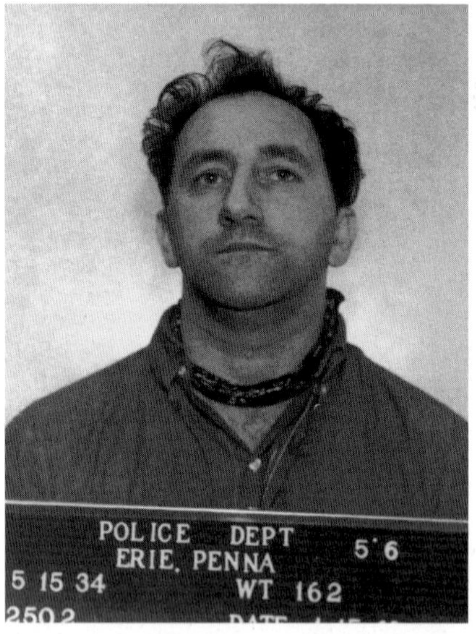

Joseph Scutella, Jr. caught 15-to-30 years in prison for masterminding the arson fire at his family restaurant, Pal Joey's, the sentence to be served on top of his 25-year term for dealing cocaine. (Courtesy of Erie Police Department)

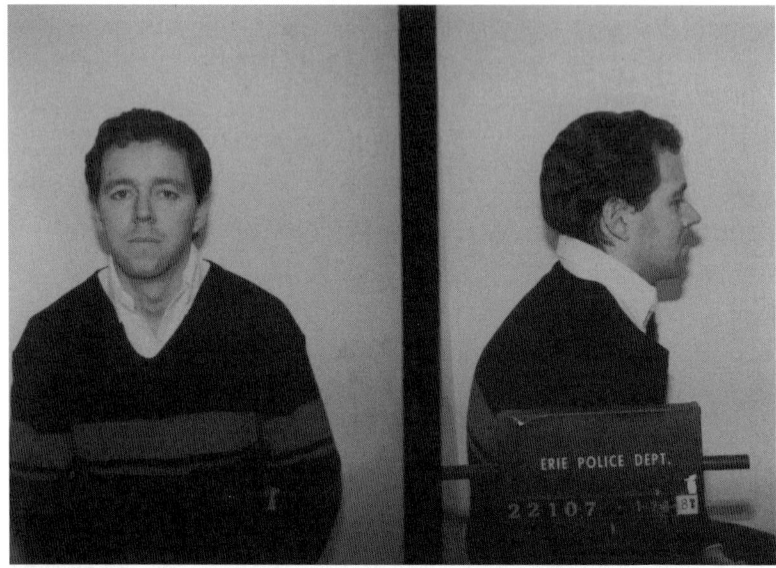

Daniel Scutella, a convicted felon, assisted his father in the arson fire and was sentenced to serve seven-to-18 years in prison. (Courtesy of Erie Police Department)

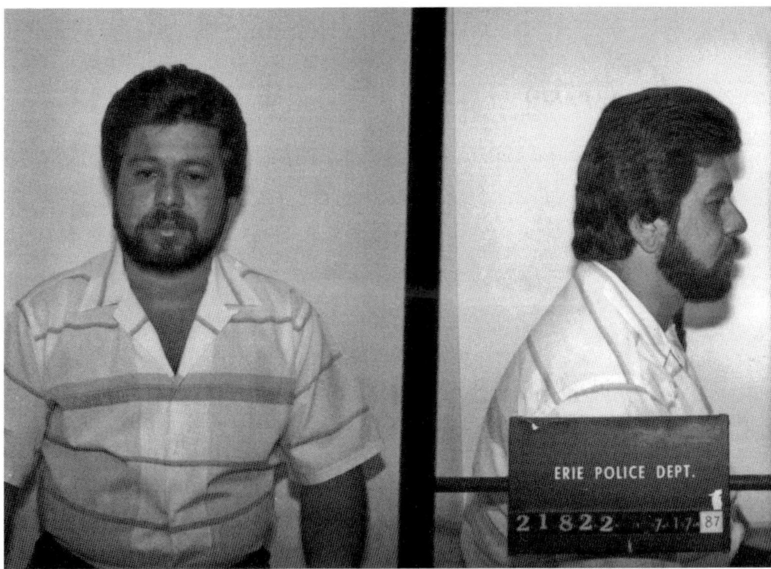

Rick Cimino was hired by Joseph Scutella, Jr. to torch Pal Joey's restaurant. Set up by Scutella, Cimino received only third degree burns for his efforts. (Courtesy of Erie Police Department)

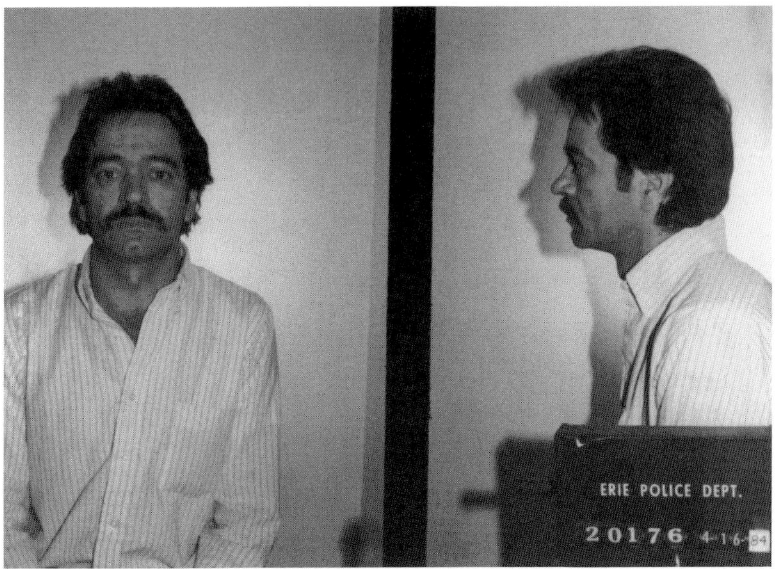

Darrell Steiner, Cimino's wheelman the night of the fire, turned state's evidence as an unindicted co-conspirator. (Courtesy of Erie Police Department)

John Fasenmyer (middle facing camera), said to be a wannabe wise guy, tried to steer DiPaolo away from Cimino by bribing the officer. Fasenmyer was charged was bribery and illegal wiretap, and ultimately pleaded no contest to the wiretap count in return for prosecutors dropping the bribery charge. (Courtesy of Erie Police Department)

CHAPTER 23

Darrell Steiner had been talking fast and now he paused for a moment, gulped and drew in a deep breath. DiPaolo could tell he was scared and besides, he was in way over his head.

He allowed for a few moments of silence while Steiner continued to breathe deeply. "Then what happened?" DiPaolo probed, but this time a little more gently. DiPaolo was experienced enough to know when to turn up the heat, and when to turn it down.

Steiner said he laid low, keeping out of sight for several days, reading news coverage of the arson fire in the *Morning News* and *Erie Daily Times*, listening to reports on local radio stations and watching Erie's television news. He told the Erie detective he felt somewhat relieved in that it appeared nobody at or near the scene of the arson had seen him or Ricky Cimino. A few days later, he continued, he began visiting Cimino at Cindy's apartment.

"Ricky was still in a lot of pain, but he seemed to be getting better," Steiner said, adding that Cimino stayed in bed, naked, as the arsonist could not physically tolerate wearing even loose-fitting clothing. Think of your worst, blister-popping childhood sunburn and how it felt to wear even a baggy shirt. This was worse, much, much worse.

Steiner also said Joey Scutella had arranged for a physician to visit Cimino at Cindy's apartment and treat him there, rather than risk going to a doctor's office or to one of Erie's four hospitals. When

Cimino appeared to be recovering and feeling better, Steiner, on one of his visits, finally broached the question.

"Ricky, when do I get my money?" he asked the badly burned man. "He said Joey told him the insurance company would not pay until the company knew for sure the Scutellas didn't have anything to do with the fire."

"And how did you respond to that?" DiPaolo continued to question.

"I told him that's bullshit," Steiner said. "That it might take months. Fuck that!"

"And how did Cimino react?" DiPaolo asked.

"He said, 'Hey, what the hell do you want from me?'"

Steiner told DiPaolo as time passed he was becoming more and more upset that others had not upheld their part of the deal with him. About a week after the February 1, 1985 torching, Steiner said he got up enough nerve – or stupidity – to actually telephone Scutella.

"I said, 'Hey, I ain't waiting forever, man. I want my money!'"

To which an incredulous Scutella replied, "What the fuck you talking about?"

"Either I get my money or else!" Steiner brazenly threatened the career criminal. Another deep breath. DiPaolo waited. Then, to the detective Steiner said, "I guess I really fucked up. He hung up on me."

DiPaolo withheld the urge to say, "Hel-lo-o-o?" But instead, he kept his "duhs" to himself, just smiling inwardly.

A short time after the heated telephone exchange, Steiner, who was then living with Karen Briska, had an unexpected visitor at their apartment. It was Cindy Northrup.

"I'm supposed to tell you that Joey Scutella wants to see you right away . . . like now," Cindy said. "He is in the car!"

Now Steiner was worried, but still foolishly believed he would somehow be paid the $12,500 drivers' fee that Cimino had promised him. He was in for an unpleasant surprise.

"Open your fucking shirt!" Joey Scutella ordered when Darrell Steiner got into the car. It was a rude introduction to the man Steiner had foolishly threatened earlier.

Steiner complied. He knew Scutella was concerned with the possibility that he was wearing a wire. Honor among thieves? Ha. No one trusted anyone.

"Look," Scutella tried to explain. "Rick owes you. I don't owe you."

End of meeting. Steiner told DiPaolo that after the hastily arranged car conversation with Scutella, he immediately drove to Cindy Northrup's apartment to confront the still ailing arsonist, Ricky Cimino. But it was Cimino who did all the confronting.

"He was screaming like a wild man," Steiner said of Cimino. He was yelling, 'You are going to get us both killed! Why in the fuck did you call Scutella? You don't tell someone like him to give you your money or else!'"

For the first time Ricky Cimino told Steiner that the Scutellas previously had no knowledge that Steiner was involved. Now they knew. Big mistake.

"He said he was supposed to have done it alone," Steiner said. "He told me Scutella was pissed because I had brought someone into it."

"Now what?" Steiner asked the recovering Cimino, the gravity of the matter finally apparently beginning to sink in.

"He told me, 'Get the fuck out of town before something happens – like he kills you! I'm lucky I'm still living. You don't think he wanted me to survive, do you?'"

Darrell Steiner said Cimino handed him a paltry $200 in cash and said, "Call me in about a month. I'll send the rest to you wherever you are. But I'm serious, man. Get the fuck out of Erie."

Steiner stopped again and took another deep breath, then continued.

"That's why I'm here (in Florida) with Karen. And I never called Ricky back for the rest of my money. Jesus, I don't want him to know where I'm at. Hey, that Scutella family is nuts!" (The reference was to the implied threat.)

"Only Karen's family and my folks know where we are, and that's the truth."

A few months earlier, Steiner continued, Karen Briska's sister telephoned her to say Joseph Scutella had been sentenced to serve a lengthy prison term on the cocaine charges. He had been sentenced in U.S. District Court in Erie to serve 25 years in connection with the West

Virginia drug conviction and was incarcerated at the Sandstone, Minnesota federal penitentiary.

Still, it didn't alleviate Steiner's fears. Despite Scutella's imprisonment, Steiner was concerned over what could happen to him if he returned to Erie.

"We're still not going home," Steiner insisted, mustering some degree of defiance.

Then Steiner thought for a few moments before almost begging.

"I don't want to get charged. I'll testify against all of them. I promise. Just don't charge me."

DiPaolo was silent for what must have seemed forever to the deeply inhaling Darrell Steiner.

"Well then, you know you'll still have to come back to Pennsylvania for a grand jury appearance," DiPaolo matter-of-factly said. This time, there was no pause.

"I'll do it," Steiner said.

Another break.

DiPaolo couldn't believe the success of his Miami trip after Darrell Steiner implicated Ricky Cimino and, more importantly, Joey Scutella, in the as yet unsolved Pal Joey's arson fire.

The road to Frank "Bolo" Dovishaw's killer was a winding, twisting and unpredictable journey. There were speed bumps all along the way. But there were also successes. And with Darrell Steiner's coming clean about his role in the arson fire, this was definitely one of the moments to savor.

After interviewing Steiner, DiPaolo placed a long distance telephone call to Pennsylvania Deputy Attorney General Bill Connelly. The Deputy A.G. had been assigned to the Dovishaw investigation and other unsolved Erie crimes related to the local underworld.

"I want to give this Steiner guy immunity in return for his full cooperation with us," DiPaolo told Connelly. Connelly had been aware of DiPaolo's trip to Miami, and he understood all too well the Erie officer's point. Steiner was not a major player, but he could put the entire arson case together for investigators and prosecutors – and perhaps even lead to more breaks in the Frank "Bolo" Dovishaw case further down the road.

"Give me a number," Connelly directed DiPaolo. "Call you right back."

DiPaolo waited. And while he did, he brought Miami cop Santorma up to speed on Steiner's confession, then thanked her for the assistance and cooperation of the Miami Police Department. "We owe a lot to you," he said. "Maybe someday we can return the favor."

Before she could reply, the phone rang.

It was Deputy A.G. Connelly finally getting back to DiPaolo. The state prosecutor got straight to the point and outlined the proposed Steiner deal:

"We fly Steiner to Pittsburgh and he testifies before our special grand jury. He testifies truthfully. When arrests are made, he will testify at their trials if we need him. As an un-indicted co-conspirator, he walks. That's it."

Sounded more than fair to DiPaolo as he pitched the proposed deal to Steiner. "Do you want to talk with a lawyer before you decide?" DiPaolo asked.

Steiner's response was immediate. "Dom, I have no reason to disbelieve you. Everyone knows how you play this game. I will do it."

And now it was the Erie cop who was breathing easier. Much easier.

But then, Steiner spoke again. "Just one thing."

DiPaolo suppressed an involuntary groan. "Yeah?" He was now the tough cop again.

"Can I bring Karen up to Pittsburgh with me?"

The cop didn't want the complication of dealing with a significant other, yet he wasn't about to jeopardize this star witness' deal, either. He sighed.

"Sure. I don't see a major problem with that. When we get back to Pennsylvania, I'll call you with the grand jury date. Just make sure you're ready."

At that point, DiPaolo signaled Santorma, who had been waiting outside the interrogation room.

"I think we're ready to head back to the hotel, and you can have someone take this guy home," DiPaolo said.

"What about the traffic warrant?" Steiner asked the Miami cop Santorma.

With a wink in DiPaolo's general direction and a shrug, she said, "Geez, I can't find it. In fact, it's already out of the system. I guess this is your lucky day. Just don't go through any more red lights."

No, she's wrong, DiPaolo smiled to himself. *It was my lucky day.*

A month later, Steiner and Karen arrived in style at the Greater Pittsburgh International Airport. There, DiPaolo awaited the couple, along with Erie Patrolman Vinnie Lewandowski, who assisted the detective sergeant throughout the entire Dovishaw murder and Pal Joey's arson investigations.

Leaving the airport with Darrell and girlfriend Karen in tow, the cops drove 25 miles east to North Huntingdon, Pennsylvania, in Westmoreland County, where the Commonwealth's investigating grand jury was seated and hearing testimony. Once there, Darrell Steiner kept his end of the deal. And it is strongly suspected that members of the grand jury listened all so intently.

DiPaolo knew the noose around Joe Scutella, Jr.'s neck was slowly being tightened.

Back in Erie a short time after Darrell Steiner's secret, but suspected eye-popping testimony before the grand jury in Westmoreland County, DiPaolo began the tedious process of closing loopholes and tying up loose ends.

He first telephoned a prominent Erie physician friend, Dr. Forrest Mischler. "Doc, I've got a special request for you," DiPaolo began.

"Sure. Shoot," Mischler good naturedly responded.

"I need you to examine a man with serious burns to his body. I need you to determine the exact type of burns and whether they were caused by a fire or by some other source."

Mischler readily agreed. "Sure, Dom. If the burns are prominent enough I can determine what degree and possibly even how long he's had them."

That's all the cop needed to hear.

Sometimes, search warrants are routine. Other times, they border on the unique. Other times, they are even quirky. The "body" warrant DiPaolo prepared for Erie County Judge William E. Pfadt to sign swung the pendulum all the way toward the bizarre. The search warrant was for Ricky Cimino's buttocks and his back.

Yet Judge Pfadt, a soft-spoken and longtime jurist who had once been the county's elected chief prosecutor, barely raised an eyebrow as he signed the warrant. DiPaolo thought it was as though he signed search warrants for people's asses every day.

But when Ricky Cimino read the warrant, he did more than raise both eyebrows. He was stunned. And not because a warrant had been issued for his somewhat gross posterior. For when he read the warrant and came across the name "Darrell Steiner, Informant," Cimino knew his days of freedom were numbered.

Indeed, it was a very strange assemblage that gathered that day. All had come together at the behest of a search warrant in Dr. Mischler's West 2nd Street office to check out one Ricky Cimino's infamous behind.

Detective Sergeant Dominick DiPaolo was in attendance, of course, as was Erie Police Department Identification Section Specialist Raymond King, assigned the unenviable task of photographing Ricky Cimino's back side. Also present with Cimino was his lawyer, Erie criminal defense Attorney David Hunter.

Dr. Mischler spoke first, instructing Cimino to remove his shirt and trousers. Cimino, with an affirmative nod from lawyer Hunter, complied.

In silence, Mischler examined Cimino's buttocks, back and upper leg areas.

"How did you get those burns?" Mischler asked.

Hunter remained mute.

"I fell asleep under a heat lamp trying to get a tan," Cimino unconvincingly lied.

Hunter was still quiet. That he didn't advise his client to remain silent when questions were posed greatly surprised DiPaolo, whose experience with defense lawyers ran to the contrary. It also spoke volumes about the defense strategy.

Taking notes throughout the examination, Dr. Mischler finally said, "Okay, fine."

His findings? Third degree burns, the most serious of the three degrees. These burns were from a fire, not from a heat lamp.

While Cimino was dressing, DiPaolo ventured, "I want to talk with you, Ricky."

At that point, Hunter finally spoke, according to DiPaolo.

"He ain't talking," the mouthpiece said.

How ironic, DiPaolo thought. After incriminating himself in front of many witnesses, now he's not talking?

"Fine," the cop smiled. DiPaolo knew Cimino's day was fast coming. It might take a few more weeks, or even months. But the detective knew he would eventually break him. DiPaolo could wait.

Besides, there was still much remaining to be done in the Bolo Dovishaw murder investigation. And soon, just like a piece in a jigsaw puzzle, another unlikely source would surface.

CHAPTER 24

A WEEK AFTER RICKY CIMINO'S BADLY BURNED BUTT WAS EXAMINED and photographed, Erie wannabe wise guy John Fasenmyer telephoned Detective Sergeant DiPaolo. It wasn't a courtesy call, DiPaolo knew, for he had long considered Fasenmyer to have many if not tight, than at least loose connections with heavy hitters in Erie's underbelly of organized crime.

Fasenmyer longed for others to think of him as someone important, a tough guy with a deep, gravelly voice, but the cop considered Fasenmyer to be mostly just another wannabe.

So it was shortly after Mischler's examination of Cimino that Fasenmyer telephoned DiPaolo requesting a face-to-face meeting with the detective. DiPaolo had no idea what – if anything useful – Fasenmyer had to offer. But the cop agreed to meet him at a local used car sales lot known in some circles as Fasenmyer's favorite hangout.

Fasenmyer was already waiting when DiPaolo walked into the car lot's office.

"Sit down," Fasenmyer half-smiled, indicating a worn, cloth-covered chair.

DiPaolo eased himself into the chair, his eyes checking out the surroundings. Dingy, dusty, with a damp, musky smell. A few grease-stained calendars on the wall. Piles of paperwork stacked unevenly on the desk.

"Coffee?" John Fasenmyer seriously attempted, but failed in another smile. DiPaolo shook his head. This wasn't a social call.

"What's up, John?"

Fasenmyer shifted somewhat uncomfortably in his chair behind the desk.

"Well, Dominick," he began as though they were dear, old friends. "Everyone knows you're like a fucking bulldog when you get into something. But you're really wasting your time on Ricky Cimino." DiPaolo was silent. Fasenmyer plowed on.

"Ricky didn't do nothing. Now, I can't say that for Joey Scutella, but it wasn't Ricky. You got the wrong guy this time."

"No shit!" DiPaolo feigned exaggerated surprise. "Tell me, will you. Who's the right guy?"

"C'mon, Dominick! You know me! I ain't no snitch. But Ricky's my friend and it ain't him. I know! So why don't you lay off him? You're making him real nervous and for no reason."

DiPaolo couldn't help his grinning. "Well, John, if he didn't do anything, he shouldn't be so nervous, wouldn't you say?"

Suddenly, Fasenmyer took a totally different tack, one that even surprised DiPaolo.

"Dominick, you like golf, don't you?" It was more of a statement than a question.

"What the fuck does that have to do with any of this?" the detective asked.

Fasenmyer attempted another benign smile. "Well, you know Johnny, the guy who owns this lot, and the mayor, Lou Tullio, and me, we go golfing all the time at the Lake Shore Country Club. Why don't you join us sometime? You know it can't hurt, you golfing with the mayor. And if he knows you're friends with us, well, maybe we can talk to him about a promotion for you."

DiPaolo had an immediate visual image of Fasenmyer golfing with Tullio and Johnny Bizzarro, a former middleweight contender in the 1950s and 1960s who now owned Fleetwood Auto. Bizzarro had been one of the mayor's financial supporters. Johnny's younger brother, Louie, was an outstanding boxer himself. He went 14 rounds with world champion Roberto Duran until the "Hands of Stone" wore Louie down. Louie is a successful businessman, owning car lots and the locally famous "Ringside," a bar and restaurant popular with politicians.

DiPaolo knew a veiled bribe when he heard one, and was having difficulty remaining professional.

"What else do you want to tell me?" DiPaolo asked, his voice rising somewhat.

"Hey, I'm just trying to look out for you," John Fasenmyer was suddenly being extremely defensive, every cop's friend, the salt of the earth.

"Yeah, I'm sure you are. Who put you up to this?" the cop demanded.

DiPaolo thought about his relationship with Lou Tullio, one that had cooled many years ago and had finally frozen over to the extent DiPaolo knew that golf or no golf, a promotion was as likely as the cop taking command of NASA's next Space Shuttle mission.

"Dom, believe me, nobody put me up to anything!" Fasenmyer insisted. Then, he shifted gears and again changed to an altogether new subject.

"Hey, I hear Ray Ferritto is making a ton of money off Bolo's book. You hearing that, too?"

Now, for the first time since Fasenmyer had begun talking, DiPaolo was genuinely pissed off. For this meeting he had driven nearly a half hour to Edinboro, a small college town just south of Erie. The time expended, he suddenly knew, was as productive as taking out the garbage. But the cop managed to collect himself.

"John, listen and listen good. I do my job. If it turns out it's not Ricky Cimino, then it isn't. But I know it *is* him. So stop with the bullshit. And while you're at it, fuck golf. Fuck Lou Tullio. And fuck Ray Ferritto. I got work to do. See ya."

As DiPaolo rose to leave, Fasenmyer tried in futility just once more. "We can still talk to the mayor for you?"

What a stand-up guy, DiPaolo thought. He almost spit out the words. "I don't want a promotion from him. Save it." And the cop walked out in disgust.

CHAPTER 25

By April 1987 – more than four years after Frank "Bolo" Dovishaw's execution-style murder – the still unassembled pieces of the mammoth puzzle compiled by Detective Sergeant DiPaolo were slowly starting to fall into place. DiPaolo's team had guided many witnesses through the legal maze of the Commonwealth's special investigative grand jury, which in turn handed up a series of indictment-like actions formally termed "presentments." As a result, the tenacious cop's initial plan finally began to bear the fruits of his often frustrated labor. The idea was to bury his nemesis, longtime criminal figure Caesar Montevecchio, with so many serious criminal charges that even if he walked on some, those that stuck would mean additional prison time tacked onto the 15 years he was already serving.

Also informally called "shot-gunning" in the criminal justice community, it was DiPaolo's intention that any additional time meted out to Montevecchio on these new charges would be tantamount to a life sentence. And nothing loosens lips as does the vision of spending the rest of one's days behind bars in a state penitentiary.

Based upon insider information from "Fat Sam" Esper, DiPaolo prepared warrants charging Walter "Skip" Tracy, Michael Farbo, Charles "The Hawk" Serafini, Billy DeSantis, Susan's brother, James and Peter Russell, and Pittsburgher Fredrico Maggio, aka Freddie May, with multiple counts of burglary, theft and conspiracy. Tacked on were charges under Pennsylvania Corrupt Organizations statute, Section 911, one count for each offense. Pennsylvania's Corrupt Organizations law is similar to the federal Racketeering Influenced Corrupt Organization Act, also known as R.I.C.O.

Two of those charged, Walter "Skip" Tracy and Peter Russell pleaded not guilty to two separate burglaries that netted them and "Fat Sam" more than $95,000 in cash. Esper did his Joe Valachi impression by testifying against them and both were bound over to court. Tracy cut a deal with DiPaolo, and was willing to testify against all the other co-defendants if needed, and then plead guilty to all the burglaries and robberies he was charged with in exchange for a reduced sentence. On July 12, 1984, he entered his plea and got five-to-ten years for all his crimes. And then, on January 30, 1985, just over six months later, his sentence was suspended for "good behavior" and he was put on probation for four years.

Russell, however, took another path. Instead of showing up for his trial in Erie County Court on September 12, 1984, Peter went to Shade's Beach on the shores of Lake Erie in Harborcreek Township, just east of Erie, piled his clothes in a neat stack, and left a Bible, a photo of his son and a letter to his mother – which read: "What I am about to do, many people may not agree with, and I do not condone this, but basically everyone is lying on me." It was a suicide note. Peter Russell was gone, but not forgotten: He turned up in San Bernardino, California 10 years later, where he was arrested and extradited back to Erie, pleading guilty to the burglary counts from 1984. He got only two-to-five years in prison, followed by 10 years on probation and 500 hours of community service. After being released, more charges were later filed against him and at the age of 61 he was found in Las Vegas, arrested and sent back to prison.

As for Montevecchio, DiPaolo's up to now elusive big fish, Caesar was charged with 32 criminal counts. DiPaolo knew the initial 32 charges were just for starters.

There would be more, plenty more.

When DiPaolo had exhausted information from "Fat Sam's" stool-pigeoning, he turned to the claims made by Cleveland's now-cooperating Robert Dorler. The Ohio man had provided enough eyewitness accounts to safely charge William Bourjaily, George Meeks and Montevecchio with the home-invasion armed robberies, burglaries, criminal conspiracies, and solicitation to commit homicide against Aziz Michaels, who survived 11 bullet wounds in the Uzi attack.

Again, the detective tossed in one count each of Corrupt Organizations for every criminal charge filed. Montevecchio, as the result of the barrage of presentments and warrants, was now facing 56 separate and distinct charges – and those were separate from what DiPaolo believed would be an ultimate coup de grace: Enough credible evidence to arrest Caesar in connection with Frank "Bolo" Dovishaw's January1983 murder. But that would have to wait.

The current charges, all totaled, amounted to more than $2 million in house jobs racked up by Montevecchio and his team of co-conspirators. As a result of so many charges being filed in such rapid succession against so many defendants, DiPaolo's crime clearance rate, already in record territory, was now headed off the charts.

But there were still more to come. The last set of charges was filed by DiPaolo on information provided by getaway driver Darrell Steiner against the badly scorched Ricky Cimino for arson and conspiracy in the Pal Joey's blaze. DiPaolo also filed three additional counts of aggravated assault in the case. Those charges arose from the three Erie firefighters who were injured while battling the raging inferno in downtown Erie that cold February night.

But once again, DiPaolo still wasn't quite finished. He filed even more charges in the arson fire, including risking a catastrophe and reckless endangerment, as well as tacking on Corrupt Organizations counts for each. The Pal Joey's arson was merely a speed bump for the veteran cop as he moved closer to nailing Montevecchio for Bolo's murder. Nonetheless, a rewarding and satisfying speed bump, DiPaolo thought.

On February 4, 1987 in Harrisburg, Pennsylvania Attorney General LeRoy Zimmerman swore-in DiPaolo as a Special Agent of the Attorney General's office. At the time, he was the first non-attorney in the state to be allowed into the Grand Jury Room while testimony was being taken. While DiPaolo was busy with the grand jury presentments and drafting arrest warrants, Caesar Montevecchio was now settled in to his new home at the federal penitentiary at Terre Haute, Indiana. Cleveland's William Bourjaily, meanwhile, was plying and honing his culinary talents as a trustee cook at the Milan, Michigan, federal penitentiary. So it was with a somewhat perverse sense of delight that the Erie cop mailed each prisoner copies of the grand jury presentments, along with the warrants, advising both they had 60 days to waive extradition to Pennsylvania – or DiPaolo would come after them and bring them back. As for the other wise guys and wannabes, they were easily rounded up in Erie, Pittsburgh and Cleveland, creating much local media buzz over the number of arrests. But still, as some annoyingly pointed out to DiPaolo, no homicide charges were filed. It would be Montevecchio, strangely, even surprisingly, who would be the first to crack.

In June 1987, DiPaolo learned Montevecchio had waived extradition and would be returned to Pennsylvania to face the bevy of new criminal charges against him. DiPaolo knew he could have easily arranged for U.S. Marshals to transport Caesar from Terre Haute to Erie. Montevecchio was still a federal prisoner, so such an arrangement with the U.S. Marshals Service would be proper. DiPaolo had waited for five years for this day, and he wasn't about to allow the opportunity pass without milking this career criminal for all he was worth. Instead of escorted federal transportation, Caesar Montevecchio would get very personalized chauffeur service from Dominick DiPaolo.

As soon as travel arrangements were made and the waiving of extradition papers signed, the Erie detective and an agent from the Pennsylvania Attorney General's Office made the tedious and boring eight-hour drive through the flat country of Ohio and Indiana to Terre Haute. Arriving the night before, DiPaolo and his partner checked into their motel rooms. The front desk clerk was more than pleased to suggest an eatery, a recently opened establishment a few miles away in French Lick, Indiana, called "33 Brick Street." When they reached the restaurant, they found it decorated with Boston Celtics' memorabilia. The prominent restaurant colors were Kelly green and white, with a Red Auerbach Banquet Room and even a Bob Cousey Room; the former referred to the former legendary Boston coach, the latter to the Celtics' great floor general.

Just as the two officers sat down at their table, a tall man approached and thanked them for being there. Obviously, he had the bearing of being the owner, approaching other tables with the same "thank yous." DiPaolo immediately recognized the guy as Larry Bird – formerly the Celtics' famous No. 33. When Bird later learned the two men were cops on business, he sent over complimentary drinks. DiPaolo had been a Celtics fan since he was a mini-kid.

"Too bad we don't have a camera," he told his partner.

"Why? Who was that guy?"

"That's Larry Bird – Mr. Celtic!"

"Who's Larry Bird? And how do you know him?"

After a groan, DiPaolo said, "Let's just eat."

The next day, after being led to one the federal penitentiary's prisoner holding areas, DiPaolo was struck by Caesar Montevecchio's deteriorating physical appearance. The cop had last seen Caesar about a year earlier, but the man he now observed appeared to have aged more than a decade during the short intervening period of time.

Montevecchio remained mute, not uttering a single word of greeting. Still in federal prison garb, Caesar was shackled as he slowly walked to DiPaolo's waiting vehicle at the main gate. The dark green, plastic garbage bag containing Montevecchio's alternate clothing was tossed into the unmarked police car's trunk. Within minutes, the trio was speeding east, back to Erie.

"Dominick, I'm surprised to see you." The car had only traveled a few miles from the prison gate, yet it was the first time Montevecchio opened his mouth to speak since DiPaolo and the A.G. agent entered the penitentiary. Montevecchio had been the first to break the silence. And now, DiPaolo could tell Caesar was riled.

"I thought the marshals would move me, or you would have sent one of your guys down here. Funny, I didn't know you do your own leg work."

With not a little sarcasm, DiPaolo managed a half-smile and said, "I do everything."

For the next 20 miles or so, Montevecchio was silent as the A.G. agent drove and the mundane Indiana scenery flashed past them in a blur. Then suddenly, Caesar blurted out, "You really want to hurt me, don't you?"

DiPaolo waited just a moment for the right effect before responding. "What do you mean by that?"

"With all these charges, it sure as hell looks like you're trying to give me a life sentence." That prompted a warm feeling from the deepest place inside the detective's gut. The mass filing of charges had certainly touched a nerve and made a point with Caesar Montevecchio.

The cop waited a few moments for effect. Then DiPaolo turned somewhat to face Montevecchio in the back seat. The cop mustered up the coldest stare possible for him. Looking directly and unblinking into Caesar's steel gray eyes, DiPaolo left no doubt as to his intentions.

"I *am* trying to give you a life sentence. Hopefully, when I get done with you, I'll have you in the electric chair where you'll fry. And I'll be there to watch."

For a moment, Caesar looked as though he was about to faint, DiPaolo thought.

"You hate me that bad?"

"Shut up and enjoy the scenery. It's going to be the last you'll see for a while, maybe forever." DiPaolo managed a smile.

Caesar thought about the police officer's words for several seconds. "You know, it wasn't me who wanted to hurt you. You know it was the other guy. You know who I mean," Montevecchio insisted. The reference was clear as to the "hit" that was put out on the investigator.

More non-descript Indiana terrain melted away as the car sped forward. DiPaolo held his temper, which wasn't an easy task as he remembered the probing questions from his family about their police escort during that horrible time. But he managed not to say a word, baiting Montevecchio into again finally breaking the silence.

"Do you think we can deal on these charges?" Caesar asked, apparently in earnest. More silence. Then from Montevecchio an offer: "I'm willing to cooperate with you if we can strike some kind of a deal."

As much as DiPaolo hated to admit it to himself, Montevecchio was seriously whetting his interest. But DiPaolo also had an uncanny sense of timing. And he knew that the moment, which might never come again, was perfect for him to strike. Not surprisingly, he did!

CHAPTER 26

To say that Erie Police Detective Sergeant Dominick DiPaolo did not trust Caesar Montevecchio would be the greatest of understatements. The Erie cop had had too much previous professional experience with this career criminal, the man who once boasted and swore that he'd someday make John Dillinger look like a choir boy. Now as DiPaolo motored through the flat and boring terrain of northern Ohio, returning Montevecchio from Indiana to Erie, the cop's very natural inclination was to become highly suspicious when Montevecchio held out the possibility of a plea deal on some 56 felony counts stemming from a series of home invasion robberies and even racketeering charges he was facing.

Yet, forever on DiPaolo's mind was the January 1983 slaying of Erie sports betting kingpin Frank "Bolo" Dovishaw – that and the nefarious probability that Caesar Montevecchio was in some way behind that execution-style murder.

Montevecchio was now claiming he wanted to cooperate. DiPaolo was determined to discover just how far Caesar was prepared to go to save his himself from what would undoubtedly amount to spending the rest of what had been a pathetic life behind bars.

"Before you say anything more, I'm going to read you your rights," DiPaolo instructed. "And only then, if you still agree to continue to talk with me and you also sign the waiver, then and only then do we talk."

Montevecchio responded immediately. "Okay. But it's not necessary for me to sign anything. Just give me my rights."

DiPaolo briefly stared for a long, hard moment at his prisoner, mostly for effect. Then he reached into a folder from which he produced a pre-printed form. The police officer ticked off the oft-repeated Miranda warning from memory, as he had done hundreds of times during his many encounters with suspected criminals. Then, he dated and recorded the time of day on the official waiver form, holding out the document and a pen to Montevecchio to sign.

"Sign," DiPaolo ordered.

"I don't have to sign it. I understand my rights," Montevecchio insisted.

"No, you *don't* understand. Either you sign the waiver or we don't talk. Now what the fuck is it going to be?"

"Shit, man, you just don't trust anybody, do you?" Montevecchio almost sighed.

"I trust a lot of people," DiPaolo shot back. "But you're sure as hell not one of them."

Another almost sigh. It was close as Montevecchio could come to that human expression of emotion. Caesar took the paper and pen, peered up at DiPaolo, then scrawled out his name.

"There. Satisfied? Jesus!"

"Go ahead," DiPaolo instructed, trying to hold back an involuntary grin. "Talk."

Suddenly, Montevecchio was feeling not quite so shrewd. He had signed himself into a tight corner. And now he was beginning to have second and possibly third thoughts about it.

"Wait a minute, Dom. Wait a fucking minute. If I start talking now, then what the hell happens to all these fucking charges against me?"

"Nothing," DiPaolo shrugged nonchalantly.

"Nothing? Nothing? Jesus! Then why the fuck should I talk?"

"You're the one who brought it up. Not me."

For another 30 miles or so of non-descript interstate highway, the inside of the unmarked police car was silent. It resembled an intricate game of chess, but with each man waiting for the other to blink first. It was a game Caesar Montevecchio lost.

"Okay," Caesar finally said somewhat exasperated. "I give you all the burglaries, robberies and drug deals I was involved in. I also give you Joe Scutella for the fire. And I'll give you Bolo's murder."

DiPaolo did his best poker face impression, not speaking, not showing any emotion. Montevecchio continued.

"I'll give you some things out-of-state – shootings, all kinds of good shit," Caesar said. "Now, what do you say? Do you think we can deal?"

DiPaolo knew he was in control. He intentionally paused a maddening minute or so for even more effect while Montevecchio desperately pretended not to hold his breath. Finally, the cop spoke.

"What about giving me who you were with in all of the jobs? And also, you must testify against all of them?" DiPaolo countered.

"Sure, Dom, sure. If you want me to, I will."

DiPaolo sensed Montevecchio was being much too agreeable considering the circumstances. But he knew Montevecchio well. A lot more than Montevecchio suspected, perhaps even better than Montevecchio knew himself. At any rate, Dominick DiPaolo silently vowed to himself he wouldn't be conned by this con.

At the same time, DiPaolo's heart rate had increased significantly, the cop realized. All this time trying to get to Bolo's killer was about to pay off. But he wouldn't let Montevecchio know what he was thinking or feeling, not now. DiPaolo wouldn't give him the satisfaction. The cop forced himself to remain not only calm, but almost indifferent, as though this were just another matter-of-fact, routine wrap-up to a case.

"Without naming names right now," the investigator thoughtfully began, "I want you to tell me all about Bolo Dovishaw and all about what part you played in his untimely demise." DiPaolo again paused a moment for effect, then casually tossed out his bluff. Let's see if savvy Caesar Montevecchio will bite on this one, the cop thought. "Let's start off by allowing me to finally determine whether you're being straight with me. As you might know by now, I've already compiled much information and have quite a bit of that puzzle solved."

Montevecchio, never one to shy away from a good game of cat and mouse, especially with a cop, smiled wryly. If he had any inclination at all that he was about to become the mouse, he didn't let on. He never did.

"I know you have a lot of pieces," Montevecchio said. "But you don't have them all. Not by a long shot. And face it, man, you need me to put them all together for you."

"Then let's hear it."

What DiPaolo had been waiting to hear since that cold January day of 1983 was finally about to unfold in graphic detail and Technicolor. And, Montevecchio had surely been right on that one count. DiPaolo by no measure was even close to having it all. But now DiPaolo, hopefully with Montevecchio's assistance, was about to put all those many little pieces together and solve this perplexing puzzle.

As Caesar Montevecchio began to talk, DiPaolo knew he had been right all along about the involvement of the all-time MVP of Erie crime figures when it came to the Bolo Dovishaw murder case, and how important Montevecchio would be in solving the case that had stumped the cop for so long.

"There were three people involved that I know of for sure," Montevecchio began.

"Go on," Dom DiPaolo encouraged when Montevecchio paused briefly.

"There could have been more involved, but I didn't talk with them. Someone else did." He drew in a deep breath.

"Oh, yeah? Explain," DiPaolo directed.

"Well, there was one person who wanted Bolo wasted. And, there was one other person who set it all up. And, there was also one other person who was the shooter. The other person who I think I know was involved, but never ever talked to, didn't actually get involved until the day after Bolo bought it." Montevecchio was breathing deeply now, and his words were coming more quickly as he continued, "There was another person who wasn't involved in the hit, but who knows where the gun went. I can have him cooperate with you, too. Dominick, the truth is I can put the whole case together for you."

It was clear Montevecchio was now pleading with DiPaolo for this deal. Then Caesar offered again, "Look, I can put the whole fucking case together for you. I'll plead guilty to my part and all the other charges. But I want a deal on paper – and before I do anything, I have to talk first with my family."

The two men were quiet for a few minutes as the flat country farm scenery rolled by. DiPaolo's silence was paying off. It was a good tactic, most cops and even newspaper reporters knew. Just create an awkward period of "dead air" and the interviewee feels somewhat compelled to fill the quiet space. So, Montevecchio still wasn't done talking.

"Actually, I can't give you Joe Scutella, but Ricky Cimino sure can. And all I got to do is talk to Ricky and tell him I'm going to talk and I know that he will, too." In reality, DiPaolo knew a lot more about the Pal Joey's fire than Caesar ever suspected, but it was a good check on Montevecchio's truthfulness and credibility to let this desperate guy ramble on.

Another pause for effect.

Then Caesar said, "And I'll give you something else that you probably don't even know."

"Yeah?" DiPaolo raised his eyebrows conveying his disbelief. "What's that?"

"Did you have a conversation a little while ago with Fasenmyer about Ricky?"

"If you're asking," the cop coldly said, "then you obviously already know the answer, don't you? You know I had the conversation with Fasenmyer. How?"

"Fasenmyer taped you. And now they're playing the fucking tape all over town. That's how."

DiPaolo felt himself grow flushed. "So, exactly how did you know that while you were cooling your heels in the joint?" DiPaolo probed.

"Hey, not that hard, Dom. I called someone in Erie and they told me Ray Ferritto has a copy of that fucking tape with you on it. So, what do you think? Do you believe me now?"

Finally, DiPaolo was sold. For the most part. But he knew there were still holes in Montevecchio's story to fill. Gaping holes.

Caesar Montevecchio was about to get his deal. But it would come at a high price for many of his pals who had trusted him. Ah, so much for honor among thieves, Dom DiPaolo thought to himself. There never was any such honor. When they were cornered, they all flipped on their buddies.

Before the productive road trip from Indiana to Erie had ended, DiPaolo assured Montevecchio he would speak with the prosecuting attorneys assigned to the case. "But I'm going to need names to give them."

"They'll have them," Montevecchio assured the cop."But what about me? What the fuck happens to me in return for all of this cooperation?"

"If you weren't the shooter at Bolo's place or the shooter in any other murder, I can tell you now that a deal can be arranged," DiPaolo promised. It really wasn't that much of a promise since DiPaolo already knew Caesar had a tight alibi for the night Bolo Dovishaw was murdered.

Montevecchio weakly nodded. The long time wise guy appeared to be very well aware that for the first time in his criminal career he was about to blow in many of his soon-to-be former pals.

DiPaolo, also in thought, wasn't all that surprised. Sooner or later, he mulled to himself, they all do the same, every last one of them. Indeed, after many years of getting away with often unspeakable atrocities, the wheels had finally fallen off the Caesar Montevecchio Express. His bus was about to crash and many others thrown under its wheels.

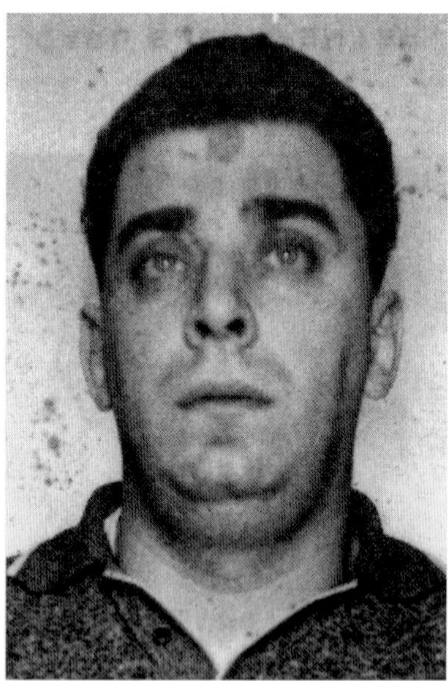

Frank "Ash Wednesday" Dovishaw, also known as "Bolo," was executed in his west Erie home January 3, 1983. The kingpin of local illegal betting, Dovishaw's brushes with the law were early in life and often. That he would die a violent death surprised few. (Pennsylvania State Police Photo)

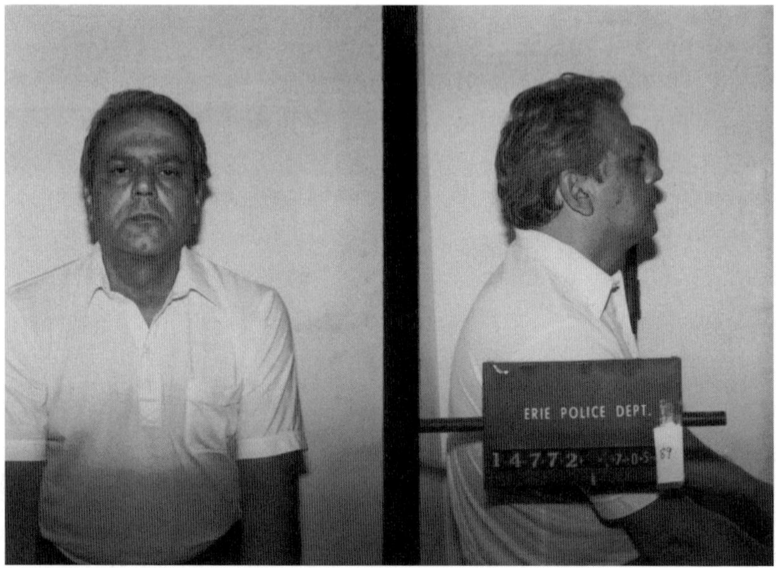

Anthony "Niggsy" Arnone owned an Italian import business in Erie's "Little Italy." He was charged with masterminding the "Ash Wednesday" murder. (Courtesy of Erie Police Department)

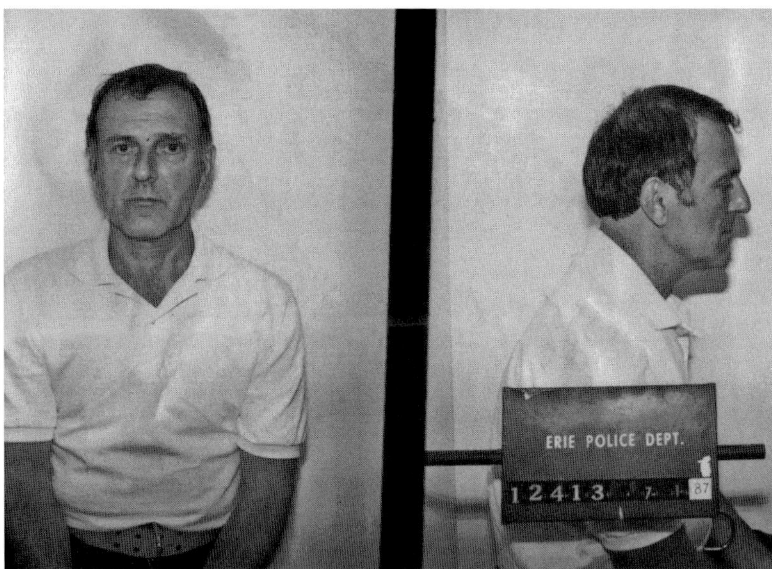

Caesar Montevecchio was charged with being the middleman in arranging the hit on Frank Dovishaw. He was also a suspect in an attempted hit on Det. Sgt. DiPaolo. (Courtesy of Erie Police Department)

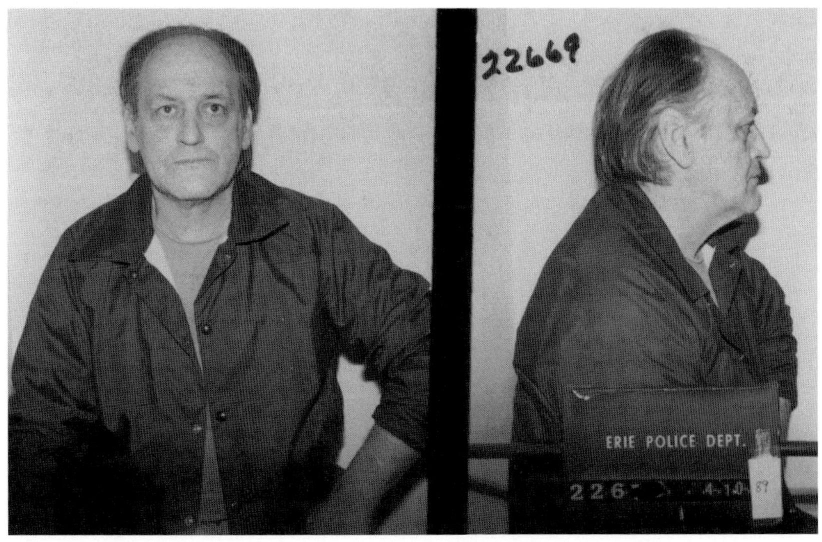

Robert Dorler of Medina, Ohio, got $20,000 for killing Dovishaw on January 3, 1983. He was also charged in an Ohio mob hit. (Courtesy of Erie Police Department)

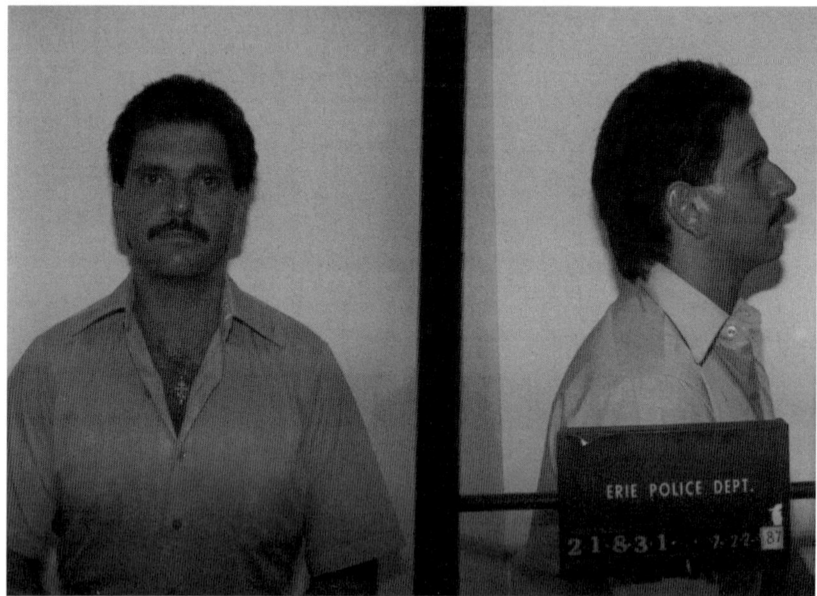

William "Billy" Bourjaily of Parma, Ohio, by chance became Dorler's wheelman after the Dovishaw murder and was charged with conspiracy. (Courtesy of Erie Police Department)

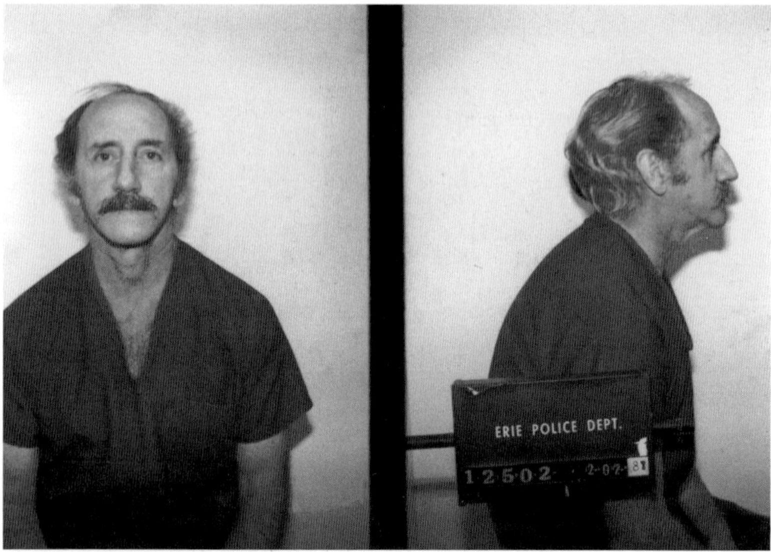

Joseph "Little Joe" Scutella, Jr., put out a separate contract on hit man Raymond Ferritto for the night of the Dovishaw hit. Scutella's job also was to get wise guy Anthony "Cy" Ciotti out of "Ash Wednesday's" house the night of the killing. (Courtesy of Erie Police Department)

Raymond Ferritto, aka Ray Marciano, an admitted hit man in Cleveland's Danny Greene murder, and reputed to be involved in many other murders, was a partner with Dovishaw in a lucrative bookmaking operation. (Courtesy of Pennsylvania State Police)

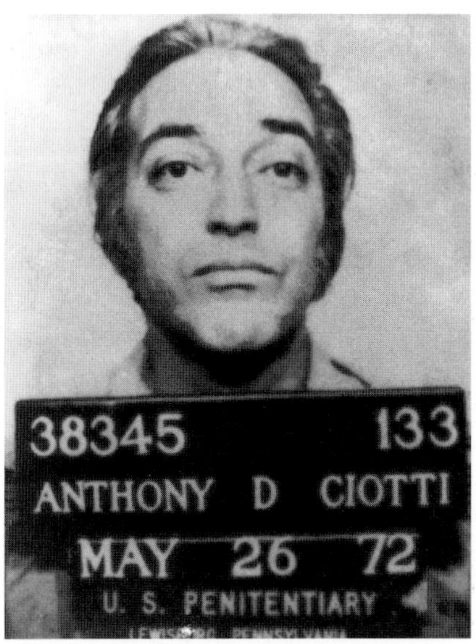

Anthony "Cy" Ciotti, Jr., is a convicted felon who was advised to leave Dovishaw's home before the murder. (Courtesy of U.S. Penitentiary, Lewisburg, Pennsylvania)

Phil Torrelli (facing camera in suit and tie) was also a partner with Dovishaw and Ferritto in Northwestern Pennsylvania's largest bookmaking operation. (Courtesy of Erie Police Department)

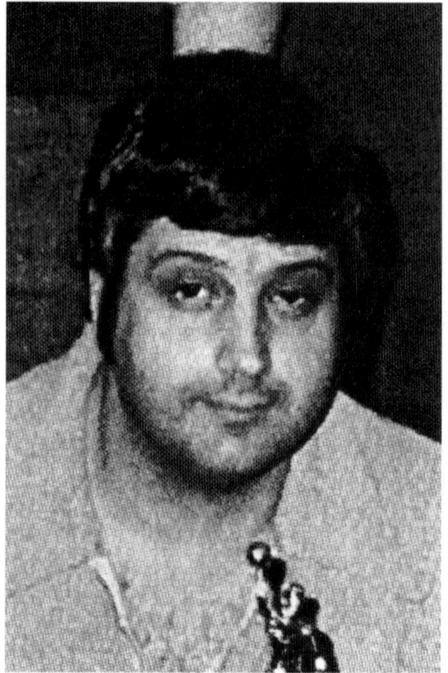

Frank Rotunda is the dirty cop called to Dovishaw's house by the wise guys to "find" Bolo's body. (Author's Private Collection)

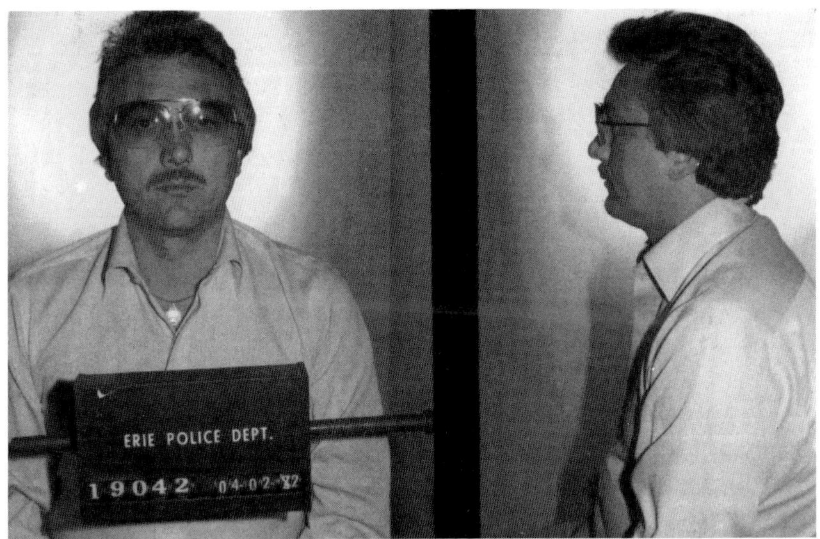

Vincent DiPasquale helped Ferritto find Ciotti after the murder, but before Dovishaw's body was discovered. (Courtesy of Erie Police Department)

Hit man Raymond Ferritto (tan coat, middle of casket) and Cy Ciotti (dark coat behind Ferritto), pall bearers for "Ash Wednesday." (Courtesy of Erie Police Department)

"Ash Wednesday's" body, covered with bed sheets and a rug, in Dovishaw's basement. (Courtesy of Erie Police Department)

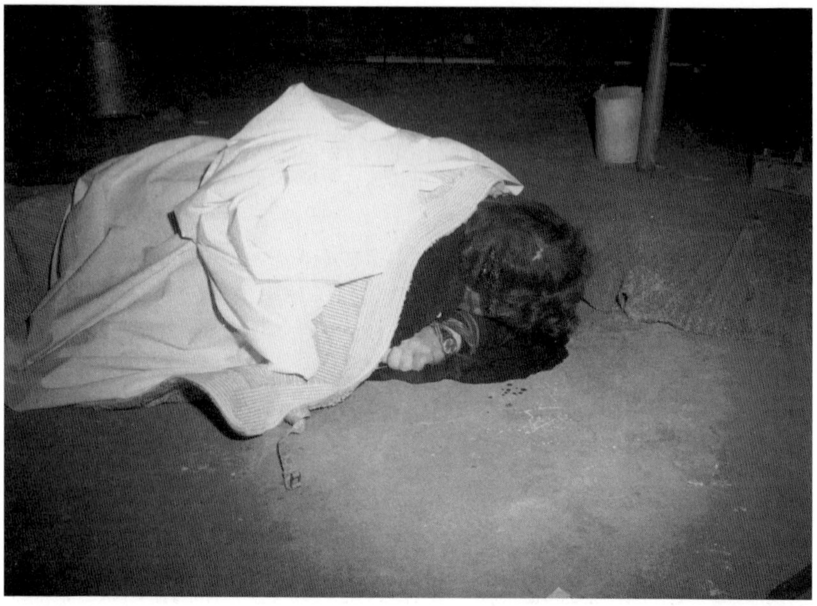

After sheet and rug removed, "Ash Wednesday's" body in a pool of blood, with a bullet wound to his head. (Courtesy of Erie Police Department)

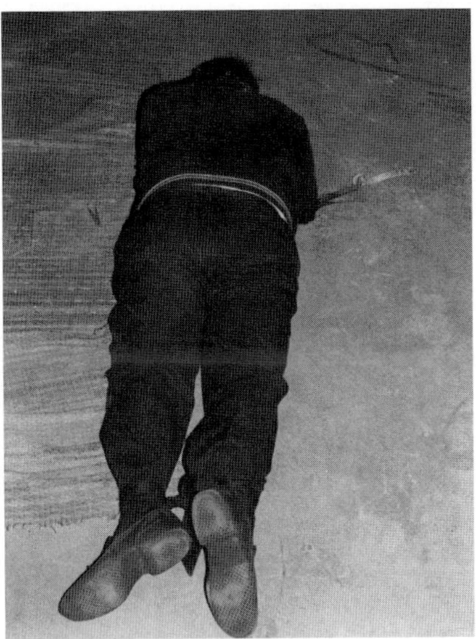

Dovishaw's body with hands and feet bound. (Courtesy of Erie Police Department)

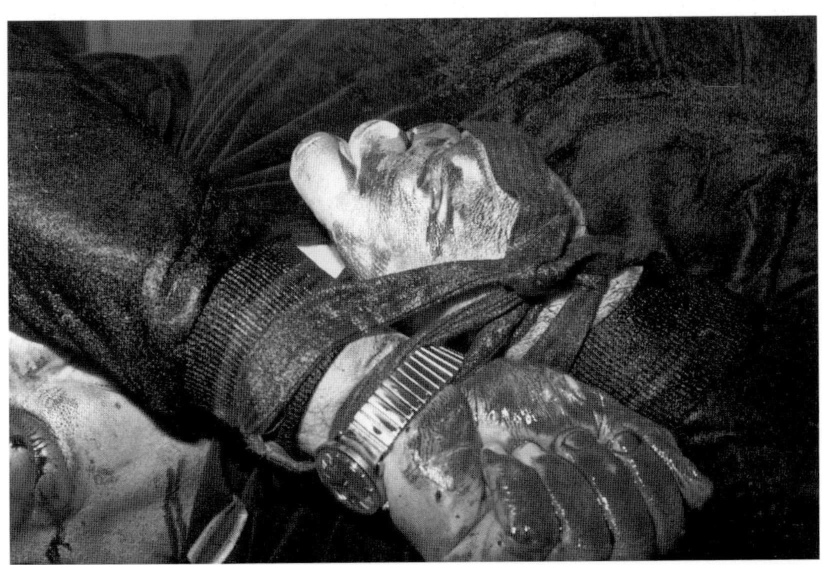

Dovishaw's blood-covered hands, bound with woman's cloth belt. (Courtesy of Erie Police Department)

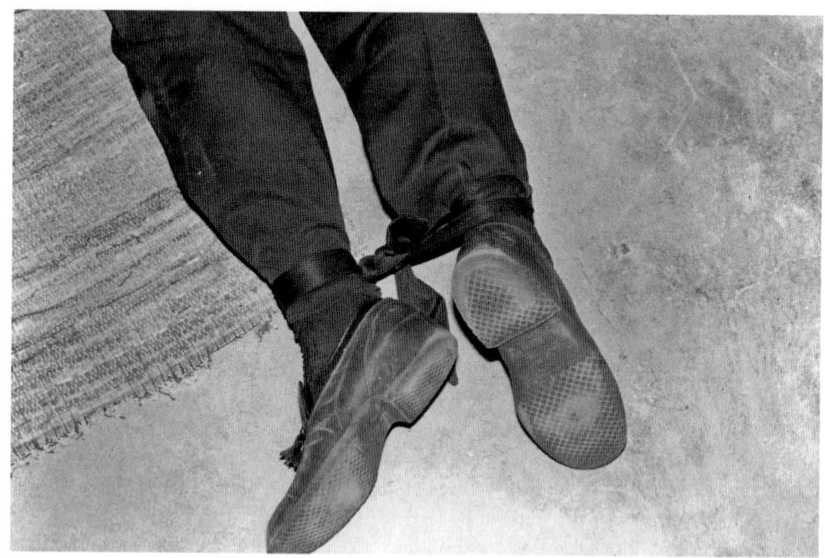

Dovishaw's feet, bound with woman's silk belt. (Courtesy of Erie Police Department)

Hit man Dorler dumped "Ash Wednesday's" green 1979 Cadillac in the parking lot at Holiday Inn South. (Courtesy of Erie Police Department)

PennBank vault safe-deposit boxes. Dovishaw's box, 449; Mastrey's 450. (Courtesy of Erie Police Department)

Arnone's box, 509; Dovishaw's 503. (Courtesy of Erie Police Department)

Dovishaw's box, 424. (Courtesy of Erie Police Department)

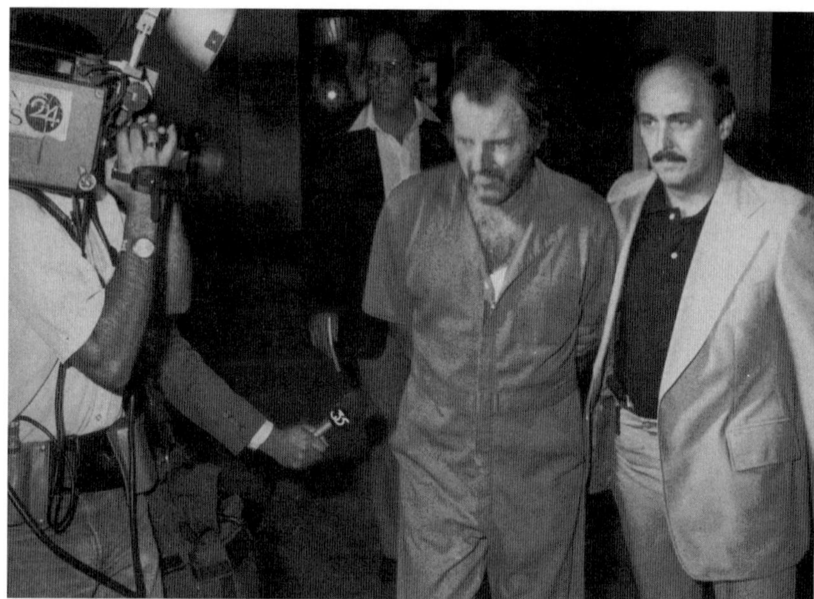

Detective Sergeant Dominick DiPaolo and Detective D.C. Gunter arrest Caesar Montevecchio in the Frank "Ash Wednesday" Dovishaw murder. (Author's Personal Collection)

DiPaolo arrests Anthony "Niggsy" Arnone and charges him with the contract hit on "Ash Wednesday" Dovishaw. (Author's Personal Collection)

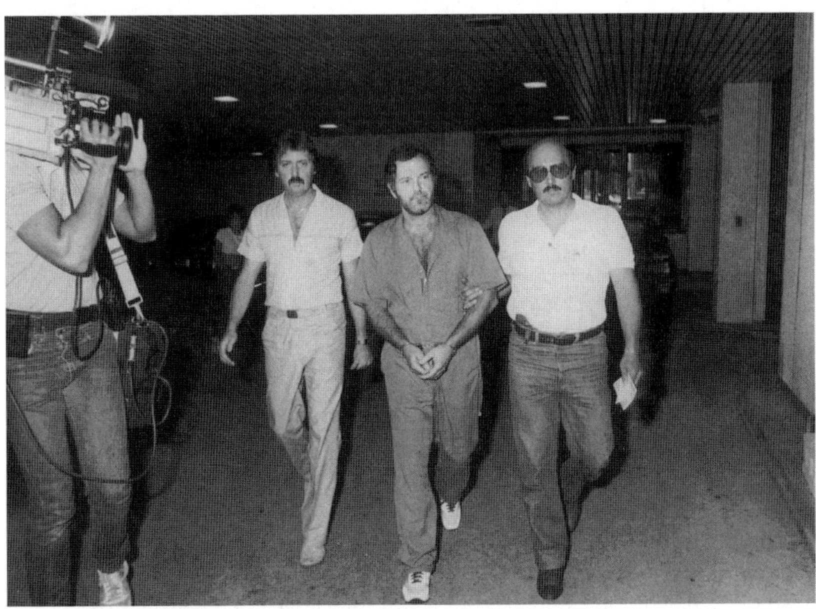

Detective Sergeants DiPaolo and Grassi escort Montevecchio to the Dorler trial, where Montevecchio testified against the hit man. (Author's Personal Collection)

The "Ash Wednesday" Dovishaw murder

Frank "Ash Wednesday" Dovishaw was found dead in the basement of his home at 1634 West 21st Street on January 4, 1983. He had been murdered one day earlier. The events that took place shortly after the murder:

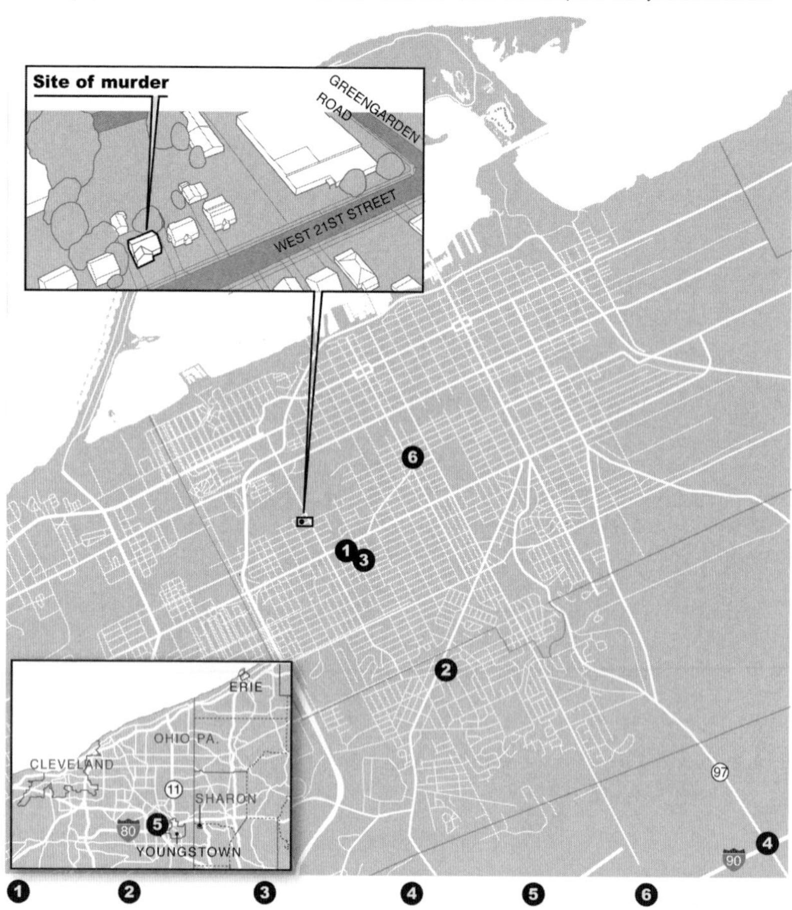

1 Caesar Montevecchio establishes an alibi January 3 at the Sports Page, 1527 West 26th St.

2 Hit man Robert Dorler of Ohio gives the safe-deposit box keys of "Ash Wednesday" to Montevecchio in Station Restaurant parking lot, 4900 Peach St.

3 At a laundromat at 1470 West 38th St., Montevecchio passes the keys to an Erie businessman who Montevecchio later says ordered the Dovishaw hit.

4 Dorler dumps Dovishaw's car in the Holiday Inn South parking lot at Interstate 90 and Route 97.

5 William Bourjaily drives Dorler back to Ohio, discarding the murder weapon while crossing a bridge over Meander Lake.

6 Admitted mob hitman Raymond Ferritto leaves his home at 724 Brown Avenue January 3 to search for Dovishaw. He and several others discover the corpse of "Ash Wednesday" the next day.

Part Four

KEYS TO A MURDER

CHAPTER 27

Once back in Erie, Detective Sergeant DiPaolo wasted little time in putting a different set of wheels in motion – wheels that would begin to confirm the Montevecchio deal.

At this sensitive point in the negotiations, DiPaolo knew Montevecchio couldn't afford to allow anyone to know he was talking to his previous archrival, the Erie cop, or that he planned to turn Commonwealth's evidence and testify for the government. That held doubly true, DiPaolo thought, for keeping Caesar Montevecchio's longtime legal voice, criminal Attorney Leonard Ambrose, in the dark, at least for the time being. Ambrose had reportedly collected an astounding fee to represent Montevecchio in 1983, according to DiPaolo, money that had been turned over by Caesar's brother, Albert, a successful New York businessman. Yet despite the hefty legal price tag, Montevecchio had been shocked with a 15-year sentence for concealing cocaine in his golf bag.

Fast forward to now. When these new indictments and charges had been splashed all over Erie's two daily newspapers, Ambrose telephoned Montevecchio's wife, Bonnie, to assure her that he was on the case and would rescue her husband, she later testified in open court.

Attorney Ambrose instructed Bonnie Montevecchio, "Don't worry. I'll do my best to get him out of this. Just have him call me when they bring him back to Erie," Bonnie later testified.

Montevecchio himself believed that Ambrose might pose a problem for him and his proposed deal, which Caesar foolishly was prepared to negotiate all by himself. He told DiPaolo, "I've got to call him, you know. Because if I don't call Lenny, then he'll automatically know that something is up."

After thinking over the situation, weighing the options and finding not many to consider, DiPaolo allowed Montevecchio to place the call to Attorney Ambrose.

"Hey, these are bullshit charges," Caesar told his lawyer. Ambrose appeared concerned with his fee, Montevecchio later said. Ambrose is said to have asked Montevecchio if he could get $100,000 from Albert – up front – so he could begin preparing the defense case – according to what Caesar told DiPaolo. Later, Montevecchio conveyed the gist of the telephone conversation with Ambrose to DiPaolo.

"I told him that I had to talk with my brother first," Montevecchio said. He explained to DiPaolo that Ambrose's response was, "Well, when you do, call me."

The cop had to chuckle. DiPaolo was thinking it should be Ambrose who was paying Montevecchio for getting him the 15 plus years in the slammer.

Next, DiPaolo and fellow investigators met with Dennis Pfannenschmidt of the Pennsylvania Attorney General's Office. Pfannenschmidt was now assigned to the overall investigation. He was also responsible for the state's special investigative grand jury. Together, investigators and prosecutors began to sort out the particulars, weighing the benefits and risks of dealing with the slippery and often questionable Caesar Montevecchio.

Caesar had asked for a *coterminous* sentence to run with the 15 years he was already serving on the cocaine charges. It was legalese, a technical concept akin to a concurrent sentence. Under Montevecchio's proposal, he would plead guilty to all charges against him. He would also cop to one new count stemming from the Frank "Bolo" Dovishaw murder, and would receive a maximum sentence of 15 years. That was the deal.

And it was acceptable to DiPaolo solely because Montevecchio was the only wise guy who could give him the person who was believed to have ordered the Bolo Dovishaw hit, along with the "why," and then give him the actual shooter.

No one else could.

And so it was on July 7, 1987, the Pennsylvania Attorney General's Office in Harrisburg confidently authorized a plea bargain arrangement with Erie's most notorious career criminal, Caesar Montevecchio. But there was a stipulation from on high: The first time Caesar was caught in a lie, any lie, the attorney general's office insisted, the entire deal would be terminated and all Montevecchio previously confessed to would be used against him – and with no *coterminous*! All totaled, just one lie would more than double his sentence to decades in prison.

Now, it was all up to Montevecchio.

DiPaolo hastily arranged for Caesar to meet with wife, Bonnie, so that Montevecchio would have a private moment to break this new development to her. Bonnie, however, knew something was up. When she entered the office of the Pennsylvania Attorney General situated in Erie's downtown Griswold Plaza Post Office building, her eyes were already noticeably reddened, her mascara running from crying. As soon as Caesar revealed his intentions to her, she sobbed uncontrollably again.

Then Caesar Montevecchio wept.

As for Dom DiPaolo, he felt no compassion – only cold contempt for this career punk who spent a lifetime destroying not only what was once his own promising life, but the lives of so many innocent victims. The veteran Erie cop listened intently as Montevecchio, for the first time, admitted to his wife the crucial role he had so easily played in the Bolo Dovishaw hit. Somehow, the detective felt Bonnie suspected it all along.

Following Caesar's emotional confession, Bonnie Montevecchio dried her tears somewhat, then turned to Dom DiPaolo with raised eyebrows. "You've been after him for such a long time – for years. Can we trust you now?" she asked.

"Let me explain something to both of you," DiPaolo replied. "I knew your husband was involved with Bolo Dovishaw from day one. He denies he had a contract out on me, but insists it was his buddy, 'The Hawk.' But now I know the truth about what happened. And I could be in a position to stick it to Caesar big time. But I still have a job to do and my only concern right now is to clear all these cases and move on. As for trusting me, well, you're going to have to trust me. There's no alternative. You don't have a choice."

For a while, there was total silence. Then, Bonnie, her eyes still red and teary, hugged her husband and reluctantly left the building.

Caesar, apparently deciding he could do nothing other than trust the cop, began talking. He gave up the burglaries, the robberies, the Aziz solicitation to commit murder, all the many cocaine transactions. And the best part of all was that Caesar Montevecchio was finally naming names. All those who were involved in every job, every hit, every snort of the bright white powder – Caesar was giving them all up.

It took five hours. Five hours of robberies and burglaries and drug deals and enough names to fill the cop's notebook two times over and even then some. Finally, Montevecchio and DiPaolo arrived at the "Golden Moment" for the Erie detective: The Frank "Ash Wednesday" Dovishaw murder.

But now, almost characteristically, DiPaolo thought, Caesar was beginning to balk.

"You just don't know how hard this is for me to do," Montevecchio started to whine.

DiPaolo showed no pity. "Fuck the drama," the cop said with as much rancor as he could muster. He reminded Caesar of the bargain, the deal. And, he reminded Caesar of Bonnie and the kids.

Again, softly, this hardened local John Dillinger wannabe began to weep. DiPaolo waited.

"If I didn't have all these charges against me, I would never give him up. Never! But I want to see my kids again."

Now Montevecchio was sobbing.

But DiPaolo still wasn't having any of it. "I'm waiting," the detective finally said with deliberately conveyed and obvious impatience. Settling down somewhat, Montevecchio sucked in a deep breath and expelled the name in a single rush of air:

"Anthony! *Anthony*. He's the one."

Believing he actually knew who Caesar was finally fingering, DiPaolo was nonetheless stunned with Montevecchio's sudden brazen revelation. But just to make sure he wasn't mistaken, he asked Montevecchio directly: "Anthony *who*?"

Caesar Montevecchio, now completely wiped out by his confessed betrayal, seemed slightly surprised with the question. "Arnone," Montevecchio sighed. "Anthony Arnone!"

DiPaolo smiled knowingly. He had been right. He long suspected Arnone, especially with the Mastrey connection and his friendship with Montevecchio.

Anthony Arnone! "Niggsy" to the all those in Erie's Little Italy neighborhood – and the wise guys and wise guy wannabes beyond the immediate area. The pieces were beginning to click together in DiPaolo's skull. It was all making so much sense to him now! Arnone owned an Italian import company at West 18th and Cherry Streets, the same building where Montevecchio had visited sometimes daily during various undercover police surveillance operations since Dovishaw was murdered in 1983.

Niggsy's father, Liborio Arnone, also known throughout the neighborhood as "BoBo," died several years earlier. The senior Arnone left the importing business to his son Niggsy. Niggsy had been relatively clean, as far as Erie cops knew. Unlike many others who grew up in Erie's west side Little Italy neighborhood, wise guys or wannabes, Niggsy Arnone's only previous run-ins with the local law had been with illegal gambling and, as a young man, that 1957 fake robbery at Dee's Cigar Store. Niggsy had been indicted by the feds in 1974 – along with 22 of his closest friends – for bookmaking, but served only a few years on probation.

Arnone was also known to be addicted to the ponies, as well as the ongoing, prevalent illegal numbers game in Erie. Word on the street had it that Niggsy would bet the $100 window at various tracks for multiple tickets a race. He was known to have frequented Thistledown in nearby Cleveland, Ohio, at least twice a week, while visiting the local Off Track Betting parlor almost every day, sometimes with Caesar, a Commodore Downs employee would later testify. If ever a person was addicted to gambling, it likely was he.

It now made perfect sense to DiPaolo that sooner or later, Niggsy Arnone, despite the income from his father's importing business, was going to have cash-flow problems. Eventually, DiPaolo thought, Arnone was going to find himself in the same precarious straits as many other compulsive gamblers: He was going to be desperate for more money, extremely desperate.

But Arnone had a history going back many, many years with Dovishaw as well – and that history would inextricably link the two in life, and in Bolo's death.

To many, it might seem like ancient history. But to Dom DiPaolo, who knew the genesis of every wise guy and wannabe in Erie since the 1940s, the 1957 phony robbery at Dee's Cigar Store was as fresh in his mind as the day he reviewed the now yellow-tinted official police records so many years ago. Now, as Caesar Montevecchio was fingering Niggsy Arnone as the one who set up the Bolo Dovishaw hit, DiPaolo again recalled that Frank "Bolo" Dovishaw, then only 20, but already with his eye cast toward the easy money of Erie's dark underworld, hatched his own plan for committing that "perfect" crime. At the time, Bolo thought it was ingenious. And so did Arnone, his longtime, boyhood pal from Little Italy. DiPaolo remembered that an integral part of Frank "Bolo" Dovishaw's plan to get away with robbing Dee's Cigar Store called for the co-conspirators to deposit a large chunk of their illegally-gotten booty in a bank safe-deposit box.

It was illustrative of Bolo's penchant for safe-deposit boxes to hide dirty money, a habit that would eventually and ultimately lead to his violent death. Dom DiPaolo was perceptive enough to figure out that this seemingly small footnote in well-worn newspaper clippings from the 1950s, would 26 years later provide the germ that hatched the conspiracy to kill Dovishaw. The use of bank safe-deposit boxes to stash illegal money would become Dovishaw's lifetime habit – an M.O. remembered by the man eventually suspected of contracting for Bolo's murder. Few could know that Dovishaw kept hundreds of thousands of dollars in gambling receipts in safe-deposit boxes. That Bolo Dovishaw kept the keys to those bank safe-deposit boxes concealed on his person was known to even fewer. Niggsy Arnone knew, DiPaolo believed. He was so certain he was prepared to bet his reputation on it. Niggsy Arnone, a central figure in the botched phony robbery years earlier, who would later take over his family's food-importing business but could not stay out of heavy debt because of his apparent addiction to horse-racing, was one of the few who knew of Dovishaw's stash.

It must have been so very tempting, DiPaolo thought. Arnone probably knew full well how to get at that stash: The keys. The keys Bolo always carried with him. Even more, DiPaolo believed Anthony "Niggsy" Arnone knew exactly how to obtain the keys to Bolo's riches. If it was him indeed, Arnone had an "insider" at the bank – Montevecchio said it was "a woman" – who could help him get to and then open Dovishaw's safe-deposit boxes.

But first things first. First, he had to get the keys. And, DiPaolo speculated, Frank "Bolo" Dovishaw, Arnone also probably knew, would only give them up if he was dead.

Dom DiPaolo, by nature, was not an excitable guy, either on the job or in his private life. Yet with this revelation from Montevecchio, it was difficult for DiPaolo to hide his excitement. Some 30 years after the phony robbery, Caesar Montevecchio was fingering Anthony Arnone as the planner, the arranger of the death of Frank "Bolo" Dovishaw. DiPaolo listened intently as Montevecchio spoke, telling of being approached by Arnone early in 1982.

"Niggsy tells me he's planning to hit Bolo," Montevecchio related calmly, in nonchalant tones, as though he was explaining a pastor's church sermon to an old pal. "He says we can make some really big money."

Caesar said he asked Arnone, "Yeah? How you going to do that? How you going to kill him? And just where's the money coming from?"

"What was Arnone's answer?" DiPaolo asked.

"He said, 'That pig has over $400,000 in cash in his safe-deposit boxes at the bank. And I got an "in" at the bank. All we do is get the keys, then kill the pig, hide his body to give me time to get in there at the bank, and we'll hit the fucking jackpot.'"

Montevecchio told DiPaolo that Arnone promised him a percentage of the take for helping set up the killing and key-snatching. As always, trying to downplay his role, Montevecchio swore to DiPaolo he told Arnone, "'You're fucking sick, man. You better see a doctor.'"

Arnone, however, was persistent, Montevecchio insisted as he continued to outline how they allegedly planned Dovishaw's killing. "'Well?'" Caesar quoted Arnone as asking, "'What do you think?'" Montevecchio told DiPaolo he conveyed to Arnone that he was still skeptical. But Arnone, unwilling to abandon the idea, plowed forward, Montevecchio told the cop.

"'Hey, I rented a safe-deposit box at the same bank,'" Arnone revealed to Montevecchio. "'And whadaya know, it just happens to be right above the pig's box!'"

Montevecchio quoted Arnone as telling him, "She already helped me out with that one," apparently in reference to the "woman."

In life as in death, Bolo didn't get much respect from his contemporaries. "Pig" was Arnone's characterization of Dovishaw. But, sadly for Bolo, Arnone wasn't alone in disdaining Erie's big-time sports betting bookie.

"That's when I knew he was serious," Montevecchio told the cop. "But, y'know, what the hell. It started to seem like a good fucking plan. And who didn't need the money?"

Several days after that first meeting in 1982, the two met again, Montevecchio said. And once the wheels began to turn, it appeared the course was set and Dovishaw's destiny fatefully sealed. During that second meeting, Montevecchio continued, Arnone was full of new details for the murder plan. With the help of the "woman" at the bank, he had it worked out in his mind, Montevecchio said. But he needed Montevecchio. And as long as it involved an easy payday, Caesar Montevecchio wasn't at all bashful in helping carry out the plan.

"'I'll give you $10,000 upfront,'" Arnone promised, according to Montevecchio's recollection of their conversation during that second meeting. "'And the shooter gets $20,000. You handle it. You find the shooter. And don't tell me who. I don't want to know.'"

Before even approaching Montevecchio and presenting the murder plan to him, Arnone knew Caesar would not be the gunman, Caesar told Detective DiPaolo. "That's why he asked me to find someone else. Niggsy knew I had plenty of connections from the old days. He knew I could come up with someone." Ironically, DiPaolo knew that to be true as he recalled Montevecchio's phone call to Giacalone about taking out the cop.

It was almost as though Montevecchio was proud of those connections and his assistance, DiPaolo thought. Even now, facing additional prison time, Caesar's still proud of his long cesspool of a life.

"Okay, I get it. You weren't to be the shooter. You were to find the killer," DiPaolo reiterated somewhat impatiently. He had waited a long time for this. "Then what?"

"We were pulling off a lot of jobs at different joints at the time," Montevecchio shrugged. "After one of them, I asked Bob if he'd consider a hit for twenty big ones."

"Bob?" DiPaolo wanted to make sure of the details, in particular that he was getting all the names right.

"Yeah, Bob. Fucking Bob Dorler. Dorler says, 'Well, yeah. Put the money up front. Sure. Why the fuck not?'"

Montevecchio said he told Robert Dorler he'd have to get back to him later. Then, Caesar went straight to Arnone, Montevecchio said.

"I got someone who needs the money up front," Montevecchio told Niggsy.

"'Oh yeah?'" Montevecchio said Arnone replied. "'Well, fuck him. When it's done, he gets paid. You know damned well that's how we do it. If not, get somebody else.'"

And so, the strategic planning began in earnest.

CHAPTER 28

NOW – AS THOUGH THEY WERE GETTING PREPARED FOR A FIRST Communion or wedding celebration – the murder planning was set firmly in motion. Montevecchio told DiPaolo he and Arnone agreed the Bolo hit would take place on a Monday during the late fall of 1982, hopefully on a night when Frank Dovishaw was busy at home taking action on a Monday night NFL game.

Later, Dorler agreed to accept his payday after the hit was a *fait accompli*. What the hell, Dorler had agreed, either way $20,000 was $20,000. As the planning and preparation process progressed, Dorler drove to Erie and, with an eager Montevecchio, did a drive-by on Bolo's house. "Make sure, now, that you put Bolo's body in the trunk of his own car – the green Caddy – and drive it back to Cleveland before you abandon the car," Montevecchio instructed.

DiPaolo was fascinated at the meticulous detail that went into one killing. "Then what?" was all he could impatiently ask when Montevecchio paused briefly.

"So then I told Dorler about the money Bolo kept in his house under that vanity in the bathroom. And I also told him to be sure he searched Bolo's car as well. Bolo always keeps a stash there, too."

He told DiPaolo that "Chuckie Serafini and Bo Baumann hit Bolo before and got big money – $50,000-plus – from the vanity." Then Montevecchio said something that chilled the Erie cop like never before. "I told him, 'Get his bank safe-deposit box keys! Make sure you get two of them. And Jesus Christ, be sure that you get them before you waste fucking Bolo.'"

DiPaolo let out a breath. "And what did Dorler say to that?" the Erie cop probed further.

"He just said, 'Okay.' Oh, yeah . . . and then he smiled."

On a Monday night in December of 1982, Medina, Ohio's Robert Dorler was to meet Caesar Montevecchio at West 38th Street and Washington Avenue in Erie at exactly 6 p.m. The plan was for Caesar to drop off Dorler within an easy walk of Dovishaw's house. During the winter, however, "easy" becomes a relative term – and much dependent on Erie's always fickle and quickly changing weather conditions. Plus, the drive from Ohio on a winter's night had to be considered iffy as well. The plan called for Dorler to quickly pull off the hit, get money from the house, and possibly the car, but most importantly he would collect the valuable keys to Bolo's bank safe-deposit boxes. Next, Dorler was to load Dovishaw's body into the green Cadillac's spacious trunk and drive west to Cleveland, where he would abandon the vehicle in a location where it was unlikely to be discovered for days or even weeks.

But even before Dorler could come to Erie that night, Montevecchio said he was forced to call off the hit. "Cy Ciotti's car was parked in Bolo's driveway. Cy had been staying with Bolo. I felt, geez, no fucking need to complicate things even more."

Caesar told DiPaolo a new date was set, one in which Ciotti would be told to be away. It was to be a red-letter day sometime after the holidays, but not too long after: Monday, January 3, 1983.

CHAPTER 29

WHILE CAREER CRIMINAL CAESAR MONTEVECCHIO CONTINUED to wax elegant in his talkative mood, Dominick DiPaolo wasn't about to do anything foolish to slow him down. No, not at this stage in the investigation! DiPaolo had worked too hard, had waited too long, had been through too much with his own family, to risk a single miscue or misspoken comment at the wrong time to skew Montevecchio's often rambling confession. Caesar was putting together the January 3, 1983, Bolo Dovishaw murder in a way even the veteran Erie Police investigator had not allowed himself to dare dream possible. All of the months and years of work were finally coming together and paying off.

DiPaolo was content to let Caesar talk. And talk he did, almost non-stop. Once started, it was like an advancing powerful locomotive – difficult to brake to a stop. And now, Montevecchio actually was getting close to the moment of truth. The new date for the "Ash Wednesday" hit finally had been selected.

It was at that time, however, when Caesar found it necessary to first meet with his old pal, Joe Scutella, who would soon become infamous in his own right for arranging to torch his family-run restaurant in the heart of downtown Erie. For starters, Montevecchio wanted to make damned sure this time that Cy Ciotti was out of the house when Dorler arrived to accomplish his mission. Ciotti's presence had spoiled the intended hit once, and Montevecchio was ensuring there wouldn't be a repeat performance by instructing Scutella to advise Cy it would be in his own best interest to not be around that night.

Scutella quickly agreed, but had some inquiries of his own for Montevecchio, Caesar informed the cop. "Joey wanted to know who the shooter was," Montevecchio matter-of-factly told DiPaolo, much in the same way co-workers often share Monday morning boring and mundane events with each other after a long weekend. But Montevecchio wasn't talking about barbecues or family outings. He was nonchalantly discussing the snuffing out of a human life, the life of a man Montevecchio had known almost since early childhood.

When Montevecchio met with Scutella, however, Caesar was careful to hold his cards close to his vest, he told DiPaolo. The set-up man had been intent on not revealing too much, even to his longtime partner in crime, Pal Joey.

"I didn't want anyone to know it would be Bob Dorler who was wasting Bolo," Montevecchio disclosed. "Not Joey. Not even Niggsy. Nobody would know, period." And so Caesar would later say in open court.

Montevecchio took in a deep breath and smiled. It was that sardonic, cold smile DiPaolo knew so well. "So I told him it was Louie Raffa, you know, we call him 'Lumpy Lou.' He would never know the difference, anyway, so why should I give up that kind of valuable insider information? Better, I thought, if only I knew who the shooter would be. What difference would it make to Joey anyway? And, shit, man, he would be no worse off for not knowing."

It was then, Montevecchio said, Scutella made an interesting, yet not all that surprising proposal. It wasn't surprising to DiPaolo, who had by now come to expect such thinking from the lowest of Erie's low.

"Scutella tells me, 'Tell your hit I'll give him $10,000 more if that fucking Ray (Ferritto) is there.'"

"Ray?" Caesar Montevecchio repeated the name, as though merely for effect. "'Fuckin' A,' Scutella said. 'I would love to finally see that cocksucker dead.'"

The hit man Ferritto, whom DiPaolo knew all the way back to his high school days, was feared and hated in almost equal doses by most of the Erie-based wise guys or wannabes. It was the nature of the beast for those at the top of the underworld heap; always someone wanting to step up by having the kingpin knocked off. On the surface, perhaps they all got along famously in their many illicit endeavors. But behind-the-scenes, the chinks in Ferritto's armor were obvious. Still, although he might not have the respect of the wise guys, Dom DiPaolo knew they were wise in at least one sense: To the man, they all feared Ray Ferritto.

Montevecchio said he promised Joey Scutella he'd pass along the offer to the shooter. Shortly after, just as he had promised, and while Montevecchio and Dorler were working out final details for the killing of the Erie bookie, Caesar broached the Raymond Ferritto "bonus" hit with the Ohio shooter. Robert Dorler didn't have to be asked twice. A two-fer! the shooter thought. An extra 10 grand. Nice payday, indeed. Sure he would do it.

Monday, January 3, 1983, the last day of "Bolo" Dovishaw's wasted life, dawned in Erie cold, gray and ugly. The day was almost as ugly as the hearts of those who would kill him for his money – almost, but not quite. The co-conspirators who plotted to murder Erie's numbers and illegal gambling leader had already placed their plan into motion. This time, there would be no more screw-ups and innocent bystanders in the way. This time, all involved knew, there would be no going back.

The day started, according to Caesar Montevecchio's confession to Dom DiPaolo, with a long distance telephone call from Cleveland to Montevecchio. "Billy (Bourjaily) called me trying to score some cocaine," Montevecchio said. He was going to drive here from Cleveland," Caesar told the detective, on just the chance Caesar could secure cocaine from his local source. At first, Montevecchio thought the timing, given the events that would transpire later that night, was out of sync. But then, he reconsidered, partly because of his greed to perhaps make a profit on the coke, and partly because he was watching his own back.

Montevecchio didn't want William Bourjaily to know anything about the planned Dovishaw hit scheduled for later. Still, Caesar shrewdly figured, he could "kill two birds with one stone." He'd meet Bourjaily in Erie on the cocaine score, while at the same time developing a solid alibi for himself should circumstances eventually dictate he would need one.

"It seemed a pretty slick move at the time," Montevecchio proudly boasted to the Erie police officer. "It would boost me in two ways. First, of course, the coke score, and then I'd have a perfect alibi. So I figured, why the hell not?"

With Bourjaily still on the phone, Caesar silently calculated the timetable for Bolo's planned murder before telling the Ohio man to meet him in Erie and at what time. "I told him to meet me at exactly six o'clock at The Page," Montevecchio told DiPaolo.

The "Page," short for "The Sports Page," was a popular west Erie neighborhood bar known for its reasonably priced beer and tasty hot pizza. The bar was owned by Pete Pallotto, DiPaolo's cousin, and Richard Carideo. DiPaolo was known to hang out there, too, especially during the summer months as he ran The Page's softball teams for many years. The bar was frequented by a varied clientele that included lawyers, Erie School District administrators, cops, judges, newspaper writers, and those representing most of the professions, along with a collection of neighborhood regulars from the politically active Sixth Ward, all comfortably mixing in conversations of politics and athletics with their Miller and Bud Lites and pepperoni and cheese pizzas. A local crime figure, such as the bookie "Big Al" DelSandro, would occasionally meet his old-time buddy Dominick Padovani, aka "Uncle Paddy," for a drink at The Page. Uncle Paddy resided in a room at the Nomad Motel.

Montevecchio had also figured that The Page was situated along busy West 26th Street, with an easy access to Interstate 79 as well as Interstate 90, the shortest, quickest and most direct route between Cleveland and Erie. What could be better? Montevecchio thought with some satisfaction.

Once the meeting with Bourjaily was set, Caesar continued, he telephoned Joey Scutella to make sure the downtown restaurant owner had gotten Cy Ciotti out of Bolo Dovishaw's house. With Anthony "Cy" Ciotti's presence at Bolo's house in December still weighing heavily in Montevecchio's mind, Caesar didn't want yet another execution rescheduling. Considering himself to be a "detail man," Montevecchio told DiPaolo that he made damn sure to take care of this final lingering detail. "Joey did his job. He got Cy out of there over the weekend, which is just what we needed to happen," Montevecchio said, obviously pleased with his social planning skills. Joey had learned Cy was in Covington, Kentucky, and headed to Pittsburgh. So Joey got Cy's phone number from Vinnie DiPasquale and had the message delivered.

Caesar added, ironically, there was no honor among thieves. "Bolo was Cy's meal ticket for many, many years and he just stepped aside as Bolo was going down."

Montevecchio also advised Arnone that day that he would call him later. Caesar said Arnone told him again about the safe-deposit box keys and said, "The Pig had to get new boxes because he'd lost his fuckin' keys, but the new boxes are in a great area. Get those fuckin' keys!"

At this point, Dom DiPaolo felt the need to interrupt, asking Montevecchio whether there was more conversation about whacking Raymond Ferritto while Dovishaw was being hit. The cop always had been intrigued with the inner-workings of the local wise guys, and who was "in" or "out" of the loop at any given moment.

"Well, it was looking good for us," Montevecchio continued. "So, I asked Joey if he still wanted Ray killed if Ferritto happened to be in Bolo's house when the shooter arrived. And he says 'fuckin'-A' he did."

Montevecchio also had a secondary, self-serving reason for telephoning Scutella.

"I told him that I'd need some stuff, y'know, the coke, for later that night," Montevecchio said.

It was another admission DiPaolo wisely tucked away just in case he needed the valuable information for future reference. The bragging Montevecchio had just told the cop that Joey Scutella was Caesar's supplier of the white powder. And now, it was DiPaolo's turn to smile to himself.

By 6 p.m. that night, as was expected for a January evening, the temperature had dropped noticeably. Most native Erieites didn't mind, however. They were used to hard winters. Although sub-freezing temperatures are a natural phenomenon for January in northwestern Pennsylvania, Caesar worried most of the day that the notorious Lake Effect weather – the kind that often dumps feet, not inches, of snow on Erie – would pre-empt the plan to kill Bolo Dovishaw. Lake Effect snow often involved a wider area from Cleveland to Buffalo. So far, however, the night was just cold, frigid, and the snow was limited to occasional flurries.

The plan, Montevecchio now told DiPaolo as his words came somewhat faster, called for Robert Dorler to meet him at the Laundromat at West 38th and Washington Avenue, a few miles south of ground zero – Frank "Bolo" Dovishaw's residence. It was a small, coin-operated self-serve facility directly across the street from the popular all-night Panos' Greek restaurant, which served up daily doses of heartburn with its tasty patented Greek 'burgers, 'dogs and 'fries.

Dorler arrived on time, dropped off at the almost vacant corner Laundromat in southwest Erie by his wife, who quickly turned the car around and immediately headed back to the safety of Medina, Ohio.

"Here's how it was supposed to work," Montevecchio continued to relate to the fascinated cop DiPaolo. "After the hit, Bob was supposed to meet me and give me the safe-deposit box keys. Then he was supposed to drive Bolo's Caddy back to Cleveland and dump it there with Fat Boy's body nicely tucked in the trunk. It would have taken a really long fucking time for someone to finally find the car." Caesar sighed, "But, as you already now know, it didn't fucking work out that way. No, not by a fucking long shot it didn't. Thanks to fucking Dorler."

DiPaolo nodded knowingly, but he decided to remain silent, thus using the non-verbal pause to encourage Caesar Montevecchio to continue. Montevecchio remained silent for a long moment, too, as though he had somehow been magically transported back in time to that early 1983 January night. He seemed almost lost in thought. But with another deep breath, Montevecchio must have felt that compulsion to continue.

"Well, Bob Dorler was really dressed for the role," Montevecchio said with a shrug. "He was wearing a suit and tie under a black top coat. He was also carrying. But you know already that."

DiPaolo nodded, then interrupted. "Sure I know that. But tell me, what was he using?"

"A Beretta. Small caliber. It looked like a .32, I think. Somehow, for some weird reason, he preferred Berettas. Definitely, it was his favorite make."

"Then what happened?" the detective quietly probed to keep the confession moving forward.

"We talked again about the plan, y'know, just to make sure we were on the same page. I'd drop him off in Bolo's neighborhood on West 21st Street, then meet him about an hour later at the Station on Peach Street." Montevecchio said the plan called for Dorler to be driving Dovishaw's car.

"He knew how to get to the Station." The Station Restaurant was not far from the Laundromat at Peach Street and Washington Avenue. From there, it would be a straight shot along Peach Street south to Interstate 90 and the return trip for Dorler to Medina, Ohio, with a stop in Cleveland to dump Dovishaw's green Caddy.

"He would get the safe-deposit box keys from Bolo, then kill him, put the body in the trunk of Bolo's Caddy, then meet me at the Station in about an hour to drop off the keys. At least that was the plan, anyway. It seemed really good enough to work. Only Dorler couldn't get the fat pig Dovishaw into the fucking car. That's when all the problems started."

Going back to just before the murder, Montevecchio said he dropped off Dorler in Dovishaw's neighborhood as planned, then drove straight to The Sports Page bar several blocks away. Once there, he said he patiently waited for William Bourjaily to arrive. Early on a January Monday night, "The Page" wasn't crowded. Die-hard patrons were just beginning to drift in, and Caesar greeted the few of them he knew by their first names. One was Ray Kovalesky, a Tech High School teacher who attended the University of Detroit, and, like Montevecchio, it was almost his alma mater. (DiPaolo later described Kovalesky as getting extremely loud when drinking.) As soon as the teacher saw his old pal, he made a beeline for him. Kovalesky would be a good witness corroborating Montevecchio's story. But he refused to get involved – a move that not only infuriated DiPaolo, but resulted in DiPaolo seeking a subpoena forcing the testimony. DiPaolo went to Tech High School and served Kovalesky in his classroom. Kovalesky went wild. About a year later, DiPaolo walked into The Sports Page after a slo-pitch game and from across the bar, Kovalesky yelled, "You mother fucker! I hope you die for what you did to me." DiPaolo ignored him, but the large crowd of onlookers began to laugh at Kovalesky, who became louder and louder. Finally, Rich Carideo, The Page's owner, said, "That's it Ray, get the fuck out and don't come back again." Kovalesky left, and was not seen again at The Page.

But now, on that fateful evening, as far as anyone at The Page knew, it was just another routine Monday night for Caesar who was out for a beer.

"I was only there for a few minutes when Billy Bourjaily walked in," Caesar told DiPaolo. "As soon as he showed up, I tried to call

Scutella from the bar phone. But his daughter, Kelli answered and said Joe wasn't home. But she said she would tell her dad that I was looking for him."

While Montevecchio killed time with Bourjaily, the two men ordered drinks and exchanged small talk with several bar patrons, Caesar said. One of the "regulars," "Benny Zoom" Szumigala, who owned Teresa's Deli, bought Caesar and his buddy drinks. (Several months later, in May 1983, Benny's dad's house was broken into. When Caesar and "the boys" were arrested for the burglary, Benny later told DiPaolo, "I bought that piece of shit a drink the night he was in The Page when they killed Bolo, then he robs my father. The next time you see him, spit in his face and tell him it's from Benny." Then Szumigala laughed.)

Montevecchio continued his story: "Then, I tried to call Joe again. It was probably a quarter to seven. This time he answered. I told him I was looking for that stuff. But he really wanted to know whether Porky was still breathing, if you know what I mean. I said I didn't know. But I told him I'd try calling him later with whatever news I might have had at the time." According to what Montevecchio told DiPaolo, he returned to Bourjaily, telling him the cocaine was a "no-go" for the time being. By 7 p.m., Caesar was getting antsy. He knew it was time to meet the killer Dorler at the Station Restaurant and told Bourjaily they needed to leave. "So, we took off right away," Montevecchio said. "I told Billy to follow me in his car to the Station."

As it turned out, Montevecchio thought later than night, it was a probably a great stroke of good luck for all of them that Billy Bourjaily was in town. He would be needed to drive the shooter back to Ohio.

When Caesar Montevecchio pulled into the Station's parking lot on upper Peach Street, Robert Dorler was unmistakable, still dressed in black. Dorler arrived a short time before Montevecchio. He was standing in front of Bolo's large green Caddy, stomping his feet to keep warm, waiting impatiently, Montevecchio related. "I approached him and we began to talk about what happened at Bolo's," Montevecchio said. "He started to tell me, but stopped short when he saw Billy pulling into the parking lot and then getting out of his car. Actually, he got pretty pissed at the sight of Billy."

Montevecchio thought a moment, then continued, saying Dorler demanded, "What the fuck is he doing here?"

"I told him Billy was here on a coke deal and to never fucking mind him. I was only interested in what happened at Bolo's. I mean, that's why we were there, y'know."

Montevecchio paused again, as if to catch his breath. But these now frequent pauses were beginning to annoy DiPaolo. He wondered whether the pauses were the result of Montevecchio trying to keep his facts straight, or because he couldn't believe he was actually about to confess to a cop about being party to a premeditated killing. Either way, DiPaolo, prodded again. "Go on," DiPaolo said with determination and authority, "what did Dorler tell you?"

"Well, Dorler says, 'Bolo is dead.' Then he says, 'Here are the keys.' It was like, you know, so far so good. He hands me both safe-deposit box keys. So I think everything is fine and we're home free. But then he says he couldn't lift Bolo and get him into the trunk. So he just left him there. Dead. In the basement."

Even though it was years later, Montevecchio was still incredulous as he retold the story to DiPaolo. "What a dumb fuck!" Caesar lamented. "And I told him so, too. I told him he just fucked everything up. But he kept insisting Porky was just too big for one person to lift. And he thought everything would be okay because he covered Bolo's body with a rug and with some clothes he found in the basement. So much for all that good fucking planning."

Standing there in the cold, Caesar Montevecchio said, it didn't take the group of three very long to come up with what they believed was a solid "Plan B."

"We all agreed the best thing was to dump Bolo's car where it wouldn't be found at least right away, and then get those two – Bob and Billy – out of town as fast as possible." The new plan, Caesar explained to the cop, was to leave Bolo's car in the rear parking lot at the Holiday Inn South at Route 97 and Interstate 90.They couldn't take the chance of driving the car to Cleveland in case the body was found and his car reported stolen, Caesar said.

Dorler would drive Dovishaw's car to the Holiday Inn, and Bourjaily would follow in his own car. Once Bolo's car was abandoned, Bourjaily would drive Dorler back to Medina. Considering all that had gone down that night, it seemed like a good alternative, Montevecchio said.

"So that's what they did," he continued. "They dumped the car at the Holiday Inn in the rear lot in between a few other parked cars and then they headed back to Ohio."

"What were you doing while they were dumping the car?" DiPaolo asked.

"Well, you know, I had to report what had gone down to Anthony."

"Arnone?"

"The very same."

"How did you contact him?"

"I just drove back to the Laundromat at 38th and Washington and then called Niggsy from the pay phone there. I told him he could find me right there at the Laundromat because, you know, we sure as hell didn't want to actually talk about what happened over the phone."

"Did Arnone immediately agree to meet you there?" DiPaolo asked. "Or, was there more conversation about it?"

"Oh yeah, he agreed to come. And it didn't take him long to get there. As soon as he showed up, I handed him the safe-deposit box keys. But then I had to tell him that Bolo's body was still in the house, that he weighed too much for the shooter to move him all by himself."

"And how did Niggsy respond to that news?"

"Pretty much the same way I did. He was pissed. Very pissed. He started complaining and bitching that we were all going to end up in jail."

Suddenly, Montevecchio stopped talking. For the first time, it now apparently dawned on him that Arnone had been right on that first night so long ago as rigor mortis was just starting to set in to Bolo Dovishaw's body. Ironically, Detective Sergeant DiPaolo was thinking the exact same thought.

As the two men allegedly huddled outside one of Erie's countless coin-operated laundries that frigid January night in 1983, at least one of them had an inner sense that their perfect murder might be beginning to go awry. They had managed to successfully whack Erie gambling giant Bolo Dovishaw. They had even gotten the keys to his safe-deposit boxes and were eagerly looking ahead to the treasures inside them. But the Ohio shooter, Robert Dorler, could not budge the overweight Bolo, let alone get all that dead-weight of his corpse up Dovishaw's cellar steps and into the Cadillac's trunk. So Dorler left dead Bolo in the basement, covered with an old rug and dirty laundry.

Caesar Montevecchio, the middleman in the complex murder plot, continued to relate the intimate details of that night's activities to DiPaolo, particularly Montevecchio's later meeting with Erie businessman Anthony "Niggsy" Arnone, who Montevecchio insisted had arranged for the killing. Arnone, Montevecchio told DiPaolo, was still fuming after learning Bolo's body was not driven to Cleveland as planned, but abandoned at his house, and his car dumped in the parking lot of a local Holiday Inn. Now Arnone was fearing the worst, Montevecchio told the veteran Erie cop.

"So, we're standing there and he's saying that we're all going to end up in prison," Caesar Montevecchio continued. "But hey, I was pissed off, too. But I told him, 'Just go do your thing with those bank safe-deposit boxes and let me worry about everything else.'"

DiPaolo could tell that even at that early juncture, with Bolo's body not yet cold in the basement, the conspirators' careful planning was coming apart. Montevecchio said, "I still thought we were pretty much home free, especially if everyone kept their fucking mouths shut. I was looking ahead to a nice fuckin' payday. We almost got away with it. Look how many years it took you to get to me." Montevecchio would later testify to all of what he told DiPaolo.

CHAPTER 30

THE NEXT DAY, JANUARY 4, 1983, DAWNED JUST AS COLD AND GLOOMY as the previous day, the day of Dovishaw's last meatball sub.

"I called Niggsy at his place about noon," Montevecchio disclosed to DiPaolo. "All he said was, 'I have something for you. Stop over.'"

"Did you meet with him?" DiPaolo asked.

"Yeah, but first I called Dorler in Ohio. I told him I'd meet him at that pancake house along Interstate 90, you know the one, 'Mr. C's' or something like that. It's right off the Ashtabula and Warren exit."

"What was that all about?"

"Well, I was thinkin' that after I met with Niggsy, I'd have something for Dorler. You know, get it over with so there would be no more loose ends for us to tie up," as he would later say in court.

Arnone's Italian import business at the corner of West 18th and Cherry Streets was just down 18th Street from the popular Sons of Italy Club and the National Club at West 17th and Cherry, with a favorite Italian funeral home, St. George, close by, as well as the Calabrese, LaNuova Aurora and Knights of St. George Clubs and many other businesses reflecting Westside Erie's Italian ethnicity and culture. When Montevecchio arrived at the importing business shortly after noon, a nervous Anthony "Niggsy" Arnone quickly ushered Caesar to a long-vacant second floor apartment in the century-old brick and frame building, Montevecchio said.

"When we get up there, he tells me there is much less than he had thought there would be in Bolo's safe-deposit boxes," Montevecchio said. "Of course, that wasn't what the fuck I wanted to hear."

"Then what?"

"Then he hands me a brown paper bag filled with cash, a lot of cash. He says, 'That's for the shooter. Twenty grand. Just like we agreed to. I'll get the rest to you later. Fuck, this has already cost me thirty seven thousand dollars!'"

Arnone, fidgeting uncharacteristically according to Caesar, also handed over to Montevecchio, Dovishaw's bank safe-deposit box keys and issued a new set of instructions.

"He says, 'Put the fuckin' keys back into Bolo's car, wherever the hell you have it stashed.' I still wanted to know more, y'know, like when I'd get the rest of the money. But he just wanted everything to go away. Including me."

Fascinating how these wannabe big shots acted when they were scared, DiPaolo thought to himself, but decided against commenting to the talkative Montevecchio.

"So Niggsy tells me to leave. He says, 'Just get the hell out of here. I'm fuckin' nervous enough as it is already. Just leave, plant the keys in the car, and we'll talk later.' So, I left. With the money and the keys."

With dry road conditions, the drive west along Interstate 90 to Mr. C's Pancake House, strategically situated almost exactly halfway between Erie and Cleveland, took Montevecchio slightly less than an hour. The road conditions were excellent for the dead of winter, so Montevecchio made good time, even though he was cognizant about speeding. It would make no sense to get stopped and ticketed by either Pennsylvania or Ohio state troopers, he knew. The restaurant itself was located directly off the exit ramp. It had long been a popular roadside eatery for locals and travelers alike, including long-haul truckers. The prices were cheap enough and the food relatively good. Especially popular was the all-day breakfast fare.

"Both of them were already there I when I pulled in," Caesar Montevecchio told DiPaolo.

"Both?" DiPaolo asked for clarity.

"Yeah, the both of 'em. You know, Bob Dorler and Billy Bourjaily."

"Hmmm, were you surprised that Bourjaily was with Dorler at the time?"

"Not really. Actually, I kinda expected it."

"What happened next?"

"I gave the bag of money to Dorler. He just nodded. But then I gave him the safe-deposit box keys. I told him he needed to get the keys back into Bolo's car, you know, so it wouldn't look like anything was missing when the car was eventually found by the cops or whoever." Montevecchio paused, took a deep breath and became somewhat pensive.

After a minute, maybe two, DiPaolo again prodded, "So, okay, how did Dorler respond to that?"

"Not very well. At first he just flat out fucking refused to do it. He says, 'You want the keys back in the car, then *you* put the keys in the car. No way in fuckin' hell I'm driving all the way back into Erie. The car's at the Holiday Inn. The one off I-90.You fucking do it.'"

Now it was DiPaolo's turn to pause for a moment. "So how'd you convince him to change his mind?" the Erie detective finally asked.

"I told him to go fuck himself. I was yelling at him. I shouted, 'Fuck you! That's part of the deal, man. You know I can't go anywhere near that goddamned car! Are you outta your fuckin' mind?'"

"So Dorler took the keys after all? Reluctantly?"

"Yeah, I guess you could probably say that. Reluctantly. He wasn't at all happy, but he took them and he agreed to get them into Bolo's car." Without there being much left to be said, the three men parted company, Montevecchio said.

Prior to driving to meet Dorler and Bourjaily at "Mr. C.'s" restaurant, Montevecchio told the detective, he had made a recognizance drive by the Holiday Inn parking lot where Bolo Dovishaw's car had been abandoned just the night before.

"There was nothing there. No activity. Nothing," he said. "Just an occasional car coming or going."

Then, once again, on Caesar Montevecchio's return drive back to Erie from the Ohio pancake house, he also felt compelled to cruise past the hotel parking lot. "Still quiet. Nothing," he told the cop.

But later, about 11 p.m., while driving past the intersection of Greengarden Road and West 21st Street, a location from which Montevecchio could easily observe Frank "Bolo" Dovishaw's home, the scene was now anything but tranquil.

"It scared the shit outta me," Montevecchio said. "There were fuckin' cop cars everywhere!"

The next day, Wednesday, January 5, 1983, was again cold, but now snowy. As Montevecchio continued his account of the days immediately following Frank "Bolo" Dovishaw's murder, Caesar said the snow didn't stop him from driving to Arnone's import business and warehouse in Little Italy.

"When I walked into his office, I could see right away that Niggsy was not only worried, but now he was clearly upset. Apparently, he had a major problem at the bank where Bolo had his safe deposit boxes."

"Yeah? What kind of a problem would that be?" DiPaolo wanted to know. Although the detective was already very familiar with some parts of Montevecchio's account, others he was now hearing for the first time.

"He said that when he walked into the bank, there were too many people around. He got scared and left. Then later, when he came back to the bank again, he said there were still way too many customers around. So he says he took out a loan to 'make it look good,' you know, to give him some kind of a legitimate reason for being there at the bank, but the dumb fuck had to sign his name for the loan. I mean, how fuckin' stupid can you be?"

During their conversation, Montevecchio said, as Niggsy discussed his contact at the bank, Caesar said Arnone mentioned "she" at least several times. Now DiPaolo was getting information that could lead to a game of connect the dots as he believed the noose was beginning to tighten on Niggsy Arnone. Yet still nonchalant, DiPaolo asked, "Yeah? So who's the woman?"

"Like I told you at first, I don't know, at least not for sure. Arnone never told me or anyone else who it was. But I'm thinking it had to be Theresa. Theresa Mastrostefano Mastrey. You know, Niggsy's first cousin who works right there at the bank. They're *cuginos*." Niggsy Arnone's mother, Rose Giamanco Arnone, and Theresa Mastrey's mother, Anna Giamanco-Altadonna Palilla, were sisters.

Even more important, DiPaolo believed, was that Theresa Mastrey, the assistant bank manager where Bolo Dovishaw kept his sacred safe-deposit boxes, could be an integral part of Niggsy Arnone's scam, although she consistently denied any involvement.

"Was that all that transpired during your meeting with Niggsy on the 5th?" DiPaolo asked, hoping Montevecchio would not detect how fast the cop's heart was beating.

"No, there's a little more. Niggsy wanted me to get rid of those bank bags he snatched from the safe deposit boxes."

"Well, did you?"

"Fuck no! I don't know why he didn't dump them himself. But he said he would get 'The Hawk,' you know, Serafini, to do it for him."

"Why the hell would Serafini agree to put himself squarely in the middle of something that could come back and bite him in the ass?"

"Money. Because he ain't got none," Montevecchio replied. "Then he told me it was the Hawk," adding that Arnone often treated Serafini like a little brother.

The interview with Caesar Montevecchio was proceeding even much better than DiPaolo had initially hoped. It appeared to DiPaolo that at last Montevecchio was truly telling all he knew about Frank "Bolo" Dovishaw's murder on January 3, 1983, even disclosing his own role in allegedly arranging the hit for Erie businessman Anthony "Niggsy" Arnone. But DiPaolo had learned long before from practical experience to be skeptical, even cynical, even in the best of circumstances when dealing with any career criminal, especially Caesar Montevecchio. Montevecchio was no longer the innocent altar boy and high school football hero of so many years earlier. A pathological liar who was willing to do anything dishonest for money, Montevecchio would not be one to reform overnight, DiPaolo knew. That's why the cop was wary of anything passing Montevecchio's lips. Still, DiPaolo was prepared to listen as Caesar continued to relate his version of Dovishaw's untimely death and unseemly aftermath. Montevecchio continued:

Two days after their January 5 meeting, Caesar said, Arnone telephoned Montevecchio at his home wanting to set up yet another meeting. "He wanted to meet again at the warehouse," Montevecchio said. When Montevecchio got there, just a short drive from Montevecchio's own home, Caesar said Arnone was beside himself, seething with anger at none other than one Dominick DiPaolo.

"He says, 'That fucking DiPaolo went to the bank, then drilled Bolo's boxes and found the money and some jewelry. But he don't suspect nothin' about us." Montevecchio said Arnone told him he had been tipped off and warned by the woman, who cautioned Niggsy the tenacious pain-in-the-ass detective was now "asking a lot of questions" at the bank branch where she worked. "But Niggsy said she told him nobody saw nothin' and that he thought we were still pretty much home-free. Arnone told me he left something like 10-to-20 grand and jewelry that was Bolo's mother's, so that there would be no suspicions that the boxes had been scored."

DiPaolo knew the only female he dealt with at the bank since the investigation began was Mastrey, the assistant manager. It was such a fine bit of rich irony, the detective thought to himself. With Arnone taking money from the bank boxes and giving some of it to Robert Dorler, Frank "Bolo" Dovishaw had in reality unintentionally paid for his own execution. Montevecchio would later say as much in court.

"Anything more?" a now weary Detective Sergeant DiPaolo asked Caesar Montevecchio when it appeared Montevecchio was nearing the end of his long, often rambling narrative of greed, betrayal and murder.

"Well, yeah. After Bolo was hit, when I was in jail on all the other stuff you threw at me, Arnone often gave Bonnie money. I knew it was Bolo's money he was giving, but at least she was getting something. A couple of times it was a few grand. So, you know, I feel pretty bad about all this, about shitting the bed on Anthony."

But Caesar did not feel bad enough to cover for his one-time friend, Niggsy Arnone, DiPaolo thought. Montevecchio still wasn't done. He related what he knew about the Aziz hit in Cleveland later the same year Bolo was killed and a call he received from the Dovishaw hit man, Robert Dorler.

"Just before I was arrested in 1983, Dorler called me. He wanted me to be a part of the hit on Aziz in July. But I begged off – too many things were happening. So I was glad to just hook up Dorler with 'Fat Sam.' You know, everything Fatso told you back then was true. Even the cocaine I got for Esper came from Dorler."

It had been an exhausting 10 hours for both Montevecchio and DiPaolo. They agreed to take a break until the next day. DiPaolo needed the time to reflect on Caesar's confession. But he knew he still had more to do. Much more.

He needed to confirm everything Montevecchio claimed, Caesar's entire account of the Dovishaw killing, including why Cy Ciotti was sent out of town for the weekend before the hit. Quickly, however, it all checked out. Montevecchio's account of the money and jewelry left in the bank boxes was also accurate – $10,000 to $12,000; relatively little compared to what Dovishaw had taken in, plus his mother's valuables.

But still, DiPaolo would have to wait to learn if Montevecchio's final promise – that Bourjaily would sing as well when he was returned to Erie – would become reality. And more, Montevecchio also insisted that Ricky Cimino would reveal all that transpired in connection with the Pal Joey's fire. At this point, DiPaolo was finding little reason to doubt Caesar.

What remained to be done was comparing how Dorler's statement, related to DiPaolo at the conclusion of the killer's first visit to the state grand jury in Westmoreland County, matched up with Montevecchio's rambling tale. The job of tying it all together, DiPaolo knew, was just beginning.

Just as Caesar Montevecchio was giving up so much, Erie County ADA Tim Lucas phoned DiPaolo at the Attorney General's Office. "Dominick, good news!" Lucas said. "The Superior Court reversed (Judge) Nygaard. All the original charges are reinstated! Didn't I tell you Nygaard fucked up! I already talked with your buddy Veshecco and he and I would like to package these charges with Caesar's others and have him plead to these with the same deal. Could you arrange that with Caesar and the Office of the Attorney General?"

"No problem!" the cop replied. "Do you want to call Lenny – or do you want me to?" DiPaolo added with a wry smile.

DiPaolo told Montevecchio about the reinstated charges, offering him the same deal by pleading guilty to the burglary charges that were dismissed in 1983. Knowing when he was beaten, Montevecchio replied, "Whatever I have to do I will."

Now that the 1980 Nardo burglary was back in play, DiPaolo demanded a full explanation from Montevecchio about who was involved and where the stolen goods ended up. The statute of limitations had expired on anyone else's involvement, but now DiPaolo was thinking of toying with some of those "who broke my balls" way back when.

Montevecchio began by saying the Louie Nardo house burglary and safe job was "the craziest" with which he was ever involved. Montevecchio termed Tony DeMauro one of his best 10-percenters – the man who first put Montevecchio onto the Nardo score.

How did it go down? First, after learning of this sweet deal, Caesar telephoned his pals in Warren, Ohio: Amil and Jimmy Dinsio. The Dinsios drove to Erie to scope out the job. Although Bob Bocci was originally supposed to join them on the job, Montevecchio said, he backed out at the last minute.

According to Montevecchio, DeMauro wanted Nardo to be hit on a Tuesday night. But Montevecchio said that would not go down well as he played poker every Tuesday and "it would look funny if all of a sudden I wasn't at the game." He hosted the game at his late mother's home.

It nonetheless turned out to be a Tuesday that late November of 1980 while he was playing cards that Tony DeMauro walked in and announced the burglary was going down that night. Montevecchio initially disputed DeMauro's claim, saying Nardo's wasn't supposed to be hit until the following Wednesday.

Just then, several men walked in and sat nearby, so the conversation of the Nardo burglary came to an abrupt end. Montevecchio told Bocci, "Let's take a ride." The two got into Bocci's car and drove to Nardo's Glenwood Estates home. After exiting the car, as Montevecchio cautiously approached the house, he first spied the wide open front door. The next thing he saw was a bright gold pocket watch lying on the sidewalk near the front door. Stooping to scoop up the watch as he headed for the door, Montevecchio was momentarily stunned when someone inside the house fired off a gun shot at him.

Bocci immediately took off in the car, with Montevecchio now running in the street to catch up. Eventually, Bocci circled back and picked up Montevecchio.

"What a mother fucker! They were shooting and the crazy fucking Bocci left me there. I didn't know what the hell was going on," Montevecchio said in his statement. After being picked up, the two drove back to the card game at Montevecchio's mother's house and quickly pulled Tony DeMauro aside. Tony told them he had set up the burglary with the Dinsios because it was raining that night – with nobody out walking around, less chance of being observed by nosy witnesses – and that he arranged for the burglars to take the loot to Carl Stellato's farm house, just southwest of Erie in McKean Township, where it would be divvied up among the participants.

It was then that Montevecchio learned Amil Dinsio had shot at him in front of Nardo's house. Dinsio, not knowing who was approaching the house, said he thought Montevecchio might have been another intruder or even a cop.

The next day, Bocci traveled to Pittsburgh, Montevecchio said, where he met up with his fence, Harry Fleming, to sell the stolen loot from the Nardo job. Fleming, as it turned out, had done a stint for murder in the early 1960s. Bocci befriended Fleming while both were serving time at Western Penitentiary near Pittsburgh. Robert Bocci was doing his stretch there for his part in a burglary.

Meanwhile, Bocci convinced Montevecchio to toss the gold pocket watch down a sewer, so there would be no evidence to link Caesar to the break-in. As for DiPaolo's part, he wasn't about to let all this good information go to waste: He arrested both Stellato and Fleming to pressure them for whatever information they might be able to provide about the Owen and Dovishaw investigations. They were joined by Bob Bocci in cooperating with the cop, and charges against all of them eventually were withdrawn in return for said cooperation.

Harry Fleming was an old time slug with many connections to powerful attorneys and politicians, mostly in Pittsburgh. One such attorney was the recipient of a $5,000 woman's necklace that Fleming gave him instead of the cash he owed the lawyer. The attorney's wife was said to have been a recipient of a necklace, which came from the Nardo job. After questioning Fleming on where the jewelry and coins had gone, Fleming was let out of jail on bond and began making phone calls.

Eventually, DiPaolo teamed up with a Pittsburgh burglary detective. They went from pawn shop to pawn shop when the Pittsburgh cop got a radio transmission with a phone number for DiPaolo to call.

DiPaolo did not recognize the Erie phone number, and was slightly miffed that someone knew he was in Pittsburgh and attempting to contact him through the Pittsburgh Police Department. When DiPaolo called the number, he found himself speaking with Erie Attorney Jess Jiuliante, later to be President Judge of the Erie County Court of Common Pleas.

"Hey, Dom," Jiuliante began, "just to let you know, I got a call from an attorney friend in Pittsburgh and his wife doesn't have any necklace from the Nardo job. He would be more than happy to talk with you."

"Jess," DiPaolo asked, "how does your buddy know I want to talk with him?

"Gee, I don't know. I'm only trying to help out."

Suddenly, it became obvious to DiPaolo that Fleming had called his lawyer pal, who in turn called Jiuliante. If there had indeed been a stolen necklace in the possession of a prominent Pittsburgh lawyer's wife, DiPaolo knew it was now gone. Later, however, some of the stolen goods from the Nardo job were found at the pawn shops Fleming had given up. Fleming was sent to prison on new burglary charges, and died shortly after.

Meanwhile, DiPaolo is still amazed when he thinks of Bocci, who simply could not stop talking. "He wouldn't shut up! He gave up everyone he knew and then cried – he didn't want to go back to jail, he told us," DiPaolo recalled of his interview with the talkative Bocci.

Eventually, it was determined that the total take from the Louis Nardo burglary and safe job was valued at more than $700,000 in jewelry and cash. Two years later, Nardo was again a victim of an armed robbery at his home perpetrated by Caesar Montevecchio and his gang. Another case of history repeating itself.

Some eight years earlier, Amil Dinsio made national headlines when he hit a bank in trendy Laguna, California. That gig resulted in a movie, a book and a television documentary. While serving a stint at Leavenworth for the California job, Amil Dinsio met Caesar Montevecchio. The relationship resulted in a crime partnership that led to the Nardo break-in barely two months after Dinsio's release from prison on October 6, 1980.

On Thanksgiving weekend 1980, more than eight years after the California job, Louis Nardo's house safe was broken into in the same way – bypassing the alarm system, drilling holes, filling the safe with water and using blasting caps to gain entry. But by the time in 1987 that Montevecchio confirmed it was Dinsio who hit Nardo, the five-year statute of limitations on felony burglary had run out. It meant the Dinsios and others involved in the Nardo job could not be charged.

Montevecchio, in his statement, also told DiPaolo that in 1980 Dinsio constructed a fake steel bank night deposit box which could be installed directly over a real bank deposit box. Customers' keys appeared to unlock the fake night deposit box, although there was no lock mechanism involved. Once the customers thought they had access to the night deposit box, they dropped in their bank bags. The phony night deposit box even had the name of the manufacturer, "Diebold," engraved on the front to further add to its authentic look.

Twice, Montevecchio used the phony bank box in Erie, he claimed to DiPaolo. He would install the phony box at a bank on a Friday evening, then remove it by Sunday night, he said. Each time, the fake box was jammed with bank bags, over 100 of them, according to Montevecchio. Caesar said he took the bags to the Westside home of Charles "The Hawk" Serafini, and they, along with the Hawk's girlfriend, opened the bank's bags with scissors and knives. After splitting the cash, Montevecchio said, the trio then burned the checks and the bags. Montevecchio swore to DiPaolo he only employed Dinsio's fake night deposit box twice.

Although the statute of limitations had expired on the Nardo break-in and the fake night deposit box endeavors, Montevecchio's confession provided DiPaolo insight to the culture of crime in Erie, as well as a new understanding of what some consider an entitlement to the belongings of others. He became aware of an almost total lack of remorse by those who would take a human life.

As for Amil Dinsio, at 74 years old he's serving 25 years for armed robbery and won't be released until 2018 at the earliest.

CHAPTER 31

WITH CAESAR TALKING, PIECES OF THE BOLO DOVISHAW MURDER puzzle were fast falling into place. DiPaolo knew there would be only a short window of opportunity to get the key players to roll over on each other. He also knew he needed to move speedily, but without upsetting what was now in place with Caesar Montevecchio and several others.

DiPaolo thought back a few months to February, 1987, when he made that arduous drive from Erie to Milan, Michigan, to meet with William "Billy" Bourjaily at the federal penitentiary there. The Michigan prison systems, both state and federal, were now almost as familiar to DiPaolo as Pennsylvania's wide-spread Department of Corrections.

When DiPaolo introduced himself to Bourjaily, Billy only smiled and asked, "Jesus, Dominick! What took you so damned long to get here?"

DiPaolo didn't answer, knowing Bourjaily knew how to work the system.

"C'mon, man! I got the word on you. I've been waiting."

DiPaolo suspected Bourjaily had more smarts than Dorler or even Montevecchio. But how smart is someone residing in a federal slammer?

"First, I read you your Miranda rights," DiPaolo said.

"Dominick. No disrespect man. But I ain't signing nothing. You came to talk. So, fucking talk to me."

"How many times have you been to Erie?"

"Erie?" Bourjaily feigned surprise. "Where's that? Ohio? New York?" Now he was laughing.

"Where your buddy Caesar lives," DiPaolo reminded him, refusing to even crack a smile. "Sound familiar now?"

"Let me tell you something. I've been to Erie a lot. And I know you didn't come all this way just hoping I'm going to give you something. Besides, I know you probably got the answers to the questions already. Right?"

"Such as?"

"Such as this – if you can get Caesar to roll, then I will roll, too. And you'll find out just what you want. And, believe me, man, I do know exactly what you want. As I said, you didn't come up here all this way just to see me because you enjoyed the frigging ride, correct?"

"So, that's it?" DiPaolo asked.

"Sir, believe me, and again, no disrespect, but that's all I'm saying. If I keep talking, you are going to put me in a jackpot (street talk meaning compromising position that could nail him for a crime). And I just can't let that happen."

That was in February – it was now July – and Caesar was already rolling as the vise tightened!

Shortly after that February chat with Bourjaily, DiPaolo again turned to Robert Dorler. A month after DiPaolo's eye-opening Michigan meeting with Billy Bourjaily, on March 10, 1987, Dorler was moved from the Rochester, Minnesota, federal penitentiary to Pittsburgh, and then to North Huntingdon, just east of Pittsburgh. The large North Huntingdon Township municipal government building was the site of Pennsylvania's fourth statewide grand jury investigating the January 3, 1983, execution-style murder of Erie bookie Frank "Bolo" Dovishaw.

It was almost strange to see so many of northwestern Pennsylvania's law enforcement professionals, lawyers and wise guys all gathered in one place, but some 140 miles from home. Dorler had previously agreed to testify under a grant of immunity from prosecution for any crime he committed in Erie, with the exception of homicide. That meant that no matter what he said about any crime he committed in Erie, he could not be charged or prosecuted for it. The only exception was murder.

Earlier, Dorler had told state prosecutor Dennis Pfannenschmidt about each Erie crime in which he was a participant. Burglaries, robberies, drug deals. He provided the prosecuting attorney with multiple names, places and details of the crimes. Included were the names of other key participants in the crime spree: Louie Raffa, George Meeks, Fat Sam Esper. Without hesitation, Dorler gave up all his Erie partners in crime.

As part of the deal with prosecutor Pfannenschmidt, Dorler was expected to now do the same before the statewide investigative grand jury. Everyone in law enforcement knows grand jury testimony is secret. At least, such testimony is *supposed* to be kept secret. Yet, it was later publicly reported that Robert Dorler spent more than four hours on the witness stand before finally being asked by Pfannenschmidt, "What do you know about the Dovishaw murder?"

At the time it was reported that Dorler, somewhat rattled with the question, simply replied, "I refuse to answer that question on the grounds that it might tend to incriminate me. So, I'm taking the Fifth." If those public media reports of this segment of Dorler's grand jury testimony were true, it meant Dorler had unwittingly given up the Dovishaw murder. If true, it meant DiPaolo had perfectly maneuvered Dorler into an inescapable corner months before Caesar's confession!

DiPaolo thought about the message Dorler was sending, intentionally or unintentionally. He was refusing to testify against Montevecchio about a crime he had previously denied having knowledge of, yet he had availed himself of his Constitutional right to evoke the Fifth Amendment against self-incrimination in connection with that very crime.

During every previous conversation between DiPaolo and Dorler, the career criminal insisted he knew nothing about the Dovishaw killing. So why not tell that to the grand jury? Like TV's famous Sergeant Schultz? *I know nothing!* But if true, Dorler had – by "taking the Fifth" – unintentionally acknowledged he either played a role in Bolo Dovishaw's murder, or at least had important information about it.

Immediately following his testimony and once outside the grand jury room, Dorler angrily accused DiPaolo, "You fuckin' tricked me!"

"No homicides?" DiPaolo blamed the question on a prosecutorial mistake. "Geez, he wasn't supposed to bring it up," the Erie cop innocently said.

"Fuck you!" Dorler shouted. "Now I don't talk on Caesar. How do you like that!"

It was more than an implication. And the comment was heard by news reporters in the corridor outside the courtroom.

With each outburst, it seemed clear to DiPaolo that Dorler was digging a deeper hole. Still fuming, Dorler was taken to his holding cell to await transport back to the Minnesota federal prison. Since the U.S. Marshal Service could not move Dorler back to Minnesota for at least two more days, DiPaolo believed this was another opportunity! DiPaolo drove to the North Huntingdon municipal lockup to tell Dorler of the delay in travel plans.

"You're fucking with me on purpose because I won't talk," Dorler screamed.

But DiPaolo, calmly and truthfully reported, "I have no control over the U.S. Marshals. They operate according to their own schedules. So you're stuck here."

It was beginning to look to DiPaolo like fate was sending a perfect hand his way. And now, all he had to do was play it straight, while allowing Dorler to hang himself.

The next morning dawned somewhat reluctantly with murky and gray skies and a chilly mist. March was definitely no paradise in Pennsylvania.

The ringing phone in DiPaolo's hotel room startled the cop awake. "Jeezus," he groaned, staring at the night stand clock. It read shortly before 6 a.m. On the phone was Officer Vinnie Lewandowski, who DiPaolo had placed in charge of his transport team. Lewandowski and Officers Bill Leamy and Bob "Goody" Goodwill were moving the key players back and forth between their lock-ups and the grand jury in this western Pennsylvania town. Lewandowski had received a phone call from the North Huntingdon lock-up.

"The guards there say Dorler wants to see you at once, like right now! They say he wants to give up Bolo's murder," Lewandowski told DiPaolo. That quickly got DiPaolo's attention, and he was suddenly alert and wide awake. DiPaolo showered, shaved, dressed and drove the short distance to the North Huntingdon city lockup in minutes.

As soon as he saw DiPaolo, Dorler blurted out: "I'll tell you what you want, but you gotta put it all together and get me the fuck out of here!"

"I'm listening," DiPaolo said. "But just start from the beginning. The very beginning. I want to know everything."

"Look, I have some pretty direct knowledge about the Bolo hit. But I'm not the shooter. And I didn't arrange it, either."

"Yeah? So, who was involved?"

"Billy Bourjaily and two other guys. I'll give you all the details. But I want immunity. For me. And for Billy."

DiPaolo thought for a moment.

"Was Billy the trigger?" he asked.

"I'm not going to answer that," Dorler said.

"Well, what the hell!" DiPaolo shot back. "You've got to give me a little more than that for me to go to bat for you and Billy on the immunity. You've got to know that, right?"

Now it was Robert Dorler's turn to slowly ponder and consider his next move.

"Okay. The gun used on Bolo was a .32 caliber Beretta. Caesar was the one who supplied it. I know because I got rid of it outside of Pennsylvania in a body of water."

"Oh?"

Dorler went on to explain that all the weapons used in the armed robberies during 1982 and 1983 were supplied by Caesar Montevecchio.

"What else?" DiPaolo pried further.

"The last thing I tell you is that Bolo's hit had something to do with bank safe-deposit box keys. But that's it, DiPaolo! Get me and Billy immunity and then take me back to the fucking grand jury."

"I need to ask you one thing," DiPaolo said. "Just what do safe-deposit box keys have to do with all this, with Dovishaw? Tell me that."

"Should be obvious, for Christsake! Bolo couldn't be killed until he gave up the fucking keys. And Ferritto – he was supposed to be hit, too. But he wasn't there. That's it, man. Right now, I'm done fuckin' talking."

It was exactly what DiPaolo needed. The ride from North Huntingdon Township to Erie took less than three hours. But it was well worth it for DiPaolo and every other law enforcement type who labored for so long on the Dovishaw murder case.

At the Pennsylvania Attorney General's office in the Griswold Plaza, Robert Dorler finally formally gave a statement on Bolo Dovishaw's murder. He continued to beg off on who the killer actually was, but he sure gave winking and nodding hints it was his pal Bourjaily. What would later (in July) surprise DiPaolo most was how well Dorler's account (minus the shooter information) would mesh with Caesar Montevecchio's story. Although some of the minor details given by the two men varied somewhat, Dorler and Montevecchio were remarkably on the same page when it came to outlining key components of the premeditated hit. According to Dorler, Bolo Dovishaw's key movements had been scoped out for almost an entire week before the January 3, 1983 murder.

"Monday after the New Year's weekend was picked because of all the bowl games because we knew Bolo would have one of the biggest weekend takes of the year," Dorler said.

Dorler told DiPaolo the plan was indeed to kill Dovishaw, get his safe deposit box keys and any money stashed in Bolo's "secret" bathroom hiding place.

"Yeah, and if Ferritto was in the house, there was an extra ten grand for the shooter for hitting him, too. That payoff was supposed to come from Caesar's coke dealer friend." Sometime after that, Dorler said the information came to him from Montevecchio that the extra hit money would be paid by Joey Scutella.

He related the events of the night of killing in details as chilling as Erie's January weather.

"Apparently, from what I was told, the second Bolo answered the door, it was over for him," Dorler said with a smile. With the 32-caliber pistol (loaded with Norma brand ammunition) held almost touching Bolo's head, Dorler told of how the shooter forced Dovishaw face down on the floor while patting him down for possible hidden weapons. Still with the cold, .32 caliber pistol touching Dovishaw's skull, Dorler told of how the killer calmly directed the petrified bookie to the basement and again ordered him face down, this time on the concrete floor.

"He apparently grabbed a couple of belts from some lady's dresses on a laundry rack and tied up his feet and hands. Bolo was crying and pleading with the shooter, saying things like, 'Take whatever you want.' The shooter also asked if Dovishaw had any cash in the house, but Bolo said there wasn't any. But the shooter knew about Bolo's secret hiding place in the bathroom and Bolo tells him there's just a couple of bucks there, that's all. Caesar told the shooter to get the fucking safe-deposit box keys and the guy says Bolo just gave them up easier than shit. They were, like, in his pants pocket. The guy just took them. Then the shooter has to know where the car keys were and Bolo tells him they're on a table near the front door. So, that's it. The guy gets what he wants and then he wastes him."

"Shit, I need more than that," DiPaolo said, shaking his head. "A lot more."

"Okay, okay. If you really got to know!"

"Yeah, I do!"

"Okay. The shooter actually has Bolo get on his knees. He tells him, like Don Corleone, 'Hey, nothing personal Bolo. It's just business.' All the time I hear that he's still crying his eyes out. Oh, yeah – there was supposed to be this throw rug at the bottom of the steps. So the guy folds it and puts it against Bolo's head. He puts the .32 right up to the rug, like it was touching it, then shoots the fat fucker just once. Just one time."

"What did you *hear* happened then?" DiPaolo asked, emphasizing "hear."

"Well, fuck, I guess Bolo just dropped like a sack of goddamned potatoes. So the fuckin' guy gets a sheet from a laundry basket down there and covers him up and puts the rug over him."

Dorler described how the killer found the bathroom hiding place and pocketed the few thousand Bolo previously had hidden in the vanity. "He went through the rest of the house just to see if there was anything else worthwhile to boost. But I guess there was nothing but the car keys."

Back in the basement, Dorler continued, the killer pulled the rug and sheet away from Bolo's body. "What the fuck! He thinks Bolo is alive! Every time before, this guy says, they would shit and piss themselves when they died. But not Bolo."

No one had come up with this information before, not even Caesar. This obviously wasn't the killer's first rodeo, DiPaolo thought.

Dorler told how the shooter described returning to the kitchen and discovering a paring knife in counter drawer, then returned to the basement. "He grabs 'Ash Wednesday' by his hair and pulls his head way up, then he just jams the fuckin' rusty knife into his eye as hard as he could. All the way in. He waits a few minutes and sure enough, Bolo shits and pisses himself. And then the guy knows for sure he was dead."

Dorler, like others in his underworld circle, knew that "Ash Wednesday" was another of Frank Dovishaw's nicknames, acquired from his Catholic childhood friends because of the unsightly blemish in the center of his forehead, the place where parish priests apply the ashes from the previous year's burned palm leaves.

Dorler confirmed to DiPaolo that the initial plan had been for the killer to place Dovishaw's body in the green Caddy's trunk. "Fuck, no matter how hard the guy tugs and pulls, he can't fuckin' budge the fat fuck. So he's thinking, Jeezus, what now?"

According to Dorler's account, before the killer could decide what to do, however, there came a yelling and banging at the front door. The killer couldn't have known it then, but it was Kenneth Wisinski, father of Dovishaw's 13-year-old newspaper carrier, Michele, trying again in vain to collect the $21 Bolo owed his daughter. Wisinski perhaps never knew how close he came to sharing the same fate as the man from whom he was attempting to make good on the debt to daughter Michele.

Dorler told DiPaolo the killer pulled out the pistol and waited, prepared to whack whom he believed to be Ferritto or whoever else might try to gain entrance to Bolo's house. But the crisis quickly passed. "So, the guy waits for a while and when he's sure that whoever was banging on the door had gone, he goes back downstairs."

Once again, the shooter attempted to move Dovishaw's body, Dorler said. And once again, he had no success. "Apparently, there was just no way he was going to get that heavy bastard Bolo upstairs, let alone even budge his body."

With no curtains or drapes over the basement windows, the killer was concerned the body would be visible to anyone happening to be looking in, Dorler told DiPaolo. "Caesar woulda gone nuts. The last thing any of us wanted was someone peeking in and seeing Bolo's rotting corpse down there in the cellar. So, the guy covers him up again and then just kicks the knife under the rug. Anyone looking in the windows would only see a big pile of clothes on the basement floor."

Within minutes, the killer left the now quiet house through the side door and was tooling Dovishaw's 1979 Deville toward the pre-arranged meeting place – the Station Restaurant at West Gore Road and Washington Avenue, Dorler said. And it was where Caesar Montevecchio soon would be waiting for the shooter, Dorler said, again hinting at Bourjaily.

"I guess there weren't that many cars there in the back lot that night," Dorler continued. "But the shooter parks near a few, then pops the trunk. Wanted to check for a bank bag or more. But no such luck. Nothing there but a half-empty case of booze and a couple of empty brown paper sacks." No one else knew this but the police, DiPaolo thought. Had the killer looked further, he would have discovered more. Much more.

Not very bright, this cold-minded killer, DiPaolo thought with a smile.

Finding nothing in Dovishaw's car, the slightly disgruntled hit man waited for Caesar Montevecchio to show up at the pre-arranged time of 7 p.m.

"When Caesar gets there, the shooter gives him the bad news about Bolo still being in the basement of the house."

"So, how did he take it?" DiPaolo asked, already knowing the answer.

"Holy shit! Pissed! Was he ever! But the guy tells him Bolo was just too goddamn heavy to lift. There wasn't much Caesar could do about it, not then, anyway. Nobody was about to go back there to the house, for Christsakes. It was over and done with and that was that. He just needed to move forward from there. What the fuck, it wasn't the end of the world, just the end of Bolo."

"What about the bank box keys?" That *was* the motive, after all.

"Oh, yeah. Almost forgot! The guy gives Caesar the bank keys. Then Caesar says he'll call the guy the next day about his payday. I guess that was about it."

DiPaolo tried to imagine all the chaos that getting rid of the car would have entailed for Caesar and the killer.

"So they take off and dump Bolo's Caddy at the Holiday Inn on Interstate 90. It's off the eastbound lanes. With Bolo's car stashed there, the shooter heads back west toward Cleveland, fast, but within the speed limit. Despite the change in plans with the body and everything, what the hell, they still felt things seemed to be going okay."

(To make his version sound plausible, Dorler said he was with Caesar at the time, while the shooter had his car stashed at the Station

Restaurant. The shooter arrived at the Station in Bolo's car, then drove it to the Holiday Inn South, with Dorler following him there in the shooter's car. Once Bolo's car was dumped there, the shooter drove his own car, with Dorler aboard, back to Cleveland.)

"I mean, he nailed Bolo. Got the damned bank box keys for Caesar. And the shooter even collected a few grand more from the bathroom hiding place. Everyone had been hoping there would be more in the car. But all in all, still not a bad fucking night. The big thing was not to get pulled over heading back to Ohio."

A good night, DiPaolo thought, following Dorler's warped sense of accomplishment. "Anything I need to know about your trip back to Ohio?"

"Oh, yeah. That's when the .32 Berretta was ditched!"

"Where?" This was turning out better than expected.

"In Ohio. I told you."

But now DiPaolo was starting to get pissed. "Don't fuck with me Dorler. Just give it to me straight, and with all the details."

On their way back to Cleveland, Robert Dorler said he and the shooter didn't go straight home. They took a short detour. About 15 miles after crossing from Pennsylvania into Ohio, Dorler said, as they approached the Youngstown exit, Dorler instructed the shooter, "Get off here. Take Route 11."

It was the road heading somewhat southwest through Mahoning County, infamous for its reputation as a hotbed for organized crime in the Youngstown-Warren-Niles region that sat nicely midway between Cleveland, Buffalo and Pittsburgh, with Erie in the center of the crime triangle.

"Stay on 11 for a while," Dorler said he ordered the shooter. It took about 40 minutes along the secondary highway before they came to the Meander Lake Bridge just outside of Youngstown. "As we crossed the bridge, I told the shooter to slow down just a bit. I rolled down my window and tossed out the .32 clip first, then the gun. It's a good place to ditch hot hardware. Shit, I've done it many times."

Dorler told DiPaolo that Lake Meander wasn't quite frozen over yet and that the murder weapon likely ended up on the bottom with God knows how many other weapons used in scores or even hundreds of illegal activities.

"Then what?" DiPaolo issued his standard prod after Dorler became silent.

"Nothin' – the shooter just drove me home to Medina and then drove himself home. That's all."

Medina, Ohio, is slightly west of Cleveland. As a result, the shooter had to by-pass his own residence, drop off Dorler, then drive back east back to Cleveland. If Dorler was indeed dropping the dime, it was apparently on Billy Bourjaily. It was the end of a busy day, but one that would occupy DiPaolo's time and attention for years to come.

So far, Robert Dorler's rambling story was pretty much following the same course and story lines as Caesar Montevecchio's account of the night Frank "Bolo" Dovishaw was murdered. DiPaolo knew it was important that while their recollections of that night didn't need to coincide perfectly, they must be on the same page, especially with the important details of how the killing went down. DiPaolo envisioned defense attorneys like that Lenny Ambrose, delighting in poking holes in the prosecution's case and tripping up witnesses. So far, so good, DiPaolo thought as Dorler continued to give up himself and his buddies.

Dorler said that the next day, January 4, 1983, Caesar telephoned him and they agreed to meet at 7 p.m. at that same Interstate 90 intersection – Exit 34-Warren – where Dorler and the shooter had taken their gun-ditching detour. They would meet at Mr. C's Pancake House, a busy place for truckers and travelers alike.

"Caesar was right on time. And he was alone."

"Were you alone, too?" DiPaolo asked, knowing that Dorler had company.

"No, I got there with the shooter a few minutes earlier just to scope out the joint and make sure there was no set-up, if you know what I mean. Not that I thought there would be. Just being careful, y'know?"

Dorler said the shooter got into Montevecchio's car and was immediately handed a brown paper bag stuffed with cash. The exchange, he said, only took a few minutes. Dorler said Montevecchio headed back to Erie, while Dorler and the shooter were quickly driving toward Cleveland on the familiar Interstate 90. This time, there were no detours.

But there was a missing detail, DiPaolo recalled. Dorler didn't mention the part about the argument with Montevecchio over taking the bank safe-deposit box keys back to Bolo's car at the Holiday Inn near Erie. Yet, he was content to let it slide for now, taking note of the discrepancy between Dorler's and Montevecchio's accounts.

In the car, Dorler said, the shooter counted the money in the brown paper bag. "Exactly twenty grand," he said. "Just what they agreed on. So the shooter counted out fifteen thousand for himself and then gave me five grand for the rides."

"That was generous of him," DiPaolo said. "Anything more to add, or is that pretty much what happened and the way everything went down?"

"That's about it as I remember that night. Y'know, it *was* a while ago, but you got all the important stuff. Our plan was to just lay low for a few months. You know, no phone calls. No contact at all. It seemed like a good plan."

While Dorler made his new revelations in March, by July DiPaolo – thanks to Caesar – knew exactly who the shooter was. Dorler had confirmed the entire story. But he substituted Bourjaily for himself as the shooter.

Where Dovishaw kept his stash; other murder puzzle pieces fall into place

Frank "Ash Wednesday" Dovishaw kept perhaps hundreds of thousands of dollars from his illegal sports betting operating stashed in a bank safe-deposit box. Other crimes in the Erie area helped Erie Police Detective Sergeant Dom DiPaolo string together enough clues to effect arrests in the murder case.

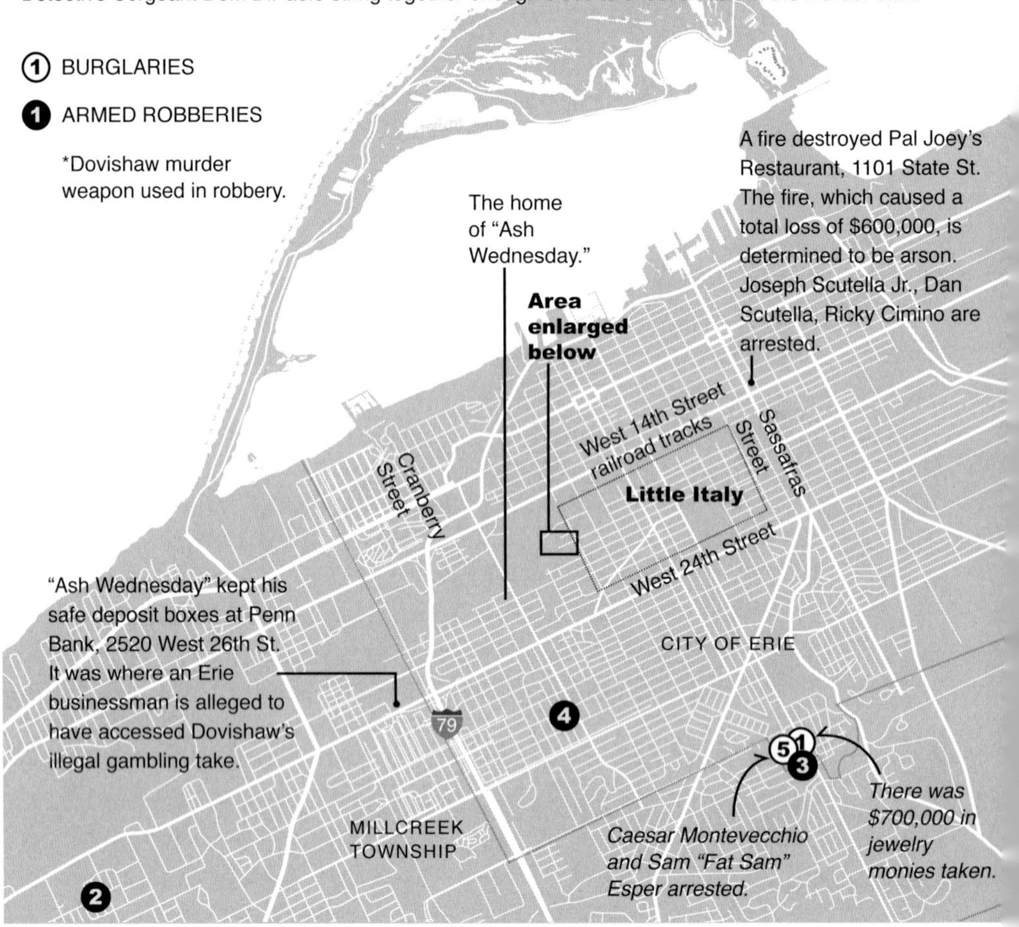

① BURGLARIES

❶ ARMED ROBBERIES

*Dovishaw murder weapon used in robbery.

The home of "Ash Wednesday."

Area enlarged below

A fire destroyed Pal Joey's Restaurant, 1101 State St. The fire, which caused a total loss of $600,000, is determined to be arson. Joseph Scutella Jr., Dan Scutella, Ricky Cimino are arrested.

West 14th Street

railroad tracks

Sassafras Street

Cranberry Street

Little Italy

West 24th Street

CITY OF ERIE

"Ash Wednesday" kept his safe deposit boxes at Penn Bank, 2520 West 26th St. It was where an Erie businessman is alleged to have accessed Dovishaw's illegal gambling take.

79

MILLCREEK TOWNSHIP

Caesar Montevecchio and Sam "Fat Sam" Esper arrested.

There was $700,000 in jewelry monies taken.

① *November 27, 1980*
Louis Nardo home at 605 Hilltop Rd.

❷ *April 19, 1982*
Jack, Jean and Grant Miller's home at 2913 Madeira Dr.*

❸ *May 7, 1982*
Louis Nardo and Evelyn Faye robbed at 605 Hilltop Rd.*

❹ *May 12, 1982*
Frank Scalise's home at 3504 Oakwood Ave.*

⑤ *July 28,*
Home at
Hilltop Rc

1980 Erie Police Corporal Robert Owen murder still a mystery

The murder site of Owen was a secluded place for Erie police officers to gather. The spot was an open lot with some warehouses nearby. At right, the crime scene on a modern map.

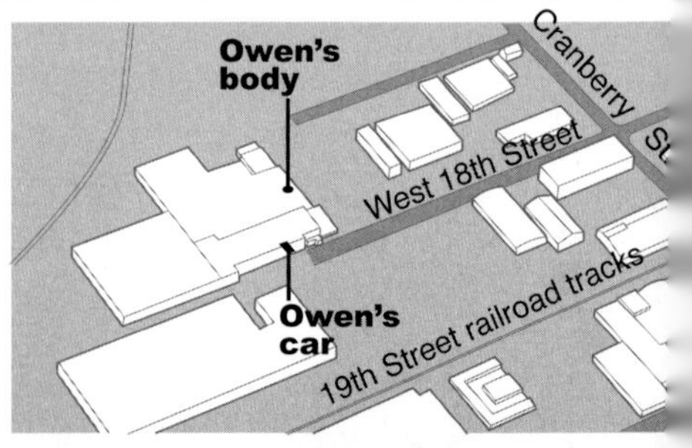

CHAPTER 32

CHARLES BOWERS, SR. WAS THE FORMER ERIE CHIEF OF POLICE, later to be followed by two sons in the post.

After retirement, the prematurely white-haired Bowers, a Yonkers, New York native who still spoke with a heavy accent, landed one of those plum jobs as head of security at Security Peoples Bank, which later became PennBank. Better to have a former cop there as opposed to a stuffed-shirt corporate type, Dom DiPaolo knew. He also knew he could count on Charlie Bowers for any help if he needed it. And help he got.

DiPaolo learned from Bowers that Theresa Mastrey, the assistant branch manager cousin of Niggsy Arnone, had been transferred to a PennBank branch at East 8th and East Avenue from the Super Duper West bank branch on West 26th Street. Bowers advised DiPaolo of the transfer and later so testified in court. The transfer made DiPaolo's investigation all the easier, not having Mastrey there at the original branch.

DiPaolo's continuing investigation, with help from the former police chief, showed that in May 1982, Frank Dovishaw was using bank safe-deposit boxes Nos. 503 and 610. On May 12, 1982, the investigation revealed, Anthony "Niggsy" Arnone signed up to use Box No. 509. Arnone's box was physically situated directly above Bolo Dovishaw's box. Coincidence?

The bank officer who signed up Niggsy was *Cousin Theresa.* This was admitted by Mastrey to DiPaolo. It also demonstrated to DiPaolo that the plan to murder Frank Dovishaw apparently was hatched nearly eight months before his early 1983 demise. DiPaolo thought there was no way Montevecchio could have known any of this, but from Niggsy – and that Mastrey made it happen.

During one of his many past drunken episodes, Bolo Dovishaw lost the keys to both safe deposit boxes. It had been in November 1982 and the boxes had to be drilled open, after which he was assigned new boxes by bank official Theresa Mastrey. Now Dovishaw was in possession of boxes numbered 424 and 449. Neither of the new boxes were near Niggsy Arnone's bank box. But the plan to murder Dovishaw was nowhere near breaking down. Box No. 449 was directly adjacent to Box No. 450. Box No. 450, it was later determined by bank records, was rented by Theresa Mastrey. Mastrey told DiPaolo the proximity of the safe deposit boxes was a coincidence. With 1,200 safe deposit boxes in the vault, what a coincidence! DiPaolo thought.

Leg work and compiling paper trails are among the most tedious as well as arduous tasks of police work. Just ask any cop. What happens on TV crime shows is rarely the model for real life police work. But these mundane tasks were anything but daunting for DiPaolo. He relished the satisfaction of fitting the pieces together, just as an experienced puzzle-worker might at completing a complex jigsaw puzzle.

DiPaolo compiled a paper trail for all entries into Bolo's bank safe-deposit boxes. Bank records showed that on 90 percent of Dovishaw's visits to his bank boxes, Theresa Mastrey was listed as the bank's attendant. Most of the other times, Diane DiRenzio-Amendola was the attendant.

The situation – with Cousin Theresa on the inside – could not have been better for Niggsy Arnone, DiPaolo speculated. He thought, "If Theresa hadn't worked at the bank, Bolo would still be making book."

The paper trail also extended to Arnone's visits to the bank's Super Duper Store branch office. According to the entry card for Arnone's bank box, Niggsy had access to his box on May 12, 1982. The bank attendant, according to the card, was listed as "T.M." Mastrey, who confirmed this to DiPaolo and she later so testified. The next time Arnone visited his safe deposit box, according to bank records, was eight months later on January 4, 1983. The day after "Bolo" Dovishaw was slain. Another coincidence? The bank attendant that day? No initials were listed on the card. No one, not even a suspected co-conspirator, would be that foolish to sign their own initials, DiPaolo thought.

But Arnone's paper trail of renting the box in May, telling Montevecchio about it, then not going back until eight months later, further helped to unravel the puzzle, DiPaolo thought. But there were more pieces. Montevecchio claimed in a statement and in later testimony that Arnone told him he signed his name to the safe deposit box card on January 4, complaining bitterly about it, while Mastrey left the bank attendant line blank. Arnone did in fact take out a loan that day, a move the cops believed was to cover his appearance at the bank for other purposes – namely Bolo Dovishaw's bank boxes.

With the borrowed $4,000, Arnone went directly to Erie Bianchi's Lincoln dealership and purchased a new Town Car. The car was for himself. He used his trade-in, along with $3,900 of the borrowed money, to pay for the new wheels.

Circumstantial evidence confirming Caesar Montevecchio's account of the 1983 Dovishaw murder continued to mount. During a check of PennBank logs for January 4, 1983, DiPaolo learned 17 customers had accessed their bank boxes that day. Each safe deposit box card was signed by the customer and initialed by a bank attendant. All except one: Anthony Arnone's. DiPaolo also learned that Mastrey, as one of the managers, rarely went into the vault with customers accessing their bank boxes unless she personally knew the individuals, such as Bolo, Mastrey's admission to DiPaolo, bank records and trial testimony showed.

Following the paper trail, DiPaolo thought, was making Montevecchio's statement – if not Montevecchio himself – even more credible. For example, Niggsy Arnone, bank records showed, borrowed heavily on his business in 1981, 1982, 1984, 1985, 1986 and 1987. The only year with no loans, with the exception of the January 4 borrowing of $4,000 – was 1983. Another coincidence? But, from January through April of 1983, Arnone not only purchased vehicles and paid off outstanding loans, but also took out certificates of deposit totaling some $82,791.50. In addition, Augustine Matson, a CPA, later testified that from 1983 to 1986, Arnone made cash deposits in his account of more than $140,000, which was unaccounted for in his records, according to trial testimony and newspaper accounts. More coincidence?

Arnone's deli business could have sold tons of salami and perhaps extra virgin olive oil that year, DiPaolo mused with some sarcasm.

DiPaolo also learned that heavy losses at the track were financially strangling Arnone. With the exception of the 1983 banner year, through 1987 Anthony "Niggsy" Arnone had amassed debt totaling $312,550.98. But there was no Bolo Dovishaw to come to Arnone's financial rescue.

Arnone had pulled off the scam of scams, according to what seemed obvious to DiPaolo from his findings. If the accusations were true, Arnone had paid the shooter $20,000, plus another $10,000 to Montevecchio. Arnone, if these charges stood, had used "Bolo" Dovishaw's own money to pay off the shooter and the arranger. As for the others who might have been involved on the inside or outside, only Arnone allegedly knew about who was paid off, DiPaolo thought. Perhaps that explained the $37K already spent that Arnone allegedly complained about to Montevecchio? Again, DiPaolo thought, if all this was true, Frank Dovishaw had actually made payment on his own hit.

Dom DiPaolo was getting very familiar with the drive from Erie to various state and federal prisons in Michigan. With evidence – circumstantial and eye-witness – falling into place, in July 1987, DiPaolo drove to the federal penitentiary at Milan, Michigan. There, he retrieved William "Billy" Bourjaily – the last minute getaway accomplice for the killer Robert Dorler more than four years earlier.

Some of DiPaolo's most important information had come during conversations with prisoners going to or coming from incarceration in Michigan. The drive back to Erie was no different. Once on the open road, Bourjaily was eager to begin the conversation. "I read that grand jury presentment," he began. "It was very interesting."

"Oh, yeah?"

"Yeah. For instance, it's all wrong. Isn't that interesting?"

"Yeah? Like how?" DiPaolo played along, noncommittal, keeping a poker face.

"For starters, Bob Dorler isn't telling you the whole truth. I don't need immunity for any murder. That's because I didn't do any murder." Bourjaily also denied, despite statements from others, that he played a role in the Louis Nardo armed robbery. "Hell, I was in Florida when that went down and I can prove it. That one is total bullshit," he said.

"I know it was George Meeks, not you," DiPaolo said.

"Well, what do you know? I guess that maybe Dorler does remember it right."

DiPaolo smiled, then shook his head.

"What's so frigging funny?" Bourjaily asked.

"No, Dorler didn't get that one right. He said it was you. It actually was Caesar who said it was Meeks."

Bourjaily appeared surprised. "Oh? Caesar talking now?"

"Yes. Yes, he is!"

For several miles of white dashes along the interstate, Bourjaily was silent. "Can I get a deal?" he quietly asked.

"Maybe," DiPaolo tormented his prisoner. "Maybe. If you have what I want."

This time Bourjaily wasn't the least bit hesitant. "The hit on the bookie," he blurted out. "I'll tell you how Dorler told me he did it and how it went down. I can even show you where the gun went. And, what the fuck, I'll testify. Is that what you want?"

DiPaolo nearly bit his lip to stop the huge grin from exposing itself. *Man*, he thought, *after being cornered, these guys are so easy. After all this time, it's now like a race to see who shits on whom first.*

When DiPaolo arrived back in Erie with prisoner William Bourjaily and with Bourjaily already doing 10 years of hard time, a deal had to be quickly struck:

- Bourjaily would plead guilty to all the armed robbery charges;
- He would offer state's testimony in the Bolo Dovishaw murder trial or trials; and
- He would give up the gun, or its location, to DiPaolo.

In return, Bourjaily would receive only five years maximum time for the Jack Miller armed robbery on top of the sentence he was already serving. Bourjaily took the deal. For without it, upon conviction of the additional robbery charges, he could have wound up dying an old man in prison.

"Okay," DiPaolo began somewhat slowly. "Where's the fucking gun?"

Bourjaily easily related to DiPaolo the ride back to Ohio the night Dovishaw was killed and how Robert Dorler, riding shotgun, disposed of the murder weapon.

"It was a .32," he said. "We took a slight detour off of 90 and tossed it into Lake Meander near Youngstown. You must have heard of that place, Dominick. It's the traditional gun dump for the mob."

DiPaolo telephoned the Mahoning County, Ohio, Sheriff's Department to inquire about the Lake Meander gun dump. He spoke with a deputy sheriff.

"You say the murder was in 1983?" the deputy asked. "Hang on a minute."

When the deputy came back on the line, he stunned DiPaolo with his revelations. "Hell, we drag the lake every year. We might even have your gun. In fact, we have 372 on display right now."

DiPaolo was having difficulty grasping his new-found good fortune. "How many?" he asked.

"You heard me right. Three hundred and seventy two."

Bourjaily was right, the Erie detective thought. Youngstown, Ohio's Lake Meander had to be the mother lode of all illegal weapons dumping sites. The next day, DiPaolo, accompanied by an agent from the Pennsylvania Attorney General's Office, anxiously drove the 90 miles to Youngstown – again, long considered the mob crossroads between Pittsburgh, Cleveland, Buffalo and Erie. At the downtown Mahoning County Sheriff's Department headquarters, in all their dredged up glory from the depths of Lake Meander, were nearly 400 recovered weapons – guns of all makes, sizes and calibers. On display were perhaps every caliber of handgun ever made. Every caliber, that is, except a .32 pistol. Still, despite his disappointment, DiPaolo did not give up hope. He was convinced his stoolies were telling the truth. The gun that killed Frank "Bolo" Dovishaw had to be in the water somewhere near the bridge over Lake Meander. And the Erie cop was determined to find it.

Within several days, DiPaolo returned to Mahoning County and the overpass from where Dorler tossed Bolo Dovishaw's murder weapon. With DiPaolo were members of the Erie County Sheriff's Department Scuba Team. Amid so much hope, however, luck abandoned DiPaolo and the divers. After a day of fruitless diving in the murky Lake Meander water, DiPaolo ordered an end to the search. It had been seven hours in the sub-freezing cold and snow. The small, .32 caliber pistol that ended the life of Erie racketeer Bolo Dovishaw continues to rust, undisturbed, somewhere in the silted bottom of Lake Meander.

The big break with the murder weapon, the one that tied up all the loose ends, had come out in the fight, before the Dovishaw murder, that old man Frank Scalise had with his assailants when the accidentally ejected shell was found at the scene and determined to be from the same gun that killed Bolo. Jimmy Wandless, who was Scalise's step-son-in-law and DiPaolo's childhood friend, told Dom that ol' Frank was hoping to get the gun away from his attackers – nobody was going to take *his* money! DiPaolo thought, only God knows what would have happened had Frank managed to wrest the gun away from them!

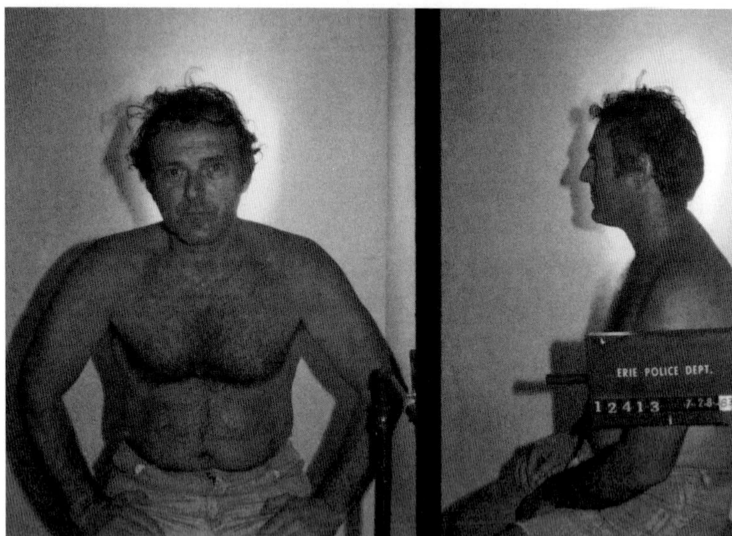

Caesar Montevecchio, a legend in Erie crime and sports, began his organized crime spree in the mid-1950s as a "set-up" man for armed robberies, burglaries, bank robberies and murder in Pennsylvania, Ohio and Michigan. Sentenced early on to up to 70 years in prison, he was paroled after serving only a fraction of the sentence and began a new crime spree. (Courtesy of Erie Police Department)

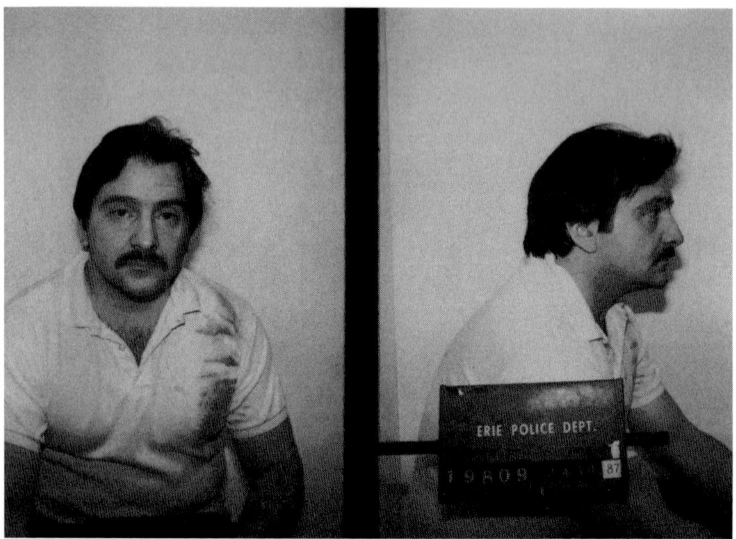

Charles "The Hawk" Serafini was a follower of both Caesar Montevecchio and Anthony Arnone. He was also a suspect in an attempted hit of Det. Sgt. DiPaolo. (Courtesy of Erie Police Department)

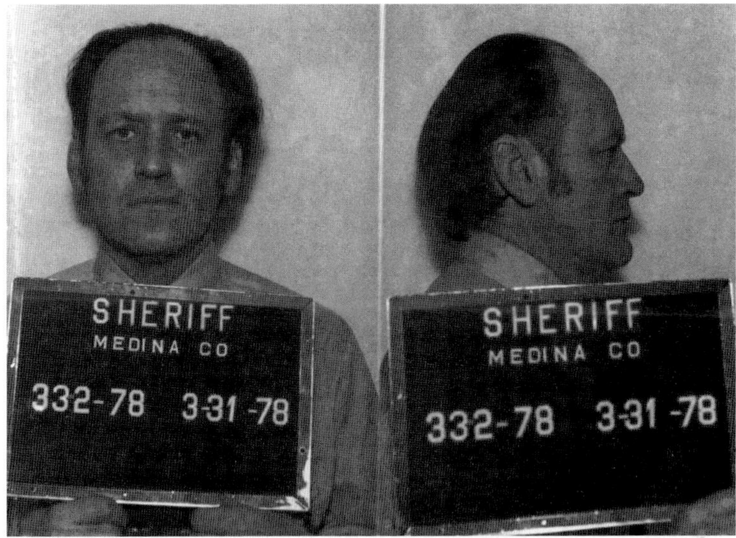

Robert Dorler of Medina, Ohio, convicted of killing Dovishaw and later admitted to an Ohio mob hit. Dorler also was involved in the Erie armed robberies of Jack Miller, Louis Nardo and Frank Scalise. Was sentenced to two concurrent terms of life imprisonment without parole. (Courtesy of Medina, Ohio, Sherriff's Department)

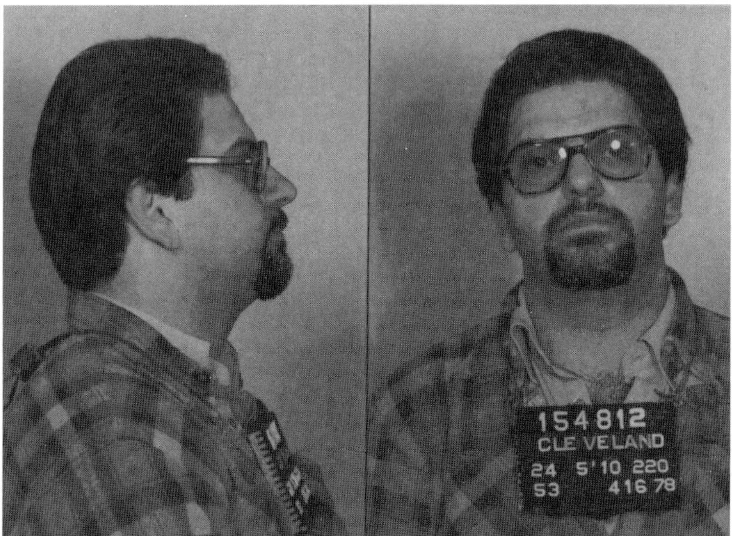

William "Billy" Bourjaily of Parma, Ohio, a convicted drug dealer and Dorler sidekick involved in Erie robberies, was Dorler's wheelman back to Ohio after the Dovishaw hit. Sentenced to 15 years for conspiracy in connection with the "Ash Wednesday" slaying. (Courtesy of Cleveland, Ohio, Police Department)

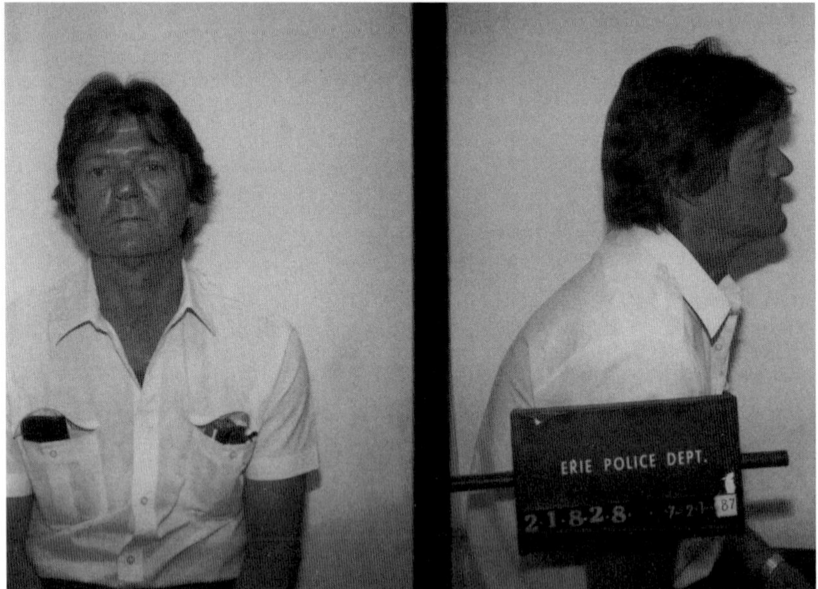

George Meeks of Brooklyn, Ohio, is a convicted felon used by Dorler in armed robberies in Erie. Sentenced to 10 years in prison. (Courtesy of Erie Police Department)

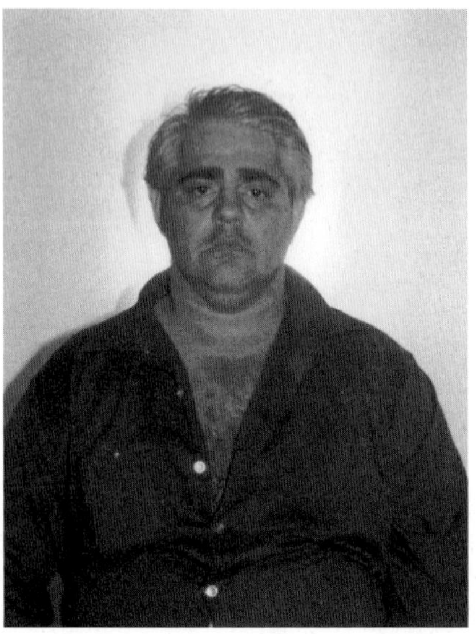

Samuel "Fat Sam" Esper also ran with Montevecchio's gang, but dodged prison by testifying against his pals and was placed in the witness protection program. (Courtesy of Erie Police Department)

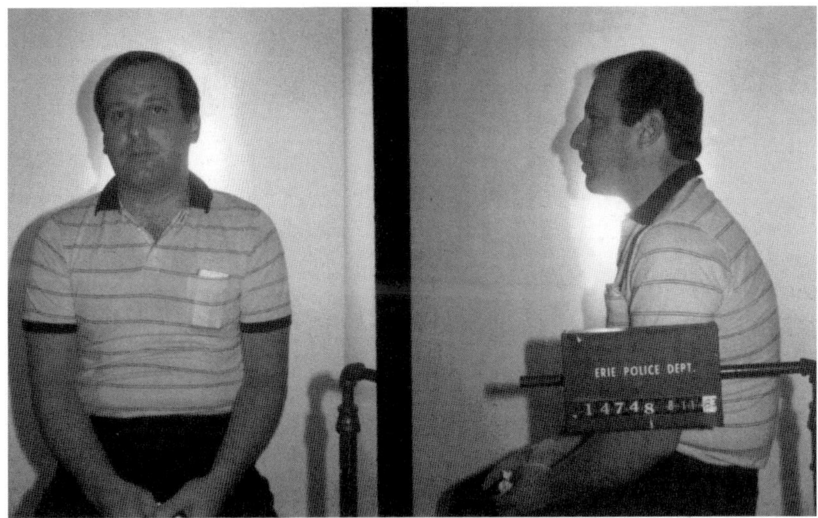

Carl Stellato, aka "Satch," had $700,000 in stolen items from the Nardo burglary at his farmhouse before the loot was taken to Pittsburgh. (Courtesy of Erie Police Department)

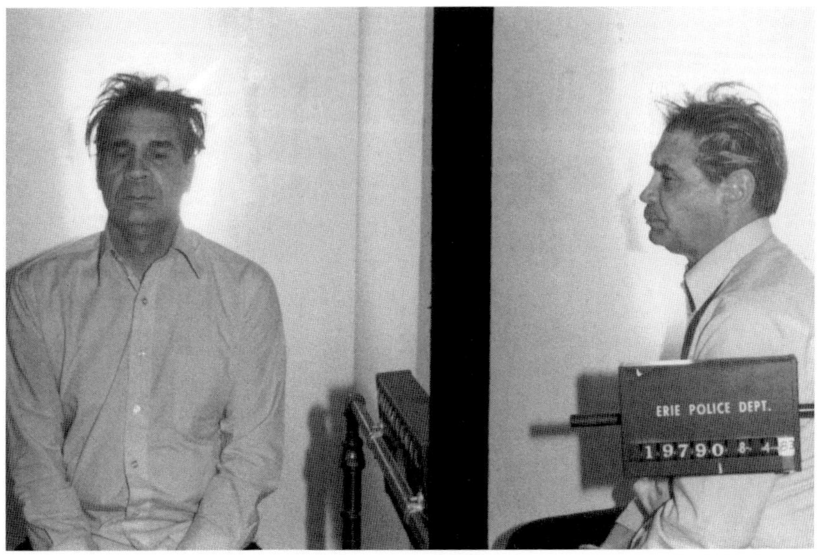

Fredrico "Freddy May" Maggio, a burglar with Montevecchio and Esper, transported some stolen items from the Nardo break-in to be sold in Pittsburgh. (Courtesy of Erie Police Department)

Robert "Bob" Bocci, along with Montevecchio, transported most of Nardo break-in loot to Pittsburgh to be fenced. (Courtesy of Western Penitentiary, Pittsburgh, Pennsylvania)

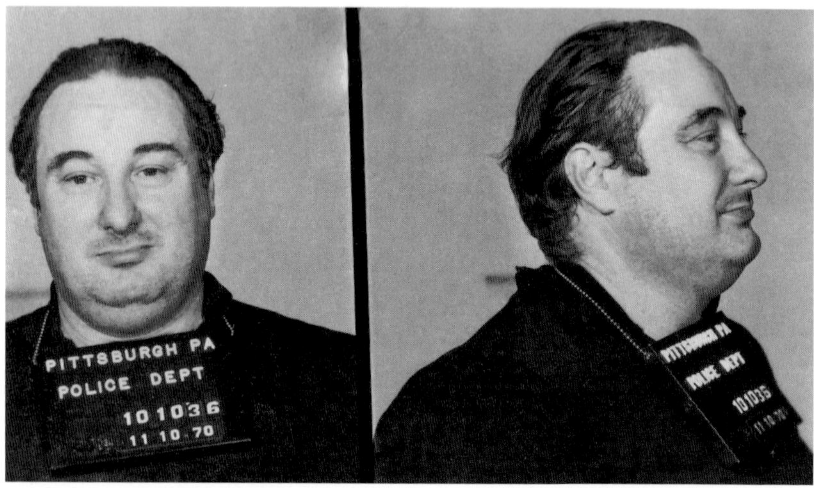

Harry Fleming of Pittsburgh, convicted of murder and burglary, fenced the stolen loot from the Nardo burglary. (Courtesy of Pittsburgh, Pennsylvania, Police Department)

Part Five

THE STAND-UP GUYS FORGET *OMERTA*

CHAPTER 33

With Caesar Montevecchio and Billy Bourjaily both cooperating and talking freely, Dom DiPaolo took an extraordinary step: He helped arrange for legal counsel for both. The move was a shrewd one. It showed DiPaolo wanted no legal foul-ups with his two star witnesses. It also effectively served to eliminate the person DiPaolo considered his longtime chief legal opposition, Attorney Leonard Ambrose, from the overall big picture.

Ambrose had already made life difficult for DiPaolo several years earlier when the lawyer stopped Montevecchio cold from talking with detectives about the Dovishaw murder as well as the 1980 killing of Erie Police Corporal Robert Owen.

At the time, Caesar Montevecchio had been meeting secretly with members of the Pennsylvania Attorney General's strike force, including DiPaolo, as well as agents from the Federal Bureau of Investigation. Erie County District Attorney Michael Veshecco had informed Ambrose of the sessions. Ambrose quickly closed them down. At the time, Montevecchio had not been officially linked to either killing, but police already had in their possession those tape-recorded conversations between Caesar and his pal, "Fat Sam" Esper. The recorded conversations gave a strong indication that Montevecchio had information that could be valuable to police investigators about both cases.

Montevecchio was negotiating for himself and told DiPaolo he did not want his lawyer to know about his deal, DiPaolo told the news media, explaining that Montevecchio had been "Mirandized" and had formally waived his right to have an attorney present during his interrogation. When Ambrose learned of the questioning from Veshecco, however, the criminal lawyer moved immediately to stop the meetings. Joseph Kownacki, then Erie County Public Defender, agreed with Veshecco's actions. But a former prosecutor, Erie County Judge Shad Connelly, was quoted in the same newspaper article as saying there was no legal obligation for a prosecutor to inform the defense attorneys when the defendant has initiated talks with the prosecution and signed the proper waivers.

Whatever the opinions, however, it brought a promising process that could have tied up the Dovishaw case, and perhaps others, years before they were actually adjudicated, to a sudden halt. DiPaolo wanted none of that now. That's why he was prepared to find alternative representation – other than Attorney Leonard Ambrose – for Montevecchio and Bourjaily. Besides, it was best if DiPaolo knew the opposition well. And, both defendants needed legal counsel to help walk them through court appearances on plea bargain dealings as well as represent them at sentencing.

First, DiPaolo telephoned one of his best friends, professionally as well as personally, Attorney Tom Agresti, who had been an assistant district attorney, but was now in private practice with his father, highly-respected Erie Attorney Dick Agresti, and his uncle, Attorney Joseph Agresti. The elder Agresti brothers, and now their offspring, Dick's son, Tom, and Joe's son, Chuck, represented one of Erie's most famed legal families. Dick had founded Boys Baseball, Inc., during the 1950s and had also become a legend in Erie sports as well as local political circles.

"Hey, Dominick, I appreciate you wanting to throw me a bone, but my dad will have a fit with me being involved with the wise guys, you know. So I've got to take a pass on this one," Tom Agresti told DiPaolo.

DiPaolo was disappointed. He had worked with Tom Agresti, now the Chief Federal Judge for Bankruptcy in Northwestern Pennsylvania, on Agresti's first murder trial as an assistant district attorney in 1980, a case in which Agresti won a first degree murder conviction. Glenn Puckett had used his car to run over his wife, who was riding her bicycle home after her night nursing job at Metro Health Center. DiPaolo had put together the Puckett case within days of the murder.

"Then, I'll try Frank Kroto," DiPaolo told Agresti. Kroto was another pal and as experienced in criminal law as any Erie lawyer. Agresti concurred Kroto was an excellent choice.

DiPaolo had worked with Kroto a decade earlier in the successful prosecution of Donald Lee Chism, an Erie father who wiped out his entire family by murdering his children, wife and wife's uncle, five in all, Erie's most notorious mass murder.

"Sure," Kroto said without pause upon receiving the request. "Ten thousand dollars." That was about one-tenth of what DiPaolo believed Ambrose would have charged. DiPaolo knew Montevecchio was getting the biggest bargain of his life.

Caesar had told DiPaolo that his brother later informed him that dumping Ambrose and hiring Kroto saved him $90,000.

DiPaolo believed Ambrose had been phoning Caesar's wife, Bonnie, at home ever since Montevecchio was returned to Erie. The cop believed Ambrose was urging her to have Caesar "hang tight" and "not fold." He urged Bonnie Montevecchio to "call Albert" for the hundred grand, DiPaolo said he later learned from Bonnie Montevecchio. At one point, Bonnie related to DiPaolo that Ambrose had told her, "Get the money from Albert. I'll get him (Caesar) off." Later trial testimony also related the conversation.

"Fuck Lenny," Montevecchio told DiPaolo. "I'm facing 56 fucking charges. If he gets me off on 55, I still do life.

Next, DiPaolo asked Erie County Public Defender Michael Palmisano to represent Billy Bourjaily, walking the Ohio man through court proceedings as well. Palmisano, another former prosecutor (and later a Common Pleas Court judge), readily agreed to take Bourjaily as a private client for $10,000.

DiPaolo and Palmisano had a long history together, dating back to the 1977 murder of Erie newspaper night side printer Bill Berry. Berry was shot to death in his car and it was DiPaolo who developed a suspect in the case. Louis Allessie, apparently upset after his girlfriend broke-up with him, began stalking her. The night Berry was murdered was unfortunately his first date with Allessie's ex. Allessie waited for Berry in Berry's car, ordering him at gunpoint to drive to an east Erie ball field. It was there Allessie executed Berry. Det. Sgt. Walter "Butch"

Gajewski and Detective David Bagnoni worked with DiPaolo on the case. Allessie was convicted by a jury.

After the killing, Allessie's pal, William Rothstein, drove the killer back to his car, and got rid of the gun. Rothstein was later given immunity in return for his testimony against Allessie. Mike Palmisano prosecuted the case while Allessie was represented by a young Michael Dunlavey, who not only became a U.S. Army General in the intelligence field in charge of the "Gitmo" prison, but also a Pennsylvania Common Pleas Court judge in Erie County. (Rothstein would later be involved in Erie's infamous Erie "Pizza Bomber" case during which Brian Wells died when a collar bomb around his neck detonated. Rothstein died of cancer before the Feds figured out his involvement in the case, but the person many considered to be his wacko girlfriend, Marjorie Diehl Armstrong, was convicted in the bizarre bank-robbery/murder case.)

DiPaolo's relationship with Palmisano was one of mutual respect and trust. While he had Palmisano on the line, DiPaolo hinted he would toss him one more client. But the cop did not at the time disclose the client's identity – Ricky Cimino. There was still more leg work to do before the arsonist Cimino fell into DiPaolo's wide-cast net. But now, Cimino – burned ass and all – was finally willing to see things from DiPaolo's perspective.

It was the hot July of 1987, four and a half years after Frank "Bolo" Dovishaw was laid to rest with a bullet hole in his head and a paring knife penetration from his eye to his brain. How different the weather conditions were that July day than the January 1983 night when Bolo died, DiPaolo thought. Weather aside, there were also other extremely significant differences: Key conspirators, including the triggerman, were rolling on each other. And now, finally, Ricky Cimino, a bit player turned arsonist, was about to flip as well.

Cimino, who had been arrested and charged in the February 1, 1985 Pal Joey's fire based on statements from Darrell Steiner, telephoned DiPaolo, not once, but twice, from the Erie County Prison. Cimino wanted to talk. This was the first opportunity DiPaolo would have to interview Cimino, and he now vowed to make the very best of it.

On that muggy day, Cimino was transported less than a block, from the Erie County Prison on the 5th floor of the courthouse to the Erie Police Detective Division on the 1st floor of Erie's City Hall. Patrolman Vinnie Lewandowski, who had been helping DiPaolo all along in the complex investigation, transported Cimino. DiPaolo knew Lewandowski could be trusted.

During their initial session, Cimino quickly cut to the chase: He would cooperate and give up everyone who had anything to do with the arson fire, including his role in it. He also would give up the dirty Erie cop who, albeit unknowingly, had helped to set up the faked finding of bookie Bolo Dovishaw's body. He would produce the tape of DiPaolo's conversation with John Fasenmyer. And, Cimino promised, he would diagram Erie's vast cocaine distribution network and how all the moving pieces fit together and worked for DiPaolo.

According to what Cimino told DiPaolo, federal agents had visited Ricky at the Erie County Prison with a deal. They asked that he testify before a federal grand jury probing cocaine distribution in Erie.

"Those lying fuckin' Feds told me that if I talked on Merchie Calabrese and his son, John, that then maybe, just maybe, my charges would go away."

"What did you tell them?" DiPaolo asked.

"Nothing. But if you want me to talk on Merchie, I will."

"Let's worry about what *we* are doing and fuck the Feds," DiPaolo said. Merchie Calabrese was the son of former Erie Alderman Merchie, Sr., and a longtime wise guy often connected with the activities of Caesar Montevecchio in the late 1960s when they were involved in those many bank jobs along the East Coast.

DiPaolo thought to himself, "So typical of the Feds. Local cops do all the work to get these fuckers behind bars, and then the Feds go and talk to them about their own cases, and lie to them about how they can make the state charges go away. Only they can't! Any wonder why I can't trust them!"

In return for his cooperation with DiPaolo, Cimino wanted a get-out-of-jail-free card. And he also wanted his bail-bond reduced to an attainable level. And, of course he wanted a deal on the eventual sentence he would receive. Incredulously, he actually thought he could receive a sentence of probation, amounting to less than a slap on the wrist.

While DiPaolo was contemplating what appeared to be an outrageous plea-bargain demand, Attorney David Hunter – Cimino's lawyer – telephoned police headquarters and insisted he be connected with DiPaolo. When DiPaolo eventually answered Hunter's call, Hunter said, "I hope you're not talking with my client without me there."

"No," DiPaolo sighed convincingly. "His right hand fingers didn't turn out on the original prints. So we're reprinting him."

"Yeah? Then let me speak with him."

"Sure," DiPaolo said. "Hold on."

Learning Hunter was on the phone, Cimino said, "I don't want him for a lawyer no more. Fuck him."

"Then just tell him you're getting printed," DiPaolo suggested to the arsonist. Cimino followed instructions. DiPaolo wanted to hear more from Cimino while the cop mulled the deal the arsonist set forth. He listened as Cimino spoke candidly about the Scutellas, the ones who owned and operated Pal Joey's Restaurant, and about their involvement in the spectacular torching of their own business, purportedly to collect the big insurance pay-out.

Cimino also spoke about Erie Police Detective Sergeant Frank Rotunda, whose desk, ironically, was positioned directly adjacent to DiPaolo's in the Detective Division at Erie Police Headquarters. Cimino spoke of Rotunda's participation, not only in cocaine trafficking, but also in burglaries with Erie's wise guys and wannabes. Frankie Rotunda, DiPaolo thought, the same dirty cop that hit man Ray Ferritto and Cy Ciotti called upon to "find" Bolo Dovishaw's body in the basement of the West 21st Street house January 4, 1983. DiPaolo, though he loathed Cimino and those of his ilk, nonetheless knew the importance of such valuable witnesses who could help to bring down so many other occupants of Erie's slimy underside.

"Let me take this to the prosecutors," DiPaolo said. "No promises. I'll get back to you."

Dennis Pfannenschmidt, the special prosecutor from the Pennsylvania Attorney General's office, considered what in legal terms was called Ricky Cimino's "proffer" – the tendering of the plea deal he proposed to DiPaolo.

"Full statement," Pfannenschmidt countered. "Full testimony on everyone involved. No objection to bond reduction. And one and a half to three years away from anyone he talks on."

It was a straight-forward counter-offer, but one that still provided a measured response in the punishment meted out to Ricky Cimino. No one was about to allow an arsonist off the hook scot free. Translated, this meant Ricky Cimino would be required to give a full and truthful statement, and then testify against every person he named in his statement. And, there would be no objection to his making bond. But in the end, Cimino must enter a guilty plea and then receive prison time in a different institution from any of those he had testified against. However, without his full cooperation and testimony, Cimino was told, he was looking at a possible maximum sentence of 15 to 30 years in a state penitentiary.

Pfannenschmidt's counter-offer was not exactly what Ricky Cimino had envisioned. He had allowed himself to believe that he could talk his way out of any hard time.

"Let me sleep on it," he told DiPaolo.

"Don't sleep too long," DiPaolo warned. "This deal's not forever. Others are flipping, too."

Ricky Cimino clearly wanted out of jail. On July 27, 1987, he made a decision. As it turned out, it wasn't really that difficult, after all. "Okay," he told Dom DiPaolo. "I'll take your deal. But you got to get me a new lawyer. And I don't want Hunter to know."

Immediately, DiPaolo phoned back the Erie County public defender, Michael Palmisano. "As I mentioned before, I have one more for you," DiPaolo said with a smile. "But we have to meet. The three of us."

Mike Palmisano agreed. During the hastily arranged gathering at Erie Police Headquarters, DiPaolo outlined his demands. "When you get Cimino out on bond, Ricky has to wear a wire on Rotunda."

Cimino, now in a cooperating mode, had no objection. Then, in Palmisano's presence, Ricky Cimino gave his promised full statement. He recounted his first conversation in 1984 with restaurateur Joe Scutella about the torching of Pal Joey's in the heart of downtown Erie.

"I was running the Pickwick Club at the time and doing coke with Joe Scutella, the old man," Cimino began. "I think it was in April or May of 1984 when he told me something like, 'Them fucking kids are running Pal Joey's into the ground.' His idea was to torch the rear of the building, then collect on the six hundred grand in insurance, and somehow then still stay open."

According to Cimino's statement, during the next few months of 1984, Scutella occasionally brought up his arson hopes for the failing restaurant, but he had established no solid plans. It was, at that point, Ricky Cimino said, just talk. But then, in January of 1985, Cimino continued, Scutella finally told him, "Fuck it, man. We have to do it. We're taking a beating."

Cimino said Scutella asked him to set the fire. "I told him I had no idea of how to go about burning down a whole fucking building, or even part of one." But Scutella reassured him, Cimino said, and he quoted the senior Scutella as saying, "Hey, I'll set the place up. You just walk in, throw a cigarette down. That's it. And I'll give you 25 grand for just doing that."

It sounded like pretty easy money, Cimino told DiPaolo while Palmisano listened. Cimino readily agreed to Scutella's arson proposal. Such a simple plan, however, became much more complicated than just the tossing of a lighted cigarette. During the next few weeks, Cimino said, Scutella told him about his nephew traveling to Jamestown, New York, to acquire metal containers colored red, white and blue. The containers, Cimino continued, were to be filled with accelerants. Scutella told Cimino the containers from Jamestown would be attached to timing devices.

"He told me, 'But you know, you still have to light it to get it started,'" Cimino said. Now Cimino was speaking in rapid bursts. He told of an actual "dress rehearsal" late the night before the real event. "We met about 1 a.m. the night before the fire was to be set and Scutella showed me where the cans full of the accelerant would be, and where and how I was to enter the building."

To Cimino, it sure looked like the perfect set-up. So how did it go so wrong?

Monday, January 31, 1985, 10 p.m. The streets were snow-covered and almost deserted. But life was about to heat up in frigid downtown Erie that night.

Ricky Cimino, as he was now relating to Dominick DiPaolo and Public Defender Mike Palmisano two-and-a-half-years later, was with his pal, Darrell Steiner at downtown Erie's popular Plymouth Tavern. The Plymouth was situated on the same side of the street and just a few buildings south along State Street from the soon-to-be-torched Pal Joey's Restaurant.

By 1 a.m. the morning of Tuesday, February 1, 1985, and with courage acquired from several hours of downing the less expensive draft beers from the Plymouth's impressive tap collection, Cimino said he told Steiner he needed to leave for just a few minutes, but would soon return. Cimino said he walked through the night's light snowfall the short distance to Pal Joey's.

"Joe's son Danny was inside bartendering," Cimino said, adding that Peter Vella was seated at the bar. DiPaolo knew Vella to be another wannabe wise guy. (Later, 1988, Vella would be indicted for drug trafficking cocaine and marijuana and caught 15 years in prison.) Hanging out with Vella, Cimino said, were Ernie Scutella, Dan's cousin who worked for the state, and another barroom character who Cimino did not know. He also said the house band, a husband/wife duo called Fire and Ice had played a last set and was leaving. *Fire and Ice*, DiPaolo thought with some irony, how appropriate for a hot event about to unfold on a cold night.

"Near the back bar area, I saw the red, white and blue cans," Cimino said. "It sure looked like the joint was already set up for the fire. So I told Danny I'd check out the upstairs." But when Cimino got outside and approached the East 11th Street side door leading to the second floor area, he said he found the door securely locked. "I went back inside and told Danny the damned door was locked. So he phones his father somewhere. Then, as soon as he hangs up, he calls his sister, Kelli, and tells her to bring him the key to the side door in a hurry."

Cimino soon left to return to the Plymouth and Steiner, but as he was departing Pal Joey's, he said, he nearly bumped into Kelli Scutella, who was rushing through the front door. Apparently, she had followed directions, bringing her brother the key to the restaurant's side door. This was later also established during trial testimony.

Back at the Plymouth, Cimino quickly filled in Steiner, then instructed Darrell to park his car on the south side of West 11th Street, and just across State Street from the targeted Erie restaurant. Cimino said he was supposed to light the fire on the second floor, then escape down the steps and out the side door onto East 11th Street where

Steiner would pick him up and they'd quickly be gone into the snowy night, heading east on 11th Street. At 1:55 a.m., Cimino continued, the pair left the Plymouth together, but split up as Steiner moved to position his car as instructed, while Cimino walked slowly north to the now nearly deserted Pal Joey's.

"Go upstairs!" Cimino quoted Danny Scutella as saying as soon as Scutella spotted Cimino. "Then wait until I tell you I'm leaving before you light it!" Cimino's account was also repeated during trial testimony. (Dan, who was later charged, did nine years after being found guilty during a jury trial.)

Cimino, who walked to the side outside door, said this time the door popped open after he first pushed hard against it. Once on the second floor, he said, he quickly eyed the five red, white and blue cans scattered about the area, just as they were downstairs in back of the bar near the kitchen. Yes, Cimino again thought to himself, they were well-prepared to burn this building to the ground.

He waited. Ten minutes passed, maybe more. Then, Danny Scutella yelled up through the floor vent grating from below: "We're leaving!" He apparently was referring to Vella, Ernie Scutella and the unknown barroom patron. For Cimino, the moment of truth had arrived. What could go wrong? Everything was set for success. Cimino said he found his way through the dark to the back of the building.

He lit a single match. But while it still flickered between his fingers, and even before he could toss it, he was nearly deafened by two loud, booming explosions.

In a nano-second, Ricky Cimino's world turned into the inferno of hell.

Everything was ablaze. Including Ricky Cimino. Terrified and on fire, Cimino told DiPaolo and Palmisano, both mesmerized by the confession, that he dashed down the stairs and burst through the side door to the outside as Pal Joey's Restaurant became a raging conflagration behind him. He was aware the clothing on his back was aflame. He could feel the sharp, stinging pain as he intuitively rolled in the cold, wet slushy sidewalk snow to extinguish the flames.

Still screaming in agony as he forced himself into Darrell Steiner's waiting car, he said he heard Steiner say something about driving to a hospital. Pal Joey's was located about halfway between Erie's two major medical centers, Hamot and Saint Vincent. But Cimino, even in excruciating pain, knew better than drawing any more attention to himself. "No! No! Just take me to Cindy's!" he ordered his driver in agonizing shouts, referring to the apartment of Cimino's girlfriend, Cindy Northrup.

Northrup and her roommate, Tammy Winiecke, lived not far from the multi-alarm blaze now consuming what had been Pal Joey's Restaurant and before that the popular "Erie Restaurant" decades earlier. Both Northrup and Winiecke had been asleep at that wee hour of February 1, Cimino said. But when he and Steiner arrived, both tried to help Cimino, gently bathing his charred and blistering burns with wet towels and cold water.

DiPaolo recalled that after he returned from Florida with Steiner's confession, both Northrup and Winiecke had lied to him. They denied they had treated Cimino for burns that night. Cimino simply was not there. And they never even heard of Steiner. During their later testimony before the same grand jury in which Steiner was also a witness, they issued the same denials – even after the search warrant on Cimino revealed his serious burns. They brought perjury charges on themselves.

Cimino continued his confession: Cimino telephoned Donna Costello, Joe Scutella's squeeze of the moment, about 4 a.m. the morning of the arson fire from Northrup's house, trial testimony later indicated. "When she answered, I said, 'Donna, let me talk to Joe!'" Cimino said. "I heard her say, 'Rick's on the phone for you, Joe.' Then I heard Joe say, 'Yeah. Right. Don't break my balls.'" He never guessed that Cimino had survived.

When Scutella was finally convinced it was indeed Cimino on the phone, he picked up the receiver.

"Hello?" he said.

"I need help!" Cimino said he pleaded with Scutella. For what seemed an eternity, there was only silence from the other end of the line – as though Scutella was indeed surprised to be hearing from the arsonist. Finally, Scutella asked, "Where?"

"Cindy's!"

Scutella hung up. Within 10 minutes he arrived at Northrup's. "What happened?" Scutella asked. He listened as Cimino recounted his tale of woe, of trying to set the blaze, of lighting the match, of the instantaneous explosions, and of being horribly burned.

"Yeah? You must have done something wrong," he quoted Scutella as responding.

"Fuck it!" Cimino said. "Get me a doctor!"

"Yeah. Okay. I'll get someone. Maybe I'll get my doc (an Erie physician) to come over," Scutella said. And then he was out the door. Cimino waited. In pain, in excruciating pain, Ricky Cimino waited. He was unable to sleep except in small exhaustive snatches, and could only think about the pain.

Finally, about 8 a.m. – an eternity for Cimino – wise guy wannabe Pete Vella telephoned. Vella had been one of those hanging out at Pal Joey's bar the previous night. Vella quickly got to the point, Cimino said (and this account was later presented during the trial). Scutella's physician pal would not attend to Cimino's medical needs. But Joe Scutella, Vella told Cimino, had some kind of a physician relative in Canton, Ohio, who would treat Cimino's burns. Canton was a two-and-a-half hour drive. Cimino knew, even through the pain, that his face, hands, back, buttocks and legs were so severely burned that he could never travel by car for two-and-a-half minutes, let alone more than two hours. Or, he wondered, would it be a one-way ride?

"I guess that's when I realized this cocksucker Scutella had set me up," Cimino told DiPaolo and Public Defender Michael Palmisano. "Right then and there I knew that I wasn't supposed to come out of there alive. And then I remembered Scutella's comment to Donna on the phone that morning – that 'Yeah. Right. Don't break my balls.' remark. It now all made sense to me. Scutella was in no way expecting me to call because I was supposed to be burned up!"

When Cimino replayed the conversations in his mind, he said, it all added up. He had been told to remain on the second floor for 10 to 15 minutes after Danny Scutella left the premises. And now he recalled hearing a "click" sound, as though a furnace was clicking itself on. But the sound was actually created by a timing device, Cimino now understood, a device set to detonate and quickly spread the accelerants. Ironically, Cimino had never actually started the blaze. But if the Scutellas' plan had worked as plotted, Cimino would have been blamed for the arson, it was testified to during the later trial. It made Cimino cringe now to envision how his charred remains would have been discovered in the burned out skeleton of what was once Pal Joey's. The Scutellas would have likely claimed to have had a beef with Cimino and that Ricky was attempting to retaliate against them by torching their restaurant, he said.

It would have been convincing to police. But more importantly, it would have been more than convincing to the insurance investigators. DiPaolo, however, had not only screwed up the Scutellas' plan, but had brought the insurance claim to a financially crushing halt. The cop harbored no doubts Cimino was set up to die in the fire. Cimino was now confessing and giving up the Scutellas without feeling even remotely guilty about betraying them. They had betrayed Cimino, and had done so in the most basic of ways.

"I feel relieved," Cimino told DiPaolo. "All Joe Scutella did for me was deliver some salve and lotion while I was in bed for four weeks healing."

Just like the stock market, criminal activity is driven by greed and fear. Not surprisingly, both impulses were coming in full force to Darrell Steiner. Not long after the Pal Joey's arson blaze that nearly burned Ricky Cimino to a crisp, greed kicked in for the impatient get-away driver, Darrell Steiner.

Steiner wanted his money. It was no insignificant sum: half of the $25,000 that had been promised to Cimino. Still relating details of Joseph Scutella's bizarre attempt to cash in the $600,000 insurance policy on Pal Joey's Restaurant in downtown Erie, Cimino told DiPaolo of Steiner's bold, but foolish approach to Joe Scutella.

"He went to Joe about getting paid," Cimino said. "But Scutella had no idea that Darrell was part of my deal. Let's just say that Joe was pissed and leave it at that."

When an outraged Scutella came to Cimino about Joe's encounter with Steiner, Cimino said he told him, "Hey, we got to live with it, that's all."

Scutella blew up. "No! Fuck that! *You* got to live with it," Scutella roared at Cimino. "Just give him some goddamned money before he opens up, you stupid fuck."

"Where the fuck am I going to get it?" Cimino said he asked Scutella.

Scutella grudgingly peeled off five $100 bills from the wad he carried and reluctantly handed over the cash to Cimino. "Pay off Steiner," Scutella ordered.

A short time later, Cimino said, he met with Steiner and paid off the get-away driver with the $500 he got from the angry Joe Scutella. "I told him to get the fuck out of town. And that it was not only stupid, but really fucking dangerous to mess around with Joe Scutella." Interestingly, Steiner had told DiPaolo he got only $200 from Cimino. DiPaolo could only wonder: Did Cimino pocket the remaining $300?

"Tell me who else was involved that you know of for sure," DiPaolo instructed.

"Well, Joe was the only one I talked with, other than Danny telling me he was leaving and Kelli who brought the key down to open the door. I went upstairs, too. That's all I know about." The "nephew" who delivered the Jamestown cans was never named. Tri-Tella, Inc., the legal name of the business that operated the restaurant, was technically owned by Joe III, Danny and Margie Scutella, since, as a convicted felon, Joey could not legally own a liquor license.

As the evidence in the case developed, DiPaolo could not establish any involvement in the arson-set fire by Ernie Scutella. Still, it was more than a godsend to have Cimino on the right side now. The cop knew all about the domino theory in law enforcement. Find a chink in the armor and before long, all the players begin to topple, one by one by one. And Cimino was a good chink.

Ricky Cimino continued his marathon confession to DiPaolo by next discussing the audio tape being played around town for Erie wise guys by John Fasenmyer.

"You actually heard the tape?" DiPaolo asked.

"That's no shit," Cimino said.

"Yeah? Well, what exactly did you hear?" DiPaolo pressed Cimino.

"I heard his offer of a promotion for you. And Ray Ferritto heard it, too. Fasenmyer also gave the tape, or a copy of it, to Margie Scutella, Joe's wife, and then she played it for the whole damn family." Cimino's allegation was also included in his formal statement to police.

"Who else?" DiPaolo asked, managing not to show how pissed he was.

Now laughing, Cimino said, "I'll tell you. Fasenmyer gave it to Johnny Bizzarro (former Erie boxer and used car lot owner) and even Tullio (Mayor Louis Tullio) heard it." (Tullio later acknowledged he heard the tape, but said the offer was not true, he had nothing to do with it, and was shocked his name was being used in such a way.)

"How can I get a hold of it?" DiPaolo asked, again with nonchalance.

Cimino thought for a moment. DiPaolo waited, again trying to hide his frustration with the many clowns, and worrying he wasn't doing a very good job of it.

"Well, I can have my father (Bob Cimino) call Fasenmyer and pick it up. He can tell Fasenmyer that (Attorney) Hunter wants it as part of his defense plan for me. My father will bring it to you."

DiPaolo didn't have to think for long. "Make the arrangements," the detective instructed. "And do it fast."

The next day, Bob Cimino dutifully showed up at Erie Police Headquarters with the tape. DiPaolo was also the recipient of an unexpected telephone call that day from Mike Salarino, another wannabe and friend of both Fasenmyer and Cimino. Salarino would later die a lonely death in prison. But now he was calling DiPaolo at the behest of his pal, Ricky Cimino. Salarino and Cimino had spoken about John Fasenmyer and the controversial tape recording the night before at the Erie County Prison. Salarino told DiPaolo that Cimino asked him to call with this new information about John and the tape.

"Let's hear it," DiPaolo sighed, wondering what possibly could be new information about the tape.

"Apparently, before Fasenmyer talked with you, he came to my house and asked my wife, Arlene, whether she had a small tape player," Salarino said. "You know the kind, one that also records cassettes."

"Did you own a recorder?" said DiPaolo.

"Yeah. Well, our daughter did. So Arlene agrees to let him borrow our daughter's tape player and recorder."

"What else did he tell her?"

"Fasenmyer told her that he only needed the machine for that day and that he would return it immediately, as soon as he was done using it."

"Then what?" DiPaolo asked, now feeling himself becoming more and more pissed off with that asshole Fasenmyer – the whole bunch of assholes, actually.

"He brought it back later when I was there. Fasenmyer said, 'I tried to put DiPaolo in a jackpot (compromising position) but it didn't work.' That's all. I figured out what it was all about later when the tape was being passed all over the place. Dom, I want you to know it sure as hell wasn't my idea. We, none of us, had no frigging idea of what he wanted that tape machine for."

Salarino was one of Cimino's best and closest friends, DiPaolo knew. Then, on May 3, 1987, about two weeks prior to Cimino's arrest, Salarino got his 15 minutes of fame when he was written up in the *Erie Daily Times*. At the local Commodore Downs horseracing track, Salarino had scored the largest twin trifecta win in the track's history. Together with Cimino, Salarino had hit for $195,000.

And I'm actually making less than 20 grand a year chasing these nitwits around, DiPaolo mused to himself with no little sense of irony. But he wouldn't have it any other way.

All during his interview with Ricky Cimino, in the back of DiPaolo's mind was the dirty cop – Frankie Rotunda. As much as DiPaolo hated wise guys for muddying the reputation of honest, hard-working Italian-Americans, the detective sergeant detested the very thought of just one dirty cop even more. That the short, baby-faced Frankie Rotunda was also of Italian heritage only made DiPaolo despise him more vehemently. DiPaolo vowed that if nothing else, he'd see the weasel-like detective rot in prison. In fact, he'd take delight in putting him there! And now Cimino, during his long confession, was finally getting to Rotunda.

"Rotunda was into cocaine big time," Cimino said. "And now he's doing house jobs, too."

"House jobs? Really? For example?"

"Frank and Vinnie DiPasquale did a house on Pine Avenue. They got a ton of jewelry. Vinnie took it to Buffalo to fence and got $28,000 for it."

"What else?"

Cimino paused again, trying to sort out in his mind what was relevant and what wasn't. "Well, Frankie Rotunda and Ronnie Thomas got into a really major beef over Thomas' claims that Rotunda ripped him off over a kilo of coke. You interested in something like that?" Ricky Cimino asked.

What the fuck! DiPaolo thought. "Of course I'm interested! What kind of quantity are they dealing with?" he asked.

"Jimmy and Larry Troop are running the stuff for Rotunda and Thomas. They're moving kilos at a pace of maybe two and three times a month. That's big bucks any way you look at it," Cimino explained, as though DiPaolo, the ex-narc, was totally ignorant about the value of illegal drugs. Yet, despite his many years on the Drug Squad, DiPaolo did not rebuke Cimino. He was content to allow Ricky to talk as much as he wanted.

DiPaolo had long been acquainted with the Troop brothers, two thugs from Erie's eastside who made minor names for themselves in high school athletics, but quickly went south after their glory days had ended.

"What else?"

"Well, Frank Rotunda is convinced that because of his close personal relationship with that Berardi guy that he's untouchable," Cimino said. Art Berardi was Erie's police director, appointed by Mayor Tullio to oversee police operations. Even the police chief reported to Berardi. And Berardi reported only to the mayor. DiPaolo was also aware of Berardi's relationship with Rotunda, and that the two occasionally dined together.

"You know," Cimino ventured somewhat cautiously, "that Berardi guy doesn't like you all that much. One night, when they were having dinner, Berardi tells Frank that you don't like Italians. That you only lock up Italians and that you're not very much of a team player."

Seeing red, DiPaolo nearly lost it. He had never been a big fan of the police director. *Too bad Fasenmyer didn't bring up Berardi's name on the tape. I could've mother-fucked that wannabe cop!* DiPaolo thought. *That would have given all of them pause.*

DiPaolo did not respect either Berardi, a former Pennsylvania State Police officer, or Erie Mayor Louis J. Tullio. Recalling that Berardi had gotten himself caught up – but never actually implicated – in a cheating scandal over state police promotions, DiPaolo knew the police director had been under intense pressure to retire from the state police when Tullio hired him. In connection with the cheating scandal, Berardi was mentioned in a PSP book, "75 Years of the Pennsylvania State Police." If for nothing else, DiPaolo would forever have bad taste in his mouth for the way Berardi upset the family of a cop who died several years after retiring. Berardi stopped former Detective Rito Woolis' family from burying him in his Erie Police uniform, saying only active officers can be so-honored at burial. To DiPaolo, who knew better, Berardi's denial – and the hurt it caused – were unforgivable.

Later, members of Erie's Fraternal Order of Police accused Berardi of making statements detrimental to Erie police and their FOP organization. He was suspended from the Pennsylvania State Police FOP in which he held membership. His appeal to the state and national FOP lodges was denied.

"Berardi was right about one thing," DiPaolo told Cimino. "I would sure as hell never want to be on his or Lou Tullio's team."

After a moment or two of awkward silence, DiPaolo directed that Cimino continue with his narrative.

"Well, just before I was arrested, Frank asked me if I was interested in doing a house job with him. It seems he had been assigned to investigate a case involving some old lady who was ripped off by a gypsy in one of those roofing scams going around now. Rotunda says the woman is in her upper-70s and lives alone. He says her dead husband had owned some kind of a machine shop and made a lot of money, and that the old lady had a walk-in safe in their house."

"What then?"

"Rotunda says the safe had to be loaded. But I got busted and never got to do it with him."

Now it was DiPaolo's turn to ponder Cimino's revelations about Rotunda. The way it stood, it would be Cimino's not-credible, unreliable word against that of a police officer. Never a good match up, even in the best of circumstances, to put a criminal's word against that of a cop's. Defense attorneys always want to know whether jury members will give more credence to a cop than an average citizen. And prospective jurors usually give the politically correct answer that all witness testimony will be weighted evenly. But everyone knows that jury members give the most weight to cops, correctly, or innocently, believing police officers are supposed to be the good guys. No, DiPaolo knew he needed more.

"Let's say I get you out on bond and the offer is still good," he began. "Will you wear a wire on Rotunda?"

"Dominick, I don't want to go to jail," Cimino said "Whatever you want, man. If you want me to wear one on the mayor or on Berardi, you got it."

"Don't fucking tempt me with Tullio and Berardi. But we'll definitely talk about that later."

With Cimino's bail-bond set at $500,000, DiPaolo needed to know how much bond the now-cooperating witness could make. "Give me a reasonable number," DiPaolo said.

"One hundred grand," Cimino quickly answered. "I know I can come up with that."

"Okay," the cop said. "We'll make it happen. But first, there's more for you to talk about. Much more."

Ricky Cimino was a font of information, a one-person Erie crime scene directory. As he continued his interview with DiPaolo, Cimino highlighted his cocaine connections and those with whom he was affiliated and dealing. At that time in the mid-1980s, high quality coke had a street going rate of $2,400 an ounce. That put it way above the price of most everything, including gold.

Suddenly, Cimino recalled a home invasion robbery pulled off by the Troop brothers and the Detective Frank Rotunda. Not only did Rotunda drive the get-away car for the Troops, but he had his son, Tim Rotunda with him. "Another Joe Scutella 'bring-your-kid-to-work-day,'" DiPaolo thought. Tim Rotunda later pleaded to the crime.

"They beat the fuck out of a guy and his wife and sons," Cimino said.

DiPaolo had been given similar information earlier by other sources, including from the victim who said the Troops were responsible for the beating and that a cop was involved as well. But the guy would not testify. DiPaolo made an indelible mental note to follow up on this dirty cop later. Something more was bothering the Erie officer. It gnawed in his gut: A detective sergeant had used his official assignment to plan the victimization of an elderly woman who had already been victimized once before. DiPaolo thought, cops are supposed to be the good guys. But not this one! It was behavior so foreign to DiPaolo he would never understand. Never.

CHAPTER 34

Although he wasn't exactly thrilled with working with Ricky Cimino, as expected, Detective Sergeant DiPaolo made good on his promise. He phoned Erie County Public Defender Michael Palmisano and asked that a court motion be filed for reduction of Cimino's bail-bond. What DiPaolo didn't know, however, was that Palmisano and Attorney Hunter had previously filed such a motion to get Cimino's bond reduced – and the motion was promptly denied by the sitting judge.

"Who was the judge who turned it down?" DiPaolo asked Mike Palmisano.

"Shad Connelly."

"Let me call him before you re-file."

Erie County Judge Shad Connelly was a former prosecutor, a dyed-in-the-wool "Law and Order" type who hated the bad guys as much as DiPaolo did. DiPaolo's relationship with Connelly went back to the early '70s when DiPaolo moonlighted at the Cally Club. Late one night around the holidays, Connelly, home from law school, tried to get into the club, but had no membership or sponsor. Just seconds before, DiPaolo turned down another person trying to get in and for the same reason. This person was still lingering in the lobby when Connelly appeared. After DiPaolo explained to Connelly at least three times why he could not allow him to enter, Connelly made the mistake of saying, "I'm going in and I don't see anyone who is going to keep me out!"

As the future lawyer, prosecutor and judge started to walk around DiPaolo, the cop grabbed him, a scuffle ensued, and Connelly found himself in the Erie Bureau of Police lock-up on a charge of disorderly conduct. Soon after, Attorneys Chester and Richard Vendetti, Connelly's first cousins, contacted DiPaolo, asking that the cop give Connelly a break and withdraw the charges. They thought the charges would hurt the law student. DiPaolo agreed. The charge went away. Connelly became an attorney and after landing an assistantship in the Public Defender's Office, a second confrontation took place, this time in a courtroom.

DiPaolo was testifying and the young public defender was trying to get under the cop's skin with the defense questions. "Have you ever been suspended from duty?" Connelly asked.

Before Assistant District Attorney Bernie Siegel could object, DiPaolo calmly stated, "Never, Mr. Connelly."

President Judge Edward Carney called the attorneys to a sidebar at the bench and said, "I don't know what you're trying to prove, but don't you ever again do that to a police officer in my courtroom, Mr. Connelly. There is no need for that. You have a lot to learn!"

After the jury went into deliberations, DiPaolo explained to Siegel why Connelly had asked the question. When the jury members returned barely an hour later, they found Connelly's client guilty. Leaving the courtroom, Connelly apologized to DiPaolo. Later, after Connelly became an assistant district attorney himself, he and DiPaolo became close personal friends, attending each other's kids' graduation parties and weddings.

Connelly and Frank Scutella, as assistant DAs, were required to support their boss, Bob Chase, when Chase ran against Mike Veshecco in 1980. DiPaolo was a strong supporter of Veshecco and when Veshecco won the election and planned to clean house in the DA's office, it was DiPaolo who convinced him to keep Connelly and Scutella, as both, in DiPaolo's mind, were excellent prosecutors. Veshecco agreed to keep the two on, but only for a few months while he had the opportunity to observe them and determine whether they fit in with his operation. Both turned out to be Veshecco's go-to prosecutors – both were kept on permanently.

DiPaolo recalled all this in his mind as he spoke briefly with his old pal before telephoning Public Defender Palmisano. "Re-file the motion," he told Palmisano.

There were still more calls for DiPaolo to make that morning. One was to Ricky Cimino's father, Bob Cimino. "If you want your kid out of jail soon, better start rounding up $100,000 bail-bond," DiPaolo instructed the senior Cimino, who assured the veteran Erie cop he could put together the required bond.

And so on July 27, 1987, the multi-faceted hood Ricky Cimino – now police snitch extraordinaire – was released from the Erie County Prison after posting the reduced $100,000 bond. The money had been put together like a brokered stock deal with help from Bob Cimino, his buddy Mike Salarino, his cousin Ronnie Sciarrilli, his aunt Isabella Abbatto, and his good friend, former Pennsylvania State Representative Bob Bellomini. Such information about bail bond is always a part of the public record, and was reported in the newspaper as well.

Bellomini, known best as "Bells" to the west-Erie crowd of Democrats that put him in office, had just been released from prison following a five-year stint for graciously receiving kickbacks while in office. In Erie's dark underbelly, everyone was somehow related. Damn near incestuous, DiPaolo often thought.

The next time Dom DiPaolo and Ricky Cimino met, Cimino was a free man, at least temporarily. DiPaolo skipped the informal pleasantries and was rather direct in his warning: "I helped get you out," he said. "Fuck with me, and know that I'll bury you."

Cimino nodded cooperatively.

"I'll give you a couple of days to come up with information I need. Start hanging around. I'll expect you to call me in two days. Two days! Got it?"

Cimino started to protest the lack of time, but DiPaolo interrupted him. "You've got two days. Don't make me regret this."

But Ricky Cimino, burned ass and all, turned out to be good to his word. Two days after his release from jail he telephoned the cop who helped get his bond reduced. "I just left Frankie Rotunda," Cimino told DiPaolo. "We had a few drinks at Lombardo's Tavern, where we hang out."

"And?"

"And he wants me to help him do a job at a rich widow's house over the weekend. I told him I wanted to think about it and would let him know later."

DiPaolo smiled.

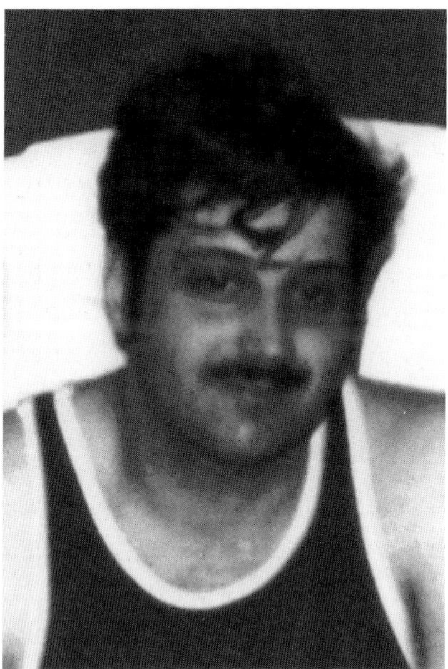

Former Erie police officer Frank Rotunda was sentenced to serve 18 years in prison for armed robbery and solicitation to commit murder in connection with hiring men to kill his cocaine partner. (Author's Personal Collection)

Ronald Thomas, a convicted cocaine dealer, was the target of Rotunda's murder plot. (Courtesy of *Erie Times News*, Erie, Pennsylvania. Photo by Rob Engelhardt.)

Larry "Yogi" Troop was hired by Rotunda to kill Thomas, but reported the plot to police. A year later, DiPaolo arrested Troop and his brother, James, for multiple armed robberies. The Troops were sentenced to serve 25-to-50 years. (Courtesy of Pennsylvania State Probation and Parole)

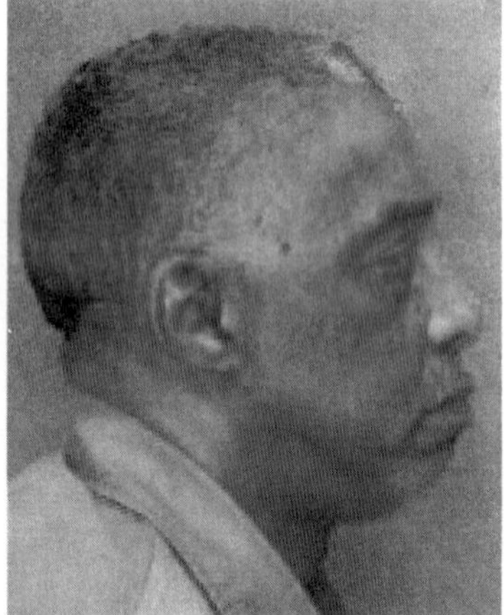

Inmate Number: **AJ2812**
Name: **Troop, James**
Photo Date: **2/25/2013**

James Troop, Larry's brother, also hired by Rotunda in the Thomas murder plot, but went to police and was given immunity. Later, he was sentenced to serve up to 50 years with his brother for multiple armed robberies. (Courtesy of Pennsylvania Penitentiary)

DiPaolo reacted swiftly to this new information.

The next Saturday, Ricky Cimino found himself wired for sound. Wearing the body wire, Cimino was meeting Erie Police Detective Frank Rotunda at the Lampe Marina, situated along Erie's east bayfront. When the time came, DiPaolo, the surveillance cops in the van and Cimino in the car waited some 45 minutes. But Rotunda remained a no-show and finally the cops called it a night. (The only activity the surveillance team observed was an Erie Police Detective Sergeant boarding a boat at the marina with a female attorney friend. DiPaolo recalls the rocking boat and the raucous laughter of the surveillance team members as being the only highlight of the evening's stake-out.)

DiPaolo, however, was not finished with Cimino. In fact, the cop was far from finished with his new snitch. "Just make sure you call me immediately after your next contact with Rotunda," DiPaolo warned.

Cimino nodded dutifully.

While DiPaolo was keeping Cimino on a short leash, another event transpired that greatly worried the cop. And he would soon become uncertain and skeptical of whom he could trust – even the supposed good guys: The cops.

It was the following Monday morning when Erie Police Director Arthur Berardi telephoned DiPaolo at the Pennsylvania Attorney General's Office where DiPaolo was assigned to work. The content of the call somewhat stunned DiPaolo, who was not easily surprised by anything.

"I just want you to know – in case your investigation is going in that direction – that the feds are going to take down Frank Rotunda today," Berardi explained. DiPaolo could not help but wonder whether Berardi had been tipped off about what he and Cimino were up to in relation to Berardi's pal, Rotunda.

"Rotunda?" DiPaolo feigned surprise. "Hell, I'm not doing anything on him."

"Well just remember," Berardi warned the detective, "hands off on Rotunda."

It was almost too much of a coincidence, DiPaolo thought after they hung up. The call represented the first time Berardi had ever contacted or even ever spoken to DiPaolo about anything. Suddenly out of nowhere, DiPaolo was being told to lay off Berardi's good buddy? And the cop could only wonder if anyone in the AG's office was perhaps talking way too much out of school.

Later that same day, DiPaolo learned from the Pennsylvania Attorney General's Office in Harrisburg that state investigators had received what was termed a "courtesy call" from federal agents about Rotunda. The feds had known all along that Rotunda's name surfaced during the Frank "Bolo" Dovishaw murder investigation. And the feds had now been tipped off – by whom, DiPaolo was not told – that DiPaolo was running a wire on Rotunda with authorization from the state AG's office. As a result, the feds, long untrustworthy in DiPaolo's eyes, telephoned Police Director Berardi. They told Berardi they were going to take down Rotunda and they didn't want some local dick like Dominick DiPaolo interfering with their plans. Berardi assured the federal agents that he held enough of a position of authority within the Erie Police Department to call off DiPaolo. Later, DiPaolo was told by the FBI that investigators did not ask Berardi to call him. So, it was a toss-up as to who was lying, DiPaolo thought: Berardi or the FBI.

That afternoon, Erie police detective Frank Rotunda, a short man who reportedly wore lifters in his shoes, a man whose five foot four frame might not have met police height standards if not for getting a pass from Mayor Louis Tullio, made his family proud again. FBI agents arrested the cop on a charge of criminal solicitation to commit murder. The intended target had been Ronnie Thomas, the same Ronnie Thomas long involved in illegal drug and underworld activities. The same man Cimino had fingered to DiPaolo in earlier conversations.

The Troop brothers, when pressed, had given up Rotunda after they were approached by the cop to kill Thomas. They also confessed to the home invasion robbery involving Rotunda and his son, along with at least several large cocaine deals. Rotunda knew he was done. He quickly caved. Within two months he pleaded guilty to the charges and was sentenced to serve nine years in prison. But knowing the feds, DiPaolo suspected he would be out in no time.

What DiPaolo also knew was that the ex-detective would become Queen of the Hop in prison, with a dance card filled nightly. Could not have happened to a better guy, DiPaolo thought. In fact, while Rotunda was waiting to be shipped to a federal slammer, and while he was housed in the county jail at New Castle, Pennsylvania, he was tuned up by other inmates – and on Thanksgiving! Cops in prison rarely fare well. But he still didn't think Rotunda got enough time!

As for the Troops, they got a "kiss" from the feds and were quickly out on the street again and up to their old illegalities. Rotunda's son, Tim, who had been along with him on the armed robbery, was arrested for tossing the guns used in the robbery, guns owned by his father, into Lake Erie. The kid pleaded guilty to a felony count, but since it was his first offense, he caught a break – three years probation.

DiPaolo was later assigned to investigate a rash of armed robberies. He quickly developed the Troops and their pals as prime suspects. After DiPaolo served search warrants at homes where the Troops were known to stay, the brothers fled town. A short time later, while DiPaolo watched the local evening news, he learned the owner of a Meadville, Pennsylvania, jewelry store was shot, along with a customer, during an armed robbery. After hearing the description of the robbers, the Erie cop contacted Meadville Police. The robbery M.O. was similar to that used by the Troops. He did not hesitate to arrest the brothers. On January 9, 1989, the Troops were convicted of the Erie armed robberies and sentenced in Erie County Court to serve 25-to-50 years in a state penitentiary, and also slammed again in Crawford County Court for the Meadville armed robbery and shootings.

Unlike the feds, DiPaolo refused to cut the Troops a break, even after they begged for leniency. In court, the Troops tried to say that DiPaolo hated them for what they did to his buddy, Frankie Rotunda. Little did they know, DiPaolo was happy they took Rotunda down – he was never DiPaolo's friend. According to Jimmy Troop's testimony to the judge, "Me and my brother both stand over six feet tall. But if the description was two white midgets doing the robberies, he (DiPaolo) still would have arrested us." The judge told Troop he heard enough, and gave him a new home for up to 50 years.

Meanwhile, the Pal Joey's arson probe ended with Joe Scutella and his son, Dan Scutella, both being convicted following a week-long trial. The old man got 15-to-30 years and his kid caught nine-to-eighteen years. Ricky Cimino did almost two years, and Darrell Steiner was back in Florida basking in the sun, another stoolie who skated. Cindy Northup and Tammy Winiecke, who initially "didn't know anything," were charged with perjury and false swearing and eventually came to their senses and pleaded guilty. The general assumption was that they were used and scared, each got five year's probation.

An interesting and unexpected development in the Pal Joey's investigation occurred when John Fasenmyer pleaded no contest to a charge of wire-tapping a conversation with DiPaolo. Fasenmyer, in exchange for his plea, was cut a break and sentenced to a year of probation and fined only $300. Also in return for the plea, a charge of attempted bribery was dismissed. Fasenmyer had been represented by a good drinking buddy, according to DiPaolo, the future Erie County District Attorney, Brad Foulk. It was DiPaolo's own observation. DiPaolo, who earlier in his career had moonlighted at the downtown Erie Holiday Inn, recalled seeing the two together often.

Although not a central figure or defendant in the arson fire that destroyed the downtown restaurant, it was Fasenmyer who talked with DiPaolo at a used car lot, offering him a promotion if DiPaolo would drop his investigation of Ricky Cimino.

The Pennsylvania Attorney General's office had accused Fasenmyer of illegally wiretapping his conversation with DiPaolo, and with criminal conspiracy to commit bribery in offering to use his alleged influence with two Erie businessmen and Mayor Lou Tullio to get DiPaolo the promotion. So, all along the way, key and peripheral figures on Erie's crime scene were dropping by the wayside as DiPaolo forged ahead with his Dovishaw murder probe.

CHAPTER 35

THE DATE TO BRING DIPAOLO'S INVESTIGATION INTO THE DOVISHAW murder before a grand jury was fast approaching. It was already August, and the statewide grand jury was set to meet in September in North Huntingdon Township, just east of Pittsburgh. There was still much legwork to be done, DiPaolo knew. But he also knew he would be ready to help the A.G.'s office make a case before the investigative grand jury. Part of DiPaolo's plan was to make his stars – Caesar Montevecchio and Billy Bourjaily – more credible before the jury panelists when they testified.

DiPaolo telephoned Greg Orlando, Erie County Court Administrator, longtime close friend from DiPaolo's youth and godfather for the DiPaolos' daughter, Dawn Marie. DiPaolo asked Orlando to coordinate a plea arrangement for Montevecchio, Bourjaily and Cimino, but keep it under wraps so that even the media would not know until the day of the plea. DiPaolo knew he could trust his life-long friend – and Orlando complied.

On August 20, 1987, Montevecchio and Bourjaily pleaded guilty to all they had been charged with – including third degree murder in the Dovishaw killing nearly five years earlier. Caesar had been charged on 56 criminal counts, including the Nardo burglary and other crimes, charges that had been reinstated from 1983 by the Pennsylvania Superior Court. Bourjaily was charged with 19 offenses. DiPaolo arranged to have the Louie Nardo armed robbery charges dropped after determining

Bourjaily was not present for it. After all the media coverage, it was obvious to all that Montevecchio and Bourjaily had made significant plea-bargaining deals with police.

Within an hour of their guilty pleas in open court at the Erie County Courthouse, DiPaolo had search warrants prepared and executed on Anthony "Niggsy" Arnone's safe-deposit boxes at the PennBank branch where Arnone's cousin Theresa Mastrey served as a bank officer.

At the West 26th Street branch, Box No. 509 was drilled open. The box rented by Arnone was empty. But the signature card revealed two entries: One of them, May 12, 1982, when Arnone first rented the box, was initialed by the bank official "T.M." On January 4, 1983, the day after Frank "Bolo" Dovishaw's murder, Arnone entered the box again for the second and final time. Absent were the initials of any bank representative. The information, or lack thereof, was nonetheless telling, DiPaolo thought.

DiPaolo's investigation was now showing Niggsy Arnone to be concerned about Bonnie Montevecchio's well-being. In the days prior to and leading up to DiPaolo's securing search warrants and drilling Niggsy Arnone's bank safe-deposit box, and prior to Caesar Montevecchio's guilty plea, DiPaolo learned Arnone was phoning Bonnie Montevecchio almost daily with offers of help.

"He called her almost every day," Montevecchio told DiPaolo. "He kept asking whether she needed anything or whether I needed anything. He also brought food to the house and kept asking Bonnie why I was not calling him anymore."

Bonnie apparently told Arnone that her husband's telephone use while in prison was limited to calls to her and to his defense lawyers.

"Tell him to stay tough," Arnone had instructed Bonnie, according to Montevecchio. "Tell him not to worry, that things will work out."

DiPaolo now wondered whether Arnone had become suspicious about Caesar's possible cooperation with police. Especially since Anthony "Niggsy" Arnone was suddenly paying so much attention to Bonnie Montevecchio and the Montevecchio family's welfare. But all the attention came much too late. The deed was done. No amount of salami, prosciutto, capocollo, cannoli, provolone or pseudo family concern could keep Caesar from talking on Arnone. Perhaps Arnone knew what was coming, perhaps not. Either way, it now didn't make much difference to DiPaolo. One-by-one, the dominos were falling.

The Erie police detective sergeant was on a roll with his now busy power drill. Safe-deposit Box No. 450 was being drilled open. The box was owned by Theresa and Donald Mastrey. And Dom DiPaolo couldn't wait to look inside.

DiPaolo's anticipation of the contents of Box No. 450 proved worth the wait. Inside, police found an assortment of currency, starting with John F. Kennedy half-dollars, coin proof sets, U.S. mint sets, Canadian currency and even U.S. Savings Bonds, now almost obsolete. Police also found three white envelopes addressed to Mr. and Mrs. Donald Mastrostefano, one to Mr. Liborio Arnone, one to Mr. and Mrs. Frank Palilla and Mr. and Mrs. Liborio Arnone. All the envelopes contained U.S. currency. Added together, there was $17,000 in cash stashed in the envelopes.

But there was more. DiPaolo found another $35,000 in seven neat $100-bill stacks of $5,000 each. As an officer for a bank, DiPaolo pondered, one would figure Theresa would have thought better of leaving all that money laying idle. Why not collect interest through an IRA, CD or any of dozens of instruments of investment? he wondered. DiPaolo thought of her Box, No. 450, being next to Bolo's, No. 449. And he recalled what Caesar said Arnone told him about Bolo's new box being in a "great area."

All the contents of the box had to be inventoried. Photo copies of all the documents were made. And the inventories were left with credible bank officials.

Once the busywork was completed, DiPaolo drove straight to Arnone's Import Warehouse at West 18th and Cherry Streets in Little Italy.

"Hey, Dom! How ya doin'?"

If Niggsy Arnone was surprised, or even upset to see the Erie police detective in his place of business, Arnone never let on. At least not then.

"Great, Niggsy!" DiPaolo responded with a wide grin. "And you, Niggsy?"

"Fine, fine! But wassup?" Arnone asked, starting to appear somewhat concerned with all this good cheer coming from Erie's leading criminal investigator.

"Can we talk someplace?"

Also present were Frank Ferrare and Salvatore Palilla, Theresa Mastrey's brother, who worked at Arnone's. Neither man offered a word of greeting, although both knew DiPaolo quite well. Now Arnone was starting to look very concerned about the unexpected visitor. Quietly, he led DiPaolo and an agent from the Pennsylvania Attorney General's Office away from the others and to Arnone's private office. DiPaolo was savoring the moment.

After what seemed like a lengthy awkward silence, DiPaolo finally advised him: "We've just drilled your safe deposit box at Theresa's bank." With much fanfare, he handed Arnone the search warrant and the box's inventory sheet.

"Read it!" DiPaolo instructed.

Arnone blanched, turning ghostly white. It was obvious he was shocked by this new development.

"My box?" he stammered. "My box? For what?" He snatched the search warrant and box inventory list from DiPaolo's outstretched hand, fire burning in his eyes.

"Read it!" DiPaolo ordered again, but this time with a smile.

DiPaolo never prided himself much on his writing skills. But he was positive this search warrant was one of the best he had ever produced – all 12 pages from start to finish. It spelled out all the details of woe that transpired years earlier. And now Niggsy Arnone was reading all about it. Caesar. Dovishaw. Ferritto. Mastrey. Palilla. All in black and white. Arnone's hands shook as he read.

After nearly 10 minutes of eerie silence, Anthony "Niggsy" Arnone finally looked up from the warrant and began to bellow, "Caesar Montevecchio told you this!"

Now Arnone was becoming furious. He threw the search warrant to the floor and demanded, "Get this fuckin' shit out of here! This cocksucker is a deranged person! That's who you're fuckin' dealing with, an extremely deranged person!"

Niggsy Arnone was now visibly shaking so badly that DiPaolo thought he was going to pass out. But the cop couldn't help but further make his point to the man he now believed orchestrated "Ash Wednesday's" murder years earlier.

"Hey, wait a minute, Niggsy," DiPaolo said. "This 'cocksucker, deranged person' is the same guy you're bringing food to his house two, three times a week? And you're calling this deranged person's wife every day to see how she is? And how he is? Geez, Niggsy, are we talking about the same 'deranged, cocksucker' here?"

Now Niggsy actually was screaming! "Yeah! I haven't heard from him, okay? So I called her to see how the fuck he was! I feel sorry for him, y'know! I feel sorry for his kids. What the fuck!"

DiPaolo paused for a moment for effect. Then, in measured tones he told Arnone, "Well, Niggsy, Bonnie Montevecchio does not want you calling her any more. And she does not want any more of your food. So just stay away from her. Got it?"

"Yeah? Well fuck her, too!" Arnone shouted.

DiPaolo started for the door, but then he stopped, looked back at the warrant on the floor and said, "You might want to save that search warrant. You know, so you can show it to your lawyer? You're going to need one."

All Arnone could do was fume.

And then DiPaolo was gone. He had a bank to revisit. And an Arnone cousin to question.

DiPaolo had that feeling he experienced many times before in his career – a feeling not unlike the one he experienced when he was really on his golf game, a contentment kind of feeling that everything was finally going his way and all was right with the world. It had been years in the making, but all the pieces of the puzzle, all the players, great and small, were at last falling into place.

It was mid-afternoon that Friday, August 21, 1987, when the Erie cop and a local agent from the Pennsylvania Attorney General's Office walked into the PennBank branch office at East 8th and East Avenue, directly across the street from Wayne Elementary School and not far from Erie's storied East High School, where DiPaolo's son, Pat, would just a few decades later become principal.

East Avenue had been the heart of the city's Polish-dominated lower east side, just as West 18th and Liberty Streets represented the cross hairs of Little Italy. But just like Little Italy, East Avenue, once a thriving business district of restaurants, shops, offices, well-kept residences and churches, had now fallen on hard times.

The bank branch was one of the few modern structures to occupy the street that ran from the lake front south to the adjoining Millcreek Township.

"How can I help you?" asked Theresa Mastrey as DiPaolo approached her. Mastrey was not the branch manager, but held somewhat of a position of authority at the bank that once had been locally owned and operated as the Security Peoples Trust Company. Still, it was one of Erie's most popular banks, with branches throughout the entire county. Mastrey had been transferred from the West 26th Street branch.

As for Mastrey, her demeanor, DiPaolo noted, was confident and professional, as though she had nothing to hide, not a worry in the world. Really, a bring-it-on attitude, DiPaolo thought to himself.

"I have a couple of questions for you," DiPaolo said, skipping the formalities since Mastrey obviously knew who he was and, more importantly, why he was there. "Is there someplace private we can talk?" he asked.

"S-sure," she responded with just a hint of hesitation, no longer quite as confident or carefree. Perhaps chinking this tough woman's armor would be easier than previously imagined, the top Erie homicide investigator thought. A few minutes later, in Theresa Mastrey's windowless private office, DiPaolo, never one to beat around the bush, got directly to the point of his visit.

"As you know, we're investigating the murder of Frank Dovishaw," he said. "Our investigation has led us here and to you in regard to your safe-deposit box at the West 26th Street branch."

DiPaolo had had her safe-deposit box and Niggsy's box at the West 26th Street branch, where she was working at the time of Bolo's murder, drilled open. She had no idea the boxes had been drilled.

"Okay," Mastrey said, stiffening a little. "But what's Bolo have to do with me?"

DiPaolo paused for a moment, more for effect and to let the silence become awkward more than for anything else. It was that same interrogation strategy he had honed well over many years of interviewing criminal suspects. After what must have seemed an eternity to the bank employer, he asked, "Well, if you were to open your safe deposit box right now at this moment, would you have any cash inside of it?"

She thought for a moment. "Probably," Mastrey said. "But not a lot. Definitely not a lot of cash."

"What does 'not a lot' mean?" DiPaolo sought clarification of such a vague term, one not relevant.

Mastrey again paused, then said, "Oh, about ten thousand maybe. Why?"

Suddenly, without warning and much to DiPaolo's chagrin, it happened: The special agent present from the Pennsylvania Attorney General's Office blurted out, "Yeah, but what about adding about $35,000 to that figure?"

Theresa Mastrey's faced drained of blood and turned white. Immediately, she became if not defiant, then definitely confrontational.

"How would you know that?" she hissed back at the AG's representative.

DiPaolo was pissed. He wanted to continue this game of cat and mouse with Mastrey, not revealing how much he knew while hopefully trapping Mastrey into disclosing more than she had originally intended to tell the law enforcement officers. But now the AG's agent had pretty much blown the game and DiPaolo had no other option or recourse than to slam her with the truth and then just hope for the best.

"We just drilled your box," he said quite matter-of-factly, as though he was merely asking a teller for a receipt. But now, Theresa Mastrey had a meltdown.

"Who has my money?" she screamed, loud enough to startle and attract attention from others in the branch office. "And when do I get it back?"

DiPaolo remained calm, but still ticked off at his sidekick from the AG's office.

"Here's the search warrant," he said extending the document to Mastrey, who snatched it from his hand. "Read it," the cop ordered with a definite sense of autocratic authority.

The papers shook in the assistant branch manager's hands as her eyes grew wide.

After a few minutes of reading and re-reading the search warrant, PennBank's Theresa Mastrey managed to collect herself and her thoughts. DiPaolo and the agent from the Attorney General's Office waited patiently in silence, DiPaolo aware he had Mastrey exactly where he wanted her: Angry, confused and frightened. Finally, Mastrey cleared her throat and spoke to the two law enforcement officials.

"Look, I'm a respectable business person," she began. "I don't know why I'm being treated this way. This is really bullshit. Really it is. Besides, this is not my money."

"Oh, yeah?" the veteran cop asked. "Then exactly whose money is it?"

Mastrey sucked in her breath. "I can't say."

"Then you better get yourself a lawyer . . . and fast!" DiPaolo advised her. Clearly, DiPaolo observed, Mastrey was beginning to lose it again.

"Well, what about my money?" It was more than a question. It was almost a plea.

"But Theresa, you just said it wasn't yours," DiPaolo couldn't help but grin. Theresa Mastrey was silent as the officers left her bank.

It had been a productive Friday, for sure, Dom DiPaolo thought. And it was about to get even better. That night, Alfred DelSandro telephoned the Erie detective sergeant. He phoned The Sports Page and asked whether DiPaolo was there. It just so happened that DiPaolo, his wife, Janet, and other team members and their wives had just arrived from a Slo-Pitch game.

DelSandro and the slain "Ash Wednesday" Dovishaw had been considered two of the biggest bookies with the most profitable operations in Erie. But Al DelSandro was getting old. His health was failing. And, aside from occasional cranky grumbling, he was not nearly as active – and, in some cases as feared – as the old man with mob connections had once been. DiPaolo had not only known DelSandro most of the police officer's life, but their families were inextricably linked, as many of Erie's Italian-American families were. Al's deceased brother, Valdo, was DiPaolo's godfather. And the cop's godmother, Rose DelSandro, was still living. What's more, Rose and Dom's mother, Mary "Babe" Pallotto DiPaolo, were close friends from childhood, remaining that way until both died in their late 90s. At this point in time, August

1987, both were still living and playing cards in a club at least twice weekly. Dom's godfather Valdo, meanwhile, had run a few watering holes over the course of his life. Tim and Del's, for example, was a popular tavern that DelSandro ran with his son-in-law, Andy Timko. DelSandro was also once the operator of the equally popular Weigeltown Inn in Erie's Sixth Ward.

"You grabbed that Palilla girl today," DelSandro didn't beat around the bush, either, as he referred to Theresa Mastrey by her maiden name.

"I didn't actually arrest her," DiPaolo advised. "But I did confiscate her money."

"That fucking money is mine!" the old man DelSandro proclaimed with some authority.

"What?" DiPaolo drew out the one syllable word so it sounded incredulous.

"My daughter-in-law, Roseann Giamanco-Altadonna DelSandro, well that is her cousin Theresa Mastrey. And the IRS has a lien on me." He paused a moment to let it sink in with DiPaolo, then continued again. "So I gave that money to her, to Roseann, to keep for my grandson. She tells me that her cousin Theresa is a big shot at the bank and so the money would be, you know, fucking safe there."

DiPaolo, always the skeptic, asked, "How much? How much money was she holding for you?"

"Thirty-five thousand. And fuck, it's mine."

If true, DiPaolo thought, no wonder Mastrey was a little jumpy at losing Big Al's nice stash. But then DelSandro sweetened the pot considerably, more than DiPaolo could have ever hoped for.

"Listen, Dominick, here's something just for you. My daughter-in-law told me they were at a wedding the summer before Bolo got hit."

"Yeah? So what's up with that?"

"Listen, will you? Niggsy was there and they said he got all fucked up and was telling Theresa they needed to figure a way they could get into the Fat Pig's bank box."

"Yeah? So?" DiPaolo tried to remain calm. "Would your daughter-in-law talk with me about that?"

"I dunno, maybe," DelSandro said. "All I can do is ask her. She told me they (Niggsy/Theresa) were laughing."

"Good. Very good. Call me Monday at the police station, Al."

DelSandro promised he would. All he wanted was his money back. All DiPaolo wanted was a more solid case against Anthony "Niggsy" Arnone. Both would get what they wanted. Or so it seemed.

The following Monday, August 24, 1987, Al DelSandro did not call. But his daughter-in-law did. Roseann Giamanco-Altadonna DelSandro telephoned DiPaolo at the station exactly at 9 a.m. and agreed to meet shortly with the Erie police detective sergeant. Talk about a family affair! Roseann's father, Niggsy Arnone's mother, and Theresa Mastrey's mother, were all siblings. *All first blood*, DiPaolo mused.

A short time later, Roseann met face-to-face with DiPaolo at Erie Police Headquarters to explain the strange money exchange that led to all that cash in Mastrey's safe-deposit box. "It's true, the money came from my father-in-law," she told DiPaolo. "It all came from Al DelSandro. I've been giving the money to Theresa at different times to put away for my son, Al's grandson."

"When did all this start, this giving Theresa Mastrey all that money?" DiPaolo asked.

"Probably in 1980 or maybe 1981," Roseann quickly answered.

"How do you go about giving the cash?" DiPaolo asked.

"I would give her like three hundred dollars, or four hundred or a thousand, always in denominations of fives, tens, twenties and sometimes even hundred dollar bills. And she would put it away for me."

But by now DiPaolo knew it wasn't Al DelSandro's money. There were no fives, tens or twenties. Everything in Mastrey's box was in one hundred-dollar bills. The others were simply conning him, presuming that if DiPaolo believed the money was DelSandro's, he might return the cash to the local mobster. DiPaolo sensed when he was being used. And that was confirmed after asking Roseann, "What about this wedding where Niggsy and Theresa were talking about getting into Bolo's bank box?"

"Hmmmm. I never heard that," she answered with surprise and thoughtfulness. "Al's getting old. Sometimes Al forgets and gets confused."

Now DiPaolo feigned confusion. "You mean you never told anyone that Theresa turned down the deal and said 'no'?" DiPaolo asked. "You mean you never told Al that?"

"Dom, Al's getting old, you know. Nowadays he just doesn't understand that well."

But DiPaolo knew from other investigations over the years that DelSandro was hooked up with John LaRocca, boss of the Pittsburgh La Cosa Nostra, and laid off his bets to LaRocca's organization. DiPaolo now believed Roseann was attempting to scam him, either to get the money back or set up some kind of a defense for Cousin Theresa and Cousin Niggsy. They never suspected that DiPaolo knew that Theresa had four other bank safe-deposit boxes at different PennBank branch offices throughout the region. And ol' man DelSandro's money obviously was in one of them. Too bad for DelSandro, the $35,000 was confiscated by the state at a forfeiture hearing during which DiPaolo testified. If it was truly DelSandro's money, then the headache was now Mastrey's. And, DiPaolo wondered to himself, did Big Al's grandson ever see the money Al gave Roseann, and she gave to Mastrey?

It was turning into a busy Monday morning at Erie Police Headquarters that hot August day. Shortly after his meeting with Roseann Giamanco-Altadonna DelSandro, a worried banker, Theresa Mastrey, telephoned about 11 a.m.

"I want to meet and talk with you," she said. It almost sounded like a plea.

"Yeah? So what's the problem?" DiPaolo asked.

"Well, my lawyer is in Florida and he won't be back until Thursday."

Mastrey asked DiPaolo whether she should meet with the detective then, or should she wait until her lawyer returned in three days. DiPaolo knew that if she lawyered up, he would have an ethical obligation not to talk with her without her attorney present.

"You better talk with him about that," DiPaolo advised, knowing he now had many sweating – and it wasn't just because of the typical August weather. To be honest, he was loving it. An hour later, there was a long distance telephone call from Florida. It was Erie Attorney Jay D'Alba asking whether he could bring in his client, Theresa Mastrey, for a chat Thursday morning.

"Sure," DiPaolo cheerfully answered. "Why not!"

"Is she a target?" the lawyer wanted to know.

"You bet she is."

There was silence on the other end of the line.

"Hmmmm. Still there?" DiPaolo asked.

"Are you willing to negotiate to give Theresa immunity from prosecution," D'Alba tried to broker some kind of a deal for his client over the phone.

"Not my call to make," DiPaolo said. "Let's hear a proffer and go from there."

DiPaolo was now eagerly anticipating Thursday. Especially since it gave all concerned three more days to sweat.

That Thursday, Attorney Jay D'Alba showed up at Erie Police Headquarters at 9 a.m. He was alone. Detective Sergeant DiPaolo motioned him to a standard office chair. "Well?" DiPaolo asked, getting straight to the point. No reason to engage in small talk.

"Theresa did not do anything wrong!" D'Alba blurted out.

DiPaolo raised his eyebrows, but didn't speak. He rather enjoyed handing out the silent treatment.

"Besides, that search warrant of yours is really nothing but a big piece of shit."

DiPaolo was silent, expressionless. He motioned with his hands for the lawyer to continue.

"Her name was never given to Caesar Montevecchio by anyone," D'Alba said. "And so what if she is Niggsy Arnone's cousin? She's got lots of cousins." He asked again, "Will you give her immunity?

Now it was DiPaolo's turn to let the screw slowly turn. He was silent for several long minutes, all the while transfixing his cold stare on the increasingly uncomfortable appearing criminal defense lawyer. What DiPaolo was thinking was this: *He calls my search warrant a piece of shit – and now he wants immunity?*

But what DiPaolo actually said was this: "Immunity? You've got to be kidding! Immunity for what? You just got through saying she didn't do anything wrong. So why are you asking for immunity? Are you now saying she's done something that would require the granting of immunity?"

D'Alba, now clearly uncomfortable, squirmed a little more before answering. "Well, hypothetically, what if she took care of Arnone that day? And, still hypothetically, what if after he was in the vault, he took the master key from her and then told her to take a walk?"

Interesting hypothesis, DiPaolo thought.

D'Alba paused for effect, then said, "So, if it turns out that if all that were the case, could you then give Theresa some kind of a deal?"

DiPaolo was silent again for another long moment. "Well, we'll definitely need more details," he speculated. "And please remember, I don't make the calls on immunity. But it all has to come from her, not you? Do you understand?"

"Yeah, I understand. But I'll have to get back to you," D'Alba said.

What a cast of characters, DiPaolo thought. *If not for the brutal murder, much of this actually would be hilarious.*

Later that day, D'Alba again showed up at the Attorney General's Erie office. But this time he had Theresa Mastrey in tow. Quickly, DiPaolo began to read Theresa her Miranda rights as a prelude to signing the standard waiver form in which defendants agree to talk with police. It's called "Mirandizing" interviewees. He thought that if Mastrey wanted to give up Arnone as D'Alba "hypothetically" indicated, then the cop could prove Arnone was in the vault with the master key, along with Bolo's keys. It would be the jackpot, and make Caesar Montevecchio's testimony golden.

"You have the right to remain silent," the detective sergeant began slowly. "Anything you say can and will be used against you in a court of law . . . "

"What about if what Theresa says is not all that incriminating?" D'Alba suddenly screamed out. "Are you going to tell the jury that, too?"

DiPaolo was patient. "Mr. D'Alba, please let me finish."

"No, fuck that! Let's do this fuckin' right. Just tell her you're going to tell the jury everything that's not incriminating as well."

To DiPaolo, it appeared D'Alba was becoming unhinged. As for Mastrey, she remained quiet, motionless, but the unusual expression on her face seemed to be shouting out, "Jay, what the fuck are you doing?"

"I *am* doing this right," DiPaolo said. Now he was getting just a little warm under the collar as well. *Jesus, this guy is acting like a fucking nitwit!*

While DiPaolo was still pondering what had gotten into the lawyer, unexpectedly D'Alba leaped up and pulled the neatly typed waiver form from DiPaolo's grasp, totally catching the cop by surprise and actually ripping the waiver.

"I'll put it in. I'll put in what you'll tell the jury," D'Alba was now loudly yelling, although only three of them were in the tiny police interrogation room.

Now it was DiPaolo's turn. "Take your fuckin' client and get the hell out of here before I do something I'm going to be sorry for!" he ordered the defense attorney.

"Jay," Mastrey pleaded, "please!" And then, "Settle down!" she urged.

"We all have rights, you know!" the lawyer continued to scream at nobody in particular.

"Get the fuck out of here," DiPaolo roared. Then, in angry strides he left the room. D'Alba and his client could do nothing else but follow in embarrassed silence.

That same day, Theresa Mastrey's lawyer tried just one more time. But it was a fruitless effort. D'Alba telephoned the Pennsylvania Attorney General's Office, asking to talk with DiPaolo. But the cop, after Jay D'Alba's last disruptive appearance, wasn't having any of it. He flatly refused to take D'Alba's call.

D'Alba sighed. But just before hanging up, he told the office secretary, "Okay, then serve her (Mastrey) with a subpoena for the grand jury. She'll talk then."

Several days later, Attorney D'Alba apparently got his grand jury wish for his client. Theresa Mastrey was served with a subpoena ordering her to appear before the special investigative Pennsylvania grand jury.

During the roughly two-week period between the time Mastrey was served with the subpoena and her actual grand jury appearance, Dom DiPaolo was not idle. He set out to learn as much as possible about Theresa Mastrey's financial activities, particularly those that occurred following the January 3, 1983 murder of Frank "Bolo" Dovishaw.

For instance:

- On January 5, 1983, the day after Arnone allegedly got into Bolo's boxes, Detective Sergeant DiPaolo learned Mastrey purchased a $4,000 Individual Retirement Account (IRA) using cash.

- Two months later, on March 21, she opened a new safe bank deposit box;
- On April 21 of that year, Theresa Mastrey bought a $5,000 savings bond, once again paying for it with cash;
- On May 10, less than a month later, Theresa's husband, Donald Mastrey, was on record as opening safe-deposit box Number 455, and the next day purchasing a $5,000 bond using cash;
- Then, on June 17, the couple purchased another $5,000 bond with cash.

Following the money has always been good advice for police detectives and journalists alike. The cash trail revealed that between January 5, 1983 – the day after Niggsy Arnone was accused of opening Bolo Dovishaw's bank box – until June of that year, a grand total of $19,000 in cash was used by the Mastreys to purchase bonds. DiPaolo recalled the January 5, 1983 conversation between Arnone and Montevecchio at the time Montevecchio allegedly collected $20,000, and Arnone was to have said the event already cost him $37,000 – and less than 24 hours after Niggsy allegedly got into Bolo's boxes with help from "her."

Furthermore, DiPaolo learned that after not having visited their safe deposit boxes at all during the previous four years dating back to a 1979 entry, from March to June of 1983, the husband and wife had visited their boxes six times – all relevant to the Erie cop's probe.

DiPaolo also discovered that while in December 1982 the Mastreys' monthly checking account balance was about $3,000, the monthly average between January 1983 and January 1984 jumped to $15,000. How such a difference in the checking account average monthly balance would be explained was what DiPaolo was anxious to learn.

As mentioned before, Theresa was transferred from her employer's Millcreek branch to the East 8th and East Avenue bank branch on Erie's lower east side in 1984. Once there, she opened two safe deposit boxes, DiPaolo learned. Then, she opened two boxes at the Millcreek branch of PennBank, and one at the 18th and State Street office. DiPaolo learned the Mastreys had one box which had not been entered in four years prior to Bolo's murder. Now Bolo's *morta*, and they open seven more boxes at various banks, entering them multiple times in three months? DiPaolo thought that maybe even millionaires don't have eight safe-deposit boxes.

During the late afternoon of Friday, August 21, 1987, DiPaolo presented a search warrant to Mastrey. The time was exactly 4:35 p.m. Even though it was so late in the day, at 4:55 p.m. DiPaolo learned Mastrey accessed her safe deposit box at the East Avenue branch office. And she entered the box again on the following Monday, August 24, at 4 p.m. The next day, Tuesday at noon, PennBank Security Chief Charles Bowers, the former Erie Police Chief, walked into Barney's Restaurant on East Avenue, just south of the bank branch where Mastrey worked, and spotted Mastrey with her cousin, Niggsy Arnone. When they saw Bowers, they quickly left. It was obvious to Bowers and then to DiPaolo that something was up. And the day after Mastrey's September 16 grand jury appearance, she visited her safe-deposit boxes at the 18th and State Street, Millcreek and East Avenue bank branches, then promptly closed out all six of them.

At times, it often occurred to DiPaolo, the internal daily battle at Erie Police Headquarters was just as draining and daunting as the war against crime and the scum haunting the streets of the City of Erie. Sometimes even humorous, the seasoned cop was forced to acknowledge that even a Pulitzer Prize-winning novelist would be hard-pressed to fictionalize many of the real-life daily events within Erie's Police Department. DiPaolo would admit to cracking a smile or two at the strange goings on there. It was against this background of the culminating days of the Dovishaw murder investigation, a mind-numbing, years-long probe that was now producing results, that DiPaolo was called into the office of Deputy Chief of Detectives Dennis Tobin.

Tobin wasn't mincing words. He was clearly upset with his star investigator, Dominick DiPaolo. DiPaolo recently had been quoted in the *Morning News*, the more aggressive and crusading of the two Erie dailies operated for many years by the family-owned Times Publishing Company, about a far away murder case. Actually, it was a fictional case, the focal point of the extremely popular soap-like program *Twin Peaks*.

With the television drama's finale scheduled to air that very night, an enterprising Erie newspaper reporter interviewed several well-known local law enforcement figures seeking their "professional" opinions on just who would be finally revealed as the *Twin Peaks* killer.

The reporter interviewed the Erie County District Attorney, a Pennsylvania State Police officer, and Erie Police Detective Sergeant Dominick DiPaolo, locally known as Erie's top homicide investigator. All were asked if they had figured out the identity of the killer on *Twin Peaks*.

Like every day on the job, DiPaolo showed up early in the detective squad room that morning, grabbed his first cup of coffee and a smoke, and began reading the overnight police and crime reports. It was at this point that Deputy Chief of Detectives Tobin, slightly ashen-faced after his usual morning meeting with Police Chief Paul DeDionisio and Police Director Arthur Berardi, summoned DiPaolo. With the door to Tobin's office slightly ajar, and a dozen nosy detectives, maybe more, eavesdropping at their nearby desks, Tobin loudly tore into DiPaolo.

"Who in the fuck assigned you to that murder case in Johnstown, Pennsylvania?" Tobin yelled. "DeDionisio and Berardi just finished chewing out my ass. They said I have no control over you and that you do whatever the fuck you feel like doing. What have you got to say for yourself?"

DiPaolo was trying hard not to laugh. Still, he played dumb with the boss. "Murder? Johnstown? What murder in Johnstown, Chief?"

"Don't play fucking games with me! You know what the fuck I'm talking about! The article in the paper this morning. Where you were quoted as saying you know who did it, but wouldn't say who. That one! Just who assigned you to that case?"

Simultaneously, the entire squad room erupted into uproarious laughter. It seemed like the detective chief, as well as Berardi and DeDionisio, were the only ones in the Western World who didn't watch and apparently never even heard of *Twin Peaks.*

"Dennis, did you actually read the article?" DiPaolo calmly asked, biting his lower lip to suppress his own urge to laugh out loud at his superior officer.

"Part of it," Tobin admitted somewhat tentatively.

"Just part of it?"

"Well, they told me about it," Dennis Tobin said defensively, referring to Police Chief DeDionisio's and Police Director Berardi's chewing out session.

"What the fuck! It's about a TV show! Are you guys all crazy?" DiPaolo asked.

He paused while Tobin thought about the comment and DiPaolo's words sunk in. Tobin rose from his chair, his face still bright red, but now from embarrassment, and stomped out of his office. He stopped briefly in the squad room, where at least a few of the detectives were on the floor, holding their guts, crying out in laughter. The other cops in the room were simply doubled over at their desks. The Deputy Chief of Detectives looked around the room, then stormed out.

This was simply another footnote in Dominick DiPaolo's long police career. But now, he thought, there was work to be done that was no laughing matter. At least not to the family and friends of Frank Dovishaw – no matter how useless Dovishaw's life might have been. It still would be nearly two more years before the final figure in the Dovishaw murder investigation was brought to trial.

CHAPTER 36

FIVE AND A HALF YEARS AFTER FRANK "BOLO" DOVISHAW WAS GUNNED down in his west Erie home, DiPaolo and the Pennsylvania Attorney General's Office finally arrested the suspected shooter.

On September 7, 1988, Robert Dorler, Sr., 53, a Medina, Ohio hit man who would do anything for a buck, was charged with homicide and conspiracy in the January 3, 1983 execution of Erie's well-known gambling kingpin and bookie Dovishaw. At that time, Robert Dorler, considered to be a cold-blooded killer without conscience or emotion, was serving a five-year stint in the federal penitentiary in Lewisburg, Pennsylvania, on counterfeiting and arson charges stemming from his many previous criminal activities in Cleveland, Ohio.

Pennsylvania Attorney General LeRoy Zimmerman and Deputy Attorney General Dennis Pfannenschmidt, who supervised the state and grand jury investigations involving the Dovishaw case for the previous 18 months, made the announcement of the charges against Dorler in a statement to the local news media. The two Commonwealth prosecutors accused Dorler of being the actual triggerman who carried out the contract hit for a $20,000 cash fee. Also in their announcement, the Attorneys General accused notorious Erie crime figure Caesar Montevecchio of recruiting Dorler for the job. What's more, in a story below the Erie *Morning News* headline reading "Con charged in Dovishaw hit murder," Zimmerman was quoted as saying he'd seek the death penalty against the suspected killer Dorler. According to the Attorney General,

"Evidence indicates this was a carefully planned contract murder, carried out in cold blood for profit."

The law enforcement officials also disclosed publicly for the first time that a third person – in addition to Dorler and Erie's favorite son of crime, Caesar Montevecchio – was also under investigation in the Dovishaw murder. Reports of how the planners and plotters wanted to get to the cash in Dovishaw's bank safe-deposit boxes now began to emerge publicly in the media as well as details about another offered contract killing that had been put out on the 46-year-old Dovishaw's bookmaking partner, acknowledged mob killer Raymond Ferritto of Erie.

According to the *Morning News* story that day, "The grand jury presentment (state grand juries issue presentments; federal grand juries issue indictments) alleges that Dorler also had a contingency contract to kill another reputed bookmaker, Dovishaw's alleged partner, Raymond Ferritto. The grand jury contends that the contingency contract worth another $10,000 was put out by someone other than the person who paid for Dovishaw's killing. That unnamed Erie crime figure was more interested in taking over Dovishaw's lucrative bookmaking operation, but needed Ferritto out of the way, too . . . " the newspaper story speculated.

Media members could not know at the time that Joe Scutella, Jr., was the one being accused of putting out the "contingency contract" on Ferritto, but the newspaper story did in fact point out that Ferritto's life was spared only because Dovishaw was alone in his 1634 West 21st Street home when Dorler assassinated him that frigid wintry night in January 1983.

As published in the newspaper, the grand jury presentment, the legal term also used to outline the case, said Dorler "went to Dovishaw's house alone and overpowered Dovishaw after he answered the door. He took Dovishaw into the basement and tied his hands and feet, whereupon Dovishaw begged him not to kill him. He told Dovishaw to stop begging and to be a man, then ordered him on his knees. He then shot Dovishaw in the back of the head. When he saw that Dovishaw had not emptied his bowels, Dorler stabbed him in the eye to be sure that he was dead."

Such matter-of-fact reporting describing a knife that was stabbed into the victim's eye socket, of course, had a more than chilling, eye-opening effect upon the newspaper's horrified readers that morning. After the killing, the newspaper article continued to report, Dorler fled from Bolo's west Erie home in Dovishaw's car, then met Caesar Montevecchio and gave Montevecchio two keys to Dovishaw's bank safe-deposit boxes. Dovishaw's car was then abandoned, the newspaper reported, in the parking lot of a hotel along Interstate 90 just south of Erie. An acquaintance, William Bourjaily, the story also reported, then drove Robert Dorler back to Ohio. There, a .32 caliber Beretta, the murder weapon, was tossed into a lake.

The state grand jury's presentment, as outlined in the morning newspaper story began for the first time to unravel for the citizens of Erie the cold and calculated brutality of the horrific and gruesome murder of Frank "Bolo" Dovishaw a half decade earlier. It was a public glimpse of how those who occupy the slimy underbelly of Erie, combined with their equally loathsome counterparts in other cities and states, demonstrate a total absence of mind and heart for the sanctity of any life. Odd, DiPaolo, with his strong family upbringing, often thought. Especially considering that many of Erie's hoods came from solid Italian-Catholic roots where, like Caesar Montevecchio, they served as altar boys and faithfully attended Saturday morning Catechism instruction as well as Sunday morning and most Holy Day masses. Odd that these men would turn out so horribly and without feeling as they grew up surrounded by extended families of loving grandparents from the "old country" as well as a wide assortment of aunts, uncles and cousins, often times all under the same roof in Erie's "Little Italy" neighborhood.

The newspaper article went on to describe how Dorler collected his $20,000 fee from Montevecchio the day after the slaying. The story told of how Caesar Montevecchio then returned Bolo's bank box keys to Dorler, who later planted the keys in Dovishaw's car, which was at the time still parked in the back lot at the Interstate 90 hotel. Speaking of Montevecchio's appearance before the statewide grand jury, the newspaper article related that Montevecchio acknowledged he had been the middleman in the plan to kill "Ash Wednesday" when he was at home taking bets during an NFL game.

The newspaper account told of how Dorler, several days later during that January of 1983, visited Bourjaily, showed him a newspaper report of the murder and said he wouldn't be captured based upon what was reported, according to the presentment. So much for Dorler's reasoning ability, DiPaolo thought.

In other statements to law enforcement officials presented to the grand jury, according to the September 7, 1988, newspaper article, Dorler admitted that he had direct knowledge of Dovishaw's murder, but the career criminal vehemently denied killing Dovishaw.

These fascinating facts finally released to the public were the result of DiPaolo's years of toil. He was ultimately credited in the very last paragraph of the newspaper story as being on special assignment and having "aided" the Attorney General's Bureau of Criminal Investigation in the Bolo Dovishaw murder probe. But DiPaolo didn't mind what others might have considered a slight. It was more important to him that the investigation was moving forward and there were concrete results to show for the years of effort. Besides, he was well aware the investigation was still far from over. It would be months before there would be a final arrest.

Hindsight is always 20-20. That's why, in retrospect, it might have been a tactical error to brag. At least at that point in time. But in late September 1988, that's just what Pennsylvania Attorney General LeRoy Zimmerman's office did.

The *Erie Daily Times* reported that a grand jury was told of the Erie businessman who ordered the "Ash Wednesday" hit, but that Zimmerman wanted enough evidence to win the case before he arrested the man.

A spokesman for Zimmerman, the newspaper said, disclosed that the Attorney General wanted to tie up the Dovishaw case, but not until he believed prosecutors would be successful. The words were anything but prophetic, DiPaolo, the lead investigator in the case, would eventually know.

The newspaper explained that Zimmerman's office, the result of a special grand jury probe, already arrested Montevecchio and Dorler, pointing out Montevecchio's admission and guilty plea to third-degree murder. Zimmerman, the paper reported, would seek the death penalty for Dorler.

But the article aroused even bigger interest in what it didn't reveal – the actual identity of the man the paper claimed was behind the hit, again pointing out the Erie businessman was still on the loose and wouldn't be arrested until the AG's office believed it could win in court.

Famous last words, DiPaolo would later think.

It would take another five months. But it finally happened in late May of 1989 – and more than six years after the horrific, brutal murder.

When Erie businessman Anthony "Niggsy" Arnone was shockingly outed as the alleged mastermind behind the Frank "Bolo" Dovishaw hit, it was by his former underworld pal, Erie's longtime career criminal Caesar Montevecchio. Arnone's name finally surfaced publicly during a preliminary hearing for the ruthless Dovishaw triggerman Robert Dorler Sr., of Ohio, who was months earlier charged with criminal homicide and criminal conspiracy.

During that balmy May Day hearing, it was Montevecchio, who, while testifying against Dorler, identified Arnone as the man who allegedly hired him to arrange for the January 1983 slaying of the Erie gambling kingpin Dovishaw. Arnone, who was living in the upscale Colonial Avenue neighborhood of Millcreek Township just west of the City of Erie, was at the time the president of Arnone & Sons Food Importers on Cherry Street.

In *Erie Daily Times* reporter Jim Thompson's article about the hearing, an Arnone employee said his boss was making an out-of-town delivery and not available to comment on Montevecchio's damaging testimony.

The story reported there was tight security for the Erie County Courthouse hearing, and that the name of the man who hired Montevecchio to arrange the Dovishaw killing was revealed publicly for the first time that day.

Caesar Montevecchio had already pleaded guilty to third-degree murder for his involvement in arranging Dovishaw's murder, and was still awaiting sentencing at the time of Dorler's preliminary hearing. Montevecchio was called to the witness stand to testify by lawyer Skip Ebert, Pennsylvania's chief deputy attorney general. Ebert wasn't one to waste questions or deal with informal chit-chat with his witnesses. He quickly got down to the business at hand, asking Montevecchio whether he had been hired to arrange for Dovishaw's death.

Caesar answered affirmatively in terse fashion.

Ebert wanted to know who did the hiring. Montevecchio paused, then quietly gave up Anthony "Niggsy" Arnone.

DiPaolo had waited six and a half long years for those words to be uttered in court. But now, on this day, and in this court, the words rang almost hollow and anticlimactic.

Montevecchio's testimony continued. He said at first Arnone offered him 20 to 30 percent of the money held in Dovishaw's bank safe deposit boxes. But he said he hesitated to agree to such a deal because he had no idea how much – if anything – was in those boxes. In his testimony, just like in earlier interviews with DiPaolo, Montevecchio said Arnone eventually offered him $10,000 in cash for arranging the killing. Caesar Montevecchio accepted the offer, he told the court.

Furthermore, Montevecchio said, Arnone didn't want to know the identity of the actual killer. He recounted how he met Dorler in the summer of 1982, had spoken with him about criminal activity, and Dorler later agreed to kill Dovishaw.

After January 3, 1983 was settled upon for the murder, Montevecchio testified that Dorler went to Dovishaw's home alone, then met up with Montevecchio about an hour later in a restaurant parking lot, according to court records and the newspaper account.

Montevecchio had been a good witness, a very good witness, a credible witness. Even though he was betraying longtime friends for a break in his own sentence, there appeared to be no real doubt that the Erie hood might have been lying. His words, to cops and courtroom observers alike, had a ring of truth to them. Montevecchio's and Dorler's long and filthy criminal careers were about to be ended, DiPaolo was convinced. With the investigation still proceeding on schedule, it would be the Erie businessman Anthony "Niggsy" Arnone's turn to begin to sweat. And sweat he would. DiPaolo would make sure of that. For at least a few more months.

The Fourth of July might very well be the best-known American national holiday. But for DiPaolo, it was two days later in 1989 – on July 6 – that became such a red-letter day. For it was on that day when Anthony Frank "Niggsy" Arnone was finally arrested for what was believed to be his alleged role in organizing the January 3, 1983 brutal murder of Erie bookie Frank "Bolo" Dovishaw. It was DiPaolo's pleasure, he would later remember, to personally drive from Erie to Arnone's Millcreek Township home in the suburbs and serve the arrest himself.

It was about 6 p.m. on one of those absolutely beautiful summer afternoons in northwestern Pennsylvania. DiPaolo found Arnone outside, enjoying the balmy day in a lawn chair. As Niggsy read the local sports page, seemingly without a care in the world, DiPaolo thought at the time, the Erie cop rudely intruded upon the serene pastoral scene. "Anthony, I have a warrant for your arrest," DiPaolo proclaimed.

Before the stunned Arnone could respond, DiPaolo read the suspect the murder warrant and advised him of his Miranda rights. If Arnone was upset, he did not let on. He remained cool. collected.

"Call my lawyer," Arnone ordered his wife, in quiet, measured tones.

All the while, DiPaolo would later recall, Arnone continued to remain calm, even as the detective hand-cuffed him and drove the suspected murder-arranger to Erie Police Headquarters, and then to the on-call district magistrate to be formally arraigned. It was in obvious stark contrast to Arnone's alleged nervousness when Montevecchio came calling at his business six-and-a-half years earlier, and even when Detective DiPaolo initially started snooping around Bolo's bank safe-deposit boxes.

At the conclusion of the arraignment – basically a formal reading of the criminal complaint – and with no bond allowed on murder charges in Pennsylvania, Arnone was ordered committed to the Erie County Prison. Arnone, however, had reason to be calm. He had been smart enough to retain a high-profile criminal lawyer from Philadelphia – Attorney Joseph Santaguida.

The headline in the Erie *Morning News* the next day shouted, "Erie man charged in Dovishaw 'hit.'" The story was accompanied by a large photograph of DiPaolo leading Anthony "Niggsy" Arnone by the arm as they exited from the magistrate's office.

The suspect was still wearing the white, short-sleeved pullover shirt and faded black jeans he had on when arrested at his home. Setting the judicial process in motion, Arnone was sent to prison to await a preliminary hearing before District Justice Ronald Stuck, filling in on Erie's

Westside, the jurisdiction that covers the geographical area in which the murder occurred, specifically Dovishaw's West 21st Street home.

The crime had occurred in District Justice John Vendetti's district. But Vendetti had recused himself from hearing the case partly because his father had booked illegal numbers just as Niggsy Arnone did in years past. The elder Vendetti, known as "Jiggs," had been previously arrested and convicted for his illegal numbers operation. This information was also contained in federal court dockets and newspaper accounts. Vendetti phoned DiPaolo to say he also had to get out of hearing the case because he had been friends with Niggsy and some of the others involved. DiPaolo said, "John, do what you have to do."

Again, DiPaolo marveled at Erie's intertwined criminal relationships, the few degrees of separation between respectability and dishonor.

During the preliminary hearing less than a month later, it must have appeared to Niggsy Arnone that the bottom was starting to fall out of his life. Niggsy listened intently as his former pal, career criminal Caesar Montevecchio, fingered the Italian food import business owner with arranging bookmaker Dovishaw's murder. Montevecchio, speaking in quiet tones that at times seemed to trail off into nothingness, told District Justice Ronald Stuck that Anthony Arnone paid him to hire an Ohio killer in 1982 to murder Dovishaw. According to Caesar, he was acting at the request of Arnone when he hired Robert Dorler as the killer. Montevecchio testified that Arnone had wanted the keys to Dovishaw's bank safe-deposit boxes at an Erie bank branch. Montevecchio went on to describe how he met with the killer Dorler before and after the arranged hit at Dovishaw's home January 3, 1983.

But there seemed to be more of a dark cloud over Montevecchio's testimony against Arnone than when Caesar earlier testified against Dorler. At least, that's what a newspaper writer speculated in his article. According to the story in the Erie *Morning News* describing the preliminary hearing, Montevecchio's testimony did not appear as strong to the reporter as the middle man's earlier testimony against Dorler. The story reported that Arnone's lawyer, Joseph Santaguida, attacked Montevecchio's character and criminal history.

"'You are a thief. Is that correct?'" the reporter quoted the lawyer as asking Montevecchio.

"'I have been a thief,' Montevecchio replied.

"'You are a robber. Is that correct?' Santaguida continued.

"'I have been a robber,' came the slow reply.

"'Is being a robber when you get a gun and say to someone, give me all your money?'" Santaguida scornfully asked.

"'That's what a robber is,'" Montevecchio agreed."

Under that same line of questioning, the newspaper reported, Montevecchio acknowledged having been a burglar, dope dealer, participant in a murder, as well as a liar. And the lawyer ultimately got Montevecchio to reveal that he first told police that Joseph Scutella, not Arnone, was the one responsible for Dovishaw's murder. Montevecchio told the lawyer and Stuck that he made up the story about Scutella before he began cooperating with police, that it was at a time when he did not intend to fully cooperate with authorities.

"'Was he responsible?'" Santaguida asked," according to the newspaper article.

"'He (Scutella) was responsible for getting Cy (Anthony Ciotti) out of Dovishaw's house.'

"'Was he responsible for the death?' Santaguida demanded loudly. 'You know what I'm talking about!'"

Montevecchio admitted that Scutella was not responsible for the murder and that he only told Scutella about the proposed hit because he wanted someone to warn Ciotti to move out of Dovishaw's house. Caesar did not want Ciotti to get hurt during the crime. Montevecchio also said that he had tried to implicate Scutella to win a release from prison.

"'I didn't tell them anything that was true,'" Montevecchio was quoted in the newspaper story and court records.

"'I know that!' Santaguida responded sarcastically. 'You've never told anything true yet.'"

The merciless grilling continued. Now the lawyer was asking Caesar if he recalled telling Federal Bureau of Investigation agents that two Cleveland mobsters murdered Dovishaw in reprisal for Dovishaw's alleged minor role in the killing of a Cleveland underworld figure, Danny Greene, years earlier. Montevecchio said he had no recollection of such a conversation with FBI agents.

"'It's not foreign to you to implicate someone in this who was not involved, is it?' Santaguida demanded. 'You are capable of implicating someone else . . . You're willing to lie to help yourself, isn't that correct?'

"'I also told you I wasn't in a position of helping police at that time,' Montevecchio replied.

"'So you told them something that was not true?'

"'I think at that time I would have told them anything,' Montevecchio replied," according to the lengthy Erie newspaper article.

Caesar Montevecchio also testified he stopped talking to the cops when it appeared to him the police wanted him to connect him to the hit and with the Louis Nardo break-in.

As Attorney Santaguida continued his hostile cross-examination, Montevecchio freely acknowledged several more details relating to incorrect information given to Erie police investigators in the Dovishaw case. That prompted Santaguida, according to the newspaper article, to chide, "You should be writing books rather than being a thief, a drug dealer and a murderer."

When asked by prosecuting attorney Skip Ebert why Montevecchio thought police would believe him years later when he fingered his friend Niggsy Arnone for arranging the murder, Caesar shrugged and said, "I knew they would (believe him at that time) because I was telling the truth and they could check it out."

DiPaolo was also called to testify and provided testimony in support of Montevecchio's account of how the murder was put together and came to be.

The detective sergeant told of Arnone's safe deposit box that was situated in the same bank where Dovishaw had his safe deposit boxes. He testified that Niggsy Arnone got his safe deposit box through Theresa Mastrey, the assistant manager at a PennBank branch.

When Ebert asked if Mastrey was related to Arnone, according to the newspaper article, DiPaolo responded that Mastrey was Arnone's first cousin.

DiPaolo also testified that when bank boxes were searched by police in 1987, Arnone's was empty, but some $60,000 in cash was found in Mastrey's boxes.

DiPaolo said the last recorded visit by Arnone to his safe deposit box was January 4, 1983. It was the same day "Ash Wednesday's" corpse was found, the newspaper reported.

It was not unusual for a defense lawyer to attack the prosecution's witnesses and evidence during a preliminary hearing, and also to withhold defense witnesses or arguments, instead holding both back until the later trial. Why reveal strategy before it was necessary? Santaguida followed the accepted defense procedure of the day – and did not present a defense case.

District Justice Stuck, apparently satisfied the state had made a *prima facie* case against Anthony "Niggsy" Arnone, bound over the defendant to criminal court on all charges.

Part Six

THE TRIALS: *"PARTNERS IN CRIME, DEALERS IN DEATH"*

CHAPTER 37

Now it was time for Theresa Mastrey's 15 minutes of fame. And, it was also time for Dominick DiPaolo to marvel again at the stranger-than-fiction aspect of the world of criminal justice. Especially in the "big small" town of Erie, Pennsylvania, where no aspect of a cop's life ever could be taken for granted.

The Dovishaw murder investigation, with all the characters who inhabited it, was proving to be no exception to the weird rule. Mastrey, angered that her name had surfaced prominently during the preliminary hearing for Anthony "Niggsy" Arnone several days earlier, held a press conference in the office of her lawyer, Joseph J. D'Alba.

It was August 3, 1989, another typical summer day in Erie. Mastrey, according to another story in the *Morning News*, was claiming that prosecutors unfairly harmed her reputation and good name within the Erie community. D'Alba appeared to be comfortable on his own safe turf, DiPaolo thought. Not only did D'Alba point out that his client fully cooperated with police in the Dovishaw probe, but also that Mastrey was never charged with a crime.

"What the government has done to Mrs. Mastrey is both unique and unfair," Attorney D'Alba proclaimed in the newspaper account.

D'Alba, according to the newspaper story, claimed that by linking Mastrey's name to the murder investigation, prosecutors had placed his client in a bad light. He said she must now vindicate herself, even though she had done nothing wrong, nor had she been charged with any kind of a crime. It had been DiPaolo who linked Mastrey's name to the murder case based on information from Caesar Montevecchio about the "her" mentioned by accused murder arranger Niggsy Arnone. It was DiPaolo who testified that bank records showed Arnone last had entered his own safe deposit box on January 4, 1983, the day after the gangland-style killing and the same day Dovishaw's lifeless body was discovered in the basement of his west side Erie home.

As for the $60,000 in cash DiPaolo had testified he discovered in Mastrey's own personal safe deposit boxes, the ex-bank official told the news media that the amount was not anywhere near that sum.

"If someone invested that money I'd like them to invest the rest of my money. It's really grown since they've taken it," she is quoted as saying with no small degree of sarcasm. Still, Mastrey would not say exactly how much money police found.

For his part, when DiPaolo was contacted by reporters, he refused to be drawn into the Mastrey controversy, a good move for a wise cop who knows when not to try his case in the local media. All he would say is that his investigation was continuing and he would not comment. He knew a public debate over the issue would serve no purpose.

During her press conference, Mastrey did not deny that she might have been the person who opened a safe deposit box account for Arnone, her first cousin, at her bank.

According to the newspaper story, Mastrey acknowledged that as a bank officer she was able to issue safe deposit boxes, but didn't know if she handled Arnone's request for a box. She maintained that she cooperated with police since the start of the probe, underwent much questioning, and even testified before two grand juries.

D'Alba, meanwhile, told the media Mastrey voluntarily submitted to questioning by police five times, and that that her grand jury testimony was without immunity.

D'Alba told the media his client accounted for all of her personal finances and that he believed police investigators were satisfied with her openness. He also revealed that Mastrey had undergone a lie detector test with passing results that should have easily cleared her beyond suspicion. But the lawyer wasn't finished. "What more can she do?" D'Alba asked the media. "The government is trying to fulfill the story that Caesar Montevecchio is trying to convey to the public, and to do that they must speculate about other people."

Montevecchio, D'Alba said at the press conference, has yet to have his version of the murder corroborated by anyone. In her opinion, Mastrey told the *Morning News*, the government's case was a lie. Yet Montevecchio had never said it was Mastrey who was involved, just that someone Arnone referred to as "her," according to what Montevecchio told authorities.

Mastrey said she was angry and weary of being a victim. But Theresa Mastrey wasn't done yet. Within a month, she'd again be making tons of noise in the media. Whether that would be good or bad for the murder investigation, DiPaolo could not be certain.

"Arnone witness sues PennBank to regain job." The *Erie Daily Times* headline on September 6, 1989 screamed for attention. And attention is what it got; for Theresa Mastrey wasn't yet done with her new-found fame!

With Detective Sergeant Dominick DiPaolo busily helping the prosecution prepare for multiple criminal trials in the 1983 murder of Erie bookie "Ash Wednesday" Dovishaw, such headlines and stories were becoming distractions.

Mastrey, also known as Theresa A. Mastrostefano, had filed a major lawsuit suit in Erie County Court seeking monetary damages from the bank that employed her for many years, and reinstatement to her management position. The bank had suspended her without pay since the previous January and now she wanted past due salary and her job back. Mastrey had been an assistant manager at the Millcreek branch of PennBank, the newspaper story explained. She was responsible for supervising the safe deposit box area where murder victim "Bolo" Dovishaw kept money from his illegal gambling business. Mastrey's cousin, Niggsy Arnone, had also opened a safe deposit box there, and it was situated in close proximity to Dovishaw's boxes.

Theresa Mastrey alleged in her lawsuit that she had complied with all subpoenas to testify before state grand juries and cooperated fully with the investigating authorities. She also reiterated in the suit that she had not been accused of any wrongdoing. According to the court filing, Mastrey began working for Security Peoples Trust Company, which later became PennBank, in 1956. It was a much simpler time, then, when Erie's banks were home-owned and managed. It was before mergers and acquisitions gobbled up or snuffed out smaller financial institutions in favor of the regional and national giants. It was a time before computers, when banking was more personalized, and, in Erie, when bankers knew their customers by their first names, as well as the names of family members and friends.

The lawsuit said Mrs. Mastrey was promoted by the bank several times over the years until she eventually became an assistant branch manager. But when the Frank "Bolo" Dovishaw murder investigation became linked with the bank and its safe deposit boxes, Theresa Mastrey's professional life rapidly went south, the suit indicated. First, Mastrey was required to take a leave of absence with pay from the bank. That occurred on September 4, 1987, after police searched her safe deposit box and after her first appearance before the state grand jury. Then, in December 1987 and January 1988, the suit said, Mastrey was notified by bank officials that she was suspended indefinitely and without pay because of the duration of the probe.

In the suit, it was alleged bank officials indicated she would receive back pay for the time she missed once she was called back to work. Yet, despite several requests for reinstatement, the suit said, the bank refused.

According to the suit, Mrs. Mastrey was not either accused or charged with wrongdoing connected to the murder probe. The suit went on to say the employment termination was a "wrongful discharge" and punished Mastrey for answering a legal summons to testify before the grand jury.

All of this was reported in the *Erie Daily Times* story, as well as Mastrey's demands for damages, for alleged misrepresentations that she would be reinstated and for the treatment of this loyal 25-year bank employee. The suit also claimed the usual maladies, including loss of income, loss of management position, loss of pension and other benefits, loss of professional reputation and humiliation, and mental suffering.

It was DiPaolo's opinion that as far back as 1982, had Mastrey refused to listen to her cousin Niggsy's plan to get into Bolo Dovishaw's safe deposit boxes – had she told him "No!" – then Bolo would still be alive and Mastrey would still be an official at the local bank branch. No, DiPaolo believed, and opined all along, Mastrey only had herself to blame for allegedly going along with the conspiracy in the first place.

As DiPaolo's opinion went: Without a bank connection, Bolo would be still breathing. Bolo would not have been killed unless someone could get into his boxes; just having Bolo dead would benefit only Ferritto, who would take over sole ownership of the book; where would the plotter get the $20,000 to pay the actual killer, if not from the boxes? The entire plot could not have been pulled off without a bank insider. And finally, the plotter could trust only a close relative at the bank, no other employee. This was DiPaolo's thinking and opinion. During Mastrey's first meeting with DiPaolo and Gunter at the bank after the murder, she volunteered information without being questioned, saying things like, "Bolo was a big mouth, bragging to the tellers about his money in his boxes. If I pick-up some info, I will call you." DiPaolo thought she was setting herself up as a helpful bank employee, but in a way, he later believed, she was actually giving cops the motive for the killing.

As if a harbinger predicting what would soon come, a short time after Theresa Mastrey's grand jury appearance near Pittsburgh, an Erie man kidnapped his girlfriend, holding her and police at bay for several hours. Police officers on the scene eventually talked the man out of the building. The man released his girlfriend unharmed, and then gave up to officers. In time, the man – a lawyer – had his law license suspended and was ultimately sentenced to prison. It was Jay D'Alba – Mastrey's attorney. D'Alba, after being released from prison sometime later, was able to get his law license reinstated, but again he his judgment apparently lapsed. In 2008 he was convicted for indirect criminal contempt stemming from a violation of a protection from abuse order that a woman had filed against him. In 2012, the Pennsylvania Supreme Court ordered another law license suspension, this time for one year.

But now, DiPaolo couldn't be distracted by Theresa Mastrey's woes. He had a murder case to prepare – and win. And first up was the ice-blooded Ohio hit man who shot Bolo Dovishaw in the back of his head as the bookie begged for his life, Robert Dorler.

In just two months, Dorler's trial would begin with state prosecutors seeking the ultimate punishment – death by electric chair at central Pennsylvania's Rockview penitentiary.

Partners in murder. Dealers in death.

Strong words. Even for a prosecutor. Robert E. Dorler was a central figure in such a partnership and dealership, Deputy Pennsylvania Attorney General M.L. Ebert told an Erie County criminal court jury on Friday, November 14, 1989, the long-awaited opening day of Dorler's capital offense murder trial.

Ebert began by saying he actually had no direct evidence to link Dorler, 53, of Medina, Ohio, with the January 3, 1983 killing of Erie's Frank "Bolo" Dovishaw. But Ebert insisted that the information put together by investigators over the past nearly seven years – including Dorler's own incriminating statements – would be enough to prove his guilt beyond a reasonable doubt and send him to Pennsylvania's electric chair.

"When you hear those words, you're going to know that Mr. Dorler knew about this case, that Mr. Dorler participated in the crime and that Mr. Dorler was a partner in murder," Ebert told the Erie County jury. At the start of the two-week trial, the state prosecutor told jurors in Erie County Judge George Levin's courtroom that the evidence against Dorler would be so overwhelming they must convict him of first degree murder.

However, the *Erie Daily Times* reported that day in its afternoon editions that defense attorney John H. Moore would use Ebert's own witnesses to acquit his client.

In Moore's opening statement to the jury the defense attorney said he would attack the credibility of key prosecution witnesses, many of them career criminals themselves. Moore said he'd show that these criminal witnesses were ratting against Dorler out of vengeance and to help themselves get reduced sentences on a wide array of felony charges they themselves faced.

"I ask you above all, when any witness testifies, to ask yourself if that witness has anything to gain by coming into this courtroom," Moore said to the jury of eight women and four men.

Moore was not a typical well-coifed courtroom criminal defense lawyer. He differed in appearance from many of the slick, more well-known and sharper-dressed criminal defense attorneys in town. Tall and bespectacled, he was overweight and frumpy-appearing, often with ill-fitting clothes. Sort of like a modern-day image of Clarence Darrow. His appearance belied a sharp, clear defense-attorney's mind, and also hid vast previous experience as a criminal prosecutor himself. While

DiPaolo had faith that Ebert's prosecutorial abilities would not betray DiPaolo's long, tenacious murder investigation, the cop still knew that Moore's defense ability mustn't be taken lightly.

Under Pennsylvania law, the trial phase must be followed by a penalty phase should there be a first degree murder conviction. It means that upon conviction, a separate proceeding must immediately follow during which the jury would consider other evidence – "aggravating" and "mitigating" – before determining whether the penalty is death or life in prison.

Judge Levin, a former trial lawyer, was an experienced, if sometimes unorthodox jurist, who appeared to look at different ways of interpreting the law. During a murder case a decade earlier, for example, he believed that a morgue photo of a female stabbing victim was too graphically inflammatory and emotion-producing for the jury to view in its entirety. While the defense and prosecution fought over admission of the photo of the victim sprawled on a slab in the morgue, Levin directed the courtroom tipstaff to produce a pair of scissors before he neatly and surgically removed the women's head from the photo, allowing only the image of the stab wounds to her upper torso to be admitted into evidence. With neither side particularly pleased with the ruling, neither objected. Both sides believed it was a fair, if not unusual, solution. (The District Attorney at the time, Robert Chase, later walked around the courthouse for weeks after the trial proudly displaying to employees the severed head portion of the photo.)

But now Judge Levin was presiding over his first truly mob-related case. With all the media attention, his judgment in the Dorler murder trial would have to rival that of the legendary Solomon.

In his opening remarks to the jury, Prosecutor Ebert strung together the facts, in his eyes, of what was to be the state's compelling case against Dorler. Ebert told jury members they would ultimately learn about the slimiest side of Erie's underbelly, along with influence and assistance of Ohio mobsters who would do anything for a buck. Even murder. Especially murder. The prosecutor promised the jury members he would prove that the evil Robert Dorler, along with longtime Erie crime figure Caesar Montevecchio, Erie businessman Anthony "Niggsy" Arnone and Ohio criminal William Bourjaily, were all members of the same conspiracy that carefully planned, then carried out Dovishaw's murder. He was already cautioning the jury that many of the witnesses would not be pretty, but probably offensive to most honest, law-abiding folks.

"I'm going to tell you right now, I'm not overly proud of some of the people the Commonwealth is going to call in this case," Ebert declared right off. Saying that those in the know about murder conspiracies are often as not criminals themselves, "Contract killings don't take place in front of school teachers."

Ebert was trying to set up the panel to not only accept, but also to believe Caesar Montevecchio and his testimony. All involved knew this case hinged on Montevecchio's credibility with the jury, and while Ebert wasn't about to convince anyone that Caesar was still a choirboy, the prosecutor did need to plant the seeds of Montevecchio's credibility early on in the minds of skeptical trial jurors.

Defense attorney John Moore was having none of Ebert's platitudes toward Montevecchio. And Moore especially wasn't about to allow Ebert's words to the jury to pass unchallenged. Moore, in his opening remarks, pointed out that although Caesar Montevecchio and Billy Bourjaily pleaded guilty to criminal charges several months earlier, neither of them had as yet been sentenced. The comment was meant to raise the jurors' suspicions and create doubt. The defense attorney assured the jury that both men had been promised they would be handed either minimum prison sentences or time to be served concurrently with prison terms they were already currently serving. "In other words," Moore said, "Caesar Montevecchio would not serve another day for the murder of 'Bolo' Dovishaw. In other words, Caesar Montevecchio was given a free ride."

In yet another bizarre twist to an already bizarre tale, Moore told the jury he would demonstrate during the trial that Montevecchio, in wiretapped conversations several years earlier with government witness "Fat Sam" Esper, freely acknowledged that it was he who had killed Bolo Dovishaw at the behest of Pittsburgh's Frantino crime family. The reason the Frantino family wanted Dovishaw wasted, Moore skillfully argued, was because the Pittsburgh mobsters wished to take over 'Bolo' Dovishaw's lucrative Erie gambling business.

Moore's attempt was to demonstrate to the jury vengeance, that Montevecchio and Bourjaily turned on Dorler in the Dovishaw probe because Dorler had gone before a grand jury, and also because

Montevecchio and Bourjaily were trying to get lighter sentences for themselves.

Confusing and slightly twisting the facts even more, which good defense lawyers have an uncanny knack for doing, Moore related to the jury that Montevecchio, in an earlier statement to Federal Bureau of Investigation, also implicated Joseph Scutella as the man who ordered the slaying, with the two Ohio men getting the twenty grand for the hit. "We will prove that the Commonwealth's case was put together solely to justify the plea bargains with Caesar Montevecchio and William Bourjaily," Moore concluded.

The opening statements were widely reported in the Erie media, and jurors must have found them to be mind-numbing as they were delivered by skilled lawyers on both sides of the courtroom. But now the time had come for the lawyers' spinning their cases to cease, and the actual testimony of the witnesses to begin.

Prosecutor Ebert began cautiously on that first day of Dorler's murder trial, slowly building his case with credible witnesses. It had been a long-proven prosecutorial technique that first, you had to ascertain that yes, Virginia, a crime had been committed. Once the jurors were convinced of the actual authenticity of wrongdoing, the prosecutor could feel more comfortable going for the jugular.

Testifying on that first day were those who could beyond the shadow of a doubt convince the jury that Bolo Dovishaw died not from natural causes, not from old age, not accidentally, not from his own hand, but as the direct result of the conspiracy and foul play of others

First was former Erie Police Detective Sergeant Joseph Weindorf, who had been the first investigator on the scene, even before Dom DiPaolo got the assignment the morning after Bolo's murder was discovered. Weindorf, who later became Erie's public safety director for a short period, and then the controversial Erie County Director of Public Safety, was a college-educated cop who had the respect of other officers and those operating within the area's criminal justice system. He told the jury the Erie Police Detective Division received a telephone call shortly before 8 p.m. the night of January 4, 1983. The call was from a former Detective Sergeant, Frank Rotunda, who told his colleagues on duty that night about a possible homicide. (Many were aware by that time of how Rotunda was led to find Dovishaw's body by the elite of Erie's criminal underworld. But that's getting way ahead of events as they were presented by state prosecutor Ebert that day to the jury in Judge Levin's courtroom.) As a result of Rotunda' call, Weindorf told the jury, he was dispatched to Dovishaw's West 21st Street home.

The former *Erie Daily Times* newspaper reported on the testimony, saying that Weindorf was let into the house by Rotunda (later to serve a prison sentence for murder solicitation in a drug case). Present in "Ash Wednesday's" house were admitted mob killer Ferritto, "Cy" Ciotti, Torrelli and Dovishaw's estranged wife, Joan. Weindorf said he recognized the three men from past experience, telling Rotunda to keep them at the house. Weindorf testified Rotunda said there could possibly be a body in the basement. Weindorf did in fact find Dovishaw's corpse in the basement, saying it was covered by a sheet and a rug. Weindorf also told the jury that during his initial investigation he learned Dovishaw's car, later discovered in the parking lot of the Holiday Inn South along Interstate 90, was then missing.

Next to take the witness stand was Dr. Halbert Fillinger, a Philadelphia region forensic pathologist affectionately known in law enforcement circles as "Homicide Hal." In those pre-*CSI* days, Fillinger was as close as Erie County law enforcement would get to a real-life scientific crime scene investigator. Many of the autopsies performed on Erie County murder victims were the work of general hospital pathologists who picked up extra money for their post-mortem work. Fillinger had been an assistant medical examiner in Philadelphia County, and, at the time of his testimony he was chief deputy coroner for Bucks County. Now accepted as an expert witness in the Dovishaw case, he testified that he had inspected the crime scene and performed an autopsy on Dovishaw's body on January 5, 1983. According to Fillinger's often graphic courtroom testimony, Dovishaw died from a gunshot wound to the right rear portion of his head. The physician said that based on crime scene observations, it was likely Dovishaw died where he was found, probably in a kneeling position when fatally shot, with hands and feet bound.

"Homicide Hal" told the jury the victim also had been stabbed in the corner of his left eye. But because of damage from the bullet, Fillinger could not determine whether the stabbing occurred prior to or following the gunshot. Furthermore, Fillinger said the pool of blood found near Dovishaw's body suggested that Dovishaw was alive when he was shot, and likely lived for perhaps a half-hour after the shooting.

With Thanksgiving only several weeks away, and Judge Levin wanting this trial over by then, the first day of testimony concluded late that Friday afternoon. But Monday morning, following a relatively peaceful weekend, would bring even more explosive revelations.

CHAPTER 38

EVEN DRESSED IN A LIGHT-COLORED SUIT, WHITE SHIRT AND conservatively striped tie, Robert E. Dorler Sr. appeared just the opposite of a businessman or regular Sunday churchgoer. Dorler had a cold, ugly look about him. A look, some would say, of one who would commit murder without a second thought. With his receding dark hair slicked down and combed straight back from a wide forehead, Dorler's deep sunken eyes flanking a pointy, Nixonesque-like nose seemed to speak ominously of the character within, a character thoroughly, hideously contaminated throughout with unmitigated evil.

By the third day of Dorler's murder trial in Erie County Court, observers got the feeling jury members were thinking the same thing about the defendant's deep, dark countenance. Appearances shouldn't matter, we're taught early on. Books shouldn't be judged by their covers, we're told in grade school. But in the real world, most know image is often considered more important than substance in perceptions of others. In Dorler's case, there was more than just an uneasy feeling about him, more than a feeling of never wanting to encounter him in a dark alley.

The long line of prosecution witnesses did as much damage to Dorler as did his own mean appearance, as jurors were beginning to put together a clear image of how Erie bookie Frank "Bolo" Dovishaw spent his final moments on earth nearly seven years earlier. The latest witness to help law enforcement tighten the prosecutorial noose was a former partner-in-crime, now turned state's evidence for his own benefit.

William Bourjaily, 36, of Cleveland, was another of the career criminals called to the witness stand to testify against Dorler. Both were from the Cleveland area, where the brotherhood of criminal activity often runs deep. Fellow criminals worked with or knew of each other, and often their productive criminal relationships lasted for many years.

Called to the stand by M.L. Ebert, prosecutor from the Pennsylvania Attorney General's Office, Ebert quickly, albeit reluctantly, established that Bourjaily was not to be heralded as an ideal witness performing a civic duty. No, William Bourjaily was anything but honest, decent and upstanding in his community. Bourjaily was compelled to admit during his testimony that he was serving a federal prison term on drug charges. Yet, as dirty as Bourjaily might have been in the eyes of the law, he was an excellent witness who spoke with authority and with the ring of truth in implicating Robert Dorler in Bolo Dovishaw's murder.

Bourjaily began by telling the jury he had traveled from Ohio to Erie that fateful night early January 1983 to meet with longtime Erie underworld figure Caesar Montevecchio in an attempt to score a source of cocaine for Bourjaily to market in Ohio. When asked just how he came to know Montevecchio, Bourjaily said they became acquainted a year earlier when Montevecchio set up several Erie-area robberies for Bourjaily to help commit. But on January 3, 1983, the prosecution witness testified, the Montevecchio bunch graduated from armed robbery to murder. It was on that night that Bourjaily met Montevecchio at The Sports Page bar on West 26th Street about 6 p.m. to talk about an Erie-Cleveland drug connection. But Bourjaily said Caesar couldn't make the drug hook-up. Yet, as they left the bar, when Bourjaily still insisted on trying to make the connection, Bourjaily said Montevecchio said to follow him. It was at the Station Restaurant, then, where they met Dorler, Bourjaily said. He said he knew Dorler from previous Erie and other crimes.

In Bourjaily's testimony, he said Dorler was driving a Cadillac that night, and that he asked Bourjaily to follow him, and then give him a ride home, back to Ohio. Bourjaily said he drove behind Dorler from the Station Restaurant on Peach Street to the Holiday Inn South along Interstate 90 where Dorler abandoned the vehicle in the popular hotel's rear parking lot. When Dorler got into Bourjaily's vehicle for the ride back to Cleveland, Bourjaily said, "He (Dorler) was pretty nervous."

During small talk along the way, Bourjaily asked Dorler what he had been doing in Erie that cold night, Bourjaily testified. "Leave it alone," Bourjaily quoted Dorler as telling him at first. But later, Bourjaily said, Dorler acknowledged he had killed a man in Erie.

"When I asked him what he was doing there, he told me he killed a guy named 'Bolo,'" Bourjaily said. During the ride from Erie to the Cleveland area, the two men took Interstate 90 west to Route 11 in Ohio, and then headed southwesterly on Route 11 toward Youngstown, Bourjaily testified. As the car crossed a bridge at Meander Lake, Bourjaily said, Dorler directed him to slow down. He said Dorler opened the front passenger-side window, then pulled out a .32 caliber automatic Bourjaily recognized as Dorler's, then tossed it out the open window into the lake.

He recognized the weapon, he said, because he previously borrowed it from Dorler to rob Erie businessman Frank Scalise on May 12, 1982. According to Bourjaily, it was Dorler who loaned him the .32 caliber handgun used in the Scalise robbery. He also said he returned the gun to Dorler very soon after the Scalise stick-up. The testimony helped put the jig-saw puzzle of a case together for jurors and nail down ownership of the gun that killed Dovishaw: It was Dorler's.

Jury members listened intently, apparently fascinated with the vivid and compelling up-close-and-personal behind-the-scenes descriptions of the aftermath of the cold-blooded slaying. But William Bourjaily's damning testimony against Dorler would become even more compelling – for both jurors and even for longtime courtroom observers. The witness said Dorler told him "Bolo" had been a bookie in Erie who was partnered with Erie hit man Raymond Ferritto. Bourjaily testified Dorler told him he had entered Dovishaw's house at gunpoint that night, forced the terrified victim into the basement, bound his hands and feet, and then shot him once in the head.

"He said Mr. Dovishaw begged for his life, and he told him to die like a man," Bourjaily told the quiet and stunned courtroom. Bourjaily said Dorler also told him he had stabbed Dovishaw once in the eye after shooting him.

Aside from scores of raised eyebrows and an occasional involuntary gasp, one could have heard the proverbial pin drop in the silent courtroom. It was a key moment in the trial. Especially for the jurors. It was testimony that could not be easily shaken or challenged. But Bourjaily still wasn't done. The damning, incriminating testimony from this now credible witness, despite his own unbroken lifelong record of criminal activity, continued: The next day, Bourjaily said, he accompanied murder defendant Dorler to a popular pancake restaurant – "Mr. C's" – along Interstate 90 at the Ashtabula, Ohio exit. The restaurant was an innocuous place for hoods to meet. There, Bourjaily and Dorler met with Caesar Montevecchio, who handed Dorler a brown paper bag Bourjaily suspected contained the $20,000 payment-in-full for the Dovishaw hit, he testified. Adding much credible detail to his testimony, Bourjaily told how he and Dorler left the restaurant meeting with Montevecchio, then drove back to the Holiday Inn South outside of Erie. There, in the parking lot, Bourjaily said, Dorler returned safe-deposit box keys to the car he had ditched there the previous night.

But defense attorney John Moore showed the jury that he wasn't buying any of it. During Moore's cross examination, he went straight to the heart of Bourjaily's credibility, especially in getting the witness to acknowledge that he had been a cellmate with Caesar Montevecchio, prosecutor Ebert's second key witness. Also, Bourjaily acknowledged under Moore's relentless questioning, that he had lied to investigators probing the sensational murder, having initially told them he did not even know anyone named Caesar Montevecchio. It was the best Moore could do, but the damage to his client Dorler already had been done.

William Bourjaily's testimony was indeed damning; he was one of the bad guys, yes, but still his fingering of Robert Dorler was potent evidence in the prosecution's death penalty case for this contract killing. It was the kind of testimony that average folks who serve on juries only encounter while watching television crime dramas or at cops-and-robbers movies. But now, here in the Erie County Courthouse, they were hearing the cold-blooded, often chilling details of a real-life crime that would rival any appearing on any major television network's detective or lawyer shows. It had been testimony that members of the jury would recall during their deliberations days later – and perhaps for the remainder of their lives. But the most compelling testimony of all would come from the man who was rapidly becoming an Erie cult-like figure, Caesar Montevecchio.

Montevecchio finally got his chance to talk. And talk he did that Monday in Erie County Court. The jury in Judge George Levin's courtroom got their eye-popping, jaw-dropping primer on Erie's underworld that day. Even Judge Levin seemed somewhat taken back by the depth of Montevecchio's, nonchalant, matter-of-fact testimony.

Yes, Montevecchio freely testified, almost bragging, he was the one who hired Robert Dorler to whack Dovishaw. But not so fast, argued Dorler defense Attorney John Moore. For it was Moore who knew that at all costs he must attack Montevecchio's credibility during the defense cross-examination. And attack it he did! For more than two hours.

Montevecchio began his testimony patiently explaining that the murder plot actually was hatched during the spring previous to the Dovishaw killing. In compelling testimony easily matching Bourjaily's, Montevecchio said he was approached in the spring of 1982 by Erie businessman Anthony "Niggsy" Arnone. Montevecchio said Arnone, who was yet to stand trial, had devised a plan to kill Dovishaw so that the keys to Dovishaw's bank safe-deposit boxes – where all suspected Dovishaw's gambling loot was stashed – could be stolen. But because Arnone was offering Montevecchio a mere percentage of what was found in the bank boxes, Montevecchio testified, he was initially reluctant to participate in the scheme. But he did decide to get involved when Arnone said he would give the shooter $20,000 and Montevecchio another $10,000 for being the arranger.

Eventually, Montevecchio testified, he contacted the right man for the job: Dorler. The Ohio man had previously taken part in a number of Erie robberies set up by Montevecchio, he testified. Now, Dorler eagerly accepted the terms of the contract Montevecchio had offered on Arnone's behalf, Caesar testified.

According to what Montevecchio described for the jury, he had several discussions with Dorler about the murder previous to the actual killing. They also talked about other activity, Montevecchio said. Worried that law enforcement officials would tap his home phone, Caesar testified that it was usual for him to telephone Dorler's Ohio home, then have him return the call to a pay phone in Erie.

State Prosecutor Ebert, attempting to corroborate Montevecchio's testimony, introduced into evidence Caesar's telephone records from November 1982 through February 1983. The records showed several calls to Dorler's home during the time the Dovishaw murder was being planned and immediately after the crime. Montevecchio said the events didn't go exactly as planned. Initially, the scheme called for Dorler to get into Bolo's house, kill him, get the bank safe deposit box keys, meet and hand over the keys to Montevecchio, then transport Dovishaw's body in the trunk of Dovishaw's Caddy back to Cleveland where the car would be abandoned.

Because of Dovishaw's weight issues and Dorler's lack of strength conditioning, the corpse remained in the basement at the exact spot of the killing. In further testimony, Montevecchio said Dorler traveled to Erie to commit the murder in early December1982, but that attempt was aborted because noted Erie crime figure Anthony "Cy" Ciotti and his girlfriend were living with Dovishaw at the time and both were in the house the night Dovishaw was to be killed. As the *Erie Daily Times* paraphrased, "Montevecchio said he told Joseph Scutella of Erie about the scheme and asked for his help in having Ciotti leave the house . . . He did not further identify the Scutella man. He said Scutella agreed, and also asked that Ferritto be killed. Montevecchio said Scutella offered $10,000 more for Ferritto's death, indicating it was in retribution for testimony given by Ferritto against friends of Scutella's who were involved in a Cleveland mob slaying."

If the jury members were not previously confused by the wide assortment of underworld characters whose names rapidly were being introduced into evidence, along with myriad crimes they were accused of committing, by now their heads must have been swimming – Ferritto, Scutella, Montevecchio, Bourjaily, Dorler, Arnone, Greene, mob hits, other felonies. Was everyone in Erie and Cleveland a wise guy? Some must have wondered.

When Montevecchio's testimony resumed, he told the jury of discussing the Ferritto "option" – like it was an accessory to be considered in new car purchase negotiations – with Dorler. All in all, it was becoming one of Erie's most riveting murder trials. And it was just beginning.

Sure, Dorler would whack Erie mob killer Raymond Ferritto for an extra ten grand, Caesar Montevecchio testified. Who wouldn't! But only if Ray Ferritto was actually physically in the bookie's house when Dorler was there murdering his primary target, Dovishaw. Montevecchio, however, said he was aware in advance that Ferritto would not be there at the time Dovishaw was killed, so the second murder and payment by Scutella became moot.

But now it was time for the nitty-gritty – for Montevecchio to get down to actual specifics in his state's evidence testimony against Robert Dorler. Despite Montevecchio's reputation as one of Erie's most disgusting criminals, his testimony had just enough of a ring of truth to it to convince the jurors of his veracity. On January 3, 1983, Montevecchio said, he met Dorler near West 38th Street and Washington Avenue shortly before 6 p.m. On this night, unlike another false run in December, there would be no going back. The wheels of the murder plot were then set unalterably in motion. In his testimony, Caesar Montevecchio said he and Dorler agreed to meet about an hour later at the Station Restaurant at Peach Street and Washington Avenue, not far away. After that initial meeting of the night, Montevecchio went straight to what was Dom DiPaolo's favorite hangout, The Sports Page bar, to set up his alibi for the evening.

Although Dovishaw's body was supposed to have been dumped in Cleveland, and that's what Montevecchio thought would happen at the time, he also knew the exact time of death would likely be placed by forensics experts as sometime after 6 p.m. that night. Also knowing that so-called gambling clients' calls to Bolo's numbers and football-betting business would go unanswered after 6 p.m., Montevecchio testified he made sure he stayed at the Sports Page bar until 7 p.m., thus clearly establishing an alibi for himself. Montevecchio's testimony was later backed up by Anthony Gambatese Jr., aka "Tony Gams," of Erie, who told the jury he took sports bets for Dovishaw. That night, Gambatese said, he once strolled past the innocent-looking Montevecchio at the bar to place a call to Bolo in an attempt to learn of that Monday night professional football game's "line" (point spread) shortly before 7 o'clock. Gambatese said there was no answer at Bolo's, but Victor Ferritto picked up on the relay. Montevecchio knew why. The bookie was already dead. Shot once in the head. Stabbed once in the eye.

In his testimony, Montevecchio said William Bourjaily of Ohio joined him at the bar. Bourjaily was trying to hook up with an Erie cocaine dealer for distribution in his native Ohio. Montevecchio testified, however, that he told Bourjaily he was finally getting out of the cocaine business, but would try to arrange a connection for the Ohio man with Montevecchio's longtime partner in crime, Joseph Scutella, one of Erie's largest distributors of coke. What came next was Caesar Montevecchio's first-hand account of the second meeting of the night with the killer Dorler. It was an account that clearly and convincingly demonstrated for the jury that Montevecchio was telling the truth. Jury members appeared fascinated. And so were readers of Erie's newspapers, which had reported the case faithfully from the beginning and now treated said readers to extensive trial coverage.

That Monday, November 13, 1989, had dawned dark and dreary in Erie, a perfect day for a murder trial with all the dramatic and violent underworld elements of greed and revenge, double-dealings and betrayal. It was a perfect day for Robert Dorler, 58, of Medina, Ohio, to be on trial for his life. November "doom and gloom" – an annual cold, rainy and dingy forbearing of northwestern Pennsylvania's long winter to come – was clearly in the air at the Erie County Courthouse as Caesar Montevecchio told of the minutes and hours immediately after the arranged murder of Dovishaw seven years earlier.

When he left The Sports Page, Montevecchio testified, he told Bourjaily to drive behind him as he drove to the Station Restaurant a short distance away and met for the second time that night with the killer Dorler. The first time they met, he said, it had been to drop off Dorler near Dovishaw's west Erie home. During this second meeting, Montevecchio said, the killer had showed up driving Dovishaw's green Cadillac. But there was no body in the car's trunk as was previously planned. It was the first sign that the perfect Erie murder was not so perfect. Dorler begged off, telling Montevecchio that the overweight Dovishaw had been too heavy to lift, so he left the lifeless body in the basement, where Dorler had fulfilled his part of the unholy bargain, having murdered Dovishaw. Instead of Dorler driving Dovishaw's car and body to Cleveland to be ditched there, the plan was changed. He would now drive the Caddy to the Holiday Inn South along Interstate 90, abandon it in the hotel's side/rear parking lot, and William Bourjaily would drive him back to Ohio. Before leaving Montevecchio, however, Dorler gave him two keys – the keys to Dovishaw's bank safe-deposit boxes. Bourjaily's appearance, then, had turned into a stroke of luck.

Montevecchio's sworn testimony continued: He telephoned, then met up with Anthony Arnone to deliver Dovishaw's bank box keys. Arnone was to visit the boxes the next morning.

And the next day, Caesar said, he met with "Niggsy" Arnone again, this time collecting some $20,000 for the killer Dorler, but only $1,000 of the ten grand he had been promised for being the middleman and arranging the murder. With the money, Montevecchio said, he drove from Erie half-way to Cleveland along Interstate 90, meeting and then paying off Dorler at "Mr. C's" pancake restaurant near Ashtabula, Ohio. After paying the blood money to Dorler, he said, he also returned the bank box keys to the killer, instructing him to drive back to the Erie area and place the keys in Dovishaw's car in the Holiday Inn South parking lot.

Now it was defense attorney John Moore's turn to try to destroy, or at least diminish, whatever credibility Caesar Montevecchio had established with the jury. During the lengthy cross-examination, Moore repeatedly tore into Montevecchio over discrepancies from his previous testimony.

As the *Erie Daily Times* reported, "Moore also pointed out Montevecchio's involvement in a number of crimes, including Dovishaw's murder, and a deal that would recommend he receive sentences concurrent to a 10-to-20-year term he was now serving on drug charges . . . When asked about several apparent holes in the plan," the newspaper account continued, "such as how Dorler was alone to move Dovishaw's body, why Bourjaily was brought into the plan or how Dorler was to enter Dovishaw's house, Montevecchio admitted he made several errors in the plan."

Moore was quick to point out what he considered to be additional discrepancies in Montevecchio's testimony, specifically when Montevecchio told Arnone that Dovishaw's body could not be moved. Moore also insisted that Montevecchio's testimony that day sharply differed with accounts given during his previous grand jury appearance.

"You were just checking your stories out to see which one worked better?" Moore asked somewhat sarcastically.

"No," Montevecchio answered. "I was probably confused."

Why then, Moore asked, did Montevecchio tell investigating FBI agents that it was Joseph Scutella who arranged Bolo Dovishaw's demise but was now claiming it was Arnone and Dorler who were involved in the murder plot? Montevecchio answered he was lying when he spoke with the FBI. But he insisted, in that manner reminiscent of his once-innocent Catholic altar-boy days of yesteryear, that he was not lying to the Erie County Court jury now.

One of the Robert Dorler murder trial's most titillating witnesses was admitted local mob killer-for-hire Raymond Ferritto. Ferritto, and his well-known ferocity, which DiPaolo had experienced firsthand as a teenager so many years earlier, was already a legendary Erie crime figure. Not that he was admired for his profession, but he was looked upon with a morbid, macabre kind of fascination the way one gazes with trepidation at a bizarre, stinging insect, or the way rubber-necking passersby drive slowly past accident scenes.

Ferritto was called upon by the prosecution to testify about "Ash Wednesday's" last day of life – which involved Ferritto in a very personal way. But, as DiPaolo recalled, "the slime ball, as always, held a gun, per se, to the head of the prosecution to make sure he helped himself first."

In 1987, for example, two years before the trial began, the Pennsylvania State Police Organized Crime Unit arrested Ferritto, his buddy from Pittsburgh, Manuel "Mike the Greek" Xenakis, and Jeannie Thomas (wife of cocaine dealer Ron Thomas, who dirty cop Frank Rotunda wanted killed) and a big earner in Bolo Dovishaw's booking operation. They were charged with pool-selling, bookmaking, criminal conspiracy and participating in a corrupt organization, all stemming from the multi-million dollar gambling operation connected to Pittsburgh's LaRocca/Genovese crime family. Ray Ferritto was represented by Attorney John Garhart, a successful criminal defense lawyer who once hired a limousine to transport himself to the site of the statewide grand jury probing the Dovishaw murder in Westmoreland County where Ferritto had been called to testify.

Garhart, later a Pennsylvania Common Pleas Court judge in Erie County, had phoned DiPaolo, advising him that Ferritto received his subpoena for the Robert Dorler trial, but in exchange for his testimony, he wanted the gambling charges to go away. DiPaolo, even given his knowledge of how cold and jaded criminal elements could be, was nonetheless amazed that Bolo Dovishaw's best buddy and gambling operation partner would not testify against Bolo's killer without a deal. *What a piece of shit,* the cop thought. DiPaolo swallowed hard and explained to Ferritto's lawyer that it would be up to Skip Ebert, the prosecutor handling the Dorler trial, to approve the deal.

On September 29, 1989, Garhart and Ferritto sent a proffer (detailing what Ferritto would testify to), to Pennsylvania Assistant Attorney General Lawrence Claus. Although such a deal on the testimony was distasteful to DiPaolo and prosecutors, they needed Ferritto, not only at Dorler's trial, but also at Arnone's trial to substantiate the amount of money previously contained in Dovishaw's safe-deposit boxes. As a result, a deal was eventually struck that Ferritto's sentencing judge, Roger M. Fischer, would be made aware of Ferritto's "outstanding" cooperation with the Dovishaw investigation.

In his Dorler Trial testimony, Raymond Ferritto acknowledged he had spent much of the day of the January 1983 murder with Dovishaw. Admitting he was partners with Dovishaw in their lucrative sports betting operation, Ray Ferritto told the jury he and Bolo ventured out earlier that Monday evening to make "business collections." Those collection stops ironically included one at Anthony "Niggsy" Arnone's Italian food importing business, Ferritto said.

Ferritto, calm and collected, spoke to the jury in his patented deep, throaty intonations. The killer of who knows how many testified he last saw Dovishaw just before 6 p.m. that day. He said he received at least several telephone calls from bettors that night who told him they were concerned that they couldn't reach the popular Erie bookie. After telling the jury of his own attempts to reach Dovishaw later that evening, Ferritto testified he was one of several of the local crimeland's heavy hitters to pay a visit to Dovishaw's house the next day, only to discover Bolo's lifeless body in the basement, bound, shot and stabbed.

Prosecutor Ebert questioned Ferritto about the lucrative gambling business he operated with Dovishaw. Ferritto's deep-voiced, raspy monotone never changed.

Ice for blood.

The chilling expression on his face, almost totally devoid of human emotion, remained the same as he told of the business making some $89,000 in gambling profits that sports-betting weekend. Not a bad take for two who had never toiled for long at legitimate labor or business practices. When Ebert asked Ferritto about Bolo Dovishaw's bank safe-deposit boxes, Ferritto said the bank boxes never contained less than $50,000 in cash.

Then, the prosecutor moved on to the highly unusual courtroom topic of Bolo Dovishaw's eventual funeral. The special prosecutor wanted to know whether Raymond Ferritto was actually a witness to Montevecchio being at the funeral home, and, if so, what Montevecchio's demeanor had been at the time.

Ferritto acknowledged that Montevecchio was there, then added Caesar had appeared to be very uncharacteristically nervous. "He wanted to have a private talk," Ferritto disclosed of Montevecchio at the funeral home. Then Ferritto told the jury that Montevecchio asked him whether police had been talking to Ferritto or anyone else about Montevecchio.

There was a moment of silence in the courtroom.

"Did you suspect him (of the murder)?" Ebert asked Ferritto.

"Yes," came the chilling response.

Perhaps even the cool Ferritto would be surprised, however, to learn how much cash was actually shoved into his partner's bank safe deposit boxes. (Later, on the new gambling and conspiracy charges that were part of the testimony deal, Ferritto got another judicial "kiss" when he was sentenced to six months in the Erie County Prison, but released to one year of probation after serving one whole day behind bars. He was also assessed $3,000 in fines and costs.)

The next trial witness would stun just about everyone.

A few weeks before his murder, one Erie bookie Frank "Bolo" Dovishaw's bank safe deposit boxes contained as much as $300,000 in cash. PennBank loan officer Diane DiRenzio-Amendola's estimate of the gambling loot took a few minutes to sink in for many courtroom observers. It also became clear in many minds why the co-conspirators were so eager to get their hands on Dovishaw's bank box keys. Bookmaking was apparently a very lucrative business!

DiRenzio-Amendola's testimony had an expected, volatile impact on Judge George Levin's courtroom that November 14. She had been called to the witness stand by state Prosecutor M.L. Ebert and first played for the jury a videotape of the bank's west Erie branch office. Dovishaw had two safe deposit boxes at the same branch, she testified. She said she only knew Dovishaw as a customer and that occasionally she helped him with access to the bank vault and one of his boxes.

According to DiRenzio-Amendola's testimony, she had last helped Dovishaw on December 17, 1982. She assisted him in getting to the larger of the two safe deposit boxes. Apparently because she had acted so professionally friendly toward Dovishaw, she testified, he had allowed her to view the contents of the box.

"In addition to some jewelry and papers, there was a large amount of fifty- and one hundred-dollar bills."

"It was about halfway filled and about three quarters of the way to the top" with cash, the bank employee testified, estimating about $300,000 in the box. However, following the "Bolo" Dovishaw murder when police officials had the bank safe deposit box drilled open, they found various items, but only about $18,000 in cash, according to earlier trial testimony. As if for dramatic effect, the prosecutor held up what he indicated was an amount similar to the $18,000 in the same fifties and one hundred-dollar bill denominations. The stack was *only* several inches high. Then Ebert placed the money in a safe deposit box and allowed DiRenzio-Amendola to peer inside and examine the contents.

"That's not what I saw," she said.

"There was a lot more money in this box?" Ebert asked the bank employee.

"Yes," she said.

But under cross examination from Robert Dorler's lawyer, John Moore, DiRenzio-Amendola was obliged to acknowledge she was not an expert at estimating cash.

Earlier in her testimony, DiRenzio-Amendola told the jury she had processed a loan application for Arnone on January 4, 1983, the day after Bolo Dovishaw's murder. She said she was witness to Arnone entering the bank vault, where the safe-deposit boxes are stored, that same day. Arnone also had a safe-deposit box at the bank that he had rented the previous May.

Then, as reported by the news media, DiRenzio-Amendola got down to explaining the nuts and bolts of safe-deposit box rentals for the benefit of jurors who might not have been familiar with exactly how the rental process works at most financial institutions. She said that two keys were needed to access bank safe-deposit boxes. One key is provided by the bank to the customer. The customer holds onto that key and brings it to the bank whenever the box is to be opened. The second key is held by the bank. Under normal circumstances at that time, a bank employee accompanies the customer to the vault. Both customer and employee simultaneously insert their keys into separate sides of the box, then turn the keys in the locks to retrieve the box from the vault. Sometimes, the customer gives the key to the bank official, who would simultaneously turn both. Without both keys being turned simultaneously, the box cannot be unlocked. But that was under *normal* circumstances at that time. And this was not normal; it was far from normal, all involved agreed.

"You didn't see anyone go in with him (Arnone)?" state prosecutor Ebert asked DiRenzio-Amendola.

"No," she responded.

"So, he was in the vault alone?" Ebert asked.

"Without a doubt," she replied.

CHAPTER 39

THE HIGH FINANCE TESTIMONY APPARENTLY LEFT AN IMPRESSION IN the minds of jury members. When DiRenzio-Amendola's testimony was completed, Prosecutor Ebert then recalled lead investigator Dominick DiPaolo to the witness stand.

Much of what he testified to was reported in great detail by Erie's news media as the icy facts surrounding the 1983 cold-blooded killing trickled out.

DiPaolo continued his earlier testimony about the long investigation into the Dovishaw's executive-style slaying and how the veteran cop was led to Caesar Montevecchio as the prime suspect in the murder case. For the first time publicly, however, the Erie cop told of how on several occasions during the first half of 1983, Montevecchio's phone calls had been monitored by law enforcement officials. These were the days long before now-common high tech communication practices, so the calls involved only Montevecchio's home telephone. DiPaolo said the monitoring revealed several of Caesar Montevecchio's calls during that initial period from April through July 1983 were made to Anthony "Niggsy" Arnone.

The Erie homicide detective testified that during the normal course of his visual surveillance of Montevecchio, the investigator once observed the Erie crime figure with the current murder defendant, Robert Dorler of Ohio. The sighting was on the day prior to Montevecchio's arrest on several robbery charges and the same day state's witness

Samuel "Fat Sam" Esper wore a "wire" to tape-record Esper's conversation with Montevecchio.

Much of DiPaolo's testimony, however, had more to do with focusing on the early days of the investigation, rather than on the actual defendant Dorler himself. He described the initial steps he took in the murder investigation, including ordering police identification teams to spend up to four days processing Dovishaw's house and lifting perhaps 100 latent fingerprints from various interior surfaces.

The fingerprints belonged to five individuals, all of whom could explain their presence in Dovishaw's house. The Erie police investigator told about finding the many sets of fingerprints at Bolo Dovishaw's house following the murder, but he again pointed out that those whose prints were found in the home were later ruled out as suspects. Neither Dorler nor others linked to the case were identified solely because of fingerprints found at the murder scene, DiPaolo testified.

The detective said that during the course of his investigation he attempted to piece together the last hours of Frank "Bolo" Dovishaw's life on January 3, 1983. He did this, he told the jury, by interviewing those whom he knew last saw Dovishaw alive that day. The list included Al Damore and noted Erie mob killer Raymond Ferritto, Dovishaw's business partner in the bookmaking and sports betting operation. It was then that defense lawyer Moore apparently had enough and objected to the cop telling the jury what Damore and Ferritto had told him. Moore correctly argued that both men had already testified themselves as to what they knew about the case.

Prosecutor Ebert, undaunted by such a sustained objection, switched gears and began to question DiPaolo about other areas of his investigation, including where Dovishaw kept the illegal proceeds from his gambling business. DiPaolo said he determined that Dovishaw kept most of his money in three bank safe-deposit boxes, two at what had been the Security Peoples Bank (later merged with PennBank) branch on West 26th Street in adjoining Millcreek Township, and one at a Marine Bank branch at East 38th and Pine Avenue in Erie. DiPaolo said that armed with search warrants, investigators had those boxes drilled on January 7, 1983, four days after Erie's notorious killing. In addition to jewelry and documents, police found about $18,000 in cash in each of the boxes at PennBank, DiPaolo said. The third box was determined to have been co-leased by Dovishaw and his gambling pal Phil Torrelli, at the Marine Bank branch. Only Torrelli had the keys to this box, used for paperwork, including bettors' names.

Next DiPaolo, as reported in the Erie media, provided the jury with more inside information about Dovishaw's abandoned car, the green Cadillac in which the murder victim took so much pride.

The Caddy, found in the Holiday Inn South parking lot January 5, then searched by police, yielded some $6,400 in cash and several checks, DiPaolo testified. He said two bank bags with checks and $5,200 in cash were discovered in the Cadillac's trunk. A secret compartment in the car's dashboard held another $1,200 in cash and three checks. One of the checks was endorsed by Erie businessman Anthony "Niggsy" Arnone – Arnone, the suspect accused of organizing the hit on Dovishaw to get to the safe-deposit box stash of illegal gambling loot. That check had been dated "1-6-82," nearly a year before the killing. But DiPaolo later determined that the date was actually a mistake. The check was supposed to read "1-6-83," which would have been just three days after the murder and only one day after Bolo's Caddy was found. Another check for $685.75 was signed by David Colegrande, who operated Arnone's Italian Store. It was made out to A. and G. Food, also operated by Arnone.

The next day, the vise tightened somewhat in the prosecution's case against murder defendant Robert E. Dorler. It was then that the weapon that killed Frank "Bolo" Dovishaw was directly linked to the Ohio man on trial for his life. Dorler, as usual, showed little or no emotion when the Pennsylvania State Police ballistics forensics expert made the positive connection between two crimes linked to the single weapon.

State Police Sgt. Virgil "Butch" Jellison was one of those picture perfect prosecutorial witnesses: Three-piece fitted business suit, trim, clean-cut, sit-up-straight military demeanor, and the confident aura of one who thoroughly knows his subject matter and isn't at all bashful about sharing his knowledge about it. That was Butch Jellison. Sgt. Jellison was the kind of expert witness prosecutors love. Juries usually admire such witnesses as well. Defense attorneys rarely can shake their testimony, and in the end their credibility is often impossible to challenge.

Answering with those terse, crisp "yes sirs" or "no sirs," the state police expert spoke directly to the jury in explaining that the microscopic examination of two shells – one cartridge found near the body of Erie bookmaker Dovishaw and the other discovered at an Erie armed robbery scene eight months earlier – showed that the shells came from the same handgun. The microscopic markings made by an ejector mechanism came from the same .32 automatic pistol, Jellison testified. One cartridge was found near Dovishaw's lifeless body in January 1983, the other at the scene of a May 1982 robbery of Erie businessman Frank Scalise. An entire bullet had apparently come from the robber's gun during a scuffle between Scalise and the attacker during the armed robbery, Jellison speculated.

For the jury, it was beginning to appear that Dorler wasn't the only bad guy involved in this case – but it was the Ohio man who was on trial, not the other characters in Erie's own version of *The Gang That Couldn't Shoot Straight.*

Now it was the defense's turn. Lawyer John Moore immediately dropped a murder trial bombshell. Moore's first witness was convicted drug dealer and arsonist Joseph Scutella, Jr. Scutella promptly swore that it was his old pal, Caesar Montevecchio, who had murdered Erie bookie Frank "Bolo" Dovishaw. So much for friendship. So much for honor among crooks. Caesar and Joey had been pals for ages, but apparently no longer.

Before dropping the dime on Montevecchio, at the urging of Attorney Moore, Scutella recited the long list of crimes for which he was then currently serving time in prison. Let's see now, the witness seemed to be thinking, rubbing his chin in deep thought. First, there was the 20-year sentence under the federal Racketeering Influenced Corrupt Organizations Act (RICO) for crimes associated with heavy drug trafficking in West Virginia. And when that time was served, Scutella testified, he would begin another sentence of 15-to-30 years for arson and crimes related to the fire that destroyed Scutella's former family business, Pal Joey's Restaurant. So much punishment – so little time! As it turned out, Joey Scutella would succumb to an insidious cancer long before he would pay his debt to society. But on this day, he was the star defense witness in the Robert Dorler murder trial.

Moore wanted to know if Montevecchio had ever contacted Scutella prior to January 3, 1983, the day Dovishaw was killed. Moore specifically inquired whether Montevecchio had asked Scutella to warn Erie crime figure Anthony "Cy" Ciotti to keep away from Bolo Dovishaw's house on the day of the killing. Montevecchio admitted that he made such a request of Scutella in his earlier testimony for the prosecution. Montevecchio also squealed on his friend Scutella during that testimony, claiming that Scutella asked him to also kill Dovishaw's bookmaking partner, mob murderer Raymond Ferritto. Now on the witness stand, Scutella emphatically denied both of Caesar Montevecchio's claims.

The defense lawyer, according to a report in the *Morning News*, then asked Joey Scutella to describe the events of the night of January 3, 1983. Scutella said he started out that night making plumbing repairs at the west Erie home of his wife. Upon leaving, he drove the short distance past Dovishaw's residence on West 21st Street. About a block from Dovishaw's home, Scutella testified, he spied a gray, four-door sedan with Ohio plates in front of the house. He said that as he approached Dovishaw's home, the car pulled away, leaving a man standing in the street, Caesar Montevecchio.

"I yelled to him by his nickname, 'Chaz,'" Scutella testified. "He gave me a sign to go ahead. He started jogging east." Half an hour later, Scutella said, he arrived home after retracing his original route. Passing Dovishaw's house again, he said, he watched Bolo's green Caddy backing out of the driveway. "I thought it was Bolo. I was going toward the car. Being mischievous, I was going to lay on the horn. I was going to talk to him. He was looking the other direction, but when I blew the horn he looked right at me. It was Caesar Montevecchio."

While the jury was trying to absorb new information that flew in the face of what all the state prosecution witnesses had presented, Scutella continued with his stunning testimony. "He was startled," Scutella said of the driver he claimed was Montevecchio. "He pulled out and headed toward Pittsburgh Avenue (west of Erie)."

Scutella also said he saw Montevecchio once more that night. It was about 9 p.m., Scutella said, as he left his wife's home. He said Montevecchio drove up in a car to talk with him. "He said, 'Look, forget where you saw me and I'll explain later. I'm in a hurry now. You understand?' I said yes. I thought he'd just robbed Bolo because he'd done that previously."

Two days later, Scutella continued, after he learned that Montevecchio had tried several times to telephone him, Scutella returned Caesar's call. According to Scutella, Montevecchio asked Scutella to meet him late at night in a restaurant parking lot during that phone conversation. Scutella said Dovishaw's body had already been discovered at that point in time.

"What did Mr. Montevecchio tell you? (at the meeting)" Attorney Moore asked.

"Something to the tune of, 'I just took Bolo out. I made the score of a lifetime.' He (Montevecchio) said he was going to take over this town for bookmaking. Little-by-little he unfolded the events."

As Scutella continued with his account, DiPaolo could not help but wonder what Scutella hoped to gain by falsely fingering his longtime partner in crime, Montevecchio. After all, Montevecchio had already admitted his part in the crime.

What was in these lies for Scutella? DiPaolo wondered. The prosecution couldn't help him. Even the defense couldn't do much to help him. Perhaps there was another motive? Perhaps one reason, DiPaolo guessed, was that Joe Scutella's daughter worked for defense attorney John Moore as a "runner." That was at least one connection. Or, was it to get back at DiPaolo, who put him and his kid in jail? But DiPaolo didn't care. He knew Scutella was lying and there was no way the jury would buy it.

But Scutella wasn't done yet. His further testimony would be even more perplexing.

It was clear Joseph Scutella, Jr. was enjoying his own 15 minutes of fame on the witness stand. As a defense witness who was single-handedly rewriting the history of this case, it was not immediately clear whether the jury was buying any of it. If anything, the prosecution was finding the career criminal's version vaguely amusing, if not unadulterated BS, DiPaolo thought. There must have been much rehearsal, he speculated.

After first telling the jury that Caesar Montevecchio admitted killing Dovishaw and making "the score of a lifetime," Scutella was now saying that Montevecchio also fingered William Bourjaily in the hit. It was Ohioan Robert Dorler who was on trial for his life in the Dovishaw slaying, but Scutella was now naming two other crime figures as the killers. Montevecchio had been the prosecution's primary witness against Dorler, while Bourjaily, also of Ohio, had been what the judicial system calls a "secondary primary" witness – used mostly to corroborate Montevecchio's key testimony.

According to Scutella, Montevecchio never mentioned either Dorler or Erie businessman Anthony Arnone, who Montevecchio claimed initially contracted for the bookmaking kingpin's death. When asked by defense attorney Moore what else Caesar Montevecchio told him, Scutella said, "It seemed like he was on a roll. He was all excited. He had said Bourjaily had taken the gun and thrown it in a lake in Ohio." Playing with the facts in creative ways that actually had some kernel of truth to them, Scutella said Montevecchio indicated to him that the original intent was for admitted killer Ferritto, Dovishaw's bookmaking partner, to be blamed for the Dovishaw killing. "He (Montevecchio) thought what a break he had," Scutella continued, "that they were going to blame Ray Ferritto for the murder. I told him that would be silly, that they (police) knew he (Ferritto) wouldn't do it. They were partners."

Scutella paused for a moment, then plowed on. "He thought they were going to blame Ray because he's an admitted hit man. I disagreed with him." According to Scutella's claim, Montevecchio bragged to him that he had found "in excess of a couple hundred thousand dollars" in Dovishaw's bank boxes.

It was powerful testimony, all reported in Erie's newspapers and emphasized by Moore to capture maximum jury attention after the methodical case presented by state prosecutors against Dorler. But Scutella had a look of deceit about him, one in which even his closest friends would have difficulty believing anything he might utter.

Now it was time for cross-examination. And Prosecutor Ebert wasted little precious time verbally ripping into this defense witness. Ebert began by requiring Scutella to recite for the jury all the charges for which he was presently serving hard time in prison. Ebert also got Scutella to acknowledge he had a deep-seeded grudge with the prosecution's "ethics" in his own case, but the witness denied he was personally upset with Detective Sergeant Dominick DiPaolo, whose relentless investigation in the Dovishaw murder had also put Scutella behind prison bars. Scutella claimed to be somehow related to DiPaolo through marriage. The loud groan of disgust the jury heard came from the Erie cop.

Sure, Joey Scutella finally acknowledged, he received "a raw deal." But he said that was of no influence on his courtroom testimony that day. Prisons are filled with those who got "raw deals" for dealing cocaine and arranging to torch their businesses for insurance money, DiPaolo ironically thought.

Next, under Ebert's questioning, Scutella provided a unique glimpse at the goings on and relationships in Erie ugly criminal world. For example, the state prosecutor wanted to know whether Joseph Scutella considered the notorious Raymond Ferritto to be his enemy. No, Scutella said, adding that he had always considered Ferritto to be a friend.

"You didn't like Ray Ferritto," Ebert lashed out.

"That's not true," Scutella shot back. He said he and Ferritto had been friends all their lives.

"You're friends with this big hit man?" Ebert asked, his voice dripping with sarcasm.

"Yes," Scutella said, attempting to stay cool.

Ebert wanted to know whether it was true that Scutella had once slapped Ferritto's son's face.

"I didn't slap his son! I hollered at him because he was disrespectful to me," Scutella replied. "I don't think I'd be here if I slapped Ray Ferritto's son's face."

But DiPaolo knew the truth. The truth was that Scutella *did* slap the kid, and Ray told him, "If you ever touch my kid again, you're dead!" Ferritto said this in front of a large group, some of them snickering, further embarrassing Scutella, who was forced to take the verbal abuse. DiPaolo knew that's why Scutella hated Ferritto and wanted Bolo Dovishaw's shooter to take him out for another ten grand.

Next, Ebert required Scutella to again describe in great detail Scutella's version of the night of the Dovishaw murder, in particular his chance meeting later with Caesar Montevecchio. While Scutella's account of those events remained much the same as his description during Moore's direct examination, the prosecutor sought to challenge every minor deviation from Scutella's original testimony. Ebert wanted to know whether Scutella had questioned Montevecchio when Montevecchio supposedly described Dovishaw's death two days after the killing.

"I'm not going to ask him any questions . . . I think he's a madman," Scutella said. Yet DiPaolo knew Scutella was still doing coke with this "madman," as the cop had the two on surveillance tapes following the murder.

Didn't Scutella think that seeing Montevecchio three different times on the night of Dovishaw's murder amounted to too many coincidences? the state prosecutor suggested. Sure he did. It was the only time Scutella agreed with Ebert. But when asked about his testimony under oath before a federal grand jury in 1984 during which Joey Scutella claimed he knew nothing about Dovishaw's slaying, the witness now freely acknowledged that he had been lying.

Now Ebert was angry. Or, at least he seemed to be. He lashed out at Scutella, demanding to know why, after so many years of knowing police were investigating the murder, he refused to come forward with his supposed information until now.

"Probably misplaced loyalty for a code of honor that no longer exists," Scutella said without emotion. "I didn't want to compromise my principles, good, bad or indifferent."

But in the end, it turned out Joey Scutella was no better than Sammy "The Bull" Gravano. Once a snitch, always a snitch, DiPaolo thought with a smile. So much for *omerta* (silence). *Omerta* – the Sicilian Mafia code – went out with the garbage for Little Joey, DiPaolo mused.

DiPaolo could not help but think, this convicted felon Pal Joey had suddenly acquired scruples? It was much like cons finding God in prison.

On re-direct examination, Attorney Moore asked Scutella why he chose to testify for the defense, especially knowing that the defense could not offer the convict any kind of a deal to lighten his lengthy terms in prison.

"It's just something that's gone too far and it's something that I don't want on my conscience," Scutella replied, "seeing an innocent man go to the electric chair."

Please! thought DiPaolo. Erie's most highly-rated career criminal now had a conscience?

Scutella then testified he never met Dorler, having seen him for the first time on television during one of Dorler's many perp walks before the cameras.

For Dorler, there would be more perp walks. His case was about to go to the jury. His life soon would be in the hands of 12 complete strangers. After all the ups-and-downs, all the incalculable hours of police investigation, all the road trips to Michigan and Ohio and flights to Florida, it now all boiled down to five hours on a late November Sunday afternoon.

The jury deciding the life-or-death fate of murder suspect Robert Dorler could not reach a decision during 15 hours of deliberations that Friday or Saturday. So Judge Levin had called for a rare Sunday deliberations session. The panel of five men and seven women already had been sequestered and away from their families and homes for the previous 11 days. They would endure at least one more. Levin instructed the jurors not to rush their decision. They could take all day if they chose to do so, he instructed. They were to carefully consider all the evidence, all the testimony in the nearly two-week long murder trial.

They took just five more hours. And when they returned to the courtroom, their verdict fell upon a roomful of emotionally drained participants and spectators like a lead weight.

Guilty of first degree murder.

Two of the jurors broke down in tears as their decision was read. Each member of the panel was required to stand and individually voice his or her verdict. Under Pennsylvania criminal law, such a verdict in a criminal case had to be unanimous. The 58-year-old Ohio defendant listened stone-faced to the first degree murder verdict, perhaps one of the few in the courtroom who showed no emotion. Just as his countenance showed no traces of human emotion when he rammed a paring knife into Frank "Bolo" Dovishaw's eye nearly seven years earlier so that he could watch the urination and defecation at the moment of death, Dorler was now neither somber nor perplexed nor angry with the verdict. Veteran courthouse observers would later comment that the Ohioan had listened to the guilty verdict with almost detached interest, even boredom.

Judge Levin, along with several others, had also appeared somewhat shaken by the verdict. But the judge still had a courtroom to run and quickly he recovered his composure. "Your job has been a difficult one and you certainly accepted the responsibility," the judge solemnly intoned to the grim-faced jury members, some of them still teary-eyed.

Meanwhile, Robert Dorler, wearing a white sweater with a colorful design over an open-collared shirt, was led out of the courtroom by Erie County Sheriff's deputies and to the elevator that would whisk him to the Erie County Prison, then situated on the top two floors of the courthouse building. On the way to the elevator, news reporters pressed the convicted murderer to comment on the minutes-old verdict that could lead to the death penalty.

He told the reporters he had nothing to say, adding several no comments to their persistent follow-up questions.

But the jury, however, still wasn't done. Its work ahead, according to Pennsylvania law, now required the panel to decide Dorler's fate – life in prison or death by the electric chair, not quite the "Old Sparky" of State of Florida fame, but just as lethal. But that would have to wait until the next day. Monday would begin a new work-week for the jury, a new hearing and a new decision. And just like Dorler's decision involving Frank "Bolo" Dovishaw – this one would also be life vs. death.

CHAPTER 40

SENTENCING HEARINGS IN CAPITAL CRIME TRIALS ARE AMONG THE strangest phenomena within Pennsylvania's criminal justice system. After spending days or weeks arguing a defendant's innocence during the course of the trial, defense attorneys are virtually forced into acknowledging the guilt of their clients while pleading for mercy and for the convict's life.

Such was the case in Erie County Court following the Sunday, November 19, 1989, first-degree murder conviction of Robert Dorler for killing bookie Frank "Bolo" Dovishaw. Even the defendant himself, who did not testify on his own behalf during the murder trial, had something to tell the jury – including a half-baked tale about a pie-stealing hobo and the severe punishment of an innocent puppy.

Only juries can send a convict to Pennsylvania's electric chair. Not judges. Not lawyers. Only the jury panels that convict defendants of capital offenses can make those life/death decisions. It was up to the defense to prove "mitigating" circumstances – that is, events that would spare the convict from the ultimate decree – the death penalty. The prosecution's obligation, conversely, was to present to the panel "aggravating" circumstances, information the DAs hoped would clearly indicate that, under Pennsylvania law, the defendant justly deserved to perish in the chair. Now, this new phase of the trial, commonly called the "sentencing phase," began with Dorler on the stand.

"I, too, believe in the justice system. Particularly the judicial process," Dorler told the jury that convicted him and was now considering his fate – death in the electric chair or life in prison without the possibility of parole. Sure, he said he was not Dovishaw's killer. And he admitted that he refused to testify in the trial even though his attorneys had strongly recommended he do so.

While judges warn jurors they should not read anything into a defendant's reasoning for not taking the witness stand, saying defendants have an explicit right under the law to not testify, those same jurors, nonetheless, are forever taken aback when said defendants do not look them in the eye and swear they are not guilty of the crime which they are accused of committing. In other words, many in the judicial system know judges' cautionary warnings on these matters are often useless. Sometimes, defense attorneys will only withhold their clients from testifying when they know said clients will likely make a mess of the defense by blabbing information that should not be blabbed, or when the prosecution case is so weak that there is nothing to be gained by allowing a client to testify in the first place. Besides, defense attorneys know that when defendants testify, prosecutors are given much wider latitude in cross examination to go beyond the scope of what was covered in direct examination.

"Against the advice of counsel, Miss (Renee) Remek and Mr. Moore, I declined to take the stand in my own defense," Dorler told the jury. "I guess now that was the wrong decision," the convicted murderer was acknowledging.

Speaking with about as much passion as he could muster, given his cold, emotionless demeanor during the trial, Dorler said, "You, the jury, are now faced with an even harder decision. I only ask that you listen closely to both sides."

It seemed ironic, perhaps surreal, that a man convicted of shooting another in the back of the skull, then jabbing a paring knife into the victim's eye to make sure he "shit and pissed" himself and was dead, would now relate an almost folksy, home-spun tale to the jurors. Yet, astonishingly, that's exactly what happened.

As reported by Erie's newspapers, it was a story Dorler had once read about a farmer's wife who baked her husband's favorite pie and left it on the windowsill before an open window to cool. While she was away, as Dorler related the story to the jury, a hobo wandered by, spotted the pie and began to devour it. However, when the hobo heard the farmer's tractor approaching, the hobo quickly departed, leaving the half-eaten farmer's delight on the porch. When the farmer saw the mess on the front porch and his puppy nearby, the angry man kicked the dog with so much force that the innocent puppy was seriously injured. So went Dorler's analogy.

Speaking in lawyer-like tones, Dorler then said, "Sometimes, such things happen when we rely on circumstantial evidence."

Most veteran prosecutors would much rather deal with a case solidly layered with circumstantial evidence than on one that depended upon largely unreliable eye-witness testimony. Besides, it's rare that capital crimes are ever committed in public before dozens of such witnesses. But in closing, the defendant managed to praise the jury for its hard work.

"You are truly a fair jury and I do respect you," he said. It was the old "flattery will get you everywhere" pitch. But would it work on this jury?

Predictably, the wounded puppy story didn't carry much weight with the jury, especially since the tale was nearly identical to a well-publicized one told by a defense lawyer during a federal drug trial in Erie at the U.S. Courthouse several blocks away.

Prosecutor M.L. Ebert, however, used Dorler's comments against him, telling the jury that the convicted murderer was most definitely not the puppy of his story. Not that Dorler's cold, hard appearance and icily emotionless demeanor made him appear anything remotely resembling a person with puppy-like qualities. Lashing out at Dorler, Ebert demanded, "A puppy has nothing to do with this pie, does it?"

Dorler agreed it did not.

"Did you know Caesar Montevecchio?" Ebert asked.

Of course. Dorler said he did know the notorious Erie career criminal Caesar Montevecchio.

"Did you know about this crime?"

Of course. Dorler indeed knew about the contract murder of Frank "Bolo" Dovishaw.

"Yet, you never went to the justice system you love so much except to help yourself, did you?"

"I wouldn't say that," Dorler responded.

"Isn't not doing crime a civic responsibility?" Ebert continued to pound away at the witness.

"I didn't say I believed in civic responsibility," Dorler said.

"You don't believe in civic responsibility?"

"I didn't say that."

"Do you?"

"To a certain extent. Not fully."

Ebert cut to the chase in claiming that his case had proven three essential aggravating circumstances in the Dovishaw murder:

- The crime was a contract killing;
- The crime was committed during the commission of a felony (armed robbery); and
- The perpetrator – that would be Robert Dorler – has a long history of violent criminal behavior, including convictions in Ohio for armed robbery, arson and aggravated assault.

"It's a human life for a few dollars. Let's lay it right up there!" Ebert pounded on the prosecution table. "That's what Francis Dovishaw's life was worth."

Ebert asked the jury, rhetorically, why the three aggravated factors are important. "Because the criminal justice system says enough-is-enough. You're not going to continue to hurt people," the prosecutor answered his own question. "You can't approach this emotionally," Ebert urged the panel. "You've got to do your duty now," he said as he again asked the jury to return with the death penalty for Dorler.

The prosecutor said there were absolutely no mitigating circumstances for the jury to consider in sparing the Ohio man from the electric chair, even though Pennsylvania law requires the jury to dutifully consider any circumstance it believes might reduce the penalty.

"Why? Our system of justice has some compassion, unlike a group of people who put a gun to a human being's head, pulled the trigger and extinguished his life," Ebert said. Dorler, Ebert said, knowingly committed the murder. Furthermore, the prosecutor emphasized, it was not a crime committed under extreme duress, either. "Having a payday to kill a human being is not extreme duress," Ebert said in an attempt to remove one of the factors that could be used as mitigating. Ebert readily agreed that Montevecchio and his fellow prosecution witness, William Bourjaily, were no better than Dorler. But the prosecutor said he still used them as witnesses because without them there would have been no justice for the bookie Frank "Bolo" Dovishaw. "But for these crumbs, Caesar Montevecchio and Billy Bourjaily, the whole group walks free. Nothing happens and a human being lies dead in his basement and becomes just another statistic in a crime that's never solved."

News reporters scribbled all of this in their notebooks as fast as their transcribing skills would permit.

Defense lawyer John Moore still found the means to use Ebert's own closing argument to claim there was at least some degree of reasonable doubt Dorler had committed the murder. Moore told the jury that the prosecution's belief that its key witnesses were also involved in the killing, yet will someday go free, was reason enough not to send Robert Dorler to his death. He said the jurors could not justify sending Dorler to the electric chair when they knew deep inside that others involved in the murder, others like Montevecchio, escaped more serious punishment by dealing with law enforcement authorities. Saying that Montevecchio could not be trusted, Moore asked the jury, "Can you rely on what this man says to send Mr. Dorler to his death? Are you convinced beyond a reasonable doubt that Dorler and only Dorler fired the shot that killed Mr. Dovishaw?"

The defense lawyer also asked the jurors to consider the same questions that kept them deliberating their original guilty verdict for more than 20 hours, and also to consider that it wasn't Dorler who had initially arranged for the murder. Again, referring to prosecution witnesses, Moore said, "They saved themselves and they want you to take Robert Dorler's life to prove they were right. Only life, not death, is justified in this case. Only that will permit you to leave this courthouse knowing you've done what is just, done what is fair, and done what is right."

And then, the lead defense counsel added, "We're talking about life in prison. No one's asking you to let Robert Dorler off. There is no proof beyond a reasonable doubt that he fired the shot that killed Bolo Dovishaw."

After the sentencing hearing, Dorler told news reporters that he hoped Caesar Montevecchio someday would tell the truth. But when asked about the verdict, he said he would abide by the jury's decision, as though he had a choice, but he hoped that the truth would someday come out.

As far as DiPaolo was concerned, however, the truth had already come out. It came out during the trial over and over again. DiPaolo was pleased with the outcome of his years of toil so far. But there was still Dorler's sentencing to sweat out – and then, the biggest trial of all, the one for the man DiPaolo sincerely believed set in motion the Dovishaw murder.

But . . . .

Hopelessly deadlocked. That's how the jury members found themselves that Monday afternoon after four hours of deliberating 58-year-old convicted murderer Robert Dorler's fate. The 7-5 deadlock (in favor of capital punishment) spared the Ohio man from death in the electric chair for the 1983 contract killing of noted Erie bookmaker Frank "Bolo" Dovishaw.

"The verdict slip is not signed," Judge George Levin said after the jury returned to his courtroom at mid-afternoon that day. "Does this mean you are deadlocked? Hopelessly deadlocked?" Judge Levin asked the jury foreman.

When the foreman indicated the panel was indeed at an impasse, the judge had each juror stand and publicly state they believed the deadlock could not be resolved. Each member of the panel, then, slowly rose and indicated that was indeed the case. What it meant, Levin told the jury, was that Dorler could not be sentenced to die.

Dorler, just as he had been throughout the trial, remained cold and distant as the drama played out between the judge and the 12 jurors who had convicted the Ohioan of first degree murder and conspiracy. However, several jurors were clearly in tears, just as they had been a day earlier when the guilty verdict had been announced in Levin's courtroom.

"The deadlock ended an 11-day ordeal for the jurors that included seven days of trial testimony, three days of deliberations and Monday's penalty hearing about deliberations to decide whether Dorler would be sentenced to die or spend the rest of his life in prison," reported the *Erie Daily Times.* The verdict, as the newspaper reported, was the end of one chapter DiPaolo's seven-year probe that began with the discovery of "Ash Wednesday's" corpse.

It's not often that DiPaolo was quoted in the news media, but after a verdict and the sentencing phase, news reporters sought out the veteran Erie cop.

He expressed pleasure with the guilty verdict, thanked the State Attorney General's Office for its work in the case and Ebert for getting the conviction. He credited many law enforcement agencies for teamwork, as well as his Erie Bureau of Police co-workers.

Ebert, who was also happy with the conviction, said in the newspaper, however, "I'm a little disappointed in the verdict in the penalty phase." But he added that the deadlock was not unexpected, given the heavy, ultimate life and death nature of that decision placed on the jury members' shoulders. "You saw the anguish in those people's faces," Ebert said, explaining that it's often not difficult for many to favor the death penalty, but very different when called upon to decide whether a defendant will live or die, according to the newspaper report.

John Moore, lead attorney on Dorler's defense team, was pleased his client would not face the death penalty, but still disappointed Dorler had been convicted in the first place. Of course lawyer Moore planned to appeal, which had come to be fairly standard procedure in any case involving a first-degree murder conviction. Moore said he would base his appeal on pre-trial rulings by Erie County Judge George Levin, and on several evidentiary rulings made by the jurist during the trial.

"It's apparent that the jury worked incredibly hard, harder than I've ever seen a jury work before," Moore told news reporters at the conclusion of the penalty phase.

Strangely, the jury also got a friendly nod from the killer Dorler, who had taken the stand not to profess his innocence during the trial, but only during the penalty phase. The murderer from Medina, Ohio, told the panel he had been the one who chose the individual jury members for the defense before the trial began, and that he respected their work and would abide by their decision. As though he would have a choice in the matter, DiPaolo again later thought with a touch of amusement.

"As each of you were questioned (at the start of the trial), I searched for intelligence, morality, human understanding and awareness of civic responsibility," Dorler told the men and women who would make a life or death decision on his behalf. "Leave this courtroom with no self-incrimination," he told the jury. "Leave with your heads held high. Be secure in knowing you are truly a fair jury and I do respect you."

Later, while being escorted from the courtroom to his cell in the Erie County Prison, Dorler was questioned by news reporters who again asked whether he was still claiming to be innocent of Dovishaw's murder. "Yes I do," he was quoted as saying in the *Erie Daily Times*. "I'm only guilty of accessory after the fact." He said he learned details of the murder only after the capital crime was committed. "Well, Caesar Montevecchio will need help," Dorler cryptically said. "He'll need help and he'll probably come up with the truth."

Exactly what that truth was, Dorler wasn't saying or speculating. But he did say that his former partner in crime and pal Caesar Montevecchio not only knew more about the Dovishaw killing, but also that Montevecchio had information about the death of Erie Police Corporal Robert Owen in December of 1980. That death still remains a mystery in law enforcement circles today, although DiPaolo is now fairly certain he knows who killed the cop and why.

Some believe that Owen was murdered. Others say it was suicide. Police investigations into Corporal Robert Owen's death, including those by DiPaolo and others, only managed to reach dead ends. But, as discussed previously, DiPaolo has more than an inkling of who murdered Owen. Proving it at this point, however, would be difficult. Montevecchio had confided to DiPaolo what he knew based on street talk. But it also confirmed the cop's theory.

As the Erie newspaper reported that Tuesday afternoon, neither DiPaolo nor Ebert had much time to celebrate the victory. Jury selection would begin in a week in the murder trial of Erie businessman Anthony "Niggsy" Arnone, who was accused of ordering the hit on Dovishaw.

One more trial to go, DiPaolo thought that day. And this time, it would be *the* big one.

CHAPTER 41

DECEMBER OF 1989 WAS NOT A REMARKABLE MONTH AS FAR AS extreme weather in Erie. Weather had been worse. Far worse. A little cold, a little snow, a little slush. Same old/same old for those who knew Erie's weather well. But as cold as it might have been outside, inside the Erie County Courthouse in the heart of downtown Erie on that first Monday of the month, the action in Common Pleas Judge Fred Anthony's courtroom was already heating up.

It was nearly seven years, Erie Police Detective Sergeant Dominick DiPaolo reflected while arriving early on that December 4 and stomping the clinging, dirty slush from his shoes. Seven years since bookmaker Frank "Bolo" Dovishaw was gunned down, execution style, in the basement of his west Erie home on January 3, 1983. Seven years of painstakingly toppling one Erie or Ohio felon after another as the criminally-constructed house of cards slowly tumbled. Seven exhausting years of ups and downs in a murder investigation that was often detoured for police investigators through ongoing robberies, burglaries and even one sensational underworld arson fire. Seven years of putting up with state and federal investigators, state and federal grand juries, state and federal prosecutors, and enough criminal defense attorneys to constitute a sizeable law school cohort.

And now, that entire, often grueling seven-year investigation was all boiling down to what would begin this Monday morning before a panel of 12 jurors, strangers to each other, and in a courtroom not too terribly distant from the scene of where it all had begun on that cold January night in 1983.

Seven years could have been the blink of an eye, DiPaolo thought. Or, it could have been an eternity. Either way, it was all coming to a culmination, a day of the beginning of the end. DiPaolo was experiencing a wide spectrum of emotions. He always did as a case he investigated was about to finally come to trial. It was a rush, almost a high. But this one was different. This one case representing seven years of his professional life was about to be decided by 12 individuals he knew mostly little or nothing about. *Scary*, he thought, this putting it all into the hands of strangers who, thanks to defense maneuvering, might not even get to know even a fraction of the information DiPaolo had developed and lived with over those seven years. But, he was forced to acknowledge, although somewhat reluctantly, that this was our criminal justice system. For better or worse he had taken an oath to uphold that system. It was more than just a crap shoot, DiPaolo knew. He was, after all, confident that his efforts those many years would pay off in big dividends in this final trial to bring down the last of the co-conspirator murderers of Dovishaw.

At last, DiPaolo thought, the system would prevail and he would win the hoped for conviction of Anthony "Niggsy" Arnone – the businessman he believed arranged the killing.

"The truth will come to light. Murder cannot long be hidden."

It seemed almost out of place that the prosecutor would use a quote from William Shakespeare in the opening address of a murder trial. But that's exactly how the chief of prosecutions for the Pennsylvania Attorney General's Office began his opening address to the jury that morning in Judge Anthony's packed courtroom.

Prosecutor M.L. Ebert was trying to make a point in his trial-opening salvo against the defendant, 50-year-old "Niggsy" Arnone of nearby Millcreek Township, the Italian deli owner and imported food dealer who was accused of master-minding the gangland-style killing of Bolo Dovishaw. Arnone was charged with murder, criminal conspiracy and robbery. He sat emotionless at the defense table while Ebert made him out to be a horrific, evil monster.

Acknowledging the prosecution was unable to present "direct" evidence against the defendant, Ebert subtly added, "The only person (Dovishaw) who knows who killed him is not here." However, the prosecutor who several weeks earlier won a capital murder conviction against triggerman Robert Dorler in the same case, said he would rely on the testimony of Caesar Montevecchio, the middleman who Ebert said arranged the killing for Arnone to get the sports betting proceeds inside Dovishaw's bank safe-deposit boxes. Ebert went on to say that Montevecchio, one of Erie's best-known career criminals for decades, would outline the scheme to kill Dovishaw to retrieve the keys to the bank boxes and rob the bookmaker of more than $300,000 in illegal gambling money.

This second Dovishaw murder case trial was also widely reported by Erie's news media; it was in the Times Publishing Company's newspapers and on the air multiple times a day. Much of what was reported during the trial is paraphrased, and taken from court records below:

Laying out his case for the jury in brief fashion, Ebert said Montevecchio would testify exactly how Arnone came up with the murder plan, and how Montevecchio eventually hired a crony in crime, Dorler, of Medina, Ohio, to kill Dovishaw. Ebert also patiently explained to the jury panel how he would introduce evidence that directly linked Arnone to the murder, evidence showing that Arnone visited the bank where two of Dovishaw's safe-deposit boxes were located on January 4 prior to the discovery of Dovishaw' body.

Ebert said it was " . . . a bank where that man's first cousin, Theresa Mastrey, worked and had access to the boxes," pointing his finger at Arnone.

Also acknowledging that important evidence would, by necessity, come from career criminals like Montevecchio, Ebert emphasized that police investigators could only uncover the surreptitious and stealthy conspiracy to murder Frank "Bolo" Dovishaw through those who actually took part in planning and then, ultimately, carrying out the brutal crime.

Prosecutors are fond of explaining to jurors that most crimes are not committed before reputable witnesses. They like to point out that investigators are often forced to make deals with those they would never otherwise consider even inviting into their homes for dinner. "When you hear all the evidence in this case, you will find Mr. Arnone guilty of murder in the first degree," the confident prosecutor insisted that morning.

However, it was obvious to all present from the start that the lead defense attorney, Joseph Santaguida, was having none of it. Also delivering a brief opening statement (the defense has the luxury of following the prosecution in all things *except* the closing argument), Santaguida asked the jury members to carefully examine and scrutinize the testimony of the prosecution witnesses, especially that of unsavory Caesar Montevecchio. The experienced defense lawyer argued that the career criminals involved in this case made the best deals they could for themselves, and those deals were not in the best interests of either truth or justice.

Santaguida told the jury members that the prosecution's version of the crime depended upon too many doubtful variables for that version to be successful, such as whether the safe-deposit keys could be found or even whether Dovishaw's body could be hidden. "The evidence will show that the Commonwealth's case, if this wasn't so serious, is almost laughable," Attorney Santaguida told jury members who were now hanging upon his every word. "It would be laughable if not for what this man is facing," the lawyer said, pointing to his client at the plain oak defense table, the businessman Anthony "Niggsy" Arnone. Only a not guilty verdict, Santaguida insisted, would ensure that justice is carried out.

Although brief, it was an effective opening statement, most courtroom observers agreed. It was a defense opening cleverly designed to attempt to establish reasonable doubt in the minds of the jury members even before the first witness was called. While defense trial strategies differ from lawyer to lawyer, and while some attorneys actually reserve the right to make their opening statements later in the trial after the prosecution rests, Santaguida was wise to get his licks in early on in the Arnone defense.

It was only the start of a two-week trial. For the jury, it would be two weeks of the inconvenience of cold, take-out meals from restaurants and sequestration from family and friends in a local motel.

Even before the trial testimony began, DiPaolo had an uneasy, almost queasy feeling in his gut. He wasn't feeling uncomfortable about his investigation or the solid evidence he had developed. But nonetheless, he had a nagging inner-feeling, that cop's intuition that served him throughout his career, that perhaps all was not about to go well. However, whether or not this premonition was accurate would nonetheless take two long weeks to determine.

One of the initial witnesses that first day of the Anthony "Niggsy" Arnone murder trial was as memorable in the minds of the jury members as he was notorious locally. Murderer Raymond Ferritto, his voice deep and raspy, represented for most decent folks a chilling vision of humanity gone wrong. Dark complexion and sunken eyes, which gave him an even more sinister look, Ferritto's presence on the witness stand, as was his normal countenance, was almost defiant.

Ferritto and DiPaolo had a history that went back many years, all the way to the cop's youth. DiPaolo couldn't help observing that Ferritto hadn't changed much in all that time. Just like Ferritto, and like in the Dorler trial, the mob killer had worked a deal for himself on his recent gambling arrest. This was the last part of his deal, to testify truthfully against Arnone.

He had become almost a cartoon caricature of the stereotypical syndicate figure. Almost a joke. That is, almost funny if this caricature wasn't such an icily mean caricature of himself. First, during his fascinating courtroom testimony, Ferritto publicly acknowledged that he had been Dovishaw's partner in the lucrative illegal sports betting and gambling operation the two had successfully operated for several years. Then he calmly told of how he, along with Anthony "Cy" Ciotti and Phil Torrelli, found Dovishaw's lifeless body in the basement of Bolo's West 21st Street home. The date they found the body was January 4, 1983, the day after the killing.

Perhaps the most bizarre portion of Ray Ferritto's testimony came when he told the jury how he had asked Dovishaw's widow, Joan, for her permission to examine Dovishaw's corpse in the casket at the funeral home before Bolo was laid to rest. Ferritto wanted to determine, in the most macabre way imaginable, whether his pal Bolo Dovishaw had been tortured before he had died, Ferritto testified. In the now hushed courtroom, Prosecutor Ebert asked Ferritto to explain for the jury the significance of torture.

"It could've been a hit by organized crime," Ferritto responded, adding that torture would have meant Ferritto himself was also in danger of being tortured or whacked for the illegal sports betting operation's proceeds. But Ferritto said that while examining Bolo's body at the funeral home that evening, he found no evidence whatsoever that Dovishaw had been tortured.

Ah, what a relief for the admitted killer of many, DiPaolo thought with a wry smile.

While the jury was still pondering Ferritto's remarkable testimony, Ferritto's longtime good friend, convicted drug dealer Ronald Thomas, another name from Dom DiPaolo's storied law enforcement past, was called to the witness stand.

But it was almost the testimony that wasn't! Earlier that morning, an Erie County Prison officer telephoned DiPaolo to say that Thomas was refusing to testify. DiPaolo better get over to the prison pronto, the guard said.

Just what we need, DiPaolo thought as he hurried to the facility's prisoner holding room. DiPaolo didn't have to wait long. As soon as Thomas was escorted into the room, the detective had to suppress a laugh. Thomas' appearance was different than the last time the two had met.

"No fucking way I'm going on the witness stand without my wig," Thomas protested.

It took a few minutes for DiPaolo to flesh out the story, but eventually he learned that when the U.S. Marshalls picked up Thomas at the federal penitentiary for transporting to Erie, they inadvertently left behind Thomas' toupee in a bag at the prison's booking center.

He's worrying about people seeing his bald head and not that he's a stool pigeon trying to save his sorry ass? DiPaolo thought to himself, again trying not to laugh out loud. Thomas had requested that DiPaolo call his barber, Frank Romeo, where Thomas got his toupees, and buy another wig for him. Out of the question, the cop advised Thomas. After Thomas settled down somewhat, DiPaolo laid it all on the line:

"No testimony, no deal. Take your fucking pick. I don't have time for this shit."

It was a gamble, the cop knew. But the odds were in DiPaolo's favor. He was fairly certain that Thomas was more interested in reducing his prison time than he was in his own vanity. So that's how, albeit somewhat grudgingly and with an extremely bare head, Ronald Thomas showed up at the Erie County Courthouse that morning.

In its own way, Thomas' testimony was significant, implying in no uncertain terms, if Thomas could be believed, that bad blood had previously existed between Dovishaw and Arnone prior to the murder. According to Thomas' testimony, he witnessed the two men – Niggsy and Bolo – arguing about four months prior to Dovishaw being murdered in his own home.

At the time of his testimony, Thomas was serving a 10-year federal prison stint for selling cocaine. He testified that he first became acquainted with Frank Dovishaw through mutual gambling interests; eventually the two gamblers became friends. Thomas said that in either September or October of 1982, he was in a car with Dovishaw when the two visited Arnone's importing business in Erie's Little Italy. Thomas said Dovishaw asked him to wait in the car while Bolo entered the building to talk with Arnone. After a short time, Thomas told the jury, Dovishaw and Arnone came out of the building together. It was obvious they were arguing, he said.

After Dovishaw got in the car, Thomas said Bolo told him the dispute with Arnone was over a considerable amount of money that Niggsy still owed the bookmaker. "I asked him (Dovishaw), 'What could he owe you, twenty thousand?' He said, 'More than that.' I said, 'Forty thousand?' He said, 'A little more than that.'"

The testimony demonstrated that Dovishaw not only knew Niggsy Arnone, but also that Arnone was seriously in debt to the murdered Erie bookmaker.

Thomas' newly found courtroom glory, however, wasn't about to last for long. Immediately, Arnone's lead defense lawyer went on the attack, questioning Thomas about his own criminal record and attempting to cast a credibility doubt in the minds of the jurors.

"Aren't you the guy who sold drugs?" Attorney Santaguida demanded .

"Yes," Thomas said. "I made a lot of mistakes in my life and that was one of them."

But the Philadelphia lawyer wasn't done. He continued to push hard against the witness, asking whether Thomas was also the one who actually took a couple's inheritance in payment for drug debts.

Thomas acknowledged the allegation was true.

Attorney Santaguida got Thomas to admit he had testified for the prosecution in two other criminal drug trials, and that he was hopeful his current cooperation would get him a reduction in the 10-year maximum federal prison term he was then serving.

Santaguida then revisited the alleged Bolo Dovishaw-Niggsy Arnone quarrel, asking whether Thomas actually believed that any professional gambler – such as Dovishaw – would allow a client to amass more than $40,000 in gambling debts.

But Thomas said he believed a "professional" would at least allow a bettor to "get even." He also testified that although he knew much about gambling, he was considered to be an "amateur."

"Your wife was arrested for bookmaking, wasn't she?" Santaguida asked with no little amount of sting to the inquiry.

"Yes," Thomas acknowledged. (Ironically, she recently had been arrested with Ferritto.)

"So your wife was arrested for bookmaking and you don't know anything about it?" the attorney asked.

"*She* was the bookmaker," Thomas replied, heavily emphasizing the "she."

"Ah, I see," Santaguida said, laughing somewhat sarcastically at the ease in which Thomas was so quick to give up his wife, and in such a public way.

State Prosecutor Ebert, however, endeavored to continue to use Thomas' testimony to demonstrate to the jury that Arnone did in fact owe money to Dovishaw, and he used other witnesses to establish a relationship of sorts between Niggsy Arnone and Ebert's prime witness, Caesar Montevecchio.

DiPaolo himself was a key witness for the good guys, testifying of personally watching several visits Caesar Montevecchio made to Arnone's Cherry Street business in the spring of 1983.

CHAPTER 42

AS IF THE PREVIOUS EXPLOSIVE TESTIMONY WAS NOT ENOUGH, THERE was another important witness for the prosecution that day. It was Caesar Montevecchio's emotion-choked wife, Bonnie Montevecchio.

In halting testimony, Mrs. Montevecchio told jurors of the friendship that once existed between her career-criminal husband, Caesar, and the Erie businessman, Anthony "Niggsy" Arnone. According to Bonnie Montevecchio's testimony, Arnone had given her family gifts of food and money while Caesar was imprisoned, and in general demonstrated what appeared to have been concern for the Montevecchio family's well-being.

Described in Erie newspaper accounts as "a slight, attractive woman with a voice that often quavered as she testified," Bonnie Montevecchio claimed she knew nothing of her notorious husband's numerous criminal activities for many years after they were married. She told of Caesar Montevecchio working at Erie's Hammermill Paper Company, and, when he wasn't on the job he was generally spending quality time at home with his family.

Most career criminals, even murderers, love their families and pets, DiPaolo thought. Many times, that vicious criminal behavior is not apparent in their home element.

Bonnie Montevecchio also testified that when talk and allegations of Caesar's criminal activity began to surface in the early 1980s, she refused to believe the myriad negative things being said about her wonderful husband. At her request, she strongly emphasized to the jury, Montevecchio had even ended a weekly poker game that he had hosted in their Erie home. *What a guy!* DiPaolo was compelled to smile to himself.

Anthony Arnone, she said, often had been involved in the once-a-week poker games. "I stopped the games," Bonnie testified with resolve. "I didn't like it. I realized money was involved. I had children in the home. I told Caesar." She said that after she complained about the game, she thought it was moved to a different venue.

After Caesar was arrested and imprisoned in July of 1983 on charges not related to Dovishaw's murder, she said Arnone, obviously concerned, telephoned her. "Anthony called me shortly after Caesar was arrested and reassured me. He said Lenny Ambrose was an excellent attorney. That he'd beat the charges."

Bonnie Montevecchio added that, speaking of the charges against her husband, "He (Arnone) said none of this was true, that DiPaolo was out to get Caesar and everything would be all right."

Montevecchio, his wife's testimony continued, remained jailed until early in 1985.

Bonnie told the jury of Arnone's visits to the Montevecchio home during that time frame. According to Mrs. Montevecchio – obviously an extremely frightened woman who was still testifying in halting, almost introverted tones – it was Arnone who often brought her family food and, on three occasions, gave her about $500 in cash while her husband was imprisoned locally. Although she testified she didn't feel quite right in accepting either the food or the cash gifts, her family nonetheless had been in need of both. When Caesar Montevecchio was later jailed on criminal drug charges in 1987, Mrs. Montevecchio again testified that Anthony Arnone had telephoned her.

During cross-examination, Mrs. Montevecchio acknowledged that she appreciated Niggsy Arnone's assistance during her husband Caesar's stints in prison. She also said she believed that at that time that Arnone was sincerely concerned about the welfare of her family, and that his only motivation was one of deep personal friendship with her dear husband.

It was when Montevecchio was returned to Erie from the federal penitentiary that she said she learned for the first time of his alleged complicity and possible role in the Frank "Bolo" Dovishaw murder, and then about her husband's ultimate cooperation with Detective Sergeant Dominick DiPaolo. Strangely, it was an awakening of sorts for the long-time wife of Erie's infamous career criminal.

During that time, she continued, Arnone had telephoned her again, but this time to inquire about whether Caesar was attempting to make a deal with DiPaolo. The implication was that Niggsy was indeed extremely concerned, even worried, that his pal Montevecchio was co-operating with DiPaolo in the Dovishaw murder investigation. And, as it turned out, he had expressed such concern and worry with very good cause, as Montevecchio was indeed talking to DiPaolo about the entire scam, which Caesar insisted, was Niggsy's idea.

But, when she was asked whether she or any member of her family had ever been threatened by Arnone, Bonnie responded quickly that they had not been. This key trial witness did say, however, that she had received a telephone call from Caesar Montevecchio's former lawyer, Leonard Ambrose, that she believed conveyed a sense of danger. "He told me to talk some sense to Caesar," Mrs. Montevecchio testified, "that Caesar was trying to play lawyer again. He said the people he (her husband) was dealing with were not nice and the kids and I might be in danger because of it."

As Santaguida continued his cross-examination of the woman, she began sobbing. Judge Anthony, now somewhat frustrated, finally directed one of the courtroom tipstaffs to fetch a box of Kleenex for Mrs. Montevecchio. But that's when Attorney Santaguida quickly wrapped up his questioning and Bonnie's ordeal was over and she was finally permitted to leave the witness stand.

The jury members, some of them with mouths still agape, veteran courtroom observers would later speculate, were blown away by such an inside look at Erie's organized and disorganized crime machinations. Bonnie Montevecchio, as the innocent and trembling wife, had made an indelible impression in the minds of these jury members, that much was easily speculated upon. But would it be enough to combine with the other testimony and win state prosecutor Ebert his second conviction in the Dovishaw murder case? No one in the prosecution side of the courtroom was breathing any easier yet.

Finally, on that first frenetic day of testimony in Niggsy Arnone's murder trial, an official of the Ohio Bell Telephone Company was called to the stand to confirm the telephone records of William Bourjaily of

Parma, Ohio. Such records would have linked Bourjaily to Dorler and ultimately to the cast of Erie hoods – the usual suspects in so many criminal cases over the years.

All in all, it was an explosive day of testimony, but one that led DiPaolo to feel just slightly better about the chances of winning a conviction. Perhaps he didn't have to worry after all. Still, there was more testimony to come. Much more.

Although the Anthony "Niggsy" Arnone murder trial was about the man who allegedly arranged the killing, it was becoming as fascinating to onlookers and newspaper readers as the capital murder trial of the actual ice-blooded killer, Robert Dorler, that preceded it several weeks earlier. Clearly, the jury was awed with this behind the scenes look at Erie's criminal underbelly, as was the local news media, the broadcast and print reporters who covered daily virtually every word of testimony.

As Caesar Montevecchio took the witness stand, all eyes focused on the almost legendary Erie criminal – a man who had squandered an excellent private Catholic school education and even a full-ride football scholarship at a Division I university in favor of a life of organized, sometimes disorganized, crime.

Montevecchio and his family, all could now firmly agree, would eventually pay a high price for his carefully chosen field of illegal endeavor. Now Montevecchio had center stage in Judge Anthony's courtroom. And he was about to make the most of it. As though they were watching a great movie, the jurors, onlookers and media would not be disappointed!

"The first time we talked about it was at his office at the warehouse," Montevecchio began, indicating that he was initially approached by Arnone during the spring of 1982 with a plan to kill the bookie Bolo Dovishaw. (DiPaolo had earlier confirmed that in May 1982, Arnone opened his safe-deposit box.)

The warehouse that Montevecchio had spoke of was Arnone's food importing business at West 17th and Cherry Streets in the heart of what was fondly known as Erie's "Little Italy" district – perhaps a one square-mile predominantly Italian haven in the town's central west side. It was a high traffic area, that part of Erie, where not only thousands of hard-working Italian-Americans lived and worked, but also where organized crime took root and thrived and flourished there.

"He (Arnone) told me he was informed that there was a lot of money in Bolo's safe-deposit box and that it'd be a good idea to kill him and get the money from the box," Montevecchio said in almost matter-of-fact tones, as though such conversations about brutal killings for hire were more the norm than the exception.

"We kicked it around a little bit and basically I told him it wouldn't work," Montevecchio said, nodding his head for emphasis, as if he was a court-certified expert on the topic. But Montevecchio said he was assured by Arnone that if Montevecchio could get the bank box keys, the plan would indeed work as Arnone had an "in" at the bank.

To sweeten the deal, Montevecchio testified, Arnone offered Montevecchio a percentage of what was found in the bank safe deposit box. But Caesar Montevecchio was no dummy. He knew better than to grab for the percentage in such an uncertain deal. He wanted an offer that would fix his take in a definite, more tangible sum from the start. Forever the shrewd money negotiator, or thinking of himself in that way, Caesar rejected the offer of a percentage, he told the jury.

He explained that if Arnone got into the bank box, Arnone would then be the only one who knew exactly how much money was there. In other words, there was no way Montevecchio was going to trust Niggsy Arnone to disclose exactly how much money had been in the bank box. Honor among thieves? Forget it!

Instead, Montevecchio continued, Arnone offered him $10,000 to arrange the killing. And the triggerman was to get $20,000 for knocking off Bolo Dovishaw.

"After the set amount was offered, did you agree to do it then?" Prosecutor Ebert asked Montevecchio.

"At that time, yes," Caesar freely admitted.

Then Caesar Montevecchio told the jury about the aborted Bolo Dovishaw murder attempt in December 1982. He added that the Ohio-based killer, Robert Dorler, eventually agreed upon a new date, January 3, 1983, as the time for the next attempt on the bookie's life and his banked gambling proceeds stash. That one was successful, Montevecchio said. When dealing with the warped sense of values that were Montevecchio's for so many years, it was difficult for many to understand a definition of successful in regard to a cold, calculated contract killing.

No one could be completely sure, but some courtroom observers still swear that when Montevecchio told the jury that the second murder attempt was met with such success, they detected a slight smile on his then, up-curled lips. Others who were there in the courtroom said they heard in Caesar's voice a most definite sense of great pride, even accomplishment. It *was* his craft.

CHAPTER 43

PERHAPS DIFFICULT TO BELIEVE, BUT IT SEEMED THAT EVEN THOUGH Caesar Montevecchio knew he would be doing hard time despite his cooperation with police, he was nonetheless still enjoying his moment in the spotlight. It was as though he had found the bright lights to finally match his huge criminal ego. While in prison in Michigan 20 years earlier, Caesar had demonstrated a unique flair for the dramatic when he became the sports editor of the penitentiary's newspaper. He proved to be a pretty fair writer at that, especially since he understood sports and the lingo of jocks from his glory days as an Erie high school star athlete, although he never reached those heights in his aborted college athletic career at Detroit.

Now in the courtroom, he repeated much of the same testimony he gave during the Robert Dorler murder trial several weeks earlier. Montevecchio, in response to prosecutor Ebert's skilled questioning, told the members of that Anthony "Niggsy" Arnone murder trial jury that he personally contacted and contracted Dorler, of Medina, Ohio, to kill Mr. Dovishaw. Rattling off those same eye-popping, mouth-dropping details as in the previous trial, Montevecchio again claimed that it was Arnone who first hatched the scheme with the basic idea, he underscored in his testimony, to get the keys to Dovishaw's bank safe-deposit boxes. But Caesar also said he at first had turned down the offer, rather than work on the contingency basis allegedly proposed by Arnone.

Montevecchio described his life-long pal Arnone as a "10 percenter," just one of many in Caesar's arsenal in a miserable criminal life. Such a person fingered potential burglary and robbery targets for Montevecchio to scope out and then later hit with all the professionalism acquired over the years. In return, the person got 10 percent of the "profits."

Immediately following Dovishaw's murder, Montevecchio met Dorler at Erie's Station Restaurant on upper Peach Street, Caesar said. It was there Montevecchio received the bank safe-deposit box keys from the killer, he testified. Then he met with Arnone, handing off the keys directly to Niggsy. Just one day after the murder, Montevecchio continued, he again met with the defendant, Arnone. This time the meeting was at Niggsy's warehouse in the heart of Erie's Little Italy. There, Arnone returned the bank keys, which were to be placed back inside Dovishaw's abandoned car at the Holiday Inn South hotel. Arnone also gave Montevecchio a brown paper bag containing the blood money – $20,000 in hard cash – which Montevecchio said he later delivered to Robert Dorler at the popular Interstate 90 pancake house restaurant not far from Ashtabula, Ohio.

It was during this testimony that Montevecchio acknowledged that sometime later in 1983, the murderer Robert Dorler asked Caesar to kill a man in Cleveland. Montevecchio said that after he initially declined Dorler's offer, Dorler asked whether Caesar's longtime partner in crime, "Fat Sam" Esper, might be interested in doing the Ohio hit. Why not keep it all in the family, the warped thinking of those involved went. Montevecchio said the two met with Esper, and on July 28, 1983 and he bragged to Esper that he had killed Dovishaw to "pump him up" for the Cleveland killing Dorler was now seeking from Esper. Montevecchio was not aware at the time that Esper was wearing a police wire. As a result of the wired conversation, Caesar Montevecchio was arrested a short time later and charged with committing a series of burglaries, and also with possession of cocaine. It was becoming obvious to all there was little Caesar Montevecchio would not do for a buck.

The witness admitted on the stand that he lied to police during his prison stint when he claimed that Joseph Scutella, now of Pal Joey's arson fame, had actually planned and carried out the killing of Bolo Dovishaw and the would-be hit on the ruthless Raymond Ferritto of Danny Greene bomb-blast fame. It was Caesar's futile attempt to get himself released from prison for Christmas, he testified quite earnestly, trying to explain away the reason for his many lies to authorities. He even blamed the Frantino crime family in Pittsburgh, which he later acknowledged had nothing to do with this killing. But he added that he had never actually signed the admission statements that police had requested that he autograph for them, and ultimately he was not given his Christmas holiday that year.

After DiPaolo arrested him on additional drug charges in 1986, and after he learned Robert Dorler was supposedly cooperating with police about other crimes, Montevecchio rationally assumed the Cleveland murderer would attempt to cut a deal for himself regarding the Dovishaw slaying. Such a deal would not go very well from Montevecchio's perspective. Montevecchio said that in July 1986 he decided once-and-for-all to fully and honestly cooperate with the police investigation and come clean about the murder of Frank "Bolo" Dovishaw. DiPaolo was wearing him down, he said. He had no other way out.

It was then, Caesar Montevecchio said, that he finally named Anthony "Niggsy" Arnone as the man who ordered the killing of the Erie bookie Dovishaw. Also during the direct examination from the prosecutor, Montevecchio revealed for the first time that he had accepted groceries from the defendant, Arnone, as partial payment for Montevecchio's part in arranging to hire Dorler, Bolo Dovishaw's killer. Arnone, as president of Arnone and Son Food Importers, had vast access to specialty foods. That would prove helpful to Montevecchio and his family. According to Montevecchio's testimony, he permitted Arnone to owe him $9,000 of the ten grand Caesar was supposed to have collected for being the middle man in the murder. He said he often received groceries from Arnone, who did not charge him for the food, but deducted the cost of the groceries from the total amount he owed Montevecchio for arranging the Dovishaw hit.

"I was in jail. What was I to do? Nobody else gave my family food or money."

During the relentless cross-examination, defense Attorney Joseph Santaguida was incredulous with the prosecutorial star's thus far damaging testimony against his client, Arnone.

"You killed somebody for some salami and capocollo? Is that what you're telling me?" Santaguida harshly, loudly demanded while some of those in the courtroom fought to hold back chuckles.

"That is partially true, yes," the straight-faced Montevecchio managed to answer.

"Getting paid off for a murder with $50 worth of groceries?" the blustering attorney continued.

"That is correct," Montevecchio said. "That was part of it."

Then Montevecchio explained that he wouldn't exactly characterize the exchange of groceries and reduction of the amount of blood money owed as the killing of someone for a salami. He tried to explain that Niggsy Arnone simply deducted the cost of the groceries from what Arnone owed Caesar.

"You, the burglar, the robber, the dope dealer, and you do a murder and get paid for it in groceries?" Santaguida seemed to chide the infamous criminal Caesar Montevecchio. "Just answer yes or no. Is that true?"

"That's partially true, yes sir," Montevecchio again responded with that typical chilling calmness that used to drive DiPaolo crazy, but was now actually becoming amusing to the police officer.

This back-and-forth courtroom banter between Santaguida and the witness was particularly contentious throughout the defense counsel's deliberate, often sarcasm-laced cross-examination of Montevecchio. But Montevecchio just didn't seem to mind. He seemed to be enjoying it all.

Like the rapid-fire staccato of a submachine gun, Santaguida blasted and peppered Montevecchio with a barrage of questions for more than three grueling hours. At times, the lawyer's courtroom theatrics provoked the anger of the normally patient Judge Fred Anthony. But through it all, Caesar Montevecchio stayed cool, his courtroom demeanor and composure seemingly unshakeable. He did have plenty of previous life-experience nonchalantly brushing off cops' and lawyers' questioning. Indeed, for Caesar, a lifetime avocation.

Santaguida became frustrated, it seemed, at times lashing out in diatribes laden with his personal opinions of Caesar's unseemly character, unholy reputation and prior lack of truthfulness. DiPaolo, smiled to himself, knowing full well that this lawyer, frustrated as he might seem, was right-on in his presumptions.

As reported in the *Morning News*, at one point during the heated exchange, as Ebert leaped to his feet at the prosecution table to again object to the questioning, Judge Anthony finally had had enough. With a sharp rebuke and scathing criticism of the defense attorney, Judge Anthony said, "It's improper and you know that, Mr. Santaguida, and I expect you not to do that again."

Santaguida calmed down just a little, but his questions to Montevecchio were delivered just as hard, and with the same vitriolic sarcasm. When Arnone's counsel asked about inconsistency between Montevecchio's preliminary hearing testimony and what he was now telling the jury members during the murder trial, Erie's professional hood again refused to become rattled.

"My answer to that question during the preliminary hearing was not correct. I was confused."

"What's the difference between a lie and confusion?"

"A lie is intentional. Confusion is not intentional," Montevecchio convincingly explained, and obviously apparently with some authority on the subject.

"*You* were confused?" the defense lawyer asked with dripping sarcasm.

"You had successfully confused me."

"So let's admit you're a liar! Then I'll be successful and we'll all go home!"

Yet as they continued, Montevecchio, responding to the lawyer's questions, acknowledged he lied to his wife, to police, to the Federal Bureau of Investigation and even to his one-time criminal crony and partner in crime, "Fat Sam" Esper, while the two were actually on their way to committing a house burglary.

Santaguida emphasized Montevecchio's habit of hiding his long-time criminal activities, including many first degree felonies, from his wife, Bonnie. The lawyer also pointed to the many different accounts Caesar had given to the police, including implicating Joseph Scutella in the Bolo Dovishaw killing. "He was your partner. You lied to him?"

"Yes."

"You lied to your wife?" Santaguida pressed.

"Yes."

"You lied to the authorities before, didn't you?"

"Yes."

"And, we have to believe you're not lying now?"

There was a pause for effect. And then there were still more questions.

Santaguida asked how Robert Dorler could have been expected to single-handedly move Dovishaw's heavy body from the home. Montevecchio replied that Dorler insisted that moving the body alone could be done.

The lawyer also wanted to know how Dorler was expected to find the elusive safe-deposit box keys, which had to happen before anyone could have a pay day. Montevecchio said that Dovishaw had shown others the keys following a previous robbery to demonstrate he didn't keep much cash on hand in his home.

Santaguida asked how and why Billy Bourjaily considered becoming part of this murder scheme after the fact. Montevecchio acknowledged it was his own mistake.

And why, Santaguida continued, was Joe Scutella told about the plan? Wasn't Caesar worried Scutella would tip off Dovishaw that his life was in danger? But Montevecchio, as he always did, had an answer for every query. He said he implicitly trusted his pal Joey because of the two Erie criminals' long-standing friendship and relationship in mutually beneficial criminal activities. Caesar had pulled his first burglary with Joey and his father, Giuseppe, way back in the 1950s.

While Dorler was promptly paid the twenty grand for the evening's "work," why was Montevecchio satisfied to receive only $1,000 as a down payment? Santaguida continued. Caesar said it wasn't odd that he would allow Niggsy Arnone to owe him the remainder of the $10,000 he was supposed to receive for arranging the murder.

Santaguida questioned why "a smart guy" like Caesar could plan a hit such as Bolo Dovishaw's, but not want to learn how the hired killer would perform his end of the murder contract.

"My deal with him (Dorler) was to kill Bolo, get rid of the body and get the safe deposit box keys," Montevecchio replied. "How he did it was up to him."

The defense lawyer asked why Dovishaw was not murdered prior to January; why not perhaps in the previous fall, after the scheme was first hatched? Montevecchio shrugged it off, saying he didn't know.

"Weren't you the big planner, the big genius in this whole thing?" Santaguida hammered away.

"I don't think there was anything genius about this, but I had a hand in the planning." To deny anyone involved was a genius was perhaps the smartest and most ironic trial testimony to date. Although it had taken the better part of seven years, Dovishaw's killer and those associated with the actual crime had still gone down, one by one. Still, DiPaolo was becoming concerned that this trial jury was not in the mood to accept as gospel all that Montevecchio was saying, as the Dorler trial jury had done. Maybe it was time for the cop to worry a bit.

As if he understood that the cold-blooded Caesar Montevecchio needed somehow to be humanized before the Niggsy Arnone murder trial jury, Prosecutor Ebert now called upon a familiar witness, Dennis Pfannenschmidt, the former deputy Pennsylvania attorney general who had initially okayed the deal allowing Dom DiPaolo to bring Caesar down.

Pfannenschmidt told the jury that Caesar had broken down in tears in 1987 as he implicated his lifelong buddy Niggsy Arnone in the Dovishaw murder. The former prosecutor said he had been in another room when Montevecchio finally agreed to come clean, be truthful and cooperate with DiPaolo, the lead Dovishaw murder investigator.

"I began to hear these noises," Pfannenschmidt told the jury. "I was in one office and Mr. Montevecchio was in another." The courtroom strategy seemed to be working. The jury appeared hooked on Pfannenschmidt's compelling trial testimony, its members leaning forward in their seats so as not to miss a word.

"I went over near the door and looked in and saw Mr. Montevecchio at the table. His head was in his hands and it appeared to me that he was sobbing."

Compelling for the jury, perhaps, yet defense lawyer Santaguida wasn't buying any warm and fuzzy sympathy stuff for Caesar Montevecchio. The attorney made fun of Pfannenschmidt's description, again employing his own dripping sarcasm.

"You said you saw *him* crying, is that right?" Santaguida asked the former state prosecutor. Again, there were a few muffled courtroom snickers.

"That's right," Pfannenschmidt said with sincerity, managing to keep his face straight and emotionless.

Judge Anthony's courtroom wasn't the only place where legal action – at least the tongue-wagging kind – was taking place during the sensational

Niggsy Arnone murder trial. Away from the bright lights and somber courtroom, there were plenty of words being exchanged.

According to a report in the Erie *Morning News* on December 6, 1989, a day after Caesar Montevecchio's testimony, an Erie lawyer and an Erie police lieutenant were claiming Montevecchio lied at least once during his lengthy testimony. The criminal lawyer was Attorney Leonard Ambrose, the cop, Lt. Donald Levis.

The day before, during Ebert's direct examination of Montevecchio, Caesar testified that he was told by his former lawyer, Attorney Ambrose, that police officers were watching him. According to Montevecchio, Ambrose had learned of the claimed police surveillance from Erie Police Lieutenant Levis. When asked by Ebert whether he knew he was still under police surveillance when he was released from prison early in 1985, Montevecchio testified that he was told he was being watched by the cops.

"I had a call from my attorney, Lenny Ambrose. He had information from Donald Levis that I was to be under surveillance," Montevecchio said.

When interviewed by the Erie *Morning News* later that day, Ambrose unequivocally said, "That's ridiculous. I never talked to Donald Levis about this case. In the first place, Levis was never involved in Caesar's case." Ambrose did say he had many conversations about the case with DiPaolo, the investigating officer.

Lieutenant Levis, in an interview with the newspaper separate from Ambrose's, also flatly denied Caesar Montevecchio's allegation. "I don't ever remember talking to Len Ambrose about Montevecchio," Levis told the newspaper. "I had nothing to do with Montevecchio's case. I'd have no reason to talk to Mr. Ambrose."

Levis did say, however, that he recalled having information about a police surveillance on Montevecchio on one occasion, but indicated that was at least several years prior to the Dovishaw slaying. But Levis said that even then he didn't remember talking to Ambrose about it.

Since the counter allegations and denials of Ambrose and Levis would have tainted the jury by implicating Montevecchio in what might have been a major lie, none of the reported interviews got to the jury panel considering Niggsy Arnone's fate in Judge Anthony's courtroom.

As the top cop in the case, Dominick DiPaolo was steaming at what he considered behind the scenes, out-of-court maneuvering. Any information that an attorney would have about surveillance on any suspect would have to have come directly from within the Erie Police Bureau, DiPaolo believed.

There were a number of officers aware of the surveillance. DiPaolo knew Lt. Levis and Police Chief Paul DeDionisio were in Police Director Art Berardi's office when DiPaolo requested a detail of Erie officers for the Montevecchio surveillance. He also knew there were others within the Erie Police Department who had known about the Montevecchio surveillance request from the very beginning.

The surveillance team had been hand-picked by DiPaolo – the same officers he chose to work on "Fat Sam" the entire time they protected him. DiPaolo believes he knows exactly where the leak came from: While the surveillance went on, one officer, Vinnie Lewandowski, advised DiPaolo several times, "Dom, something is up! I know that he didn't make us because of what *we're* doing, but yet his actions are very strange – like he knows."

DiPaolo thought at the time it was strange for the entire two-week surveillance that Montevecchio went to church every morning, and never even once went to Niggsy Arnone's place, a Barbute game, or hooked up with any of his cronies. It was like Caesar Montevecchio was again the altar boy of his Erie youth. Montevecchio, DiPaolo had long suspected, actually had known he was being tailed all along. His testimony in court indicated an awareness of the police tail – and DiPaolo believed Montevecchio was telling the truth, at least in this instance.

When the newspaper reporter covering the case telephoned DiPaolo for a comment after Levis and Ambrose alleged that Montevecchio lied about each of them, DiPaolo told the newsman to ask Chief DeDionisio about he and Levis being present in Berardi's office when the request for surveillance was made. When the reporter did contact the chief of police, DeDionisio said he could not comment as the case was still current and in court.

It wasn't the first time DiPaolo found himself at odds with Levis. Four years earlier, while DiPaolo was the chief investigating officer in a gun theft case against former Erie Police Chief Sam Gemelli. Levis, a longtime friend of the criminally-charged police chief, had been a star witness for the defense during Gemelli's trial.

According to the newspaper account the morning of October 5, 1985, "Erie Police Lt. Donald Levis testified Friday that former Erie Police Chief Samuel Gemelli once ordered him to investigate Detectives Dominick DiPaolo and David Bagnoni on allegations they gave heroin to police sources."

Levis testified it was before DiPaolo began his investigation of Gemelli that the chief had ordered the probe of the two drug squad detectives. At the time it was a defense attempt to discredit the chief investigator by somehow tarnishing DiPaolo's well-known image as a tough-talking, crime-fighting cop. The implication brought by Levis' testimony at the time was that DiPaolo had had an ax to grind with the police chief and launched the stolen weapon probe against Gemelli. Levis' testimony in the Gemelli case had come nine full years after that 1976 heroin investigation which resulted in a determination of no merit in the allegations and no charges being filed against the two Erie officers. The two had been exonerated by an independent police investigation headed by respected Detective Captain Thomas Stanton, who determined Bagnoni, on the night heroin was to have been given to the source, was on vacation in Florida, while DiPaolo was conducting a raid in another part of town with Captain Charles Erickson and Detective Sergeant Patrick Shanahan. The source, Stanton determined, was not even arrested on the night in question.

There was also another incident in which DiPaolo and Levis were at odds. It was in 1981 after DiPaolo's and Don Gunter's six month probe into the late-1980 death of Erie Police Corporal Robert Owen determined the killing to be a homicide. It was Levis' opinion that Owen had committed suicide, a theory supported by the FBI.

It had long been DiPaolo's belief that Mayor Louis Tullio wanted the cause of death to be suicide to take the heat off the Erie Police Bureau. There was much rumor, innuendo and speculation that a cop killed Owen – and a suicide ruling would stop payment of the insurance money to Owen's widow. Levis was permitted to travel to Quantico, Virginia, headquarters of the FBI Academy, where he met with and supplied information about the case to a behavioral specialist. Once the information was provided, the Feds came up a psychological profile, which DiPaolo believed was more akin to a Ouija Board than science.

After the FBI's lengthy study of the information by Levis, the feds determined the death was probably a suicide, but could not be 100 percent sure. The FBI also commented on the ruling of a world-renown blood spatter expert, Dr. Herbert MacDonell, who ruled the death a homicide, saying the expert's tests were inconclusive. Levis' public request for a Coroner's Inquest and ruling of suicide was denied by Erie County Coroner Merle Wood, who said that the evidence presented made him certain the death was a homicide and no new evidence existed that would cause a change in his ruling.

A month after two Erie councilmen, Mario Bagnoni and Bernard "Babe" Harkins, criticized Mayor Tullio for holding up the insurance payment to Jane Owen, the money was finally paid. To this day, the Owen case is still an open and unsolved homicide. Over the years, cold-case investigators from different law enforcement agencies in Pennsylvania studied the thousands of documents and reports to try to determine whether new information could be developed. At least four different investigative teams studied the case in the more than three decades since the police officer's death. Not one concluded the death was a suicide, including the latest investigation in 2013.

Once again, DiPaolo surmised, the public split had pitted police officer against police officer, helping the credibility of neither and doing little in the way of resolving the Owen investigation.

Back at the Bolo Dovishaw murder trial, where Anthony "Niggsy" Arnone was accused of master-minding the January 1983 hit on one of Erie's best-known bookies, DiPaolo believed Caesar Montevecchio was now telling the truth when he testified he knew all about the police surveillance on him.

Ironic, DiPaolo thought. Twenty years earlier, even DiPaolo wouldn't have imagined that he would one day take the word of this John Dillinger wannabe over fellow Erie police officers.

CHAPTER 44

DESPITE THE OUT-OF-COURT GOINGS ON, THERE WAS STILL A MURDER trial underway.

Detective Sergeant Dominick DiPaolo was determined to focus his attention on the trial, rather than the extracurricular activities in the local press. Nearly seven years after the killing, the culminating trial in the seemingly endless Frank "Bolo" Dovishaw murder investigation was finally underway and winding down, much to DiPaolo's satisfaction.

The shooter – Robert Dorler of Medina, Ohio, and the middleman, Erie's Caesar Montevecchio, had already fallen. Now, in DiPaolo's mind, there was only one person remaining to fall, the man on trial for plotting the hit, Anthony "Niggsy" Arnone. The Erie cop had given the investigation his best shot – but now it was out of his hands. It was a helpless feeling, but DiPaolo understood how the system worked, and he knew he would live with the outcome, no matter what it turned out to be.

State prosecutor M.L. Ebert, representing the Pennsylvania Attorney General's Office, began calling his final witnesses on December 6, 1989, in an attempt to nail down the theory advanced all along that Niggsy Arnone had orchestrated the 1983 killing to get into Dovishaw's bank safe deposit boxes.

With the alleged assistance of a relative employed at the bank, an allegation maintained by the prosecution throughout the trial, authorities claimed Arnone had helped himself to more than $300,000 in Bolo's illegally gained gambling loot.

On the other hand, Arnone, 50, steadfastly maintained his innocence.

Now the prosecution needed to back up its contention that Dovishaw, one of Erie's most notorious bookies, was killed out of greed for his ill-gotten loot. Prosecutor Ebert called to the stand Augustine Matson, a former special agent with the United States Internal Revenue Service. Matson, who was now in business for himself as a Certified Public Accountant, testified he was hired by investigators and prosecutors in January 1988 to examine Arnone's tax, business and banking records, now a part of the official trial transcripts.

"We couldn't find enough sources to explain funds going into those accounts," Matson said. The gist of the former IRS agent's testimony was that after examining Arnone's financial records he could not explain the presence of some $140,000 in deposited funds from 1983 through 1986. Stated differently, there was more than $140,000 in Arnone's accounts over and above the money that had been available to him during the time period in question. Jury members appeared amazed.

Dragging out a large chart to make the figures more understandable for the jury, Matson testified that Arnone had deposited amounts of money that were over and above the money that was available to him in each of the four years from 1983 to 1986.

"In 1982, I found, there was enough sources of money to explain what was in the account," the Certified Public Accountant said. "But in the years 1983 through 1986, I didn't have enough known sources to explain what was in his account."

Lead Defense Attorney Joseph Santaguida, however, began his cross-examination of the witness by attempting to discredit several of the accountant's financial assertions. Santaguida attempted to show the jury Matson had never been given complete figures representing Arnone's finances during the years in question. Plus, the witness never interviewed or spoke with Arnone or Arnone's accountant.

"In effect, you were trying to put together a puzzle without all the pieces?" Attorney Santaguida asked Matson.

Matson denied that assumption. Instead, Matson said, he was in possession of all of Arnone's financial information for the years 1983 and 1984, although he also acknowledged some of the information for the two remaining years was incomplete.

Santaguida scored jury points several times when he got Matson to acknowledge he didn't interview Arnone or his accountant, nor did he speak with Arnone's wife. When Santaguida asked whether interviewing both Arnone and his accountant should have been standard operating procedure in such investigations, Matson indicated that he believed those interviews were not called for.

It was then that Santaguida brought forth material that Matson had used himself in teaching classes on the topic. The Matson teaching documents introduced by Santaguida called for such analysis of financial records to include at least interviews with the subjects of the investigation.

"Did you do that?" the lawyer asked, referring to interviews with either Arnone or Arnone's accountant.

"No sir," Matson responded.

Now Santaguida wanted Matson to tell him and the jury about various methods accountants use so they can find different deposits from "unknown sources." He used the example of a gambler depositing $1,000 into a bank account, then withdrawing it, then again depositing $1,000 into the same account. Although the records would show $2,000 in deposits, as his example went, just the same $1,000 was involved.

Matson acknowledged such an instance was possible, but said it did not fit the pattern of Arnone's regular deposits of varied amounts from $100 to $500. Matson was a prosecution witness. It wasn't his job to help Santaguida defend Arnone. So it wasn't all that unusual that there would be some push back during cross-examination testimony. Using Santaguida's example of a gambler withdrawing and re-depositing funds, Matson explained Arnone wouldn't have needed to take cash from his account for gambling because cash was easily available to him at his business.

Santaguida also attempted to show that some income could have been from repayments of loans Arnone had made. But again Matson said the frequent small deposits over a lengthy period tended to indicate otherwise.

Asking Matson whether deposited money could have come from increased profits from Arnone's importing business, Matson again acknowledged that was possible.

But he also said that Arnone's business tax records had showed no dramatic increases in profits during the years involved.

Later testifying for the defense was Joseph Bressan, Niggsy Arnone's accountant.

After Santaguida produced for Bressan several instances of business payments Arnone had made from his personal bank account, Bressan said such payments were accounted for at the end of the year while determining business earnings and expenses.

Whether or not the testimony of the financial experts hurt or helped either side was up to interpretation, depending on which side of the courtroom one was sitting. For DiPaolo, it wasn't time to push the panic button. But he was forced to admit that Santaguida was proving to be a much more formidable courtroom opponent that the Erie cop was accustomed to facing.

The next prosecution witness was getting to be no stranger at the Erie County Courthouse. Less than a month earlier, PennBank loan officer Diane DiRenzio-Amendola had testified in the trial of Robert Dorler, helping to convict the triggerman in the Dovishaw murder.

Now, as DiRenzio-Amendola again found herself a witness for the prosecution she testified that the last time she had seen the inside of the largest of the two safe-deposit boxes Dovishaw rented at her bank branch, it held "lots of money, papers and jewelry." During her earlier testimony, she had told the Robert Dorler trial jury that she saw the box stuffed with $50 and $100 bills, perhaps as much as $300,000.

DiRenzio-Amendola had known Frank Dovishaw only as a customer. But occasionally, she had testified, she had helped him with access to the bank vault and one of his boxes there. She had last helped Dovishaw on December 17, 1982, she told the jury. At that time, she assisted him in getting into the larger of the two safe deposit boxes. Apparently because she had acted in a friendly way toward the customer Dovishaw, she testified, he had allowed her to view the contents of his safe-deposit box.

"It was about halfway filled and about three quarters of the way to the top," she said during that earlier testimony.

When DiPaolo drilled open the box after Bolo's untimely demise, he found only about $18,000 in cash. Hardly the amount anyone would expect to find as the sacred stash of Erie's leading sports-betting figure.

Now, during the Niggsy Arnone trial, Ebert asked the witness if, at the request of the prosecution, she had filled a like-sized box as Dovishaw's with 50s and 100s.

Acknowledging she had done so, she told the jury that it took $300,000 in the test box. Her testimony appeared to have the same incredulous impact on the Anthony Arnone jury as it did on the Dorler panel. It would be easy for most on the panel to understand the motivation for a killing that came with a 300 grand payday, DiPaolo hopefully thought to himself.

DiRenzio-Amendola also told the Arnone jury, just as she had done before the Dorler jury, that she had processed a loan application for Anthony "Niggsy" Arnone on January 4, 1983, the day after Bolo Dovishaw's murder. And again she testified to having seen Arnone enter the bank vault, where the safe-deposit boxes are stored, on that day. Arnone had been alone as he entered the vault area, DiRenzio-Amendola told the jury members. Arnone also had a deposit box at the bank that he had rented the previous May.

In her previous testimony, DiRenzio-Amendola had explained that generally it takes two – the holder of the box and a bank employee, each with a key – to open safe-deposit boxes. During that previous testimony, referring to Arnone entering the vault area alone, Ebert had asked the witness, "You didn't see anyone go in with him (Arnone)?"

"No," DiRenzio-Amendola had replied.

Further painting a vivid portrait of Anthony "Niggsy" Arnone as a heavy bettor, and perhaps even a gambler in deep debt, the prosecution called an eye-witness to Arnone's betting habits. Daniel Berlin, a public school math teacher who worked his summers selling pari-mutuel tickets at Erie's Commodore Downs Racetrack from 1973 to 1982, was quick to identify Arnone to the jury as a "regular" at the track.

When asked if he could identify Arnone by sight – given it was seven years since he worked at the track – Berlin slowly visually examined those seated around the defense table, carefully checking out each man there. Then, Arnone raised his hand to identify himself. Berlin said he recognized Arnone by sight years earlier because his visits to the racetrack appeared to be almost every night. And usually he was in the company of Caesar Montevecchio.

"Most every race he'd bet between $100 and $200," Berlin said. "Typically, not always." Berlin explained that 10 races were run each night, and the season during some years lasted 100 days.

When defense lawyer Santaguida asked Berlin if there was something wrong with visiting the racetrack or betting, Berlin said he had no such beliefs. Berlin also testified he had no idea how often Arnone won in his betting because the winner windows were situated apart from the selling windows where Berlin had worked.

Based on the numbers provided by Berlin, Arnone could have bet anywhere from $100,000 to $200,000 a season.

The jury was doing the math. Impressive.

Seemingly saving its best shot for last, as if to add an exclamation point to the courtroom proceedings, the prosecution summoned one more time as its primary police witness, Detective Sergeant Dominick DiPaolo.

DiPaolo had been through this drill before. Many times. And he was eager to get this trial, the entire Bolo Dovishaw murder investigation, behind him. But first, he would be sworn in a last time, promise to tell the truth, and then relate an account all too familiar to him for the nearly seven long years of the Dovishaw investigation. Since DiPaolo was chief investigator, it would be important for Santaguida to try to poke as many holes in this cops' testimony as possible. It was a defense lawyer's obligation, DiPaolo well knew.

From the start, Santaguida repeatedly interrupted DiPaolo's testimony, objecting, according to one published report, some 11 times during the first hour. But DiPaolo was steady and stayed on message as he got his story out. The police investigator told jurors that searches of Bolo Dovishaw's home after the murder turned up about $600 in cash in a jacket pocket. The jacket had been draped over a chair near the front door. Police found another $600 inside a bank envelope in a bookcase in the home, DiPaolo said.

Later searches of Dovishaw's Caddy, when it was found two days after the murder in the parking lot of an Interstate 90 hotel, turned up some $5,200 in cash that had been hidden in the spare tire well under the trunk carpeting. More cash and even checks were found hidden beneath the car's dashboard. One of the checks, DiPaolo testified, was made out to defendant Anthony Arnone. Arnone, DiPaolo said, admitted turning the check over to Dovishaw before Bolo's murder. Arnone did not say why he gave the check to Dovishaw. The check was dated January 6, 1982, but Arnone told him the check should have been dated January 6, 1983, explaining it was meant to be held and cashed three days after Dovishaw died.

In further testimony, DiPaolo patiently, dutifully told the jury members of how investigators found nearly identical sums of money amounting to $18,000 in each of Frank Dovishaw's bank safe-deposit boxes at the PennBank's Millcreek Township branch office. His testimony jived with the theory advanced by the prosecution that larger amounts of money were removed from the boxes, while some sizeable sums were then left behind to confuse officers.

Then the prosecutor shifted gears. "During the course of your investigation, did you ever find the murder weapon?" M.L. Ebert asked the officer.

"No, sir," DiPaolo said. DiPaolo said that investigators, assisted by divers, thoroughly searched the bottom of Meander Lake near Youngstown, Ohio, for the murder weapon. "There were 254 weapons recovered," the detective said. "But not ours."

The answer drew nervous laughter from some of the spectators who understood the significance of the large number of lethal weapons found in the lake beneath a bridge not far from a seat of organized crime. The weapons had been recovered from the lake during investigations between 1980 and the late-1987 search involving Dovishaw's murder. But the latest search struck out in terms of finding the murder weapon, DiPaolo said.

The cop's investigation of Anthony "Niggsy" Arnone as part of the Dovishaw murder probe, he testified, began in July 1987 when Caesar Montevecchio agreed to cooperate and then fingered his longtime friend. DiPaolo said that when he took Montevecchio's official statement implicating Arnone in the crime, tough guy Caesar Montevecchio wept.

During his cross-examination, Santaguida asked whether DiPaolo instructed Montevecchio to telephone Arnone over a monitored telephone line in an attempt to record incriminating information from the defendant.

DiPaolo said he had not.

Santaguida managed to work into his cross examination information that police had successfully used similar investigatory methods when "Fat Sam" Esper was wired with a recording device to lure Montevecchio into making incriminating statements against himself. But DiPaolo explained that instance involved a "body wire" Esper wore when he was with Montevecchio. Montevecchio never wore a wire, nor was he asked to.

The prosecution finally rested its case following DiPaolo's six hours of testimony over two days. Now it would be Santaguida's turn.

DiPaolo, for all his confidence in what he believed to be a solid case, still felt uneasy, queasy, as the defense stepped up to the plate. As most of his gut feelings went, this one would also prove to be accurate.

CHAPTER 45

ATTORNEY JOSEPH SANTAGUIDA WAS THE *DEFENSE* LAWYER. BUT HE immediately took to the *offense* when the time came for Anthony "Niggsy" Arnone to defend himself against murder charges in Erie County Court. Santaguida knew he must come out swinging hard if Arnone was to escape such a seemingly solid prosecution case alleging the import food business owner planned the January 3, 1983, killing of Erie illegal sports betting bookie "Ash Wednesday" Dovishaw.

The first defense witness was an angry one. It was Niggsy's *cugino*, Theresa Mastrey, the former PennBank officer that authorities implicated, although she was never charged with any crime,

According to the *Morning News* newspaper story that 1989 December day, Mastrey "described herself as the victim of unjust persecution and said she liked and trusted Arnone, but never helped him commit a crime." Her anger obvious and temper rising as she testified, Mastrey told the jury members that large sums of cash found when police opened her own bank safe-deposit box in 1987 actually belonged to the young grandson of the late Al DelSandro, another alleged reputed Erie gambler.

Niggsy Arnone leaned forward intently at the defense table, just as he had throughout the trial, his attention focused directly on the witness stand. Arnone was particularly interested in Theresa Mastrey's testimony. It was Mastrey who worked at the bank where Bolo Dovishaw kept his safe-deposit boxes, the newspaper article pointed out, adding and emphasizing that Mastrey had not been charged with any crime.

Mastrey's appearance on the witness stand followed five days of testimony by 26 prosecution witnesses called to testify by the state prosecutor, M.L. Ebert. Now, the 51-year-old Mastrey was the lead-off witness in attorney Santaguida's defense of his client.

As her testimony unfolded, many of the facts were not in dispute. For example, Mastrey did work as an assistant manager at the PennBank branch where Frank "Bolo" Dovishaw had kept two safe-deposit boxes.

How did Theresa Mastrey know Niggsy Arnone? the defense attorney asked. She said Niggsy was her cousin, and also a bank customer. She testified she had handled bank loans for Arnone, but that all the transactions were well within the bank's regulations. All of the loans, she said, were approved by the bank because of Arnone's excellent loan repayment record. The only question asked of her, DiPaolo thought, was did she handle loans for Arnone; it seemed to DiPaolo's cop's mind she was overly defensive in her response.

Under further deliberate questioning from Santaguida about access to the bank's safe-deposit box vault, Mastrey patiently explained the keys to the vault were kept at the teller's station nearest to the vault. But all bank employees, she said, were authorized to give customers access to their bank boxes.

When asked if she could have allowed her cousin Niggsy into the vault without making Arnone sign the vault's log, she answered, "Sure, I could have. But I didn't and I wouldn't."

She had testified she would never help Arnone to commit a crime, DiPaolo thought. And, when asked by Santaguida whether she could have allowed Arnone into the vault without logging it in, she said she could have, but didn't. Now DiPaolo recalled lawyer Jay D'Alba's request for Mastrey's immunity under the hypothetical theory she allowed Arnone into the vault, then took a walk. Close, DiPaolo thought, to what Santaguida had asked.

Mastrey was also asked about the $37,000 in cash in her own safe-deposit box that came to light when police drilled and opened that box in 1987 some four years after Dovishaw's murder. Mastrey said the money was the property of Roseanne DelSandro's young son. When asked why DelSandro had given it to her to put into her bank box, she hesitated. "Prompted by Santaguida," the newspaper story read,

"Mastrey said Roseanne DelSandro's father-in-law, the late Al DelSandro, had given Roseanne $30,000 to place in safe-keeping for the child. She said Roseanne added smaller amounts to that sum as time passed. Mastrey estimated that she had the money, or most of it, since 1978 or 1979," the newspaper reported.

"Did you tell the police this?" Santaguida questioned.

"Yes, they knew this from the start," she replied with apparent anger, her temper somewhat flaring. "I testified in front of two grand juries. I was interrogated I don't know how many times. I even took a lie detector test! They knew it (the money) belonged to Roseanne DelSandro. They knew it."

"Why did they know it?"

"Because Dom DiPaolo . . . ," she began, but was stopped by a loud objection from the prosecuting attorney. DiPaolo, listening to her testimony, recalled that the information had come not from Mastrey, but from DelSandro.

The opposing attorneys were summoned to the bench, where they held a brief whispered huddle with Judge Fred Anthony. The quickie sidebar conference was presumably about the defense attorney's line of the questioning, before all sides returned to their tables.

"Did you ever assist anyone with getting into Frank 'Bolo' Dovishaw's safe-deposit boxes?" Santaguida concluded his direct examination.

"No, I wouldn't do that. I would jeopardize my position," Mastrey answered, her previous anger now subsided.

DiPaolo thought the witness had been well-prepped prior to her testimony. Yet, her anger quickly percolated to the surface and boiled over during Prosecutor M.L. Ebert's probing cross examination. Ebert questioned Mastrey about her finances, her alleged dislike of "Bolo" Dovishaw, and about statements the defense witness made during previous Dovishaw murder investigation hearings.

Ebert asked about $19,000 in investments she had made in 1983, including a $4,000 IRA opened January 5. That specific date was mentioned because it followed Dovishaw's murder by only two days. But Mastrey testified that each of those investments was previously explained to police investigators. She said the investments were mostly made with funds she rolled over from her previous investment accounts.

Next, Ebert attempted to show that the thousands of dollars found in Mastrey's bank safe-deposit box were hers, not Roseanne DelSandro's son's money as the family previously claimed. (DelSandro was another cousin. Between Erie's large Italian west side and Polish eastside communities, and frequent intermarriages between east and west as well as the town's original German and then Irish immigrants, the city was noted for its many extended families.) Since DelSandro's late father-in-law, Al, had been a bookie, Mastrey said he didn't want the money for his grandson in any regular or normal bank account. Pertaining to ownership of the money, Mastrey testified, "I thought I had a note in there."

Whether or not a note was found, the prosecutor pressed on, leaning heavily on the angry defense witness. Through it all, however, Mastrey refused to be intimidated and angrily pushed back. Exactly who was benefiting by the angry positioning between the two sides in a trial where the stakes – a man's life – were heavy, no one could know for sure, or even speculate.

Ebert was now pointing to legal documents filed after investigators confiscated the money from her bank box, documents indicating Mastrey wanted the return of "her" property. Mastrey replied that she was seeking the return of property that had been placed in her custody.

The prosecutor also probed Theresa Mastrey's repeated approval of loans to her cousin, Anthony Arnone, through intense questioning. She said Arnone obtained those loans from another bank officer before her later approval. Yes, she approved the later loans, she said, because of Arnone's continued good record of loan repayment and because of her cousin's credit-worthiness.

Ebert's line of questioning took another tack. How many safe-deposit boxes did Mastrey keep over the years? And why was it that she needed more than one box after DelSandro gave her the large sum of money?

"Mr. Ebert!" Mastrey said, her frustrated anger returning. "I've done nothing wrong! That money doesn't belong to me!" DiPaolo thought she didn't answer the question. He knew that between Mastrey and her husband, there were seven boxes at multiple bank branches.

Ebert remained nonchalant "Ma'am, have you been charged with anything?"

"No! Yet you're using that money like I did do something wrong! God! Two years I've been persecuted over this!"

When she was asked why her safe-deposit box was situated next to Dovishaw's, she responded that customers selected their own boxes based on what was available in the bank at the time the boxes are rented. As such, and under that caveat, Dovishaw selected the location of his own bank box.

"You didn't like Mr. Dovishaw, did you?" Ebert probed.

"I didn't dislike him."

"You never called him a pig?" The question was a courtroom eyebrow raiser.

Mastrey denied having ever called the murder victim by any such name.

"You were upset with him when he left town and let your husband get arrested, weren't you?"

Mastrey now appeared surprised, even shocked, by the prosecutor's question.

"I beg your pardon?"

But defense attorney Santaguida quickly objected, forcing Ebert to ask instead whether Mastrey's husband had ever been in the illegal bookmaking business with Dovishaw. He also asked whether that relationship had led to a police search of Mastrey's home that resulted in her husband being "taken away" while Frank Dovishaw skipped town.

Mastrey appeared to tightly clench her teeth. Her anger again flaring as she replied that her husband had once taken only a handful of betting slips from where he worked to Dovishaw. It was in 1970, she testified.

"I never knew Mr. Dovishaw left town," she lashed back. "And my husband wasn't taken anywhere. I don't know why you're trying to make me look dirty. I've lived a clean life. I've worked hard!"

"You've never done anything wrong?" he asked.

"No!" Mastrey firmly said as DiPaolo involuntarily sighed.

As if for dramatic effect, Ebert slowly returned to the prosecution table and opened a file folder. Jury members' eyes followed Ebert's every move, and were now glued to the folder.

"Did you put another woman's name on a signature stamp without permission?" Ebert asked.

Again, the witness appeared stunned by the question. "Yes, I did," she said, explaining it was because the person whose name she stamped was not immediately available. In other words, she said, it was a favor for a person who needed immediate notarization.

"Then you forged her name!" Ebert accused.

"Boy, that's really rotten," Mastrey charged back. "Yes, I did do it! Is that the sum of what you find that I've done wrong in my life, Mr. Ebert?"

It a dramatic case of courtroom give-and-take, these vitriolic exchanges between the witness Mastrey and the prosecuting attorney Ebert. But no one keeping tabs on the trial, at least not the objective observers, could be quite sure who came out on top throughout the many nasty exchanges.

Mastrey had come across as indignant, often bitter and angry. Would the jury sympathize with the innocent victim characterization she painted of herself? All that remained to be seen as the witness and evidence portion of the murder trial wound down.

Santaguida was almost done with his brief, but succinct defense of import food business owner and murder defendant Anthony "Niggsy" Arnone. After Theresa Mastrey's fiery testimony and all the contentiousness entailed between witness and prosecutor, the defense lawyer called Roseanne "Roe" Giamanco-Altadonna DelSandro to the stand.

DelSandro was called as a corroborative witness aimed at backing up Mastrey's explanation of where all that money in her safe-deposit bank box had come from. Yes, DelSandro readily testified, the money was hers. But more exactly, she noted, the money actually belonged to her young son. She said she did not put the money in a bank account or in a bank box of her own because her father-in-law, Al DelSandro, her son's benefactor, had asked that she not. She said the money was all in 100-dollar bills. Yet, according to DiPaolo, the money he found there was in fives, tens and twenties, as well as C-notes.

Also testifying that final day of the defense case was the defendant's wife, Bernadine Arnone. Mrs. Arnone said she and her husband acquired several undocumented personal loans over the years.

Santaguida used her testimony to explain away the findings of a government witness, accountant Augustine Matson. It was Matson who had testified that some $140,000 in Arnone's bookkeeping records could not be accounted for through normal sources of income.

Mrs. Arnone was the last witness. And then, Santaguida rested his case.

Anthony "Niggsy" Arnone did not testify in his own defense. Once again, there are many valid strategic arguments on both sides of the legal fence over the impact of defendants who choose not to face juries. Defense lawyers often use the strategy of not calling their clients to testify, saying prosecutors must prove their cases and it's not for defendants to prove their innocence. The judicial system does not require defendants to answer a prosecutor's probing questions before a jury. The burden is always on the prosecution. Plus, as earlier stated, defense lawyers know judges are inclined to allow much wider latitude in prosecutorial cross-examinations of murder defendants as opposed to the other testifying witnesses. Thus, the reluctance of many defense attorneys to subject all but the best-prepared clients to the rigors of an aggressive district attorney's probing questions. Yet, in many post-trial interviews with jurors, both men and women acknowledged defendants' refusal to testify adversely influenced their decisions to convict.

In the Arnone murder trial, without the defendant's testimony, the prosecution called no rebuttal witnesses. The jury would get the case after Santaguida and Ebert made closing arguments to the panel. Both experienced lawyers were well aware that this was the time when cases could be won – or lost.

CHAPTER 46

FRIDAY, DECEMBER 8, 1989 WOULD BE A MAKE OR BREAK DAY FOR ERIE businessman Anthony "Niggsy" Arnone. It was a day during which his attorney would make the ultimate lawyer's plea – one that would either succeed and ultimately free the man accused of planning a horrendous murder, one who had been held in the Erie County Prison since his arrest – or it would be a day he would fail to make an impression on the 12 jurors who would send Arnone to Pennsylvania's electric chair or a state institution for perhaps the rest of his life.

Either way, while it might not have been the actual decision day for the jurors, it was nonetheless a day that would lead to that final decision and resolution of a homicide case that had festered in Erie for too many years.

Arnone, on trial for first degree murder, indeed was putting his life in the hands of defense lawyer Joseph Santaguida. Attorney Santaguida, in a courtroom strategy that would long be discussed in local legal circles, had called only three defense witnesses before resting his case. Three and done. Not surprisingly, Arnone was not one of them. Santaguida had decided to keep his client from testifying in his own behalf – and for good reason. When asked by a newspaper reporter why he didn't put Arnone on the witness stand, Santaguida replied, "He carries with him the presumption of innocence." Standard question from courthouse reporters. Standard response from defense lawyers.

With no rebuttal witnesses testifying, the defense lawyer was now quickly pressed into immediate action. He needed to present his final argument, his version of the case, to the jury.

Pennsylvania's criminal justice system favors, or at least gives the benefit of the doubt, to the defense in most legal circumstances. The burden of proof, for example, is *always* on the prosecution, not the criminal defendant. That presumption of innocence, as Santaguida had told the Erie newspaper reporter, is always present, always constant and only ends upon conviction. Even more, the case against the defendant must be proven not beyond a shadow of a doubt, for virtually few things can be so proven, but beyond what is legally termed "a reasonable doubt." If there is reasonable doubt, explained by judges in different ways, but essentially as a doubt that would give pause to any prudent person considering a major decision, the jury would not be wrong to acquit.

Further benefiting the defense is the requirement in Pennsylvania that any conviction must be a unanimous decision by all 12 members of the jury. Criminal trials differ significantly from civil trials. Civil cases require only a "preponderance" of the evidence, and even then, verdicts need not be unanimous.

As a result, the deck is clearly stacked by the Pennsylvania Constitution on the side of the defense in all criminal matters before the courts. The old adage still rings true, "Best to free 1,000 guilty men than to convict one innocent man." Cops, attorneys, and even the judges all are well aware statistics show most of those appearing before the bar of justice are indeed guilty. But the defense is still given this benefit of presumption of innocence, and often to the accused's advantage.

The prosecution, for example, must present its case first, giving the defense the clear advantage of responding to all witnesses and allegations before deciding whether it would put on its own case. The defense gets to present its case second, allowing the jury members a fresher understanding of the most recent facts being presented to them and thus a fresher understanding of the defense position before deliberations begin.

However, there is one advantage given to the prosecution in criminal trials, a significant one. The prosecution has the opportunity, and the very distinct advantage, of presenting its closing argument to the jury last. In this instance only, the defense must go first in arguing its case. The state's advantage, then, is to counter any defense claims in presenting a version of the trial that will be remembered last in the minds of the jury members.

So, on this cold December day, it was Attorney Santaguida who was called upon to deliver the murder trial's first "summation" to the jury. It would have to be good enough, powerful enough, to make a lasting impression on those who would consider his client's fate. For not only would the jury get to hear the prosecution's forceful response after Santaguida's argument, but also the jury members would be required to absorb an incredible amount of law and legal definitions provided by the trial judge's "charge" before they could begin their private deliberation.

Santaguida knew this was his last best opportunity to make a positive impression on the individual members of the jury. He immediately went into attack mode. As expected, the lawyer unapologetically questioned the Commonwealth's case against Anthony Arnone and jumped with great force upon the credibility, or lack thereof, of the central prosecution witness, Arnone's former pal and alleged co-conspirator, Caesar Montevecchio.

"Without Caesar Montevecchio, what case do they have?" Santaguida posed the question. Jury members listened with rapt attention. "It boils down to the believability, the credibility of Caesar Montevecchio."

The defense attorney, as many courtroom lawyers have often done, implored this jury to use its own common sense in figuring out the honesty, or absence of it, among the many trial witnesses, including Montevecchio. Suggesting that jury members examine the witnesses' "track records," Santaguida urged them to use those same thought processes they successfully use to make their own important decisions in everyday situations.

Santaguida also reminded the panel that Montevecchio's testimony was part of the overall plea deal that had been arranged between Montevecchio and the prosecution team. He said Montevecchio faced only maximum prison time of some 10-to-20 years as opposed to the hundreds of years he would have likely been sentenced to serve without his favorable testimony for the prosecution. The lawyer also pointed to witness Ron Thomas, a convicted drug dealer, whom he indicated would also probably get a reduced sentence in return for his testimony.

Blame the prosecution – that's what successful defense lawyers have a knack for doing. It wouldn't take much for jury members to conclude for themselves that Montevecchio and Thomas had personal interests for testifying. Yet, it is fairly standard practice for the defense to try to discredit prosecution witnesses, raising concerns about their credibility and casting as much doubt on them as possible.

"Guys like Ronald Thomas, Caesar Montevecchio, they lost their right to be believed a long time ago," Attorney Santaguida insisted. It was a good point, many thought. Challenging the believability of career criminals was considered a given. "Ladies and gentlemen, you are the last bastion of fairness!" Joseph Santaguida implored.

Santaguida reminded jury members of the promises they had earlier made to acquit his client unless the evidence proved otherwise, and beyond a reasonable doubt.

"This is pay-up time," he said. "This is time to be true to your promises. A man is arrested and accused of a crime. What's it mean? Nothing." He told the jurors they must find Arnone not guilty if they had any reasonable doubt whatsoever.

"Imagine, reasonable doubt about this case!" he chided somewhat and with great sarcasm. "There's walking, talking, screaming reasonable doubt!" Santaguida was blustery, loud and animated as he continued in his 90-minute summation.

It was a masterful argument, perhaps one of the best heard in many years in Erie County Court. Not too long as to bore and tire jurors, yet long enough to cover the complex information now tied directly to Arnone's life or death fate.

The state built its case against Arnone on a "garbage theory," the lawyer claimed as he kicked at the boxes of evidence on the courtroom floor. "This is all window dressing," he pointed at the evidence boxes. "What's it got to do with this case? Nothing!"

Santaguida did concede, however, that the Commonwealth's ongoing analysis of financial figures relating to Arnone's food and importing business raised many questions about the actual fiscal health of the company. But he said that while the figures might indicate "an income tax problem, an IRS problem, it doesn't make him a murderer." Furthermore, Santaguida insisted that the government's allegations that Arnone stole thousands of dollars from Dovishaw's bank safe-deposit boxes, but continued taking out business loans "makes no sense."

Again pointing at government witnesses who themselves were acknowledged criminals, his voice rising to decibel levels loud enough to be heard in the corridors outside the courtroom, Santaguida lashed out, "Give me a break! Give me a break with this whole case . . . the whole theory of this case!"

He reminded the jurors that even prosecutors had called a law enforcement witness who testified that Caesar Montevecchio earlier lied in the Bolo Dovishaw murder investigation. Santaguida wanted to know how the jury could be expected to put a person in the electric chair based upon the testimony of a liar such as Montevecchio.

Erie Police Detective Sergeant Dominick DiPaolo, the longtime lead investigator in the case, also took much of the defense attorney's abuse and bashing during Santaguida's closing argument.

Another tried and proven defense tactic is to blame the messenger. "Dom DiPaolo is the orchestra leader to this whole chamber of horrors," Santaguida lashed out.

Without a doubt, it remained an impressive closing argument, DiPaolo acknowledged to himself – concise, to the point, and putting the blame on others, even the cops!

But it wasn't a closing argument that couldn't be countered by the prosecution, a closing that could match Joseph Santaguida's point-by-point. That's what DiPaolo hoped would be the case. DiPaolo's years-long tenacity had gotten the case this far. The detective's never-give-up investigatory style, often against formidable odds, had already resulted in arrests and guilty pleas in the murder case. Courtroom success or failure was mostly out of his hands, dependent upon others.

CHAPTER 47

One of those others was the prosecutor. It was M.L. Ebert's turn before the jury panel.

The Deputy Pennsylvania Attorney General was also keenly aware his case would hinge upon the believability of Caesar Montevecchio's testimony. What an unenviable task for any law enforcement official, trying to convince a jury that Caesar Montevecchio was a credible, reliable witness, one to be believed. And how does one go about such a herculean task when one doesn't totally believe himself that former choir boy Montevecchio had any redeeming qualities? Still, Ebert would give it his best shot.

First, he patiently reiterated much of Montevecchio's damaging testimony against Arnone. Then he explained that while Montevecchio might have lied earlier in the investigation, once he began cooperating with Detective Sergeant DiPaolo in 1987, his statements were confirmed by physical evidence uncovered by criminal investigators. For example, how could Montevecchio have even imagined such a story that he related in his testimony if he did not first know that the defendant Arnone had a safe deposit box at the same bank where Dovishaw had rented his bank boxes? It was opened in 1982 and next to Dovishaw's box. DiPaolo thought about a 1982 wedding during which "the Pig's" bank boxes were discussed – coincidence? Or, how could Caesar have even known, if not for Niggsy Arnone himself, that Arnone had visited the bank vault on the day after Frank Dovishaw was murdered?

Or that Arnone had signed the vault entry slip that same day? Valid questions to ponder, all of them.

Despite the creativity, embellishment and even the cleverness, Ebert indicated, Caesar alone could not have dreamt up those facts. Ebert pointed out Montevecchio's account had been fully corroborated by the physical evidence found by police as the case slowly unfolded over the years with glacier-like, but steady speed. And Ebert disputed Santaguida's characterization of the alleged murder plot as "stupid," saying the defense version was not accurate. Then Ebert turned again to his key witness, the one person upon whom this murder case would rise or fall. Montevecchio, although he was not then still physically present in Judge Fred Anthony's courtroom, got center stage prominence.

"You have a right to believe Caesar Montevecchio," Ebert insisted with volume and flare equal to Santaguida's previous dramatic summation. Dom DiPaolo was indeed impressed in the way Ebert responding to all the allegations made during Santaguida's summation.

Then the prosecutor added, "Now, maybe you're saying, M. L. Ebert, you need reality therapy. Caesar Montevecchio is a scum, a rat, a criminal. But, he was part of that murder plan! And as stupid as Mr. Santaguida says it was, it almost succeeded, didn't it?"

Jury members now clearly pondered Ebert's words, much in the same way they had considered what Santaguida said earlier. It was turning into a good argument and Ebert now clearly had the attention of six transfixed men and six equally mesmerized women. No one's eyes were glazing over. This was fascinating stuff.

"If Caesar Montevecchio hadn't come forward, everyone would have skated!" Ebert said.

Ebert addressed motive, perhaps the most important factor in any murder trial in jurors' minds. They want to know, why did he do it? Ebert told them what he believed was overwhelming evidence against Arnone, including testimony about Arnone's then failing business, and a series of loans and gambling debts, some of which were said to be owed to Dovishaw himself.

"In one respect, Anthony Arnone and Caesar Montevecchio are identical," Ebert said of the one-time friends. "Both were driven to this job by their gambling. One compelling drive got to them." Arnone's need for cash resulted in his coming up with a plan to get that cash,

Ebert told the jury. Money is always a strong motive to introduce, and one in which jurors can relate. “They executed a plan. They executed a human being.”

Ebert paused once more for effect, but then said, “You now know what the last moments of Dovishaw’s life were like. And for what?” Ebert’s words hung heavy in the packed courtroom. “For another poker game? Another night at the track? There’s only one just verdict in this case.” He pointed at Arnone, saying, “That man is guilty as charged.”

It was indeed as powerful a prosecution summation as DiPaolo had seen, the cop at the defense table thought. DiPaolo had seen many closing arguments, and even a few trials where attorneys presented no summations. Ebert’s surely ranked with the best of them. But would it be good enough to sway the jury’s collective decision? Would it be good enough for a unanimous verdict sending Niggsy Arnone to the electric chair or life in prison? DiPaolo sighed. Once again, he thought, the decision was out of his hands.

CHAPTER 48

IF ANY OF THE NIGGSY ARNONE MURDER TRIAL JURY MEMBERS WERE at all physically tired that afternoon, they did a masterful job of covering it up. There was not even a post-lunch yawn, even a stifled one. How could there be? They had just been privy to a double performance of heady stuff. No TV or movie drama, but real life!

After nearly a full day in court, 12 Erie County citizens evenly divided along gender lines, each having sworn to do their best to render a fair, impartial verdict, began deliberating Arnone's fate shortly after 3 o'clock. There would be more than eight hours in their small jury room before calling it quits for the night. Yet, at several key points as the evening unfolded, it appeared almost certain to many that a verdict in the murder case might be close-at-hand.

For example, at 10:45 p.m. jurors returned to the nighttime courtroom to ask Judge Anthony to again explain each of the state's criminal charges against Arnone. Specifically, the jury wanted to know legal definitions, under Commonwealth law, for murder, robbery and criminal conspiracy.

It wasn't an unusual request. Jurors are forced to absorb as much "legalese" during the span of just one morning or afternoon as many bright students get to study during entire semesters at schools of law. No one could blame them for wanting clarification of the law. Later, Dominick DiPaolo would clearly recall at that moment that Attorney Santaguida cautioned his client, "They got you on one of them." DiPaolo thought both lawyer and client appeared ill.

Then, just 15 minutes later, at 11 p.m., the jury foreman indicated the panel would deliberate an additional 15 minutes. Veteran courtroom observers assumed jurors were preparing to conduct a final vote on the charges. But after those 15 minutes ticked off and at exactly 11:15, the foreman asked Judge Anthony to adjourn court for that night. Anthony, a jurist of several decades experience and a man who knew when not to push a panel beyond its limits, ordered that the jury, already sequestered throughout the case, would spend at least one more night at a local hotel and recessed court.

Before jurors departed, Anthony repeated many of his daily instructions, that they not discuss the case outside the jury room, watch TV trial coverage or read newspaper accounts of it. He directed the panel to return to his courtroom fresh and alert at 10 o'clock Saturday morning.

A new day often has the impact of battery-recharging for juries. Historically, verdicts often come down quickly after the start of Day Two deliberations. And when that memorable Saturday morning dawned, this jury panel returned to the courtroom ready to issue its verdict in the highly-publicized homicide case, a case of greed, betrayal and guilt. But not for all.

CHAPTER 49

It was a cold, gray Saturday morning when the tipstaff in Judge Anthony's courtroom advised the defense and prosecution teams that the jury had reached a verdict.

Next, the staffer called her boss, Judge Anthony, who was still at home.

Now, he was on his way to the Erie County Courthouse for the conclusion of the murder trial that had captivated local newspaper and television reporters, as well as their vast audiences. In the back of the courtroom, before the jury was brought in and while the judge was en route, Attorney Joseph Santaguida met with Niggsy Arnone's family and supporters. Quietly, he advised them there *might* be a guilty verdict, and he cautioned that if they acted out in an unruly way, they could be arrested.

As Anthony Arnone was led into the courtroom by sheriff's deputies, he was met by his supporters. Some wept in anticipation of the verdict, some said, "I love you, Anthony," and others urged, "Stay strong!" It was then that Santaguida asked Erie County Sheriff's Deputy Toby Rigazzi, a former Erie detective, for permission for Arnone to meet with his wife in a courtroom across the corridor so the two could have a private moment together before the jury rendered its verdict. Leaning over to Prosecutor M.L. "Skip" Ebert, Santaguida whispered, "In case he doesn't see her for a while." Ebert did not object.

Santaguida appeared convinced that with the questions posed by the jury members Friday night about defining the degrees of felonies, his client could be convicted of something serious.

All the testimony, all the summations, all the deliberations, and all the waiting finally was over. Now, it was the jury's turn.

When jurors returned to the courtroom, the first words uttered that drab Saturday morning from the deputy clerk of courts reading the long-awaited jury verdict did not immediately sink in.

The follow-up words, however, the ones that came from the defendant, gave Erie Police Detective Sergeant Dominick DiPaolo a horrific hollow sensation in the pit of his gut: "Ahh! My God! My God!" shouted Anthony "Niggsy" Arnone for all to hear. The murder defendant's shouts came nanoseconds after the jury's verdict was read in Judge Anthony's courtroom not long after deliberations resumed.

"Not guilty." Just two words. Not "innocent" – but in legal terminology according to Commonwealth of Pennsylvania law, simply "not guilty."

The two words had a powerful impact on all present. After Arnone's spontaneous outburst at hearing the acquittal, defense attorney Joseph Santaguida of Philadelphia was the next to respond. "Wow!" he said approaching his client Arnone, half in pleasure, half in what seemed to be surprise and perhaps even some disbelief in what he had just heard. He was still recalling the jury's questions the night before, the ones that seemed to indicate his client might not walk away a free man. But now, everything was changed. And in a way DiPaolo had not expected.

A gathering of Arnone's family members and friends, keeping vigil in the courtroom during the weeklong trial, broke into tearful cheers as realization of the verdict's ramifications become clear in their collective consciousness. It was a purely emotional moment, and clearly Niggsy Arnone's to savor.

Yet, it was also a moment for the prosecutor, M.L. Ebert of the Pennsylvania Attorney General's Office. Ebert was stoic and philosophical in eyeing what was obviously an unexpected defeat, at least to the prosecutorial team.

The prosecutor didn't have the same huge chunk of his career and life wrapped up in the Dovishaw murder investigation as DiPaolo had. For DiPaolo, it was a bitter and sudden end to an investigation that had consumed seven years of his life, representing more than a third of his police career. The cop's steadfast investigation had netted the Ohio man, Robert Dorler, who had executed Dovishaw in cold blood. DiPaolo's investigation had even claimed Erie career criminal, Caesar Montevecchio, who helped to arrange the Dovishaw killing. But with the jury's verdict, the man DiPaolo had charged with plotting the killing was free. DiPaolo's only thought: *Who would have thought Arnone could beat this murder rap!* Still, DiPaolo had been a cop at prosecution tables long enough to know there were no sure bets on verdicts or the ultimate decision of juries. That was the country's criminal justice system, and whether the verdicts were liked or not, whether considered just or not, DiPaolo supported the system.

As these initial moments after the verdict passed and the lead investigator was forced to ponder what it all meant, it was Arnone who seized the moment. He took two steps toward the prosecution table and, as the *Erie Times-News* reported in its December 10, 1989, Sunday morning editions, Anthony "Niggsy" Arnone pointed at DiPaolo and accused the detective sergeant of trying to frame him. DiPaolo didn't even blink.

Many in the courtroom remained fixated on the drama unfolding before them, but DiPaolo stayed calm, never flinching at the accusation and staring coldly at Arnone. This cop had been in tougher situations. Arnone was saying that justice prevailed and that the jury did not believe the lies.

DiPaolo, in his own thoughts, debated briefly whether to respond to Arnone, especially to the "frame him" accusation. But he knew the time was not right. Not then. But he *would* have something to say later.

Aftermath & Epilogue:

NOT GUILTY/ INNOCENT ARE NOT SYNONYMOUS; ONE MORE JURY TO FACE

CHAPTER 50

THE TRIAL'S AFTERMATH, AS WITH THE MAJORITY OF MAJOR COURTROOM cases, dealt mostly with the victors. Just like in life, the victors reap the spoils. And the losers, well, they lick their wounds and, hopefully, prepare for another day. The Anthony "Niggsy" Arnone murder trial was no exception to this unwritten, but universal rule about courtroom winners and losers.

"A jubilant Joseph Santaguida credited the common sense of the Erie community and the intelligence of 12 particular members of that community for Saturday's acquittal of his client, Anthony 'Niggsy' Arnone," the *Erie Times-News* reported in its day-after-the-trial Sunday morning coverage.

"I think we had a very intelligent jury," Attorney Santaguida said. Perhaps the jury would not have been considered as such by Santaguida had the verdict gone the other way? "The jury said 'Don't bring us this kind of witness. Bring us real evidence,'" the defense counsel was quoted in the Erie newspaper, referring to several prosecution witnesses, not the least of which was Caesar Montevecchio, whose criminal past and his current motives for testifying were at best questionable. But prosecutors don't get to pick and choose witnesses the way many defense lawyers do. Like them or not, prosecutors are stuck with whom they have.

In apparent good humor for the first time since the trial began a week earlier, the Philadelphia lawyer commended the Erie County jury for its difficult efforts and careful consideration and deliberation of the facts presented in open court. Referring to Montevecchio as the prosecution witness presenting key evidence, Santaguida said, "It was unreliable. A person lies once, he lies twice . . . Why should they believe him now in the most serious forum, the court of law, where a life is at stake?"

Another jury had believed Montevecchio when it convicted Robert Dorler, the man Montevecchio claimed he recruited to murder Dovishaw on behalf of the now-acquitted Arnone. But that conviction was old news – and was now less than important, or so it seemed, in this latest jury verdict that culminated the Bolo Dovishaw murder investigation.

When the jury selection began in the Arnone trial, the *voir dire* questions were straight forward. The would-be jurors were asked whether they knew any of the attorneys in the case, any of the police officers involved in the arrest, or anyone else from a lengthy list of potential trial witnesses read aloud in open court.

Other questions were posed as the jury members were being empanelled. "Do you know Anthony Arnone or anyone in his family?" and "Have you ever conducted business at his store?"

One person in the jury pool was known to DiPaolo from his investigations, but he and prosecutors felt the relationship was not significant enough to keep the person from serving on the Arnone jury panel. Eventually, this person was retained on the final list of 12 jurors who decided Arnone's guilt or innocence. Several months after the not guilty verdict, out of sheer curiosity, DiPaolo approached a friend who also knew the juror in question. DiPaolo asked that he approach the juror and ask that they meet off-the-record with DiPaolo. The cop wanted to get the person's take on how the Commonwealth had failed to prove what the prosecution thought was an airtight case.

Jim Miller advised DiPaolo the juror's initial response was, "No! Absolutely not!" And then, "It's over and I'm not talking to anyone!"

"Mills," who for years played slo-pitch with DiPaolo, said, "Dominick, I think you're on to something. This person acts nervous and out of character every time I see them." Mills also told DiPaolo that others, out of curiosity, attempted to speak with the juror about the trial, but the juror didn't want to talk with anyone.

"I'll give it some time, and then give it another shot," Mills said.

"No, leave it alone," the cop responded. "The last thing I need is to be accused of putting pressure on a juror!" But DiPaolo thought it strange indeed that the juror would refuse to meet with him. And stranger still, he thought, that the response was so emphatic and emotional. It aroused the cop's radar-like, built-in suspicions and DiPaolo attempted to talk with several of the juror's work-related acquaintances. They were just as ardent as the juror in refusing to speak with him. He learned from others that these co-workers were doing much talking among themselves. They were aware, for example, that although the juror might not have actually known Arnone personally, the person ran a number of organizational fundraisers that purchased pizzas from Arnone's Italian importing business.

DiPaolo, upon further probing, also learned that the juror's uncle was heavily involved in the illegal numbers game allegedly operated for many years out of a family-run Italian food warehouse near Pittsburgh. However, with this information coming second and third-hand, there was little else DiPaolo could do.

Throughout the years that followed, it wasn't lost on DiPaolo that this same juror did much to avoid him whenever they were in immediate proximity of one another.

"This jury member always put their head down to avoid even eye contact," DiPaolo would later say, careful not to refer to the juror's gender. Just a guilty feeling? DiPaolo would wonder to himself. Or something else? DiPaolo believes he will never know. And, even now, so many years later, he won't comment on the juror's identity.

Still, immediately following the Arnone verdict one could ponder why the Niggsy Arnone jury and the Robert Dorler jury saw many of the same facts presented by prosecution and defense in different ways.

In his interview with the Erie newspaper, Attorney Santaguida had claimed that the prosecution's evidence was often contradictory. "It just doesn't make sense," he said, referring to prosecution claims that Arnone stole hundreds of thousands of dollars from Dovishaw while still taking out several bank loans and owning a business in financial difficulty at the same time.

Santaguida wasn't bashful about indicating that the victory was sweet. "I would compare it as one of my more favorable cases," he said. He cited another highly publicized case he had a part of winning, along with several other lawyers. It was a Philadelphia mob trial involving members of the Nicodemo Scarfaro family. While there were multiple lawyers and defendants, "Here, where it's one defendant, you feel maybe you were the one to sway the jury," he said in reference to his own impassioned defense of Arnone. His attacks on several prosecution witnesses had to have had an impact in the minds of at least some jury members, even the now questionable one of DiPaolo's later curiosity.

It wasn't the sought after culmination to the many long years of often drudgery and daunting police legwork that DiPaolo had been hoping for. But the jury had spoken. It was a tough pill to swallow, but DiPaolo, perhaps as much as, or even more than anyone involved, still believed in the system. And it was the only way the cop could look at it without getting nauseous.

CHAPTER 51

AT THE ARNONE HOMESTEAD THAT SATURDAY AFTERNOON, NOBODY was getting nauseous. It seemed that the entire neighborhood shook with a boisterous victory party already underway.

It was there that Santaguida again spoke on behalf of the acquitted defendant and his family members, and was quoted in the Sunday newspaper, "All he wanted was a fair trial," the defense lawyer said. "He feels he got it and thanks God that justice was served. A jury of his peers heard the charge and didn't believe it. He feels he has been vindicated."

Speaking now from the winning side's perspective, and perhaps momentarily forgetting the pre-verdict concerns, Santaguida said his client had sincerely believed that the case would be resolved in his favor. "It's been a tremendous ordeal for his family and loved ones," Santaguida said. What he didn't add was what most on the law enforcement side of the fence already knew: In criminal cases, it is the defendant's family that often suffers. Ask members of Caesar Montevecchio's long-tortured family.

Prosecutor Ebert, while telling the *Erie Times-News* that he was disappointed with the verdict, said he nonetheless still believed justice was indeed served. "When it's 'not guilty,' the system has been served. I am happy for Mr. Arnone's family." He did add, however, that his disappointment over the verdict extended to the police officers who labored long and hard for seven years.

"I certainly don't feel bad for taking this case to trial," the state prosecutor said. Ebert apparently felt compelled, and justifiably so after Attorney Santaguida's fairly harsh and critical public comments, to defend the prosecution's use of the career criminal Caesar Montevecchio. Even Ebert had earlier called Montevecchio "a scum, a rat, a criminal."

Caesar Montevecchio, an openly-acknowledged participant in the crime, had to be used by the state in the prosecution of the alleged co-conspirators. The state had no other alternative than Montevecchio as its leading Arnone murder trial witness. "It's not a question of anything to rethink," Ebert said when asked by a newspaper reporter about his decision to use Montevecchio as the key prosecution witness.

DiPaolo believed that if the verdict had gone the other way, Mastrey would have been next up on the court docket. *She caught a big break,* the detective thought. Ebert and DiPaolo had talked prior to the trial about filing charges. But now, there would be no more prosecutions in connection the Dovishaw killing.

Niggsy Arnone was now free to operate his food importing business.

Confessed murder arranger Caesar Montevecchio, despite his cooperation with police and prosecutors during two murder trials, pleading guilty to the murder charge and over 60 other crimes, including the Nardo burglary and the charges reinstated from 1984, went to jail. It could have been life in prison without the deal. But DiPaolo put aside any bias he still harbored in connection with the "hit" Montevecchio put out on him.

But the tale continued for convicted Dovishaw triggerman Robert Dorler of Medina, Ohio. He was serving his life prison sentence with no parole when it was discovered "Ash Wednesday" wasn't Dorler's only hit. When Dorler starting talking to DiPaolo about Erie crimes in 1986, the Ohioan told the detective sergeant about a mob war in Youngstown, adding that if DiPaolo let him out of jail, he would try to find out about contract hits in the Ohio city on Joey Naples, Joey DeRose Sr., Joey DeRose Jr., Dominick Senzarino Jr., and Jim Cononico, aka "Peeps." But DiPaolo, not trusting Dorler, wasn't about to put him out on the street again, especially without any guarantee of success.

Ohio armed robberies dating back to 1954 had Dorler in and out of prison, often doing hard time. During a stint at the Marion State Penitentiary, Dorler's roomie was Ronald "Ronnie Crab" Carabbia, who, along with his brothers, Charles "Charlie the Crab" Carabbia and Orlie Carabbia, ran the Youngstown mob. (It was "Ronnie Crab" who in 1977, along with Erie's Ray Ferritto and Pasquale Cisternino, murdered Cleveland's Danny Greene.) Dorler, released from prison in 1981, immediately hooked up with "Orlie" Carabbia and began working for the Youngstown mob. Because he wasn't Italian, Dorler never would be a "made man" in the Mafia, but he was a faithful soldier for a while.

That year, "Orlie's" cousin, Junior Senzarino, double-crossed the organization over bookmaking money. Along with "Skinny Sam" Fossesca, a made man, Dorler was offered and accepted the "hit" assignment on Orlie's cousin.

One night as Senzarino pulled into his garage, Dorler followed him inside, hiding behind Senzarino's car after the garage door closed. Using a sawed-off shotgun, Dorler plugged Senzarino twice, once in the head, and again in the chest. But finding himself trapped in the garage, Dorler panicked, punched out a window and leaped through it, severely cutting his arm and face in the process, and leaving a blood spatter trial inside and out. Police not only found blood on the window curtain, but also a blood-soaked hankie outside.

In 2001, more than two decades later the Ohio Organized Crime Task Force, checking out cold cases involving Youngstown mob murders and so-called "Freelance Hit Men," got a DNA match between Dorler and blood at the Senzarino home. Dorler was indicted and snitched, as Dorler usually did when cornered, this time on his buddy "Skinny Sam" Fossesca. (Fossesca was indicted for killing Joe DeRose Jr.) Dorler pleaded guilty to the Senzarino hit, and was rewarded with a life sentence to be served concurrent with the Dovishaw killing. "Charlie the Crab" went missing in 1981, never to be heard from again. "Ronnie Crab" continues to do life without parole for the Greene murder, while Orlie, the eldest of the brothers, passed of natural causes.

Thinking back to 1986, DiPaolo mused that con-man Dorler actually really *did* know the Youngstown hit men. He had been one of them! It would not have surprised DiPaolo to learn Dorler was also involved in the Corporal Robert Owen murder, but DiPaolo quickly determined the Ohio man was in prison at the time. Dorler never did serve out his concurrent life sentences for ending the lives of "Ash Wednesday" and Senzarino. The killer was found lifeless one November 2008 morning, *morta* in his cell of a massive heart attack.

Meanwhile, Billy Bourjaily would serve his time for being an accomplice to murder, plus the robberies.

Daily life in Erie continued as usual – both at the downtown Police Headquarters and in the city's west side "Little Italy" neighborhood that spanned the likes of crooks like Montevecchio and cops like DiPaolo.

"This chapter in Erie's history is closed," Ebert said with a great sense of finality, if not outright relief.

CHAPTER 52

"YOU TRIED TO FRAME ME!"

That's what Erie and regional newspaper readers woke up to the day following the verdict. As the Sunday morning headlines in the *Erie Times-News* December 10, 1989, screamed Niggsy Arnone's accusations against an Erie police officer, a smaller headline, also on Page One, gave context and the perspective from the other side – the longtime investigating cop's side.

In a smaller side-bar to the main story, the newspaper speculated that next to the defendant, Dom DiPaolo might also have had the most riding on the jury's verdict.

No "might" about it, DiPaolo thought as he reviewed what seemed like a lifetime investigation with its many turns, twists and characters, angelic and evil. He had invested countless hours in this investigation and indeed had much riding on its outcome.

The newspaper story also said the verdict was DiPaolo's first ever loss in a capital murder case. It was a distinction that did little to cheer DiPaolo in those post verdict days.

"There's no doubt it's a little disappointing, on the last link of this chain, not to get a conviction," the 20-year police veteran told the newspaper. "In looking at this investigation from its inception and going through the years with the people involved in this case, you take the best type of case that you have to the jury."

The police officer expressed some degree of satisfaction that the prosecution was not a complete loss, telling the paper the Dorler trial jury members saw the evidence differently than the Arnone jury. He emphasized that dependence upon a jury of one's peers is what makes our criminal justice system great. His sincere belief in the criminal justice system, which he had long and faithfully served, came through to any would-be doubters. Eyeing his involvement philosophically, he said he wasn't sorry about any aspect of the investigation. Looking back, he said, he wouldn't change any aspect of his probe if he had it to do again. He pointed out that the prosecution took the case to the grand jury and to court, adding that juries make decisions that they have to live with.

If jury members second-guessed their own verdict, it would not be known, at least not publicly. Although DiPaolo later unsuccessfully attempted to engage one of the jurors, more out of professional and personal curiosity than any residual hard feelings, he would never learn what went on inside that jury room during the hours of deliberations between the 12 strangers.

He said the investigation was especially difficult for him because he was well-acquainted with, and in a few cases even related to, several of those who surfaced in the lengthy murder probe. It would be difficult to have grown up of Italian descent in Erie and reached adulthood without knowing and/or being related to hundreds of others of extremely similar life circumstances and backgrounds, DiPaolo thought, but did not articulate to the Erie newspaper reporter conducting the post-mortem Arnone trial interview. But softly and with a sigh, he did tell the reporter it was an often difficult investigation for him because he personally knew many of the participants and their families.

Despite those sometimes close or casual friendships and relationships, the cop DiPaolo above all had been sworn to serve and protect the City of Erie's residents, so he did what he had to do, he told the reporter.

Even with the loss, DiPaolo insisted to the newspaper reporter that he had become a better officer and person because of the results of plying his craft during the ongoing and lengthy murder probe. He said the experience of working any case makes one a better police officer, and that with all cases being different, cops learn from each.

DiPaolo acknowledged that with the culmination of the long "Bolo" Dovishaw murder probe, he was prepared to move on in his professional and personal life. The time had come. He was prepared to take on new challenges. But first, he told reporters, his priority would be to take a short vacation to recharge his batteries. Then he would return to the work-a-day life in the Erie Police Detective Division, where each day brought on new challenges on behalf of the citizens of his city – eastside, west side, Little Italy – they all represented Erie, and he represented all.

No matter what cases would be thrown his way in the coming months and years, he mused to himself, he would not quickly forget the Dovishaw case, or the failed plot on his life and all his family endured.

DiPaolo at times was criticized for investing so much into solving an undesirable racketeer's murder. Dovishaw, a well-known Erie bookmaker and gambler, lived an entire life of crime and was often disliked by many.

But he concluded his interview saying nobody, no matter what some did with their lives, should die as "Ash Wednesday" did. It was a good statement, and one that probably said more about the cop himself than about any facet of his years-long homicide investigation.

CHAPTER 53

FOLLOWING THE SPLIT VERDICTS IN THE BOLO DOVISHAW MURDER trials, life in the City of Erie in the northwestern-most corner of the Commonwealth of Pennsylvania returned to relative normalcy. That included Detective Sergeant Dominick DiPaolo's life.

He continued coaching the Sacred Heart boys high school basketball team in the Catholic Youth Organization league. Between football and basketball, he coached for 25 years, along with Wally Coughlin and Rick "Snowy" Herbstritt, in 1991 winning the Pennsylvania C.Y.O. basketball state title with 29-1 record. Father John Detisch, Deacon Craig Heuser, and Sister Nancy Fischer, team spiritual advisors, good naturedly took credit for the championship run! DiPaolo continued to be player/manager of The Sports Page slow-pitch team every summer, taking enormous pride that his son, Pat, who started off as the team's bat boy 17 years earlier, led the team in hitting the last three years the team played together. The highlight of Dominick's athletic career was playing alongside his son.

The return to normalcy included sweaty summers and snowy, shivery winters. Two seasons, mocking Erie people are fond of saying, winter and road work. For the first time in a quarter century, a new mayor, Erie's first woman to hold the office. Then, the death of the legendary Lou Tullio. Life and death. Both went on as usual.

Most of the stars of the Dovishaw murder era quickly faded into obscurity behind the steady and daily onslaught of new criminal activity.

Street gangs and street crime. "Organized crime" per se, evaporated with the times. The actual headliners of the Dovishaw and other investigations became hazy memories. Their time under the bright lights – Bolo's, Caesar's, Ray's, Cy's, Ricky's, Joey's – their time had passed, only to be replaced by a new generation of criminals. Rookie bank robbers, burglars, home-invaders. But not organized like their predecessors.

With the Dovishaw case in the past, Caesar Montevecchio served a few years in prison, was released, and led a mostly quiet life compared to his once-legendary, incendiary and volatile Dillinger-like past until suffering a debilitating fall down the stairs, a home accident that mostly confined him to his house, just another sick and tired old man with memories of ill-gotten gain, but not glory. Never glory. A life wasted. And now, for the first time in their marriage, Bonnie Montevecchio would always know exactly where to find her once on-the-go, career-criminal husband. DiPaolo often wondered whether Bonnie remembered asking him in 1987 if she and Caesar could trust him. She asked if they would grow old together, or be separated. And now, the answer is evident. DiPaolo did not lie to them.

"Set-up" man Anthony "Cy" Ciotti would live out the rest of his life in a nursing home. At age 86, the convicted drug trafficker, burglar, forger, robber, gambler, among other listings on his five-page rap sheet, was still up to his former life's ventures. He had been in another nursing home previously, but allegedly was thrown out for having whiskey and wine brought in, then selling it to the home's residents. Early in 2013, Carol Pella, who DiPaolo credited as being one of Erie's finest investigative journalists from the 1970s through the 1990s, was suffering from the final stages of Lupus and respiratory failure. Under Hospice care, Pella was admitted to a nursing home. On her first day, still the reporter, she phoned DiPaolo – a longtime friend – saying, "Dominick, this is unbelievable! My room is right across from Cy Ciotti! Can you believe this!" Still mentally sharp although her body was wracked with disease, she recalled that after Ciotti had been convicted of the Record Bar robbery in Erie and was led by cops on a perp walk, he spit at her when she tried to interview him. One day at the nursing home, Pella and Ciotti passed each other in the corridor. She told DiPaolo that Ciotti pointed at her, telling his nurse, "Keep her away from me!" Pella died that March at the age of 62. DiPaolo recalls her famous investigative "I-Team," as well as her great friendship.

As mentioned earlier, the murderously-motivated Ohioan Robert Dorler served hard time in prison until he died there, alone in his cell, in 2008. For him, there would be no mercy.

Mob killer Ray Ferritto moved to Florida with his wife, Susan DeSantis Ferritto, in hopes of living out his golden years in relative peace. Once there, as though by judicial decree from on high, he was totally and fatally consumed by an insidious cancer. Ferritto perished in a horrible death many believed was too good for the admitted hit man who had plied his craft on innumerable victims, perhaps some as evil as himself, but also those who could be considered innocent.

After three years of being baby-sat by Erie police, on July 8, 1987, "Fat Sam" Esper, who had been kept in various "safe house" apartments and hotels throughout Erie County, was finally accepted into the Federal Witness Protection Program. It was that date in 1987 when Dominick DiPaolo and U.S. Attorney Don Lewis drove Fat Sam to meet U.S. Marshals, who took him to a secret destination to spend the rest of his life. DiPaolo thought the drop off/exchange point was almost poetic – it was off Exit 34 off Interstate 90 in Ohio at Mr. C's Pancake House – the same restaurant where Caesar Montevecchio met Robert Dorler and Billy Bourjaily on January 4, 1983, to pay them for the hit on Bolo Dovishaw.

As life moved on, Arnone's defense lawyer, Joseph Santaguida continued his successful criminal defense practice in Philadelphia. In May 2011, the Associated Press reported that Santaguida was representing a "Godfather"-like reputed crime boss and mob leader named Joseph "Uncle Joe" Ligambi.

After his trial, Anthony "Niggsy" Arnone returned to his West 18th and Cherry Street food importing business, eventually participating in opening a restaurant across the street in the heart of Erie's equally legendary "Little Italy." As life in the slow lane moved on, many forgot about his close brush with the law and the murder accusations against him. After two decades of freedom, Niggsy, like his pals Ray Ferritto and Joey Scutella, died of cancer at the age of 71 on September 1, 2010. His obituary in the Erie newspaper was full of kudos and praise for the man who once had a try-out with the New York Yankees, who passed "after a courageous battle with cancer." Obituaries in Erie's newspaper were not news stories, but paid ads. Yet, when DiPaolo got the news of Arnone's death, he called a confidante and left this short voice mail message: "Niggsy is with Bolo. Do you think they're in the same barbute game?"

Meanwhile, Theresa Mastrey was fired by PennBank for her conduct as assistant manager – hiding almost $40,000 in cash for her cousin in her own safe-deposit box. The money, it was determined, came from illegal gambling proceeds. She had also admitted forging the name of a notary public while working for PennBank.

She later filed a civil lawsuit against the bank to get back her job along with two years' back-pay. During the jury trial, under cross examination by the bank's lawyer, Attorney Roger Taft, Mastrey said the testimony about the illegal gambling money in her safe-deposit box came from other witnesses in the Arnone trial.

DiPaolo testified for the bank about the Dovishaw investigation, Arnone's and Mastrey's safe-deposit boxes, including the contents. He told Taft during a trial recess that Mastrey must have forgotten about her Aunt Amelia "Maya" Giamanco, her two daughters, Theresa "Tree" Giamanco-Altadonna Miller, Roseann "Roe" Giamanco-Altadonna DelSandro, and Roseann's husband, David DelSandro. All were arrested for booking illegal numbers for Big Al DelSandro, who Mastrey said was the source of the money. When the trial resumed, Mastrey testified that it was Attorney Ebert who had made the comment about the notary forgery during the Arnone trial; she had only agreed to it.

The jury returned immediately with a verdict for the bank. There was no appeal. DiPaolo thought those jurors saw her in a different light than the Arnone panel.

Later, Cousin Roseann petitioned the court to get back her $40,000 and two silver wedding bands. But prior to the hearing, an agreement was reached between the parties: The rings were returned to Roseann. The state kept the loot.

Other Erie crime figures and cops also faded away with the passage of time. They were replaced by a new breed and generation of even more un-organized criminals, along with cops who knew precious little about Erie's previous ruling underworld leaders. In a phrase, the "institutional memory" of the law enforcement branch of Erie government had evaporated – gone were such post World War II law enforcement mob experts such as Eddie Allen, Jim Kinnane, Frankie Schwartz and several others who started their careers in the 1940s, 1950s and 1960s.

DiPaolo, was one of the few left who knew of the past and how it related to the present. For example, several months after Niggsy passed, an Erie police leader phoned District Court Judge DiPaolo to ask, "Dominick, I know I sound pretty dumb, but can you please tell me whether the Dovishaw case is still open? The FBI just called to ask whether the case is open, and, hell, I couldn't even tell them."

"No," DiPaolo told one of Erie's top cops. "No, that case was closed years ago." And then DiPaolo thought, *imagine that, the FBI not knowing what's going on!* Yet today's crime-fighting police officers, if ignorant about the subtleties of Erie's long and storied and almost rich underworld past, at least do know something about street crime, gangs and the brand-new cyber offenses.

DiPaolo continued with the Erie Police Department, still handling most major crimes as they were committed and reported, and still specialized in homicides. He also became a training officer for rookie detectives. Some made it; some didn't. One of his trainees, Frank Kwitowski, would later become captain and the head of the Detective Division. DiPaolo headed four more homicide investigations and was again successful with guilty verdicts returned, including life in prison for two men, in the cases that went before juries.

The last homicide DiPaolo investigated was the beating death of 44-year-old James "Shorty" Stanley, who had been left for dead in an alley behind the boarding house where he resided. Stanley and his friend, Allen Garfield, 41, were beaten by Anthony Paolello, 45, after a woman who had been raped by Paolello in another room of the boarding house ran to Stanley's and Garfield's room for help. Paolello, along with Daniel Funt, 20, who also lived there, and Anthony DeFranco, 28, known as "Tone Capone," beat the two men because of the possibility they would report the rape to police. The assailants also took $70 from Stanley. Garfield made it to a nearby bar before he passed out. Bar patrons called for an ambulance, which apparently saved his life. After 20 days in intensive care, Garfield was well enough to tell DiPaolo and his partner, Detective Gerald McShane, who had beat them.

Paolello was found guilty of first degree murder and sentenced to death, the penalty later revoked and converted to life without parole. Funt got up to 55 years for third degree murder and robbery. Tone Capone was offered a plea deal to third degree murder. In return, he would have gotten 20 years in prison. But Attorney William Weichler, Attorney Ambrose's law partner, turned down the plea offer. His client was convicted of second degree murder. Leaving the courtroom, the defendant sneered at DiPaolo. Capone was sentenced to life in prison with no parole. He rolled the dice and got snake eyes, DiPaolo later said, also recalling he had been the guy who was proud to say Caesar Montevecchio was his idol.

But DiPaolo's time as a cop also began running short – this of his own choosing. As much as he relished locking up the bad guys, he had been interested in politics for many years. He managed to craft and hone that interest into an art form. Some of it was in his genes, passed on by his dad, a popular west Erie ward healer. For DiPaolo, Erie's Sixth Ward politics represented a love and a fascination. But wherever his interest originated, it was more than a passing fancy. He was an elected committeeman, and Sixth Ward Democratic Chairman for 14 years.

By 1993, just four years after the Arnone murder trial ended in an acquittal, the political bug finally bit into the Erie cop – and hard. With all the confidence of a rookie politico, but a confidence bolstered by his "Inside Baseball" knowledge of Erie's stormy political scene, DiPaolo tossed his hat into the five-candidate race for district judge in the huge and politically motivated Sixth Ward – one of the City of Erie's largest political subdivisions. It was a major decision, running for public office, as DiPaolo had to take a leave of absence from the Erie Police Department. It meant no pay. No health care insurance. With two kids in college, a mortgage and car payments, DiPaolo had to hope and pray what he was doing was right. But in politics, it's all about the timing and DiPaolo had no doubts the time for him to run for office was right. After a few loans, much breath-holding and a tough four months, the DiPaolo family got through the campaign.

Of the five candidates in that 1993 election for Sixth Ward District Judge, DiPaolo easily won both the Democratic and Republican nominations, demolishing the field, including the sitting incumbent district judge.

Dr. David Kozak, Professor of Public Policy at Gannon University, a presidential scholar and perhaps Erie's foremost political observer and commentator, told DiPaolo after that primary election that he considered it "amazing" DiPaolo pulled the number of votes he did in a five-person race, especially since it was suspected a large number of Italian families in the Sixth Ward were working against him – Arnone, DiNicola, Scutella, Cimino, Calabrese, Mastrostefano, Ciotti, Serafini and Giamanco-Altadonna, to name a few – all those he had dealt with during his police career.

The Friday night before the May primary election, DiPaolo and a group of his volunteers ended up at The Sports Page for pizza and suds after campaigning all evening. Before long, exhausted Dom and his wife, Janet, bid goodnight to the volunteers and left for home. A short time later, son Patrick, then studying at Thiel College, arrived in town with his buddies to help with the final days of his dad's campaign. Also helping out was the DiPaolo's college student daughter, Dawn, who was home with her friends to campaign for Dom. Both DiPaolo kids had gone directly to the "The Page," hoping to surprise their parents, only to learn from part-owner Rich Carideo that the DiPaolos left minutes earlier.

As the entire group enjoyed beer while waiting for their pizza, a young woman approached Pat DiPaolo and asked, "Are you Dom DiPaolo's son?" When Pat responded in the affirmative, the woman spit in the young man's face, then walked away. The rest of the group, stunned, could only stare in disbelief. Pat, meanwhile, went to the men's room, where Carideo brought him a fresh towel and apologized for the incident. Daughter Dawn, and her friends Kara Schlosser, Jenny Kupczyk and Renee DeRose, wanted to approach the offending woman, but Pat would not hear of it and directed the group to leave. Several days later, Carideo told DiPaolo how impressed the others were with Pat's actions, with all knowing that just four days before the election the woman wanted to provoke an incident. Only later, DiPaolo said, did he learn the woman was Kelli Scutella, daughter of Joe Scutella. DiPaolo said she was working on the committee of the incumbent that DiPaolo that was running against. But in the end, it was DiPaolo who enjoyed the satisfaction of winning on election night. Years later, Rich Carideo and Peter Pallotto still talk about the pre-election incident at The Page, and about how Pat, who starred in football, wrestling and baseball in college, walked away from a potentially explosive and embarrassing situation that could have harmed his dad's chances in the election. The DiPaolo kids, unlike some families at the time, others said, had values and respect.

And so it was in January 1994, after 25 years of exemplary service with the Erie Police Department, Det. Sgt. DiPaolo became District Court Judge DiPaolo and a leading member of Pennsylvania's minor judiciary.

Before DiPaolo left the service of the City of Erie, he was honored by Erie City Council as the most decorated police officer in Erie's

200-year history. The citation pointed out that DiPaolo was not only the recipient of the "Policeman of the Year Award," but also the Erie County Bar Association's prestigious "Liberty Bell Award," the Erie Insurance Club's "Dedicated Public Service Award," and Mercyhurst College's coveted "James Kinnane Law Enforcement Award," named to honor Erie's long-serving Federal Bureau of Investigation Special Agent in Charge. Among many honors, DiPaolo was inducted into the National Police Hall of Fame in Miami, Florida. During a quarter-century police career, he had amassed 2,006 criminal arrests. He investigated 32 murders. Many of those murder defendants are still serving life terms.

DiPaolo had also been successful in 185 jury trials that ended with convictions, as well as seemingly countless cases that culminated with the defendants understanding the hopelessness of their situations and pleading guilty. Hearing the word "guilty" from the jury had always provided DiPaolo with a motivating rush. In his entire career, only two homicide cases had culminated with acquittals by juries.

The Niggsy Arnone acquittal was a bitter pill to swallow. A stinging loss after such a long and meticulous investigation that spanned the better part of the eastern United States.

The other acquittal involved Louis DiNicola, a roofer who in 1979 was charged with torching a house in Erie's Little Italy. The motive for the fire allegedly was that a woman who lived in the home had spurned the defendant's affections. The woman's two small children and an adult man who lived elsewhere in the two-apartment house had died in the resultant inferno that swept through the structure.

DiPaolo and Detective Donald Gunter later arrested DiNicola, charging him with one count of arson and three counts of homicide.

Attorney Bernard Siegel, a former Erie County First Assistant DA, was brought into the case as a special prosecutor after the Erie County District Attorney's office recused itself from participating in the prosecution. The recusal reportedly occurred because in 1979, then Assistant District Attorney Tom Ridge, spoke about the case to Ron DiNicola, brother of the defendant, while Ron was a student at Harvard, Ridge's alma mater. Because of the perception of a possible conflict, Attorney Siegel was brought in to prosecute.

Despite the almost entirely circumstantial evidence presented by Special Prosecutor Bernard Siegel in 1980, the jury panel convicted DiNicola of all the charges that DiPaolo had brought against him. DiNicola was sentenced to serve three life terms, plus another 20 years, in a state penitentiary. The jury had 46 minutes before returning to the courtroom with the stunning guilty verdict.

In 1994, some 15 years after the crime and DiPaolo had ended his police career, DiNicola's new attorneys won a new trial for their client. The Pennsylvania Supreme Court granted a new trial based upon just one line of improper testimony out of the many hundreds of pages of testimony. The new defense team was headed by DiNicola's brother, Ron, a prominent lawyer who staunchly defended his client with brotherly motivation and love. Other members of new dream team included former U.S. Attorney General Ramsey Clark, former legendary New York City police officer Frank Serpico (portrayed by Al Pacino in a movie of the same name), and Dr. Cyril Wecht, the controversial Allegheny County coroner who helped investigate the deaths of luminaries such as Elvis Presley, Marilyn Monroe, and even President Kennedy. Wecht was indeed the medical examiner for the stars. Several local attorneys were also a part of the defense. The group was considered as much a "dream" legal team then as the lawyers who later represented O.J. Simpson during the former NFL and movie star's murder trial in Los Angeles.

Dom DiPaolo was standing outside of Erie County Judge Richard Nygaard's courtroom, waiting for the start of a bond hearing requested by the "Dream Team" when Hyle Richmond, longtime courthouse reporter and evening news anchor for WICU-TV, Erie's NBC affiliate, stopped to say, "Wow, Dominick! This is a real high show today with all these heavy hitters!" Just then, a man in his early 50s, thin, with a full beard and wearing a suit that appeared two sizes too large and with no tie, asked, "Excuse me, are you Dominick DiPaolo?" When DiPaolo acknowledged that he was, the man extended his hand, saying, "I'm Frank Serpico. Heard a lot about you!"

Slightly stunned, DiPaolo said, "Heard a lot about you, too."

The men shook hands and after polite small talk, Serpico said, "Hey, nice meeting you."

"It's an honor," DiPaolo said. "Read your book. Saw your movie a few times and I believe you are a very honorable man. I respect you for what you did, and I'm sure that once you get in to this case and determine what really took place, you will be testifying for us."

Smiling, Serpico said, "I appreciate your kind words and will definitely talk with you later!"

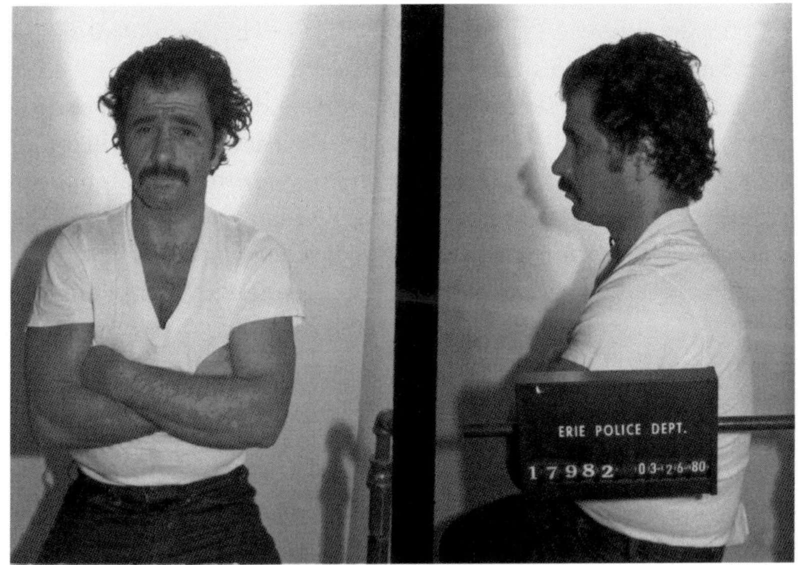

Louis Paul DiNicola was convicted in 1980 on three counts of murder and one count of arson and sentenced to three consecutive life terms. Fifteen years later, he was granted a new trial on appeal and found not guilty. (Courtesy of Erie Police Department)

DiPaolo believed Frank Serpico was in Erie for the media. He did not testify. There was nothing for him to add to the defense. But, by the time the second Louis DiNicola trial began in Erie County Court, one key witness had passed away, and several others had changed their stories. Also, one of the hired defense witnesses in the trial, Dr. Cyril Wecht, established doubt in the minds of the jurors by introducing forensic evidence with which DiPaolo disagreed.

(In 2008, Wecht was indicted in Pittsburgh by overzealous Feds, DiPaolo believes, including U.S. Attorney Mary Beth Buchanan. Wecht was charged with 41 public corruption counts as the government spent over $200,000 to bring him to trial for supposedly improperly using $1,700 in his public position as Allegheny County Coroner. After a federal jury was declared hung, Buchanan announced she would re-try Wecht. She assigned Leo Dillon as lead prosecutor for the second trial. Dillon, an Allegheny County assistant district attorney in the early 1980s, had tried Wecht for theft. Wecht was acquitted. As a result of this new trial, however, the U.S. House Judiciary Committee investigated

Buchanan and others, as there was new concern about select prosecution in the Wecht case and others. Out of the 365 cases Buchanan prosecuted, 298 were against Democrats and 65 against Republicans. In the Wecht case, she was accused of intimidating former jurors by sending agents to their homes and work places to determine why they did not convict the Democrat. Former Pittsburgh Mayor Tom Murphy said the charges and trial were examples of excessive prosecution by the feds, adding they were driven by ideology rather than truth and justice. Buchanan and Dillon backed off. Wecht was not re-tried on the federal charge. Buchanan resigned in 2009.)

Combined with the high-powered defense team, the death of witnesses, a less-than-supercharged prosecution team that wasn't the A-Team from the first trial, DiPaolo had an intuition that this case was in jeopardy. It was. At the second DiNicola trial, just as DiPaolo had predicted, 15 years after the fatal fire, DiNicola was acquitted and then ultimately released from his incarceration.

There was one other homicide DiPaolo and Gunter investigated that both hoped would have had a different outcome: On December 10, 1980, Roger Kent Hamilton, 38, a maintenance worker at an Erie McDonald's, was gunned down while taking out trash at 2 a.m. Later, from the spent casing found at the scene, it was determined Hamilton was shot with a .22 caliber weapon. Sam Covelli, the restaurant's owner, posted a $25,000 reward for information leading to the arrest and conviction of the murderer. Several days later, a witness reported Hamilton had argued with another man at the restaurant's rear door. When the victim fell to the ground, the other person fled. But the witness observed neither a flash from a discharging weapon nor did he hear the gun's report.

The witness agreed to undergo a polygraph exam and also hypnosis, an investigative tool used at that time. The witness was placed under hypnosis by William Vorsheck of the Erie Institute of Hypnosis, who helped DiPaolo previously and was used in many police investigations. Results from the lie detector and the hypnosis were positive and conclusive.

After identifying the murder suspect as Richard Armstrong, 34, the detectives and Assistant District Attorney Frank Kroto agreed Armstrong would be picked up and a search warrant issued for his apartment. When the officers approached Armstrong, he said of Hamilton, "Fuck him. He had it coming!" Then he lawyered up.

During a photo line-up, three other witnesses identified Armstrong as being at McDonald's at the time of the murder and Armstrong was charged with the crime.

A short time later, while Millcreek Township Police were investigating an armed robbery and homicide at the Ponderosa Steak House, just west of Erie, 45- and 22-caliber spent shell casings were found at the scene. Mark Taft was shot several times in the back and while he was on the ground. DiPaolo arranged for Pennsylvania State Police ballistics expert Sgt. Virgil "Butch" Jellison to compare the .22 shell from the Hamilton murder with that found at the Taft homicide scene. DiPaolo and Gunter still had serious reservations about the Hamilton murder and wanted all possibilities checked. Jellison had no doubt the .22 shells matched. The charges against Armstrong were dismissed after this new evidence was reported to ADA Kroto.

Through Millcreek Police, John Peter Laskaris was identified as a suspect in the murder, robbery and an attempted bank job, and arrested in West Virginia. Just several years earlier, Laskaris was involved in a homicide investigation surrounding the death of Erie Strong Vincent High School student Debbie Gama, who was killed by her teacher, Raymond Payne. Laskaris agreed to a deal, testifying against Payne. who was convicted and sentenced to life in prison without parole. (In the early 1970s, DiPaolo had received information from Al Bilotti, an Erie school police officer, that Raymond Payne was providing students with marijuana. Police Chief Sam Gemelli advised the school superintendent of what Payne was doing, but Payne denied the accusations and the investigation was dropped. "If we, along with Bilotti, could have continued to investigate Payne, maybe Debbie Gama would still be alive," DiPaolo later observed.)

In the Hamilton investigation, Millcreek Police Detective Sergeant Richard Nagosky advised DiPaolo that more information could be available from Laskaris and Edward Palmer. DiPaolo and Gunter traveled to Fairmont, West Virginia, where the two were being held on other charges. The detectives learned Laskaris and Palmer had planned to rob McDonald's the night in question. They had inside information from an employee dating Laskaris that no bank deposits would be made over the weekend and the safe would be stuffed with cash. As the two approached the parking lot, Armstrong and Hamilton were either talking or arguing at the rear door, which Laskaris' girlfriend left unlocked. Laskaris and Palmer were upset the other two were in their way; one shot was fired from a .22 automatic fitted with a silencer. Hamilton dropped to the ground, Armstrong ran, and Laskaris and Palmer quickly drove away.

A month later, Laskaris, while robbing the Ponderosa, killed Taft. Laskaris was convicted in West Virginia and in Erie on a number of armed robberies, and the Mark Taft murder. Laskaris got life in prison with no parole, plus 60 years. Palmer, who cooperated with authorities, got five years. It appeared that the eye-witness, whose observation originally resulted in the arrest of Richard Armstrong, was correct all along: He saw the argument, then Hamilton go down and Armstrong running away. He did not see Laskaris, or hear the shot because of the silencer. The witness passed both the polygraph and the hypnosis because he had been telling the truth, DiPaolo and Gunter later explained to ADA Kroto. In 1987, District Attorney Veshecco and DiPaolo went at it again when DiPaolo learned Veshecco would not prosecute Laskaris on the Hamilton murder, apparently deciding, to DiPaolo's dismay, that one life sentence was enough. Meanwhile, Richard Armstrong's days were numbered. He died following a fall. He had been another of Marjorie Diehl's lovers.

Even to this day, after DiPaolo won his fourth and possibly final six-year term of office on the bench, the former cop remains philosophical about his only two courtroom losses.

"The juries in the 'Niggsy' Arnone and Louie DiNicola cases spoke and I respect their decisions," DiPaolo easily says without a hint of rancor or bitterness. "Even more, I respect the system that allows juries of one's peers to function unimpeded in our society. That's our system. And win or lose, it's the best system and we live by it. It's often well-intentioned guesses that the juries render."

Yet, after some contemplation over the lost murder cases, recalling the grand jury sessions, arraignments, preliminary hearings, trips to Florida, Ohio, West Virginia, Indiana and Michigan, he still manages to add a final thought based on this public servant's deep religious convictions: "Someday – and that day has already come for Niggsy – I truly believe that each man will have one more jury to face. Let's see if He believes them."

That's Dom DiPaolo. An Erie guy with deep roots in his community.

First a cop. Now a judge. Tough, but fair.

And that's exactly what his life stands for: Justice for all.